THE COMMUNIST INSURGENT INFRASTRUCTURE IN SOUTH VIETNAM:

A STUDY OF ORGANIZATION AND STRATEGY

by

Michael Charles Conley

Research and writing completed: November 1966

CENTER FOR RESEARCH IN SOCIAL SYSTEMS
The American University
Washington, D. C. 20016

Operating Under Contract With
The Department of The Army

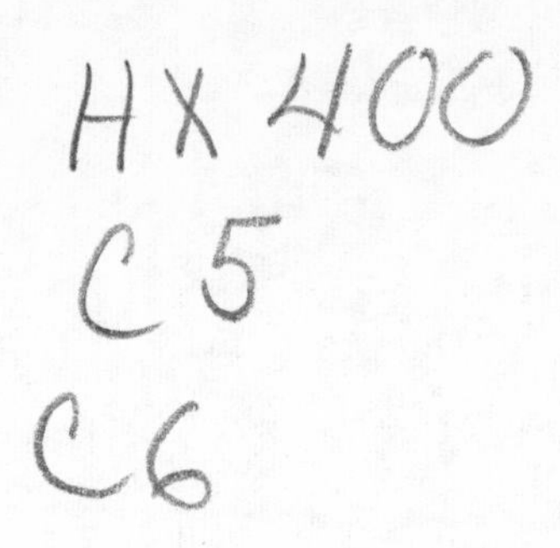

This research is accomplished by the Center For Research In Social Systems at the American University, a nongovernmental agency operating under contract with the Department of the Army.

FOREWORD

This report on the Communist organization in South Vietnam was produced for ODCSOPS, Department of the Army, under a contract between the American University and the Office of the Chief of Research and Development, Department of the Army. During the work on this study the author was granted access to documents captured on the battlefields of South Vietnam. Translations of some of these are to be found in the report. The documents should provide both substantiation for this work and background for further investigation on the part of those interested in events in South Vietnam. Other first hand accounts, available from books, journal articles, and informal conversations, were also used.

This report describes and explains the functions and structure of an extremely complex and labyrinthine set of organizations that have been collectively and commonly called the Viet Cong. It also presents the thesis that the organization and operating procedures of the Viet Cong have precisely followed previous Communist teaching and practices, that the Viet Cong organization offers "the classic synthesis" of Communist principles and procedures from the past half-century.

PREFACE

This study seeks to achieve three major goals. First, it attempts to describe the infrastructure of the Communist-dominated insurgency in South Vietnam which evolved during the period 1954–1965. Second, in the light of the organizational composition of that movement, it analyzes the strategy pursued by the insurgents on the political, sociopsychological, economic, and paramilitary levels in their effort to displace the formal government of the country with the agencies of a new administrative structure upon which a future totalitarian regime might be constructed. Last, the study attempts to place the more conventionally military content of the conflict in context by examining it in terms of the spectrum of organizations and highly varied activities which collectively constitute the reality of the threat that has been generated in the course of the last decade.

Generalizing from the specific and the unique, the emphasis is placed upon identifying those essential features of the Communist insurgency movement which repeatedly occur in the villages, districts, provinces, and interprovincial zones of South Vietnam. The mass of primary source data available often permitted the separation of one group of practices, organizational arrangements, and conceptual principles which appeared to be uniform from a second group which held only for restricted areas. Consequently, the picture drawn generalizes from the specific; however, it is not pure abstraction, since it contains relatively precise data on party organizations in specific regions of South Vietnam at particular moments in the recent past. In a situation where the details of organization and operation are in a state of continual flux, the alternative to an attempt to seek out the principles that lie behind the reality of the moment is to view all as chaotic and transitory. The blend of principles and concrete examples attempted here constitutes one possible resolution of the admittedly unsolvable problem of precisely describing the insurgency in all its parts on a countrywide basis.

The sources employed in the study may be divided into two major categories and several subcategories. The first consists of verbatim English-language translations of Vietnamese sources falling into four subcategories, i.e.:

(a) Documents intended exclusively for inner-party dissemination, frequently at levels no lower than district party committees, outlining policies and their priorities for execution in extra-party organizations.

(b) Documents of party origin, but intended for unrestricted distribution in civil mass organizations and/or military units, involving standards of behavior expected, justifications for tactics employed, rules and regulations of "popular" associations, constitutions, bylaws, public announcements, etc.

(c) Written inner-party self-criticisms both on single individuals, conducted during cell meetings, and on larger groups, civil or military, e.g., reports to higher party or party/military committees accounting for performance during specified periods and providing explanations, frequently of a markedly candid character, for failures acknowledged.

(d) Articles appearing in the North Vietnamese Communist publications *Hoc Tap* ("Studies") and *Nhan Dan* ("The People"), governmental declarations and speeches, radio broadcasts emanating from North Vietnam, and English- and French-language publications of the Hanoi Foreign Languages Publishing House.

In the second category fall secondary sources which may be differentiated into three subcategories:

(a) Intelligence reports, intelligence evaluations attached to captured documents, debriefings, and evaluated interrogations of enemy personnel who were captured either in uniform or without visible military insignia or authenticated military backgrounds.

(b) Books, monographs, and periodical literature on Vietnam and the conflict in the South since 1954, including the extensive polemic literature on the sources of the conflict and the rationale for our presence there.

(c) Selected literature on Communist external and subversive activities during the last sixty-odd years.

Of these multiple groups of sources, those receiving the most extensive use are the first three groups under the first category and the documents of group (a) in the second category. While it may be asserted that the circa five hundred documents of widely varying length finally employed in the present study are indeed representative of the much larger body of material examined during the initial phase of work, it has been impossible to ascertain whether they are representative of either (1) the total mass of primary documentation generated by the several elements of the insurgent organization in South Vietnam during the last decade and a half, or (2) that portion of this material translated into English by various agencies during the same period of time. The author is inclined to believe that an investigation of the total literature—an impossible task today since substantial numbers of these documents either in Vietnamese or English translation are now permanently lost to us—would show his sources to be representative. He is encouraged in this conclusion, first, by the internal consistency over an extended period of time found to obtain among the documents examined, and second, by the substantial agreement which exists between these sources, on the one hand, and primary sources coming from earlier insurgencies, on the other hand. However, it is necessary to note here that in practice sampling was restricted by the immediate issues of (1) accessibility and (2) the original determination of the offices charged with translation as to what should be rendered into English. Regarding the second of these limitations, it should be added here that documents translated by various agencies were available to the author in abundance.

The documents of definitely North Vietnamese origin were utilized primarily to determine the party and government status of several individuals significantly involved in the direction of the insurgency from north of the 17th parallel. The secondary literature on Vietnam was utilized as a source of area background and means of gauging the impact of insurgent operations as perceived by outside observers. Outside of the references to the literature of international communism appearing in the introduction to appendix A documents falling in the final subcategory figure in the bibliography at the end of the text are intended as a guide to the reader who wishes to explore more closely the extra-Vietnamese origins of the phenomenon in process inside Indochina.

An attempt was made to screen the information contained in the extensive documentation by utilizing only data for which corroborating evidence was available in additional records. In no case were data employed which were not supported by at least one additional source. Discussions of the principles underlying insurgent practices are invariably based upon a wealth of substantiating information drawn from documents captured at different dates and from widely separated regions of the country. Given the mass of documentary evidence available, confirming information was normally readily available even in matters of detail. Where the data assembled on a given practice or procedure appeared to originate exclusively within a single delimited area, the issue under investigation was considered distinctive to that restricted area and no attempt was made to generalize from the specific situation. Where a validating commentary was available, the commentary itself was treated as equivalent to a corroborating source and no additional confirmation was deemed requisite, although every effort was made to find supplementary information where possible.

It was especially critical in this study to adhere rigidly to methodological principles of the order used here, due to the fact that it has not been possible to place the reader in a position where he can investigate independently all of the sources quoted or otherwise employed in the investigation in order that he might arrive at the conclusions presented. Throughout the text of this document, quoted material appears without attribution.

It is hoped that the reader's understandable interest in the types of sources employed can be satisfied in part by the selection of English-language translations of a group of the documents utilized in the study. These documents are intended to facilitate the reader's further understanding of the South Vietnamese insurgency, but also offer a means by which he may more adequately examine for himself the nature of the materials which served as a major source of information in the preparation of this study.

By introducing the appendixes to the study with an extended essay which examines the general properties and procedures of Communist parties globally and relates the observed or recorded behavior of Vietnamese Communists to this body of information, it is possible to concentrate upon an analysis of specifics in the text and yet provide a framework in which the reader may pursue the larger subject of the norms of international communism. In a broader sense, both of these subjects are of direct relevance to an adequate grasp of the immediate subject of Communist insurgency in South Vietnam.

Another methodological issue has confronted the author throughout the work: the inability uniformly to determine, from the orders and directives that have fallen into our hands, the extent to which the insurgent was successful in concrete terms in approximating the goals he set himself. Some insight into this matter is provided by the reports penned by responsible insurgents which were intended exclusively for the eyes of superior party officials. The extensive self-criticisms revealed in these documents provide us with considerable insight into the difficulties confronting the movement; although even here complete frankness could hardly be expected where the future of the report writer himself was at stake.

Another source that defines the close correlation between intent and accomplished fact can be found within the extensive secondary literature on the subject, produced by free world journalists and their counterparts from Communist bloc countries and free world Communist parties, which affirmed on the basis of personal observation that the bureaucratic structure called for in party directives actually existed, and that the types of tactics outlined in operational orders were in fact implemented.

Finally, there is yet another body of literature which helps to substantiate the fact that one is dealing here neither with fiction nor with wishful thinking. It is the body of information provided in scholarly studies, journalistic accounts, and primary documentation on the earlier Communist attempts at subversion which followed strategy lines similar to those in South Vietnam. (While this body of literature from the past, like that on the current conflict, fails to provide definitive answers, the correlation between word and deed which can be substantiated is significant enough to support the conclusion that de facto success on the part of Vietnamese Communists in organizational work among civilians and soldiers is not atypical of previous efforts of a comparable character.) That is to say, there is a body of historical data to support the contention that the procedures followed by Communist insurgents actually work and can be employed repeatedly with the substantial likelihood of meaningful results.

In any definitive sense no wholly satisfactory solution can be given to the issue of the disparity between the goals sought by the insurgents and the results achieved. If it is not possible to achieve accuracy in the seemingly clear-cut matter of a body count of enemy killed in action, how much more perplexing is it to try to determine quantitatively the level of effectiveness of political action, conducted clandestinely in an environment frequently hostile to the polltaker and among a population not in a position to appreciate fully what is happening to them or able to grasp the dynamics of the phenomenon of which they are a part.

This lack of quantitative statistics on the efficacy of organization and operation, however, does not vitiate the utility of the present study, which first of all seeks to generalize from the specific and deal with the principles at stake rather than with the exact force levels of the opposing camps, and which secondly deals with an insurgent organization that in fact grew markedly in competence and sharply increased the numbers of its adherents during the period up through December 1965 (the cutoff date for the research in this study).

Among the assumptions underlying this study is the belief that the effectiveness of the steps taken by those charged with the defeat of insurgent forces is meaningfully dependent upon the precise information of an organizational character on the movement to be combated. To be useful, a statement of this order must distinguish clearly among the component elements of the insurgency, and it must concurrently show, with a sense of discrimination, the manner in which these several elements are organizationally integrated and tactically and politically coordinated. These issues are adjudged to be of such a nature that their examination must precede an investigation of grand strategy. To study grand strategy without the prior study of organizational matters would rob it of much of its meaning. Consequently, beginning in chapter 1, attention is turned to an extended investigation of the ordinary and pragmatic matter of who runs whom. Thereafter, grand strategy may be treated in the context of the distinctive organizational interrelationships which evolved in Vietnam and which not only facilitate strategy but also delimit the alternatives open to the Vietnamese Communist strategist in his planning and staff work.

To the concern for matters of organization and structural interrelationships among specialized agencies and echelons of the movement must be added a second major characteristic of this study: its attempt to approach the phenomenon of insurgency, not so much in terms of what is perceived by the outside observer as in terms of the perception of the movement which might be attributed to its own leaders. Clearly, any number of objective difficulties stand in the way of an empathic projection of this sort.

This is not to suggest that available secondary literature conceived in a dissimilar frame of reference is consciously ignored; but it is to assert that the effort to understand the insurgency from the perspective of one of its own conflict managers, together with attention to organizational matters, sets off the present study from the reportage of a primarily journalistic character that has been produced thus far on the Vietnamese conflict.

Such an approach to the study of this insurgent movement carries additional consequences in its wake. Precision in the identification of the movement's many parts and extreme care in providing these several elements with appropriate nomenclature become issues of critical importance. For the insurgent leader assigned command functions and held responsible for the maximum utilization of a highly varied body of personnel specialized in a myriad of distinctive activities, the use of a terminology which fails to discriminate in detail between the multiple agencies and types of operations conducted would render the efficacious and rapid commitment, movement or redirection of forces difficult if not impossible. And as precision of designation becomes a critical factor for the insurgent leadership, it likewise becomes important in the study of that leadership and its organization. For this reason the facile phrase "Viet Cong" is not employed in the text of this study.

The seeming arbitrariness of the decision to avoid using the term "Viet Cong," given the currency it has acquired in general usage, is understood if one considers that the phrase has acquired its present popularity primarily through the writings of persons more concerned with what the United States and the RVN are doing than with what the opposing movement is. To be sure these journalistic accounts of the conflict have brought genuine insight and even scholarly erudition to the study of the phenomenon. Nevertheless, if one's analysis of the hostile formations is cast in the context of a report intended for the consumption of the American public which is primarily interested in the nature of the U.S. commitment and the character of our current operations in Vietnam, the incentive to spend any great amount of time on the specifics of insurgent organization is slight. However, the use of "Viet Cong" would defeat the ends set for this study, for the term is utterly devoid of precise meaning in any organizational context. And it is a phrase which one will seek for in vain in documents captured from the insurgents.

We are told that "Viet Cong" means "Vietnamese Communist." If this is the case, then it would be imprecise to use it in referring to the extra-party formations, military as well as civil, examined at length in this work, in which the bulk of the participants are, *by Communist design*, non-Communist. On the other hand, to use the term to mean, rigidly, the membership of the Vietnamese Workers' (Communist) Party is likewise unsatisfactory, for that apparatus consists of two operationally distinct portions, each with its own official name as determined by the geographic location of the party member in question. North of the 17th parallel, a Vietnamese Communist belongs to the Dang Lao Dong (DLD) and to the south of that line, he is, by fiction, an adherent of the Dang Nhan-Dan Cach Mang or People's Revolutionary Party (PRP). Given this distinction, critical to the present work, one would be continually obliged to explain to the reader which "Viet Cong" is under discussion.

There is an even more compelling reason for not using the term. In popular usage, its Communist connotation is ignored and it tends to be equated with the armed and military forces of the insurgency. And with respect to this one segment of an insurgent structure which contains a wealth of other elements, it discourages conscious discrimination as to the various types of armed elements which have been activated. All of them together are, popularly, guerrillas, and Vietnamese "guerrillas" are the "Viet Cong." The use of the term in such a manner utterly vitiates any attempt to understand the opposing combatant structure, to say nothing of the insurgent movement as a whole. Further, in its grossest form, the "Viet Cong," so defined, is set off against the "National Liberation Front" which is conceived as an autonomous body of persons, distinct from, but sympathetic to, the goals after which the guerrilla is striving. It is hoped that the following analysis will throw into proper perspective the reality of the interrelationships among these several bodies, but it will be impossible to achieve this goal if the extremely imprecise term "Viet Cong" is employed. It can only get in the way of an analysis, not assist it.

The author is indebted for the completion of this work to the sympathetic assistance received from a number of colleagues in the Center for Research in Social Systems of The American University who have willingly interrupted their own demanding working schedules to read and criticize the original drafts of the present work. In particular, thanks must be extended to three persons: John LeNoir, who served as research assistant during the first half of the year 1966 prior to his departure for Vietnam to examine the situation there at first hand; Richard Dabney, who, in editing the text of the following chapters, served as both a most severe critic and a most sympathetic supporter; and Dr. William Hanna, whose antitheses served as constructive catalysts during various revisions of the manuscript. Finally, many substantive improvements were brought to the study by the advice of consultants outside of CRESS who also gave much time to the examination of this book. Mr. Slavko N. Bjelajac, Special Operations Directorate, Office of the Deputy Chief of Staff for Military Operations, Department of the Army, Mr. Marshall Andrews, and Dr. George K. Tanham, Special Assistant to the President of the RAND Corporation of Santa Monica, California, should be mentioned. Responsibility for the conclusions presented here, however, remains exclusively with the author.

DESCRIPTIVE TABLE OF CONTENTS

Chapters 1–6 (Part One) deal with the Communist Party in South Vietnam. *Chapter 1* gives the historical background of South Vietnam, including a history of the Communist Party there. It also summarizes the current public debate regarding the causes and interpretations of the conflict. *Chapter 2* describes the activities of the PRP (the Communist Party in the South) at the interprovincial level and delineates the critical elements in its infrastructure. *Chapter 3* details these activities at the provincial and district levels. *Chapter 4* describes the party control apparatus, which is operated at all levels through the principle of reverse representation. *Chapter 5* details the activities of the crucial youth organization of the PRP. *Chapter 6* sets forth the vulnerabilities and weaknesses of the party apparatus.

Chapters 7–9 (Part Two) treat the civil mass associations under the control of the PRP. *Chapter 7* describes the general principles of how Communists use civil organizations in subversive insurgencies. *Chapter 8* shows how these principles were put into practice by the PRP in the control of popular organizations, special interest groups, and guerrilla self-defense units. *Chapter 9* shows how Communist-dominated mass associations are federated into "fronts" for the effective conduct of the insurgency.

10–12 (Part Three) discuss the Communist-controlled military forces of the insurgency. *Chapter 10* describes the origin of the forces of the Vietnamese Communist Party in the South. *Chapter 11* details the military command structure at the interprovincial level. *Chapter 12* describes the individual military unit and how it operates.

Chapter 13 (Part Four) describes how the party manipulates the civil and military components in the overall conduct of the insurgency.

Chapter 14 (Part Five) shows how these strategic principles are applied by the PRP operating in the Saigon-Gia Dinh Special Region.

SUMMARY OF THE TEXT

I. Objective

This work describes the infrastructure and concept of operation of the Communist-dominated insurgency in South Vietnam during the period 1954–1965, giving particular attention to matters of organization. Political, sociopsychological, and paramilitary factors are analyzed to determine their impact upon the strictly military aspects of the conflict. To the extent that the basic phenomena treated here occur in other insurgencies, this document may serve as an introduction to the general field of Communist insurgency.

II. Conceptual Framework

(1) Several alternate approaches are available to Communists striving to seize the instruments of political power in a nation. Among those historically most frequently employed have been (a) the coup d'etat—primarily an urban phenomenon—followed possibly by a civil war; (b) the subversion of a national coalition government within which the Communist Party is initially but one among a number of parties supposedly cooperating the administration of state affairs; and (c) the protracted social revolutionary conflict—that form of aggression in which the party most frequently spawns guerrilla forces. The decision by the party to use any one of these specific approaches obliges it to make determinations of a highly distinctive character with regard to organizational forms, campaign platforms and slogans, and political allies.

(2) Though the strategy approach taken determines the organizational forms to be evolved, it does not necessarily follow that the party's concept of operations must be treated first in an analytical investigation of the South Vietnamese insurgency. The issues of form, propaganda content, and political alliances are not self-evident, but are characterized by the indirection which the Vietnamese Communist has inherited from his fraternal predecessors. The latter three matters must be thoroughly clarified if the concept of operations to be grasped adequately. Through an examination of the substantive content of these three components, the observer can identify the guidelines within which the party operates. Particularly, the practical organizational work within the civil population, which determines the movement's form, deserves the greatest attention. The approach taken is inseparable from all three of the factors listed, but mass work must be assigned first priority because the organizations it brings into being provide the operational base from which strategy unfolds and set limits to the alternatives open to the party at any given moment.

(3) The party specialist assigned to attract substantial numbers of persons into party-controlled mass organizations must carefully adjust his tactics and temper the speed with which he moves to blend in with local conditions if he is to exploit to the maximum the attitudes and trends which prevail in the society he is attempting to reshape.

(4) In the light of these considerations, an understanding of the dynamics of the South Vietnamese insurgency presupposes an approach which aims to acquaint the reader with the following subjects: (a) the recent past of Vietnam and its peoples; (b) the intricacies of the directing party organizations; (c) the precise manner in which the party merges with and then gradually alters the cultural patterns of the people among whom it works. Consequently, the following study proceeds inductively from an investigation of the parts (party, civil, and military—the indicators of strategy) to the whole (the movement as the physical expression of a highly sophisticated form of political warfare).

Following the analysis of the Communist movement's organization and concept of operations, the study is concluded by investigating the distinctive situation obtaining in the Saigon-Cholon-Gia Dinh area, drawing together the several previously examined facets of the problem.

III. Assumptions

(1) The distinctive doctrine of political warfare employed by Communists in their attempts to subvert non-Communist governments in the 1960's is the product of a period of theorizing and experimentation by Communists extending over the first six decades of the twentieth century. A chronological examination of the manner in which each of the component elements of current party doctrine was elaborated, tested, and then integrated within the existing body of knowledge on subversion reveals a continuity of basic concepts throughout this entire era. The man who set the parameters within which this doctrine prospered through trial and error, and reached its classic expression in the current South Vietnamese insurgency, is Vladimir Ilyich Lenin. The study of his thought is assumed to be the key to understanding current doctrine, since it sets forth the guidelines within which the doctrine evolved.

(2) It is believed, further, that there exists currently a body of principles and operational procedures applicable to the handling of protracted subversion by Communists under the most varied of environmental conditions, and which is readily available to the leadership core of Communist parties in widely scattered areas of the world. The efficacy of any one of these practices varies from one culture to the other and all of them have produced results which, when utilized in combination, are sufficiently positive in the eyes of international communism to raise them to the status of general principles.

The nature of these precepts, transferable from one milieu to another, can be identified through the comparative study of Communist-dominated insurgencies in different parts of the world. By a general grasp of these principles the dynamics and essential goals of the South Vietnamese insurgency become more readily identifiable, and speed is acquired in sorting out patterns that are typical of insurgencies falling into this category and in highlighting the distinctive aspects of the present protracted conflict.

(3) Both the French Indochinese War, 1946–1954, and the history and

ethnology of the several distinctive peoples residing within Vietnam clearly bear upon the subject of the Communist-dominated insurgency in South Vietnam after 1954; the first chapter herein is devoted to focusing this study through the lens of that background.

(4) The social restructuring in process within Vietnamese society in areas responsive to the Central Government is a subject distinct from the main theme of the present study. While social changes are of importance to the formulation of U.S. long-term policy in Indochina, an effective treatment of the Communist-dominated insurgency in the South may be made without a parallel study in depth of the process of change apparent within the government's camp.

IV. Methodology

The materials employed in this study were drawn from English-language translations of captured enemy documents, data emanating from North Vietnam, from intelligence and interrogation reports, the contemporary secondary literature, and selected primary sources derived from the literature of international communism during the several decades of its history.

The information contained in the extensive documentation that has fallen into our hands was screened by utilizing only that data for which corroborating evidence was available in additional records. In no case was data employed which was not supported by at least one other source. Discussions of the principles underlying insurgent practices were invariably based upon a wealth of substantiating information drawn from documents captured at different dates and from widely separated regions of South Vietnam.

Given the mass of documentary evidence available, confirming information was readily available even in matters of detail. Where the data assembled on a given practice for procedure appeared to originate exclusively with a single delimited area, the issue under investigation was considered to be distinctive of a restricted area and no attempt was made to generalize from the specific situation. Where a validating commentary was available, the commentary itself was treated as equivalent to a corroborating source and no additional confirmation was deemed requisite, although every effort was made to find supplementary information.

The chapters were prepared approximately in the order in which they appear in the present text and the chapter on strategy followed the analyses of the several distinctive components of the movement.

V. Conclusions

A. Structure

(1) The Dang Lao Dong (identified south of the 17th parallel after 1962 as the Dang Nhan-Dan Cach Mang, or People's Revolutionary Party) is the strategic center of the insurgent movement. If it did not initiate the effort toward the subversion of the RVN—a question still open to debate—

it very quickly dominated the movement, permitting it to (a) build an infrastructure through which it has contended for power and (b) dictate the strategy to be implemented throughout the multiple echelons of the movement.

(2) The party consists of a hierarchy of committee branches and their sections and subsections, paralleled by an organization within the organization which is cellularly structured and ready to resume its clandestine character at the slightest provocation. This system is further elaborated by the existence of a party youth structure and a separate system of commissars assigned to the supervision of youth work in this inseparable party affiliate. All of these structures, in turn, are imbedded within civil organizations, which have additional control channels of their own, and within armed units which currently maintain quasi-conventional military command structures and reporting channels.

(3) Across the board, the insurgent structure is characterized by the absence of voluntarism, no matter what the organizational level, the intensity or activity, or the phase of escalation may be. It is particularly important to stress this point with respect to the civil associations—the so-called "popular" mass organizations activated by the party's cadre. Under no circumstances will the command cadre willingly allow itself to become dependent upon freely extended civil support. Although the party welcomes such support, it never formulates its operational plans on the assumption that those plans will be carried out by individuals retaining the right to change their minds.

(4) The significance of the paramilitary organizations activated under party guidance at the village and hamlet level (e.g., the Du Kich) can be most readily grasped if one evaluates them as the elite mass associations at the local level. The distinction between the members of the liberation peasants' association and the village guerrilla unit is one of degree, following from (a) the latter's greater prestige and (b) the heavier demands placed upon the personnel of the latter body. The guerrilla's weapon is a status symbol as well as an instrument with which to kill government personnel. The party is aware of this and assigns a more important role to the indoctrination of these persons than to those enrolled in the ranks of other village liberation associations.

(5) The armed units of the insurgent movement, the Po Doi Dia Phuong and the Quan Doi Chu Luc, are the instruments which provide the party with the ability to contend with the security forces of the RVN and the United States.

(6) Fighting is no end in itself, but is one of a series of means toward the total control of the population. The determination of which means will be utilized at any given juncture or in any locale is a matter for party decision. The military services participate in making such determinations because they are commanded by high-ranking party members who exercise influence as a consequence of their positions within the party itself.

(7) A study of the infrastructure in the Saigon-Cholon-Gia Dinh area

—in contrast to the obtaining in the five other interprovincial commands—demonstrates the flexibility with which the cellularly structured People's Revolutionary Party may modify both party and extra-party organizations and vary operational procedures to conform with distinctive field conditions. Divergences from the norms elsewhere do not reflect a different basic strategy in urban areas. Rather, they must be viewed collectively as tactical adaptations requisite to the pursuit of one and the same approach in a unique environment.

B. Concept of Operation

(1) Protracted social revolutionary conflict—the third strategy identified in paragraph 1, section II, above—is the form employed in South Vietnam. It calls for the insurgent to (a) build an infrastructure dominated by party members who constitute the nervous system of the revolution, (b) engage in both overt and clandestine or underground activities, and concurrently (c) activate a complex of armed elements and a competitive national administrative system. Many of the insurgent's hopes for success are based on his conviction that this strategy cannot be successfully countered.

(2) The insurgent will use both the armed units and the whole infrastructure to destroy the nation's class structure and administrative machinery. He will use the civil elements of the front to provide the populace at large with the prototype of an alternate national administration.

C. Counterinsurgency Recommendations

Since the prime concern of the Communist insurgent leadership is the domination of the Vietnamese civil populace from which it recruits and within which it hides the agencies of the party hierarchy, the most effective way to reach and destroy the party is through the population which must be provided with the organizational means through which it can identify itself with the government and actively participate in the identification of the insurgents. Subordinating this phase of operations to a campaign strategy which concentrates upon the destruction of the enemy's armed forces allows the party to continue with the activation of new elements or, at best, buys success at the sacrifice of economy. The People's Revolutionary Party organization itself should be dealt with immediately, and the purpose in committing troops to combat is to gain access to the people. The only way to stop this insurgency is to crush the PRP beyond any hope of recovery.

CONTENTS

Page

CHARTS

MAPS

PART ONE
THE PARTY AND ITS OPERATIONAL PROCEDURES

CHAPTER 1
INTRODUCTION AND BACKGROUND

SUMMARY

The Vietnamese Communists, under the direction of Ho Chi Minh (alias Nguyen Ai Quoc), progressively came to dominate all organized dissidence directed against the French colonial regime in the 1930's and against the Japanese occupation during World War II. They built their organization upon the body of principles and practices evolved by the Communist International or Comintern (1919–1943) for Communist parties throughout the world. Conflict between the resistance forces that emerged from the war and the representatives of France who returned to Indochina following the cessation of hostilities in 1945 launched the protracted war concluded by the Geneva Accords of 1954 and set the stage for the initial phase of the current insurgency in the South.

Considerable disagreement exists regarding (1) the assignment of responsibility for the gradual escalation of the South Vietnamese insurgency after 1956/1957 and (2) the essential character of this conflict. The factual evidence examined in this study has led to the adoption of that interpretation, among the possible distinctive viewpoints, which assigns to the Vietnamese Communist Party the pivotal role in the intensification of the struggle. Ngo Dinh Diem and his family did indeed exacerbate frictions present in various elements of the populations as a result of serious errors of judgment and this, in turn, simplified the Communist Party's task of winning adherents; however, the evidence does not support the attempts that have been made to compound still further the blame placed upon Diem and his family.

Chronologically, the era of insurgency in the South may be divided into three periods; 1954–1960; 1960–1965; 1965 to the present. The initial phase is characterized by terrorism and sporadic organizational efforts among the peasants in scattered areas. During the second period the insurgent movement achieved its most sophisticated organizational form with the establishment of (1) a national front and (2) significant armed combat units. Regarding these two extra-party structures, two basic principles persistently obtained: First, they were operationally interdependent; neither could prosper without the assistance of the other; but equally important, both were under the direction of the party which antedated them by three decades and which assumed the guise south of the 17th parallel after 1962 of the Dang Nhan-Dan Cach Mang (People's Revolutionary Party—or PRP).

The Historical Framework

Vietnam is that portion of the Indochinese peninsula bordered on the north by China and on the west by Laos and Cambodia, and is the source of some 2,000 years of continuous cultural and political history. Although the region was reduced to a dependency of the more powerful Chinese for extended periods, its peoples have persisted in retaining their separate identities. Its most recent conquerors were the French, who dominated the region for nearly 80 years. French rule ended with the Geneva Agreements of 1954 after eight years of internal warfare, and since then the country has been divided at the 17th parallel into two distinct political entities. In the North a Communist government, headed by Ho Chi Minh, has ruled since the Geneva Accords; the South has had a succession of non-Communist governments. The eight-year regime of Ngo Dinh Diem (1955–1963) lasted the longest.

Until the arrival of the French, Vietnamese society was traditionalist; clusters of families engaged chiefly in the cultivation of rice constituted the base of the social order. These cohesive social units prescribed the conduct of their individual members, while formal administration became the function of a stratum of wealthy families reared in the mandarin traditions acquired during Chinese rule.

The bulk of the population in modern times has been ethnically Vietnamese, a Mongoloid people like the Chinese, who originally dwelt together with other, similar tribal peoples in southern China before the Christian era. In the South, in the territory of the Republic of Vietnam (RVN) this stock constitutes some 85 percent of the population, or more than 12 million persons. The remaining major ethnic groups are the Chinese, a million strong in the South; the Cambodians, roughly 350,000 in number; and a variety of distinct indigenous tribes, collectively referred to as the montagnards. These latter peoples, the original inhabitants of the country, were forced into the mountainous regions of the country by the Vietnamese peoples as they moved south. Estimates of the numbers of these mountain peoples vary between 500,000 and 700,000. Hostility between them and the Vietnamese has been sustained to the present.

During the French colonial era, the systematic exploitation of the agricultural potential, particularly in the Mekong Delta, produced an extremely wealthy class of Vietnamese landowners who emerged as a new element in domestic society. They introduced all of the abuses of absentee landlordism into the daily life of the Vietnamese, but were also the avenue through which the country became acquainted with Western literature and science.

Though traditional patterns were gradually undermined through the changes introduced by the French, hostility to alien rule persisted. Spokesmen of discontent arose from that stratum of the population most deeply influenced by French institutions and thought. A small, growing number of French-educated Vietnamese began to use the body of Western political literature as an ideological basis for criticizing the colonial regime. By the 1920's opposition reached the stage of open agitation. When authorities responded with repressive steps, the opposition abandoned open political organization in favor of conspiratorial leagues. The best-known of these early clandestine bodies was the Vietnamese Nationalist Party (Viet Nam Quoc Dan Dang—VNQDD). This organization was virtually destroyed when it was ruthlessly repressed by the French in 1930 following the Yen

Bay mutiny, in which the VNQDD had taken part. Thereafter the leadership of the nationalist resistance to colonial rule fell to the Vietnamese Communists.

The Communist Party of Indochina (ICP), which became a member party of the Communist International, was founded in 1930 at Hong Kong by Ho Chi Minh (then known as Nguyen Ai Quoc). As in many other countries, so in Vietnam, the party was constructed through the fusion into a single disciplined apparatus of several Communist and left-radical splinter groups, each with its separate history from the period of the 1920's. After 1930, the members of the ICP were subjected to the rigorous controls evolved by Lenin and his disciples during the preceding two decades. In contrast to the VNQDD and other unsuccessful nationalist organizations, the ICP was highly effective in the conduct of penetration procedures, agitation and propaganda, and other characteristic Communist activities. It fed avidly upon the discontent widespread in Vietnamese society, providing direction to dissidence and heightening ideological impact.

Paul Mus, noted French scholar, adjudged the unrest of the years 1930–31 and the associated transfer of leadership among anticolonialist groups from parties of the VNQDD type to the ICP as the reflection of a basic "cleavage" in the indigenous opposition to French rule.[a] There remained, on one hand, vestiges of the dilettante of revolution, a product of the literati's conspiracies; on the other hand was a new foreign-trained leadership concerned with the routine matters of operational doctrine and organizational work.

The attempts of the French Sûreté to crush the ICP were unsuccessful. Strikes, demonstrations, and peasant-supported uprisings became the order of the day, and on one occasion two provinces were seized outright. Given the ICP's staying power and the aggressiveness of its tactics, together with the effective suppression by the French of the more moderate organizations which could have provided alternate forms of leadership for Vietnamese nationalism, it is readily understandable how Ho Chi Minh and his close associates could have acquired control over the resistance movement against Japanese forces during the Second World War.

Nationalist Chinese activities in Vietnam were to be conducted through a new coalition organization of all major Vietnamese nationalist groups called The League of Vietnamese Revolutionary Parties (Viet Nam Cach Minh Dong Minh Hoi—usually abbreviated to Dong Minh Hoi). In fact, a single element of this combination became dominant, the party of Nguyen Ai Quoc, who in May 1941 took the name of Ho Chi Minh and concealed his Communist identity by operating through an organization which contained non-Communist nationalists as well as the membership of the the old ICP.

The new organization was called the Vietnam Independence League (Viet Nam Doc Lap Dong Minh Hoi—better known as the Viet Minh). Money received from the Chinese Nationalist Government to support intel-

[a] Paul Mus in Foreword to Gerald Cannon Hickey's *Village in Vietnam* (New Haven: Yale University Press, 1964), p. xix.

ligence operations plus a small additional amount of aid from U.S. sources was used to strengthen the Viet Minh structure, bringing it increasingly under the control of its Communist membership. Vo Nguyen Giap—also a Communist—activated guerrilla bands which made only minor contributions to the military operations against the Japanese but nevertheless came to constitute the only genuinely significant indigenous military force. By the end of the war, Communists totally dominated the new Viet Minh organization.

In March 1945, the Japanese interned the Vichy French with whom they had collaborated during the preceding four years and provoked the Emperor Bao Dai into proclaiming Vietnam an independent nation under Japanese "protection." A capital was established at Hue in the central portion of the country. During the same period, however, Ho Chi Minh was also busy. He renamed the guerrilla formations of Vo Nguyen Giap the "National Liberation Army" and made himself the president of a "Committee for the Liberation of the Vietnamese People." On 23 August 1945, Bao Dai, Emperor and Chief of State, ignorant of the true nature of Ho's new committee, abdicated his position as Emperor in the committee's favor and accredited it as Vietnam's responsible government. Less than two weeks later, on 2 September, Ho, in turn, proclaimed the "Democratic Republic of Vietnam" and established a provisional government. The heart of the provisional government was the Viet Minh and the core of the latter body was the Communist Party. In public statements, however, Communist themes remained untouched and the virtues of bourgeois democracy were widely celebrated.

After World War II the first French troops to reach Vietnam landed in Saigon in the middle of September 1945 and a new resistance movement in defense of the proclaimed independence began in the southern portions of Vietnam (old Cochinchina). The struggle initiated then was never to be completely stamped out at any time during the next two decades. In the North, where French troops reappeared in numbers only after February 1946, the Communists were originally obliged to negotiate with a Chinese Nationalist occupation force provided for by the Allied powers at the end of the war. Given the Chinese Nationalist opposition to a return of the French, a modus vivendi became possible. Elections were held for a National Assembly in which remnants of the Dong Minh Hoi and the old VNQDD were represented and an ostensibly nationalistic, coalition government was formed, headed by Ho Chi Minh. In return, the Communists declared the ICP dissolved (November 1946).

When the Chinese Nationalists acquiesced in the return of the French, however, the encouraging political developments were placed in jeopardy and negotiations with Paris commenced. In March 1946, the French recognized the "Free State" of the Democratic Republic of Vietnam north of the 16th parallel. The new state was to manage its own finances and maintain its own armed forces. A plebiscite in Cochinchina was to determine whether that region would be included in the union. The question remains debatable whether the French negotiated in good faith. In any case, a study deterioration of relations led to shooting breaking out in Haiphong, the port city for Hanoi, in November 1946 and the subsequent bombardment of the port by French vessels which slaughtered a reported 6,000 Vietnamese. By December 1946 the protracted guerrilla war which was to be concluded by the Geneva conferences of 1954 had commenced.

The instruments through which the Vietnamese Communists prosecuted their insurgent conflict against the French were the Viet Minh, discussed above, in which Communists staffed all critical offices, and the Lien Viet, a front organization designed to enlist the support and talents of broad segments of the population in the protracted struggle. This second organization, according to a Vietnamese Communist high in the party, dated from 29 May 1946.[b] Officially no ICP, as such, existed between the outset of the war and the first quarter of 1951. In fact, the party was particularly active during precisely this period.[c] The decision to publicly acknowledge the presence of a Communist Party at the start of the movement was taken during the Eleventh National Congress of the supposedly nonexistent organization which 200 delegates attended on 11 February 1951. It was decided that the party should be known as the Vietnamese Workers' Party (Viet Nam Dang Lao Dong, or DLD). A public declaration to this effect followed on 3 March 1951.[d]

The same 1951 Party Congress also integrated the Viet Minh within the national Lien Viet front originally set up in May 1946 some 5 years after the Viet Minh itself was proclaimed. Nguyen Kien Giang writes of a "unification de la Ligue Viet Minh et du Front Lien Viet."[e] This determination followed naturally from the decision to distinguish openly between the party membership and their collaborators. The steps taken in 1951 accorded fully with past party practices. What the ICP had been to the Viet Minh in the early forties and what the Viet Minh had been to the Lien Viet in the late forties, the Dang Lao Dong would now become with respect to both the Viet Minh and the Lien Viet in the 1950's. In every case, the principle of distinguishing a small professionally trained elite from a large, ill-trained assemblage of followers governed organizational practice. In no case would one abandon the allies of an earlier day who might yet contribute to the party's goals, but to the maximum extent possible they were to be held far from critical party councils. In removing themselves from the nonparty elements incorporated within the Viet Minh,

---

[b] Nguyen Kien Giang, *Les Grandes dates du parti de la classe ouvrière du Viet Nam* (Hanoi: Éditions en Langues Étrangères, 1960), p. 57.

[c] Bernard Fall has aptly noted (*The Two Viet-Nams: A Political and Military Analysis* [rev. ed.; New York: Frederick A. Praeger, 1964], p. 179) that the very active life of the party during this interval is belied by the Vietnamese Communists themselves. Thus the work by Nguyen Kien Giang of 1960, released at a time when political considerations no longer required silence on the party's role in the insurgency, attributes the following actions to the ICP at this time: The release by its Central Committee of formal statements on 25 November 1945 and 5 March 1946; National Party Cadre meetings 31 July 1946, 3 April 1947, in August 1948 and January 1949, and finally, the February 1951 Eleventh National Congress of the ICP (cf. Nguyen Kien Giang, *Les Grandes dates*, pp. 52–67).

[d] Nguyen Kien Giang, *Les Grandes dates*, pp. 67–68.

[e] *Ibid.*, p. 68.

the party membership achieved a preferred organizational form without openly spurning their friends.

The fall of Dien Bien Phu in May 1954 and popular pressures in France hastened a French-Viet Minh settlement to end the conflict. The essential features of that settlement are contained in two documents, a military accord signed in behalf of the Commanders in Chief of the French Union Forces in Indochina and the People's Army of Vietnam (20 July 1954), and an understanding agreed to by voice vote by the participants in the Geneva Conference (21 July 1954).[f] The military settlement provided for a provisional military demarcation line (the 17th parallel approximately), assigned the conduct of civil administration in each of the two regrouping zones to "the party whose forces are to be regrouped there in virtue of the present agreement," and called for the removal of all hostile enclaves in either zone through the movement of the personnel so involved to the other side of the line. The relocation of personnel was to be effected within a period not to exceed 300 days. There were to be neither reprisals nor discrimination against persons or organizations so moved "on account of their activities during the hostilities." Both prisoners of war and "civilian internees"[g] were to be liberated within a 30-day period and likewise permitted to move freely across the demarcation line. Further, section "d" of article 14 provided that "civilians residing in a district controlled by one party who wish to go and live in the zone assigned to the other party shall be permitted and helped to do so by the authorities in that district."

Additional stipulations forbade the introduction of more military personnel or equipment into Vietnam, the use of either military zone as a staging area for operations by a foreign power, and the adherence of either zone to any military alliance system. Enforcement of the provisions was to be the responsibility of an International Commission, composed of representatives of Canada, India, and Poland, which would operate through inspection teams free to travel at will through any portion of the country.

The final Geneva declaration adopted by a voice vote by representatives of the governments concerned affirmed at the diplomatic level the propriety of the military determinations. It reiterated each of the major principles contained in the earlier accord, stressing two issues in particular. First, the military demarcation line was to be understood as provisional; it "should not in any way be interpreted as constituting a political or territorial boundary." Second, the line of division was ultimately to be removed as a result of general elections to be held in July 1956. From these elections, two goals were to be achieved at one and the same time. The country would

[f] For an abridged version of the relevant documents, see Marvin E. Gettleman (ed.), *Viet Nam: History, Documents, and Opinions on a Major World Crisis* (Greenwich, Conn.: Fawcett Publications, Inc., 1966), pp. 137–59.

[g] The military accord defined "civilian internees" as "all persons who, having in any way contributed to the political and armed struggle between the two parties, have been arrested for that reason. . . ." Thus activities which would otherwise be labeled "criminal" were pardonable if committed in behalf of a political goal. Cf. Gettleman, *op. cit.*, p. 145.

YEAR	PARTY DESIGNATION	EXTRA-PARTY FRONT
1930	Indochinese Communist Party (ICP) established	
1941		Viet Minh created; became member organization of Dong Minh Hoi
1945		Committee for the Liberation of the Vietnamese People announced; proclamation of Democratic Republic of Vietnam (DRV)
1946	Dissolution of ICP announced; membership controlled larger Lien Viet Front from within old Viet Minh	Creation of Lien Viet
1951	Proclamation creating Dang Lao Dong (DLD)	Fusion of nonparty Viet Minh membership with Lien Viet
1955		Establishment of Fatherland Front (in the North)
1960		Establishment of National Front for the Liberation of South Vietnam (NFLSVN)
1962	Designation of DLD members south of 17th parallel as People's Revolutionary Party (PRP)	

Chart 1. COMMUNIST PARTY ORGANIZATION FROM 1930 TO 1962 IN VIETNAM

be reunited and it would be provided with a genuinely representative, democratic government. Consultations in preparation for the elections were to be held between the representatives of the two zones "from 20 July 1955 onward."

During the months after the Geneva settlement a major movement of personnel took place, for the most part from the North to the South. According to Bernard Fall, some 860,000 refugees—more than 500,000 of them Catholics—moved south. In addition "some 190,000 Franco-Vietnamese troops" joined the exodus south.[h] In the South, close to 80,000 local guerrillas, regulars, and dependents, including approximately 10,000 mountain tribesmen, proceeded north.[i]

The disparity between the two figures was generally interpreted at the time as a popular repudiation of communism by the population at large. In fact, this was an inappropriate conclusion since "the number of people going north was held to a small total by order of the Viet Minh [read: Dang Lao Dong] which wanted its sympathizers to remain in the south to prepare for the elections." [j] Fall estimates that the political/military elite of this force which simply "went underground" consisted of "perhaps" 5,000 to 6,000 hard core guerrillas. It may be presumed that these persons in turn dominated a considerably larger force of nonparty guerrillas whose number cannot be precisely estimated.[k] They hid their weapons and radio equipment and became anonymous villagers—at least for a while." [l] If the population movement strengthened the numerical size of the openly anti-Communist segment of the population in the South, then the exchange likewise enhanced the potential of the subversive forces in the South by moving dependents of the hard core north where they could not be molested by security forces. Equally important, the raw material from which to fashion additional "indigenous" cadres for later infiltration into the South was made available to authorities in Hanoi by the tens of thousands.

In the North, the immediate post-Geneva years—1955–1960—saw the elaboration of the conventional controls of a totalitarian state based upon patterns that had become all too familiar in other Communist takeovers in recent decades. In the South, policymakers were less clear as to the course to be pursued. Initially, Bao Dai as Chief of State formed a new government, with Ngo Dinh Diem as Prime Minister.

Relations between Bao Dai and his Prime Minister deteriorated rapidly. The conflict between them was resolved by a popular referendum in 1955 in which 98 percent of the population allegedly decided for the creation of a republic of which Diem became the first President. The existence of the Republic of Vietnam (RVN) was proclaimed on 26 October 1955.

President Diem first distinguished himself not by his efforts against indigenous communism but against yet other elements of internal opposi-

[h] "How the French Got Out of Viet-Nam," *New York Times Magazine*, 2 May 1965, reprinted in Marcus G. Raskin and Bernard B. Fall (eds.), *The Viet-Nam Reader: Articles and Documents on American Foreign Policy and the Viet-Nam Crisis* (New York: Vintage Books, 1965), p. 88. Robert Scheer, *How the United States Got Involved in Vietnam*, Report to the Center for the Study of Democratic Institutions (Santa Barbara, Calif.; 1965), p. 56, gives the figures of 679,000 Catholics and 200,000 dependents of the colonial native army.

[i] Fall, *The Viet-Nam Reader*. In his *The Two Viet-Nams*, p. 358, Fall gives a figure "close to 100,000." Scheer gives the figure of 150,000 refugees who moved to the North (*op. cit.*).

[j] Scheer, *op. cit.*

[k] Relevant to the matter of the numbers involved is the point made by David Halberstam, *The Making of a Quagmire* (New York: Random House, 1965), p. 36: "One of the real problems of SVN today is that a vast percentage of the vital, able people of the country became deeply involved with the Viet Minh before they realized the full extent of its Communist role; by the time they did, they were so far along that they remained committed to what was to become the Hanoi government in North Vietnam."

[l] Fall, "How the French Got Out of Vietnam," *op. cit.*

tion, a mélange of armed politico-religious sects, semifeudal leaders, and ambitious military officers. By late 1956, he had asserted himself over the insubordinate Chief of Staff of his army, over the military forces of the Cao Dai and Hoa Hao sects, and over the Mafia-like Binh Xuyen gangster bosses who initially controlled the Saigon police. Such accomplishments demanded tough, resolute leadership from Diem and this same will to rule expressed itself in the following years through an ever more pronounced hostility to political opposition in any form. Only those political combinations which were unequivocally pro-government were tolerated.

Diem was politically an autocrat and religiously a partisan of the Catholic element of the population, estimated to constitute only some 10 percent of the population. From this element, Diem drew his most reliable supporters. Many of his principal advisers and officials were Catholics who had only recently been transplanted to South Vietnam from North Vietnam during the 300 days of free movement provided for in the Geneva Accords. Such persons were unpopular among the southerners on two counts; they were both Catholics and "aliens." That they seemingly received preferential treatment only intensified local hostility to them.

In the light of the autocratic, even dictatorial practices pursued by Diem and his police, a very serious public debate has evolved over the nature and origins of the struggle in Vietnam in the 1960's and the role of the United States in it. Several of the major points of contention in this discussion necessarily bear directly upon the problems surveyed here. Critical among these are the following:

(1) May the initial phase of the insurgency movement in South Vietnam be understood as a spontaneous peasant protest against increasingly unjust and oppressive policies pursued by a national government and its provincial and lesser administrators without regard for the interests of the bulk of the citizenry? Or was it artificially provoked by persons who seized upon the theme of maladministration simply as a pretext to cover premeditated scheming?

(2) Is the Vietnamese insurgency distinctively "oriental" and understandable as one steeps himself in the history and thought of this region? Or is it simply one more example of a technique which has been equally effective in areas far removed from Asia?

(3) May it not be argued that, irrespective of the distinctive origins of the insurgency movement initially, it is today substantially little more than a liberal reform movement seeking no more than those personal civil rights which we Americans have long celebrated?

A number of answers have been suggested to those questions posed by the different schools of thought which have crystallized in the public arena. On one side are those who answer the first of the above questions by holding President Diem and the Ngo family of which he was a member responsible for the development of the insurgency. Diem is accused of having pursued increasingly reactionary and oppressive policies designed not to ameliorate the outstanding grievances of the peasants and others in Vietnam but to enhance his dictatorial controls over government and assure his longevity in office. As his efforts bore down upon the citizenry, so the argument continues, they were obliged to take up arms in self-defense and where the government persisted in its efforts to effect total control, this resistance progressively assumed more sophisticated organizational forms.

Those who take this stand on the first question tend to respond to the second of the above questions—that involving the distinctiveness of the Vietnamese insurgency—by identifying it varyingly as "oriental" or "oriental Communist," that is to say, a resistance movement based upon traditional Asiatic patterns as modified by Communists. In the first case, the role of the Communist Party in the insurgency is necessarily treated as marginal, the party being treated as little more than simply another participant in a partisan coalition whose policies take into account the interests of groups that are quite unmoved by Marxist ideology or Lenin's opportunistic adulteration of Marxism. Those who adjudge the movement to be a mélange of Asiatic and Communistic elements assign a considerably more prominent role to the Communist, who could be acknowledged as the architect of the movement's formal organization and might be identified as the ultimate welder of authority among the assembled insurgent forces. In this latter case, the Communist is frequently understood to have taken over a movement in whose initiation he played only a marginal role. Observers who identify themselves with this position are careful to distinguish between the Marxist party in the South, the People's Revolutionary Party (PRP), and the Communist organization in the North, the Dang Lao Dong (DLD) or Worker's Party. Considerable attention is given to the fact that the PRP came into being only in 1962, that is, well after the insurgency began seriously to escalate, and stress is placed upon the microscopic size of the organization, estimated to contain as few as 500 persons.

Irrespective of disagreement among the proponents of this stand as to the authority and size of the Communist elements, most of them tend to see the resultant organization and its organizational practices as heavily influenced by the distinctive norms and customs unique to that portion of the orient which historically evolved under the continuing influence of classical Chinese culture. Even though Mao Tse-tung and his colleagues may be recognized as significant innovators, still, it is argued, the origins of the patterns they further elaborated are to be sought in such population control techniques as the *pao chia* system of feudal China. This line of argument leads easily to the conclusion that insurgency as it has been known in China, Indochina, and, to a limited extent, in Korea is not exportable, except perhaps into immediately contiguous land areas, since it presupposes a population which is already culturally conditioned to the kinds of social patterns evolved by the dynasties of historic China and spread during the centuries into neighboring states and political dependencies.

From this point of view, the "falling domino" theory suggested by President Eisenhower [m] is meaningful only in the restricted geographic region of mainland Southeast Asia. Again, for persons of this persuasion the South Vietnam insurgency can *not* be a "test case," the winning of which would constitute a go-ahead to world communism for the building of comparable movements elsewhere about the globe. Consequently, to the extent that the local "Marxist Party," the PRP, is adjudged to be free of Hanoi's real control, one might sympathize with the suggestion that peace for South Vietnam can be based upon direct negotiations between the United States and the insurgents themselves in the South.

At the opposite pole in the Vietnam debate are those who (1) place the Vietnamese Communist Party organization at the center of the insurgency, (2) consider the label "PRP" as simply a convenient name for that portion of the DLD south of the 17th parallel, and (3) stress the similarities between the activities of the DLD/PRP complex, conceived of as a single entity, and those of other Communist parties around the globe. From within this frame of reference, the current insurgency in South Vietnam becomes simply one more example of an operational procedure which has been utilized by Communists in wide-flung world theaters in their attempts to seize the instruments of political power in nation states.

Despite their personal failings and inadequacies and the lack of balance in the policies they pursued, neither Diem and his younger brother Nhu, nor the bureaucracy through which they worked, according to this view, may be singled out as the "cause" of the insurgency. Positive accomplishments, if they fell short of the goals sought, nevertheless did counterbalance many of the weaknesses that plagued South Vietnam during the latter half of the 1950's and the early years of the present decade. To deal in personalities without due attention to the problems confronting the new government is to ignore the imposing limitations that narrowed the alternatives open to Diem and inhibited effective administration at the local level.

Among the principal difficulties that particularly hobbled government efforts among the peasantry, so this argument continues, the chief one was the existence throughout the eight years of Diem's government of the rural-based, subversive insurgent apparatus controlled from Hanoi. It quickly became apparent to the government that meaningful communications and the commencement of a positive dialogue between the administration and the citizenry could only come as the eventual payoff of internal security efforts. Diem assigned priority attention to issues of public security, allowing considerations of this character to figure, for example, in his population settlement and land redistribution programs. This does not mean that he had his heart set upon the suppression of individual liberty. On the contrary, it means that he conceived of himself from the very outset as being engaged in what would later be called counterinsurgency operations.

[m] At press conference, April 7, 1954.

Determined to maintain their strength in the South, the second argument continues, the North Vietnamese Communist leadership repeatedly denied to Diem the domestic tranquility he sought to establish. This left Diem with few alternatives. He could either accept the challenge from the North or permit the progressive takeover to continue by default. For the U.S. Government, the alternatives were equally narrow: support the efforts of Diem—who had demonstrated his will to fight against the premeditated subversion of his new country—or agree to yet another territorial extension of Communist authority (which would necessarily include Laos and Cambodia as well as South Vietnam, leaving aside the ultimate consequences that would follow from such a decision).

From this point of view, there was no moment during the 1950's when one could say that the insurgency in South Vietnam commenced, for the efforts at subversion were never discontinued. The Communists' drive for power received its initial militarized form in the course of World War II following the activation of the original Viet Minh. From that moment on, it was a sustained effort which was pursued on past the mid-1950's, with no regard for the Geneva Accords. Vietnam is indeed a "test case." The free world must hold; there is no choice to make at this point.

Emerging clearly from this analysis are two fundamental and opposite interpretations. Has the insurgency assumed forms unique to a Southeast Asian environment? "Yes," say many who assign heavy responsibility to the Diem regime. "No," say those who adjudge the insurgency to have been premeditated and who approach the problem from a background in the comparative study of Communist insurgencies elsewhere. Does it display the characteristics of a spontaneous movement of liberal protest? "Yes," answers the one group. Aside from the phenomenon of systematic assassination which was probably Communist in origin and premeditated in its intent, the initial disturbances suggest individual initiative on an uncoordinated basis in direct response to immediate provocation. "No," is the rejoinder. At no time in the 1950's may one legitimately declare that an insurgency "commenced" and, when it gradually began to assume more critical proportions in the later years of the decade, it was only responding to specific orders received from outside. Has the movement taken on more distinctively popular Vietnamese forms as it grows, relegating Communist influences, such as they are, to a subordinate position? "Yes," is the one answer. The insurgents' front, as the only major political force in the South free of authoritarian government controls, authentically reflects the will of a substantial portion of the Vietnamese citizenry. "No," say those who see the Communist Party as the author of the struggle; the party is as much in control now as it was in the middle of the decade.

Between these opposite poles there are, of course, a number of possible intermediate stands, and there are a variety of additional factors which may be drawn into the debate. Thus DLD domination of the insurgency in the South from the outset does not preclude acceptance of the thesis that this phenomenon was essentially "oriental" in character and not exportable to other distinctive regions of the world. Still others who assign primary responsibility to Hanoi for the escalation of the conflict, hold Diem to have been an unconscious accomplice of the DLD by engaging in ill-conceived, oppressive measures (e. g., the forced movement of population into "strategic hamlets") which enormously simplified the task before the Vietnamese Communists by driving the population into their arms.

Adding yet another dimension to the debate is the related polemic literature more immediately concerned with the tenability and legitimacy of our current commitment, military and otherwise, in Vietnam in the light of how the affair commenced and how we became involved. Only passing notice will be given here to this aspect of the problem, since this issue lies outside the bounds of the subject matter analyzed in this book. However, it is the present author's proper responsibility to alert the reader to his stand on those several issues treated above which necessarily affect the study.

The facts adduced from the available evidence and from among various and differing viewpoints have led to an interpretation which assigns an all-critical, pivotal role to the DLD. The present study is concerned with indicating (1) precisely what the DLD party organization is, and (2) how it was able "casually" to provoke a conflict which has now been in the process of escalating for nearly a decade.

Further, on the basis of a comparative analysis of Communist-dominated insurgencies elsewhere, the current struggle in South Vietnam is found to accord in all of its parts with principles that have historically figured prominently in insurgencies in totally unrelated cultural milieus. In pursuance of those conclusions the Vietnamese Communist (Workers') Party is not only placed at the center of the stage, but is adjudged to conform fully with the principles of organization and procedure which have obtained for other Communist parties around the world during the last five decades.

Considerable importance attaches to the fact that Diem, who was operating with a grossly inadequate administrative apparatus, was obliged to undertake the job of bringing order into a society near social and economic collapse. There existed in the South no organization under government direction which could compare with the cadre organization through which Communists could communicate with the local population. This fact looms large in an understanding of the course of later events and has not received adequate attention in the literature on the origins of the present insurgency in the South.

There could be no question during the Indochina War of building a rural pro-government civil apparatus because the French, who planned to return to the countryside, would have found such an apparatus to be in opposition to those plans. The Vietnamese Communists, for their part, were in the process of preparing for eventual rule from the very onset of the conflict and one of the essential characteristics of the insurgent process itself was the progressive building of their future administrative bureaucratic structure within the civil population as they fought.

The principle at issue here will be treated in greater detail later, but it is important to note that this preoccupation with the mundane matters of daily administration was not regarded by the insurgents as a matter to be taken up after victory, but rather as one of the principal means through which victory was to be achieved. The French, in contrast, gave only the most superficial attention to the development of an indigenous bureaucracy as a means of contending with their enemy. This followed from the very purpose that motivated their operations, namely, their desire for a military victory which would allow a French-oriented administration to reestablish itself in the interior. Military defeat and political withdrawal meant not only that there would be no French administration but also that many persons earmarked for such governmental functions after the war would necessarily become a major source of embarrassment to the new government if it even contemplated using them. Further, it meant that the new government, composed of persons who had had no voice in the formulation of strategy and who had been provided with no opportunity to activate a counteradministrative cadre with which to contend with the Lien Viet for the loyalty of the peasantry, had to begin almost from scratch.

The ill-fated Can Lao Nhan Vi Cach Mang Dang (Revolutionary Workers' Party), and other organizations associated with the Phong Trai Cach Mang Quoc Gia (National Revolutionary Movement), all creations of the regime of Diem and the Ngo family, are to be understood not as the agencies of a reactionary government set upon stamping out popular liberties but as post-Geneva attempts to respond to the challenge presented to the government by a Communist control apparatus which remained in place despite the determinations of the 20 July 1954 military accord for the pacification of Vietnam.

Though the controls exercised by the subversive cadre were not readily apparent in the ostensibly peaceful years of 1955 and 1956, they remained nevertheless real. And they were exercised over elements of a peasantry which had been shaken from its passivity by the ebb and flow of the combat and political agitation that had characterized the preceding decade. The peasantry had been alerted to injustices, once largely tolerated although recognized, and to governmental indifference to local needs. The cohesive social units of an earlier epoch had broken down. In extensive regions of the South, the nórms of the past lost their attractiveness, while the failure of the Central Government to communicate meaningfully with the village and hamlet population encouraged the Vietnamese's anarchical proclivities [n] and inhibited the growth of new loyalties upon which an alternate, stable order could be built.

In periodizing the era of post-Geneva insurgency in the South, the level of organizational sophistication of the movement during any given time

[n] Malcolm W. Browne has written in *The New Face of War* (New York: Bobbs-Merrill Co., 1965), p. 186, "The Indochina area is an essentially lawless corner of the earth, never more than a step or two away from complete anarchy. Successive governments in Saigon (including those of the French colonial regime) have never controlled the Vietnamese people in a very effective way. Even at this writing, various American experts estimate that nearly one-tenth of the nation's population has probably never experienced any control from Saigon."

frame provides a highly useful means of distinguishing one phase of the struggle from the next. Proceeding from such criteria, three basic periods can be identified. Since one is dealing here with the resurgence of activity as opposed to its commencement, the first period dates from 1954 to 1959/1960 when evidence indicates a markedly stepped-up level of interest by the North in the subversion underway in the South. As Bernard Fall has noted, during this time the insurgency operated "as simply an extension of the then-existing Communist underground apparatus." [o]

The Third Congress of the Lao Dong Party (September 1960) occurred during the early stages of the second period of development. By that date substantive steps had been taken to provide the insurgent effort with a new structural form. During the Congress, Hanoi openly announced its intention to involve itself directly in the conflict "to liberate South Vietnam." This task was declared to be "a protracted, hard, and complex process of struggle, combining many forms of struggle of great activity and flexibility, ranging from lower to higher, and taking as its basis the building, consolidation, and development of the revolutionary power of the masses." [p] Concurrently, preparations were well underway for the activation of the Mat Tran Dan-toc Giai-phong Mien-Nam (The National Front of the Liberation of South Vietnam, or NFLSVN). Arrangements for this event were assigned to the North Vietnamese Fatherland Front which coordinated mass work and "popular" drives for Hanoi party authorities and operated under the supervision of Hoang Quoc Viet, a key Central Committee member of the Dang Lao Dong. (The Fatherland Front made its announcement of the front's existence on 20 December 1960.[q])

The last of the three periods, the one currently developing, dates from 1965. It is characterized by the heavy injection of major troop units of the North Vietnamese Army into South Vietnam, and by the stepped-up involvement of the United States in a counterinsurgent role. The organizational complex through which the party-dominated insurgency was prosecuted had reached its most elaborate form by the onset of the present phase of conflict. Evidence suggests that by early 1966, this structure—the subject of detailed analysis in the present study—was in the process of devolving into simpler forms necessary to survival in the current tactical environment. The effectiveness of the organization's operations at both the political and military levels, however, remained high.

Critical to the first period of the insurgency, 1954–1959/60, is the year 1957. In a periodization of the era not resting primarily upon organizational criteria, this year could serve as the moment of transition to a second phase of conflict. Terrorism and assassination calculated to isolate

---

[o] *The Two Viet-Nams*, p. 355.

[p] U.S. Department of State. Publication 7839 (Far Eastern Series 130), *Aggression From the North: The Record of North Viet-Nam's Campaign to Conquer South Viet-Nam* (Washington, D. C.: Bureau of Public Affairs, February 1965), p. 20.

[q] Fall (*The Two Viet-Nams*), in an alternate periodization, extends the first period to December 1960, presumably because of the formation of the NFLSVN. By this time, however, fundamental organizational modifications were already underway.

the population progressively from contact with government commenced in the latter portion of 1956 (once it was clear that the national elections, scheduled for July, would not occur in the South), and reached alarming proportions by 1957.[r] From this juncture on into the early sixties the number of assassinations would continue to increase each year.

During the second period, 1960–1965, all of the forms of activity which had commenced earlier continued unabated, increasingly in conjunction with large-scale guerrilla operations calculated to destroy opposing military units. To celebrate the successes of the armed units during this period Hanoi finally published in 1965 an English-language volume describing the battles at Ap Bac, Hiep Hoa, Chala, and elsewhere.[s]

Also during this period came the announcement, made in Hanoi, 1 January 1962, that the Marxists-Leninists in South Vietnam had joined together to form a new party to be known as the Dang Nhan-Dan Cach Mang (People's Revolutionary Party, or PRP). Supposedly this was an entirely new body. Its entry into the NFLSVN as a member association was to be understood as a collective decision by the Communist-oriented residents in the South now finally to band together and take up an active role in the conflict as a way of responding, once and for all, to the endless provocations engineered by the repressive Diem regime. In point of fact the PRP was simply the name to be employed henceforth by that element of the Dang Lao Dong operating south of the 17th parallel.[t] The use of this term was to be understood in no way as reflecting any organizational innovation not already planned for during the 1959–60 transitional period. The sole motivation for this step was the desire to strengthen yet further the fiction underlying the creation of the NFLSVN—namely, that insurgency in the South was spontaneous, genuinely indigenous in its membership, and representative of the will of the population at large. By acting as if the PRP were native grown rather than an extension across political borders of a totalitarian cadre organization, it presumably would further demonstrate the independence of the insurgency from foreign influences. That this was in fact the purpose behind the 1962 announcement was nowhere more clearly indicated than in a set of instructions from the provincial party committee of Ba Xuyen Province to its district committees, dated 7 December 1961. The text reads as follows:

> To D2 and K,
>
> In regard to the foundation of the People's Revolutionary Party of South Viet-Nam, the creation of this party is only a matter of strategy; it needs

[r] The correlation between incidents of subversion in the South and Hanoi's demonstrable ability to pinpoint, geographically, the areas in which they occurred during the first half of this period has been treated by Bernard Fall in an essay of 1958, reprinted in his *Viet-Nam Witness, 1953–66* (New York: Frederick A. Praeger, 1966), pp. 172, 184. He concludes from a comparison of actual locations in the South where rebel activity had occurred and the areas identified in Communist complaints to the International Commission regarding alleged violations of the civil rights of "former resistance members" that the information available to Hanoi was of such a precise nature that it could only have been acquired through "Viet Minh agents who have remained behind in the South after the armistice or who have been infiltrated into the area since." The coordination of the rebels with Hanoi, he concluded, is inescapable.

[s] Le Hong Linh *et al. Ap Bac: Major Victories of the South Vietnamese Patriotic Forces in 1963 and 1964* (Hanoi: Foreign Languages Publishing House, 1965).

[t] On this point, see further, Fall, *The Two Viet-Nams*, p. 357.

to be explained within the party; and, to deceive the enemy, it is necessary that the new party be given the outward appearance corresponding to a division of the party (Lao Dong) into two and the foundation of a new party, so that the enemy cannot use it in his propaganda. (For the rest of the text of this document, see appendix I, doc. I–5.)

Organizationally, the structure erected by the close of the second phase of the insurgency contained three major component elements: (1) civil organization, the NFLSVN, (2) a composite of armed units of varying competence and size, and (3) the increasingly able PRP. Of these three elements, the party apparatus remained the decisive channel of organization, as it had been earlier when only the prototypes of the additional echelons could be dimly perceived. From it proceeded direction, control, and supervision. Only within its councils could policy be made and strategy planned.

Formally, the PRP was structured after the fashion of a hierarchy, with committees at the village, district, province, and interprovincial or regional levels. At the base, clusters of cells functioned under the control of village committees with direction and control at the national level provided from without by the Political Bureau (Po Chinh Tri Trung-Uong), and the Secretariat (Ban Bi Thu) of the Central Committee of the Dang Lao Dong ultimately working within South Vietnam through the "Central Office for South Vietnam" (Trung-Uong Cuc Mien Nam) allegedly located in Tay Ninh Province to the north of Saigon, close to the Cambodian border.

If, in the late 1950's, the demands upon administrative know-how and tactical adaptability had indeed been high in the conduct of such party activities as espionage, open political agitation, the penetration of critical offices and organizations, and the conduct of terrorism and assassination, then the type of apparatus required to sustain those earlier activities had been relatively simple. It could consist of little more than the above described committee system and such agencies as agent handlers, strong-arm squads, and agitation propaganda personnel. In this form, the initially skeletal structure, well established only in restricted areas of the south, had fleshed out both in membership and administrative competence. However, once the extensive utilization of guerrillas had been determined upon, even in the counterpart field of political work, greater and more urgent effort had to be expended to induce broad elements of the population to participate in and to lay the foundations for a future, party-controlled alternate government and administration. While the exact organizational interrelationships of the three parallel structures—party, civil, and military—vary in detail from one insurgency to the next, their general interrelation, not only in Vietnam, but elsewhere as well tend to remain uniform. Schematically, this typical insurgent structure may be as shown in chart 2.

This stylized disposition of forces may be utilized with equal ease in the study of a number of Communist-dominated insurgencies. It becomes specifically applicable to South Vietnam if the central committee and its immediate staff agencies are understood to be situated in Hanoi and an additional vertical level of administration and control is inserted in all three hierarchies at the interprovincial or regional level, above the province-level bodies.

Clearly, such a structure will never appear full-blown at the outset of the guerrilla conflict. It can be evolved only gradually, spreading from one party-dominated area to another and from lower levels of organization to higher as the insurgent effort meets with success. Throughout, as chart 2 suggests, the party retains ultimate authority at all times by building the newly activated extra-party bodies around elements of the old "peacetime" organization which are detached from their parent unit for this purpose, or—in the immediate case of South Vietnam—sent south from "regroupment" in the North during the 300-day period of free movement provided for at Geneva.

Chronologically, the development of the lower levels in the hierarchy evolved in the following fashion:

(1) Activists from the "peacetime" party organization are dispatched to rural areas seldom frequented by government representatives where they are subjected to paramilitary training and incorporation into a regional unit.

(2) Propaganda organizers of the party are dispatched to villages/hamlets to take up residence among the peasantry and begin agitation against the national and local government.

(3) Small-scale operations are launched against rural security/administrative authorities; there are displays of strength, supported by the beginning of terrorism and assassination in villages.

(4) Intensification of agitation in villages, exploiting popular grievances and/or local apprehension provoked by military operations and terrorism; organization of village population into manageable mass organizations (i.e., peasant unions, youth groups, sports groups, women's groups, etc.) or the reactivation and strengthening of organizations where they exist at a low level of development or have fallen into neglect.

(5) Recruitment of villagers to join regional military unit, progressively expanding its size and firepower.

(6) Expanding tactical operations leading to the military domination, i.e., "liberation" of significant areas and forcing withdrawal of existing security and administrative elements to major towns, amounting to the de facto surrender of local control to the insurgents by default.

(7) Conduct of party-controlled, local elections in areas where the rural population has been drawn into mass organizations. Creation of rebel civil administration at local, district, etc., levels known as "liberation committees."

(8) Activation of battalions and regiment-sized armed units, drawing upon the organized peasants who are now subject to a "draft" by the "elected" civil government.

(9) Withdrawal of seasoned combatants from regional forces to activate main operational forces under the direct command of higher party bodies.

(10) In urban areas where the party organization can only function clandestinely, expansion of the undercover apparatus, intensification of mass organizational work, distribution of leaflets, rumor campaigns, and penetration of critical offices and installations.

Important to this process is (1) the role played by the armed forces in the elaboration of civil organizations, and (2) the critical role played by

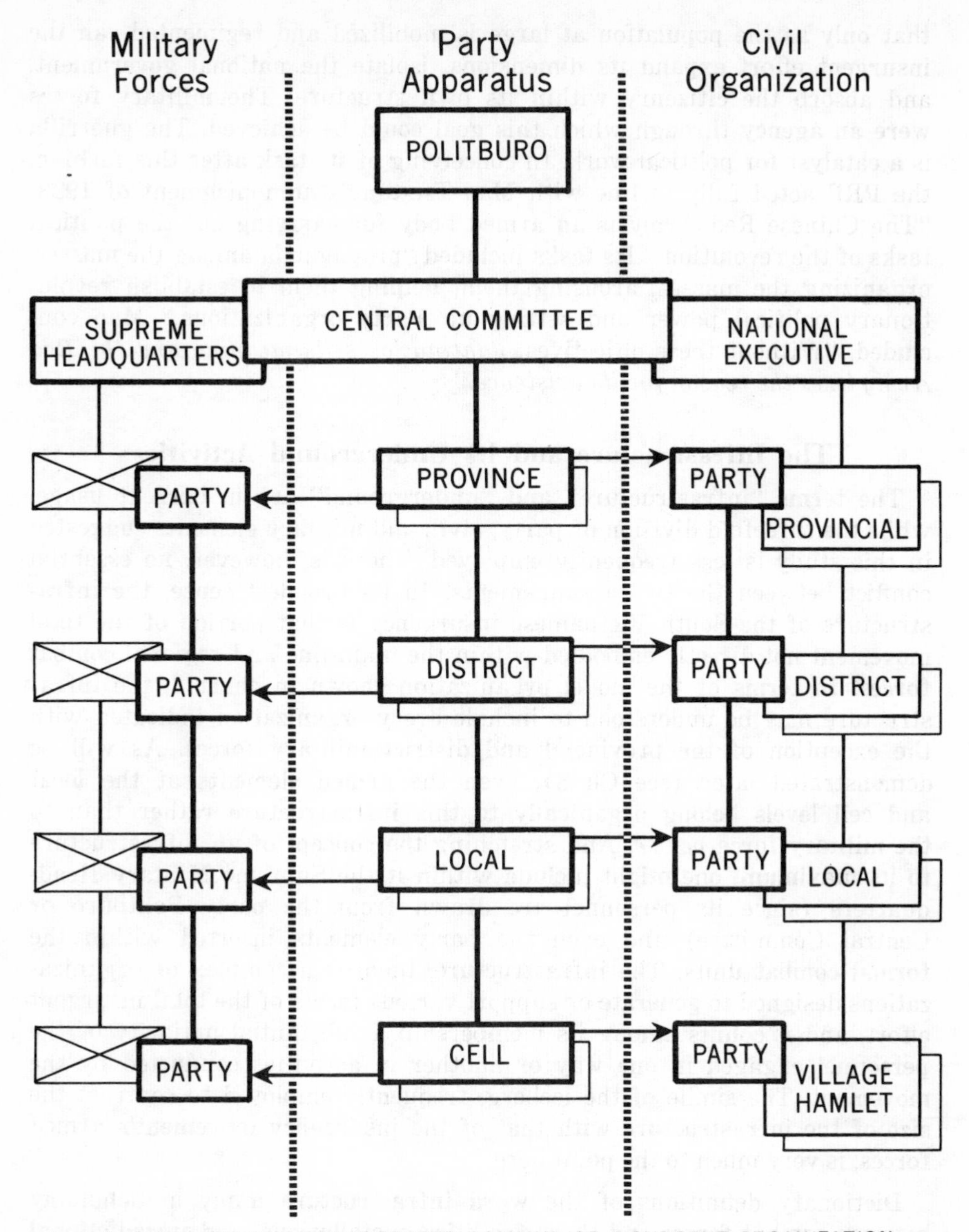

Chart 2. MODEL OF FULLY ELABORATED COMMUNIST INSURGENT ORGANIZATION

the latter structures in mobilizing the rural population to meet the needs of the combatant element. From the organized peasantry came recruits as well as intelligence and multiple forms of logistical support. It was the task of the party apparatus to initiate, accelerate, and carefully supervise this process, assuring itself that the military element duly appreciated that fighting was not an end in itself but a further means of increasing political/organizational work. It remained the party's firm conviction that only as the population at large is mobilized and regimented can the insurgent effort expand its dimensions, isolate the national government, and absorb the citizenry within its own structure. The military forces were an agency through which this goal could be achieved. The guerrilla is a catalyst for political work. In conceiving of its task after this fashion, the PRP acted fully in line with Mao Tse-tung's admonishment of 1928: "The Chinese Red Army is an armed body for carrying out the political tasks of the revolution." Its tasks included "propaganda among the masses, organizing the masses, arousing them, helping them to establish revolutionary political power and setting up Party organizations." Mao concluded, "Without these objectives, *fighting loses its meaning and the Red Army loses the reason for its existence.*" [14]

The Infrastructure and Its Underground Activities

The terms "infrastructure" and "underground" are in current usage, while the threefold division of party, civil, and military elements suggested in this study is less frequently employed. There is, however, no essential conflict between the two arrangements. In its broadest sense, the infrastructure of the South Vietnamese insurgency is that portion of the total movement not directly embodied within the main-line and regional combat forces. In terms of the model organization shown in chart 2, the infrastructure may be understood to include every organization indicated with the exception of the provincial and district military forces. As will be demonstrated later (see Ch 8), even the armed elements at the local and cell levels belong organically to this infrastructure rather than to the military force *per se*. And stretching the concept of an infrastructure to its maximum, one might include within it the Supreme Military Headquarters (since its personnel are drawn from the party Politburo or Central Committee) and even the party elements inserted within the formal combat units. The infrastructure, then, is a complex of organizations designed to generate or support various facets of the total insurgent effort, and it counts among its membership a substantial majority of the personnel engaged in one way or another in activities conducted by the movement. The simile of the iceberg, frequently employed to contrast the size of the infrastructure with that of the insurgency movement's armed forces, is very much to the point here.

Dictionary definitions of the word infrastructure imply a dichotomy between combat forces and those facilities, installations, and jurisdictional arrangements requisite to both the support and the control of combat units. In its military usage the unit commander may use the term as a loose designation for the operational procedures and structure which back him up and provide him with direction in the performance of his mission. In the NATO structure, where the term has enjoyed particular currency, it refers to (1) all fixed and permanent installations, fabrica-

[14] "On Correcting Mistaken Ideas in the Party," *Selected Military Writings of Mao Tse-tung* (Peking: Foreign Languages Press, 1963), p. 52. (Emphasis added.)

tions, and facilities required for the training or implementation of NATO operational plans, and (2) the agreements for their mutual financing.[v]

The use of such a word may seem out of place in the descriptive terminology for an insurgency where fixed or permanent installations are infrequent. Indeed, both the appearance and procedures utilized by an insurgency's infrastructure will be radically different from those of NATO. However, if one concentrates on function and purpose, it becomes apparent that the noncombatant organizational complex identified above—as viewed through the eyes of the guerrillas operating at the district, provincial, or higher level—satisfies precisely the same need that the infrastructure of NATO fills with respect to its combat forces. Both are the source of support and control. They differ from one another in the means employed to perform those functions because of the dramatically dissimilar environments in which they operate. Where in the case of NATO the word support evokes images of steamship docking facilities and railway switching centers, applied to an insurgency it refers to the backs of the peasant porters and the political mobilization work of agitation/propaganda cadre in villages. Control, instead of proceeding through SHAPE and the appropriate joint command center down through the unit command structure, flows from the party Politburo and Central Committee down through the party committee system to the cells within the guerrilla forces.

In the case of an insurgency, where one is dealing with a very large body of people (well in excess of a million in Vietnam), it is clear that the infrastructure is not and cannot be a uniformly covert, hidden complex. The simile of the iceberg ceases to be applicable at this juncture. The small party organization embedded within the numerically much larger extra-party components of the infrastructure will indeed seek to avoid the limelight and act in accordance with the principles of clandestine existence, but it would be unrealistic to expect similar behavior from untrained, nonparty participants. Among the latter, secrecy becomes important only when security becomes tenuous. In areas militarily dominated by the insurgency, the infrastructure acts openly. When the military presence declines, an increasing premium is placed on covert behavior. Since survival and effectiveness in the latter case presupposes training, the percentage of experienced cadre utilized increases as local security becomes more uncertain, and the role assigned newly won extra-party elements of the infrastructure becomes more passive.

In this context, there is no conflict between the concept "infrastructure" and discussion of insurgent organization in terms of the threefold division previously introduced. The term is useful and will be employed in the text of the following chapters where appropriate. However, it will be used sparingly when it is necessary to deal in specifics. While it may serve as a label for every phase of insurgent activity (short of small-unit tactics), encompassing the work of a substantial number of people, the term is

---

[v] The Joint Chiefs of Staff, (JCS Publ. 1) Dictionary of United States Military Terms for Joint Usage (JD), Washington, D. C., 1 December 1964, pp. 22, 33, 72, 97.

inherently inadequate where precision of identification is sought. In such situations the threefold division of insurgent structure commends itself as a more useful conceptual framework.

The work "underground" as frequently employed in free-world literature on unconventional forms of conflict as a synonym for the word "infrastructure," as defined here. Such usage is appropriate, provided that one is entirely clear about the manner in which the terms are being employed. Unfortunately, the word may get in the way of an adequate understanding of the phenomenon under analysis here for either of two reasons. First, an underground is frequently understood to be a "clandestine" conspiratorial organization. Insurgency, in the hands of professionals, is most assuredly conspiratorial but, while characterized by the organizational complexity of its infrastructure, *that infrastructure is not uniformly clandestine.* Consequently the use of the word underground may encourage a conceptual error, not of a peripheral character, but critical to the subject at hand. Second, the term is employed to identify covert resistance organizations such as those that operated in western and northern Europe during World War II; but these were not insurgencies.

Because such distinctions frequently are not drawn, one is encouraged to avoid possible confusion by avoiding the word. In this study a compromise is employed. The phrase "to engage in underground activities" will be used, but the various groups so involved will not be referred to collectively as "the underground." Instead, the author will speak of the "infrastructure" of the insurgency. Where a broad reference is made to underground activities, it will indicate involvement in any of a complex of activities of a psychological, societal, economic, political, or administrative character.

Strategy and the Uniqueness of the Case

The party leadership views the entire era of protracted conflict as a relentless series of cycles during which the insurgent moves from a defensive posture calculated to prevent the destruction of his forces—civil and party, as well as military—to counterattack his opponent once the level of intensity of the latter's thrust has declined. The time consumed in any given cycle may vary from a span of days, where the forces involved are primarily tactical military units, to periods of many months where conceived in terms of the entire insurgent structure's response to any given major counterinsurgent challenge. Because of the multifaceted character of the activities in which the insurgent organization engages during any given defensive or offensive—involving unconventional and nonmilitary efforts for which the opponent may well be unprepared—the structure's leadership believes that the disparity of forces on the opposing sides will progressively change in favor of the subversive organization. Ultimately, this trend of events will permit the insurgents to instigate a general uprising in urban centers which will reach its climax in the seizure of political power in the capital, Saigon.

Any given offensive becomes a mass drive. It will engage the maximum possible number of persons in the most varied kinds of activities, and it will be conceived of as a blending of multiple parallel efforts calculated, in combination, to achieve a predetermined set of tactical goals at the military, political, societal, and economic levels. On the defensive, strategy may likewise call for equally distinctive operations involving tricks, ruses, new stratagems and the movement or reassignment of personnel, but it can also include the restructuring of the insurgent organization itself or the interjection of fresh forces from abroad. Altogether conscious of the demonstrated survival capabilities of its clandestine cellular structure, the party may abandon its more complex committee system in any given area in favor of this more basic organization as one phase of a specific operation. Simultaneously, additional elements of the North Vietnamese National Army, PAVN, may be infiltrated to "up the ante." Both of these options are open to the insurgent leadership and must be understood as characteristics of its response to the counterinsurgent at midpoint in the 1960's.

As in the case of the offensive, the defensive may extend over a considerable span of time. Strategically, the time interval may last several years featuring possibly a series of lesser multifaceted tactical offensives as components of a preeminently defensive stance. The disposition of military forces at the commencement of 1966 suggested the onset of precisely such an era for the Communist insurgents in South Vietnam which might extend indefinitely into the future. In such a milieu, all of the insurgent's "weapons systems" would remain "go," but along with a possible devolution simpler, or more thoroughly clandestine, organizational forms, an increasing prominence would be assigned to the reported 30,000 to 50,000 political and propaganda (agitprop) forces available to the movement's leadership.[w]

If an insurgent organization such as that in South Vietnam seems highly distinctive from a Western point of view—with its parallel party, civil and military echelons, each, in turn, recognizing further structural bifurcations—then it is a matter of importance to stress that when the current model operative in Indochina is compared with the other Communist insurgent organizations which have preceded it during the last thirty years, it is found to have contributed nothing new to the Communist storehouse of experience above the most trivial tactical level. The Vietnamese experience is not distinctive from the Communist's point of view. Neither the party organization itself, the distinctive organizational practices it follows, the subsidiary organizations it has set up, nor the conceptual framework it has pursued in evolving its forces and in contending with the constituted government of Vietnam for the political control of South Vietnam may be understood as unique in any sense. In prosecuting its subversion of South Vietnam, the Dan Lao Dong has introduced no combat

---

[w] Slavko N. Bjelajac, "A Design for Psychological Operations in Vietnam," *Orbis: A Quarterly Journal of World Affairs*, X, No. 1 (Spring 1966), p. 126.

techniques, operational procedures, or political concepts which are not already known from previous Communist attempts to export subversive insurgency. My investigation of the open literature produced by Communists during the first five decades of our century leads me to conclude that the precedents and the rationale for all of the activities promoted by the current insurgent organization in South Vietnam can be identified in the past. Vietnam, then, is not the occasion for the beginning of a new type of warfare; it is, rather, the classic synthesis of a system of organizational principles and operational procedures evolved prior to the sixties.

In the following pages, each of the three major echelons of organization discussed above will be examined closely. Both the civil components of the National Liberation Front and the movement's armed forces must receive the most serious attention. Neither of these echelons of organization can be placed in proper perspective, however, until the character of the party itself is firmly grasped. Consequently, an analysis of the party precedes the investigation of both the civil and armed or military wings of the insurgent organization, and these latter two bodies are understood, literally, as projections of the party apparatus itself.

CHAPTER 2

THE INTERPROVINCIAL PARTY COMMITTEE AND THE STRATEGIC GOALS OF ITS STAFF AGENCIES

SUMMARY

In the early days of the insurgency movement, the Dang Lao Dong drew up the blueprint for a territorial party hierarchy in the South in competition with the legal South Vietnamese Government. At the highest level of the Communist Party structure an alleged National Congress of Representatives and a Central Executive Committee were said to exist. Beneath the national level, the territory of South Vietnam was divided into five interprovincial commands, and under these bodies the party provided for provincial commands, district and town commands, and finally the basic party units at the local level.

This hierarchic structure was an actual reality in the South by the mid-1960's except at the national level. The interprovincial commands were responsible to no mythical South Vietnamese "National Congress," but rather to the Central Office for South Vietnam (COSVN), an agency of the Communist North Vietnamese central committee's "Reunification Department," located in Hanoi.

Prior to March 1962 South Vietnam had been divided into two interzones —each responsible directly to an agency of the central committee of the Dang Lao Dong. During that month they were made into a single operational headquarters known as the Central Office for South Vietnam (COSVN). The COSVN remained under the control of the DLD, and supervision over it was exercised through the central committee's reunification department. At the next lower level were the five strengthened interprovincial zones and the special Saigon-Gia Dinh organization.

Supposedly these interprovincial bodies consisted of party members selected by the chosen electors of provincial bodies which, in turn, exercised their authority as a result of the decision of district, village, and hamlet party chapters. In line with this contention the summit of the organization above the interprovincial committees was declared to be the national congress of representatives of the PRP and its central executive committee. In fact, no nationwide meeting of PRP members had ever taken place. The regional or interprovincial committees were responsible to COSVN. The provincial committees, in turn, were under the complete control of the interprovincial committees, and the provincial committees, in their turn, controlled the district committees, which ultimately dominated the activities of the basic party units. Schematically, the national party structure may be represented in the manner shown in chart 3.

At each level of organization beneath COSVN itself, the committees contained at best three critical party elements (not including the military structure which will be treated in Part Three: The Military Organization):

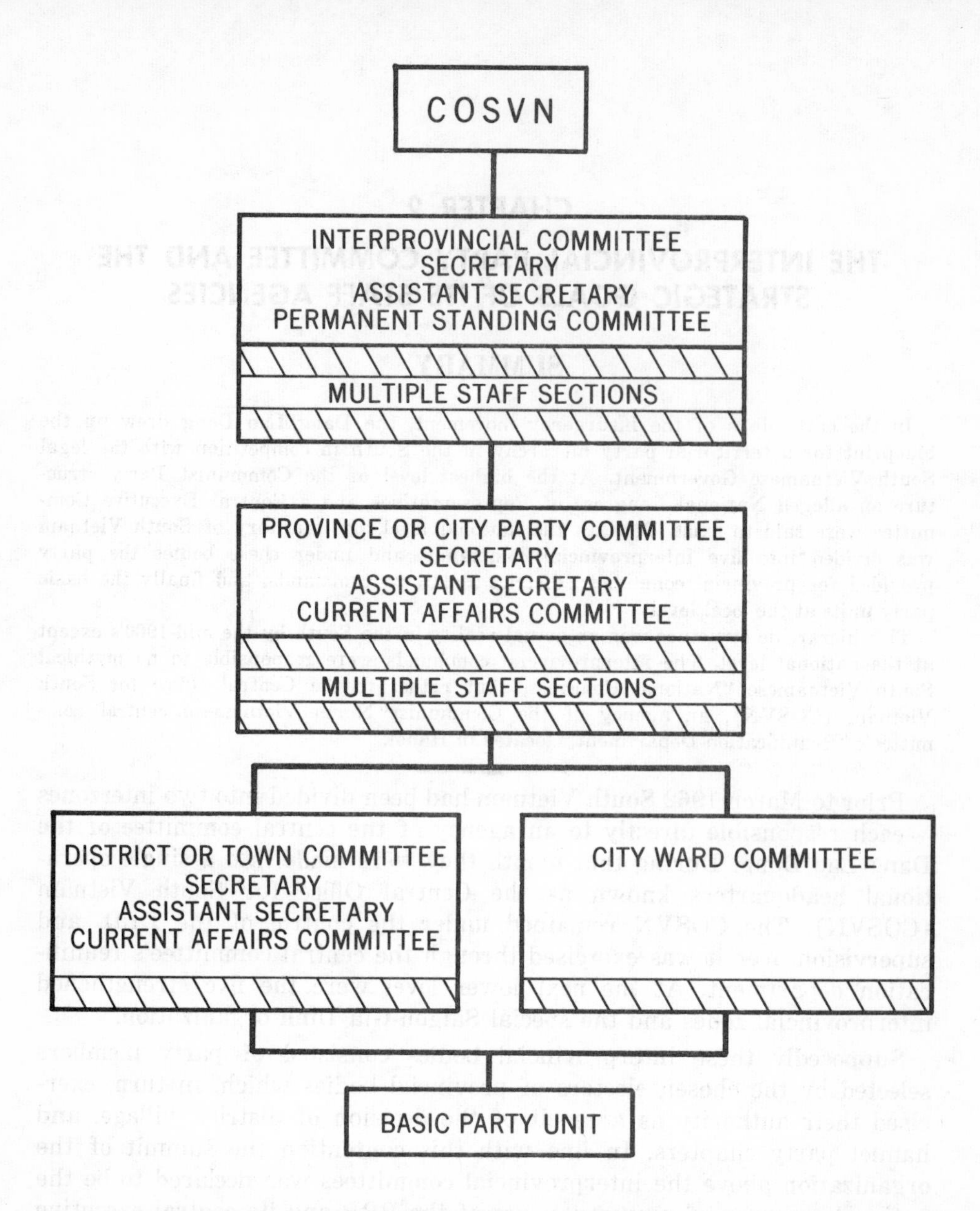

Chart 3. HIERARCHICALLY STRUCTURED COMMITTEE (BUREAUCRATIC) SYSTEM OF THE VIETNAMESE COMMUNISTS IN THE SOUTH

namely, a secretary and his assistant, a current affairs or permanent standing committee, and a system of staff offices and agencies. This structure was most complex at the interprovincial level and our detailed analysis will begin there.

The Fifth Interprovincial PRP Commissariat

The evolution of the Fifth Interprovincial Party Committee was characteristic. During the late 1950's, a skeletal organization of hard-core party members provided direction and control for the embryonic provincial and district committees. This group was headed by a cadre of the DLD party with membership in that body's central committee. Though one member of this group held the rank of colonel in the North Vietnamese Army, the role assigned to these men was essentially a political one.

By late 1960, the permanent standing committee of the Fifth Interprovincial Party Committee—a body of approximately nine members headed by a secretary general, an assistant secretary, and a routine affairs officer—controlled a group of about 150 men. Some 30 party members assigned to the Fifth Interprovincial Party Committee were deployed throughout the territory as provincial and district party committee first secretaries. The remaining personnel were assigned to the staff and administrative offices under the standing committee, providing that body with practically the entire complement of agencies through which it would still be operating five years later. Prominent among these agencies were the following bodies: the administrative branch, the communications and liaison element, the intelligence/security apparatus, medical and dispensary facilities, the training and propaganda agency, the enemy troop and civilian propaganda section, and the economics agency.

The Administrative Branch

The administrative branch of the Fifth Interprovincial Committee was headed by an alternate member of the central committee of the DLD and it translated the instructions issued by the permanent standing committee into directives sent out to provincial committees and other subordinate agencies.

The Communications and Liaison Element

The importance of this aspect of insurgent activities was asserted in a DLD statment to its courier and liaison personnel:

> The party's communications and liaison network is similiar to the blood vessels of a man. If the blood vessels stop the man will die. If communications and liaison stop, the party's work will come to a standstill.

To assure the success of communications a complex of procedures and institutional arrangements was established and the relationship between contacting agencies was made a matter of formal regulation. Detailed stipulations governed the activities of courier and protection personnel, from attire and comportment and the extent of their knowledge to the routes to be employed and the weaponry to be used. Once on the move, travel "must be minutely scheduled. Anything wrong in this schedule should put the cadre at home on guard against the capture of the cadre concerned by the enemy." Some of these rules were as follows:

> At least 2 routes should be available at all times. A permanent station must exist while other stations should be separated from each other.
>
> Prior to each departure, the liaison agents who guide cadre must see to it that the cadre are well informed of the route and prepared to take action against any emergency that may arise.

During travel, the names of rivers, mountains, and local areas should not be disclosed to the cadre. Materials such as nylon, cigarette butts, papers, etc., should not be thrown out along the route so that its position will not be disclosed to the enemy. When arriving near a station, the turning point of the route should be kept secret.

Further, the DLD provided itself with limited means of telecommunications, and broadcasts directed at the South Vietnamese citizenry were exploited for use as a cover for the transmission of DLD orders.

Building gradually, as personnel and experience increased, the administration branch of the Fifth Interprovincial Committee came to exercise direct control over the courier system and to play a supervisory role over the radio and crypto sections which encoded, decoded, and broadcast radio messages. Additionally, the administrative branch supported the related work of a parallel committee agency, known as the "control of infiltration routes" section, which supervised reception centers and all liaison stations situated along Infiltration Route No. 1 (the Ho Chi Minh Trail) in coordination with the Fifth Military Region Headquarters. This led to the administrative branch's involvement in such responsibilities as establishing new routes or closing old ones, as the tactical situation required; keeping abreast of current passwords and cover designations; developing procedures for issuing movement papers; keeping up to date on the status of personnel and supplies due in from the North; and maintaining rations for transient personnel.

The Intelligence/Security Apparatus

The security specialists in the territory of the Fifth Interprovincial Committee were trained in the rules of clandestine behavior: they were taught how to set up a secret rendezvous; they were instructed to move their contact centers at the first suggestion that a party member had been captured; and they were warned against any act of haste in approaching former commanders who were released from prison or claimed to have successfully escaped. Compartmentalization figured large in security regulations governing the life of the cadre.

He does not pose questions, speak, or find out by curiosity what he does not need to know. He should be determined not to read or talk about anything which does not have a direct relationship to his work. In the event he encounters a comrade who talks to him about something which he need not know, he should stop the cadre and remind him of the security principles.

The Communists relied upon the potential of the civil population, mobilized through mass associations, to alleviate material needs, generate combat recruits, and to serve as a mass informer network. In the light of the type of warfare conducted by an insurgent organization, the movement's leadership reasoned, "the enemy's eyes and ears can be covered only if the people are thoroughly trained in preserving secrecy; only in this way can the party's agencies and cadre be covert."
One party training pamphlet actually went so far as to define the word counterespionage" as—

consisting of basic education making our own people and the rest of the people aware of the enemy's goals, consolidating ties between the party and the people, training the people to enforce security measures, and urging the people to uncover spies who try to collect intelligence and win our cadres over to their side.

In training the people, cadres should remain composed, never panic, be neither pessimistic nor subjective, and insist on a security enforcement policy.

In the Fifth Interprovincial Committee, such efforts were the responsibility of the five-man security section, which later expanded into two major elements, a counterintelligence section and a physical security section. The first of these two agencies, in addition to performing traditional counterintelligence functions, including traffic control, was directly involved in the characteristic totalitarian practice of thought control. It reported on the political utterances of party members and villagers, paying special attention to the ideology and political viewpoints expressed by personnel from the Fifth Interprovincial Committee assigned to subordinate agencies. The physical security section, in contradistinction, was designed to exploit the successes which came with improved thought control. Its task was twofold: to develop intelligence networks utilizing the local peasantry, and to participate, along with local party personnel, in the development of civil defenses against the penetration of hostile military forces. To encourage vigilance throughout this structure, interprovincial and COSVN inspection teams moved periodically into the general zones to examine the work of district and village committees. While very much concerned with the enforcement of security regulations, these bodies would also investigate concurrent programs initiated by fiat from above.

The Medical and Dispensary Facilities

The Fifth Interprovincial Committee originally controlled medical personnel and a dispensary in 1960. By 1961, the party's military forces had evolved sufficiently to make the transfer of administrative responsibility to the armed element feasible. The dispensary and its associated specialists came under the control of the logistics division of the Fifth Military Region Headquarters.

Finally, and this was of considerable importance to the future intensification of insurgency, three additional offices evolved under the standing committee of the Interprovincial, two of them in 1960, and the third in 1961 as the efforts of the first two began to pay off by substantially strengthening the party's controls over the surrounding civil population. The two agencies of 1960 were the training and propaganda (T&P) agency and the enemy troop and civilian propaganda (ETCP) section; the third, developed in 1961, was the economics agency.

The Training and Propaganda Agency[a]

The training and propaganda agency generated propaganda and con-

[a] For a detailed Vietnamese Communist description of the complete training and propaganda structure in South Vietnam, from the COSVN down to the village and hamlet level, see appendix E, doc. E-1. (In this authentic document, the training and propaganda apparatus is identified by the alternate name of the "Propaganda-Indoctrination" organization.)

ducted political and ideological indoctrination and party training courses. The leaflets and pamphlets put out by this section attempted to popularize statements and appeals allegedly issued by the National Front for the Liberation of South Vietnam (NFLSVN).

In its capacity as the conscience and trainer of the party membership, this section "reeducated" those party members whose orthodoxy had been found wanting. It was to this section that provincial committees would turn for "technical guidance . . . on matters pertaining to propaganda." It also maintained a formal training school and carried on a continuing study of RVN propaganda, distributed magazines and posters, and made motion pictures. The training and propaganda section of the Fifth Interprovincial Party Committee completed a lengthy documentary film showing the course of a military action which occurred in Quang Nam Province in 1961.

It also summarized the reports coming from the party's offices in the several provinces and other subordinate agencies in bulletins specifically designed for general news release via radio.

The Enemy Troop and Civilian Propaganda Section[b]

In contrast to the training and propaganda branch the enemy troop and civilian propaganda (ETCP) branch of an interprovincial committee was comparatively large, and operated through a myriad of organizations erected within the civil population (and clandestinely within security forces). Its mission was to solidify pro-insurgent sympathies among the masses of the population *through organizational work.* Where the messages broadcast by the T&P branch or the military successes of guerrilla forces encouraged the belief among the peasantry or other segments of the population that the insurgents were predestined to win, it was the task of ETCP to strengthen and build upon that conviction by drawing those so oriented into party-dominated organizations where they could be set to work.

Psychological operations, for the Communist, are inseparable from organization. Those convinced will be organized, and organization means activity. One is to act as a member of a group and in a manner which accords with the beliefs one has accepted. The individual enlisted in the activities of a mass organization will gradually acquire a vested interest in the fortunes of the organization to which he belongs precisely because of the effort he expends in behalf of that body. In South Vietnam, the attempt was made to draw up a list of categories calculated to make every individual resident in the area subject to organizational work, whether it was an insurgent-controlled base area, or a marginal zone for which the opposing forces were contending, or a hostile area clearly dominated by counterinsurgent security forces. By far the most frequently appearing organizations were those for youth, women, and peasants.

[b] Insight into the activities of this branch—contrasting it with the central task of the training and propaganda branch—is provided by docs. E–3, E–4, and E–5 in appendix E.

Among the other mass organizations frequently met with were those for religious groups (e.g., Buddhists, Cao Dai, Hoa Hao, Catholics, etc.); minority groups (e.g., Cambodians, montagnards, Chinese, etc.); and there were many more.

The work of party cadres among groups of the above character was labeled "civil proselytizing" within the PRP. This effort was paralleled by a second program of psychological/organizational work which the PRP identified as "military proselytizing." Under the latter term, two types of activity were understood. Both had a direct bearing upon military operations. First, it referred to that collection of practices through which civilian youths might evade conscription by the Central Government and be induced to perform military service in the armed forces, militia, or self-defense guerrilla units of the insurgent movement. Second, it embraced party operations within or against the RVN security forces intended to (1) build up an informer apparatus in those forces, (2) provoke desertions, and (3) adversely influence unit morale. Recruitment cadres worked through the civil population to accomplish these goals. The military effort was part of the civil program, and in the absence of the latter, would rapidly collapse.

Once civil groups were organized into multiple bodies, delegates were chosen by each mass association—with the organizer's "advice"—to represent them at a local inter-mass organization "liberation committee." These "popular" bodies in which nonparty personnel substantially outnumbered known members of the PRP were drawn together into a hierarchical structure which could function at the hamlet, village, district, provincial, and interprovincial levels. At the national level—to put a roof on the structure—stood the National Front for the Liberation of South Vietnam (NFLSVN), which was thus provided with an organizational base that seemingly (1) authenticated its claim to represent the will of the Vietnamese people in the south and (2) justified its unilateral determination to "legislate" for the country at large. It was the gradual assumption of administrative functions by the "liberation committees" at their several organizational levels which legitimized the labeling of this heirarchy as a "shadow government" for South Vietnam. The precise character of the role played by this organization, its de facto power base, and the control exercised over it will be treated in Part Two: The Civil Organization and its Tactics.

The Economics Agency

This was an insurgent agency which became fully operative only as insurgent-dominated base areas emerged. While the minimum functions of this element, i.e., allocation and distribution of funds acquired from North Vietnam, could be begun early in the game, the decisive activities of this section presupposed the ability to control significant bodies of the civil population. Thus this body was to "prepare plans for production, and control the implementation of production plans by subordinate units and agencies," and was thereafter responsible for the management of crops, the control of "supplies contributed by the civilians of the base areas," their distribution, and storage.

Further, this agency was charged with "organizing handicraft shops" and "operating trading teams which procure all essentials for the region." By 1961, the economic section of the Fifth Interprovincial Party Committee controlled a paper manufacturing plant and ran several "trading teams." It was rumored to be the administrator of a textile factory. Through the provincial and district committees of the Fifth Region, it controlled a multitude of home and cottage industries.

Branches and Agencies in Other Interprovincial Committees

The organization and disposition of personnel in the Fifth Interprovincial area was paralleled in the corresponding bodies in other multiprovincial regions. As an example, the Secretary-General of the Sixth Interprovincial Committee which controlled Lam Dong, Tuyen Duc, Ninh Thuan, Phuoc Long and Quang Duc Provinces was Major General Nam, alias Tran Le, alias Hoa as of the winter of 1965. While he served as the official responsible for the entire insurgent effort in this region, he was, characteristically, trained primarily as a political officer and held concurrent membership in COSVN. In the eyes of the insurgency's supreme leadership in Hanoi, he was the COSVN "representative" in the area of the Sixth Interprovincial. (For a more detailed treatment on the principle of reverse representation, see ch 4.)

Associated with General Nam in the executive committee of the Sixth Interprovincial Party Committee were six highly trained DLD members, one of them an army officer with the rank of senior colonel.

Two of the executive committee members, one of them an officer in the PAVN, were concurrently leaders of the military affairs committee. A third combined his role as the director of the economy finance branch with the position of deputy commander of the interprovincial military headquarters. While this indicated the critical importance of combat, it also reflected the party members' determination to maintain tight controls over military policy and operations. The other critical offices of the Sixth Interprovincial were party organizational (cadre) work, and propaganda and training—locally referred to as "propaganda, culture, and indoctrination."

The Cellular Structure of Interprovincial Committees

Parallel to the channels of authority which this body had in common with any non-Communist body of comparable sophistication stood a comprehensive, seemingly duplicating apparatus which embraced every party member within a second hierarchy. Irrespective of party status, all served as active members of a formally constituted cell of three or more members. It was in the cell that the party member had his home, not in his bureaucratic office. Indeed, it was this parallel apparatus which was preeminent in the member's career and orientation.

Within the Fifth Interprovincial Party Committee, to use this particular body for purposes of illustration, the party members in each of the interprovincial's offices—including, of course, the personnel of the permanent standing committee—were grouped into several cells. Thus the party members (exact number unknown) among the 25 persons in the communications section as of 1961 were formed into two or more cells, each with a minimum of three persons. All of the other sections organized in a like fashion.

The arrangement in the permanent standing committee deserves special attention. At the time that PAVN Maj. Gen. Nguyen Don became secretary general of the Fifth Interprovincial Committee, the standing committee consisted of some 10 persons, including the secretary general himself and his assistant secretary. All of the members of this body were direct appointees of the central committee of the DLD. Most of them headed up administrative or section offices of the interprovincial, though the interests of some could not be equated narrowly with the specific missions assigned to a single subordinate group. Varied though the roles played by any one member of this group might be, from the point of view of the party leadership in Hanoi, they constituted the membership of party cells, each led by cell captain or secretary.[c]

The members of three or more cells within the interprovincial committee formed a *party group* which, in turn, elected a first secretary, an assistant secretary, and a standing committee of from five to seven persons. Normally, there was one party group for each agency. This body was the highest authority in the agency in which it was formed. Since the party controlled all agencies and this committee controlled all of the party members in a specific agency or office, it follows that the party group controlled the agency in which it was organized. Continuity between the agency and the party group could be maintained by making the first secretary of the group concurrently the chief of the agency. (By implication, if these two positions were held by different persons, the chief would be subordinate to the secretary even if the latter held a less important office in the agency.)

Finally, the party groups were represented in, or were subordinated to, an ultimated interprovincial cellular body: the interparty committee of the Fifth Interprovincial Committee. As with the party group, the interparty committee was headed by a first secretary, his assistant, and a standing committee. The first secretary of the interparty committee from June 1961 to the end of 1965 was Maj Gen. Nguyen Don, who was concurrently the secretary general of the Fifth Interprovincial Committee. It was his dual status as the head of both the party apparatus and the cellular hierarchy at party headquarters which guaranteed his authority.[d] The resultant party organizational pattern at the interprovincial level appears in chart 4.

---

[c] For an analysis of the principles of Communist Party cell organization see appendix A, chapter I.

[d] The general also held a third critical office, that of supreme military commander of the Fifth Interprovincial Region. His position in the military chain of command will be treated in chapter 11.

An understanding of the reasons behind this complex organizational structure is of the utmost importance to an effective grasp of Communist-directed insurgency. Therefore, some attention should be directed to this point.

The Cellular Structure of Communist Parties

The cellular structure of any Communist Party, whether legal or illegal, is the party's most critical element. Only in the environment of the cell is the party provided with the crucible in which to mold the new recruit into a disciplined party subject. It is within the cell that the member learns to live with criticism-self-criticism. This indoctrination progressively isolates him from the attitudes and patterns of behavior which prevail in society at large. As long as the individual is left with free time, with his hobbies and private interests, he cannot be provoked into that form of commitment which the party desires. What cannot be supplied in the system of committees and agencies is provided in the cell, which places infinite demands upon its members.

Among his fellow party members within the cell, he will find himself in the midst of an intense, dynamic environment, well calculated to absorb completely his entire being. The cell places a claim on all the energies of the individual—physical, intellectual, and moral—and demands total commitment from its members. The individual is left in perpetual doubt as to the success of his efforts to fulfill the demands placed upon him and is encouraged to believe that the realization of the goals set forth will accord with his own best interests. As a result, a built-in, permanent sense of insecurity lives in the mind of each member, spurring him on to exert himself with ever greater urgency.[e]

In the South Vietnamese insurgency, the dynamics generated in such a system of cells took precedence over the party bureaucracy at the interprovincial level, particularly in light of the fact that not all of the personnel engaged in the interprovincial's agencies were party members. (There were nonparty specialists in matters such as telecommunications, supply engineering, and manufacturing.)

In addition to their daily labors in the various offices and agencies, the cell members located in the offices of the Fifth Interprovincial Party Committee were expected to meet at least once a week for criticism (or struggle) sessions during which both the individual's work in behalf of his cell and his work in his formal office were subject to the searching examination of colleagues. Here, in the cell meeting, the orders received by the group from the interparty (which, in turn, received orders from the central committee of the Lao Dong Party in Hanoi, via the appropriate interparty of COSVN) were made known to the individual and his work norms were set. In his formal office, he might well receive thereafter a directive encompassing substantially the same determinations established

[e] For a survey of critical cellular practices and their impact upon the individual, see chapters II and III in appendix A. Also examine the "fifth lesson" in the "Study Document for Rural Party Members," included in appendix E, doc. E-4.

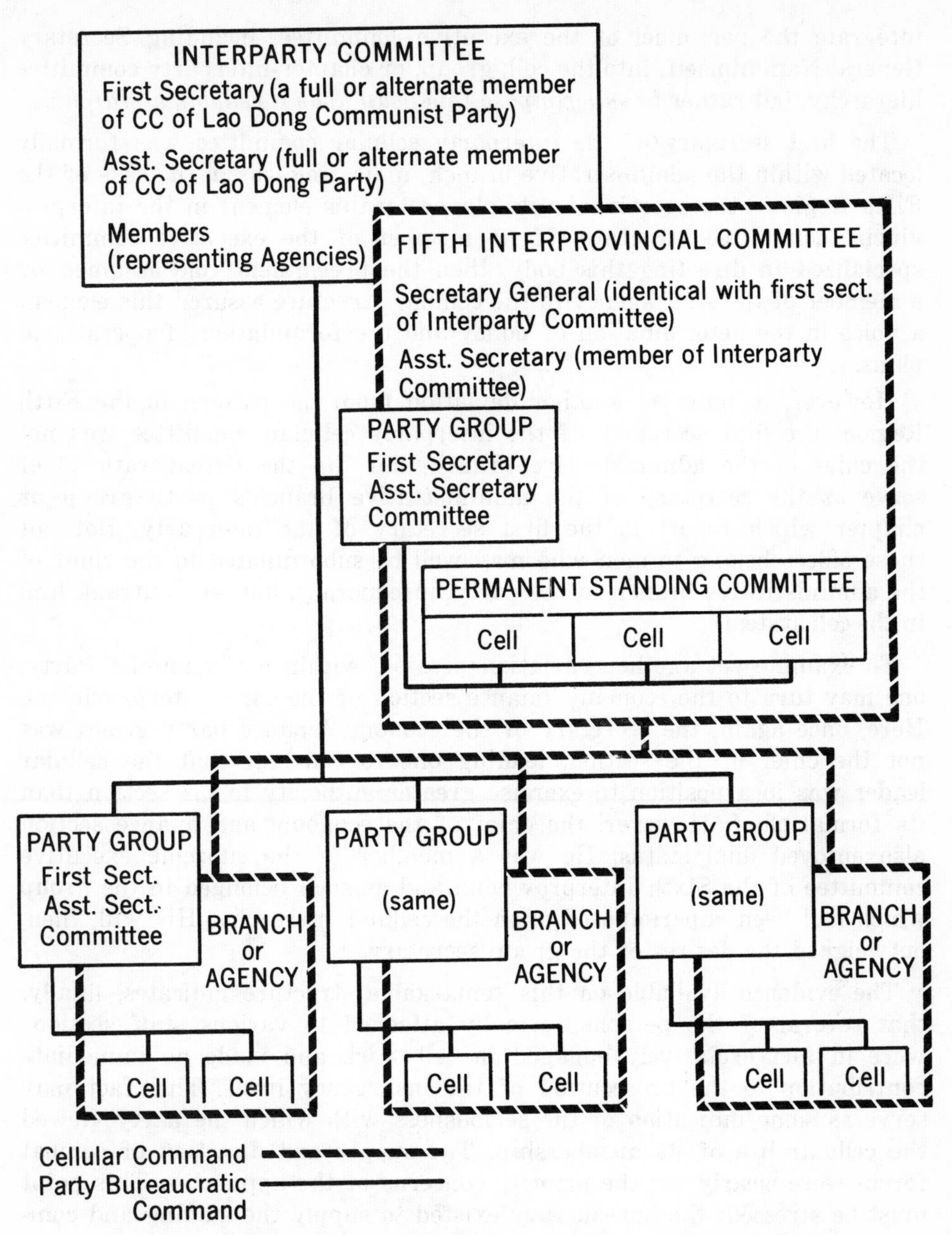

Chart 4. PARTY CELLULAR SYSTEM WITHIN THE PARTY COMMITTEE SYSTEM AT INTERPROVINCIAL LEVEL

during the cell meeting. His allegiance to his cell took precedence on all occasions over his objections to the bureaucracy.

If we return to the Sixth Interprovincial Committee structure to analyze cellular structure in a parallel party organization, a number of striking variations on the basic principles treated above can be identified. The most important deviation by far in this area was the party's decision not to integrate the personnel of the executive committee, including Secretary General Nam himself, into the cell, group, or chapter-interparty committee hierarchy, but rather *to superimpose this body upon a cellular hierarchy.*

The first secretary of the interparty cellular committee was formally located within the administrative branch, indicating—as in the case of the Fifth Region—the prominent role played by this element in the interprovincial committee structure. If no member of the executive committee specialized in directing this body, then the preeminent role assumed by a member of the staff agency in the cellular structure assured this element a voice in the determination of policy and the formulation of operational plans.

However, to note yet another deviation from the pattern in the Fifth Region, the first secretary of the interparty cellular committee was not the chief of the administrative branch, nor did the bureaucratic chief serve as the secretary of the administrative branch's party group or chapter which report to the first secretary of the interparty. Both of these offices belong to men who may well be subordinated to the chief of the administrative branch in the party bureaucracy, but who outrank him in the cell system.

To examine yet another variation possible within a Communist Party, one may turn to the economy/finance section of the same interprovincial. Here, once again, the secretary of the economy/finance party group was not the chief of the section, leading one to conclude that the cellular leader was in a position to exercise greater authority in his section than its formal chief. However, the chief of the economy and finance section also enjoyed dual status. He was a member of the supreme executive committee of the Sixth Interprovincial and as such belonged to the group which had been superimposed upon the cellular hierarchy. His will, then, outweighed the desires of the group secretary.

The evidence available on this remarkable structure indicates, finally, that several of the persons formally attached to various staff sections were in fact exclusively engaged in cell work and made no immediate contribution to the prosecution of the insurgency itself. This fact may serve as some indication of the seriousness with which the party viewed the cellular life of its membership. The supply and direction of combat forces were clearly not the priority concerns of the apparatus. This point must be stressed: the bureaucracy existed to supply the staffing and command for insurgent forces; the cellular hierarchy, in contrast, was to oversee the spiritual and intellectual life of the party member. Irrespective of military need and in the face of possible military reverses, the party made personnel available for activities which seemingly bore no immediate relationship to firepower or tactical combat successes.

The fleshing out of this complex cellular/bureaucratic structure began in earnest in the period 1959–1960. Personnel were acquired locally but also through the infiltration of regroupees from the North. In the area of the Fifth Interprovincial Region, infiltration was apparent by July/August

1960. By then it was possible to fill many vacancies in the skeletal agencies working under the standing committee. The counterintelligence section was manned and organizationally separated from the physical security branch of the interprovincial committee. The military element began to assume more concrete form, first as a military committee and, after 1961, as the Fifth Military Regional Headquarters.

The secretary general of the Fifth Region, who was called north in the summer of 1960, returned the following summer. He remained only briefly in his old post, for he had been earmarked for promotion. This was the period when the party was preparing to eliminate the Nam Bo and South-Central Vietnam Interzones and bring the interprovincial committees directly under the authority of the Central Office for South Vietnam (COSVN). The secretary general was transferred to this new command center well before its activation was formally announced. He was replaced, about June 1961, by Maj. Gen. Nguyen Don of the People's Army of North Vietnam, an alternate member of the central committee of the DLD.

CHAPTER 3

PARTY SIZE, ORGANIZATION, AND PRACTICE AT THE OPERATIONAL LEVEL

SUMMARY

The most critical of the operational headquarters was the provincial ommittee, a key center for the control and coordination of the activities of the extra-party infrastructure and the armed units. This committee, like the interprovincial committee, was headed by a first secretary, an assistant secretary, and a permanent standing committee, and was composed of multiple subcommittees, branches, and sections.

The number and nature of functional agencies of the provincial committees varied with the requirements of the area and situation. The party emphasized limiting the number of agencies to those which were essential to operations.

Agencies were established for the six vital functions:

(1) Communications
(2) Propaganda and party training
(3) Mass organizational work among the civil population and psychological operations against the enemy
(4) Economy, production, and supply
(5) Military affairs, and
(6) Security.

An effectively controlled civil population could provide the insurgents with supplies as well as military manpower resources. In many provincial commands the supply function was carried out by "worksite sections," which included such branches as a foundry, a weapons repair shop, an ammunition reloading plant, and a grenade manufacturing center. Other province supply agencies maintained specialized elements for functions such as farming, trading, manufacturing, and fishing.

Province committees were allowed a considerable measure of discretion in adding and deleting certain staff offices as a given situation required. Prison compounds, medical elements, training schools, etc., often appeared in those provincial headquarters that achieved a degree of security sufficient to justify the establishment of an elaborate bureaucracy. As necessary, such installations were secluded in forested or swampy areas of difficult access to security forces.

At the district level the number of committees and their subordinate basic units varied considerably. Flexibility in organization was more pronounced in district and village committees than at the province level. In areas controlled by the insurgent forces, the district committee usually duplicated the organizational format of the province committee.

Party organization in urban areas was distinct from that which obtained in rural areas. In order to operate in the cities, the party altered its structure. It could, for instance, desist from activating a bureaucratic committee and staff arrangement and operate solely as a cellular hierarchy.

Although the provincial and interprovincial bodies tended to resemble one another, a distinction must still be made. The interprovincial committee was primarily a planning and supervisory office; the province committee was the party's all-critical operational headquarters.

In the party bureaucracy, the leadership principle called for a provincial first secretary, his assistant, and a steering committee. This latter body normally contained fewer than a dozen members, to whom the secretary and his assistant might be added. Another officer often identified at the highest level of provincial organization was the routine business member charged with supervising the committee's many administrative functions. Although the principles of organization were rigidly enforced, the number and types of branches or agencies in a provincial committee varied with the operational circumstances obtaining in any given territorial subdivision. In any case, stress was placed not upon the proliferation of offices but rather upon their strict limitation in number for reasons of security and ease of operation.

From among the agencies mentioned above, attention will be directed here to the activities conducted in the general areas of (1) communications, (2) propaganda and party training or indoctrination, (3) mass organizational work among the civil population and psychological operations against enemy personnel, and (4) economy, production, and supply.

In none of these areas was a sharp demarcation of responsibility possible, for success in one main area was dependent on concurrent success in another. Thus the establishment of a communications network within the civil population presupposed that parallel efforts in the formation of mass organizations would have met with substantial success. Until both of these drives were in the ascendancy, an agitprop effort among enemy troops was impossible, and so was the production of materials for the prosecution of war.

Communications

The need to maintain a communications system applied to provincial committees with as much urgency as they did to interprovincial bodies. In Phong Dinh Province a knowledgeable interrogee asserted that permanent liaison stations were maintained with considerable uniformity at all party levels, usually in the homes of the local inhabitants, and were operated for the most part by women and teenagers. In addition to the transmission of written communications, these stations performed three major functions:

(1) The review of all letters of introduction;

(2) The authentication of identifying documents proffered by individuals wishing to make contact with insurgent units; and

(3) The arrangement of the necessary interorganizational contacts for those escorting personnel traveling to the next liaison station.

The technique was referred to by party personnel as "leapfrogging" and might involve, by turn, the assistance of a single private guide or a squad of heavily armed village guerrillas.

Propaganda and Training

It will be recalled that the propaganda and training branch of the interprovincial committee engaged in two groups of activities: the indoctrination of party personnel and the production and distribution of propaganda materials. These twofold functions were likewise carried out at the province level. Each provincial committee was provided with correspondents, translators, writers, painters, and printing facilities. Some provinces had broadcasting facilities.

Among the most elaborate propaganda and training sections in any provincial committee was that in Vinh Long Province. By the summer of 1965 it contained an organizational section in charge of planning and press and an entertainment element of four groups to whom a security guard force was attached. The press section included three writers, one of whom was also celebrated as a poet, and one who was identified as a reporter-photographer. The drama group of the entertainment section was headed by a stage manager, supported by a dramatist, and contained 11 performers. The dance group consisted of seven persons. But perhaps most striking were the two orchestral groups, one for modern music and—take your choice—one for classical music. Each supported a complement of a half dozen singers and a collection of instruments ranging from Spanish guitars to a maraca.

A substantial portion of the propaganda and training branch's indoctrination activities occurred within the framework of the cell and the party or unit political meeting and was pursued through the established techniques of criticism and self-criticism as provided for in the stipulations of the Lao Dong/PRP constitution. (Since the conduct of the party struggle meeting is fundamental to sustained vitality in the party, the essential organizational arrangements necessary for these practices have existed within the party since its original formation in the 1920's.)

It is this fact that accounts for the limited amount of detailed and specific information in captured enemy documents of party activity in this direction. For a good party member this is self-evident; it belongs in the very center of his daily life.

Mass Organizational Work

The ETCP branch was known by a variety of names in provincial organizations. In An Giang and Ba Xuyen Provinces, party members called it the "public relations bureau." In An Xuyen Province, it was the "peasant campaign." Elsewhere, ETCP was a proselytizing organization and could be organizationally bifurcated into military and civilian branches. These two activities, however, remained closely related and a tendency to integrate the two programs could be detected. Thus, in Quang Tri Province, the two branches were formally separated but the same individual headed both organizations.

Cadres sent out to recruit youths from the civil population were admonished to obey two basic principles: (1) to work through and with local party bodies, in order to take full advantage of such organizational work as had been accomplished in each specific location, and (2) to "mingle with the people as water is mixed with flour to bring about a consistent rising." Military cadres exercised qualified controls over committees subordinate to their own parent bodies and, in particular, over local party youth chapters.

Toward the civil population under the jurisdiction of a village chapter, the cadres from higher bodies were to show maximum solicitude, "visiting and taking care of families with relatives wounded or killed; urging the people to help the families of those who are serving in the Liberation Army." Such efforts strengthened the hands of those locally engaged in mass work and held the key to the success of military recruitment.

Mass work among civilians and within hostile military forces takes place even in those areas where the government is militarily dominant. Thus a Dinh Tuong provincial directive stressed the utility of clandestine techniques in persuading "youths in cities, towns, strategic hamlets, and weak [i.e., counterinsurgent-dominated] areas to run into our [i.e., insurgent] controlled areas for enlistment." The attempt to proselytize in these areas was always indirect. The cadres sought to provoke others into making appropriate contacts. In the absence of a party hierarchy, the cadre's first imperative was to "collaborate with the people who themselves serve as the key element in the popular movement [to be generated] around the [military troop] position." He selects local personnel, draws them together in cells, and names the cell leaders. A party document on "In-Place Military Proselytizing Cells" sets the following rules:

> An in-place cadre system will control the cell leader who controls his cell members and the cell members will control the sympathetic people. . . . The people will report to cell members; cell members will report to their cell leader and the cell leader will report to the in-place cadres.

Supply, Production, and Economy

The civil population provided the insurgent combat forces with three indispensable services: intelligence, combat recruits, and logistics. The third of these in its broadest sense must be treated in an examination of the major staff sections operating under a provincial party committee. This is the "payoff" for the insurgent organizational work and has long been appreciated as such in the literature of international communism. Thus Mao Tse-tung, in his 1938 pamphlet, "On Protracted War," declared, "To wish for victory and yet neglect political mobilization is like wishing to go north by driving a chariot south, and the result would inevitably be to forfeit victory." [a]

An extremely wide variety of activities could be encompassed within this section of a provincial committee. The supply apparatus of the Vinh

[a] *Selected Military Writings of Mao Tse-tung* (Peking: Foreign Languages Press,, 1963), p. 228.

Binh (Tra Vinh) provincial organization in the summer of 1965 was elevated to the status of a "worksite section." With its personnel gathered together in cells, each specialized in some one phase of production, this section ran a foundry, a weapons repair shop, an ammunition reloading plant, and a grenade manufacturing center. A year earlier a manufacturing site in Vinh Long employed a body of some 40 cadres, boasted of having its own electricians, and maintained a transportation subsection for the movement of finished goods as well as of agricultural products. In the summer of 1965 in the territory of the Fifth Interprovincial Committee of Maj. Gen. Nguyen Don, the finance-economy section of the Binh Dinh Province committee was an elaborate organization with multiple subsections specializing in handicrafts, trading, animal husbandry, fishing, oil manufacturing, blacksmithing, and farm production. The latter element, in turn, was further divided in hierarchical fashion into labor groups controlled through a system of some five production cells. Even greater specialization was apparent in the economy section of the Gai Lai Province committee which contained in addition to handicrafts, trading, production, and blacksmith's subsections, the following elements:

Enterprise cell
Pack transportation unit
Security guard cell
Treasurer
Medical and first aid cell
Noodle production unit

A wide variety of additional offices appeared and disappeared according to their usefulness to the party.

The District Committee

The number of district committees functioning under any specific provincial committee varied greatly. From the summer of 1960 to the summer of 1961 the party apparatus in South Vietnam was transformed from a skeletal structure, designed to sustain a DLD presence in the South, to a sophisticated command hierarchy with the trained personnel necessary for a persistent escalation of conflict. The fleshing out of interprovincial and provincial party committees through the infiltration of personnel from the North was stepped up seriously in 1960, providing the secretary general of the Fifth Interprovincial Committee, for example, with some 150 trained specialists by late 1960, 30 of whom were attached to the region's provincial committees. Lower bodies at the district and village levels seem to have been augmented significantly during the following summer with appropriately trained personnel.

Under favorable circumstances, a district committee might duplicate the offices at the province level. This was the case in the Quan Tuy Phuoc (not to be confused with the northern Tuy Phuoc) and Quan Binh Khe and in the Province of Binh Dinh in the summer of 1965. Each of the district committees was headed by a first secretary and a standing committee whose chairman also filled the function of assistant secretary. Under these executive bodies, a sevenfold division of responsibility obtained to which party youth and military affairs sections might be added. The resultant organization was complex as seen in chart 5.

One district committee, following a period of serious military reverses, identified security as its most critical problem and began to reassign to security tasks personnel who previously had specialized in three fields of psychological actions against enemy military personnel, mass organizational work (e.g., NFLSVN), and "the elimination of traitors." The reduction in prestige of the party's image in the eyes of the local peasantry following these reverses, we are informed, had produced a new crop of "spies who are emerging in the villages." "This is a temporary arrangement," the committee determination read further, "to meet the emergency. As soon as conditions return to normal, these specialists will be reassigned to their technical jobs as required." Four members of the "traitor elimination group" began security work, a fifth one assumed duties at the village level as an *ao dang* (magic lantern) cadre. Significantly, the committee's medical, supply, administrative, and communications cadres were to remain in place, while the cellularly structured "firearms parts factories" which made blowguns and bullets were upgraded to work under village rather than under hamlet controls.

The flexibility in organization which characterized provincial bodies was even more pronounced in district and village committees working directly at the grassroots level. Many factors figured in the determination of the number and size of specialized district agencies at any given time.

Another situation figured in urban areas where survival necessitated a different approach to organization by the party. An example of a specific urban party organization is provided by the Bien Hoa city committee. The Bien Hoa city committee, directly responsible to the like-named provincial committee, lacked specialized organizational staff agencies. In place of the dual command structure one found in the majority of rural committees, one could identify the elements of only a single hierarchy in Bien Hoa city, those based upon the party cell. The urban organization consisted of two identified cells of four and five men each, including their responsible leaders, an armed squad of 11 members headed by a chief, and a city secretary supported by an assistant charged with the conduct of routine business. The leaders of each of the two cells were responsible to a group chief who also directed communications and liaison. The personnel in the armed squad were likewise organized into two or three cells and their chief was their platoon leader and was also the chief of a second, group-level, cellular combination. At the top, the authority of the city secretary rested exclusively upon a party appointee as the superior of the two group leaders. This individual was the head of an interparty city committee, which included the two group leaders and the secretary's assistant.

The example of Bien Hoa city reveals graphically the competence of the PRP membership operating under adverse conditions. Where multiple committee subsections existed this example strongly suggests that in the face of an intensified counterinsurgent offensive, the party had the operational capability of falling back upon the fundamental cellular structure. Because it was already prepared organizationally for such an eventuality, the PRP could be expected to recover rapidly from pacification efforts and to continue operating from this more elusive apparatus. Imperative to such a comeback was the rigid maintenance of the cell system and the development of a body of men able to survive under conditions of illegality.

The Village Chapter

Available information suggests that basic party units seldom approached the maximum size permitted by party regulations [b] (e.g., 70 in enterprises or factories and 50 in villages). A 5- to 15-man body, organized into as few as 2 cells and directed by a standing committee of 3 or 4 persons (including the secretary) was more characteristic of party unit strength at the village level. Where this type of rudimentary organization was found, the dual hierarchy structure could not exist and as in the urban environment of Bien Hoa city the local party would consist of a group of cells integrated into a single cellular hierarchy. Party practices and regulations provided the basic unit with a framework in which it could expand or contract, compartmentalize or reintegrate to accommodate itself to the ebb or flow of the movement.

The interrogation of the security member of a district committee in Ba Xuyen Province indicated that a village chapter committee, in the autumn of 1964, could contain up to 10 staff subdivisions (i.e., front, propaganda-indoctrination, finance-economy, security, social welfare, civilian/military proselytizing, commo-liaison protection, public health, market adjutant, and labor youth, to which a "military affairs committee" might be added). A statistical analysis of organizational specialization at the chapter level in Phong Dinh Province revealed that the posts occurring most frequently in village chapters were (in order of frequency):

(1) Secretary
(2) Assistant secretary
(3) Party youth leader
(4) Agriculture leader
(5) Executive or security member
(6) Propaganda and training
(7) Military leaders or cadre
(8) Finance and supply
(9) Hamlet committees (i.e., an organizational arrangement to assume that the initiative will remain with the village chapter committee at all times in work)
(10) Youth mass organization
(11) Enemy troop and civil propaganda section

[b] An administrative form for the maintenance of personnel records on party members in appendix F, doc. F-2, gives one example of the spread of party personnel at the hamlet level.

The first 6 appeared in three-fourths of 33 chapters, the last 5 including military offices, in not more than half of them. Less frequent were such offices as those for minority elements (e.g., Cambodians), assassination and executive sections, health and welfare or communications and liaison. With respect to communications, the absence of an appropriate subsection does not, of course, indicate the absence of an interchange of information and instructions: it signifies that this function is controlled directly by the superior district committee which refuses to delegate authority. Again, though security and intelligence collection do not figure in the list, these activities were, nevertheless, conducted. Where organization was simple, these latter responsibilities constituted one of the most important additional duties of the chapter secretary or possibly his assistant.

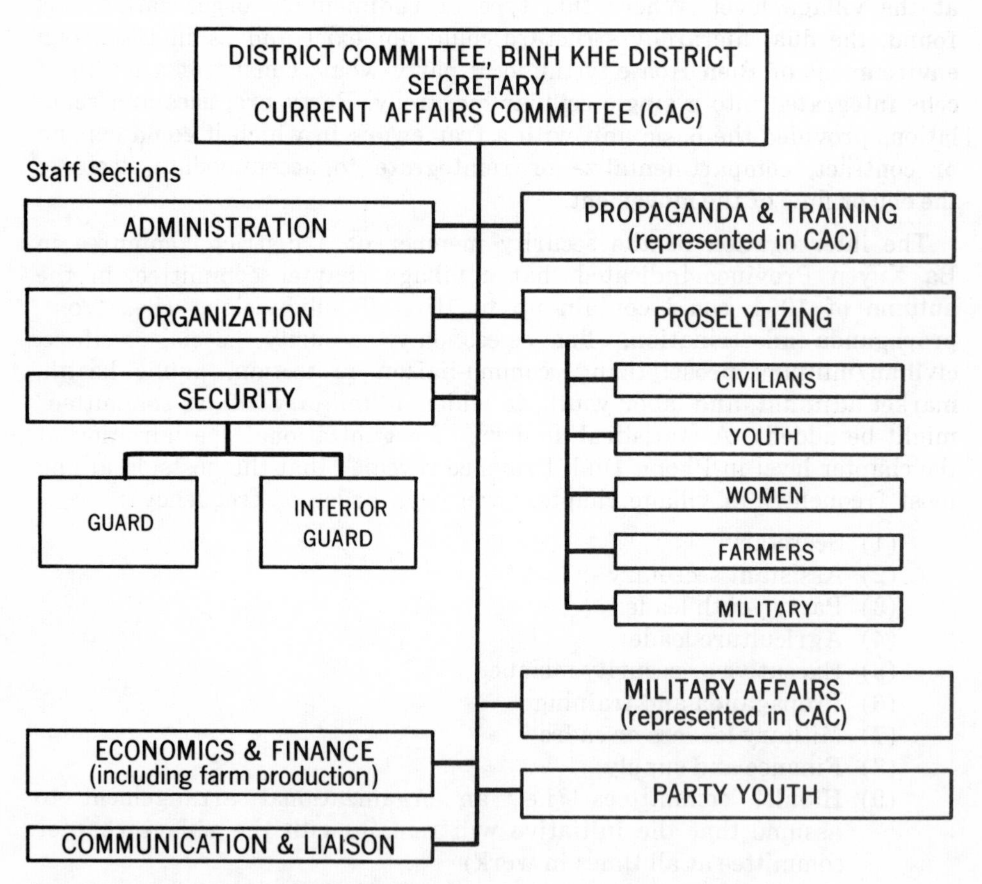

Chart 5. STAFF SECTIONS WITHIN PARTY COMMITTEE AT THE DISTRICT LEVEL

CHAPTER 4
THE PARTY CONTROL APPARATUS

SUMMARY

The fundamental principle of Communist control was a strict adherence to the principle of "reverse representation." Multiple channels of communication and surveillance, including a system of inspectorates, a security and counterintelligence apparatus, were maintained. The dual hierarchies of the party cell structure and the bureaucratic committee system also constituted channels of control over all levels of party organization.

Inspecting teams were established at command levels in the party organization to spot-check reports of subordinates. A typical interprovincial inspecting team might consist of five men specializing in such areas as mass organizational work, military organization, security, and administration. Such a team was sent out with blanket authority to inspect and intervene in the conduct of any local program. The individual inspectors were assigned to groups of villages in which they reviewed reports and questioned local party personnel.

In addition, basic party units were provided with security staffs which were responsible for supervising their fellow party colleagues while "looking after" and "educating" the local population. The district security sections usually were headed by a chief who was also a member of the district standing committe and who normally commanded a staff of reconnaissance, intelligence, and clerical personnel.

A village security section was headed by a member of the village executive committee. He might have deputy security chiefs responsible for designated groups of hamlets within the village complex. In the hamlet organization the local population elected the security agents—an example of the party's tactical realism in practice, since it was almost impossible at the hamlet level to withhold the identity of principle agents.

Responsible party officials at the interprovincial, provincial, and even district levels within the party echelon of the insurgent movement were provided with a myriad of channels and techniques through which they controlled subordinates. Attention must be directed particularly to the security or counterintelligence apparatus and to the principle of "reverse representation," and it should be noted that these were only two of the control means available to the party leadership. The system of inspectorates and the party's cellular hierarchy itself also served to make subordination a critical fact in the daily life of the party member.

The Cellular Hierarchy as a Control Mechanism

Provincial committees were subject to dual control channels from the interprovincial committee and could use the same mechanism to control district committees. The heads of district sections were responsible, through their district first secretary, to the leadership of corresponding sections at province level. Concurrently, as the leader of a party cell, group or interparty cellular committee, the Communist member of a district committee was subject to the decisions of the interparty cellular committee at the province level. The same stipulations applied equally in the subordination of village chapters to district committees.

The Inspecting Team

The party official at the interprovincial, provincial, or district level also employed the device of the inspecting team, composed of specialized personnel with the knowledge and authority to intervene in local high-priority programs. The interrogation of a Vietnamese captain, infiltrated from the north and assigned to the Eastern Interprovincial Committee until his capture, reveals the thoroughness with which this device may be employed.

The captured party insurgent was a member of a five-man body, operating from the interprovincial level, composed of specialists in youth, farm, military, security, and administrative work.

During the period of the captain's association with the inspection team, it was given the task of examining the village organizations functioning under the Binh Duong district committee in the Binh Duong Province. Suspicious of reports received through regular channels from subordinate committees, the interprovincial had selected this area as a means of spot-checking the achievements claimed by lower bodies in general and providing itself with a continuing additional source of information.

The five-man body was empowered to peer into every phase of party activities, from local agricultural policy and the size and readiness of guerrilla and militia forces to the extent of the civil populace's involvement in insurgency work and the nature of current propaganda releases for mass consumption. On the basis of the team's findings the interprovincial was expected to issue new instructions to all of its district and provincial subsections.

They commenced their work with a 5-day conference with the provincial first secretary followed by a 10-day discussion with district committee members, travelling to the seat of the district committee's offices for that purpose in the company of the provincial boss. Thereafter the provincial secretary returned to his own committee, and the four members of the visiting group spread out through the district, leaving their chief behind at district headquarters. Each inspector was assigned a group of villages to be investigated and was encouraged not only to read such reports as were presented to him but also to question village party members at length and personally to observe local activities. Each member of the team reported back to the team leader at district headquarters at the end of each month. The captain in question had already reported back in person twice when he was apprehended by South Vietnamese security personnel.

Security and Counterintelligence

The missions assigned the security officers in a basic party unit were educational and indoctrinational as well as operational, and were directed as much at the civil population at large as toward the intelligence specialist. "If village security section was to educate and look after the masses," declared a party leaflet captured in 1964, then it must likewise "educate the cadres, party members, and special armed forces of the front." The members of the committee section were to keep abreast of the ever-changing situation in the village area and maintain surveillance over "reactionary elements in order to inform the village party unit of their harmful activities in time." They were to "watch and discover mistakes and errors of the cadres and the party members." Even agents engaged in military proselytizing in hostile territory were to be kept under close watch.

The importance attached to this work within the civil population can be gauged by examining a course of instruction devised for village chapter security personnel in the summer of 1964. This document reveals the PRP's approach to the training of security cadres at the grass roots, the level of sophistication expected from the novice in the field, and the relative emphasis placed on the several aspects of security work. The program was assigned to take place during an 11-day period and was divided into 2 portions of 9 and 2 days. During the first portion, three major subjects were treated: (1) the "functions, activities, and plots" of the hostile (i.e., RVN) intelligence agency (duration 2 days); (2) face-to-face persuasion with respect to the populace at large (2 days) and with respect to key communicators (called "target personalities"), the opinion-molders and pace-setters in village society (1½ days—total duration, 3½ days); (3) craft of counterespionage, i.e., the building of agent networks and the research and investigation which had to precede it (2 days); the intelligence, particularly counterespionage, collection efforts and the treatment and final disposition ("imprisoning and judging") of suspects (1½ days—total duration, 3½ days).

This program was followed up by a general peptalk and group discussions with strong ideological overtones (1 day) and a recapitulation of the course on the final, the 11th day. Throughout, each new subject was introducted by a lecture lasting half a day and the remainder of the time was spent in a "discussion between cells" after the fashion of a party political meeting. Considering the complexities of the fields of intelligence collection and counter espionage, the party's determination to devote one-third of the available time to the subject of face-to-face persuasion demonstrates the organization's conviction that it could best achieve its goals by working through the civil populations. The novel character of this concept of security operations is brought into bolder relief if one keeps in mind that mass organizational work and face-to-face persuasion rarely are aspects of Western intelligence training, if indeed they are even acknowledged to be part of the subject.

Clearly, a population which can be approached through party-controlled mass organizations can be provoked into paying close attention to the demands of the indoctrinators and checked to determine the extent of their compliance with the policies made known to them. This fact, plus the party's admonition to the security official to "educate" the peasantry at large, necessarily obliged him to coordinate extensively with party personnel engaged in the parallel programs of the committee branches and sections. This was particularly the case with respect to training and propaganda; enemy troop and civil population; and supply, production, and economy branches of a party committee. One party document required village chapter security personnel to accept responsibilities in fields that were the primary concern of these three elements. Thus they were to "insure" that "big party operations" such as "political struggle, demonstration meetings, and sabotage" were implemented, while they were "to coordinate activities with the front and the village farmers' association to settle conflicts and to prevent abuses from occurring."

The Structure of the Security Apparatus at the District and Chapter Levels

A relatively advanced structure was provided for at an early juncture in the evolution of party organizations at the lowest levels, for it was at these levels that the success of intelligence, security, and counterespionage (as the party understood these activities) counted the most. A district security section was headed by a chief and an assistant leader. It contained reconnaissance and intelligence personnel and clerical help when available. Such bodies devoted a continuing effort to the development of an agent network and in areas along national frontiers.[a]

Village security sections were headed by a chief appointed by a superior body. In any case, it was expected that he would become a member of the executive or standing committee at his level.

Due to the precarious situation of the basic unit, particularly during its first months of existence among a population which might well be hostile, party stipulations called for the duplication of subordinate offices. "In hamlets located far from each other and where the situation is unstable, two deputy security chiefs may be appointed to take care of security affairs. In hamlets that contain many houses, the village security section can appoint two agents to look after its security."

Hamlet security agents were to be "elected" by the population. "Thus, the latter will have confidence in these cadres and supply them with any information they can get." This is one of a great number of examples of the tactical realism of the PRP. Proceeding from the propositions that the personnel operating at this low level would not be able to keep their identity a secret, and that individuals had to be assigned to this function in spite of their technical incompetence, the party sought for a means of retrieving as much of a positive character as possible from an imperfect situation. The formula hit upon was not to attempt to withhold from the

[a] Full-time security personnel from higher party bodies could be attached indefinitely to a party committee in border areas to supervise the local entry of infiltrated personnel or ordnance from North Vietnam.

public the identity of its official hamlet agents but to involve the peasantry in their selection—as accomplices—under the cover of "popular elections." Under the slogan of "democracy" the PRP popularized its security program where it could help the most while doing the least possible damage.

PRP documents concerned with security organizations made much of the point that such bodies were "instruments," which were "subordinate to" their respective party committees. They were to "closely cooperate with other branches in the district under the supervision of the appropriate party committee in the area."

The district committee's security section stood as intermediate in this separate channel of communications. On the one hand, its involvement in any but the most routine cases required prior approval by province security. On the other hand, it had to hold all village security under surveillance and it retained the initiative in defining the jurisdiction of village sections. Something of the authority bestowed upon the district section, and its de facto independence from the committee system, becomes apparent in a document entitled "Mission and Working Procedure of the District Security Section":

> (1) The district security section sets up and guides the village security section in all works concerning security.
>
> (2) Investigates enemy spies' activities in the district and takes appropriate measures against them, according to (party) committee and higher security echelon instructions.
>
> (3) Conducts investigation into all affairs that the village security section cannot solve or those coming from higher levels.
>
> (4) Ensures security for all agencies' bases and helps district forces in their task of protecting the armed forces in the region.
>
> (5) Carries out interrogations, sets up culprits' dossiers, gives judgements of district affairs, and transfers prisoners to higher levels.
>
> (6) Establishes dossiers and lists of enemy administrative and military personnel and reactionary parties within the district. Establishes dossiers of native people working for the enemy in another area.

The examination of further documents shows the prerogatives in the hands of the district security leader in directing the work of lesser bodies. The security element of every village chapter was under relentless pressure from district security sections to submit comprehensive reports on a monthly basis. Though these reports were the basis from which records were drawn up for submission to chapter committees, it is important to stress that they were not made known to the remaining members of the basic unit in the form in which they were submitted to higher security authorities.

The comprehensive nature of the information demanded is apparent in an order sent by a district security officer to the subordinate village agencies.

> As regards armed combat, how many times did the village council and district forces attack the enemy? Under which forms? Results? On the other hand, what were the results obtained during the month for other tasks such as sabotage (activity), construction of bases, development of forces, (expansion

of) people's guerrilla warfare movement, production for self-sufficiency, and what were the results obtained during the month?

In the political field, how many people attended the propaganda sessions, discussions, meetings? How many people participated in armed propaganda activities and fled (the enemy) during the month? How many persons were infiltrated into the urban area to carry out face-to-face struggle with the government in Baria city and stage strikes to demand reunification of the country)? Clearly indicate the number of persons and incidents involved as well as their influence (upon the population).

As regards military proselytizing: How many propaganda sessions have been conducted to indoctrinate the population and troops? Independents? What were the duration and number of classes conducted for various installations?

In line with the development of the party and group, of various liberation organizations and paramilitary forces, how many sessions and hours have been spent for the indoctrination of same?

In addition, all addressees must report on finances, rural administration, opposition to and destruction of New Life Hamlets, breaking up of enemy's grip, etc. . . .

District security considered that every aspect of the lives of party members, as well as the activities of the peasants, fell quite properly within its purview.[b] An additional report was demanded on the village committee's success at "collecting petitions denouncing enemy's plots and crime and to support the struggle movement of the people in Phy Huu village (Bien Hoa) as a result of recent airstrikes which brought about the death of 400 persons." The party member possessed no advantage over the secretly disenchanted peasant in his liability to chastisement and discipline. The apparatus was a means to maintain surveillance over the insurgency's own personnel and a device for the discovery and liquidation of hostile, infiltrated agents.

Special reports were to be sent to superior security offices and, in turn, restricted directives proceeded in the opposite direction. Detailed lists of persons known or suspected of collaboration with internal security forces were sent to village sections with instructions to locate, watch, or apprehend the persons listed.

Organized groups were likewise subjected to detailed analysis in accordance with orders from higher offices. Thus another order from a district committee to village agents requested the following information.

How many religious organizations are there in the villages and hamlets? What are those religions? For example: Hoa Hao, Buddhism, Buddhist laity (Tinh Do Cu Si, or Tinh-Do Tong, etc.). Approximately how many people are there in each organization? What class do most of them belong to? Who are the leaders? Where are these religious organizations located? What are their designations? If possible, all comrades will collect biographical data on these leaders (be very cautious and discreet), without causing difficulties to us.

[b] That portion of the security official's report to higher headquarters which might very well have been examined in detail by other village chapter personnel without interfering in inner party surveillance arrangements was the section dealing with the enemy situation. the same document called for the following information: "On what front—military or political—did the enemy step up their activities most strongly during the month? What type of activities did the enemy carry out most steadily? What were the purposes for which military activites were conducted (for example, conscription, concentration of the population into New Life Hamlets etc.)? On the political front, what policies did the enemy drive at (broadcasting by means of megaphones, meeting to support the "Chieu Hoi" policy, etc.)?"

Other documents upbraided local officials for laxity in security matters, provided village personnel with arguments to be used in convincing the peasantry that they dare not discuss local insurgent activities, and pointed out new techniques evolved by hostile penetration agents. In each of these sectors, the need for secrecy and exclusiveness varied substantially, and in each case the determination of the degree of restriction rested upon a separate decision.

A perusal of the "Rights of the Village Security Section" listed in another party document shows the village security officer's relations with the committee of a basic party unit. The official in question was to do the following:

> (1) Check strangers' and suspects' identification cards; a correct attitude must be shown toward them.
>
> (2) Make arrest in cases of red-handed apprehension; make preliminary investigations, draw reports, and take the suspect to the district security [branch].
>
> (3) After getting instruction from the party chapter, the security section can give direct warning to detainees who have not mended their ways, though reeducated, and to those whose activities are harmful to the village security and order.
>
> The above powers of the village security section are effective in liberated and disputed areas. The village security section, however, is not authorized to make arrests without an order from higher levels, or to torture arrested persons, and to fine or violate a person's property.

The hand of the committee—at the basic unit level—was more apparent here than in the preceding extract, but in critical matters village security still looked first to district headquarters for a ruling. The chapter required a policymaking function only where the overt activities of the section might jeopardize the mass organizational program concurrently in process. The chapter committee could level demands or exercise veto authority in a formal sense, and the chief of village security, through his affiliation with district intelligence, had the ability to discourage undue intervention in his activities. He permitted horizontal coordination, the better to carry out the orders received from above.

The Principle of Reverse Representation

The combination of cellular controls, inspection teams, and a security apparatus provided the party leadership with a series of arrangements through which individual party members could be checked for loyalty and effectiveness. In fact, the apparatus was obliged to utilize additional arrangements to guarantee compliance. Involved here was the procedure whereby a party committee would assign responsibility to committees at lower levels and hold their respective first secretaries accountable for results, rather than retain authority at its own level or—where initiative had previously been extended—withdraw the delegated authority from the group in question. This procedure may be understood as a byproduct of the party principle of democratic centralism [c] pursued to its logical conclusion, so that we may refer to it as the principle of reverse representation. If democratic centralism, functionally defined, means the subjection of any given party body to the will of the committee at the next higher level, then the principle of reverse representation—as a corollary—pursues this theme yet further by characterizing the leader of any party body as a delegate from a superior body, imposed upon a subordinated, lesser body in order to assure higher authorities that their wishes are being obeyed. The cell or chapter captain, then, did not have the function of representing the interests of his colleagues in the councils of their superiors; rather, he was the voice of that higher authority in one of its implementing agencies.

The decision to recall authority once delegated constituted a demotion for the secretary of the subordinate party unit thus affected. Such a step compounded the demands placed upon the higher body's membership and staff sections, and possibly reduced overall efficiency, but the practice went on. In most cases it determined the relationship between the district committee and one or more of its basic chapters.[d]

An example of this situation obtained among the local chapter committees of the northern Tuy Phuoc district committee in Binh Dinh Province in the summer of 1965. Despite the fact that the Phuoc Hoa village

[c] The repeated appearance of the phrase "the subordination of the minority to the majority" in party discussions of democratic centralism encouraged the conclusion that the opinions and interests of the party rank and file as expressed during cell meetings meaningfully influenced policy formulation. As chapter III in appendix A indicates, this in fact was not the function of party discussion and criticism. Rather, by those means the party sought the conscious and voluntary submission of the member to determinations reached by his superior. Only as one was brought openly to abandon heretical ideas and to subordinate himself in public, as Stalin reasoned on this subject, could one speak of "iron discipline" in the party (J. V. Stalin, *Works*, VI [Moscow, Foreign Languages Publishing House, 1953], p. 189). That reference to the minority and majority might be misunderstood in a Western context is further borne out by its uniform coupling in Communist literature with the principle of "the subordination of lower Party bodies to higher Party bodies" (cf. *ibid.*, pp. 182–83). One is dealing here with principles that derive from Lenin, who conceived the party as built "from above" rather than "from below." And it was in this form that "democratic centralism" became a requirement for all communist parties. Lenin wrote: "The parties affiliated to the Communist International must be built upon the principle of democratic *centralism* [sic]. In the present epoch of acute civil war the Communist Party will be able to perform its duty only if it is organized in the most centralized manner, only if iron discipline bordering on military discipline prevails in it, and if tis party centre s a powerful organ of authorty, enjoining wide powers and the general confidence of the members of the party." (V.I. Lenin, *Collected Works*, X [New York: International Publishers, 1943], p. 204.) For the relevant passage in Lao Dong regulations, cf. appendix B, doc. B–1, chap. II.

[d] An extensive survey of relevant captured documents revealed only one case in which a provincial committee utilized this assignment to intervene directly in village affairs. A year-end review and critique of party activities in Dinh Tuong, captured early in 1963, revealed that the provincial committee during 1962 had assigned cadres directly to several village chapters "in order to help stir up the population against the strategic hamlets" which had been established by RVN security forces and "to help the chapters study the situation and train the cadres and pary members." The youth proselytizing section of the provincial committee, we are informed in the report, had utilized this occasion "to have its cadre recruit many young men." Yet even here, the province's step may not be thought of as censure of its distinct dependencies, for they concurrently dispatched personnel of their own to the villages. "Most of the district cadres," declares the report, "were sent to the villages to lead the village activities," or "to assure leadership." The movement of experienced party personnel out to the villages and hamlets was the party's way of responding to a rapidly deteriorating situation caused by an unprecedented expansion of the party's roles at the grassroots level which brought large numbers of poorly prepared individuals into the organization at a rate which temporarily surpassed the party's competence to digest them. For a detailed analysis of the problem posed for the party in Dinh Tuong Province, see chapter 6.

chapter was provided with a first secretary of its own, a member of the standing committee at the district level actually exercised the powers normally ascribed to the head of the chapter.

This practice was even more extensively built into the organizational structure of the western Binh Dinh district committee, which operated among the montagnards and was popularly advertised as the Autonomous People's Committee or Mountainous Region Section. Here the Quan (i.e., district) authority created a series of staff subsections charged with the direction of activities in substantial stretches of the district (i.e., An Lao, Van Ganh, Vinh Thanh). In Quang Duc Province, a guerrilla cell of seven men and a leader, operating under the direct control of the Duc Lap district committee among Rhade, Bu Nong, and Buong villagers, assumed the performance of multiple parallel tasks. The interrogation of a party member and senior sergeant engaged in supervising this armed element in 1964 revealed that it was "to preserve security and order among the people, conduct liaison between villages for the purpose of circulating information on RVNAF operations and lay spike traps and tunnel traps against RVNAF personnel." In this region where party work remained weak, the guerrilla cell, then, was not only responsible to the district committee and free of controls at the village level, but it integrated into a single group three distinct types of activity which in more advanced regions were being conducted through three organizationally differentiated committee sections.

The most extreme example of the absorption of all controls by a superior committee is shown in minutes of a meeting of top district party leaders which took place in Quan Binh Phuoc, Long An Province, one week after the organization suffered military reverses. These notes reveal the extent to which village chapters were subject to the will of the "committee at the next highest level." As a consequence of the meeting, the whole district was divided into a system of six intervillages, each under the command of members of the district committee who proceeded personally to these areas to take over physical control of the party's village chapters. They were accompanied by technical personnel withdrawn from district agencies (e.g., security, front, and terrorist or traitor extermination specialists) and locally reassigned "to be directly guided and supervised by the district delegates."

In this fashion, the village chapters acquired leaders in whose choice they were not consulted, for whether their own secretaries remained in office or not, the orders for the district commissariat's delegate took precedence over the wishes of their "elected" secretaries. This meant that the membership of the district commissariat had willfully surrendered the determination of district policy to the four or five members of its standing or current affairs committee who remained close enough to meet and make decisions. And to limit the independence of even this core of the district commissariat, provincial authorities obliged the district current affairs committee to absorb into its membership a representative from the provincial commissariat.

The restriction of the decisionmaking process is reflected in the determination, recorded in the minutes of the party meetings, that the standing committee would meet every 10 days; the district committee not more than once a month.

With the arrival of the "delegate" in the village area, control from the top was further tightened by the restriction of reporting channels. Village personnel could henceforth communicate with the standing committee only through the delegate, and this also applied to the specialist sent from the district headquarters. The "technical cadres" were admonished to "consider themselves as village cadres assigned to hamlet tasks." They were informed that they would cease to report back to their parent agencies. This would be done by the "delegate" "who will report to the standing committee, instead of having the technical cadres report as was formerly the case."

To the maximum extent possible, the district committee member was to employ the technique of criticism-self-criticism to effect the ends sought, on the assumption that by provoking party members, in the presence of an assembly of their peers, to confess in detail to their errors it would be possible to keep them in line.

The member of the district committee was to assume personally the leadership of one of the local party cells and to begin a detailed investigation of the personnel of the other immediate party bodies, classifying their cadres into one of three categories: "excellent, indifferent, or those who have surrendered to the enemy and (thereafter) returned to their native areas." He was to revitalize and expand the organization. He became responsible for building up "morale, courage, and revolutionary spirit" and was admonished "to keep the program under close guidance and supervision."

> He should state the issues and let the comrades discuss them, find out for themselves the facts and conditions, figure out their ideas, their errors, faults, and weaknesses, and finally submit suggestions as to what jobs they should perform. The district delegate should then summarize the debate systematically, and point out significant points, in order to throw more light on the issues.

However, the leadership was not to rely exclusively upon this technique to effect conformity. The normative patterns sought were to be reinforced through the agency of coercion, ever implicit in the command structure of the party. So in the Binh Phuoc district, the technique of the criticism meeting was to be used in conjunction with physical duress and confinement as determined appropriate by the district committee delegate.

> The worst ones should be sent to places away from the enemy to prevent them from surrendering, or kept close to their native areas and made to support us without risking their lives. Cadres who have surrendered to the enemy and have been allowed to return to their villages should be prevented from doing any harm to the revolution and to the people. Their movements should be restricted, their contacts with the enemy, and especially their supply of information to him, should be prevented.

One is witness here to unilateral authoritarianism, and likewise to a means for the tutelage of the inexperienced who may well be dedicated, but lack education and general background, administrative know-how, a sense for party discipline, or a realistic grasp of why such distinctive inner-party practices, such as self-criticism, are indispensable to the life of the Lao Dong Party apparatus. Thus the one-sided intervention in lower party bodies by their hierarchical superiors does not proceed with monolithic indifference to the varying competence of local party elements. In the Hong Ngu district of Kien Phong Province in the summer of 1964, the district party committee did not uniformly withdraw the prerogatives initially assigned lesser committee's when work at the grassroots level failed. According to the minutes of that district's standing committee's meeting, district level functionaries were assigned control over a string of five village organizations, but one of the village chapters was singled out for less severe regimentation. If the other units were slated to lose all of their tactical decisionmaking powers, then An Vinh village was "merely to be guided."

The specific party determination, whatever it may be, is made within the context of the larger organizational principle universal to Communist parties: Under no circumstances may the individual be left to his own devices. Since Lenin's assertion of 1901 that "our task is to combat spontaneity," Communist parties have never been erected as voluntaristic associations. Evolution in that direction is synonymous with extinction. The experienced Communist becomes the teacher-master of the novice. This role takes precedence over any other.

CHAPTER 5

PARTY YOUTH ORGANIZATION OF THE PRP

SUMMARY

Parallel to the party structure of full members, but separate and distinct from it, stood the party youth organization. The PRP used this organization as a training school for future party members. This structure should not be confused with the party's mass organization for the youth at large. The latter, the Liberation Youth Association, appealed, with little discrimination, to all youth and was a relatively large organization. The former, currently known as the People's Revolutionary Youth Association (PRYA) contained considerably fewer members, who were carefully screened and from whom much more was demanded, including service for the party in minor leadership posts. In this chapter we are exclusively concerned with the PRYA. The Liberation Youth Association will be treated in the discussion of mass organizational work in chapter 8.

The party's youth organization in South Vietnam was organized into a four-level hierarchy—subcell, cell, group section committee, and intergroup section committee. The party controlled the youth organization through channels in the party cell hierarchy, not the bureaucratic structure. This supervision and control was effected by (a) attaching interparty committee members (commissars) to the two highest levels of the party youth hierarchy; (b) assigning to the party group the task of supervising the activities of the party youth cell; and (c) placing the party youth subcell under the direction of a PRP party cell.

In addition to the party supervision, members of the youth organization at the various operational levels were responsible to their superiors within the PRYA. This placed the personnel of the youth organization at any level under the dual command of the party body at the same level and the PRYA intergroup section committee at the next higher level.

The Fifth Interprovincial PRYA provides an example of the size and composition of the youth apparatus.

An indispensable subsidiary of any Communist Party around the world is its youth organization, a halfway house into which likely future party members may be drawn before they reach the required age for candidate membership in the Communist Party proper.[a] There is a fundamental difference between mass associations and the party youth. The former are instruments through which broad elements of the population may be mobilized, integrated, organized in support of the insurgency; the latter is a school of training and preparation for the assumption of party responsibilities.

Clear insight into the role played by the party youth organization in South Vietnam is provided in a PRP document.[b]

> (1) *Purpose of the organization.* This organization is the right hand of the party so that it adopts the purpose of the party and struggles to move

---

[a] For a personnel reporting form on party youth for administrative purposes, see appendix F, doc. F–3.

[b] For the rules and regulations governing the PRYA and its affiliate for still younger children, the Vanguard Youth Organization, see appendix B, docs. B–2 and B–3.

toward Communism. It fights U.S. imperialism and its lackeys in order to complete a democratic revolution of the people by which the people will achieve national unity through peace and neutrality.

(2) *Role and responsibilities of the organization.* The organization acts as a standby arm of the party. The party is the intelligent brain, and the organization is the arm that implements the policies of the party. The party works out policies and the organization carries out these policies and guides the people's activities. The youth organization is close to the party and is the vanguard in leading the various activities prescribed by the party; it assembles the various classes of youth around the party.

(3) *A reserve of resources for the party.* The organization develops progressive elements who vow to be loyal to the party, to stay united and to serve the interests of the people all their lives. When the party needs new blood, it will recruit members from the organization of labor youth, who are young and strong.

It is not only important to distinguish the party from mass organizations in general, but it is also necessary to keep it separated from the party's "popular" societies for those portions of the indigenous youth at large who could be attracted to this more narrow organization. Quite naturally the party established extra associations to attract these elements of the youth who constituted the majority of this age group.

In South Vietnam, in 1965, the principal society of the party appealing to the mass of the youth was known as the South Vietnam Liberation Youth's Association. The Liberation Youth Association was in all respects a genuine mass organization. It received considerable attention from the PRP because of its potential in society generally and was considered, more than any other mass association, as a possible springboard from which individuals might be induced to move into the party youth organization and, eventually, into the party itself.

Characteristically, the party did not ask that its followers make an irrevocable decision by transferring them directly from an unorganized and unindoctrinated status into the core of the apparatus; the plea was always qualified, and the degree of participation only gradually intensified. One moved in toward the core of the PRP through a series of concentric bands in which the demands made upon the individual gradually increased, while his freedom of action and thought was progressively restricted.

It is important to note that the party youth have always had their own organization separate from that of the regular party membership. Lenin, in 1916, already took an unequivocal stand on the importance of independently organizing the youth subsidiary. "The middle-aged and the aged often *do not know how* to approach the youth," he wrote, "for the youth must of necessity advance to socialism *in a different way, by other paths, in other forms, in other circumstances* than their fathers." For these reasons, he continued, "We must decidedly favour organizational independence of the Youth League." The youth, of course, were to be subject to the party member's complete freedom of comradely criticism of their errors—and the correction of those errors at the hands of the responsible party supervisor, Lenin might have properly added—but such intervention was to proceed through channels. If the party failed to understand its organizational relationship to the youth and failed to differentiate, Lenin concluded, "the youth *will be unable* either to train good socialists from their midst or prepare themselves to lead socialism forward."[c]

Why the importance of this distinction? It follows from the fact that one is dealing here with a body of personnel initially quite incapable of stomaching the rigorous, stringent life of the mature party member. Discipline and thought control can be achieved only gradually and will be effected with the greatest surety where the individual acquires it as a member of a group of his peers. One may not mechanically subject youth to the controls exercised over adults; rather, one must seek a balance between the condition ultimately desired and the practices which can be immediately realized. An article appearing in a North Vietnamese periodical in July 1965 tried to formulate the principles of moderation to be observed in rearing youth in the following fashion:

> We must overcome such incorrect tendencies as being too critical, attacking the deficiencies of youths, and demanding that youths practice censorship and make corrections like Party members and adult cadres, or on the other hand, of neglecting self-criticism and criticism among Youth League members and not struggling to give timely criticism to their deficiencies and mistakes, in order to help them advance. In the education of youths, building and resisting must be interrelated, with building playing the dominant role. But if we are to build well we must resist well, for resisting is also intended to achieve good building.[d]

However, moderation is not to be understood as an attempt to shelter the prospective party member. He, as senior, is to be subjected to the school of hard knocks, to the difficulties of operating in the face of concrete reality. Thus, the North Vietnamese statement cited above formulated the following proposition: "We must closely unite education to increase knowledge with the organization of sharp and lively activities to train youths." By way of elaboration on this statement, the article continued:

> The younger generation can study communism only when they have related their study to the ceaseless struggle of the proletarians and the laborers against the old society of the exploiters. The actualities of the struggle of the masses serve as a great school for youths. We must resolutely arrange for youths to participate positively in the struggle movement of the masses, in order to educate and steel them.[e]

History of the Communist Youth Organization

The Vietnamese party youth organization has had a number of names during its history. When first established in 1925 by Nguyen Ai Quoc (Ho Chi Minh), it was known as the Revolutionary Youth. During the 1930's it was known in succession as the Communist Youth Association, the Democratic Youth Association and the Anti-Imperialist Youth Association.

[c] "The Youth International" (an editorial comment published in *Sbornik Sotsial-Demokrata*, No. 2, December 1916), V. I. Lenin, *Collected Works*, XXIII (Moscow: Progress Publishers, 1964), p. 164.

[d] VuQuang, "Making Youths into Warriors Loyal to the Fatherland," *Hoc Tap* ("Studies"), a Vietnamese-language periodical, VII (July 1965), 20–21.

[e] *Ibid.*

At the beginning of the French Indochinese war, it was the Youth Association for National Salvation, and by the end of that protracted conflict it was called the Labor (Lao Dong) Youth Association. When the Lao Dong Party determined upon the fiction of changing its name in South Vietnam to the People's Revolutionary Party in 1962 and claimed that its members in the South were independent of the Lao Dong in the North, the party's youth organization was required to adopt a new name once again in order to conform to the party's new nomenclature. It was known from 1962 to 1966 as the People's Revolutionary Youth Association (PRYA).

No matter what names are used, the organizational relationship between the Lao Dong and its party youth, who ranged in age from 16 to 25, has remained constant. Article 33 of the official regulations of the DLD and article 34 of the "draft" regulations of the People's Revolutionary Party declared: "The party organization at each echelon (i.e., hierarchical level of authority) has under its command the PRYA at the same echelon which at the same time is under the command of the PRYA organization at the next higher echelon." And at the next higher level, to elaborate the organizational principle further, the PRYA committee was once again under the control of its parallel Lao Dong committee. The summit of the dual hierarchies ended in the interparty committee of the Lao Dong's Central Committee in Hanoi, or under the current conditions in the South, in the top party office of the COSVN.

The PRP's Controls Over Its Party Youth

The party leadership appreciated that until the closing phase of a successful insurgency, it had to maintain flexibility. It had to be prepared—in the face of a sudden increase in the strength or effectiveness of hostile forces—to deactivate swiftly its more complex organizational arrangements without losing its integrity and falling apart in the process. For this reason, the party's fundamental cellular character was maintained in working order at all times, and the party youth were tied to the cellular structure where control would be sustained despite losses or reverses.

In any given locality, the PRYA could contain a maximum of four hierarchically arranged structural levels from bottom to top: subcell, cell, group section committee, and intergroup section committee. The PRP controlled this organization (1) by attaching interparty committee members, frequently identified as "commissars" to the two highest levels of the party youth hierarchy; (2) by assigning the party group the task of supervising the activities of the party youth cell; and (3) by placing the party youth subcell under the direction of a Lao Dong party cell.

The "commissar" or party cell youth specialist could give orders or assign quotas to his respective youth elements and exercise right of veto over proposed projects. A PRYA group section or intergroup section committee sent orders to subordinate PRYA bodies with the approval of its attached or associated PRP members. An intergroup youth section committee at the district, provincial, or higher party committee level

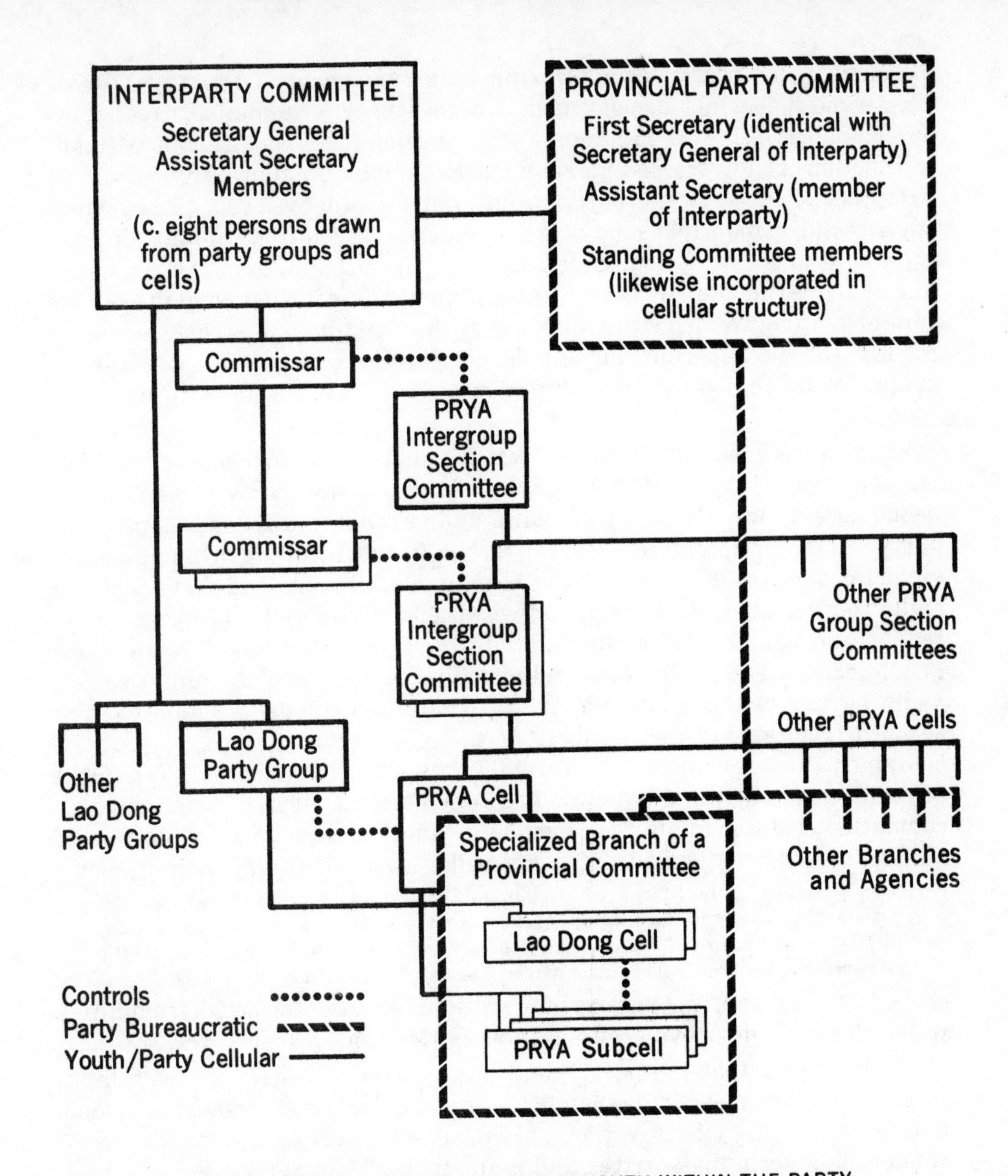

Chart 6. CELLULAR SYSTEM OF PARTY AND PARTY YOUTH WITHIN THE PARTY COMMITTEE SYSTEM AT THE PROVINCIAL LEVEL

directed the activities of a subordinate village, district, or higher intergroup youth section committee in accordance with the guidance provided by its own parallel party youth specialists. This was the meaning of the party regulation placing the PRYA organization at any level under the joint command of (1) the party body at the same level and (2) the PRYA intergroup section committee at the next higher level. Diagrammatically, the relationship may be as shown on chart 6. The reader's first reaction may be that the low level of competence, particularly among recent adherents, must make so complex a structure incapable of operating; in fact, the opposite is the case. This recognized inadequacy serves as one of the critical justifications for utilizing an arrangement of this type, for its effectiveness does not depend upon a high degree of administrative know-how at all levels. At a minimum, this multilateral structure can be made to function if duly trained personnel are available to staff only two of the party posts, those at the party group and commissar level. (The former advises the responsible party cell members on youth work and directly supervises the PRYA cell leadership.) If, in addition, effective personnel can be placed in the PRYA intergroup and group section committees, the administrative problems provoked by such a totalitarian structure can be readily satisfied, permitting the leadership to conceive of its task as primarily the indoctrination and education of the membership at lower levels.[f]

From a very extensive interrogation report of a former North Vietnamese Army lieutenant, attached to the Fifth Interprovincial military headquarters, we are provided with figures on the size and number of party youth groups at the several levels of organization in an interprovincial committee complex. At the base, a subcell contained from three to eight youths; the cell, three or more subcells. Three cells formed a group section and two or more of the latter bodies were integrated into an intergroup section. The party youth cell was directed by a cell captain, precisely as in the case of the party cell. At the group section level a committee was selected from among the members of the affiliated lesser units. Ideally, it contained five members: a secretary, assistant secretary, permanent committee member, and two attached committee members. Sometimes this committee contained only four members. Another document on the role of youth, taken from the body of a guerrilla, assigned functions as follows:

> The secretary is in charge of propaganda, training, and organization. The assistant secretary is in charge of technical matters. The permanent committee member is in charge of finance and youths (i.e., those not in the Party Youth Organization). The other committee member is in charge of production.

At the very top, the intergroup section likewise formed a committee in which all of the above group level activities were provided for.

To the extent that the party youth structure had been effectively built, it reinforced the party's capabilities to mobilize large bodies of people and provide them with direction and supervision during any of the succession of short-term mass drives and movements. Thus party youth engaged in programs for greater production by the peasants, intensified recruitment into "Liberation Associations," the erection of military defensive works (e.g., combat villages) or other immediate goals that could be realized only through the cooperation of substantial numbers of persons.

[f] Appreciating the need fo ra few highly experienced individuals at these critical levels, the official regulations of the PRYA made provisions for the retention of limited numbers of persons after they had passed their 25th birthday—when one's affiliation with the party youth normally ceased. A member engaged in a "specialized mission," serving on a group of intergroup section committee or made the subject of a special request to higher headquarters, could be held within the PRYA until he reached the age of 27. Whether retention beyond this age was possible was not apparent from the regulations. The relevant passage (paragraph 2 of article I in chapter 1) reads as follows:

> The members who are over 25 years old, or who have joined the Vietnamese People's Revolutionary Party, can no longer be group members if they are not elected to the executive committee or do not assume a specialized mission. At the request of the group, some members may remain in the group until the age of 27.

The groups which received the party youth's priority attention were the Liberation Youth Association, and the village guerrilla or militia and self-defense forces.

In each of these bodies, a representative element of the PRYA was injected in accordance with the procedures employed by the party proper itself.[g] Here, party youth served as understudies to the party members also active in the body in question, learning the trade "on the job," so to speak, while accepting direction from party members along with the general membership of the body in question. The PRYA member, however, was subject to criticism by his fellow PRYA cell members and by the party itself via a responsible, appointed party member who was expected devote a portion of his working day to this additional duty.

Statistics available on the one province of Dinh Tuong during a twelve-month period in the earlier 1960's suggest that where the party took this phase of its work seriously, the investment in time and personnel in party youth work in the long run fell substantially below that required to sustain—by way of contrast—any of its mass organizations, whether armed or unarmed. The number of party members assigned full time to PRYA intergroup, group, cell, subcell duties in Dinh Tuong was ninety-three. In contrast, the party made the following allocations of its personnel to its mass organizations according to its own figures:

Organization	*Number of Assigned Party Members*
Village Guerrilla	313
Hamlet Self-Defense	258
Liberation Youth	118
Farmers' Association	580
Liberation Women	118

The indicated allocations lend themselves to a twofold division: on the one hand, the Liberation Youth and Women's Associations which engaged the activity of only a few more persons than the party youth itself and, on the other hand, the two armed bodies and the Farmers' Association, in which a much larger allocation of party personnel was necessary. A separation such as this is further encouraged by additional information, contained in the same party report, informing us that the number of party members in the two paramilitary organizations had increased by 374 during the preceding 12 months and by 222 in the farmers' society during the same period, while no increase was indicated for the other two associations or the party youth organization.

While one must be extremely careful with such information, the discrepancies between the two groups of organizations may possibly be a reflection of the effectiveness of the party's PRYA program and the consequent party decision to rely heavily upon the PRYA to sustain youth and women's mass work—with a minimum of direct party supervision—allowing the party proper to concentrate its efforts on the more rapid activation of extensive paramilitary forces.

[g] On the technical aspects of party mass work, see appendix A, chapter IV.

CHAPTER 6

THE VULNERABILITIES AND WEAKNESSES OF THE SOUTH VIETNAMESE PRP APPARATUS

SUMMARY

The inner dynamics of the PRP heightened its susceptibility to a series of weaknesses that are not met with similar frequency in traditional Western organizations. Thus their organization, though it operated clandestinely in many portions of South Vietnam and engaged in underground activities, was irrevocably dependent upon a flow of papers, dossiers, forms, reports, autobiographies, written self-critiques, etc., which surpassed the administrative requirements of their opponents. Though this dependence on paper seemingly inhibited operations, the failure of a committee at any level of the organization to forward reports on time, constituted an even more severe problem for the organization.

Other disabilities were associated with the PRP's paper requirements. The subordinate party leader, anxious to achieve the goals set and the quotas demanded, was under considerable pressure to falsify information so as to imply that programs had been accomplished which indeed may never have gotten underway. Decisions based upon such inadequate information would necessarily be equally inappropriate. The practices through which superior bodies preempted the authority of subordinate units made the outcome of this interrelationship predictable.

Another major problem which the party could not avoid or ignore was the extreme difficulty of training the new party member, who suddenly found himself drawn up into a world of activities and practices which were quite alien to him, and for which he might lack the sophistication and background that could ease his period of adjustment. This was an even more critical problem when the period of preparation and reorientation prior to the receipt of candidate membership was abbreviated by local party leaders in order that they might claim a large figure for party growth. Since every leader wanted to display his effectiveness as a dependable cadre, the premature induction of new recruits occurred with regularity, provoking "internal discrepancies, prejudicial to operations."

The PRP had various administrative and organizational vulnerabilities. First of all, the party was unusually dependent on written reports, which required that extensive files be maintained and that a great deal of time be devoted to ensuring that reports be prepared and forwarded promptly and securely. Under pressure to produce activity and progress reports, leaders might report planned or intended progress as having been accomplished.

Another result was the relatively indiscriminate enrollment of large numbers of people into the party's ranks. Training and indoctrination for party recruits (and often for party personnel in leadership positions) was, in many cases, superficial.

Men in leadership positions in the Communist apparatus were not without human weaknesses and individual shortcomings. Many became overzealous in implementing discipline and control, thus alienating people. Terrorism could be an effective means of control but could also reverse the party's political and propaganda efforts as assassinations and brutality became less selective.

The repeated complaint was that basic party documents had "not yet been thoroughly studied," and that the novice's grasp of party principles was "superficial." Such criticisms were not exclusively directed at the grassroots level; one could also find indications of inadequate training or experience among the leading figures in the specialized branches and agencies of provincial and even higher party committees.

Continually confronted with this situation, the personnel of propaganda and training branches soon learned to set only modest goals for their students. In the captured notes of a party cadre, one finds the teacher's task formulated in these words:

> We should educate party members on what is necessary first; we should not try to teach them too much because most of them are new members. What we teach them should be related to their actual activities.

The authority associated with a leadership post in the PRP organization could give rise to another group of problems. Criminal inclinations, greed, and lust were provided with a mechanism through which they could express themselves where discipline and firm control were not maintained. While assassination, expropriation, and brutality did figure in the daily work of the party, these devices had to be used, for the most part, on a selective basis to be effective. Where control over lesser bodies weakened, terrorism tended to lose its "selective" character and boomeranged against the party and its critical mass organizations. The year-end report on party work in the provinces of Dinh Thuong and Go Cong indicated that many illicit activities were rampant during that year.

The Communist insurgents operating in South Vietnam did not necessarily recognize the provincial borderlines utilized by the RVN in its administration of the country. While some of the North's own provincial demarcation lines for the South conform with those of the Saigon government, others are totally dissimilar. The Lao Dong's My Tho Province is a case in point; it is made up of the bulk of the two RVN provinces of Dinh Tuong and Go Cong.[a]

The embezzlement of public funds, bribery, rape (most of the latter cases, we are informed, "involved Chapter Secretaries and male or female members"), "corruption and lewdness," were cited as weaknesses widespread among the party's membership.[b]

The Criticism Meeting[c]

One of the most severe problems in the training of new party members in South Vietnam was posed by the indispensable practice of criticism-self-

[a] The VC used the old French provincial boundaries. (Bernard Fall, private communication, 1966.)

[b] For a more extensive treatment of the types of problems that confronted the party among the civil population, see the authentic self-criticism reports, docs. G–1, G–2, and G–3 in appendix G.

[c] For a more extensive treatment of the criticism-self-criticism meeting, see appendix A, chapter III, as well as the written self-criticism contained in doc. C–3 in appendix C, and docs. G–2 and G–3 in appendix G.

criticism. This device was conceived as a means of inducing each member to abandon his personal interests and conform to the will of the party by focusing the collective weight of group influence upon him. The purpose of discussion was to get each member to reveal his own opinions and attitudes so that those harmful to the party's work could be identified and their possessor obliged to abandon them. The party sought to induce the member of the cell group to think in terms of the interests of the apparatus, to conceive of his private strivings as petty, to believe that only the goals sought by the organization were important, and that these goals could be realized only through the organization. There was no place for the individualist in the party rank and file and the criticism meeting was designed to break this "petty bourgeois" tendency.

For the self-willed, tradition-bound peasantry, the learning of these lessons did not come easily. The provincial leadership complained of the lack of "impartiality" at criticism sessions, of the ingress of "personal sentiments," or of the widespread formation of cliques among the village chapters." Many attended meetings reluctantly. Instead of expressing themselves during group sessions, their "critiques of other comrades often were made in private." Or worst of all—keeping in mind the intent of the struggle meeting—"they did not reveal their ideas during the discussion." Such reluctant participants would wait until after the meeting was closed "to express disapproval or criticize the resolutions taken." The report concluded: "Despite the progress obtained, we must recognize that due to the low party level of the members, the implementation of party discipline was not as proper as desired." This failure to participate in self-criticism was not restricted to recent recruits. The year-end report attacked unidentified district current affairs committee members for "not properly carrying out even their most common and routine activities such as critique and self-critique."

Recruitment Practices

Two alternative methods were employed in Dinh Tuong (My Tho) Province in recruiting party members. These were identified respectively as "recruitment in series" and "application by individuals."

The first of these techniques consisted of granting candidate status to whole groups or participants in one or another party-controlled mass organization by a single blanket determination. Such an act was followed up with "concentrated training and indoctrination for each individual involved."

The second technique was the more traditional process of "regular introduction, study of regulations and individual admission procedures," requiring (1) the submission of a request for membership accompanied by (2) an ideological biography and supported by (3) the written recommendations of two full party members in good standing.[d]

[d] For an example of these several documents, see appendix C, docs. C-1 and C-2.

It was appreciated that new party personnel acquired through the first of these techniques would be less than ideally prepared to accept the obligations of their new stations, but such an approach recommended itself in regions under effective insurgent control. There, where the population could be easily manipulated, it constituted a means of rapidly building up the party's rolls.

The latter approach, in contrast, reduced the likelihood of a high dropout rate among new party members and could be sustained in marginal or hostile areas where any open attempt at the coercion of the civil population could bring on serious retaliation. Indeed, when counterinsurgents intensified their operations in Dinh Tuong Province and weakened the PRP's controls over the peasantry, the organization abandoned "recruitment in series," and relied exclusively upon the latter technique.

The immediate occasion for the provincial organization's resort to recruitment in series was its receipt from interprovincial headquarters of a requirement to raise the number of provincial party members from the reported figures of 2,300 to 4,500 during the following 12-month period. A serious effort was made to comply and "to recruit rapidly, but carefully." Though the apparatus failed to reach its assigned goal, an increase of 1,100, or 50 percent, was reported at the end of the year. To reach this level of party membership (approximately 0.6 percent of a reported population of 593,000 [e]), the organization exploited all of the short cuts permitted by "recruitment in series." The resultant expanded party organization, however, did not escape the undesirable consequences of such an undiscriminating process of selection.

Under these conditions, the party rolls came to contain many individuals who were entirely uninstructed and were not provided with adequate supervision. The party leadership was hard pressed to make its novices understand the difference between membership in one of the controlled mass organizations and membership in the party itself, one of the most fundamental, basic principles in Communist organization. A main effort was required to stop nonparty personnel from participating in village party chapter meetings which were apparently being conducted openly after the fashion of popular assemblies. Prior to the party's intervention, wrote a provincial office, "everybody could attend such meetings."

In Go Cong district, the party was faced with the enormity of the fact that the party status of 50 percent of the organization's officials (the members of standing committees and the heads of principal branch sections) and 40 percent of its rank and file remained "undetermined." The year-end review of party work, with striking candor, admitted, "sometimes they are considered as party members; sometimes not."

A party directive, designed to bring order out of acerbated confusion, identified as "Regulation D," is more interesting for the malpractices it

[e] Official RVN statistics for this area set the population as in excess of 700,000.

revealed than for the procedure it outlined to stabilize inner-party relationships. An extract from "Regulation D" reads in part:

> During the rapid build-up of our organizations and installations, the party principles and procedures were not thoroughly observed in recruiting the members. For this reason, some members joined the party without going through the procedures. So, the province committee has decided that these members must go back through these procedures. They will be considered as new members. Those members who went through the proper procedures but who were not yet accepted into the party in an official ceremony will be considered as official members if they meet the required standards for membership. Those applicants who already had an introduction and approval but were not yet accepted as official members should go over all the procedures.
>
> The following solutions will be used for the former applicants who did not meet the party requirements for official membership, those with complicated political backgrounds or those who were preparatory members.
>
> (1) If the sponsor is a preparatory party member, the approval will be up to the district committee, and the applicant is accepted as a party member since the day of his application.
>
> (2) If the sponsor is a nonmember, or both sponsors are nonmembers, the applicant will not be accepted.
>
> (3) If one of the sponsors is a party member, the application will be accepted.

Provincial headquarters declared itself prepared to make exceptions where those who considered themselves in possession of membership refused with indignation to submit to reprocessing. "To avoid such discontent," declared the provincial committee, "each cast will be separately considered."

The Disciplining of Party Cadres

In the above compromise solution lay the essence of the party leadership's approach to the resolution of pressing party difficulties. They sought no absolute alteration of conditions, but rather, with the wisdom that comes from many years of practical experience within this unique organization, to make things better bit by bit. In the eyes of the provincial leadership, its district committees were composed for the most part of a hard core of individuals who had displayed courage, discipline, and essential loyalty, but lacked a thorough grasp of party fundamentals. Except for a certain element of "deadwood," they were "experienced in mobilizing the masses for political or military struggles" and they could be relied upon "to conduct political demonstrations, armed combat or sabotage," but some of them as yet remained "incapable of understanding party resolutions," and were "not capable of leading long-range programs." Where the reality of events left the leadership with no alternatives, the purge would be used, but if their goals could be achieved through less extreme policies, then such steps were altogether acceptable.

In Go Cong district, where village leaders had been "reluctant to take disciplinary action" against the disorderly recruits "for fear of weakening the chapters," the local committee's first secretary, accompanied by the provincial committee's first secretary, proceeded to the villages in question where they conducted indoctrination classes on the party's "conception of human life," and reinstituted the practice of "criticism-self-criticism" within the cells. "As a result, 105 members were expelled from the party, and a large number of others were criticized or warned."

The purge was no panacea, and it was employed with care and discrimination.[f] Following the first rash of purges in some villages and districts of culprits guilty of embezzlement, rape, and unspecified forms of corruption, the provincial committee intervened. Lower bodies were advised "not to consider lewdness as a transgression equal in its seriousness to deviation in policy." If the "culprits" in question accepted the party's leadership in strategy and tactics they should be retained even if they had "little chance to regain their prestige with the masses."

The more experienced members who had been released recently from prison were treated in a separate category. While it was possible that many of them were permanently lost, the party would not proceed on the basis of such an assumption. Rather they were slated for reindoctrination in small classes of five or six led by experienced persons drawn from propaganda and training branch offices of district or higher committees.

CONCLUSIONS TO PART ONE

The Indochinese Communist party, officially founded in 1930, has sustained itself under a variety of names and fronts through three and a half decades of political turmoil and armed conflict. Its leader during its entire life span has been one Nguyen Ai Quoc, known since 1941 as Ho Chi Minh, the "Enlightened One." Its first essay at establishing a party-dominated government occurred in September 1945, but the reappearance of French troops in northern Vietnam after the close of the Second World War frustrated this effort and led to the French-Indochinese war which lasted until 1954. The Geneva settlement led to the division of the country "temporarily" into two zones respectively to the north and the south of the 17th parallel. In the northern zone, Ho Chi Minh thereafter established in fact the government denied him eight years earlier. In the south he was confronted by a protagonist in the person of Ngo Dinh Diem. The second phase of the Indochinese war followed in the form of the South Vietnamese insurgency which gradually escalated during the late 1950's to become the major struggle of the 1960's.

Critical moments in the second round of conflict are the years 1959–60 and 1965–66. The first of these pivotal moments marked the commencement of the infiltration of significant numbers of persons from the North, and proclamation of the National Front for the Liberation of South Vietnam. By the latter date, the war assumed yet more critical proportions with the injection of major elements of the North Vietnamese Army into the South (of battalion and regimental size). Between these two dates, that portion

[f] Even where the party did take recourse to purging, its impact on the membership was seriously blunted by the readiness with which the party readmitted those once spurned. Thus the Go Cong district committee, after reporting that it had purged 161 members by the end of the year, was obliged to add that this number was almost the same as that of the preceding year because "most of the party members purged the year before were readmitted."

of the Vietnamese Communist Party operating in the South attempted to establish itself in the public eye as an independent party, free of control from Hanoi, by dubbing itself the People's Revolutionary Party (PRP).

By 1965, this party organization (following the precedents of the earlier French-Indochinese War), had activated parallel hierarchical structures through which it fought politically and militarily and within which it hid itself both from public attention and the vengeance of the security forces of the RVN. They were (1) the system of mass organizations and liberation committees provided with a roof by the national executive of the NFLSVN and (2) the system of armed forces having both a main line and a regional character. Control, surveillance, and policymaking, however, remained consistently with the party itself and to understand the insurgency was to understand the party.

Central to the dynamics of the PRP was the principle of cellular life. Each party member belonged to a cell of three or more persons and engaged actively in the life of his cell.

The supreme directorate of the PRP sought to make of party membership a 24-hour-a-day job for the rank and file membership, and, in the face of the difficulties of escalating a conflict in the South, found in the cell the milieu in which its goals of acquiring total commitment could be very nearly achieved. That part of the party member's daily life not taken up in staff or operational responsibilities was absorbed by his activities within his cell, where goals were set that were well calculated to stimulate still greater application on his part and to draw upon his intellectual and physical capabilities to contribute still further to the total insurgent effort. In the cell, where his immediate concern was not his field of professional specialization, but his all-round approximation to norms which the party expected from every "good party member," his conceptual framework was built and his vested personal interest in the success of the insurgency was progressively strengthened until his premonition that there was "no way out" became a certainty.

The cellular structure saw to the spiritual and emotional life of the party member and sustained the mystique and *esprit* of the movement's command cadre, and the party committee system provided the movement's supreme directorate with the vehicle through which it could capitalize upon the member's will to excel. At the interprovincial level, for example, the party member might work in any of a broad range of branches, agencies, and sections, each devised for its impact upon some element of the population. Second only to commitment, in its order of priorities, was the virtue of flexibility as the party sought to breed a corps of men with the competence to adapt rapidly to new situations. Only in this fashion could the party exploit the everchanging local conditions and maximize its impact on the civil population. "It is impossible to remain loyal to Marxism, to remain loyal to the revolution," Lenin once asserted, "unless insurrection is treated as an art." [g]

[g] "Marxism and Insurrection" (a letter to the Central Committee of the RSDLP(B), September 1917), Lenin, *Collected Works*, XXVI (Moscow: Progress Publishers, 1964), 27.

On only one count might the details of organization at the operational level be labeled rigid: where it involved the principle of cellular organization and activity. These stipulations were synonymous with "being communistic," and to forego them would be to withdraw from party membership. No compromise was possible there. Beyond this minimum requirement, however, extreme opportunism was acceptable and the task of the men who commanded elements of the PRP as first secretaries at the provincial, district, or village level was to evolve bodies best calculated to implement the insurgency's essential goals.

From the leadership at lower levels the party expected originality in the resolution of problems and in the intensification of offensive operations, and was prepared to punish those who failed to show resolution and imagination. A comprehensive system of surveillance and control reached down through all layers of the party, providing the leaders at any one level with the means to seize at will the operational control of the next lower level.

These parallel, contradictory efforts reflected an unbridgeable inconsistency between the ends sought and the means employed. Subversive warfare by its very nature places a premium on decentralized local operations in which those in immediate command may employ extreme discretion in their tactical decision; but the organization providing direction is a totalitarian movement, sharing with its historic predecessors, both to the left and the right, an inalienable distrust of private initiative, freedom of choice, and popular self-determination. The party sought creativity based upon absolute commitment.

The consequence of this distinctive situation was the appearance of a system of institutional devices and of time-honored customs such as the vertically structured security apparatus with its independent jurisdictional prerogatives, the roving inspection team, and the practice of the recall of delegated authority from the committee at the next lower level in accordance with the principle of reverse representation.

The principles of organization and control which governed the lives of those members of the Vietnamese Communist Party engaged in the insurgency in the South extended as well to the closely knit youth affiliate, which was the subject of much of the literature and many of the directives issuing from party offices. This structure constituted the school for the next generation of party members.

Two features of the party youth organizations stand out. First, its members were provided with a distinct, separate organization with its own hierarchically structured command. Second, participation in unit meetings, indoctrination sessions, and theoretical training was valid only as it was combined with assigned practical responsibilities which challenged their abilities and for which they were held responsible.

Through the commissar operating from the interparty cellular committee, control was maintained over the higher layers of the independently structured youth organization; through the party cell and group, over the lower levels in the PRYA. And within the various levels of the latter association, intensive indoctrination was combined with the practical field experience of participating in the varied activities conducted by the PRP in its struggle for the seizure of political power.

Given the complexity of the tasks the party set itself on the one side and the fallibility of the individuals to whom party membership was extended on the other, it is not surprising that the organization frequently fell short of its goal of producing the model party member celebrated in its propaganda. The problems confronting the Dinh Tuong provincial committee in the early 1960's may serve as an extreme example of the difficulties the party had to resolve during the early phases of its effort to expand substantially in size. The reverses suffered, however, may not be equated with failure. The core of reliable party personnel expanded, and the reports to superior committees offices reflected (1) the leadership's alertness to its own shortcomings, (2) its sustained aggressive will to correct these weaknesses, and (3) its possession of the administrative facilities and functional channels through which improvement could be effected. In a situation where the main thrust of government security forces and their external supporters was directed not at thwarting inner-party activities and exploiting identifiable inner-party vulnerabilities but at struggling with the military units generated by the party apparatus, the party itself remained free —behind the cover provided by those combatant elements—to seek out ever better techniques to remedy its own recognized organizational deficiencies.

A survey, then, of the structure, regulations, and practices of the PRP indicates that counterinsurgent forces were confronted with an apparatus at the center of the revolutionary struggle, which was structured in accordance with a carefully thought-out organizational doctrine and which was calculated to extract the maximum effort from these enrolled in its ranks. It presented security forces with an elusive target, easily overlooked in a conflict in which the armed guerrilla readily attracted first attention. But it was the party apparatus which spawned the armed units and the destruction of those fighting forces was not synonymous with the destruction of the party's war-making potential. A campaign plan which would lead to the destruction of hostile combatants under these circumstances was not the same thing as a pacification plan. The defeat of insurgent combatant forces provided the counterinsurgent with an environment favorable to its ultimate mission, which was the destruction of the PRP.

PART TWO
THE CIVIL ORGANIZATION AND ITS TACTICS

CHAPTER 7
THE STRATEGIC UTILITY OF CIVIL MASS WORK UNDER THE CONDITIONS OF PROTRACTED GUERRILLA WAR

SUMMARY

Mass organization work has been a fundamental activity of Communist revolutions and insurgencies since the time of Lenin. The Communist in Vietnam were fully cognizant of these practices and, following the precedents of the past, erected an infrastructure incorporating both a hard-core elite and a multitude of popular associations, fully under the control of the hard core, through which significant segments of the population could be manipulated at will. Beyond this, mass organizations served as convenient cover for the Communist Party. Activities of the insurgents were carried out in the name of these organizations. But the Communists were in control, and the mechanisms of that control were hidden from the population at large and often from the counterinsurgent forces as well. Mass organizations served as means of controlling and expanding popular support.

The PRP developed military forces through which it contended with the government for military domination of the South and a parallel organization which struggled for political control. Operating within a population where the vast majority of the people were indifferent, the party set out to (1) maintain its support through the formation and direction of mass organizations; (2) draw more of the population into these organizations; and (3) neutralize support for government pacification efforts.

Mass organization work in the South had a profound effect upon military operations by progressively undermining the base from which the government drew in defending itself, thereby redirecting the flow of national resources into the hands of the insurgent leadership.[a] Increasingly, the government had to import its own resources from abroad. Political organizational work, then, provided the insurgent with an inexpensive means of inducing protracted economic attrition.

Theoretical Background

Such an approach to internal war was not born out of the Lao Dong effort in South Vietnam; it is a fundamental characteristic of the Communist approach to the subversive seizure of political power, and was given its classic articulation in Lenin's 1902 pamphlet, *What Is To Be Done?*

---

[a] Characteristic forms of resources and manpower made available through mass work by the party for its military forces are suggested by the policy directions in appendix H, docs. H–2 and H–3.

In that work Lenin sought to strike the proper balance between a small group of highly trained professional revolutionaries and a large group of members of organizations open to the public at large. The success of the revolution depended upon accurately allocating the functions to be performed by each. Although popular associations were unsuited to tasks calling for competent clandestine behavior, without them committed revolutionaries could operate as terrorists only.

Lenin believed that a division of responsibilities between the professionals and the amateurs increased the kinds of activities which the masses could perform, while reducing the dangers attached to any one type of operation. Lenin had this to say about the division of responsibilities:

> Centralisation of the secret functions of the organisation by no means implies centralisation of all the functions of the movement. Active participation of the widest masses in the illegal press will not diminish because a "dozen" professional revolutionaries centralise the secret functions connected with this work; on the contrary, it will increase tenfold. In this way, and in this way alone, shall we ensure that reading the illegal press, writing for it, and to some extent even distributing it, will almost cease to be secret work, for the police will soon come to realise the folly and impossibility of judicial and administrative red-tape procedure over every copy of a publication that is being distributed in the thousands. This holds not only for the press, but for every function of the movement, even for demonstrations. The active and widespread participation of the masses will not suffer; on the contrary, it will benefit by the fact that a "dozen" experienced revolutionaries, trained professionally no less than the police, will centralise all the secret aspects of the work—the drawing up of leaflets, the working out of approximate plans; and the appointing of bodies of leaders for each urban district, for each factory district, and for each educational institution, etc. Centralisation of the most secret functions in an organisation of revolutionaries will not diminish, but rather increase the extent and enhance the quality of the activity of a large number of other organisations, that are intended for a broad public and are therefore as loose and as nonsecret as possible, such as workers' trade unions; workers' self-education circles and circles for reading illegal literature; and socialist, as well as democratic circles among all other sections of the population, etc. We must have such circles, trade unions, and organisations everywhere in as large a number as possible and with the widest variety of functions; but it would be absurd and harmful to confound them with the organisation of revolutionaries, to efface the borderline between them, to make still more hazy the all too faint recognition of the fact that in order to "serve" the mass movement we must have people who will devote themselves exclusively to Social-Democratic activities, and that such people must train themselves patiently and steadfastly to be professional revolutionaries.[b]

The general framework developed by Lenin was given further development by insurgents in Asia in the thirties and in Eastern Europe and Asia in the forties and fifties. These later insurgents created techniques of building civil support in countries divided in the struggle between rebels and the government. The general procedure is for the party to select from the general mass organizations persons who then constitute the membership of a "liberation" committee charged with the direction of

[b] "What Is To Be Done? Burning Questions of Our Movement," V. I. Lenin, *Collected Works*, V (Moscow: Foreign Languages Publishing House, 1961), pp. 465–66. As employed by Lenin in the above text, the term "Social-Democratic" may be understood to be synonymous with "Marxist."

civil affairs. Such a body, claiming to represent the interests of the membership of two or more mass organizations, may be called a "front." In an insurgent-dominated area, then, the front gradually assumes de facto administrative control over the local civil population.[c]

"Cover"

A byproduct of successful mass work is "cover." Mass associations draw attention to themselves and may cause observers to overlook the tightly knit, decidedly smaller apparatus which provides direction from behind the scene.

It is within this conceptual framework that the Vietnamese Communists of the sixties built multiple and diversified support associations under the centralized control of the party organization.

That the PRP in South Vietnam was fully alive to the advantages to be gained from such a structure was apparent in both inner-party statements captured by security personnel and from the choice of terms which were selected by the organization to identify itself in public. Thus one document on mass organizations justified the activities of such associations with the following words:

> To cover, protect, and insure the activities of the chapters and party members, we must organize the masses.

An even more striking indication of the PRP's appreciation of the cover provided was its determination to refer to itself in public statements as an agency of the federation of mass organizations which in fact it controlled.

The Hierarchy of Mass Organizations

To understand the extent to which the PRP made use of mass organizations as cover one must remember that the organizations erected by mass workers were drawn together into a hierarchical structure which—once fully evolved—was to function at the hamlet, village, district, provincial, and interprovincial levels, and which would be provided with a "national congress" at the top. In South Vietnam this "congress" was called the National Front for the Liberation of South Vietnam (NFLSVN).

By the end of 1965 this structure had not been completely developed. The top executive body (the NFLSVN), however, had been established in 1960 and appropriate front offices at the interprovincial level appeared in the course of the following months. By the winter 1962–63 innumerable front committees existed at the hamlet and village levels and during 1964–65 comparable bodies began to appear at the district and provincial levels, though they were not uniformly present in all party-dominated regions. Nevertheless, ever since the announcement was made that the NFLSVN

---

[c] For an imperfect but perceptive statement on the daily life of peasants who have fallen completely under insurgent control, see appendix E, doc. E–6. Notice the party's effort to engage in all of those aspects of civil administration associated with the agencies of a national, provincial, or local government. For characteristic examples of administrative forms utilized by the party in the management of the civil population via their mass organizations, see also appendix F, docs. F–2 and F–3.

existed, enough of its structure had been erected to permit Vietnamese Communists to exploit the idea in its public pronouncements.

"Liberation Committees"

It is important to note that throughout the first half of the decade of the sixties the formation of a system of "liberation committees" provided the conceptual framework for party agitation and propaganda.

The fiction at the center of all insurgent statements was (1) that the combatant forces operating in the South were brought into being by a free determination of the people's true representatives in the NFLSVN and were fully under the control of that body and, (2) that the PRP (Lao Dong in the South) was simply one among many organizations whose joint views were authentically vocalized only by the chosen spokesmen of the NFLSVN. To the extent that the PRP/Lao Dong apparat was able to make its target audiences believe this, it was able to avoid the limelight of general attention: it took cover behind an organization which was in fact its creature.

Population Control

Besides providing cover, mass organizations also helped the PRP subject the general populace to the same types of control exercised over party members in the cells. Members of popular associations were exposed to such characteristic control devices as the struggle meeting, the self-criticism sessions, and balloting on proposals on which irrevocable determinations had already been made. Through the mass organizations, one segment of the population after another was made ready for citizenship in the new world which the Communists hoped to initiate upon the consummation of a successful insurgency. Those who impeded the advent of the new era were liquidated in the name of the liberation front committee. Thus the emergence of a political opposition was forestalled prior to the hoped-for creation of the new state. According to the insurgent schedule, the entire society would have been restructured from the bottom to the top by the day when the insurgents took over the capital city.

Open Organizations and Secret Organizations

In line with Lenin's exhortation "to work wherever the masses are to be found,"[d] the PRP performed mass organizational work in areas under their control and in new areas as well. Sometimes they formed an organization themselves and sometimes they penetrated and sought to control associations already in existence. Organizations formed by the insurgents would be open or secret, depending upon the strength of the RVN's security forces, with the likelihood of secrecy being most pronounced in work among the civil population in urban areas.

---

[d] V. I. Lenin, *"Left-Wing" Communism: An Infantile Disorder* (New York: International Publishers, 1934), p. 36.

Where mass work called for the penetration of existing bodies, a distinction was drawn by the PRP leadership between (1) semiopen or semilegal bodies and (2) open or legal bodies. One party document on mass organizations identified semiopen groups as "organizations not authorized by enemy laws, but which can still operate openly because they respond to the immediate needs of the masses." Characteristic examples of the semiopen organizations were business, sports, arts, and mutual aid groups, worker exchange associations, and volunteer firefighters.

Legal associations were defined as "organizations, recognized by enemy laws" which were designed to protect the legitimate interests of one or another social class in the society. In this category were such groups as professional syndicates; women's clubs; parent-teachers' associations; linguistic, ethnic, and cultural groups; and student councils and associations. Quite naturally, this party document continued, the national government would make every effort to dominate the leadership of such bodies, but, operating covertly, the party could compete with the RVN for control of these groups. A perceptive essay distributed by the propaganda and instruction section of the Saigon-Gia Dinh Party Committee (app. E, doc. E–5) provided the following guidance on the party's work in legal and quasi-legal bodies:

> The [Party] organization must know how to use the people's struggle to defeat the enemy, regardless of regulations prescribed by the latter. Key members of the [Party] organization must develop their secret bases and do their best to win the people's support. Party cadres must know how to maintain their legal position, work together with other members to carry out their assigned mission, and struggle for the [popular] organization's interest along with other members. They must be discreet, especially the underground cadres in the executive committee [of the popular association].[e]

Methods of Mass Work

The methods to be employed in the conduct of mass work were developed into a tight body of operational doctrine, referred to as the "promotion method," which consisted of five steps: investigation, propaganda, organization, training, and struggle.

The central postulates in the Communist's work within the population, as revealed in this five-fold ápproach, were the beliefs that (1) the convictions generated in individuals via the instruments of agitation and propaganda could be sustained only as such persons were drawn into organizations activated to realize the principles articulated, and (2) that only an organization actually in operation, challenging its membership and reward-

[e] It is a matter worthy of note that both the Saigon essay and other documents on mass organization work followed up their treatment of open associations with sharply worded statements warning party members against attempting to infiltrate or subvert that group of popular bodies which enjoyed the direct support of the Ngo family in South Vietnam in the 1950's and early 1960's. Lenin's advice, in his *"Left-Wing" Communism*, to work in all associations, even the most hostile, was ignored. And the personalist Can Lao Nhan Vi, together with the National Revolutionary Movement, the Republican Youth organization, and the other bodies belonging to this group were denounced as "reactionary" and "counterrevolutionary." The mass organizational worker was informed, "We must absolutely boycott these organizations." Seemingly the leadership of these bodies was aware of Communist tactics and quite effective at combatting them.

ing or penalizing individual acts as they approximated or fell short of desired norms, would hold its membership and maintain continued interest. Thus the sequence of events in the PRP's "promotion method." Once investigation (i.e., population analysis) had determined local sources of dissidence, needs, priority interests, key communicators, and class structure, appropriately clothed themes and slogans were employed to raise members for party-controlled mass organizations.

Inside these bodies the member was subjected to more persistent propaganda and to a series of challenges, through training and struggle (i.e., operations conducted in the midst of an indifferent or hostile populace), which constituted a trial period. Through careful observation of the recruit's reactions, the party could determine the advantage of promoting him into positions of increased responsibility. No one step in this process was conceived as an end in itself and the extent of the mass worker's success at any given stage could only be ascertained at the completion of the entire process.

The United Front From Below

The successful conduct of an organizational effort conceived in such broad terms required a highly distinctive political platform—or, to use the Communists' own terminology, "strategic general line." We may identify this strategy as the "United Front From Below," or "Four Class" approach. It is one of the three alternate strategies which a Communist party may employ during an epoch in its development.[f]

A position had to be assumed that clearly identified "the enemy" and openly acknowledged his strength and resources, while concurrently disassociating the overwhelming majority of the nation's populace from any complicity in the "war crimes" of that enemy. Only as the party declared itself the friend of all classes could it build its multiple mass organization.

That segment of the population labeled as the enemy was generally restricted to government officials and the leaders of any element of the population who had clearly demonstrated their loyalty to the policies pursued by the government.

Class Policy

The central theme in party propaganda and agitational materials was that the liberation front, in contrast to the recognized leaders of society, represented the best interest of all elements of society. Therefore, party pronouncements lacked any reference to the standard themes of Marxist ideology—e.g., class conflict, the expropriation of the means of production, the liquidation of the exploiter class, and the dictatorship of the proletariat. Immediate strategy made it inadvisable to discuss ultimate goals. The party wished to create a platform which would be especially attractive to those

[f] For an extended analysis of the additional "right" and "left" general lines, see the present author's article, "The Framework of Communist Strategy," *Orbis: A Quarterly Journal of World Affairs,* IX, No. 4 (Winter 1966), 970–84.

elements which had the most to lose from the victory of the party-dominated "liberation front." If a population segment could not be attracted en masse, reasoned the insurgent, then it should be splintered into contending factions.

This policy and strategy orientation displays striking similarities with that utilized by the Chinese Communist Party in the 1930's and 1940's[g] But both the Vietnamese and Chinese approaches were nothing more than an implementation of the line called for by the Comintern at its Sixth Congress in 1928. In this document, an unblushing opportunism is commended to the leadership of the national sections of the international Communist movement. The ultimate objective was the destruction of bourgeois capitalistic society, and the immediate obligation was to confound the leaders of such capitalistic nations. To this end Communists were to "advance partial slogans and demands." These constituted "an essential part of correct tactics." Further, the "repudiation of partial demands and transitional slogans 'on principle,' is incompatible with the tactical principle of communism, for, in effect, such repudiation condemns the party to inaction and isolates it from the masses."

> Throughout the entire prerevolutionary period a most important basic part of the tactics of the Communist Parties is the tactic of the united front, as a means towards most successful struggle against capital, towards the class mobilization of the masses and the exposure and isolation of the reformist leaders.
>
> The correct application of united front tactics and the fulfillment of the general task of winning over the masses presuppose in their turn systematic and persistent work in the trade unions and other mass proletarian organizations. It is the bounden duty of every Communist to belong to a trade union, even a most reactionary one, provided it is a mass organization. Only by constant and persistent work in the trade unions and in the factories for the steadfast and energetic defense of the interest of the workers, together with ruthless struggle against the reformist bureaucracy, will it be possible to win the leadership in the workers' struggle and to win the industrially organized workers over to the side of the Party.[h]

A remarkable example of the United Front From Below is contained in "Lesson Two" of the "Study Document for Rural Party Members," dating in all likelihood from the spring of 1963 (cf. app. E, doc. E–4), in which rural class structure was analyzed in an effort to identify the PRP's potential allies in the various strata of agrarian society. The party member was informed that four classes existed in the countryside: poor peasants, middle-class peasants, rich peasants (including those with only small amounts of land to rent), and landlords. Slogans and mass work should be handled, the worker was admonished, so that none of these classes would

---

[g] For an able account of the strategy employed by the Red Chinese, see the 1962 pamphlet, published by Peking's Foreign Language Press, by Li Wei-han. *The Struggle for Proletarian Leadership in the Period of the New Democratic Revolution in China* (London: Oxford University Press, 1945). In particular, the fourth chapter of this document is instructive on the "United Front From Below" or "Four Class" approach.

[h] For the entire text of this extremely important document which remains important to international communism despite its date, see U.S., Congress, House Committee on Un-American Activities, *Hearings*, 76 Cong., 1st Sess. (Washington: Government Printing Office, 1940).

be openly alienated. To concentrate upon radical slogans which would appeal only to the land hunger of the "poor peasants" would play into the hands of the enemy, permitting him "to divide the class of middle-level peasants" and cause the revolution "many difficulties and losses." The PRP rank and file was encouraged to assume an accommodating stand before the "rich peasants" and "landlords." Thus, although "rich peasants spend a large proportion of their time in devising schemes to exploit the workers etc.," and were thought to be "a reactionary group among the peasants," still the cadre was informed that rich peasants had also been "exploited by the U.S. and Diem" and that they were for the most part hostile to their nation's leadership. Party members were told that the landlord class was not a solid bloc. "There are divisions emerging which are turning into groups which differ from each other." Among the landlords were "patriotic and progressive elements." Failure to pursue government wishes became the decisive factor in the determination of enemy status. The rule of thumb was to try to enlist neutral individuals into mass organizations or at least to encourage them to remain neutral in the conflict. Under no circumstances were persons to be unnecessarily pushed into the enemy camp.

Party documents declared that there would be no systematic slaughter of the wealthy. "When it is necessary to struggle to halt the exploitation of the rich peasants, the struggle should be limited and held firmly within revolutionary bounds and proper methods of negotiation to seize the property of the rich peasant."

When local needs required the death of a specific well-to-do person, two requirements had to be met: (1) The individual in question had to be identified as "an enemy of the people" who was guilty of specified charges which were publicly made known. He could not be killed simply on the grounds of his class origin. (2) Prior to the execution a meeting of the village population was held during which a "popular" discussion of the charges was conducted—accompanied by a vote for or against execution (if the PRP was certain that the vote would go the way it wanted it to). "The purposes of such trials," the document continued, "are to stir up the people's resentment, to enhance the people's (i.e., the front's) prestige, and to abase the enemy's prestige."

Every possible step was taken to guarantee that the show went as scheduled. The participating peasantry had to be "prepared" to reach the correct conclusion.

> Before trying a case, we should refer it to the district executive committee for approval. Then a plan should be made for education and orientation, conforming to the resolutions of the cell and of the district committee, to prepare the people, prior to the meeting, for the trial. Such education and orientation should be carried out at least within the area or the hamlet where the prisoner is to be tried. We should avoid trying a security agent or a spy in the presence of the people without previous preparation and orientation. Otherwise the people's recommendation to execute or to release a prisoner may not be consistent with our policy. This may bring about misgivings and dissatisfaction within our ranks and among the populace, or criticisms about irresponsibility which will reflect discredit on the Revolution.

Behind the party's general strategic line as well as its characteristic organizational approach to the village population during a pretrial period, lay the proposition that any segment of the population not hostile to the insurgency movement was a potential source of recruits. Another passage in the same document suggested the extremes to which the PRP was prepared to go in its attempt to recruit new members. The party did not even consider that the family of one who had been executed as an "enemy of the people" was necessarily permanently lost to the insurgent cause. "After a trial," declared the document, "the cell should continue to educate the family of the individual who has been condemned or discredited because the enemy might use such a family to fight the revolution."

In the following two chapters we will examine four interrelated phenomena of Communist civil mass work in South Vietnam. First, we will describe the party's efforts to integrate categories of persons, (e.g., women, youth, children, veterans, intellectuals, students, etc.), into appropriate mass organizations. Second, we will outline the techniques employed to make mass organizations into a civil control apparatus which as a shadow government, came to compete with the government. Third, we will show how the popular association served as a school for life which prepared its members to live under a new set of norms and values. Finally, we will show how this structure provided the party with a base from which it carried on foreign relations in the name of the citizens at large.

CHAPTER 8

COMMUNIST ORGANIZATION AND CONTROL OF CIVIL MASS ASSOCIATIONS IN SOUTH VIETNAM

SUMMARY

The Communist insurgents in South Vietnam employed three basic types of mass organizations in their efforts to overthrow the legal government: (a) popular organizations, (b) special-interest groups, and (c) guerrilla self-defense units. These three were brought together in the People's Liberation Committees. All three of these groups constituted elements of the infrastructure and engaged in underground activities. The third body, the guerrillas, were additionally involved occasionally in overt military operations.

The popular organizations were the most significant of the three, with committees at the national, interprovincial, district, village, and hamlet levels. They sought to appeal to broad segments of the population—workers, farmers, women—with special emphasis on organizing the youth.

The special-interest groups were narrower in scope, appealing to such groups as journalists, teachers, and so forth. Sometimes the front proclaimed the existence of these groups when, as a matter of fact, they did not exist.

The guerrilla militia elements were elite formations among the multiple mass associations.

All these mass organizations were controlled through party channels and were structured along the same lines as the party itself. The members of these groups were subject to control practices similar to those experienced by PRP members.

Once the party gained military control of an area the mass organizations were consolidated under People's Liberation Committees (PLC). The PLC were made up primarily of non-Communist representatives "elected" by local citizens—under tight Communist control.

Once established, the PLC took governmental control of the area. Between its plenary sessions an executive committee and staff agencies carried out the duties of governing. The party retained ultimate control through the use of party members placed in critical positions in the front structure.

Mass organizational work did not begin in an ideological and emotional vacuum. Anti-Western feelings were strongly implanted among the population in French colonial days and it took very little to rekindle these feelings, which in turn gave a sense of ethnic and political solidarity to those drawn into mass organizational work.

Most mass organizations under domination of the PRP in South Vietnam could be grouped under three general headings on the basis of the numbers of persons involved, the types of distinctive activities they performed, or the manner in which the groups were structured nationally.

Popular Associations

The most important groups were those organized nationally in a hierarchical fashion with basic units in the village or hamlet and with committees at the district, province, and higher levels. These were associations which appealed to major categories of the citizenry. There were six important ones: [a]

(1) Liberation Labor (or Workers') Association
(2) Liberation Women's Association
(3) Liberation Farmer Association
(4) Liberation Youth Association
(5) South Vietnam Vanguard Youth
(6) High School and University Liberation Student Association

Through each of these structures the Vietnamese Communists were able to draw thousands to the insurgent cause. It will be noted that three of the six are youth organizations, suggesting the importance attached to this element of the population. The Liberation Youth Association was differentiated from the last two organizations by the age bracket to which it appealed. Members of the Vanguard Youth [b] had to be between 12 and 15 years of age, and those of the Liberation Youth, from 16 to 25 years of age. The last body appealed to the same age group as the Liberation Youth Association, but limited itself to those enrolled in secondary and higher levels of education. There was, of course, yet another major organization for youth, the party youth organization, treated in chapter 4 and currently known as the People's Revolutionary Youth Association (PRYA), [c] but this body, for the reasons previously given, may not be categorized as a mass organization.

Special Interest Groups

A second major group of associations were those structured to control the activities of special interest groups (Van Hoi), such as professionals or religious and ethnic elements. Such bodies might or might not be structured on a geographic basis, depending on the number of people eligible for membership or the number actually attracted. The following bodies, as determined by intelligence evaluations, fell into this category:

Liberation Association of Writers and Artists
Patriotic and Democratic Journalists' Association
Virtue Restoration Association
Montagnard and Khmer organizations
Chinese Unity Warfare Front
People's Renaissance Front (working in Viet Hoa Dao Phat Giao [i.e., Buddhist Institute for the Execution of Dharma]
South Vietnamese Buddhist Peace Forces Association
Patriotic Army families
Peace Preservation Committee

[a] For the regulations governing membership in 1, 2, 3, and 5 in the above list, see docs. D2–D5 in appendix D. For characteristic reporting forms (bureaucratic) utilized in the administration of the Liberation Youth and Liberation Farmer Associations, see appendix F, docs. F–2 and F–3.

[b] For the rules and regulations of the Vanguard Youth, see appendix B, doc. B–3.

[c] See appendix B, doc. B–2.

Soldiers' Mothers' Association
Patriotic Teachers' Association
Employees' Liberation Committee

The character of the elements attracted to several of these bodies is evident from the names given the associations. The scarcity of information in some cases makes it impossible to determine the nature of the membership, and therefore impossible to prove categorically that all of these organizations were Communist-dominated. The number of organizations in this category changed constantly, as did the general tactical situation of which this effort was a part.

Political Parties

The spokesmen for the insurgency attempted to draw a distinction between "popular" bodies such as those mentioned above which were supposedly apolitical, and three organizations which were specifically labeled as "political parties":

The People's Revolutionary Party (PRP)
The Radical Socialist Party (RSP)
The Democratic Party (DP)

The PRP was, of course, the Vietnamese Communist Party in the South and the attempt to treat it as one of a host of organizations hostile to the Government of Vietnam was an example of the "cover" provided the command apparat. The other two organizations were not legitimate political organizations, but were composed of a few fellow-traveler intellectuals and constituted two additional Van Hoi-type organizations.

Structure of Front Organizations

Turning from the identification of the types of organizations erected through mass work to the narrower issue of how such bodies were structured, one is immediately struck by the extent to which they unimaginatively copied the organizational structure of the Communist Party itself. This was particularly the case with respect to the six largest mass associations. An examination of the constitution of the Liberation Workers' Association of the Liberation Youth Association (see app. D, docs. D–2 and D–3) revealed their cellular structure and the devices of the committee system.

Not only was the PRP's form duplicated: every significant practice demanded of the PRP member in the constitution of that organization (see app. B, doc. B–1), could be located in the constitution of the mass organization as well. The principle of democratic centralism, if implemented in a less obtrusive fashion, still determined the relationship between the leadership and the rank and file. Thus the bylaws of the Liberation Youth Association asserted that "all matters are discussed democratically," and that "the majority prevails over the minority." But in the same breath, it paraphrases the DLD party regulations to the effect that "inferiors must obey their superiors," and "local echelons obey the central echelon."[d] To facilitate the ultimate control of the mass associations by the party's command cadre, the elections of cell leaders in the former bodies were scheduled to occur every two months, rather than twice a year as in the party chapter. The brevity of the period made "democratically elected" mass cell leaders, for all practical purposes, removable at any time at the discretion of PRP members who were assigned supervisory responsibilities within the mass association in question. In organizations under Communist control, tenure of office could not be acquired by satisfying the mass membership or a portion thereof but only through conformity with the wishes of the PRP.

PRP Paramilitary Organizations

The significance of several of the paramilitary organizations maintained by the PRP at the village and hamlet levels can be readily grasped if one evaluates them as elite formations among the multiple mass associations in which the members worked overtime and not as inferior military forces which only fought part-time.

There were several peripheral groups that could, from place to place, be identified as paramilitary elements, e.g., the Veterans (or Former Resistance Fighters) Association and the South Vietnam Liberation Red Cross. More important and more frequently met with are three other bodies, the village and hamlet guerrillas or "liberation troops," the Self-Defense Forces (SDF), and the secret or "undercover" guerrillas. Of these, the "guerrilla" as the Communist insurgent understood this word,[e] was more important to the party leadership. A party document assigned the following attributes to guerrilla units. They were made up of relatively young persons who joined "voluntarily," not in the Western sense of unsolicited and spontaneous identification with some abstract cause but rather as a result of effective party work, which progressively compromised the subject's independence of decision to the point that he threw in his lot with that of the insurgents. The individual enrolled in a guerrilla unit was, to use the party's terminology, a "receptive male or female youth." The individual, further, was "trained on the spot or concentrated in an area outside the hamlet to be trained on military and political subjects." He participated in combat, but the unit to which he belonged operated only in the local area.

[d] On "democratic centralism" see the extensive discussion in appendix A, chapter III. Further, the application of this principle to the nonparty mass organization can be verified by the reader by comparing the passage in the Lao Dong regulations (app. B, doc. B–1, ch II) with the relevant sections of the bylaws of the above named associations in appendix D, docs. D–2 through D–5.

[e] In Western speech it is customary to refer to the insurgent combatant forces as "guerrillas," including under this label elite, professionally trained forces as well as local paramilitary or part-time fighters. If it is recognized that substantial differences exist in armament, training, and unit competence between varying units, then the proclivity of all of them to employ guerrilla tactics still serves as a justification for the general use of the word "guerrilla." This is not the case with the Dang Lao Dong's own terminology for referring to its military forces. For the Vietnamese Communist, a "guerrilla" is exclusively a member of a village or hamlet militia formation, the Dan Quan Du Kich. Regional (Po Doi Dia Phuong) forces and main-line (Quan Doi Chu Luc) forces are separately conceived of as constituting the regular army, (the Quan Doi Chanh Quy). A glance at doc. F–2 in appendix F, an administrative form used to maintain personnel records on the militia, shows that this element of the insurgent complex is reported on in the same manner as the other mass organizations.

Such an individual would have only a minimum of professional military training. Equally important, he lived among the local population where he was subject to the fluctuating influences prevalent among the people. His basic interests remained those with which he had concerned himself previously as a full-fledged civilian.

As distinct from the village or combat guerrilla, one party document identified the secret guerrillas as "semi-militarized forces that legally live among the common people. They live and work openly, but in reality they act secretly under the protection and concealment of the common people." Organizationally, they were grouped into teams and squads and under ideal conditions of local security could even grow to platoon-sized bodies. However, since that arm of the mobilized peasantry might consist of only highly intelligent and worldly-wise individuals—due to the secretive character of the duties they performed—it never compared numerically with the village or hamlet "guerrillas," or the SDF. In contrast with these latter bodies a very substantial proportion of the secret guerrillas were party members. Party recruits could be found in all guerrilla formations but they figured most prominently in the last body. The peasant drawn into undercover work in that organization was engaged, first of all, in intelligence and agitation work. His work at the village and hamlet level was of great usefulness to the party's security organization.

Relationship Between Military and Civil Organizations

The guerrilla's status was altered and he found himself engaged in new kinds of activities, and it was likewise the case with his neighbor who joined the peasant, youth, workers, or other mass association. Strikingly new in the lives of both individuals was the fact that they had been absorbed into organizations for which there were no precedents,[f] and were subjected to controls and social pressures that forced them to conform to alien patterns of behavior.

The distinction between the members of the liberation peasants' association and the village guerrilla unit was simply one of degree, following from the greater prestige and the heavier demands placed upon the personnel of the latter body. The guerrilla's weapon, if he was armed with a

[f] The controls exercised over the rural peasantry under the ancient *pao chia* system which once functioned under various guises in Indochina as well as in China proper have been equated with those evolved through mass organizational work. Arguing from this premise, it is concluded that the *pao chia* system (1) set the precedent for the later Communist control technique, and (2) that reliance upon such means to establish order within the population is consequently distinctively Asiatic. (See Floyd L. Singer, *Control of the Population in China and Vietnam: The Pao Chia System Past and Present* [U.S. Naval Ordnance Test Station, China Lake, Calif., November 1964].) This thesis is unacceptable on two counts. A close comparison of the two systems of control actually reveals greater dissimilarities than likenesses between them, and the Communists' ability to erect mass organizational controls among peoples with no cultural precedents comparable to those of the Orient has been historically and repeatedly demonstrated, e.g., Cuba, Yugoslavia, Greece, European Russia, and the entire satellite system in Eastern Europe, etc. In a later statement ("Pao Chia: Social Control in China and Vietnam," *United States Naval Proceedings*, LXXXXI, No. 11 [November 1965], 36–45), the same author reasserts his conclusions with little change, arriving at the conclusion that it is "obvious that the Red Chinese and North Vietnamese control systems over their respective subjects are actually variations of the original system known during the Sung Dynasty as the *pao chia*."

modern firearm, was a status symbol as well as an instrument with which to kill government security personnel. Again, both bodies were subject to controls coming directly from the same party chapter at the local village level, which had final say. The party chapter answered to district and higher party committees, not to military commanders. Main-force units were expressly forbidden to induct, indiscriminately, personnel from village political or militia bodies into combat units. "Units are not authorized to recruit all the key comrades serving in guerrilla units, the Party Chapter Committee, Party [Youth] Groups and party members [otherwise employed]." The determination of who would be recruited rested with the leadership of the party chapters and for each individual incorporated in an operational unit as a replacement, the main-force unit had to "issue a receipt to the local authorities."

Indoctrination

The party assigned to indoctrination an even more important role in the guerrilla unit than it did in other mass organizations. Through indoctrination, the influence of popular opinions adverse to the insurgent movement on the unit member could be reduced, and the guerrilla organization could be utilized as an additional device through which the local population was systematically propagandized. To maintain the paramilitary organization's prestige and hold its members together in an increasingly tight-knit operative group, military actions were undertaken in conjunction with regional or main-force units, but ultimately this structure had a greater impact on the ambient population than on government security personnel. This aspect of guerrilla operations figured prominently in inner-party correspondence and instructions, e.g.: "Guerrilla units must maintain good relations with the people, be capable of motivating them, know how to propagandize and properly carry out the party policy lines."

As substantial numbers of persons were absorbed into the PRP's mass organizations at the village level, and the loyalties of the remaining population to the traditional leaders of rural society showed clear signs of breaking down, the party's mass extensions gradually assumed de facto governmental administrative functions. "We have no laws as yet, but only policies," declared one party document from the early sixties. Those policies were implemented in such organizations as the Liberation Farmers' Association, which served as a major molder of opinion in a rural environment. The intent of this progressive usurpation of governmental powers was the total displacement of the administrative structure of the constituted government by the local instruments of a new, alernate government whose right to control the population was ultimately to be sanctioned by the de jure recognition of its supreme office, a provisional national committee, by prominent foreign countries. The seizure of actual governmental initiative in any one area would hasten this process along as the PRP fully appreciated: "The purpose of rural administration is to limit the enemy's administrative control and to extend ours."

The People's Liberation Committees

The achievement of the PRP's final goal required the formal proclamation to the world that the alternate, provisional government did exist. At the village, district, and provincial levels a formal civil administration would concurrently be organized.

Between the initial preemption of local governmental responsibilities and the final activation of a formal civil administration, there existed a transitory organizational form which solidified and further expanded de facto insurgent control, while avoiding the fateful consequence of creating a legally recognized condition of "civil war" as that term was understood in international law.[g] This halfway house on the road to the subversive seizure of political power was the front federation, or better, People's Liberation Committee or Council (PLC—i.e., soviet) system.

The prerequisites for the determination to begin with the activation of a PLC in any given area were generally listed as three in party documents. First, "our military forces are stronger than those of the enemy," and had prevailed over security forces at least to the extent that the latter had been drawn back into strongholds on the periphery of the region to be more effectively organized. Second, mass work had enjoyed success leading to a "popular disregard of enemy laws." Ideally, 50 percent or more of the population had been drawn into mass associations or, to cite one source from the early sixties, there had to be a large organized peasant association, and the local cadre had to be able uniformly to "gather together about 100 people for demonstrations." Third, the chapter party organization had to resolve the problems associated with its first major expansion of membership and had to be able to establish a viable cellular/committee structure at the village level.

The establishment of PLC's was always preceded by elections in which the bulk of the local population participated. The insurgent claimed that the individuals holding office in the system were the freely elected representatives of the people. Yet if he spoke of democracy and the free choice of the peasantry, he sought at the same time to control the resultant body. This was made possible through mass organizational work. To the extent

[g] The determination of the insurgent leadership to advance its national front to the status of a provisional government would put neighboring sovereign states—clandestinely engaged in the support of the insurgency—under pressure to extend formal recognition to that self-proclaimed new government. And such a movement on the part of the state which was, officially at least, previously neutral would, in turn, constitute an act of studied provocation, on the international plane, in the eyes of the constituted government of the country subject to internal aggression or any third country openly assisting that government. The response of the governments thus challenged, in turn, might easily lead to an expansion of the conflict territorially. Since the possible results following from such a step could be so grievous, the leaders of the insurgency will long postpone any such step, awaiting a turn of events on the international plane decidedly favorable to the insurgency before initiating a chain of events irrevocable in their consequences. Premature action by the insurgents on the diplomatic plane could boomerang and seriously jeopardize the insurgent's chances of winning rather than strengthening the likelihood of his victory. A decision by a sympathetic country not to enter into diplomatic relations, due to the dangers involved to its own territorial integrity or for any other reasons of state or local interest, would have the effect of putting on record for international attention the fact that the insurgents' own friends do not necessarily expect them to win. See further on this count, Maj. Joseph B. Kelly, "Legal Aspects of Military Operations in Counterinsurgency," *Military Law Review* (July 1963), pp. 95–122.

that the mass organizations were controlled, the PLC's could be controlled. Therefore, mass organization work had to precede the evolution of the more complex PLC system. One of the major problems standing in the way of the PRP's implementation of the strategy of the United Front From Below was the desire among major elements of the rural population to follow a more extremist, left-wing line calling for the universal expropriation of the properties of landowners. Only by thoroughgoing controls could the PRP keep in line those forces which it had unleashed.

Even so, the mere existence of a PLC did not mean that the Communist Party had control of a given village or area but only that it had made itself ready—through mass organizational work—to strive for such control.

Village Elections

To indicate to the villagers who the correct candidates were, the village chapter or its selected agents would propose a single list of candidates during a general meeting of villagers, while discouraging additional nominations from the floor by individuals in attendance. Through the mass organizations to which the individuals belonged, pressures appropriate to the occasion were then generated to assure the PRP chapter that all association members did indeed join in the voting—and made themselves accomplices of the resultant, governing body.

The individuals chosen by the party for election were predominantly nonparty persons and the party strove to make the resultant PLC a considerably larger body than the village chapter of the PRP itself. This contrast was important. The village chapter was a small organization made up of party members. Its purpose was to guarantee the conformity of "popular" organizations at the grassroots level with the designs of the party's national leadership. The PLC, in contrast, was a larger body to which the party would allow only a few of its members to be "elected." A document issued by the apparat in the Thu Dau Mot and Bien Hoa regions provided the following directions on the numbers of party members who should be directly incorporated in the PLC's.

> The number of members of those [Party] committees working overtly as members of committees of the Popular Front varies according to the degree of control over each village, but in any case the minimum number of committee members operating overtly as such should be two. The other members, although they do not operate openly as committee members, should engage secretly in propaganda activities for the Popular Front, while waiting for the time when we have extended our control over the villages and all or the majority of committee members can operate openly as such.
>
> To secure a broad base of representation within the Front, the number of Party members on committees of the Popular Front should not exceed two-fifths of the total membership. . . [h]

Diagrammatically, this phenomenon may be visualized as shown in chart 7.

[h] U.S., Department of State. Publication 7308 (Far Eastern Series 110), *A Threat to the Peace: North Viet-Nam's Effort To Conquer South Vietnam* (Washington: Department of State, 1961), p. 95.

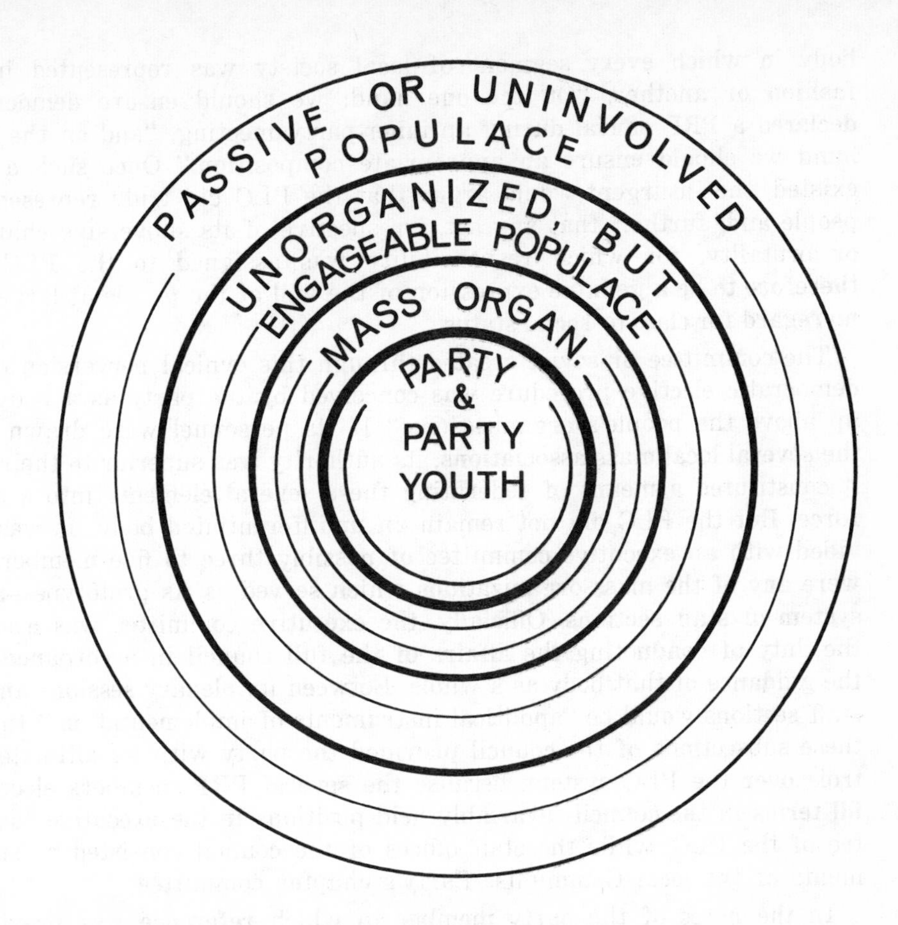

Chart 7. DEGREES OF POPULATION INVOLVEMENT

To the maximum extent possible, every ethnic, religious, social, and economic segment of the local population was represented in the membership of a PLC. The strategic word of the United Front From Below message[i] was made flesh by grouping together in a body which claimed to speak for the populace all of the interested groups in whose name the insurgency was conducted.

The PLC, then, was a transitory form of control evolving out of the mass organization technique which commenced its formal existence once the insurgent had been able to demonstrate his military preeminence in any given area. It constituted a higher level of organization, since it sought not only to control the population, but to absorb within its jurisdiction all of the multiple civil administrative tasks once performed by the local offices of the national government, or in areas where the central government previously failed to make its presence felt, to introduce governmental controls for the first time.

Finally, the PLC was, in comparison with the village PRP chapter, a large

[i] I.e., the strategy of engaging the bulk of the population in activities directed against their own recognized spokesman and leaders.

body in which every segment of local society was represented in one fashion or another. "On the one hand, we should ensure democracy," declared a PRP official during an inner-party meeting, "and on the other hand we should ensure an appropriate composition." Once such a body existed, the insurgent would argue that the PLC did truly represent the people and, further, that any act, irrespective of its subversive character or brutality, for which responsibility was assigned to the PLC, had therefore to be a genuine expression of the will of the people at large with no regard for class or social status.

The committee or soviet created through this cynical perversion of the democratic elective procedure was conceived by the party as a body "set up above the people's organizations." If its personnel were drawn from the several local mass associations, its authority was superior to theirs and it constituted a means of federating these several elements into a single force. But the PLC did not remain an undifferentiated body. It was provided with an executive committee of possibly three to five members—as were any of the mass organizations which served as its prototype—and a system of staff sections. Officially, the executive committee was assigned the duty of conducting the affairs of the full council in accordance with the guidance of that body as a whole. Between its plenary sessions and the staff sections would be "apolitical instruments of implementation." In fact, these subsections of the council provided the party with its ultimate controls over the PLC system, because the several PRP members elected to fill terms in the council invariably held positions in the executive committee of the PLC, while the staff offices of the council consisted of subelements of the local Communist Party's chapter committee.

In the notes of the party member to which reference was previously made, the following critical passage occurred:

> In areas where enemy pressure has been loosened we will assign the responsibility of rural administration to the front's village-committee; *the party branch will assume leadership*, members of the people's organizations and farmers' associations will be key-cadres and will educate the population to urge them to participate in rural administration activities. *Specialized sections of the party branch* such as military, security, economic, financial, training and propaganda, health, social action sections, etc. . . . *will function as specialized sections of the front's village committee* to make studies and set up plans. The military and security sections of the village and hamlet should be under the direct leadership of the Chapter (Party) Committee.[j]

[j] Emphasis added. This remarkable passage and the several others from the same source included in the above pages were drawn from the private notes kept by a Vietnamese Communist Party member of ethnic Chinese background—who possibly spent his youth in the Saigon-Cholon-Gia-Dinh area—during the latter portion of 1963 and in early 1964. It was his practice to jot down key words and phrases in Chinese as he listened during meetings and then transcribe them into colloquial Vietnamese at his leisure thereafter. This is indicated by his last entries which date from after 6 February 1964 but prior to 18 May of that year. These last notes were still in Chinese, suggesting either that he had not yet had time to render them into more lengthy Vietnamese prose or that the translation was made in a separate notebook not in the possession of the courier upon capture. Since the earliest notes date from August 1963, the entire collection—which fills thirty-nine pages of typewritten copy in their English translation—spans an eight-month period and provides one with a running commentary on the matters that concerned the party most during this critical stage in the escalation of the insurgency. The passage cited here above appears early in his notes taken in August 1963.

The fashion in which he expressed his thoughts and paraphrased the directions given during conferences reveals a high level of intelligence, implies extensive schooling, and clearly indicates that he

The PLC, as becomes apparent from this passage, was a body of perhaps two dozen men who lent their names, reputations, and local influence to the PRP at no cost to the latter body to provide the Communist organization with a facade behind which it might pursue predetermined goals while escaping direct responsibility for the consequences of its acts.

With this added item, we can now reassess the totality of the political/organizational responsibilities of a village chapter standing committee. It worked through: (1) a front or People's Liberation Council which lent an air of legitimacy to the governing of the populace at large, including those who had yet to be incorporated into the mass associations; (2) the system of "popular" associations of peasants, women, youths, students, etc. Legislative, executive, and even judicial functions proceeded officially from the PLC. Acclaim for the determinations of the local shadow government and demonstrations of unanimity with the statements of its overt leadership were manufactured through the mass organizations as needed. Should it be determined to liquidate a dissident in the village as "an enemy of the people," necessitating the PLC or one of its sections having to constitute itself as a "trial court" and assemble the citizenry for a "democratic" vote of guilt, then the mass organizer would be relied upon to assure that the populace voted correctly. (3) Finally, the chapter operated through its security organ, sharing its jurisdictional authority in this area with the security branches of district and higher party committees. Another entry made by the Communist note-taker mentioned above at one of his party meetings affirmed the nature and type of organs through which the chapter standing committee operated. He wrote:

> The party will give leadership to:
> the civilian proselytizing
> the security section
> the village government:
> cultural and social action
> economic and financial activities
> internal disputes

The concept of mass organization was a key element in the Communist Party's insurgency efforts. Mass organizations, as tools of subversion, fulfilled the requirements of three essential factors in conducting a systematic overthrow of an existing government.

First, through the use of mass organization, the insurgents attempted to divert and eventually replace the traditional loyalties and mores of the population. Through the ruse of frequent popular elections and apparent democratic representation of virtually all segments of the society, people were encouraged to identify themselves with the process and assume that their interests were truly represented. This was often quite effective in

---

was aware of the ultimate intent behind party policy. The themes most frequently met are ideological/organizational, not military, and involve such issues as how properly to formulate strategy for popular consumption, organizational steps to be immediately implemented, and types of activities which must be put off until a later juncture, etc. Clearly the note-taker, as well as his colleagues in attendance at these meetings, must have belonged to the Party's central command cadre and it is reasonable to conclude that this particular individual was accustomed to the exercise of authority.

areas where the existing government had traditionally neglected the populace.

The precise number of mass organizations varied from year to year and even from quarter to quarter; the entire effort in this direction was so structured that new "Liberation Associations" could be readily activated. In 1965, no one mass organization appealed specifically to rural propertied classes. Such persons as did fall into this category and did work with the PRP would be found among the members of some other one of the mass organizations in which they likewise met membership requirements. Should the PRP suddenly meet with marked success in its work among property owners as it pursued its strategy of the "United Front From Below," then it might be determined tactically desirable to set up a mass organization specifically for landowners. The erection of such a special interest group (Van Hoi) association would be quite a feather in the party's cap, seemingly substantiating their claim—*through the national executive of the NFLSVN*—of representing the best interests of all classes in Vietnamese society. The creation of such a body under these circumstances could be quickly accomplished. Landowners already involved in party work could quickly be screened out (the party maintains dossiers on all of its fellow travelers as well as its party and party youth members) and reassigned to administrative posts in the new body. Developments precisely of this character did repeatedly occur. In an effort to rapidly adapt mass work to changing tactical situations, new bodies were occasionally called into being by public announcements of the NFLSVN long before they were actually organizationally functional or provided with an identifiable leadership. Indeed, there is reason to believe that the national executive of the NFLSVN itself did not in fact exist when Radio Hanoi first announced its formation.

One set of statistics on the comparative size of the party, its mass organizations, and the population at the village level is provided by the party report on turning XB village in Kien Phong Province into a combat village (app. E, doc. E–6). There we are informed that the party and party youth together numbered 56 persons, that the total membership of the farmers, youth, and women's organizations was 543, and that through these "popular" bodies 2,000 or two-thirds of the population could be brought to "take part in party-led activities."

Second, the insurgents employed mass organizations, in conjunction with other means, as a supplementary and supporting force. The most obvious example, of course, was the use of guerrillas in support of party military activities. In addition to providing actual fire support for main force units, however, the local militias and other village organizations could likewise provide means and sources of intelligence, supply, and communications.

Not to be overlooked was the effectiveness of mass organizations as a vehicle of social pressure against the established government. Student groups, for example, often took to the streets in demonstration of protest against government policies. Less violent but often equally effective were hunger strikes and marches by women's, mothers', or religious groups. These group activities could be employed by insurgents to dramatize and give credence to propaganda themes.

Lastly, the insurgents used the ploy of cumulatively expanding the apparatus of the mass organizations in order to gradually consolidate their control over the population. In the overall context of insurgency the mass organization system is to be expanded from the village associations which involve its members in "correct" activities; to the federated fronts which embody the various local groups and assume de facto governmental control over particular areas; to the nationally consolidated front which proclaims itself to be the provisional government of the land.

CHAPTER 9
COMMUNIST STRATEGY OF FRONTS IN INSURGENCY OPERATIONS

SUMMARY

The mass organization strategy of the Vietnamese Communists called for the establishment of an infrastructure of district, provincial, interprovincial, and national federated fronts throughout the Republic of Vietnam. The front committees at various hierarchial levels and in the various provinces operated overtly or covertly depending upon the level of security the movement enjoyed in the area. While the organizational structure of the higher level fronts was considerably more complex, they had the same strategic goals as the village front federations.

The higher level fronts were composed of four elements: (1) a central committee, (2) a board of chairmen of the central committee, (3) a current affairs section of the central committee, and (4) a secretariat of the current affairs section.

The central committee comprised the representatives of the various segments of the population, giving the front of an appearance of democratic representation. The members of the central committee were usually nonparty members representing mass organizations and lower level federated fronts.

Actual authority over the fronts and mass organizations, however, lay with the current affairs section. This was the top level of the party hierarchy and it directed the operations of party members in the mass organizations' federated fronts.

Typical Communist governments afforded precedents for such an arrangement. Communist governments basically comprise two entities: (1) a parliamentary-style body of people's representatives who supposedly are responsible for the administrative bureaucracy of the state, and (2) the Communist Party with its cell and committee hierarchy. The key positions in the bureaucracy are held by party members whose first loyalty is to the party.

The main difference in the Vietnamese Communist front system in South Vietnam and the state structure of a Communist-ruled country was that in Vietnam the party was incorporated within the administrative bureaucracy rather than existing openly as a distinct and superior parallel apparatus.

Finally, the Vietnamese Communists utilized to the utmost the system of external mass organizations evolved by international communism over the decades. These bodies, whose membership was drawn from various nations, espoused the Vietnamese Communist cause on the international plane and became, in a sense, an extension of the indigenous infrastructure. Both types of organizations provided valuable military, logistic financial, technical, and political support for the insurgency.

The PLC at Higher Levels

Above the village level, district and provincial liberation committees or councils were made up of representatives who were often "chosen" through controlled elections. The members of the village PLC elected delegates to the district PLC, whose members in turn supposedly elected provincial delegates. Senior to these bodies was a group of interprovincial PLC's, one for each of the military regions of South Vietnam. At the top the central committee of the NFLSVN (Mat Tran Dan-toc Giai-phong Mien Nam, which existed before the intervening levels were established) served as a roof for the organization, providing the country with a hierarchically organized structure which paralleled the Communist Party apparatus at all levels, and claimed to speak in behalf of the population at large.

In the PLC system, control proceeded from the top down. The higher the level, the more complex the administration was, since the ultimate purpose of the entire dual apparatus was to establish an alternate government to compete with the established government for control of the country. The formal regulations of the NFLSVN, adopted at the Second National Congress which was supposedly held the first week of January 1964,[a] specified that a front committee at any level would contain four elements: (1) a central committee (CC); (2) a current affairs committee of the CC (CAS); (3) a board of chairmen of the CC; and (4) a secretariat of the CC.

The Provincial PLC

A provincial PLC was led by two individuals, either of whom seemingly might claim to be the leader of the organization: (1) the first chairman of the board of chairmen; and (2) the secretary general (SG) of the secretariat. What was one to make of this peculiar interrelationship? What were the two channels of authority?

Comparable organizational arrangements could be found only in the Communist world, and there they involved the division of authority between the party apparat and the formal government administration. *All* critical posts in Communist state administration were actually in the hands of individuals who held concurrent Communist party membership and whose first loyalty was to the party.

The principle employed within the national borders of Communist countries readily lent itself to the interests of the Vietnamese Communist insurgent organization in "liberated" or disputed areas. It helped the insurgent more than it did the party leadership in a thoroughly pacified Communist state; it solved the problem of "cover."

Only one fundamental modification was necessary in adapting the dual power structure to the Vietnamese insurgency. Rather than allow the party and the state hierarchies to stand out publicly as two separate but parallel and intertwined organizations which could easily be identified by the citizen —a situation appropriate to a country enjoying domestic tranquility—the

---

[a] See appendix D, doc. D-1.

party structure was embedded within the protostate hierarchy, with the party still holding the reins.[b]

In this context, one may see where the power lay in a provincial PLC—with the party. The regulations of the 1964 Congress of the NFLSVN suggested that this formal duality would be built into PLC's at all levels, including the village front committees. This distinctive dual structure was present even at the village and hamlet levels. The PRP attempted on the one hand to press the post of chairman upon some local, nonparty personality, while assuring itself that actual policymaking authority remained with the first secretary of the party chapter committee. At the village level it frequently happened that this interrelationship was not formally incorporated into the official structure of the PLC. Where the PRP chapter secretary played an official role in the PLC, he was often listed as one of the PLC executive committee's vice-chairmen.

The Central Committee

Underneath this duo-personal leadership were the CAS and the CC. Each of these bodies performed functions that were indispensable to the total insurgent effort.

The larger of the organs, the CC, contained the representatives of the many elements of the population which the PRP attempted to reach in pursuing the United Front From Below. The CC of the Camau liberation committee contained representatives of the following groups:

Women's Organization
Workers' Organization
Catholic Organization
Cambodian Monks' Organization
Buddist Organization
Cao Dai Women's Organization
Local Notables
Patriotic Intellectuals
Cambodian Residents
Music and Drama Teams
Refugees
Laborers
Liberation Army

---

[b] The manner in which this duality of office operates in a Communist country can be seen in the structure of the North Vietnamese state and the U.S.S.R. The 1960 Constitution of Communist North Vietnam provided for a "Standing Committee of the National Assembly" which corresponded with the "Supreme Soviet of the U.S.S.R." This body was headed by a chairman, as was its Soviet counterpart. Parallel with the party in the DLD hierarchy was a central committee which was controlled by a political bureau composed of members of the larger CC. The political bureau and its CC was headed by Ho Chi Minh with the title of Chairman of the Central Committee of the Dang Lao Dong. As in the Soviet example, all formal offices in the government structure were directly controlled or supervised by party personnel who maintained the fiction, however, that the country was ruled by the government rather than by the party organization. While the party was clearly identified in the above-mentioned constitution and credited with the leadership of the state, its true role is spelled out nowhere and it was assigned no specific function in government or any precise status vis-a-vis the government. *U.S. Army Area Handbook for Vietnam,* Foreign Area Studies Division. (Washington: The American University, Special Operations Research Office, September 1962), pp. 235–44.

The Phong Dinh provincial PLC, adjusting itself to the distinctive composition of yet another sector of the South, claimed to speak in behalf of the following elements:

Hoa Hao Buddhists
Democratic Party
Refugees
Catholics
Cambodian Residents
Liberation Armed Forces
Patriotic Notables
Teachers
Liberation Laborers' Association
Liberation Women's Association
Liberation Youth Association

Not all of the representatives serving as spokesmen for these various groups were non-Communist, but a conscious effort was made to keep the substantial majority in that category.

The Current Affairs Section

In contrast, the CAS was primarily a party-staffed office. It will be recalled from the discussion of the village PLC that the appropriate branches and agencies of the village chapter committee became the subsections of the local front's "executive" or "standing" committee. The same principle applied at the provincial level, and it was specifically from the CAS that the multiple agencies of the provincial party committee operated, providing guidance for PRP personnel secreted in similar PLC offices at lower levels and supervising and directing the multiple phases of mass work in the propaganda, agitation, and proselytizing fields.

"Cover" at Higher Levels

A point to be stressed is that these party members, and not the CC, control the mass organizations subordinated to the CC. The entire party organization, with its multiple parallel channels and supervision, lived within the front hierarchy, which assured it cover while concurrently justifying its actions. The party provided itself with an organizational framework which seemingly authenticated such arguments as the following: It was not the Communist Party of Vietnam that assassinated between 1,000 and 3,000 government officials, school teachers, and uncooperative village notables yearly but rather the peoples of Vietnam, united of their own volition in a liberation front. (In many cases the party-instigated assassination of these officials was done to respect the wishes of the people.) Since party authority was concentrated in the secretariat and the CAS, one heard the least from these two bodies. Almost exclusively, it was the board of chairmen, and particularly the front's principal chairman, who figured in news releases, public speechmaking, formal ceremonies, and official visits of front personnel to friendly foreign governments.

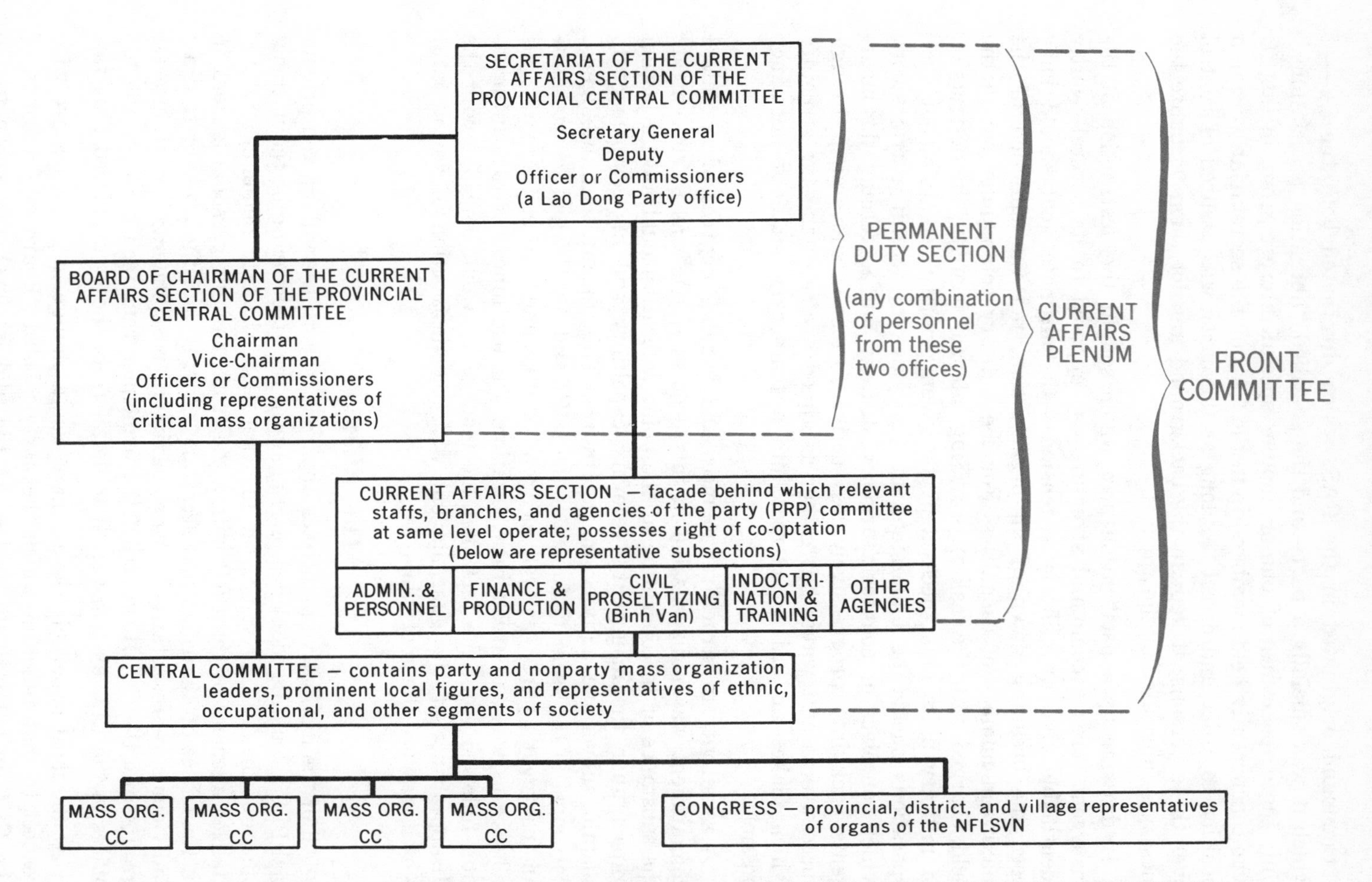
SECRETARIAT OF THE CURRENT AFFAIRS SECTION OF THE PROVINCIAL CENTRAL COMMITTEE
Secretary General
Deputy
Officer or Commissioners
(a Lao Dong Party office)
BOARD OF CHAIRMAN OF THE CURRENT AFFAIRS SECTION OF THE PROVINCIAL CENTRAL COMMITTEE
Chairman
Vice-Chairman
Officers or Commissioners
(including representatives of critical mass organizations)
PERMANENT DUTY SECTION
(any combination of personnel from these two offices)
CURRENT AFFAIRS PLENUM
FRONT COMMITTEE
CURRENT AFFAIRS SECTION — facade behind which relevant staffs, branches, and agencies of the party (PRP) committee at same level operate; possesses right of co-optation (below are representative subsections)
ADMIN. & PERSONNEL
FINANCE & PRODUCTION
CIVIL PROSELYTIZING (Binh Van)
INDOCTRI-NATION & TRAINING
OTHER AGENCIES
CENTRAL COMMITTEE — contains party and nonparty mass organization leaders, prominent local figures, and representatives of ethnic, occupational, and other segments of society
MASS ORG. CC
MASS ORG. CC
MASS ORG. CC
MASS ORG. CC
CONGRESS — provincial, district, and village representatives of organs of the NFLSVN

Chart 8. PARTY-DOMINATED BASIC COMPONENTS OF A FRONT COMMITTEE OF THE INFRASTRUCTURE AT THE PROVINCE LEVEL

Command originated in the CAS, which dominated both the CC—of which it was officially a part—and the so-called "liberation associations." Only those spokesmen of one or another special interest group in the CC who concurrently held membership in the CAS or the secretariat were in a position to order and direct. As long as the party was assured of control over these persons, it kept in the background and let them verbalize the messages fabricated by the apparat.

In drawing up a pacification plan which sought the destruction of the insurgent core or command structure—as opposed to its several overtly identifiable civil or military extensions—the ultimate goal should have been the breaking down of an organization, not the infliction of the maximum number of casualties. For the military commander out in the field, charged with the task of providing internal security, the destruction of military units must necessarily be given priority attention, but such operations should be understood by policymakers within a framework which conceives of counterinsurgency strategy not as forcing the insurgents back into progressively less active forms of subversion through successive assault waves but rather as aimed at destroying the structure which makes an orderly retreat into a temporary state of dormancy possible.

A sensitivity to structural nuances and varying degrees of organized commitment was indispensable in this process if one was to concentrate the substance of his operation at the point where it would have a lasting impact upon the insurgent's recovery capability and his competence to sustain subversive activity in the future. This meant that intelligence personnel in the security forces of the RVN and MACV had to determine an insurgent's party, as well as front, status, and within the party, his cellular, as well as bureaucratic, position. The usefulness of such information followed from the fact that the insurgency would end not with the disappearance of the guerrilla but with the destruction of the apparat which spawned the guerrilla.

The NLFSVN

All of the distinctive principles apparent in both the village and provincial PLC's could be identified once again in the structuring of the national offices of the NFLSVN; i.e., the incorporation of party elements and specialized agencies of the PRP within the front, the duo-personal leadership in the offices of chairmen and secretary general, and the attempt to draw individuals representative of the maximum possible number of interest groups into the CC. However, if the principles remained uniform, the top offices in the PLC system varied in detail from those considered thus far.

At the most superficial level, there was a change in nomenclature with respect to that function which the party labeled "Board of Chairmen of the CC," in subordinate bodies. At the highest level, one spoke to the "Presidium of the Central Committee." The secretariat, however, retained its name.

The presidium was headed by a chairman, Nguyen Huu Tho in the winter 1965/66, who was supported by six vice-chairmen and eight presidium members. The secretariat during the same period was led by Huynh Tan Phat, who likewise held a position as one of the six vice-chairmen. Beneath the SG were two deputies and two additional secretariat members. The larger CC, following the alleged January 1964 Second Congress of the NFLSVN, contained 45 seats, 34 of them filled, 11 yet vacant and slated for future prospective sympathizers whose addition would expand yet further the elements of the population represented at the national level.

The multiple mass organizations were formally tied into these permanent countrywide offices through two devices: (1) the all-national NFLSVN Congress, which was scheduled to take place every three years, and to which even a few village level mass organization members might be sent, and (2) the bestowing of membership in the formal offices of the front's top bodies upon the national officials of the several mass hierarchies for youth, peasants, women, workers, etc.

Dual Control at the National Level

At the national level each association was provided with both a chairman and a secretary general (in imitation of the PLC front system of which they were a part).[c] It becomes our task, then, to analyze the structure of the NFLSVN at the national level and to show precisely the relationship between the chairman and SG of a mass organization and the presidium and secretariat of the NFLSVN itself.

The chairman of the national executive committees (i.e., CC) of the various mass organizations tended to be members of the presidium of the NFLSVN, in two cases with the rank of vice-chairman. Where this was not the case, the chairman or one of his subordinate vice-chairmen held membership in the CC of the NFLSVN.[d] In contrast, the secretaries general of the several mass structures, tended to hold no formal office at

[c] It will be noted that little information on this aspect of mass organization was contained in the constitutions for these bodies which were distributed to propective members. Cf. appendix D.

[d] The vice-chairmen of the presidium after the second congress of the front according to the announcements of the NFLSVN were:

Vo Chi Cong	Chairman, People's Revolutionary Party
Dr. Phung Van Cung	Chairman, SVN Committee for World Peace
Tran Nam Trung	Liberation Army and People's Armed Forces, representative
Ibih (or Y-Bih) Aleo	Chairman, Committee for the High Plateau, Autonomous Movement; Ede (Rhade)
Rev. Thuong Ba Phuong Long aka Thom-me The Nhem	Buddhist Monk (Khmer)
Huynh Tan Phat	SG, Democratic Party; Chairman, NFL Saigon-Cholon-Gia Dinh Zone; SG, Secretariat of CC of NFLSVN

Source of information: "National Liberation Front's Second Congress: A Study," USIS/Saigon, 17 February 1964 (a mimeographed report), p. 5.

The person to whom the membership of a mass organization looks for leadership may hold a position at the national level in the NFLSVN inferior to that of one of his supposed assistants. Thus in the "Association of Former Resistance Members," one of the vice-chaimen with connections in the "Democratic Party" held rank as a member of the presidium while the official leader of the organization enjoys no official position at all in the several organs of the national front. Perhaps the most interesting example of this reversal of roles occurs in the national leadership of the "Liberation Women's Association," where the organization's national chairman serves simply as a member of the presidum while one of the members of that mass association's standing committee, a woman doctor, is a vice-chairman of the presidium, outranking the Liberation Women's Association's Chairman while concurrently serving as the chairman of the numerically insignificant "South Vietnamese Committee for World Peace," where she succeeded Dr. Phung Van Cung sometime after January 1964. (For an analysis of this "peace" body, cf. p. 113.)

all in the NFLSVN,[e] while the five official members of the Secretariat (Huynh Tan Phat, SG; Le Van Huan, Deputy; Ho Thu, Deputy; and Duong Bach Cu and Ho Xuan Son, members) did not, for the most part, engage in mass association work in the capacity of officers of one or another of these organizations.[f]

Central Committee Staffs and Sections (CCSS)

To these distinctive interrelationships must be added yet another peculiarity, namely, that at the national level of the liberation committee system. In contrast to the situation in all lower bodies of the front hierarchy—there are no provisions for the creation of a body comparable to a current affairs section. Immediately below the presidium and secretariat the front recognized only a single level of organization: the CC. Seemingly the national organization made no provisions to engage the competencies of the secretaries general and the current affairs sections of the supreme offices of the mass associations, but in the light of the characteristics of

---

[e] The only clear-cut exception to the general situation in which SG's did not hold formal positions in the special offices of the NFLSVN involved the person of Nguyen Ngoc Thung, presumably a party member of high competence entrusted with critical responsibilities. He held concurrently five known posts: he was (1) the SG of the Liberation Youth Association; (2) vice-chairman of the Patriotic Teachers' Association (PTA); (3) a member of the CC of the NFLSVN; (4) Chairman of the Afro-Asian People's Solidarity Committee (AAPSC), an organ of the national Committee of the NFLSVN; and finally, (5) the Deputy Secretary of the "Radical Socialist Party" (RSP). The AAPSC, which will be treated later in the text along with other similar types of bodies (cf. pp. 113–14), could not have been evaluated as a genuine mass organization. It was rather to be understood as an attempt to set up the skeletal bases for a ministerial or cabinet office in the national protoshadow government. The RSP, as has been noted previously (cf. pp. 89–90), was a small elite body of leftist intellectuals, many of whom were actually members of the PRP or Dang Lao Dong. Nguyen Ngoc Thuong's membership in both of these bodies, plus his possession of the title of SG in the youth apparat, were grounds enough to conclude that he was also a member of yet a sixth organization which provided him with guidance in his work in the others, namely, the Vietnamese Communist Party itself. That such an individual held office in the formal CC of the NFLSVN is not to be understood as vitiating the general proposition that the SG's tend not to hold offices in the presidium, secretariat, or CC of the NFLSVN. Rather it is an indication of the importance the party attached to the youth organization, leading it to make an exception in this one case in order to strengthen its controls over the mass association in question. This line of reasoning is further strengthened by Nguyen's position as vice-chairman of the PTA, a body whose primary impact was once again upon the youth of South Vietnam. By holding critical offices in both organizations, he could assure the party the coordination of the programs of the two mass associations to enhance their effectiveness. Significantly "Professor" Nguyen Ngoc Thuong has been placed not in the eyecatching, publicity-seeking, smaller presidium but in the larger CC.

[f] As there was one significant exception to the preceding generalization with reference to the position of SG's in mass organizations in the national front, so one deviation from the above statement with reference to the secretariat must be noted. Le Van Huan, Deputy SG of the Secretariat of the NFLSVN, was concurrently the chairman of the "Patriotic Teachers' Association" (PTA). Two points should be stressed here: (1) While Deputy Le may be presumed to be a party man of long standing, directly responsible through his boss, Huynh Tan Phat, and the Central Office for South Vietnam (COSVN) to the supreme Lao Dong leadership in Hanoi, he holds a civil, not a party, position in PTA; that is, he is chairman, not SG. (2) The organization under examination here is critical to the Communist as the base from which a major portion of its "popular" agitation/propaganda effort in all mass associations can be mounted, but in particular, this body is oriented toward the youth. The same imperatives which led the party to assign Nguyen Ngoc Thuong, SG of the Liberation Youth Association a vice-chairmanship in the PTA, may have led them to introduce a national secretariat member, by way of an exception, into this structure.

Otherwise, it may be noted that Huynh Tan Phat, the head of the secretariat, is also the head of the minute "Democratic Party," like the RSP a cover for a group of leftist intellectuals and no genuine mass organizations of the citizenry at large, while Deputy Ho Thu belongs to the "Central War Invalid and [deceased] Heroes Committee," again not a mass association, but rather an executive agency of the shadow government. This body, like the Afro-Asian People's Solidarity Committee (AAPSC), was the prototype of a possible future ministry of state whose formal activation would follow a Communist victory (cf. p. 113).

Communist inner-party practices such a conclusion becomes altogether unlikely.

Although the PRP made no provision for a CAS at the national level, one does hear reference on occasion to the existence of branch agencies or committees of the supreme PLC organization. While the party persistently fails to indicate with precision either the total number or exact structural position of these bodies, there are repeated references to a Central War Invalid and [deceased] Heroes Committee; to a Committee for the Consolidation of Peaceful Coexistence; to characteristic executive offices such as a Liberation Press Agency; to a finance committee and to a social welfare agency. Finally, there are a group of externally oriented bodies subject to the controls of a Committee for Foreign Relations (CFR). Among them are the Afro-Asian People's Solidarity Committees of SVN (AAPSC) and the South Vietnamese Committee for World Peace.

As a group, this collection of offices approximated a CAS as a policy-making and executive body. In a formal table of organization, however, they would be subordinated to the CC of the front in the same fashion that branches and agencies of a party or chapter committee were treated as subsections of the committee as a whole. The claim made for a CAS, that it represented yet another level of organization, could not be made in this case. Yet, irrespective of the niceties of formal organizational charts, the specific responsibilities lodged in these offices made them as a group decisive instruments of the total insurgent effort and in them, it will be argued here, one will find the SG's and their mass organization CAS personnel.

The situation which presented itself, then, was as follows: The principal national officials of the mass organizations constituted the membership of the supreme offices in the front system. The central committees of the mass associations, in reporting to their superiors, were actually reporting to the supreme executive officers of the front itself. An examination of actual practice (as revealed in both captured documents and in formal pronouncements of the front) makes it possible to identify the principles governing the appointment of specific persons to specific positions.

One could distinguish between two groups of bodies and two types of front officials; so far as the bodies were concerned one could contrast the central committee and its presidium with the staff and section offices of the front at the national level (which are treated as agencies of the CC in public statements).

Regarding the front's officials, one could contrast the chairmen and vice-chairmen of the various mass associations with the secretaries general and the CAS members of the same mass organizations. With startling regularity, the former group of officials were found to occupy positions in the CC and the presidium of the CC to the exclusion of the staff and section offices of the CC, while the latter group showed up repeatedly in these staff positions but not in the CC and its presidium.

Following the principle of the preeminence of the secretary general over the committee chairman, the following conclusions suggested themselves with respect to the top leadership of the front: (1) The CCSS dominated the CC as the secretariat dominated the presidium; (2) the guidance in accordance with which the CCSS drew up its plans and supervised their execution came from the secretariat, not the CC or the presidium; (3) the secretariat, as the supreme party office in the PLC system, took its orders directly from the Central Office for South Vietnam (COSVN), an agency of the politburo of the DLD with headquarters in Hanoi. Huynh Tan Phat, Secretary General of the Secretariat of the Supreme Central Committee of the NFLSVN, in accordance with the principle of reverse representation, was to be understood as COSVN's responsible delegate to the front system and a concurrent member of the top policymaking bodies of COSVN. Schematically these top organizational interrelationships are shown in chart 9.

Any scheme of organization separating the lines of control over the party from the channels of authority over the PLC system can only belie its author's ineffectual grasp of the dynamics of Communist organization. In the Vietnamese context, one of the front's indispensable attributes was its ability to provide cover, and its efforts could only be assured success as long as it was provided with unrelenting direction by a highly schooled cadre of party personnel. To withdraw the party from the NFLSVN would have been to destroy the front's operative capability. If the COSVN and the secretariat of the NFLSVN were the policymakers, they were concurrently the policy implementers, for they commanded the loyalties of the masses only as terrorism was supplemented by the overt efforts of "popular" bodies, appealing to the interests of every segment of the population.

The subordination of Chairman Tho and the presidium membership to the secretariat was assured through two devices: (1) Phat, like his predecessor in the SG slot, Nguyen Van Hieu, the "ambassador" of the front to Czechoslovakia, was concurrently a member of the presidium with the rank of vice-chairman. As such he was free to intervene in all matters treated by the latter body. (2) An additional vice-chairmanship was held by Vo Chi Cong, a ranking member of the Dang Lao Dong, who is openly acclaimed as the chairman of the PRP itself.[g]

---

[g] The precise relationship between Phat and Vo Chi Cong could not be determined on the basis of the available information. It was altogether possible that Vo not only coordinated with Phat, but reported as well to controls in COSVN. He presided over a convocation of the Ninth or Western Nam Bo Interprovincial PLC committee, known as the National Front for the Liberation of the West (Dai Hoi Cua Mat Tran Mien Tay) in Kien Giang Province in December 1964, attended by key party cadre from both Kien Giang and the surrounding provinces, engaged in varying phases of mass work. The agenda of the meeting suggests that Vo was less concerned with party matters, however, than with delineating policy for mass work during the following year of 1965, e.g., expansion of the PLC system, creation of people's courts, rural relief committees, education, culture and propaganda committees, taxation, etc. Given Phat's additional responsibilities in the critical Saigon area where he was concurrently Chairman of the NFL Saigon-Cholon-Gia Dinh Zone along with the fact that Nguyen Van Hieu, his predecessor at the national level, also held the Saigon job, it does seem that the SG's position called for an individual of unusual capabilities and that he was in a more important party position than Vo. For more on Phat and Nguyen Van Hieu, see the brief passage in Fall, *The Two Vietnams*, pp. 356–57.

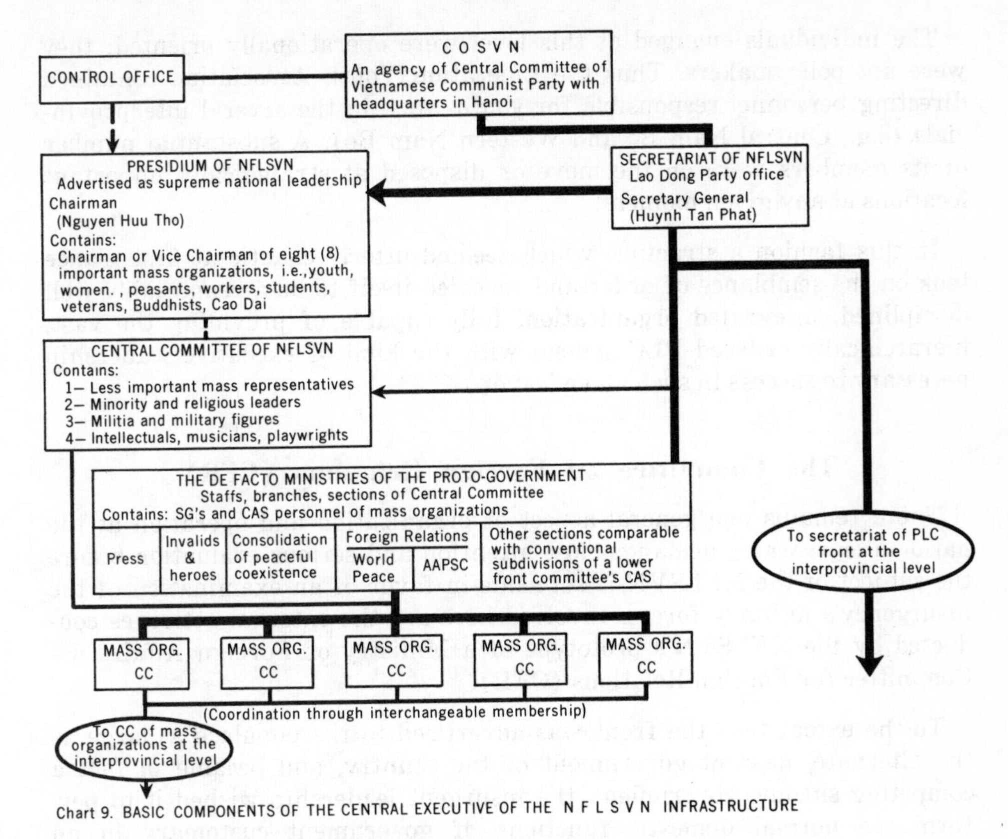

Chart 9. BASIC COMPONENTS OF THE CENTRAL EXECUTIVE OF THE N F L S V N INFRASTRUCTURE

Coordination of Control

The available evidence appears to warrant an additional group of conclusions with respect to yet other elements of the front at the national level. The lines of control at the base of the national level structure running into the CC's of the many mass associations recoupled the front's CC with its CCSS to assure a coordinated effort. The integration of mass work was further enhanced by the distinctive composition of the mass organization's own CC. The CC's of each of the larger associations were assigned personnel with extensive experience in the field and in other, parallel mass organizations, provide each of these organs with a reservoir of well-rounded experience, and with individuals thoroughly acquainted with the concurrent programs and goals in other sectors of society. Thus each CC was at once a clearing house and coordination center, and the margin of error through ignorance was cut to its minimum.[h]

---

[h] An examination of the membership rolls of the central committees of various mass associations, as they appear in both evaluated reports and unprocessed captured documents, are found frequently to list the same person as a member of two or more committees. This fact of concurrent membership in a second organization is specifically acknowledged in several Vietnamese sources of this type. More important in substantiating the above point are the evaluated reports of a biological character which identify the current activities of specific persons and list positions which they previously held. Thus the women's association CC contained a Cao Dai archbishop; an advertised representative of the Democratic Party; the principal of a Vietnamese high school; and individuals representing workers, peasants, and even "patriotic bourgeoisie."

The individuals engaged at this level were operationally oriented; they were not policymakers. Thus the Liberation Youth Association contained directing personnel responsible for youth work in the several interprovincials (e.g., Central Nam Bo and Western Nam Bo). A substantial number of its members were on the move or disposed at strategically important locations at any given moment.

In this fashion a structure which seemed utterly chaotic at first glance took on the semblance of order and revealed itself to be a remarkably well disciplined, integrated organization, fully capable of providing the vast, hierarchically ordered PLC system with the kind of executive leadership necessary to success in such an endeavor.

The Committee on Foreign Relations (CFR)

There remains one general aspect of organization and operation at the national level which demands close attention and serious evaluation before the subject of the NFLSVN is set aside in favor of an examination of the insurgency's military forces. Involved here are the external activities conducted by the NFLSVN's prototype of a Ministry of Foreign Affairs, its Committee for Foreign Relations (CFR).

To the extent that the front was advertised to the populace at large as the alternate, nascent government of the country, and became in fact a competing shadow government, the insurgent leadership wished it to perform the normal domestic functions of government customary in an ordered society—e.g., collection of taxes, assembly of vital statistics, provisioning for the general welfare—and foreign policy as well.

This activity was critical because the ability of the front to establish diplomatic relations with foreign countries strengthened the hands of the insurgent leadership in its conduct of political action and/or agitation and propaganda, both domestic and international. Indeed, in this fashion, the basis was laid from which the insurgents could negotiate their way to victory. The rebels were no more interested in fighting than the legitimate government which they opposed. They fought for a political goal. The goal was important, not the fighting. If it could be achieved through nonmilitary means, all the better.

The first delegation of the NFLSVN to a foreign country arrived in Moscow on 26 June 1962 under the leadership of Nguyen Van Hieu. Between June 1962 and June 1964, some 58 delegates of the NFLSVN visited foreign countries. Permanent offices were established in seven countries (i.e., Cuba, Algeria, Czechoslovakia, East Germany, Red China, the U.S.S.R. and Indonesia), in the form of protoconsulates, and within two international mass organizations (i.e., the Standing Committee of the Afro-Asian Solidarity Council, located in Cairo, and the Secretariat of the International Labor Unions, located in Prague; North Korea, Ceylon, and Hungary also may well accept permanent delegations in the future).

The two agencies subordinated to the CFR to which reference has been made earlier in the text, the South Vietnamese Committee for World Peace (CWP), and the Afro-Asian People's Solidarity Committee (AAPSC) were designed primarily for work in international mass organizations.

By an international mass association, one means a nonofficial but permanently established society, the membership of which is drawn from many nations, which espouses some single cause or represents some delineated international interest group or category of persons. No government will openly control the body, and its members, within their capacity as private citizens, will claim that the structure in question came into being independently and on their own initiative. In fact, there are a large number of such bodies established by Communist countries—working through their respective party organizations—and totally controlled by one or a group of them. Some of the more prominent of these international, Communist-dominated, mass societies are:

World Federation of Trade Unions (WFTU)
Afro-Asian Workers' Conference (AAWC)
World Federation of Democratic Youth (WFDY)
International Union of Students (IUS)
World Federation of Scientific Workers (WFSW)
World Council of Peace (WCP)
Afro-Asian Journalists' Association (AAJA)
International Federation of Resistance Fighters (FIR)
World Federation of Teachers' Unions (FISE)

These bodies are extremely active associations, holding frequent international meetings, issuing public statements on one or another popular issue, assisting sympathizing groups and factions within single countries, not excluding financial and technical assistance to dissident/insurgent groups (e.g., the guerrilla training school supported by the AAWC in Brazzaville, Congo). But the public pronouncements, joint communiqués, publications, and solidarity proclamations could not be considered as any less consequential in their impact upon world opinion than the technical or "hardware" assistance which those bodies could supply. By sending delegations to the congresses scheduled by any of these organizations, the NFLSVN could parade its cause on an international stage and provide other member delegations of "private citizens" with an occasion on which to issue pronouncements on the internal situation in South Vietnam—pronouncements favorable to the Dang Lao Dong's cause and conducive to the greater effectiveness of the NFLSVN's ambassadors in the so-called "uncommitted" or "neutralist" bloc of countries where continuing efforts are being made to set up permanent NFLSVN offices.

Provided with a base from which to operate, i.e., the NFLSVN and its CFR, the Vietnamese Communist Party engaged heavily in external diplomacy and mass work.[i]

Pham Van Dong, premier of the North Vietnamese formal government, speaking before the second session of the third legislature (congress) of the Nation Assembly at Hanoi in April 1965 said:

> International organizations like the World Peace Council, the World Federation of Trade Unions, the Women's International Democratic Federation, the World Federation of Democratic Youth, the International Association of Democratic Lawyers, the Committee for Solidarity with the People of South Vietnam, the Afro-Asian People's Solidarity Council, and many others have raised their voices to strongly protest against U.S. aggression in South Vietnam, and U.S. air attacks against North Vietnam, to express deep sympathy with our people, and strong support, both moral and material, for the patriotic movement in South Vietnam. The meeting of the International Trade Union Committee for Solidarity with the Workers and People of South Vietnam and the International Conference for Solidarity with the People of the Defense of Peace held in Hanoi were warm manifestations of the support extended by the world's peoples to our just struggle.[j]

---

[i] Nguyen Van Hieu, the SG of the national front before Phat, played a major role in this work, and he was not alone. He attended the tenth anniversary of the Bandung Conference in Indonesia in April 1965 as an official government representative of the protoshadow government, but others during 1965 traveled to Czechoslovakia, Russia, Peking, Cambodia, Albania, Guinea, and Havana. The CFR has sent delegations to youth meetings labor, science, student, peace, women's, lawyers' and Buddhist congresses. It has participated in one disarmament conference and engaged in several Southeast Asian, regional economic symposia.

Mao had already touched upon the principle of psychological encirclement on the international plane in his "Problems of Strategy in Guerrilla War Against Japan," *Selected Military Writings of Mao Tse-tung* (Peking: Foreign Languages Press, 1963), p. 174, but his most important formulation of this concept occurs in his "On Protracted War" in which he attempts to apply the concepts of exterior and interior lines of operations, derived from his doctrine of guerrilla warfare, to politics on the international plane. The critical passage in this latter document reads as follows:

> There is yet a third form of encirclement as between us and the enemy, namely, the interrelation between the front of aggression and the front of peace. The enemy encircles China, the Soviet Union, France, and Czechoslovakia with his front of aggression, while we counterencircle Germany, Japan, and Italy with our front of peace. But our encirclement, like the hand of Buddha, will turn into the Mountain of Five Elements lying athwart the Universe, and the modern Sun Wu-kings—the fascist aggressors—will finally be buried underneath it, never to rise again. Therefore, if on the international plane we can create an anti-Japanese front in the Pacific region, with China as one strategic unit, with the Soviet Union and other countries which may join it as other strategic units, and with Japanese people's movement as still another strategic unit, and thus form a gigantic net from which the fascist Sun Wu-kings can find no escape, that will be our enemy's day of doom. Indeed, the day when this gigantic net is formed will undoubtedly be the day of the complete overthrow of Japanese imperialism. We are not jesting; this is the inevitable trend of the war. (*Ibid.*, p. 221.)

[j] Pham Van Dong *et al.*, *Against U.S. Aggression: Main Documents of the National Assembly of the Democratic Republic of Vietnam, 3rd Legislature, 2nd Session* (Hanoi: Foreign Languages Publishing House, 1965), pp. 55–56. The following words which accompanied the above passage suggest the parameters of the impact that may result from effective and persistent mass work outside the frontiers of the country subjected to internal aggression:

> The Governments of many nationalist [in contradistinction to Communist] countries have raised their voices to demand that the United States stop its aggressive war in South Vietnam and its acts of war against the Democratic Republic of Vietnam, and to express deep sympathy and strong support for the just struggle of our people.
>
> Since August 1944, in Cambodia, Laos, Indonesia, Japan, Algeria, Pakistan, Ceylon, Burma, India, Iraq, Guinea, Mali, Ghana, Venezuela, Guatemala . . . tens of millions of people have taken to the streets to demonstrate vehemently against U.S. information halls and shouted slogans: Down with the U. S. imperailist U. S. imperialists, get out of South Vietnam.
>
> In the capitalist countries such as France, Italy, Great Britain, Belgium, Austria, Denmark, Norway, Sweden, Canada, Australia . . . the movement of opposition to the U.S. imperialists' policy of aggression and war in Vietnam has reached an unprecedented scope and degree, involving tens of millions of people and using varied forms of struggle.
>
> We are greatly moved and elated by the fact that in the recent months, even in the United States, the movement of opposition to the U.S. imperialists' attempts to step up the aggressive war in South Vietnam and to intensify acts of war against North Vietnam has been expanding steadily. This movement involves Americans from all walks of life: workers, youths, women, students, intellectuals, clergymen, Congressman, newsmen. . . . The forms of struggle are reaching a higher and higher level and becoming more and more varied: statement issued by the American Communist Party to condemn the U.S. aggressive policy in Vietnam; protest letter sent by 416 American professors and students to U.S. President Johnson; all-night demonstration by 4,200 professors and students; hunger strike by many groups of student and other people; intervention by hundreds of youths to prevent a U.S. ship from carrying troops and

CONCLUSIONS TO PART TWO

The progressive generation of a body of international opinion favorable to the insurgents' cause, of the utmost importance to the successful consummation of a conflict limited in its military aspects to a single country, was but one of the byproducts of effective mass work. Alert to the consequences of the political/organizational aspects of revolutionary insurgency, the Dang Lao Dong lavished endless, patient attention on the mobilization of the South Vietnamese citizenry and their incorporation within the infrastructure it was building. This effort lay at the very heart of strategic planning.

It has been shown that early in the insurgency, the party initiated the mobilization of the populace through the conduct of underground activities which led to the formation of associations for major interest groups or categories of citizens, making sure that the PRP held a minimum number of critical posts within the resultant body. Second, an appropriate electoral technique was developed, assuring the party control of the electoral procedure, while giving the impression that suffrage rights were freely exercised.

An electoral commission controlled the agenda and proposed candidates to be elected. Because the population knew very well that the electoral commission had the complete support of the party and the regional guerrilla units which were operating overtly, the peasantry rarely dared to propose alternate nominees. The same technique was repeated at the district, province, interprovincial, and national levels. The result was the appearance of People's Liberation Committees or councils (i.e., soviets), chosen by the citizenry. The PLA struggle and the PLC organization were developed in all parts of the country. APLF or National Liberation Front executive committee, constituting the summit of the party-dominated infrastructure, was set up to run the entire PLC network. This executive committee acted inside and outside the country as a provisional revolutionary government and as such could well be recognized by the U.S.S.R. or other socialist countries one day. The organization of the PLC's should be considered as the positive, constructive side of revolutionary warfare. While the party, along with the military organization, set out to destroy the old political, economic, and social structure and old administration, the task of the PLC's was to build a new one. For the accomplishment of this task, the PLC's acted in three different ways:

(1) *Psychologically.* The PLC's constituted an unmistakable sign for the population that the old conventional administration would be replaced by a new, revolutionary one. The sole presence of the PLC's in controlled regions and even in territory under contention had a tremendous psychological and propagandistic impact on the population.

---

weapons to South Vietnam. . . . We are deeply moved at Mrs. Helga Herz's valiant self-burning to protest against the U.S. policy of war in Vietnam, thus setting an example of noble sacrifice for peace and friendship between the American and Vietnamese peoples. The American people's movement of opposition to the "dirty war" in Vietnam has influenced many U.S. politicians. Never before has the U.S. Government faced such strong opposition by the American people. (*Ibid.*, pp. 55; 56–57.)

(2) *Politically.* The PLC's were largely "representative" bodies. At all administrative levels, from the villages up through the provinces, members of the PLC's represented multiple social, ethnic, religious, and political groups. This encouraged the impression that the infrastructure and the military forces of the revolutionary struggle represented the desires and interests not only of the CP but of the larger part of the entire population. International public opinion could be influenced and foreign powers could be induced to support the insurgents' cause. Even more, due to the carefully organized, quasi-democratic elections for the PLC's, international public opinion could be led to believe that the insurgency was not only highly representative, but also was democratically ordained.

(3) *Organizationally.* In fact, the PLC's were the nucleus of a future revolutionary government. And this nucleus, from the outset, attempted to act as a *de facto* government. The PLC built up an administration—primitive of course, but very efficient. It took over all activities in controlled territory which fell within the competence of any normal government administration. It organized and controlled economic production, trade, education, medical care, traffic, taxation, and the provisioning of food for the military forces. For the execution of all these tasks, the PLC's called upon the services of the village guard or militia made up of part-time insurgents. Where security considerations did not permit the activation of formal bureaucratic controls, the party, working through its infrastructure, attempted the closest approximation of ideal goals commensurate with the objective situation.

Behind this grandiose effort, the party organization (examined in chapters 1 through 6) was ever present—supervising, counseling, or vetoing as necessary. But while this control structure was the indispensable heart of the effort, it sought relentlessly to escape the limelight. In this protracted game of deception, provoking the enemy to attack one of one's subsidiaries, expending time, materiel, and manpower at the strategically wrong point, was elevated to the level of a grand design.

PART THREE
THE MILITARY ORGANIZATION
CHAPTER 10
THE GENESIS OF THE MILITARY FORCES OF THE PRP

SUMMARY

In a Communist-controlled insurgency, military force should be understood as being one of several instruments through which the party seeks to consummate its seizure of power. Military warfare is coordinated with activities of an underground character, e.g., agitation, propaganda, recruitment, and mass organization efforts. Ideally, all aspects of the party's insurgency efforts (military, mass organization, propaganda, etc.) would advance simultaneously through phases of development to final and total seizure of political power. If all fronts advanced in accordance with this principle, then the military forces would be in a position to destroy the government's armed forces at the time when the party's front apparatus would have consolidated enough power to assume total civil control.

There were four identifiable elements of the Communist insurgent military potential in South Vietnam: (1) the professional forces of the People's Army of (North) Vietnam (PAVN); (2) the main force units; (3) the territorial armies; and (4) the local guerrilla units.

In the early stages of the movement in South Vietnam, units of PAVN provided manpower reserves and specialists for missions in the South, obliging the Government of South Vietnam to garrison large numbers of troops in stationary defense positions along the northern border and to concentrate military training on large-scale, conventional operations instead of counterinsurgency details.

The main force was a body of well-trained soldiers, many of whom were infiltrated into the area from North Vietnam, and was considered to be a highly motivated, elite fighting force. Most of its personnel were full members or candidate members of the Communist Party or organization.

The territorial or regional guerrilla force was made up mostly of indigenous personnel and operated in delimited regions of no more than provincial size.

The guerrilla popular force was made up of local militia units. These units of villagers functioned primarily in support activities, provided the party with a manpower reserve, and served the purpose of making the militia participants unavailable to the legal government.

These various military forces were built up cumulatively. The Communist model for a military buildup, once its initial infrastructure is operational, is as follows: (a) activists in the countryside form armed propaganda teams; (b) indoctrinated teams recruit additional personnel to form regional units; (c) mass organization workers activate part-time village militia; (d) seasoned personnel from regional units withdraw to form main operational forces; and (e) personnel from village forces are "promoted" into regional forces to maintain strength levels.

Insurgent military forces are to be understood as one more instrument through which the party leadership, located in the front system, sought to consummate its seizure of power. The armed element was not the insurgency's determinative body; it was an instrument through which policy was implemented.

The Main Force

Under the generic terms regular army (Quan Doi Chanh Quy) the Vietnamese Dang Lao Dong recognized a twofold division of fighting units between the Quan Doi Chu Luc (the "main force") and the Po Doi Dia Phuong (the regional or territorial army). The former body in early 1965 contained some 35,000 hard-core personnel. It was an elite military force; its personnel could read and write; many soldiers had completed six to eight years of schooling. Most of Chu Luc were party members or candidates for membership.

The Regional Guerrillas

This body was supported in 1965 by an estimated 60,000- to 80,000-man force of regional guerrillas who operated in delimited regions of no more than provincial size in the South. Whereas a substantial portion of the personnel in the elite elements was injected into South Vietnam from the North, they were composed almost exclusively of indigenous personnel drawn from the rural population.

The Du Kich

Distinct from either of the above bodies was the Dan Quan Du Kich, the guerrilla popular army which was made up of villagers who remained in residence in their villages and were subjected to the village control apparatus evolved locally by the PRP. Persons mobilized into such organizations were expected to fight on occasion, but more frequently they would be engaged in activities of a support character. Liaison was by runners who remained subject to party authorities. As has been indicated in the preceding chapters on mass organizations, the party leadership did not conceive of the village militia as primarily a military force at all, since it was more concerned with making the militia participants *unavailable to government forces* than with shaping raw recruits into efficient fighting machines. It is in this light that one must understand the PRP's determination to concentrate 70 percent of the militiaman's rigid training schedule on political issues.

The PAVN

To be entirely realistic in his identification of the component elements of the armed forces of the insurgency under the control of the Dang Lao Dong, one must include in this category the professional armed forces (PAVN). A military force, provided its capabilities are maintained through continuous and vigorous training and discipline, constitutes a military and political factor of the highest consequence whether it is committed to battle or not. Militarily, that force was assisting the insurgency in the South in 1960 by (1) providing a manpower reserve from which specialists could be drawn for the South as required; (2) obliging the ARVN to commit sizable elements to garrison stationary defensive positions along the northern border when they could better have been employed in security and pacification missions; and (3) provoking the governmental leaders of the South to train their armed forces *for the wrong kind of war*, leaving the army with only highly restricted capabilities to respond effectively to guerrilla warfare once this type of struggle became the order of the day.

Through COSVN, leadership was provided with an agency through which the operations of "liberation" troops and militia in the South could be coordinated with or—by the middle 1960's—subordinated to, the frontline, professional infantry units. In a conflict in which military initiative was so thoroughly subordinated organizationally to political goals, the party leader's ability to command both insurgents and PAVN forces provided an excellent framework from which to plan on a long-term basis.[a]

Between March of 1962 and March of 1965, PAVN grew in size from a force estimated at circa 300,000 to one numbering 490,000 troops, the latter figure representing the maximum size of the armed forces permissible without the impairment of the country's economy.[b] The divisional strength of a regular line unit, as in traditional Western military forces, remained around 10,000 men, but the PAVN unit was acquainted with guerrilla or small unit tactics, being well tutored in such warfare by Mao Tse-tung's progeny. Between 1951 and 1953, it is estimated that up to 20,000 Chinese Communist-trained troops operated in Vietnam, and if some of the characteristics of more conventional land forces can be detected in the combat units of PAVN today, that force still can be expected to adjust rapidly to the conditions of guerrilla warfare in the South, once committed.[c]

The Classic Model for the Building of Insurgent Military Forces

The classic model for the cumulative building of military forces of an insurgent character calls for the following progression: (1) activists to the countryside to form military nuclei; (2) recruitment by nuclei to form regional units which first appear as armed propaganda teams; (3) consequent activation of part-time village militia "liberation associations" and village security squads; (4) withdrawal of seasoned personnel from regional units for formation of main operational forces; and (5) "promotion" from village forces of personnel to maintain strength levels of regional forces. This pattern of development took place in South Vietnam.

[a] On the major components in North Vietnam's military command structure and a statement comparing the principles of military organization at both the Hanoi level and insurgent, interprovincial level, see p. 130.

[b] *U.S. Army Area Handbook for Vietnam*, p. 495; statement of Senator Birch Bayh (Democrat, Indiana) of March 1965, based on information provided by the Government, quoted in Bernard B. Fall, "If Ho Chi Minh's Army Moves South in Force," *The New York Times Magazine*, 5 September 1965.

[c] *U.S. Army Area Handbook for Vietnam*, p. 500.

The Classic Model's Evolution in South Vietnam

The formation of military nuclei. In late 1959 there were only two armed platoons in the entire region of the Fifth Interprovincial body. The personnel of both units consisted exclusively of individuals who had been withdrawn to the North after the Geneva Accords of 1954 and who had distinguished themselves in the preceding war against the French. Since then they received additional training from a special mission battalion of the PAVN which ran a training center at Vinh in North Vietnam. As a consequence, the individuals in these units were qualified to use various types of weapons, mines, plastic explosives, and were trained in demolition. They were also thoroughly trained in athletic skills, concealment, sabotage, kidnaping, assassination, reconnaissance, the use of maps, compasses and binoculars, and hand-to-hand combat. Their specialty was lightning assaults on sentries. Within the party, these two bodies were known as Dai Doi (platoon companies) and the Vo Trang Tuyen (for armed propaganda).

Armed propaganda teams. Neither unit operated as an integrated body, but was broken down for operational purposes into "armed propaganda teams" frequently of no more than three or four persons. Their operations were designed to support the primarily political struggle of the party, and were calculated to build up the initial mass organizations (e.g., for women, youth, peasants, students, etc.) which later became the bases from which more ambitious military activities could be sustained. This led them to move and work throughout the interprovincial region, coordinating their activities with the agitation/propaganda/organization efforts of provincial and lesser party committees as directed by the territorial party authorities. They were equally capable of collecting intelligence and order of battle on military forces of the RVN, the assault on security forces units from ambush, and the conduct of reprisals against peasant communities and their officials. To groups of this type must be credited the thousands upon thousands of assassinations of village chiefs, schoolteachers, citizens, and government representatives.[d]

[d] By the end of 1963, an estimated 13,000 assassinations had occurred. Fall, *The Two Vietnams*, p. 360. The State Department has provided the following monthly figures for the number of casualties in the South during the single year of 1964 (*Aggression from the North*, p. 62):

Village, District, and Other Government Officials

	Jan.	Feb.	Mar.	Apr.	May	June	July	Aug.	Sept.	Oct.	Nov.	Dec.
Killed	47	34	49	30	25	31	45	36	46	48	21	24
Wounded	14	16	24	9	8	9	14	15	13	10	22	7
Kidnaped	93	113	91	67	74	132	93	103	144	69	52	100
Total	154	163	164	106	107	172	152	154	203	127	95	131

Other Civilians

	Jan.	Feb.	Mar.	Apr.	May	June	July	Aug.	Sept.	Oct.	Nov.	Dec.
Killed	111	110	138	115	105	110	181	103	132	100	66	88
Wounded	146	174	239	218	163	173	194	122	203	90	94	154
Kidnaped	694	590	1,531	647	727	483	964	834	778	477	200	498
Total	951	874	1,908	980	995	766	1,339	1,059	1,113	667	360	740

The following table shows the number of incidents of terrorism, sabotage, forced propaganda sessions, and armed attacks during 1964.

	Jan.	Feb.	Mar.	Apr.	May	June	July	Aug.	Sept.	Oct.	Nov.	Dec.
Attacks	223	217	203	220	175	140	184	113	118	83	60	96
Terrorism	1,244	1,389	1,632	1,738	1,418	1,390	2,123	1,775	1,938	1,790	1,391	1,719
Sabotage	129	201	158	169	217	176	286	315	482	480	247	318
Propaganda	174	271	167	157	140	162	224	173	178	197	109	128

Provincial armed elements. In contrast to these terrorist groups, provincial or regional armed elements (i.e., formal military bodies under the control of the party committees at the provincial as opposed to interprovincial level) in 1959 "consisted of only a few groups operating scatteredly to support political struggles." The party-controlled effort to organize the peasantry began to pay off in the late spring of 1960, at which time the provincial elements were gathered together into platoon-size units which were to operate henceforth as integral units.

Interprovincial military elements. More importantly, two additional platoons of soldiers were concurrently activated at the interprovincial level, made up, for the first time, of indigenous personnel, Vietnamese and montagnards, funneled to the interprovincial by provincial committees from among the local residents who had been "made available" through the organizational effort. The command of the unit remained in the hands of party cadre. A five-step cyclical process could be identified at this point:

(1) Organization of civilians in mass organizations
(2) Indoctrination and recruitment into military units
(3) Use of the resultant new military unit as an additional "persuader" for peasant cooperation and participation
(4) Expansion of mass organization membership
(5) Indoctrination and recruitment of yet more into military units

For insight into the early phase of organizational work among the peasantry, from a Communist point of view, see appendix E, doc. E–6.

The Military Forces of the Fifth Interprovincial Committee

The first complete cycle of these steps commenced in the region of the Fifth Interprovincial in the first half of 1960. At approximately the same time, it could be detected in the other interprovincials as well. It would be relentlessly repeated during the next 5 years, with growing success, throughout South Vietnam, producing increasing numbers of individuals available for incorporation into even larger military units—first companies, then battalions, and finally regiments. As it became possible for professional military personnel of the PAVN to concentrate on progressively more conventional forms of operations, they were not permitted to forget from where their military personnel came: *politics, agitation, and civil organization;* the cellular party structure, inseparable from the table of organization and equipment of the military forces themselves, guaranteed that this point would not be overlooked in the troop unit. By the end of 1960, three of the Fifth Interprovincial's platoons had been integrated into a company-size unit.

Infiltration from the North. Parallel with the activation of new units in 1960 came the infiltration of significant numbers of professional military personnel from the North. In December of that year, a distinct military—as opposed to party—control office for military units was established. By that date, there were two companies plus one additional platoon under the control of the interprovincial. The mission now assigned the new military committee of the interprovincial from which a military interprovincial headquarters would finally evolve was to activate the first battalion-size unit at the interprovincial level and supervise the creation of company-size units for the provinces. By late February 1961 the first regular battalion was functioning. It was composed of the two interprovincial companies and the one platoon plus forces drawn by provincial party offices out of the Tinh Quang Nam and Quang Ngai. The unit was tabbed the "Primary Battalion of the Fifth Military Region's Liberation Army," and given appropriate cover designations. Provided now with the facade of a major military unit, the personnel of which were indigenous to the area of operations, elements of battalion units of the North Vietnamese Army (PAVN) were infiltrated across the 17th parallel to provide a nucleus for yet a second, a third, and even more battalions of troops. By the beginning of 1962 even provincial committees were provided with the services of battalion-size units.

The tactical command of the Fifth Interprovincial Committee. In the summer of 1961 another office was set up, the tactical command of the Fifth Interprovincial. Personnel from the military committee, staff, political and logistics specialists, were reassigned to effect its activation. Its mission was to relieve the burden on the military committee itself for specific operations, and to provide an office through which the operations of multiple battalions and companies of troops, under the command, possibly, of both provincial and interprovincial offices, could be coordinated for a single large operation or a series of closely related operations. However, despite the substantial number of troop units available at this juncture, the party leadership still did not consider itself prepared to launch sustained guerrilla warfare. To use Western terminology, which recognizes three phases in the course of an insurgency, from its commencement through its final consummation, the PRP conceived of itself as still in phase one. Its primary task was still organization, not the destruction of hostile security units. Since the tactical command was exclusively a military operational headquarters, its utility remained marginal, its retention a matter to be determined pragmatically by the course of events. And in November 1961, the PRP leadership did indeed determine that the military units could best serve its needs as Dai Doi Vo Trang Tuyen Truyen, armed propaganda companies, intent upon influencing the peasantry in the various provinces, and not as professional military forces. Several battalion- and company-size units were broken down into lesser units and widely dispersed. The tactical command was deactivated for the time being, only to resume its role the following spring of 1962, after still additional battalions, including an artillery battalion, had come into existence following the establishment of the first regimental headquarters.

The Primacy of the PRP

With only minor variations, this was the rhythm with which the military forces of the PRP evolved in the five interprovincial divisions and the Saigon Special Zone. At the commencement of the process, no distinctive traditional military formation could be detected. The party organization alone was operative and its concerns were removed from the tactical battlefield situation. It was engaged in the initial phases of organizational work among the peasantry. In a coordinated attack upon the freedom of the individual, the party bolstered up its attempt (1) to appeal to the populace ideologically through agitation and propaganda with (2) demonstrations of its competence to retaliate against the uninterested and the hostile (e.g., terrorism, assassination, kidnaping, sabotage, etc.). The armed elements (strong man squads, toughs, physical persuaders) were strictly party groups, only later to be integrated with the professional military who were held in reserve across the border. Only as this effort began to produce results in the form of sustainable organizations could attention be given to the activation of paramilitary forces and regional guerrilla formations which, in turn, would strengthen the PRP's hand in the next round of organizational work. Success at any juncture in this process increased the likelihood of success during the next phase of mobilization. The audience toward which party work was directed grew not arithmetically but algebraically. The principle of an expanding cumulative impact came into play (see chart 10).

Diagrammatically, this process may be represented in the following way:[e]

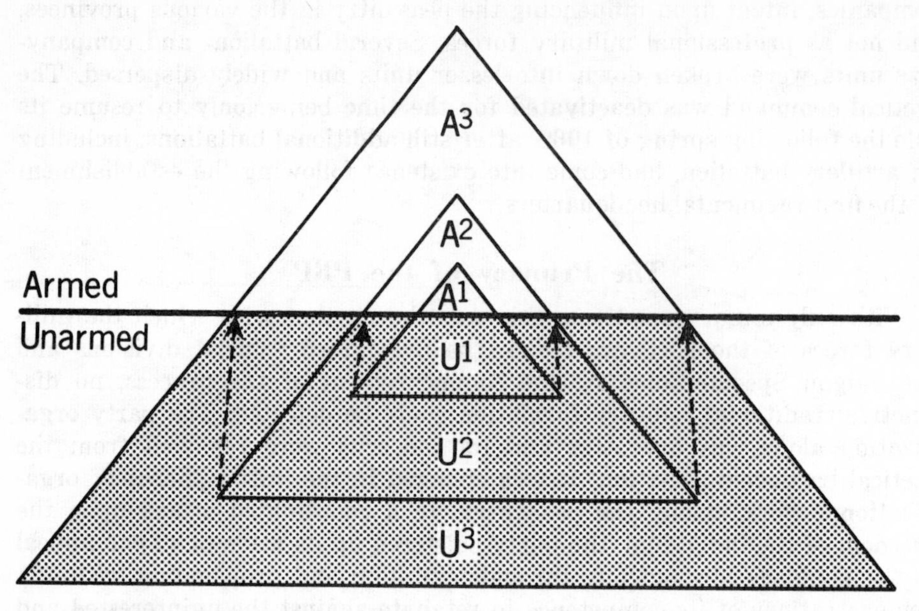

Chart 10. OPERATIONAL INTERDEPENDENCE OF CIVIL AND ARMED COMPONENTS OF AN ESCALATING INSURGENCY

(1) A small armed group A^1 organizes an indigenous civilian support U^1 which in turn supports A^2.

(2) Additional armed groups A^2 organize indigenous civilian support U^2 which in turn support A^2 and permits expansion of guerrillas into A^3 and civilian support into U^3.

(3) In practice this process can keep on going to A^4, and A^5, to U^4 and U^5, etc. Success at any given level enhances the likelihood of success at the next.

The Theorists of Guerrilla War

Extrapolating from this progression—under the guidance of Mao Tse-tung—General Vo Nguyen Giap distinguishes between three types of military tactics which evolve during the course of an insurgency, identifying them respectively as "guerrilla warfare," "mobile warfare," and "entrenched camp warfare." He does not understand these terms to refer just to alternate forms of combat. Intrinsic to each of these phases are organizational and political developments which provide the conflict with its progressive totality. At the onset of the second or mobile warfare stage, the more proficient of the irregular forces are singled out to perform more demanding missions requiring the concentration of greater numbers of combatants. The new units engage in more conventional operations . . . attacking the enemy where he is relatively exposed, advancing deeply,

[e] Modified from Slavko N. Bjelajac, "Anatomy of Counterinsurgency," a lecture presented to the Military Assistance Institute, February 1966.

then withdrawing swiftly.[f] Organizationally, the new forces assume the formal structure of brigades or regiments and though they may fall far short of professional units of corresponding size in discipline and firepower, the insurgent leadership will refer to them as their "regular troops." Politically, the movement relies upon the combat successes of these units to substantiate their assertion of being the "wave of the future."

In order to prevent discord and disunity, efforts are made to limit any interference with or any overstepping of bounds with respect to the concrete planning of a campaign or battle at the lower levels of organization. There are two factors that dictate this practice. The first is that the local units probably know the situation better than the central command, and the second is that they are probably best prepared to make decisions with respect to implementation and timing.

In his May 1938 "Problems of Strategy in Guerrilla War Against Japan," Mao Tse-tung treated the issue of command in detail, asserting:

> If any attempt is made to apply the methods of command in regular warfare to guerrilla warfare, its great flexibility will inevitably be restricted and its vitality stopped. A highly centralized command is in direct contradiction to the great flexibility of guerrilla warfare and must not and cannot be applied to it.

Mao's formula for the resolution of the problem of control versus flexibility was "centralized strategic command and decentralized command in campaigns and battles."

> Centralized strategic command includes the planning and direction of guerrilla warfare as a whole by the state, the coordination of guerrilla warfare with regular warfare in each war zone, and the unified direction of all the anti-Japanese armed forces in each guerrilla zone or base area. Here lack of harmony, unity and centralization is harmful and every effort must be made to ensure harmony, unity and centralization. In general matters, that is, matters of strategy, the lower levels should report to the higher and follow their instructions so as to ensure concerted action. Centralization, however, stops at this point, and it would likewise be harmful to go beyond it and interfere with the lower levels in matters of detail like the specific dispositions for a campaign or battle. For such details must be settled in the light of specific conditions, which change from time to time and from place to place and are quite beyond the knowledge of the distant higher levels of command. . . .
>
> If a higher level has something to say about the actual operations undertaken at a lower level, it can and should advance its views as "guidance" and must not issue hard and fast "orders." The more extensive the area, the more complex the situation and the greater the the distance between the higher and the lower levels, the more advisable it becomes to allow greater independence to the lower levels in their actual operations and thus give those operations a character conforming more closely to the local requirements, so that the lower levels and the local personnel may develop the ability to work independently, cope with complicated situations, and successfully expand guerrilla warfare.[g]

---

[f] General Vo Nguyen Giap, *People's War, People's Army* (Washington: Government Printing Office, 1962), p. 106.

[g] *Selected Military Writings of Mao Tse-tung* (Peking: Foreign Languages Press, 1963), pp. 181–83.

The guerrillas would retain a simple organizational form. They continued as before their harassment of civil and security authorities. Their political mission, however, was also important. It was their responsibility to maintain a presence among the civil population and to emphasize the omnipresence of the insurgent movement. Their relentless pressure at the local level would not only force the dispersion of security forces, but, perhaps more importantly, inhibit the populace from supplying the latter elements with needed assistance.

The intent of the insurgent leadership is progressively to intensify mobile warfare. Giap emphasizes that this may not be done at the price of allowing the guerrilla effort, locally, to fall into abeyance. A continuing effort is required to maintain a judicious balance of effort which confronts the nation's forces with a quantitatively intensifying threat on all fronts. If the phases evolve logically, one out of the other, then the mission assigned the specialized forces produced by each new stage in the process must always provide for the needs of the dissimilar units carried forward from the preceding phase of development.

The importance of maintaining both regular and regional guerrilla formations was stressed repeatedly by Giap's mentor, Mao Tse-tung. In his December 1936 pamphlet, attacking the "left" strategy which had dominated party policymakers around SG Li li-san in the 1920's Mao wrote:

> To abandon small-scale guerrilla warfare and "concentrate every single rifle in the Red Army," as advocated by the Li li-san line, has long since been proved wrong. Considering the revolutionary war as a whole, the operations of the people's guerrillas and those of the main forces of the Red Army without the people's guerrillas, we would be like a warrior with only one arm.

CHAPTER 11

THE NATURE OF THE INTERPROVINCIAL MILITARY COMMAND STRUCTURE

SUMMARY

Command over military personnel and operations was affected through four layers of authority which at the interprovincial level consisted of the interparty committee, the interprovincial (bureaucratic) committee, the military affairs committee, and the military headquarters.

The interparty committee of the infrastructure was the most influential body governing military activities on an interprovincial level. It represented the Dang Lao Dong Central Committee and its Central Office for South Vietnam (COSVN).

The interprovincial committee was the bureaucratic body which coordinated overall insurgent operations at the interprovincial level. This committee plans combined military and nonmilitary programs in accordance with guidelines established at higher levels.

The military affairs committee was the party control office at the command and staff level in the military organization. Primarily a party-oriented body, the MAC provided the critical link between the interprovincial committee and the military headquarters. The personnel of the MAC included selected individuals from the interprovincial committee and the military staff.

The military headquarters was the only body in the system which was primarily military-oriented. It provided the actual direction for military operations.

Within the military headquarters there were two separate and parallel command systems—a military hierarchy and a party hierarchy. The military channels consisted of a military staff division, a political division, and a logistics division. Each of these divisions of the military headquarters in turn commanded various sections, subsections, and operational units.

The party channels, by contrast, consisted of two interparty committees, one controlling the party members in the military staff and political divisions and the other controlling the party members in the logistics division of the military headquarters.

The Fifth Interprovincial Military Command

By mid-1962, the military structure of the insurgent's forces in the several interprovincial subdivisions of South Vietnam had reached the level of development which would make possible sustained guerrilla warfare into the mid-1960's. An analysis of the principal features of that organization in the region of the Fifth Interprovincial, where our attention was directed earlier in this study, can provide us with an understanding of the characteristics figuring in all of the military commands that finally crystallized in the early sixties.

The Military Affairs Committee of the Fifth IPC

The all-critical link between the Fifth Interprovincial Committee—one of the six major command offices of the party bureaucracy in South Vietnam for the prosecution of the insurgency, referred to in the following discussion as the Fifth IPC—and the headquarters of the Fifth Interprovincial Military Forces was the interprovincial (party) military affairs committee (MAC) of the IPC, a branch agency of the latter body.

It will be recalled from the discussion in chapter 2 that a series of agencies and branches operated at the interprovincial level under the supervision of the current affairs or permanent standing committee of an IPC (e.g., administration, communications and liaison, intelligence and security, training and propganda, enemy troop and civilian proselytizing, economics, etc.). The MAC was another critical agency of the current affairs committee of the IPC, organizationally parallel to those other specialized offices, and composed, like its companion agencies, of party members. That is to say, *this was first of all a party office and only secondarily a military body.* It was the conduit through which the current affairs committee directed the military headquarters and supervised the military units under the command of the latter body. Until the MAC approved the proposals originating in the military headquarters, the latter body was powerless to move. Ultimately, the IPC itself was subject to the controls of the supreme interparty committee at the summit of the party's cellular structure.

The Order of Authority

Consequently, at the top, military command proceeded through four layers of authority superimposed, one upon the other, from the interparty (cellular) committee, to the interprovincial (bureaucratic) committee, to the MAC of the interprovincial, to the headquarters of the interprovincial military force. Only in the last of these bodies, the military headquarters, was one dealing with a group of persons among whom individuals could be found whose orientation was primarily military.

Each of these bodies was intended to carry out specific functions with respect to the insurgency as a whole. The interparty (cellular) committee spoke with the authority of COSVN and the CC of the Dang Lao Dong within the interprovincial region. It was a final approving office with the right of veto. The interprovincial committee, in turn, was the bureaucracy through which insurgent operations were coordinated; there plans were drawn up combining military with nonmilitary programs, on the basis of instructions from above, tactically to implement strategy. The MAC was the party control office at the command and staff level in the military organization. It was the party's way of assuring itself that tactical military operations were conducted within a preeminently political context. Finally, the military headquarters was the directing center for the specific tactical operations undertaken. Here military expertise was provided with an environment in which it might function.

Individuals Holding Multiple Positions

The seemingly sharp compartmentalization of function was smoothed over in practice by assigning key figures, operating in these vertically ordered bodies, dual or multiple positions at two or more layers of the structure. Thus the MAC whose leadership was drawn from the interprovincial committee and which contained individuals from the body's permanent standing committee likewise included key staff personnel who concurrently headed up critical offices of the military headquarters. Thus, a plenary assembly of the MAC would bring together a select body of individuals who were (1) party-oriented, (2) alive to immediate military operational realities, and (3) cognizant of the totality of the current insurgent effort and the problems confronting it. Such a group of individuals was indeed best likely to represent the party's interests and needs within the military forces.

One point, however, must be stressed at this juncture and may not be missed by the reader: the fact that personnel from the military headquarters participated in the deliberations of the MAC did not erase the practical distinction between the prerogatives assigned to each of these bodies; for although a plenary meeting of either the MAC or the military headquarters would call for the appearance of a number of individuals holding concurrent membership in both organizations, the bulk of the persons attending the one gathering would not take part in the other. For the most part the composition of the one body was unlike the other and required the assembly of a different group of persons. The ability of an individual to speak with the authority of the MAC within the councils of the military headquarters was one more reflection of the principle of "reverse representation."

Another practice of the DLD which had the effect of integrating the work of the several offices under consideration was that of making the first secretary of the interparty committee concurrently the commanding general of the interprovincial military headquarters. Since the same individual was normally the secretary general of the IPC, and frequently combined this post with that of first secretary of the MAC, one person wearing four hats was in a position to resolve jurisdictional disputes where they occurred and to delineate functions on a continuing basis as the tactical situation changed. The essential reason leading the party to place these offices in the hands of one person—or allowing the first secretary of the interparty to absorb them into his own office once they become vacant—was not to effect the coordination suggested here. The first secretary would strive to control these posts in order to make his rule in the interprovincial region absolute and to provide himself with multiple alternate command channels through which he could see to it that his wishes were actually implemented. A successful effort in this direction on his part tended to encourage cooperation or at a minimum, discourage identifiable opposition. Once again, however, one must be cautioned against the conclusion that the first secretary's possession of these multiple posts rendered meaningless the distinctions between the several bodies involved. The secretary could not carry on his own shoulders the huge work load generated by these offices, but had to delegate authority. He was himself a product of such a system and was, of course, answerable at all times to higher authorities in the apparat.[a]

The Staff, Political, and Logistics Divisions

Within the major divisions and sections of the military headquarters of the Fifth Interprovincial Region, two totally distinct command systems operated parallel to one another: the military chain of command and the party hierarchy. The military channel proceeded from three major divisions (i.e., staff, political, and logistics) through sections to subsections or operational units. The party, true to its own distinctive patterns, recognized two interparty committees of the military, one embracing the personnel of the staff and political division of the headquarters, the other the personnel of the logistics division, and below this level, groups and cells. If military personnel were ultimately responsible—as professionals—to their division heads, the commanding general and his chief of staff, then the same persons—as party members—were responsible, at the highest level, to interparty committees of the military which were answerable, in turn, to the supreme interparty of the Fifth Interprovincial Committee, and significantly, it is only at this level that the two hierarchies formally joined together. An examination of chart 11 will reveal the degree to

[a] The model which provided local party leaders with guidance in determining the relationship between the Fifth Interprovincial (bureaucratic) Committee, the MAC, the military headquarters and the political division of the Fifth Military Headquarters—the last body examined in detail later in the text—was the military setup at the national level in North Vietnam itself. In principle, these four offices were the interprovincial equivalents of (1) the National Defense Council, a committee of the politburo to which selected CC members were admitted; (2) the Military Affairs Department of the Central Committee Departments; (3) the ministry of national defense; and (4) the political directorate of the ministry. These four offices were interrelated as follows:

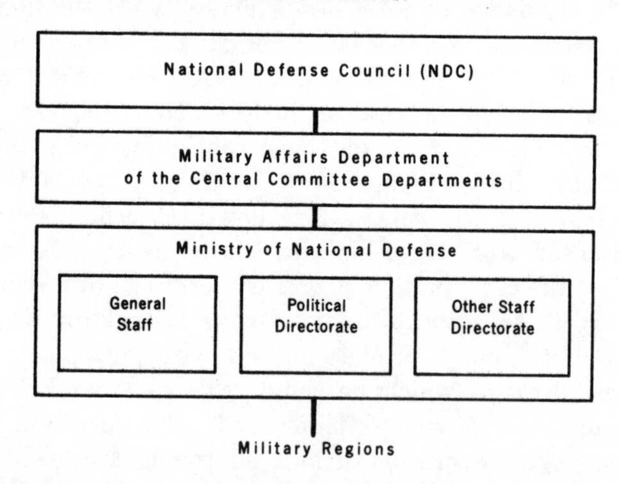

Viewed in this manner, the parallel with the interprovincial structure becomes apparent. Another parallel is suggested by the multiple offices held by General Giap, one senior position in each of the above national agencies. He was a member of the NDC, Chairman of the GPO, Minister of National Defense, and Commander in Chief of the Army (PAVN). The reason for his holding so many positions was exactly the same as that which led the PRP to allow the first secretary of the interparty to be concurrently the secretary general of the party committee, head of the MAC, and commanding general in the military headquarters.

which the party and military channels varied. In the following pages our purpose will be survey the multiple elements and units attached to the Fifth Interprovincial Headquarters and to point out the consequences that follow from the maintenance of these two alternate reporting hierarchies.

The Staff Division of the Fifth IPC

A staff division could contain a wide variety of sections, although persistent modification in detail was apparent in the study of any one such body over a period of time. However, under the conditions of phase two or three, insurgent warfare, a minimum of nine distinct sections can be identified.

The combat training and body guard (CTBG) section of the staff division of the Fifth Interprovincial Headquarters brought together two functions that need not necessarily be handled by a single office. The basic training of recruits inducted into main line units was conducted by this section; on the other hand, guard personnel adding up in numbers to a force in excess of company strength were also administered and assigned by this staff element. In a military table of organization and equipment (TOE) then, the headquarters' guard company and training school were subordinated to the CTBG section and are answerable to it for their conduct and performance. However, both of these bodies were considerably greater in size than the staff section itself and, given the heavy concentration of permanently assigned party members in each of them, the concurrent cellular organization of the PRP members led to the creation not only of multiple cells in both elements but of two higher, party "group" committees, one for each body. Such committees in military units, as in party bureaucratic organization, were headed by a first secretary, his deputy, and several associates, and such a body was answerable to an interparty committee only. Under no circumstances could it be dominated by a parallel or lesser party organization. Since the highest level of party cellular organization in the CTBG section itself was the single cell headed by a cell captain or secretary, this body, which stood above both the school and the guard company in the military hierarchy, was outranked by them in the party hierarchy.

The nature of organizational interrelationships was further complicated by the fact that the training school was removed a considerable distance from the site where the principal elements of the military headquarters of the Fifth Interprovincial conducted their work. This installation, along with the Delta Area People's Guerrilla Research Center and four operational units (two special mission companies, an artillery and an engineer company), because of the communications and movement problems associated with their activities, were accredited a distinct status within the party's cellular structure—in contradistinction to the military hierarchy—and the party group committees established in each of these several bodies were made directly responsible not to the interparty committee No. 1 of the military—as in the case of the guard company of the CTBG—but to

the supreme interparty committee of the Fifth Interprovincial Committee. The commanding officer of the CTBG was militarily responsible for the performance of the guards and the school, and the party leadership at the interparty level was concurrently provided with the means of holding this professional specialist under continuous surveillance, using an alternate command channel through which initiative could be seized at any moment and all orders countermanded.

The only way in which the section's commanding officer could acquire control over the cellular reporting channels to his own two units would be through his "election" to a top level committee in the party hierarchy. As the captain of a cell within the CTBG section, he could be nominated by higher party officials as a candidate for membership in a group committee.

Since only one person would be nominated for election to any given post, the determination of higher party leaders to select the commanding officer of the CTBG to "run for office" would constitute among the PRP membership a clear and universally recognized act of party commendation for the individual so honored. Nomination was synonymous with election and was a means of promotion. From the group committee, he might next be promoted, by "election," to interparty committee No. 1 of the military, and from there to the supreme interparty committee of the Fifth Interprovincial Region.

As he moved up through the cellular structure, becoming increasingly a "party careerist" and less a military specialist as he went, he would find himself in positions of increasing importance with respect to lower party bodies. As a member of interparty committee No. 1 of the military—provided he concurrently retained his position as commanding officer of the CTBG—he would be well situated to dominate both the military and party channels running to the guard company. In the supreme interparty, he might control the party group in the training school in addition to serving as the installation's commandant. However, the holding of two such positions in the military and party organizations as those postulated here, while it was indeed possible in theory, was most unlikely in practice. Any person earmarked for advancement to such levels of the party hierarchy would hardly be retained in a military slot of such limited importance as the CTBG, since commissioned officers in the PAVN in both the North and the South holding high party positions tended to occupy concurrently critical military appointments. Vietnamese Communists knew that a good "military" decision might be a bad "party" policy, and that if a conflict between the two should arise, then preservation of the Communist apparat had to come first. It could generate a new military organization at some future date, but the armed forces could not call a new party into being.

Psychological Dynamics

Speculations on the mentality of the members of an esoteric and proscriptive band can never escape the status of hypotheses. However, documents which give insight into the thinking of Vietnamese Communists offer a possible framework in which to understand the arrangement which set men at cross-purposes within the military structure. The following observations are offered in this context as a possible explanation of what appears to the Western utilitarian mind to be a paradox.

Mutual distrust and competition became inherent characteristics of the military organization, and from the point of view of the party leadership this was no "unfortunate but unavoidable" situation, but was an altogether acceptable condition, one to be sustained, not altered.

The party would maintain two conditions: First, policy would be implemented by persons conscious of their insecurity who would persistently attempt to surpass their past performances in an attempt to gain the approval of those in the higher echelons of the organization who alone can satisfy the personal and immediate need for recognition and sense of job security. Second, the PRP wanted to be able to intervene in the affairs of the committee at the next lower level without prior notice and without a break in stride. The PRP—as other Communist insurgent organizations before it—found that its requirements are most adequately approximated precisely through its maintenance of multiple or, at a minimum, parallel command channels such as the party and military reporting channels in the headquarters of the Fifth Interprovincial Region.

Other staff sections. In contrast to the complex situation associated with the CTBG, the staff sections concerned with support, administration, and crypto were simple organizations, and the liaison and communications section (LCS) was only slightly more complicated. Under "support," the staff division of the military organization understood only a portion of that which would fall into this category in a conventional military force. Most traditional support activities and a number of unusual programs were handled by the separate logistics divisions. The support section concerned itself with sanitation and food facilities, especially the scheduling and supervision of the farming effort, in which all of the personnel of the staff division were expected to participate, and in the transportation of food supplies purchased or otherwise acquired from the peasantry at large.

The range of responsibilities of the administration section compared largely with those of the personnel or J–1 staff position of a conventional military headquarters, while the crypto section, as in the bureaucracy of the party committee system, was a small element concerned with the decoding and encoding of messages. The highest level of party organization in all three of these sections was the cell, and all of these cells were responsible to the group committee of the staff division which was headed by the chief of that division.

The radio equipment and personnel who worked together with the crypto specialists were found under the LCS in a signal company, meaning that the LCS in practice served as a coordinating center for these two groups of specialized personnel. This placed the LCS in a situation not unlike that occupied by the administrative branch of a party committee with respect to the radio and crypto elements independently maintained within the party's own hierarchy. The military setup, however, was to be distinguished from that in the party by its larger size and preoccupation with the transmission of military orders and directives almost exclusively as opposed to party materials. The LCS and its specialized unit may be contrasted with the three sectors treated in the preceding paragraph to the cxtent that the signal company, like the guard company of the CTBG, is cellularly structured up to the group level and reports to interparty committee No. 1 of the military, while the LCS itself was organized only at the cell level and reported to the staff division group committee.

As in the case of the CTBG, the structure under the enemy situation section (ESS) was also highly complex. Narrowly, one could compare this structure with the J–2 or intelligence staff office of a major military command, but its responsibilities, like those of the security hierarchy in the party committee system, extended into areas that would not normally loom so large in the work of more conventional commands. It was within the ESS and its subordinated units that one found the personnel of the old armed propaganda teams (the Dich Van) that served as the catalysts behind the initiated mass organization of the peasantry in the late fifties and early sixties.

The PRP was fully conscious that its continuing success depended upon its ability to dominate the peasantry by combining indoctrination/organization—its positive effort—with terrorism and the threat of terrorism—the negative or destructive aspect of its two-pronged intervention in civil life. Consequently, the PRP always retained its terrorist elements. In the command structure of the military interprovincial headquarters which received its current shape by 1962, the armed propagandists of an earlier era took on the military trappings of company units of 30 to 35 men each, one identified as a reconnaissance company, the other as a special mission company of the ESS. Personnel policy in these two units indicated that they remained distinct from other military forces, for while the latter were continually expanded as new recruits became available, the reconnaissance and special mission companies remained closed to such personnel. When it was decided to expand capability in this area, the units were not enlarged, but the untested individuals made available were assigned to a second special mission company specifically activated for them and subject to control by the older special unit.

In the cellular hierarchy, the reconnaissance company reported to the interparty committee No. 1 of the military, while the two special mission companies, whose personnel would continue to operate in small groups widely dispersed over the region of the Fifth Interprovincial, were responsible directly to the supreme interparty committee of the PRP's interprovincial committee. Such a disposition within the cellular structure provided the elements of these two companies with the elasticity they needed to conduct the operations in which they specialized.

There yet remain three sections to be noted: the artillery, engineer, and militia and guerrilla sections. An examination of chart 11 reveals their structural position in both the military and party hierarchies. The nature of the functions performed by the first two of these bodies is evident from the names assigned them. A few words may be added, however, regarding the agency under the direction of the militia and guerrilla section, namely, the Delta Area People's Guerrilla Warfare Research Center.

When originally called into being, this latter organization was functionally little more than another tactical command, fashioned to coordinate the operations of two or more regional units during a specified series of maneuvers as ordered by the military headquarters. Its personnel were drawn from the military headquarters itself. However, the activities of this office were not devoid of distinctive features, for its mission was to provide designated armed propaganda squads with the supplementary military support and firepower requisite to force their way into the Quang Nam/Quang Tin border area to establish a "liberated area," set up village and hamlet liberation committees, and establish local guerrilla groups.

Successful in this initial mission, the Delta Area People's Guerrilla Warfare Research Center was maintained in existence, but its mission was altered. Its primary missions became (1) the conduct of research into and experimentation with the use of guerrilla tactics by village militia forces in the struggle against the establishment of "strategic hamlets" by the Government of the Republic of Vietnam, and (2) the conduct of training courses in guerrilla warfare. Additionally, it was to fulfill combat assignments and participate in supplementary "deep drives" of armed propaganda teams. The ultimate fate of this organization is unknown. Its campsite was the scene of government mopping-up operations, but these operations did not lead to the organization's deactivation. It is reasonable to assume that this or a comparable office still exists in the region of the Fifth Interprovincial Committee.

The Political Division of the Fifth IPC

Quite unlike the tortured complexities characterizing the staff division, the political division of the Fifth Interprovincial Headquarters presented a strikingly simple organizational picture. No one section contained party elements superior to the cell and all party members were responsible to a group committee in which the division chief was the first secretary. Thus the party and military command channels fully accorded with one another and the head of the structure held all of the reins of authority in his hands.

Such a situation strengthened the division chief's hand. The uniqueness of the top political commissar's position was strengthened further by the fact that he was concurrently the assistant secretary of the MAC, an organ of the party's interprovincial committee, and worked directly under the latter body's secretary general. Though specific information did not exist either to confirm or to refute further speculation on the party offices held by this chief political commissar, one is encouraged to see the two offices which he held as a springboard into membership on the current affairs committee of the supreme interparty committee. In any case, one was dealing here with a person of the greatest importance to the military organization, a person who had effective control over critical elements of the insurgent organization through the several positions which he concurrently held.

The Logistics Division of the Fifth IPC

In the light of the extensive discussion of the preceding two divisions of the military headquarters, little elaboration is necessary regarding the third major element of the armed forces at the interprovincial level, for a grasp of its purpose and structure requires a mastery of no additional new principles. With a few exceptions, the tasks performed by the several sections of this organization are immediately apparent from the names assigned them. The clothing items section, in addition to the role which would clearly be assigned to such an office, was the source of currency issued to military units for the purchase of clothing which the unit cannot supply. The finance section had the additional duty of providing technical guidance on farmwork. And, finally, the equipment section controlled a series of machine shops in the region of the Fifth Interprovincial. Regarding the cellular hierarchy, as a glance at chart 11 will reveal, exactly the same distinctive interrelationship obtained as in the staff division.

Wherever the party hierarchy was formed, one also found a party youth structure, which in South Vietnam was the People's Revolutionary Youth Association. Thus, throughout the many offices of the headquarters of the Fifth Interprovincial's military forces, youth subcells and cells were found at the party cell and group level subordinated to the latter bodies in precisely the same manner as in the party committee system. The principles treated in chapter 5 consequently are equally applicable here.

The Historical Function of the Political Echelon in Communist Military Organization

A second matter to be stressed regarding the political echelon of the military structure is its longevity in the history of international communism. It has performed with striking regularity the same group of functions in insurgencies occurring in widely scattered areas of the world. Communist leaders everywhere have recognized the same divisions of labor within the political structure of insurgent armed forces. The political commissar system, the policom, originated in the autumn of 1917 when the Bolsheviks were preparing for their own insurgency in Petrograd. Critical steps in its development were: first, having the Petrograd Soviet establish an inner "Revolutionary Military Committee" (25 October), "a collegium of representatives," as Trotsky described it, "to function alongside the commander of troops of the Petrograd military district",[b] and second using

[b] James Bunyan and H. A. Fisher, *The Bolshevik Revolution, 1917–1918* (Stanford, Calif.: Stanford University Press, 1961), p. 69.

the new military committee as a base from which to assign party members to military garrison units in the city as commissars. The initial motivation for this step was the desire to acquire control. Once that goal had been reached, the commissar's task became even more positive: he superintended the moral and spiritual life of his charges, both inside and outside the party. It is in this latter context that the role of the commissar in Vietnam was formulated in an editorial of the North Vietnamese *Quan Doi Nhan Dan* ("People's Army"):

> The role of the political commissars has been very clearly defined: they are responsible for the political attitude of their companies, they must look after the intellectual training of the servicemen and continually help them to develop their thinking habits. In order to carry out this task, the first and most basic thing is to give the servicemen a solid educational background, thorough understanding of their political role, and a correct view of the revolution.

Setting itself the rhetorical question, "What kind of training should be provided military personnel?" the editorial continued by citing the words of one of the army's ranking generals:

> First of all, they must clearly understand whom they fight for and what is the purpose of their fight. This understanding will produce courage, the will to fight and the determination to win. This is a problem of political education, a choice of viewpoint and of thoughts. From now on, we should give more consideration to this fundamental problem.
>
> The mind directs action. Action is right only if the mind is sound. The formation of a sound mind means first of all the strengthening of the revolutionary viewpoint which is the same as the viewpoint of the proletarian class.[c]

The institution of the commissar figured repeatedly in the Communist attempts at the export of insurgency during the decades after the Soviet revolution. It was dramatically apparent in the Spanish Civil War (1936–1939) and in the struggle of the partisan forces in eastern and southern Europe during the Second World War. It had been introduced into the Orient well before that date through the Whampoa Military Academy which was established by Soviet Party personnel near Canton in 1923. By the middle thirties, the Red Chinese Army had a fully operational political apparatus functioning from the platoon and squad levels up through all command levels as suggested in chart 12.

In the right-hand column, from the division down through the regimental level, the CCP (Chinese Communist Party) drew a distinction between the political commissar and the political department, assigning to the former policy and supervisory functions, to the latter an executive role. From the battalion down to the platoon, only the executive agency was represented, policy matters remaining in the hands of higher military headquarters. At the company level, the political indoctrination of the foot soldier was the task of a Lenin club (after 1937 called by the more innocuous name of soldiers' club), in which nonparty personnel were expected to participate along with party members and candidate members. Also

[c] "How the Political Commissars Should Fulfill Their Basic Duties as Leaders in Combat and Combat-Readiness Training" (editorial), *Quan Doi Nhan Dan* ("People's Army") (Hanoi: 11 October 1962), No. 1110, pp. 1 and 3.

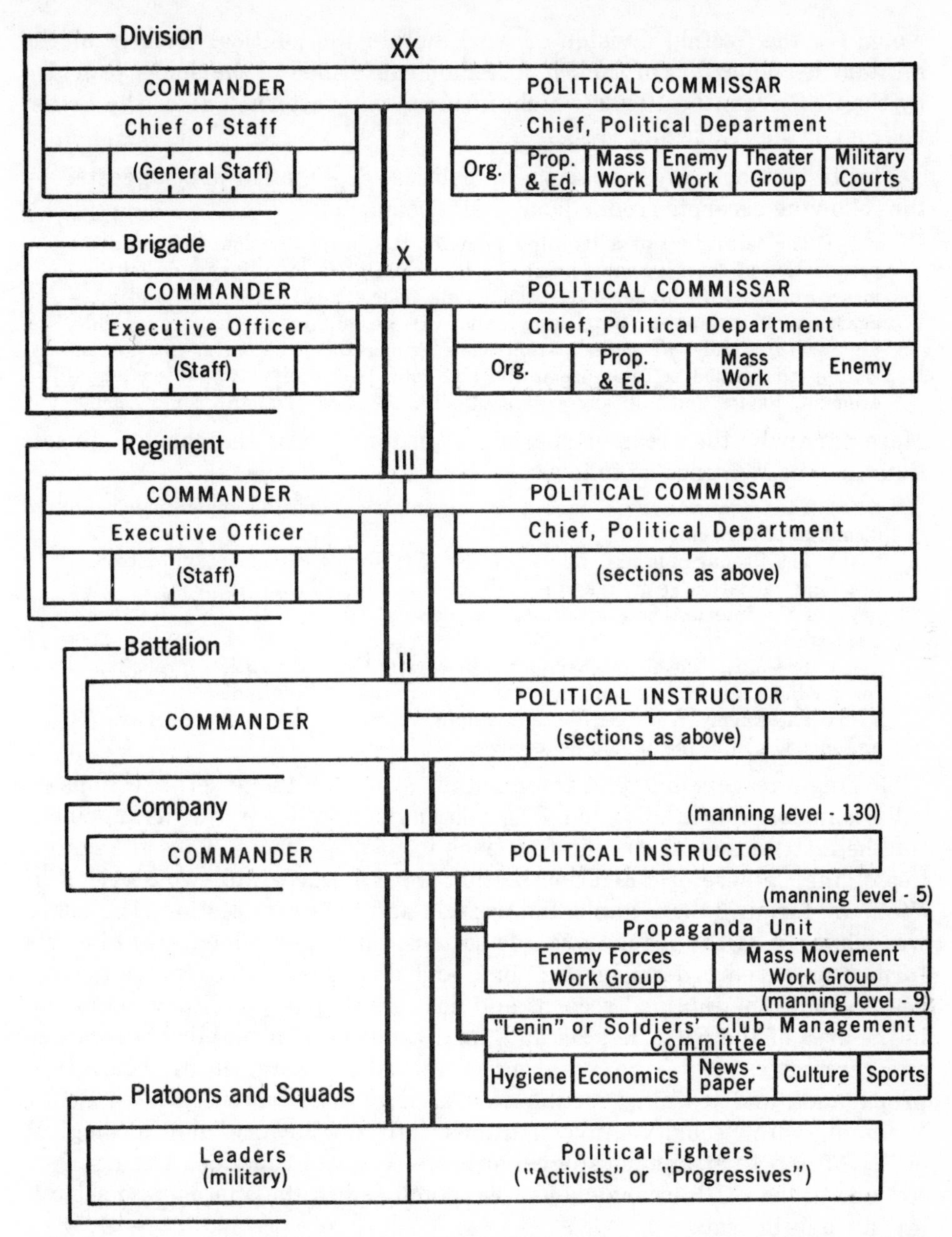

Chart 12. POLITICAL STRUCTURE IN A CHINESE RED ARMY DIVISION DURING THE 1930'S

attached to the military unit was a propaganda unit assigned a role equivalent to that of the proselytizer in the current Vietnamese insurgency.

While we shall pursue the similarities between the Chinese and Vietnamese operational unit further in chapter 12, it remains a matter of importance here to examine more closely the several sections attached to the political departments at the battalion, regiment, and brigade levels, viz.: organization, propaganda and education, mass movement work, and enemy work; for the fivefold division of work within the political division of the military headquarters of the Fifth Region conformed to the model provided by the CCP from the 1930's which, in turn, was patterned after the Soviet policom of the 1920's and 1930's.

The assignments given to a major political department are suggested by the following excerpts from official CCP documents:

> (a) The setting up of a training plan for the entire division, including the preparation of teaching materials; (b) the compilation of propaganda outlines in accordance with higher-level propaganda policies; (c) leadership and management of newspaper publishing; and (d) leadership of the propaganda, organization, and war participation work among the neighboring people, including the armed self-defense units, and joint execution with regional government, Party, and military organizations . . . of the resistance movement.[d]

More narrowly, the areas of specialization for each of the above four sections may be identified as follows:

> (a) The Organization Section: Army organization, and the appointment and dismissal of personnel.
>
> (b) The Propaganda and Education Section: ideological education of troops, practical education (e.g., reading instruction), and internal propaganda (e.g., news of the international situation, war news of China, KMT–CCP collaboration, etc.).
>
> (c) The Mass Movement Section: military-civilian cooperation, propaganda for civilians, civil organizations, and military and civilian discipline.
>
> (d) The Enemy Work Section: propaganda for Japanese and puppet troops, and instruction in the Japanese language.[e]

No single responsibility in these lists is absent in the several sections of a Vietnamese political division. The sole distinction lies in the arrangement for the distribution of specific functions to district offices. Thus the activities of the Chinese organization section were divided into two sections in Vietnam, forming the organization section and the cadre section. The latter was charged with promotions, demotions, and assignments, while the former prepared orders, instructions, and directives for party and party youth groups, maintained records and dossiers on party military personnel in the area of the Fifth Region and, finally, officiated at public observances and ceremonies (e.g., the granting of awards, honors, etc.). Again, the propaganda and training section was divided into two sections in South Vietnam, with security—investigations into the loyalty and ideological purity of party personnel—singled out as a separate function. The last two sections in the CCP arrangement were combined in the Vietnamese setting into a single bureau.

Again, it will be noted that several of these military sections were engaged in activities identical with those of several of the branches and agencies of Communist Party committees, working from the cover provided by the mass organizations or the PLC system. This situation may not be adjudged as counterproductive duplication; rather, by incorporating (1)

---

[d] Chalmers A. Johnson, *Peasant Nationalism and Communist Power: The Emergence of Revolutionary China, 1937–1945* (Stanford, Calif.: Stanford University Press, 1962), p. 82.

[e] Johnson, *loc. cit.*

training and education, (2) security, and (3) ETCP sections within military headquarters and combat units, the PRP's leadership assured for itself added capabilities for the mobilization of the citizenry in areas inadequately exploited. The appearance of these offices constituted a higher level of organizational sophistication.

At the outset of the insurgent process in Vietnam, proselytizing, indoctrination, and counterintelligence necessarily had to proceed from the party itself and its "armed propaganda teams." As mass work began to pay off, the proselytizer would move into the "popular" association, expand his staff, and move openly with greater ease. In the presence of major military forces, the agitator and recruiter were provided with another excellent base from which to operate and these latter bodies became, as Mao Tse-tung has declared, "armed bodies for carrying out the political tasks of the revolution." [f]

---

[f] *Selected Military Writings of Mao Tse-tung*, p. 52. Almost from the commencement of his insurgent operations, first in the Fukien, Kiangsi, Hunan border regions, following the catastrophes at Shanghai, Wuhan, Canton, etc., and later in North China after the long march, Mao was provided with a large body of troops. He did not begin from scratch, militarily speaking, as had been the case in South Vietnam after 1957. Provided with such an obvious resource, Mao employed it extensively as the initiator of mass organizations among the peasants, while the Vietnamese Communists, in contrast, had no alternative but to rely on terrorism and provocation, coupled with propaganda and agitation to commence their buildup. Under these circumstances, it is understandable that a fully elaborated policom system appeared organizationally at an earlier stage of development in the Chinese experience than in the Vietnamese example, and, further, that Mao placed greater stress on the mass work role of his army than has been the case among the Vietnamese Communists. Thus, the following famous statement in his 1929 essay, "On Correcting Mistaken Ideas in the Party":

> The Chinese Red Army is an armed body for carrying out the political tasks of the revolution. Especially at present, the Red Army should certainly not confine itself to fighting; besides fighting to destroy the enemy's political strength, it should shoulder such important tasks as doing propaganda [work] among the masses, organizing the masses, arming them, helping them to establish revolutionary political power, and setting up Party Organizations. The Red Army fights not merely for the sake of fighting but in order to conduct propaganda among the masses, organize them, arm them, and help them to establish revolutionary political power. Without these objectives, fighting loses its meaning and the Red Army loses the reason for its existence.

CHAPTER 12

THE MILITARY UNIT AND ITS INTERNAL PRACTICES

SUMMARY

The Communist Party in South Vietnam controlled the activities of the military forces through dual party and military command channels. Military commands proceeded down through headquarters at the COSVN interprovincial, provincial, and district levels, in each case under the watchful eyes of the supervising agencies of the respective party committees. Through tactical commands, military headquarters at the interprovincial level could assume operational control over units at the provincial level, and headquarters at the latter level, via tactical coordinating centers, could likewise preempt the command over district units. A district military headquarters, however, was barred from assuming summary control over village militia in that fashion and could assert itself only following local party approval. The lowest command level in the military was made up of teams of three soldiers each, two or more of which teams constituted a squad. These were known as military cells and should not be confused with party cells.

The Communist Party organizational structure in military units was similar to that in other echelons of the insurgency movement, but several alterations were imposed by military considerations. Thus, all the party youth members in a platoon were usually members of a single cell. Again, there was usually only one party group per company headed by the unit's political officer. Most importantly, the party group might be responsible, not to an interparty committee, but to a battalion party committee which, in turn, might report not to an interparty committee, but to a regimental party committee. The basic objectives of the party's political work were to (a) establish and maintain party control over the military units; (b) harness the talents of the indigenous middle class in building up the military structure; and (c) maintain the image of a "people's" military, drawing its personnel from all segments of the citizenry, and serving the best interests of the people at large.

Channels of Command

The main force units (Quan Doi Chu Luc) of the regular army (Quan Doi Chanh Quy) were responsible to either an interprovincial military headquarters or directly to the Central Office for South Vietnam itself, which in 1965 assumed the task of introducing entire units of the PAVN into the South and supervising their operations. In contrast, the regional or territorial army (Po Doi Dia Phuong), made up for the most part of units of no larger than battalion size, was under the control of the provincial or district military affairs committee (MAC) and its corresponding military headquarters. These latter two bodies approximated their interprovincial counterparts, but tended to be somewhat simpler in structure, depending upon the immediate tactical situation and the numbers of capable cadres available. The provincial headquarters, in turn, controlled military bodies at the district level through channels comparable to those which proceeded down from the interprovincial headquarters. The district headquarters, however, was limited in its authority over the village militia (Dan Quan Du Kich). Party channels from the district party committee down to the village party chapter had to be engaged to provide the district military headquarters with operational control over village or hamlet paramilitary units.

Tactical commands up to the level of regimental headquarters existed, and while they did not figure in all operations, they provided the combatant command with the ability to coordinate the actions of multiple units, varying from operations involving from two to six battalions of provincial or interprovincial troops down to company- and platoon-size forces at the district level. If necessary, a given company-size unit in a specific district would be moved by a tactical command into an adjoining area to reinforce, resupply, or rescue a comparable force under attack.

The actual operational units of the military organization, both main force and regional force, tended to conform in their integral military structure with traditional Western units of like size and designation. The model in chart 13 may be considered as characteristic.

Such a unit contained three infantry companies and one heavy weapons company. Signal, reconnaissance, and engineer platoons were attached to the headquarters. Additional platoon-size units could function from this level to provide for medicine, liaison with rear service agencies, special mission assignments (e.g., armed propaganda teams), and other requirements needed. The companies in turn were divided into platoons, squads, and three-man military cells or three-man elements.

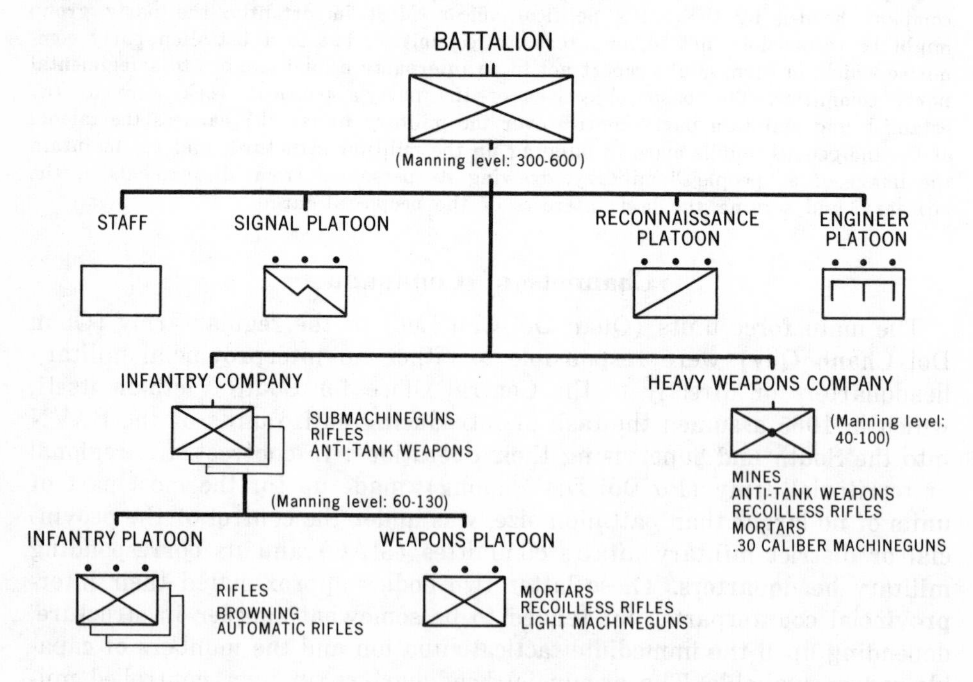

Chart 13. COMPONENT ELEMENTS OF A CHARACTERISTIC MAIN LINE BATTALION

The Military Cell

This lowest level of military organization—the cluster of three soldiers—may not be summarily passed over without attention. The military cell is not to be confused with the party cell. Its members were not necessarily party members and if they were they would belong to a party cell "in addition," *not* "instead." This cell would exist in peacetime as in war and in secure areas as well as in battle zones. On no occasion was the individual soldier to act independently, but always as a member of a group. Such a body or element, the formal institutionalization of the concept of fire and movement or the "buddy system" had immediate, obvious utility in combat. For the Communist, however, it had additional importance as a surveillance device and an organizational reaffirmation of the principle of "responsibility," inherent to the doctrine of democratic centralism, which compelled the party member to organize those under his control down to the most minute details. Never could a group, even an *ad hoc* body of varying composition, function (1) in the absence of organization, or (2) without a formally designated "responsible" leader. Neither spontaneity nor expediency would be tolerated; the variables would be held to a minimum through the structuring of all human situations.

Party Offices in the Military Structure

Outside of this table of organization—which was essentially military by design and intent—the military unit contained the entire paraphernalia of party offices, after the fashion of the Chinese structure depicted in the diagram in the preceding chapter,[a] plus a hierarchical cellular structure of party members and party youth members. In principle, the cellular organizations were of the same character as other vertical echelons of the insurgent movement, but several deviations in detail may be briefly noted here: (1) the party youth (PRYA) cell tended to be quite large, all of the youth members in a platoon-size force being integrated into a single cell.

---

[a] The political organization attached to the company in the Chinese design for a division-size force (cf. p. 141), i.e., the propaganda unit and the "Lenin" or "soldiers' club" are approximated in the insurgent unit, but they have been developed to the same level of refinement only in the larger units of the PAVN which infiltrated into the South in 1965. The functions fulfilled by the "enemy forces" and the "mass movement" work groups of the propaganda unit were paralleled in the South by the "special mission" platoons attached to the company headquarters of the primarily indigenous military unit. (It is understood, of course, that in the Vietnamese context, the task of "an armed propaganda team" drawn from a special mission platoon is to support committees, and not to supplant that effort by militarizing it as was the base in China in the 1930's. For a further discussion of this point, see part four). The proselytizing mission is organizationally provided for, and "soldiers' clubs" have apparently not been formally activated in forces of a predominantly indigenous character. This does not mean that these military units do not conduct the same kinds of programs as those figuring in the Chinese unit in the 1930's and in the Soviet unit even before then, but no single formal structure has been established to set the milieu in which such activities are conducted among those belonging to neither the party nor the party youth organization. In the PAVN unit, in contrast, one finds at the company level, not only the three-man military team and the party youth organization, referred to by North Vietnamese policoms as the "assault force in the company," but also the "soldiers' council" through which the political and ideological life of the soldier is supervised. They are "places for instruction, leadership, and popular action." Further, this body contained elements which "specialize in information and propaganda in the villages, party bases, and factories." Cf. Brig. Gen. Le Quang Hoa, "How Company Political Officers Conduct Ideological Work," *Quan Doi Nhan Dan* ("People's Army") (Hanoi: 11–14 July 1965), p. 3.

(2) A party group committee was organized for every company size unit[b] and its first secretary was invariably the company's political officer (the *chinh tri vien)* who held his office not by the fiction of "election" but openly by appointment. (The same arrangement also held at the battalion level where the battalion policom was once again the committee's first secretary.) (3) While the group and intergroup levels in the youth organization were recognized—at the company and battalion levels in the military structure—the former, the group level, may be the sole party, as opposed to the party youth cellular office, to exist in its customary form in the military organization. Where one is dealing with a military force larger than a battalion, the PRP group in the company would be responsible to the party's battalion committee. A regimental or high headquarters existed, and the battalion committee took its direction from the party committee of that headquarters. However, this was not always to be the case; if the battalion were a regional unit under the control of a provincial military affairs committee, then one or more interparty committees would exist at the battalion level and would report in the conventional manner to the supreme interparty committee of the provincial committee. Diagrammatically the several reporting channels at the company level are shown in chart 14.

Party Activities Within the Operational Military Unit

The party and party youth structures within the military unit were relentlessly engaged in the widest range of activities, calculated to evoke a political awareness in the soldier and to lead him to conceive of his military activities in an ideological and political framework. The following list of subjects which figured in the agenda of a conference of a battalion party committee suggests the breadth of operational problems with which the party itself was concerned:

Review of the status and ideology of personnel of the unit during the past, and anticipated development in the future. Corrective measures are considered.

Discussion of principles of tactics and training.

Evaluation of collective and individual efforts.

Review of the leadership in the accomplishment of policies and courses of action.

Discussion of the leadership of the party in matters of combat and other type missions.

Indoctrination, motivation, and organization of the masses of the population; review of efficiencies and deficiencies.

Improvement of the spirit of competition in the unit and utilization of individual initiative to advantage.

Discussion of nutrition and the physical condition of the personnel of the unit.

---

[b] Additionally, a party and a party youth "group" would be set up for headquarters personnel. In the case of the model battalion-size unit in the diagram on p. 124, these two "groups" would be based upon the members of the respective party bodies contained in the staff section, plus those in the signal, reconnaissance, and engineer platoons. Thus the entire battalion would produce five PRP group committees and five PRYA group committees. (Each of the five youth committees at the group level would be under the supervision of commissars appointed by the respective PRP committees. The youth intergroup, in the same fashion, would be under the surveillance of a commissar designated by the battalion committee.)

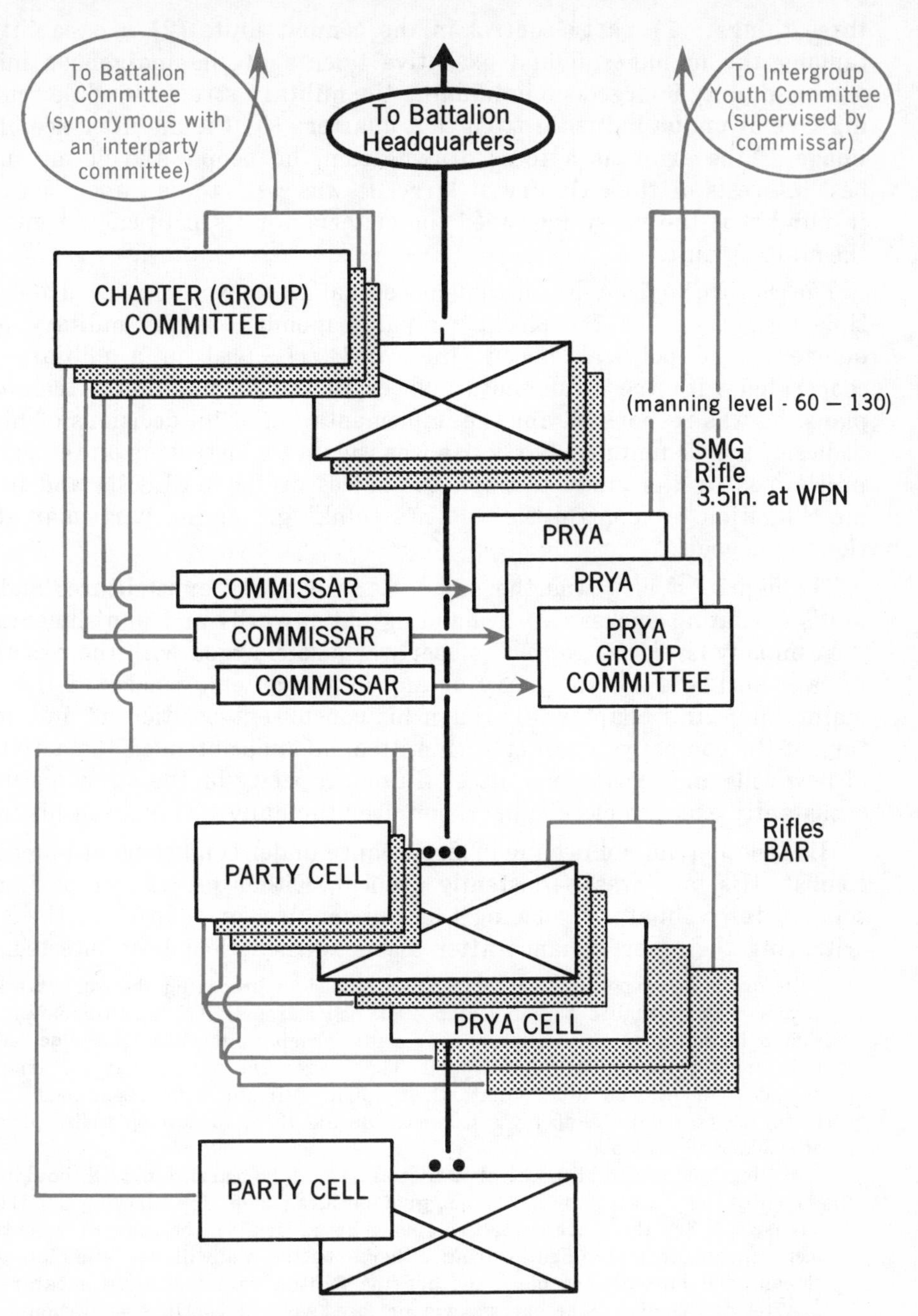

Chart 14. PARTY AND PARTY YOUTH CELLULAR STRUCTURE IN A COMBAT UNIT AT THE PLATOON AND COMPANY LEVELS

Evaluate the proficiencies and peculiarities of the various units so as to be able to take corrective action.

Discussion of new projects.

By involving themselves in matters that seemed the rightful preserve of the professional military officer, the party sought to assure itself of three things: (1) party control in the combat unit; (2) a capability of tapping the managerial and executive talents of the indigenous middle class and petty bourgeoisie in building the military structure while remaining free of undue influence from that quarter; (3) the maintenance of the image of the army as a force drawn from the people and acting in the best interests of the citizenry at large. It was with these imperatives still in mind that the party identified the criteria for its political activities in the military unit.

The political officer. From this conceptual framework followed the multiple tasks assigned the officiating party member in the military headquarters. The political officer (the *chinh tri vien)* in a military unit cooperated with the commanding officer in the formulation of campaign plans; he was responsible for the implementation of all decisions of higher bodies of the Communist Party. He was the unit's instructor on the policies proclaimed by the party through the offices of the NFLSVN and it was his obligation to "control the soldier's thinking," giving particular attention to the youth.

The *chinh tri vien* was the paymaster for party expenditures and the unit's officiating spokesman in handing out rewards and punishments. At the company level, the political officer was also charged with the recruiting of new members for the party or any of the other agencies of the PRP maintaining unit chapters. Through his concurrent position as first secretary of the company (chapter) committee, he superintended the activation of new cells and group committees. In one capacity or the other, he would "constantly exercise close supervision over the daily activities in his unit."

His function did not decline in significance under conditions of immediate combat. His task was persistently cyclical. Either he was preparing his soldiers for combat, or solacing them under fire, or counseling them and criticizing their performance after disengagement had been effected.

> Before fighting political activity should consist in preparing the combatants to make them realize the importance of political activity. The combatants should be educated on policies and precepts. Combatants should be educated to strengthen their political viewpoint. The danger and hardship in the army should be mentioned to stimulate their spirit. Stir up their resentment by telling them about the enemy's designs. Educate them to develop their spirit of solidarity in combat.
>
> During combat what political activities should be carried out? Stimulate the spirit. Give solace for hardships, give encouragement for carrying out the offensive. When there are casualties among his associates, the soldier's resentment should be stimulated. During a fierce battle, we will use stimulating slogans and have the people encourage the fighting spirit of the combatant.
>
> After the combat, whether we win or lose, we will continue education to stimulate the spirit and/or to prevent discouragement and fear. Then we will evaluate the results and analyze the reasons why we won or why we lost. After evaluation we will give rewards or punishments. Finally, we will reorganize the unit and strengthen it materially and morally. If possible we will organize a ceremony to commemorate the dead, to encourage vengeance. We will visit the families of the dead to solace them and to stir up their resentment so that they will fight with us. Then we will meet with the auto-defense forces to evaluate the results. In summary, political activity should be intensi-

fied after combat to stimulate the combatants' spirit, to reorganize and strengthen the unit, and to correct any erroneous opinions that may persist.

Behind this aggressive effort of the highest priority within the unit lay a well-articulated *raison d'être*, repeatedly confirmed by Communist experiences stretching over some four decades. In its Vietnamese guise, party work in the military unit was justified in the following words:

> The growth, success, or failure of our units depends on our political activities. Political activities are a factor that determine the success or failure of the unit; they are carried on in conformity to the policies and precepts of the Party, so that everyone may understand thoroughly his political responsibilities in accomplishing his task as a soldier of the Revolution. Political activities are useful because they help in building up our army and contribute to our victories; they are a basic factor in the development of fighting techniques. To make sure that the troops will fight successfully, we should build up the army in conformity to political policies and precepts. Without political activities we would lose our class viewpoint. Political activities aim at encouraging the people to participate in the Revolution, and at giving the combatants in the army a resolute spirit. Political activity is very important whether the troops are at rest or in combat. At this time we should strengthen our forces to destroy the enemy. This involves both strategy and tactics. Political activity is a factor which aids the strengthening of our army.

Indoctrination techniques. At the heart of the policom's task was the indoctrination of military personnel. To effect this end, he was provided with a multitude of techniques which had been evolved in the course of the global experiences of Communists. First of all, larger units, battalion size and above, engaged in the publication of reading matter for general distribution, newsletters, and information sheets, assisted by the provincial party committee's training and propaganda branch. The latter element was responsible for the release of information bulletins (cf. ch. 2) and other occasional documents, and it also served as a source of published books and newspapers imported from North Vietnam and Cambodia or reproduced locally by the party committee. All of this literature painted a single picture, reinforcing the attitudes which the party member inculcated during his discussions and conversations with the rank and file. Specific books and leaflets found by security forces ranged from Vietnamese translations of Chinese military classics to collections of short stories of military heroes and such documents as "The Story of the United States Intervention and Invasion of Cuba."

Concurrent with this program, the *chinh tri vein* was responsible for the organization of literacy programs. To this end, regular evening classes were conducted in the unit. The soldier was obliged to participate in classwork and do his daily homework assignments.

Radio Hanoi. Other sources of assistance in indoctrination work were the broadcasts of Radio Hanoi along with the transmissions of "liberation stations" claiming to be agencies of the NFLSVN. These broadcasts kept their audiences current on the tactical situation in the South, the newest "crimes" of the government, and the course of international events, and conducted special "slow-read news programs" in which the radio announcer spoke so slowly that his statement could be copied down word for word by the policom. In this fashion, the latter was supplied almost immediately with the party's "correct" line or interpretation of recent developments and could quote Hanoi authoritatively in his talks with soldiers. Beyond this, given the reproduction facilities existing in military units and party committees, the information released in this manner from the North could be in local circulation in printed form only hours after its transmission.

Idea gathering. Following broadcasts, or in conjunction with readings made available to soldiers, political discussions were led by the political officer. On such occasions, major themes were reemphasized and the individuals in the group drawn into an expression of their opinions. The practice was referred to as "idea gathering," but it was, in fact, a diluted version of the mutual criticism meeting. Where printed bulletins or newsletters were involved, it was the task of the political officer to identify the paper's "key article" and stress the principal points made in the article. As determined appropriate, it was the officer's job further to elaborate a given article with additional corroborating information. Informality was altogether acceptable and the indoctrination session could be camouflaged as a friendly conversation during leisure time, while the soldiers were smoking, or after eating when they were preparing for bed. Specifically, Communist lingo was avoided on such an occasion. Indeed, the party officer would deny that the insurgency was communistically inspired or that its command was in the hands of northerners. He spoke as a nationalist attempting to stir up the genuinely indigenous element in his forces. Exploiting the unpleasant experiences the soldiers or members of their families may have had with government officials in the past, and relying on his years of past work in agitprop which frequently dated back to the period of the French Indochina War, the *chinh tri vien* enjoyed considerable success in gaining the admiration and respect of his charges. The reports of defectors vouch for this fact.

The wall newspaper. Another traditional agitprop technique within the military unit was the "wall newspaper," consisting of a large wooden surface on which soldiers were encouraged to fasten articles, sketches, and poems composed by themselves for the attention of their fellows. Articles were to "reflect the daily activities" of the unit and might contain criticism as well as praise. The political officer exercised a certain censorship over the determination of what was posted. Most highly commended were those pieces in which specific individuals, by name, pledged themselves to overexcel in the performance of their tasks. Another type of writing consisted of ideological and autobiographical essays written by individuals either about their own past lives or some specific contribution to a recent military operation. In such pieces, the soldier was expected to bare himself before his peers, revealing his "petite bourgeoisie" or peasant inadequacies until the party, or perhaps the insurgent movement, found him out and brought him into the light of true understanding. Both the promise to overexcel and the reevaluation of one's past weaknesses were considered by the party as excellent reading fare for all the members of a military unit. In honor of special days of commemoration or specific short-term drives, the policom would encourage the soldier to prepare many articles on a single theme, from which a special issue of the wall newspaper could be composed for group reading. Every soldier was under pressure to produce pieces for this exercise several times a year, and every effort was made to provoke him into sincerely revealing his innermost thought. Articles alone did not exhaust the content of the wall newspaper: poems—ambitious one in accordance with the severe rules of oriental meter—were placed on the board.

The competitive emulation movement. Yet another device through which the soldier was fortified in his ideology was the "competitive" emulation movement. The intent was to create a competitive atmosphere in which every soldier found himself under considerable pressure to vie with his fellow combatants in arms in one area of rivalry after another. Involved might be unit or individual promises to capture a weapon from the enemy during the next battle or to heighten agricultural production by such and such a percentage. The other side of the same coin was the program for the issue of "letters of commendation" to units or—most highly praised — to individuals. Each authorized letter had an impact on more than the immediate area of its recipient's location, for the document would be reproduced in multiple copies and disseminated to all surrounding units and party offices, thus serving as a challenge to others.[c]

In addition to these multiple techniques—all of which could be concurrently utilized—the party members of the unit as well as the party youth were subject to all of the controls of party personnel anywhere (this was treated in the earlier portion of this study) and centered in the member's life in his home cell where the criticism-self-criticism or struggle meeting figured prominently.

Themes Stressed in Party Political Work

The rank and file were taught, of course, to see themselves as the "wave of the future." They were persistently confronted with the theme of "liberating the fatherland from American imperialism" and they understood the United States of America to be the ultimate enemy. Outside of these general themes that figured continuously in their indoctrination, the soldiers were instructed more closely in a series of distinct subjects which will be treated in the following pages.

First and foremost, every soldier was expected to know by heart his "soldier's oath," to which he subscribed upon entering his unit, and his "code of discipline." These read as follows in one version:

Ten Honorary Oaths of the Vietnamese People's Army

We, Soldiers of the Vietnamese People's Army on the honor of the Revolutionary soldiers, would swear under the glorious flag of the Fatherland.

(1) *We solemnly swear* to sacrifice everything for the Vietnam Father-

[c] A typical commendation letter is contained in appendix F as doc. F–1.

land, struggle for the future of the people, Democracy and Socialism under the leadership of the VN Labor Party and the DRV Government in order to build up a rich and strong VN country, achieve Peace, Unification, Independence and Democracy, and contribute efforts to the safeguarding of peace for South-East Asia and the World.

(2) *We solemnly swear* to obey higher echelon orders and make every effort to accomplish promptly and correctly any mission assigned.

(3) *We solemnly swear* to continuously enhance the patriotic spirit and the consciousness of socialism; to firmly maintain a modest and thrifty behavior; to avoid showing much pride in victory or become discouraged by defeat or by hardships and dangers. We must prove to be worthy of the People's Army tradition of resolutely fighting and gaining victory.

(4) *We solemnly swear* to exert every effort to improve our technical, tactical, and professional knowledge; to faithfully carry out all orders, to forge an organizational character, a disciplinary behavior required of a regular troop, build up an ever-powerful Army and stand ready to engage in combat.

(5) *We solemnly swear* to set an example in propagandizing the people to comply with all the policy lines of the Party and the Government, in enthusiastically participating in labor and production work in view of fulfilling the mission of a combat and active troop.

(6) *We solemnly swear* to continuously heighten our vigilance, to absolutely preserve military and national secrets. If captured by the enemy and even subjected to cruel torture, we are resolute to be loyal to the revolutionary work and will reveal nothing to the enemy.

(7) *We solemnly swear* to maintain an affection toward various social classes to love our companions wholeheartedly, to effect solidarity and mutual assistance in normal times as well as in combat.

(8) *We solemnly swear* to properly maintain weapons, our mechanized equipment and resolutely prevent them from becoming deteriorated or falling into enemy's hands. We always display a spirit of safeguarding public properties and avoiding corrupt practices.

(9) *We solemnly swear* to observe the following 3 points when contacting the people:

To respect the people
To help the people
To protect the people

and 3 commandments:

Do not appropriate the people's property
Do not oppress the people
Do not cause troubles to the people

in order to acquire the people's confidence and love and to create a concord between military and civilian people.

(10) *We solemnly swear* to firmly maintain the admirable quality of the People's Army and always make critique [of others] and self-critique. We will never do anything harmful to the honor of the Army and to the prestige of the Democratic Republic of Vietnam.

(11) *12 disciplinary articles concerning the people and the VN People's Army:*

(1) Do not take a needle or a thread of the people.
(2) Observe an equity in the trading business.
(3) To borrow anything, check with the people; the borrowed item should be returned after use, if it is damaged or lost, pay for it.
(4) Do not disturb the people when the troops take up positions in their houses. Keep the people's houses clean all the time.

(5) The ethnic minority policy must be correctly implemented. The people's freedom of belief and habits should be respected.
(6) Respect the aged people, love the children; maintain a solidarity with the youths and a decent attitude toward women.
(7) Do not intimidate or maltreat the people.
(8) Protect the people's lives and properties, common properties, and government properties.
(9) It is necessary to unite together, to respect, and to support all civilian and Party agencies and local armed forces.
(10) All policies and rules of the government should be carried out in an exemplary manner.
(11) Actively propagandize, motivate, and help the people implement all the policy lines of the Party and the Government.
(12) The Government and Army's secrets should be preserved and the people must also be instructed to preserve secrecy.[d]

Repeatedly, orders from higher headquarters emphasized the importance of assuring that every man was closely familiar with those provisions which would figure prominently among the subjects treated by the political officer.

To these precepts the party added yet a third group of regulations widely popularized in military units, the "code of secrecy preservation." The number of points covered in it vary from one formulation to another, but at a minimum it covers the following ten points.

(1) Do not disclose the military and national secrets. Do not try to get secret information which is beyond our sphere of activity.
(2) Do not maintain relations with counterrevolutionary organizations and individuals and with persons with bad political records.
(3) Do not allow ourselves to be exploited by others to do anything harmful to the interests of the Revolution and Army. The revolutionary soldier should not be involved in any dishonest act which is contrary to his ethical code of conduct and value.
(4) Do not spread false rumors prejudicial to the ideology and political lines of the people and the Army.
(5) Carefully secure documents and properly observe the policy of preserving secrecy of military documents.
(6) Protect weapons, ordnance equipment, and other properties of the Army in order to prevent sabotage, damage, or loss.
(7) Maintain law and order, observe military discipline and state law.
(8) Laboriously improve political awareness; faithfully carry out all regulations regarding military and state secrecy preservation.
(9) All indications or attempts at sabotage must be discovered in time.
(10) Properly observe the above mentioned disciplinary articles and exert every effort to do away with any ideology or act contrary to the said disciplinary articles.[e]

Yet another theme, already explicit in several of the points in the above regulation, but granted extensive additional attention as a subject on its own count, is work among the civil population. Mao Tse-tung had already, in the late 1920's, assigned considerable importance to this aspect

[d] The precise wording of this oath varies in detail from one area to another, depending on distinctive local peculiarities. See appendix F, doc. F-4, for an abbreviated alternative version circulated in PRP documents.

[e] See appendix F, doc. F-4, for a 15-point alternate to the above code.

of the soldier's life. The Viet Minh up to 1954 and the Dang Lao Dong or PRP leadership in the South since then have not been negligent in reaffirming the importance of such work. The primacy placed on nonmilitary activity among the peasants is underscored in an indoctrination booklet for main force units in which the following passage occurs:

> Because of their prestige, the members of the armed forces have great propaganda potentiality. If the fighter with a rifle in his hand knows how to make propaganda, to praise the political struggle, and to educate the masses about their duty of making the political attack, his influence may be very great. But if he simply calls on the population to join him in the armed struggle he will cause great damage. He must say, "Those who do political struggling are as important as we who fight with rifles. If you do not take up the political struggle we will be unable to defeat the enemy with our rifles." This will make our fellow countrymen more enthusiastic and will also help to promote the political struggle.
>
> For instance in one village we had a political struggle which consisted of getting a Catholic priest to request that the enemy remove a military post built near a cathedral. At the moment that the cadres were persuading the masses to join in this struggle movement, a Liberation Army unit came near the village. Its members came to the village and said to the people, "Please take up this struggle. If the enemy does not leave, it may attack our Liberation Army unit and then there will be many stray bullets flying and the cathedral will be destroyed and then the enemy will come back and set up an even stronger post. But if you struggle now perhaps the priest can get the enemy to withdraw for good from the post." So the struggle went forward and the priest was able to force the enemy to withdraw from the cathedral area, although they moved to an area not far away. However, this action gave the masses in the village great confidence in the effectiveness of the political struggle.[f]

Despite his most persistent efforts, the *chinh tri vien* was in no position to sustain *esprit* on a continuing basis. The lot of the insurgent combatant was hard, the dangers high, the frequency of defeats increasing by the middle of the 1960's.[g] The members of a fortunate unit might receive rice three times a day, and a mixture of rice with manioc or corn, or corn alone, was not unknown.

Defectors frequently revealed that they received no new clothing for periods of up to 2 years and the medical facilities, despite the organization's best efforts, were grossly inadequate. Where morale was low, displays of temper, uncooperativeness, malingering, insubordination, and desertion occurred despite all of the leadership's indoctrination. The leader of a regional force in Darlac Province complained that, recently, "of a total of twenty-three people, only eight, including myself, were able to fight. The remainder had stomachaches, fevers, or toothaches and could not fight." For one or another reason, persons would absent themselves from unit political meetings, making the political officer's task yet more difficult.

[f] Douglas Pike, "The Communication Process of the Communist Apparatus in South Vietnam" (a mimeographed study), Center for International Studies (MIT), Cambridge, Mass., pp. 39–40.

[g] Some idea of the negative impact of political indoctrination on the soldier can be gleaned from the extract from a verbatim interrogation in/ 1965 included in appendix E, doc. E–2. But considerably more important is the general political report for the year 1963, a written military unit criticism prepared for higher headquarters. From this document, one can determine not only what was wrong with the unit but also what steps were to be taken to correct the situation. This is doc. G–4 in appendix G.

Multiple reports record that individual members of units would, on occasion, leave their own units to go to join other ones located in more comfortable environments in order "to alleviate their own personal hardships," while it is not unknown that infiltrated personnel attempted to return to North Vietnam.

CONCLUSIONS TO PART THREE

The principal armed forces of the insurgent leadership in South Vietnam could be classified under three categories. The first of these elements, in terms of their combat effectiveness, consisted of the intact regular army units of the North Vietnamese army which seriously affected military force ratios in situ only after 1965. They may be confused on occasion with the 2d main line "guerrillas" which were commanded by a professionally trained corps of officers, possibly natives of the South who spent extended periods of time in the North before assuming their commands. Such units contained a significant number of personnel recruited and trained in the South. Third in order—in terms strictly of their military professionalism—were the regional forces which operated in geographically circumscribed portions of the country and to which the designation "local troops" was frequently affixed. A fourth element, which might possess modern aims on occasion, the Du Kich, was excluded from consideration in this portion of the study. In every case, these forces are to be understood as instruments through which this party organization expressed itself.

Chronologically, the third of the above forces appeared first in South Vietnam, and initially in the form of the armed propaganda team. It was the catalyst which made possible the party's first efforts to accelerate organizational work among the peasantry. Its personnel, for the most part, were members of the Dang Lao Dong (the existence of a PRP had not yet been announced) with experience in the old Viet Minh/Lien Viet complex. These units could not be understood in any conventional military sense. They were cellularly structured party elements designed to provoke cooperation where it failed to materialize under the prodding of party agitation. Following their appearance, militia units (the Du Kich) and other liberation associations prospered and the base was provided for the growth of the main line forces. That is to say, through *political activities* of a concurrently terroristic and agitational character, the insurgent generated his progressively improved military stance. The continuing presence of the armed propaganda team in the form of a regional force not only forced the nation's security forces to disperse its own forces, but provided the party with the ability to punish where members of the liberation associations, once inducted, attempted to break ranks.

Success in this effort further provided the insurgency's external leadership with the internal base onto which it grafted its more conventionally trained military personnel awaiting their cue across the border. And as success at any stage in the process enhances the likelihood of success at the next stage, so a vehicle was provided for the introduction of even larger elements of an external organization into the internal conflict.

An investigation of the command structure implanted upon the formal military structure of the insurgency readily revealed the extent to which the Dang Lao Dong went to assure its total control of the movement in all of its parts. Not only were three layers of party offices superimposed upon a military headquarters at any given level, but an additional political division was inserted into that military command center itself charged with supervising political activities among the soldiers—both party and nonparty. At the same time, an altogether distinct cellular structure, embracing exclusively party members in military organizations, was separately erected. This latter organization went over the head of the military headquarters to the offices of the supreme PRP interparty committee of the area in question. One might be encouraged to conclude that military initiative had to be stifled in this veritable sea of interdicting party jurisdictions, but our Western convention of sharply separating "the military" and "the civilian" is alien to the conceptual framework from which the well-trained Communist Party member approached conflict management. For the mature party cadre, one was first a party member, and only secondly a specialist who might perform military functions in a combat unit. In any case, the party member identified himself not with the cut of the suit of clothing he wore but with the secretary who presided over his own home party cell, group, and committee.

A byproduct of party control in a military headquarters was the strengthening of party work among the civil population, for one of the major concerns of the political division in a fully activated headquarters was to duplicate those party committee offices engaged in political organization of the peasantry. The single effect previously generated by the party committee and its terrorist affiliates was broadened by the parallel effort from a military base.

Within the military unit itself, the party organization was charged with sustaining the morale of soldiers denied the comforts of adequate food, clothing, and shelter over extended periods of time. It attempted to do this with ideas. Admittedly, this was a feat in which the odds from the outset were against the party and its spokesman, the political officer. That the effort met with less than total success came as no surprise and was rather to be expected, particularly in light of the fact that the *chinh tri vien* had to work with a body of persons, in many cases of peasant background, unschooled in concepts of government administration, unaccustomed to conceive of problems politically, and frequently illiterate.

The political officer asked himself: "How may I best utilize words to minimize on the troops under my authority the impact of factors over which I have no control?" In the resolution of this problem, the Communist displayed striking imagination coupled with down-to-earth, practical realism. Competitive emulation, the "wall newspaper," and the unit "idea gathering" session, were examples of this operational technique in action. Indeed even the basic classes in the ABC's for the illiterate could be seen in this light. Through teaching the soldier to read and write, the political officer provided the soldier with the indispensable tools he needed to participate in the exploitation of the one basic resource which would not run out.

And the ultimate consequence of this relentless effort? The building of convictions in a body of men which actually enhanced their chances for survival.

PART FOUR

THE CONCEPT OF OPERATIONS AND STRATEGY OF THE SOUTH VIETNAMESE INSURGENCY

SUMMARY

The insurgent apparatus was highly distinctive, containing a minimum of twelve parallel channels of communication and control distribution among three basic operational divisions—the party and the civil organization—constituting together the insurgency's infrastructure engaged in underground activities—and the military forces. The PRP was the pivotal hierarchy and commanding element in the complex, and authority flowed from the party body to the elements embedded within the other two structures. Indeed, the civil organization and military forces were projections of the party.

In its operations, the PRP was greatly concerned that it should not become dependent at any time upon the success of any single form of activity. Consequently it conceived of an offensive or a defensive strategy as a blending of multiple parallel efforts calculated to provoke active support from broad segments of the population, extending beyond those elements under direct party control, and integrated by a set of specific objectives which were held in common by all of the concurrently participating echelons of the movement.

Review

By way of review, we have now identified three parallel echelons of authority, each hierarchically structured, with its own multiple channels of communication and command, and tightly integrated with the other two. These structures are, in the order in which they have been treated: (1) the party apparatus, (2) the civil organizations, embacing the front or PLC system; and (3) the military forces.

Within the party, orders proceeded through the committee system at the interprovincial, provincial, and lower levels; through the cellular structure that duplicated the committee arrangement; through the security system; and through the party youth organization. In addition, *ad hoc* inspection teams could at any time be sent out by higher offices of the PRP with authority to intervene at their discretion in party activities at any level, including village and hamlet affairs.

In the civil organization, orders proceeded through the province and district offices of any given mass association down to the village. They could move through the executive committees of the front system erected over the mass organizations at any level or they could originate in the supreme secretariat of the NLFSVN and be transmitted down through the offices of the Dang Lao Dong secreted as the PRP within the mass associations.

Finally, the military structure maintained the conventional lines of command to be found in any professional military organization while also serving as a base for another party cellular structure, security apparatus, and party youth hierarchy. This means that the Communist insurgency organizations operating in South Vietnam had parallel communication and control channels, any one of which could operate independently of the others.

This complexity of channels must be kept well in mind in a closer examination of chart 15 which attempts to synthesize the several major echelons of the insurgency into a single diagram. There, only the formal military, party committee, and PLC channels are shown.

The Party and the Front

Several additional observations will assist in grasping the meaning of the diagram of chart 15. First, the supreme CC/secretariat organization of the NLFSVN was disposed to the right of the chart in a manner not altogether different from the tactical command introduced into the military picture. As such, the national offices of the front provided COSVN with an organizational device to assure the coordination of front and party activities from the top down. The controls exercised by the party offices from within the current affairs section of an interprovincial PLC were supplemented by the "popular" determinations reached by the "people's" representatives in the national assemblies of the NLFSVN. Second, the PRP structure is placed in the center of the diagram in accordance with its pivotal position in the insurgency as a whole. Its command over other echelons of the movement is indicated by the horizontal control lines to the left and right. Thus, the arrows in the diagram reaching from the branches and agencies of the party committees at their several levels into the current affairs sections of higher PLC's or the branches and agencies of the village organization at the base are intended to indicate that the party offices in question were physically housed within the PLC hierarchy itself. As has been indicated, a number of advantages accrued to the PRP through this arrangement, varying from security of person to psychological cover. Concurrently, the lines running from the military affairs committees of the party structure at its several hierarchical levels indicate the control which the PRP maintained over military forces. A political apparatus figure as one of the three major divisions of a planning headquarters and one of the two principal command heirarchies in operational units.

The Party and the Military

With respect to the military echelon of the apparatus, several types of forces were recognized. The main line or Quan Doi Chu Luc together with the regional, or Po Doi Dia Phuong, may be referred to collectively as the Quan Doi Chanh Quy. These were the "regular" military forces to the insurgency movement with the Quan Doi Chu Luc exhibiting the highest level of competence and discipline. The latter force operated either under an interprovincial committee or directly under COSVN, possibly in conjunction with the large units of the PAVN which appeared in the South in 1965.

The Po Doi Phuong operated under the control of a provincial or district committee and was more restricted in the size of the territory in which it could engage in combat.

Distinct from both these military elements was the Dan Quan Du Kich, the guerrilla popular army. This group of organizations was tied to the village or hamlet area and directly controlled by the local party chapter. In the present study this militia formation is identified as the elite mass organization of the village, a paramilitary body in which the members' mentality and orientation were still essentially peasant and civilian, not military.

Chart 15 details the supreme leadership of the South Vietnamese insurgency and indicates in greater detail the manner in which these superior offices were intermeshed with the territorial structure in the South. Control and direction proceeded from the reunification bureau of the DLD central committee, which was headed by Nguyen Van Vinh, an alternate member of the central committee itself, deputy chief of the general staff of the North Vietnamese Army, representative in the North Vietnamese National Assembly, and an instructor in the "Central Information School," the principal center for the training of agitation/propaganda cadre.[a]

The Party and the Leadership

Leadership personnel used in the South were drawn first from among the membership of the party's central committee, a body of some 42 full members and 30 alternate members, and thereafter from (1) the central research agency, an intelligence and secret police organization, well versed in the use of terrorism, and (2) the army high command to which Nguyen Van Vinh enjoyed easy access as deputy chief of staff. Many of these individuals were located within the offices of COSVN, but they could likewise assume controlling positions at lower levels.

In this picture, the council of ministers played a relatively insignificant role as a corporate entity. Those who performed serious roles in the insurgency did so in their party, not state, capacities.[b] In no case may a diagram which has been designed to show actual functional channels—as opposed to formalistic or propagandistic claims—locate this body in a position where it might interfere with command. The complexities of control, then, that characterize organization at lower levels in the insurgency hierarchy,

---

[a] *Nham Dan* ("The People"), No. 3782 (7 August 1964), p. 3. (Hanoi, CC of the DLD).

[b] Five of the six ministers (Pham Van Dong, Pham Hung, Vo Nguyen Giap, Nguyen Duy Trinh, Le Thanh Nghi) were concurrently members of the party politburo, the supreme policymaking body of North Vietnam, and as such held additional critical party posts in the North. The last minister, Phan Ke Toai, although not a member of either the politburo or the central committee, was nevertheless a senior party specialist in mass organization work, serving as a member of the presidium (i.e., highest office) of the Fatherland Front and the chairman of its membership committee. From this position, he supervised the entire mass organization in the North.

do not figure in the organs of ultimate control at the top. If jurisdictional uncertainties do indeed exist in Hanoi, then they must be primarily attributed to the personalities of the individuals who occupy the critical offices.

Insurgent Operations

There remains the critical matter of the insurgent leader's concept of operations and procedures for implementation: for example, if he were to exploit to the maximum the potentialities provided him by his multi-echeloned structure, in what ways would his offensive vary from that of a conventional tactician? What distinctive factors figured in his planning and through whom did he implement his campaign plan once it acquired its final form? This is a highly critical matter, second in importance only to a working grasp of the reality of organization itself.

The DLD leadership understood by "offensive" not a military campaign, although activity of a military character would be undertaken during an offensive, but rather a "drive" in which all the elements of the population under party control would participate. Planned defenses, as well, were of this character. The party would attempt to utilize the full potential of its controlled bodies in order to misdirect attempted mopping-up campaigns, and to sabotage the construction of strategic hamlets and other favored counterinsurgency tactics.

Planned offensives were frequently provided with a distinguishing title, e.g., the "Anti-United States Spring," which lasted from the first of March 1963 to the following April. Under this label groups of interrelated goals would be articulated. Then in accordance with the capabilities of each of the multiple elements in the insurgent structure, distinct specific assignments would be made to each of the units and a timetable would be provided for the accomplishment of successive tasks.

This timetable, with its list of interim goals to be attained, may be understood in the Western world as similar to a "production plan" in industry; for what the party leadership or any of the lesser party committees intended, when they stipulated what was to be accomplished by that date, was to set up quotas to be fulfilled, whether this was to be so many semiautomatic rifles captured by 1 April or so many covert cells to be activated in a government ministry by the same date. The essence of the insurgent's tactics under the conditions of present-day nonconventional conflict is the *blending of multiple operational principles* (i.e., weapons systems). No professional subversive insurgent would allow himself voluntarily to become exclusively dependent upon the successful execution of any single form of activity.

In the ideal situation, each "drive" involves the commitment of different types of specialized forces for the purpose of covering the entire spectrum of possible activity short of conventional positional warfare.

There would be an expansion of strongarm elements in urban areas and the activation of additional mainline forces in rural areas, intensified infiltration of mass organizations and accelerated agitation/propaganda, concurrent with raids on isolated security posts and major field engagements involving battalion- and regiment-size forces. This concept of an integrated effort of multiple dimensions was formulated as a series of slogans in one party document:

Prolonged struggle until the opportunity arises
Combined political and military activities
Legal, semilegal, and illegal activities
Close coordination of activities in rural and urban areas
Intensifying the movement of the masses to stimulate the movement of upper strata

Summarizing to this point, the Communist offensive was characterized by three very concrete and distinctive features. First, it engaged the potentials of the maximum possible number of people who could be reached through organizational channels. Second, these people were provoked into collective activities which were controlled and supervised through their organization or one of its units. Third, specific tasks, frequently numerical quotas, were assigned to each separately identifiable unit within all three of the major echelons of the total insurgent structure.

There remains yet a fourth characteristic of the insurgent offensive, implicit in the several distinctions noted above, but so important that it must be explicitly stated: both implementation and supervision remained permanently in the hands of the party organization. The insurgency grew from the party apparatus.

Within the context of the insurgent organization analyzed in this book and the distinctive concept of planning and operation which we have just examined, the leadership of the DLD was provided with the basis from which to project the long-term grand strategy of their protracted revolutionary struggle in South Vietnam. It consists fundamentally of two points: (1) survival as an organized force; while (2) progressively reducing the disparity in strength between insurgent and counterinsurgent forces. To achieve this, the insurgent organization had to be able to undergo an extended series of attacks mounted by domestic security forces and their allies so that it could respond with attacks of its own. Thus, the insurgency consisted of a series of challenge/response cycles in which the insurgents proceeded from a defensive to a counteroffensive stance, only to return to the defensive before the next onslaught.

The distinctive, unconventional aspect of this process was the character of the DLD counteroffensive, which consisted of military tactics and a complex of integrated activities embracing nontraditional levels of operations. The irregular underground aspects of the response phase in any given cycle encouraged the leaders in Hanoi to believe that the disparity of forces would be reversed. These irregular aspects included proselytizing among hostile military and civic service personnel in order to honeycomb the government's agencies with subversive cells; agitation and propaganda accompanied by terrorism and duress among the citizenry to force their collaboration and make them unavailable to the government as a source from which to draw replacements and supplies; external quasi-diplomatic activity and participation in international, Communist-dominated mass organizations, where they could be assisted in many ways—both tangible and intangible—by other national member delegations, including those from countries whose governments were attempting to assist the established government of South Vietnam. These forms of activities are every bit as much a part of an integrated insurgent defensive or offensive drive as the commitment of troops.

Something of the comprehensiveness of a party-conceived offensive is apparent from a plan drafted by the Kien Giang provincial party committee for the months of August, September, and October 1965. (For a verbatim English-language rendition of the entire document, see appendix H, doc. H–1.) The plan involved the integration of six action programs.

(1) The development of heightened ideological convictions among party members, soldiers, and the civil population.

(2) The conduct of attrition against the enemy to destroy his military forces and "New Rural Life Hamlet," combined with the building of insurgent combat villages and the expansion of the insurgent base area.

(3) The intensification of political struggle to be implemented via civil mass organizations and to include, "each month at least twenty minor incidents, including terrorism."

(4) Utilizing the dependents of soldiers in the ranks of the insurgent armed forces to carry out military proselytizing to penetrate hostile security units and break morale.

(5) The building up of the insurgents' military forces, the recruitment of youths, and the thwarting of the conscription policies of the Republic of Vietnam.

(6) The strengthening of insurgent rural areas, the sale of troop support bonds, improved security, the protection of crops, personal economy, and the frustration of American economic policies.

The final step in the insurgency as planned by DLD leaders in Hanoi—provided the process was not cut short by an unanticipated collapse of responsible government in the South, or the sudden withdrawal of external support for the government—was the climactic uprising in urban areas capped by seizure of the instruments of national power in Saigon. This was the anticipated course of events for Hanoi: first, an extended period of struggle in the countryside during which the party gradually gained the upper hand, followed by, second, a sudden coordinated uprising in the cities.

A party document captured by security forces in Dinh Tuong Province formulated this general strategy line in the following fashion:

The Revolution in the South at the present time has two possibilities:
A general uprising to seize power
A long-term armed struggle
But our final objective is a general uprising to seize power. The revolution in the South should go through *two stages* until the general uprising:
The preparatory stage, to upset the balance of power
The stage of direct revolution
When the balance of power has completely changed in our favor and when the time is proper for a general uprising, military means will be the essential means, and arming the population and our forces will be our primary task.

During the preparatory stage, in order to change the balance of power in our favor, we must exert our influence on the people in rural areas and in cities and organize the masses under the strict leadership of the Party.[c]

Hanoi was prepared for the possibility that the fortunes of its movement in the South might suffer major reverses through the introduction of fresh manpower from outside. It could respond to this altered situation in two ways: (1) by injecting additional military forces from PAVN into the South; (2) by reverting to skeletal organizational forms and clandestine procedures.

As long as either of these alternatives remained open to Hanoi in its conduct of operations in the South, security forces might take no pleasure from their tactical combat victory on the field of battle. This is to say that a singleminded or preeminent reliance upon military solutions freed the insurgent command structure to concentrate upon those nonmilitary aspects of its "offensive" upon which it counted to alter the disparity of strength in its favor. Nor may it be assumed that the party's determination to revert to less sophisticated organizational forms would either prevent it from carrying out the counteroffensive phase of the recurrent challenge/response cycle or cause it to lose hope in the possibility of ultimate victory. Regarding the first of these two points, let it be said that if the level, intensity, and choice of weapons systems would change to accord with the tactical situation, then the conceptual framework would remain intact and the insurgency would continue to be prosecuted.[d] The only distinctively new factor is that the nation's security forces might not appreciate initially that they were still involved in an insurgency. In the DLD evaluation of America's role in South Vietnam, we, beginning in 1965, were simply exploiting our best available trump card in a last-ditch attempt to regain the initiative.[e] That advantage was our expanding economy, a consequence of the fact that our "economy was not damaged during World War II," as a party document of the spring of 1965

---

[c] *Threat to the Peace: North Viet-Nam's Effort to Conquer South Viet-Nam*, II, Appendices, Bureau of Public Affairs, Department of State Publication 7308 (Far Eastern Series 110), (December 1961), p. 93.

[d] Some insight into the consequence following from the party's remarkable capability to organizationally adapt to immediate tactical situations is supplied by David Galula's account of a conversation he had with a Chinese Communist in 1947 following his capture by a Red Army unit.

> He noticed that a team of Communist civil servants immediately took over the administration of the town, which was the seat of a *hsien* (county). These officials, he was told, had long before been designated for the task and had been functioning as a shadow government with the guerrilla units active in the area.
>
> "Your forces are not going to occupy Hsinkiang permanently. What will happen to your civil officials when your army leaves?" I asked the political commissar of General Ch'en Keng's army.
>
> "They will leave, too, an dersume their clandeistine work," he replied. "Are you not afraid that they will lose their value now that they have revealed themselves?" "We have secret agents in this town who did not come out when we took it. We don't even know who they are. They will still be here when we go."

David Galula, *Counterinsurgency Warfare: Theory and Practice* (New York: Praeger, 1964), pp. 56–57.

[e] The genesis of the following argument, which is treated above only in part, is to be found in the writings of Lenin. The relevant passages from his works were drawn together into an integrated doctrinal statement by Stalin in the early twenties and constituted one of the major themes in the latter's critical 1924 Sverdlov University lectures which were thereafter published as *The Foundations of Leninism*. The argument developed by Stalin in this important pamphlet was the standard fare of party students from around the world studying in the USSR in the 1930's and 1940's. Today, it is precisely this same body of thought—disassociated from the name of Stalin—which provides the conceptual framework for the justification of Communist attempts to export revolution (i.e., subversive insurgency or "Wars of National Liberation") and it has figured prominently in the Communist apologetics of both the French Indochina War and the current conflict in South Vietnam. Cf. J. V. Stalin, *Works*, VI (Moscow: Foreign Languages Publishing House, 1953), pp. 71–196.

declared. But this economic and military predominance globally—so they reason—is only temporary. Externally, it has provoked an exaggerated competitive rivalry among capitalist countries and stimulated hostility and jealousy in the less developed, emerging nations of Asia, Africa, and Latin America. Internally, it encourages the growth of a basically unhealthy and unstable economy. Further, the multitude of economic and military commitments made around the world as a result of our dominant economic position progressively reduces the flexibility of our foreign policies. Consequently, argued the Dang Lao Dong, "the United States is rich, but not strong." But even more importantly, "we (i.e., the Vietnamese Communists) are *not* isolated," while Americans, in contrast, "cannot concentrate forces against SVN people in dealing with us." The situation, therefore, "is most favorable to us." To retain the initiative on a sustained basis, the party leadership reckoned that the United States would have to commit not several hundreds of thousands of troops but several millions. The same document, quoted above continues:

> They need at least ten million troops and would be obliged to mobilize the whole imperialist army. Since the other nations such as Formosa, the Philippines, and South Korea could not furnish troops, the United States is doomed to failure. [Following the injection of large numbers of troops] they [i.e., the United States] would seek then a political solution from a position of strength whereas we could take advantage of the talks to consolidate our position.

"We should," the PRP document continued, "continuously attack to hold the initiative. Make efforts to change the balance of forces." The goals assigned the three echelons of the insurgent structure in the spring of 1965 were fourfold:

> (1) To strive to destroy more enemy troops while developing our own forces.
> (2) To carry out revolutionary land reform policies in rural areas to heighten the people's awareness and bind them more completely to us.
> (3) In urban areas, to create instability and win over urban forces.
> (4) In the highlands, to formulate a clear ethnic minority policy and draw the population into our effort, for "the highland is a strategic springboard, a corridor for international Socialism." [f]

To achieve these goals, all elements of the insurgent movement were expected to acquaint themselves intimately with their local environment so that they might fully exploit opportune situations as they arose. "Any failure in the exploitation of opportunities will be considered as a crime."

The reaction, then, of the DLD was not that of a conventional opponent. Provided with (1) the distinctive organization with which it prosecuted its internal war and (2) the external ties provided to it through the international Communist movement, the party could well afford to reach conclusions other than those which we might hopefully have been antici-

---

[f] A second party document dating likewise from the spring of 1965, restated the above four goals in the following words:
(1) Make efforts to destroy RVNAF (Republic of Vietnam Armed Forces) capabilities.
(2) Carry out a "land revolution."
(3) Convert towns and cities into insecure areas. Rally all people under the colors of peace, independence and neutrality.
(4) The Western Highlands will be an important matter.

pating. The validity of this Communist argument depended on the correctness of a single assumption which, although not specifically spelled out, was implicit in their whole line of reasoning; namely, that we would employ the forces committed to the struggle in South Vietnam in conventional fashion and would attempt to effect a military solution prior to any serious effort on our part to respond to the more elusive aspects of the challenge.

CONCLUSIONS TO PART FOUR

The statement made in the immediately preceding pages concerning insurgent strategy and operational doctrine has been held in abeyance, for analytical reasons, until after extensive investigation into matters of organization was completed.

The reader must be cautioned, however, against reversing cause and effect as a consequence of the arrangement of this material, for, from the party's point of view, *the multiechelоned organization evolves because of the Communist's concept of operations, and not the other way around.* The Vietnamese Communist Party sought from the outset to achieve seemingly paradoxial ends. It would (1) progressively unfold an offensive, a "drive" that challenged, across the board, the forces of stability in every field of endeavor, while (2) concurrently maintaining absolute control over a movement which appeared superficially to display the attributes of spontaneity. It could realize these goals only as it called into life the several parallel echelons of organization which have concerned us extensively in this study. And it is precisely at this all-critical juncture that the DLD member today, like his Communist predecessors elsewhere in the thirties, forties, and fifties, depends most upon that body of thought and conceptual framework first articulated by Lenin. If there were variations in organization among the party insurgencies which preceded the current example in South Vietnam—and these modifications have been slight since the early forties—then the intent on every occasion has been the same: a comprehensive offensive, overt and clandestine, urban and rural, political and economic, military and terroristic. And the man who provided the modern insurgent with these guidelines to action was Lenin, the party's first "conflict manager."

Having stressed the many-faceted dimensions of insurgent campaigning, it is important to note the control that were built into operations. Thus the device of setting quotas could well serve as a stimulant to individual application and provide the governing criteria for a series of mutual-criticism meetings. At the same time it was the reflection of a distinctive Communist inclination to seek, through total planning, to exclude completely any evidence of spontaneity. Behind this procedure was the long-held party myth that an omniscient, centrally located body—the current affairs committee at the interprovincial or COSVN level—could anticipate the character of the opponent's response to the party's next round of campaigning.

The supreme offices of the NFLSVN, like the tactical commands interposed between the latter and district units, served as supplementary controls. The agencies were employed to streamline operations and were concurrently the means by which the initiative and freedom of movement, tolerated at lower levels, were restricted. It was this artful tactical blending of multiple forms of activity and, strategically, of tight centralized control that constituted the hallmark of Communist insurgency, and, at the same time, its genius.

PART FIVE

COMMUNIST INFRASTRUCTURE IN THE SAIGON-GIA DINH SPECIAL REGION

SUMMARY

The city and surrounding area of Saigon were of special importance to the Communist insurgents. The seizure of the city of Saigon would have been the culmination of efforts to assume national power and "liberate the South." To this end the Communist Party established an organization of interprovincial status to direct activities in the Saigon region.

The area was designated by the insurgents as the Saigon-Gia Dinh Special Region. As an interprovincial command it comprised the appropriate geographic/administrative subdivisions of province, district, and village, along with an all important central city command.

The highest authority in the area was the Saigon-Gia Dinh Special Region Committee. This body included various functional agencies concerned with proselytizing, mass organizational work, propaganda and training, military activities, and support and logistic facilities.

These agencies of the Special Region Committee were adjusted to the special features of the area such as the contrasting population density of the city and the surrounding area and the high concentration of ethnic Chinese in the urban area.

The proselytizing and mass organization sections were divided into departments specializing in rural or urban operations, with one agency specializing in operations among the Chinese population. The propaganda and training agencies likewise distinguished between city and rural operations and prepared propaganda messages and displays intended specifically for both rural and urban audiences.

Military units faced requirements in the central city totally different from those in the rural districts. Mobile terrorist cells operating in the city were directed by an *ad hoc* Saigon-Cholon task force command instead of the military headquarters. The support functions of communications, liaison, finance, etc., had to be performed by covert cells in the city, in contrast to the more routine operations in the rural "liberated" areas.

The party organization in the Special Region had obvious priorities in areas and activities. The capital city area command, for instance, was normally represented on an organization chart as one of three provincial committees under the special region (interprovincial) committee. The stature of the capital city command is evidenced by the fact that the leadership of the urban apparatus, for the most part, held concurrent membership in the overall Special Region Committee. The organization placed a premium on such operations as proselytizing, mass organizational work, propaganda and training, with members of the special region committee usually taking personal charge of the appropriate branches.

The Saigon-Gia Dinh Special Region was one of six geographic/administrative regions of South Vietnam established by the Communist insurgents. The SGDSR was administratively treated as an interprovincial authority by the party apparat. The region itself comprised the city of Saigon, the neighboring city of Cholon, and the surrounding districts of

Di An, Go Mon, Cu Chi Binh Tan, Nha Be, and Thu Duc (insurgent designations). The Special Region though similar in general area and size to the Republic of Vietnam's (RVN) Gia Dinh Province, was not coterminous. The overlapping jurisdictions are shown in map 2.

Whatever the administrative or jurisdictional boundaries, there are certain significant features of the area which determine how one side or the other goes about governing the area or organizing to undermine the Government.

The city of Saigon is one of the most densely populated areas in the world. Two million people are crammed into an area of approximately 20 square miles. The city's profile includes tall, modern hotels, stately buildings, and masses of tiny one-story shacks made of scrap sheet metal, wood, and cardboard. Many families even set up housekeeping in small sampans on the Ben Nge Canal which runs through the city.

The sister city of Cholon is the Chinese district of Saigon. This district reportedly is second only to Singapore in concentration of overseas Chinese. The Chinese in Cholon maintain a degree of ethnic autonomy which is clearly noticeable in both architecture and language. Signs in the marketplaces, for instance, are in two languages—Vietnamese, as required by law, and Chinese by tradition and general usage.

In the eyes of party leaders, this heavily built up area was critical for a whole series of interrelated reasons:

> This is the area where the enemy concentrates its top agencies for conducting the war in the South. A strong organization is set up here ranging from the Central Government to rural administrations. Here supplies are stored; here are located important training centers and an important seaport. The enemy is making use of this area to enhance its prestige with foreign nations. Furthermore, in the Saigon-Cholon-Gia Dinh area there is a cross section of the population. Here are found all important economic and industrial organizations. The enemy is using this area as a base for the conquest of the rural areas and for the destruction of our bases.

At the edge of the city there is an abrupt change from busy streets, sidewalk vendors, and pedicabs to vast expanses of ricefields and wooded areas. There are a number of small villages and a few rubber plantations, but all in all, the countryside surrounding Saigon is as sparsely populated as the capital city is crowded. From the party's frame of reference, it was this distinctive urban/rural area in which the final phase of the insurgency would occur; the seizure of the ultimate instruments of national power. To this end, the party was told to "prepare the population for an all-out uprising, seize the administration, oust the enemy, and liberate the South."

Under the Saigon-Gia Dinh Special Region Committee (SGDSRC), one could identify the three traditionally administrative levels—province, district, and chapter—found elsewhere in the South. However, there were variations in the organizational scheme in the special region due to the uniqueness of the area and the character of the requirements placed upon the local cadre. At the highest level of organization was a standing com-

mittee of 12 members and 2 alternate members. Eight select members of the latter comittee composed the current affairs committee, headed by a first secretary and an assistant secretary.

The functional agencies under the interprovincial committee could be grouped under four main categories—proselytizing and mass organizational operations; propaganda and the training of cadres; military and paramilitary operations; and support functions.

The agencies and sections concerned with proselytizing activities and front work were in the forefront of the party's overall activities in the Saigon-Gia Dinh Special Region. The importance of these types of operations is evidenced by the fact that 6 of the 12 members of the Saigon-Gia Dinh standing committee were identified as the chiefs of the several specialized subsections of the proselytizing agency of the Special Region. Each section has its own distinctive structure calculated to maximize impact in the Gia Dinh environment. Thus the military proselytizing section (headed by a member of the current affairs committee) was divided into branches specializing respectively in urban and rural operations. The front civilian proselytizing section, headed by still another member of the current affairs committee, was divided into four elements: branches for women, farmers, and an attached security-liaison unit. The workers' proselytizing branch made its appeal not only to the proletariat but also worked among the youth, schoolchildren, students, Chinese, and the urban middle class generally. The assistant secretary of the Special Region Committee and two other members of the current affairs committee were directly engaged in the work of this body. Finally, there was a separate youth proselytizing section in addition to the above organizations.

Through these instruments the apparat was provided with "the practical capacity to drive the enemies from a relatively stable situation in the city to a permanently unstable and passive situation."[a] To achieve their objectives in preparing for the ultimate general urban uprising, the PRP set itself a series of operational tasks, i.e.:

(1) To exploit fully legal popular organizations such as the two labor union federations, the Society for the Eradication of Illiteracy, the Federation of Students, etc.

(2) To associate with semiofficial organizations such as mutual aid societies, temple and pagoda societies, neighborhood associations, etc., in order to isolate enemy-sponsored, reactionary organizations.

(3) To promote membership in secret organizations working for the revolution, such as Liberation Young Men, Liberation Young Women, Liberation Students, Liberation Workers, etc., all of which are united in the Liberation Front (i.e., NFLSVN) which is struggling for final victory.

(4) To conduct political action followed by armed action to support the political action to an appropriate degree, and, at the same time, to conduct and direct efficient action against the enemy military.

Characteristic of the "political action" conducted through the various types of mass organizations listed above was the repeated practice of

[a] An editorial in the insurgents' *Vanguard*, the monthly organ of the South Vietnam People's Revolutionary Party, dated October 1964.

clandestinely hanging banners in the major streets in Saigon during the night, with the banners bearing such slogans as the following: "Be determined not to become a soldier and die for the regime"; "The youths in cities are joining the Liberation troops to save themselves, their families and their country"; "To be a soldier for the U.S. imperialists and to fight compatriots is to sin against the fatherland."

Second only to mass work were the party's activities in propaganda and cadre training through which it enhanced its mass work capabilities by turning out more trained cadres and printed materials. The importance of this effort was pointed up by the fact that both the chief and the assistant chief of the Saigon-Gia Dinh Special Region P&T section were members of that Special Region Committee.[b]

In order to carry out its mission of educating party personnel and producing and distributing propaganda materials (see ch 2), the P&T section of the SRC contained the following elements and subsections:

Administrative Staff	Painting and Sculpture Section
Information and Propaganda	Motion Picture Section
Writer and Artist Section	Radio (communication) and Picture Section
Entertainment Section	Metal Type Printing House
Urban Communications-Liaison Section	Mimeograph House
Urban Propaganda Network	Supply and Liaison Subsection

The information and propaganda subsection of the P&T section had two branches designated, respectively, the rural branch and the urban branch. These branches prepared weekly situation reports for their respective areas, leaving to their superior subsection headquarters the preparation of weekly bulletins of current events concerning the entire region.

The P&T section operated both a rural and an urban training school. The urban school[c] at one time was directed by the assistant chief of the propaganda and training section, who was also a member of the Special Region current affairs committee. The rural school during the same period was directed by the chief of the P&T section, a member of the larger standing committee. In these schools, party cadres studied the techniques of agitating, proselytizing, and recruiting under the conditions of the special requirements and applications of the urban/rural environment of Saigon.

The urban training unit provided 15-day intensive courses in the techniques of how to burn buildings and other sabotage operations employing grenades, mines, and explosives, along with methods of spreading rumors and disseminating propaganda leaflets in the city.

---

[b] An interesting reflection on the dual command channels, as discussed in chapter 2 (cellular and bureaucratic) is that while the chief of the P&T section was a member of the Special Region Committee, the assistant chief of the section was a member of the more select bureau within the committee, the all-important current affairs committee of the Special Region.

[c] So designated due to the nature of the curriculum. Physically, both schools were located in rural "liberated" areas.

To supplement the party's propaganda activities in the Special Region, the writer and artist branch and the entertainment branch provided musicians, playwrights, and entertainers.

The third major division of functions in the Gia Dinh region, those of a military, paramilitary, or terrorist character, were handled, much as in other areas of South Vietnam, through the Military Affairs Committee (MAC) of the interprovincial committee. However, in sharpest contrast with arrangements elsewhere, the MAC did not work through a military headquarters, but itself served as the planning and coordinating center for operations.

The three major divisions (staff, political, and logistical) of a more conventional headquarters could be understood as branches of the MAC and were subject to the control of its directing party committee. Beyond this provision, the military units of platoon size and company size in Gia Dinh, operating under the staff division, were concurrently subject to comand channels proceeding directly down from the MAC, which was free to go over the heads of staff division officials in the conduct or alteration of operations.[d] Further, both "provincial" and "district" units reported directly to the MAC. That is to say, a provincial force had no control over a district force; both reported to the same superior office, the party's military committee, which could serve as its own tactical command when two or more units were used in a single action. Finally, the terrorist, sabotage, and demolition groups, trained by the P&T section of the interprovincial committee and turned over for military command as "mobile groups," reported to the MAC through a separate headquarters, the Saigon/Cholon task force command which was not subject to control by the staff division (Cf. chart 16).

One was witness here to an attempt by the party to assume direct and immediate control over a broad spectrum of activities which elsewhere became the responsibility of subordinate agencies. The distinctive problems primarily of a security character, which necessarily figured in the metropolitan Saigon area, may be cited as the principal determinants leading to these organizational modifications. And it was beneath this extremely tight control from above that the three major divisions operated in the

[d] According to the answers to prisoner interrogations, based upon captured documents in early 1964, the military units of the Special Region attached to the staff division of the MAC consisted of one infantry unit, one combat support detachment, one special operations detachment, one reconnaissance platoon, and a Saigon task force of three mobile units. These units, with the exception of the Saigon task force, were billeted in private homes in the Cu Chi district north of Saigon. The infantry company was made up mostly of local youths from the Cu Chi area. The cadres, however, were usually ex-Viet Minh who regrouped in the north and infiltrated south.

The combat support detachment numbered approximately 50 men and was organized into 4 mortar sections, 2 heavy machinegun sections, and 3 DKZ 57 mm. gun sections.

The special operations detachment had approximately 60 men organized into two platoons. The "special operations" performed by this unit included surveillance and demolition of government defense installations. The reconnaissance platoon had about 25 men whose mission was (a) to reconnoiter government military installations, (b) to observe operating procedures of government units in order to plan ambushes and attacks, and (c) to trail government units in the field in order to mount surprise attacks against them. The Saigon task force operated in the city through small cells of dedicated individuals. Often these men held jobs and legal residence in the city. Their supplies of arms and explosives were smuggled into the city and stored in secret caches.

Special Region. The first of these—to retain the order employed in chapter 11—the military staff, was responsible for the following functions according to captured documents and interrogation reports: (a) investigating and studying battlefields, making and revising tactical operations plans for armed forces of the Special Zone, and the reviewing and approving of tactical combat plans submitted by those units; (b) investigating and studying modifications of organization, of equipment, and of training for the units within the Special Zone so that they could be adapted to local battlefields; (c) developing recruiting plans, training recruits to complement old units or create new ones; and (d) guiding the activities of the armed struggle in localities within the Special Zone helping those units to use appropriately modified tactics and techniques.

To carry out these functions the military staff had five subsections and six "assistants" to the chief of staff who were officer-level cadres and were responsible for specific functions. Directly under the military staff were the secretarial, radio communication and cipher, and cartographical subsections, a recruit training center, and a recruit reception center. The secretarial subsection was composed of five persons who handled the administrative affairs of the military staff.

The radio communication and cipher subsection was made up of the radio commo cell and the cipher cell. The nine men in the radio commo cell included a cell chief, two telegraph operators, and six men who operated the hand generator, stood guard, and delivered messages. The communications net connected the military staff with the COSVN, the SGDSRC, the military sections of the districts of the SGDSRC, and possibly other organizations. The cipher cell of six men was responsible for encoding and decoding all official documents of the military staff.

The cartographical subsection made maps and overlays as required for the military staff. Information regarding unit locations and annotations was coordinated through the intelligence section. The cartographical unit was manned by four men who had attended a 4-week training course in cartography taught by the draftsman for the COSVN.

The new recruits reception post functioned as a clearing house for inductees and volunteers who were processed and forwarded through channels. The process was as follows: the village committees would induce local youths to join the "liberation" forces. The village committee would then complete a biographical statement on those who were to be inducted, prepare a letter of introduction, and deliver the individuals to the district committee. At this point the district committee would gather the recruits from the various villages together, group them into units of from 5 to 50 men, depending on the recruiting situation, and deliver them to the new recruit reception post. At the reception post, the biographical statement on each man would be checked, clothing and equipment issued, and medical examinations given. Those whose health was bad, those with questionable backgrounds, and those with exceptional skills or education were for-

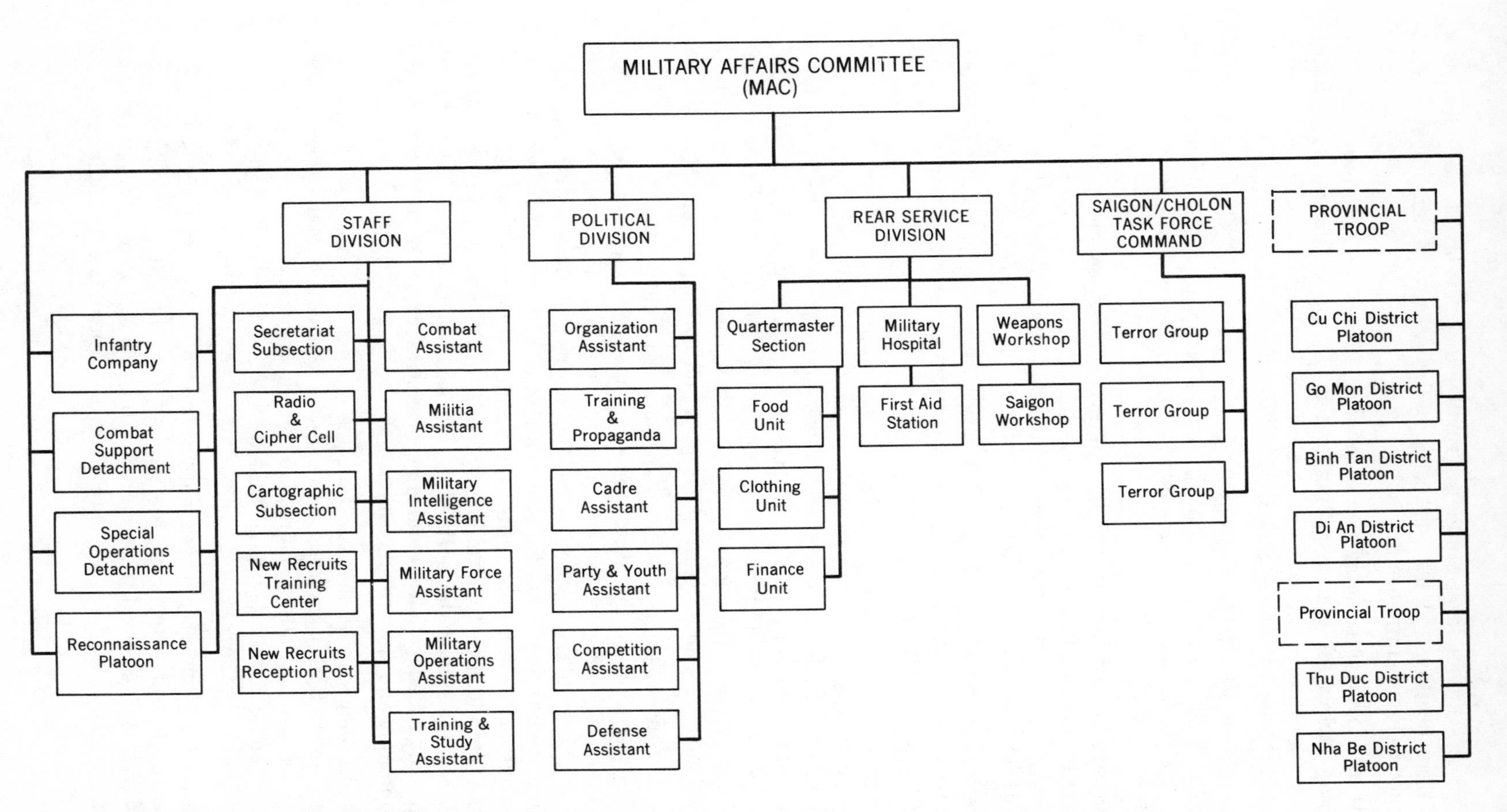

Chart 16. SAIGON/CHOLON /GIA DINH MILITARY AND PARAMILITARY STRUCTURE

warded to a higher level center for further disposition. Those individuals who were healthy and not suspected of being government agents were assigned to the training center.

The new recruit training center offered an 8-week training course in infantry tactics for recruits going to the various (main force) military units in the Special Zone. The course included instruction in close-order drill, hand-to-hand combat, and marksmanship.

The six assistants to the chief of staff were the following: combat assistant, militia assistant, military intelligence assistant, military operations assistant, military force assistant, and the training and study assistant.

The combat assistant (a senior captain) was responsible for (a) studying the battlefield, (b) accompanying and observing the units on combat missions, (c) contributing ideas in the planning phases of operations, and (d) holding critiques after each battle.

The militia assistant (a captain) observed, studied, and made recommendations to the military section on matters regarding development and operation of guerrilla militia forces.

The military intelligence assistant (a senior captain with two assistants of his own) was charged with obtaining information concerning (a) dispositions of the RVN military forces, weapons and tactics to be employed against the insurgent military forces; (b) military strength, weapons, defensive positions and internal organization of the ARVN posts; (c) mission, function, operational rules and regulations and combat potential of RVN mobilized units such as rangers and special forces units.

The military force assistant group (a senior lieutenant with an assistant) kept account of the strength, weapons, and equipment of all main force units in the region, the recruit training school, the agencies subordinate to the military section, and the district militia units; prepared research studies and recommended changes in strength, organization, and equipment of the various units; maintained records of casualties, sent letters of condolence to families of those killed, and supervised burials so that families could be notified of the location of graves; and studied and recommended policies regarding casualties in order to minimize the loss in morale and spirit of the units.

The military operations assistant maintained the journal of all (insurgent and ARVN) military activities in the region, published 10-day summaries and monthly summaries of military activity, and supplied information to higher levels so that 3-month, 6-month, and yearly summaries could be prepared.

The training and study assistant traveled to the various units to keep the cadre informed on such matters as (a) current weapons, combat procedures, and technical information of both ARVN and insurgent forces; and (b) methods of defense against these weapons and procedures.

The political office, one of the three major divisions of the military affairs committee, had as its main function the maintenance of morale and political reliability among the military units. To accomplish this the political office strove (a) to educate the soldiers in politics, directing the thoughts of the troops correctly and in accordance with Communist policy; (b) to develop the organization of the party and the labor youth group within the military units; (c) to study, organize, and implement the field competitions of the cadres in the Special Zone; and (d) to maintain internal order by taking stands against corruption, waste, obscenity, and defeatism.

The chief of the political office (a major) directed the activities of six assistants: organization assistant, training/propaganda assistant, cadre assistant, assistant for Communist Party and labor youth group affairs, and the defense assistant.

The organization assistant studied, implemented, and arranged the political activities of agencies subordinate to the military section and main force units. The training/propaganda assistant was responsible for the political education of individual members of the agencies and units of the Special Zone. The cadre assistant studied cadre policy, recommended promotions, punishments, and assignments of military cadre. The assistant for Communist Party and labor group affairs maintained files on individual party and labor youth group cadres serving in the military affairs section of the Special Zone. He also directed, evaluated, and recorded the strength and development of the party and youth group. He kept further records of party and youth group dues. For instance, he saw to it that one-third of the dues collected each month from the party and youth group members (two GVN piasters per person)[e] was retained by the basic party collecting unit for its expenses while the remainder was divided again into thirds, one-third being retained by the assistant for his expenses and two-thirds going to the central office. The assistant for competition affairs drafted instructions for individual and interunit competitions. He followed up the results of the competitions and recommended awards and commendations. Finally, the defense assistant investigated and reported on matters concerning corruption, misuse of party funds, and misconduct before the masses; made recommendations to the political officer on appropriate disciplinary measures; investigated local defenses of party installations; and applied preventive measures against individuals suspected of being anti-Communist.

The third major subsection of the military affairs section was the rear service office. Its main function was to provide supplies and support facilities for the various units in the Special Region. The rear services section was broken down into three other sections—quartermaster group, medical group, and weapons workshop.

The quartermaster section was composed of three units—food, clothing, and finance. The food unit, in order to distribute food to military units and

[e] According to official exchange rates in 1965, a piaster was worth slightly more than one cent.

other party installations in the area, operated its own grinder mill, stored ground rice in homes of local sympathizers, and coordinated the delivery of food supplies to the units. The clothing unit saw to it that the village party units got local families to sew uniforms for the military units. The local families were to sew 3 cotton suits per month, for which they were paid 10 piasters each. The finance unit distributed monthly living allowances to members of party installations and military units and allocated operational fees for special-purpose installations and activities such as the workshop and radio section.

The medical section, directed by a doctor who was assisted by approximately 13 medical specialists and nurses, operated a hospital in an adjacent province and a first-aid station in the Special Region.

The weapons workshop reportedly produced such items as mines, grenades, and rudimentary rifles. Also, spent cartridges were gathered from battlefields and taken to the workshop for reloading.

Parallel to the staff, political, and rear service divisions was the fourth office, mentioned previously, "The Saigon/Cholon Task Force Command," responsible for terrorism, sabotage, and demolitions. Operations of this type were carried out by highly specialized cells and so-called "death volunteer squads." These squads had the responsibility of creating disorders, eliminating Americans and other adversaries, and enforcing party decrees. Methods employed included sabotage of powerplants, bridges, transformers, and installations, and the use of terror strikes employing concealed explosives, boobytraps, and hand grenades.

Characteristic of their work was the attack on the Metropole Building in Saigon on 4 December 1965. The operation itself was tactically simple. A gray-paneled vegetable truck containing an estimated 250 pounds of plastic explosives was driven up in front of the building early on that Saturday morning, at 5:29 o'clock, and parked. Armed terrorists leaped, firing, from the vehicle, and placed a deadly claymore anti-personnel mine in a bag on the other side of the street. The mine was timed to go off after the first gun blast to catch those who came to the rescue of the victims of the initial explosion, the terrorists assuming defensive positions to prevent efforts to deactivate the bomb. The following fight with submachine guns forced the American guards to return to the building, allowing the terrorists to flee. The resultant explosion blew a hole three stories high in the Metropole and destroyed a number of neighboring Vietnamese shops and dwellings over a 200-yard area. Fortunately, the claymore mine malfunctioned and was successfuly disarmed. Even so, one American, one Australian, and eight Vietnamese were killed and more than 150 persons were wounded, including 52 American servicemen.[f]

On special occasions such as a national holiday or a visit to Saigon by an important American, reinforcement agents and terror "specialists" might be brought in to augment the city's paramilitary force. Such was

[f] Charles Mohr, "Saigon G.I. Billet Bombed," *The New York Times*, 4 December 1965.

the case when the party prepared to disrupt the Independence Day celebration in 1963 at a time when only 50 persons (45 male and 5 female) were locally available. Two demolition experts with a supply of mines and explosives were smuggled into Saigon for the celebration. The specialists, working in conjunction with the special task cells, were ordered to concentrate on the Independence Day military parade and the meeting of the Anti-Communist Asian League.

In addition to work, propaganda and training, and paramilitary or terrorist operations, a fourth major category of activity was noted earlier in this chapter, that involving support and administrative matters. Available information suggests that the Special Region headquarters and its immediate staff agencies were located during 1964 in the northern tip of Cu Chi district; military units were located in Cu Chi, Binh Tan district, and Saigon; and the central city executive offices were headquartered in the western corner of the Binh Tan district. The identification on a map of these wide-flung centers points up the logistics and communications problems encountered by the insurgent organization. To handle this matter special bodies were established. Among them were the following:

(a) A security section which maintained internal security in "liberated" areas;

(b) An organization section which studied and categorized party and nonparty assignments;

(c) A base security section which determined sites and emergency alternative locations for the various organizations of the Special Region, made studies of defense, and directed militia and guerrilla units in erecting fences and laying spikes;

(d) An economic and financial section which prepared annual budget estimates and saw that taxes were collected and supplies purchased for the agencies of the Special Region; and

(e) The postal transportation and communications section which directed the flow of mail and messages throughout the region.[g]

Beneath the interprovincial special committee and its associated branches, agencies, and subsections, three province-level committees functioned in Gia Dinh. They were responsibile, respectively, for the northern area, and the southern arĕa, and the capital city area. These pseudo-provinces in turn contained 10 districts. Di An, Go Mon, Cu Chi, and Binh Tan districts made up the northern area; Nha Be and Thu Duc districts formed the southern region; and interprecincts 1 through 4 formed the district level entities of the capital city area.

Of these major divisions, the party very clearly placed the highest priority on the operations in the capital city area. This was reflected

[g] A captured Communist military officer reported that each village in the Communist controlled areas had a communications and mail section manned by a two- or three-man squad. Mail service from the Special Region committee headquarters to the various sections and agents would take about three days for routine mail, one day for urgent documents, and a half day for very urgent documents. A radio communications network also was established which provided instantaneous communications among certain agencies and the Special Region Committee.

organizationally in the fact that the leaders of the several urban interprecincts were persons who were either members or alternate members of the Special Region standing committee. A study of this situation will alert the reader not to assign to the provincial and district levels of authority in Saigon-Gia Dinh the criticality which was indeed in order in evaluating the importance of comparable bodies in the insurgent hierarchy elsewhere in South Vietnam. The presence of a genuine hierarchy was made largely fictional when one considered that the party interprovincial committee was not only tied directly into the interprecincts but also (through separate channels) controlled directly both provincial and distinct units. Turning our attention immediately to organization and operational procedures within the heart of the city area proper, we find that at the beginning of the current decade, urban operations were controlled through a city executive section. This section was responsible for the following objectives:

(a) Seeking out and assassinating government officials, informers, pro-Americans, and other persons considered hostile to the movement;

(b) Placing waitresses in restaurants, hotels, and amusements parks in order to investigate persons and places and carry out sabotage where appropriate; and

(c) Infiltrating the RVN Government, spreading propaganda, and agitating among the masses.

The city executive section was originally headed by a chief, a deputy chief, a secretary general, and a five-man committee. The headquarters supervised the operations of five specialized groups.

(a) An assassination and kidnap group of ten five- to seven-man cells;

(b) An investigation and recruitment group of six cells;

(c) A sabotage group of approximately six cells;

(d) A liaison group of two cells in Saigon city proper, two cells in Cholon, and two cells in the Gia Dinh urban area; and

(e) A documentation and information group of unknown size.

By the middle of the decade this arrangement had been abandoned for the precinct and interprecinct system. The party, utilizing the precinct boundaries and designations established by the legal government, replaced the city executive section with a system of four interprecinct (pseudodistrict) committees. Supervision and control were maintained through secretaries (who, as has been indicated, concurrently held interprovincial posts). Each of the interprecinct commands maintained within its own offices all the functions previously performed by the older city executive section, confining their operations to their particular areas of responsibility.

Whatever the organizational scheme, government security measures and public intolerance forced the party to maintain a high degree of secrecy in the conduct of affairs in the city of Saigon. The headquarters facilities were located in party-controlled areas outside the city. Communications and supplies were transmitted to covert cells in the city through a system of liaison cells and clandestine mail drops.

In one such arrangement, liaison cells maintained a communication and supply line connecting the Special Region committee headquarters (located in the northern tip of the region) the city area headquarters (located approximately halfway between the SRC headquarters and Saigon), and the individual cell leaders in the city itself.

Necessity sometimes forced certain indiscretions in security, as in early 1965 when the movement was badly in need of money. One method was to establish additional cells in the city to collect funds. Responding to pressures from above, a city cadre approached an ex-cadre who had, just 3 months previously, been released from a 3-year prison term for party collection activity.

Against his futile warnings that he might be under police surveillance, the ex-convict collection agent was ordered immediately to recruit a cell and resume fundraising. The hapless collector proceeded as ordered and organized a cell consisting of himself as leader, his mother-in-law as collector and liaison agent, and his next-door neighbor as clerk-typist.

Liaison was established between the new cell and the city finance cadre through a finance section liaison agent and the cell leader's mother-in-law. The cell was provided with a typewriter, three .38 caliber revolvers,[h] receipt books, and other paraphernalia for their fundraising drives.

As the cell's collection activity got underway the cell leader's fears of surveillance were confirmed. His mother-in-law had collected only 120$VN (about U.S. $1.50) when the entire cell was arrested in a police raid.

One political cadre was to establish himself in the city and to recruit RVN government officials to the movement. He succeeded in getting a job as private tutor in the home of a very high level advisor to President Diem. Of course, the fact that the account appears in this study is evidence that the operation was less than totally effective.

CONCLUSIONS TO PART FIVE

An examination of the PRP organization in Gia Dinh emphasizes once again the apparat's capabilities for flexibility, not only in the tactics it pursued but also in the organizational forms it evolved. As elsewhere, this competence was a function of two inherent party characteristics, the first and most important of which was the cellular hierarchy, the distinctive *sine qua non* of Communist life. An underlying system of cells was the base of all of the more complex or specialized organizational designs adopted by the party. Second to the principle of the cell was the principle of reverse representation—treated in chapter 4—which granted to superior bodies the authority to alter the tactics and organization of lesser bodies, reassigning personnel and modifying mission assignments at will. One

[h] The effectiveness of the weapons was limited, due to the fact that the ammunition supplied with the .38 caliber revolvers consisted of a box of .45 caliber and a box of 6.35 mm. cartridges.

may understand the distinctive position of the military affairs committee (MAC) of the SGDSRC as in a case in point. The determination of this party body not to delegate authority to a military headquarters (resulting in the dissolution of such an office and the reduction in the layers of command by one) meant in fact that the leaders of the three major military divisions (staff, political, and logistics) were to be understood as members of the MAC itself, who served as that element's authoritative spokesmen at the next lower level of control. They did not represent the consensus of opinion in the several divisions in the councils of the MAC, but the reverse.

The relationship between the several urban interprecincts and the regional standing committee for Gia Dinh constituted an even more extreme example of reverse representation, in which the provincial level of party authority was ignored for all practical purposes—in a most unconventional manner it might be added—and the city interprecincts were treated as working directly under supreme interprovincial authorities. The persons who held positions in both bodies must be regarded as members of the latter bodies attached with command authority to the urban pseudodistricts.

However, to place stress upon the unique in the region of Gia Dinh should not lead one to see this organization as either unprecedented in past Communist experience or disassociated from the imperatives governing the strategy of other interprovincial MAC's. The Greek Communist Party (KKE) evolved a somewhat similiar structure in Athens during the years 1943–1944, its "Athens Command," which rested heavily upon the mass labor organization of the city, the EEAM (Workers' National Liberation Front).

Within South Vietnam itself, the MAC of the SGDSRC conceived strategy in precisely the same general framework as any other MAC. One may properly assert that an investigation of this distinct urban/rural structure involved a review of all the characteristic activities conducted by the elements of the insurgent organization throughout South Vietnam. If the structural disposition of forces and tactical operational procedure varied in detail, then the party still remained committed to the conduct of mass organizational work, to the building of "popular" associations for youth, students, women, peasants, and workers. The training and indoctrination of insurgents, recruitment, the building of the party youth organization, and the many other activities discussed up to this point likewise figure in Gia Dinh. Irrespective of the area of operations, the apparat would persistently attempt to structure its offensive so that every feasible form of activity which could contribute to the attrition of opposing forces was encompassed in the master plan and tactically implemented as a phase of the struggle *in situ*.

To approximate this ideal, the SGDSRC indeed evolved a highly sophisticated organization and engaged in a wide variety of activities. They lacked, however, both the intensity and versatility apparent in insurgent efforts elsewhere in Vietnam and one might, at first thought, anticipate that so complex a command would have involved itself in a considerably more dramatic effort during the first half of the 1960's. That it did not do so was a consequence, in part, of the overall role assigned this command in the grand strategy of the protracted insurgency by the central committee of the Dang Lao Dong in Hanoi.

As was the case in the World War II insurgency of the Greek Communist Party, this urban organization was intended to play its decisive role during the closing phase of the insurgency. Its ultimate mission: the seizure of the instruments of national authority once the rural apparat has displayed its superiority over the constituted government's security forces and local administration. Only as this urban fighting machine maintained intact its multiple elements would it be in a position to fulfill successfully its *raison d'être*. The SGDSRC was more concerned with survival and clandestine growth than with immediate struggle. The intent behind the operations conducted on a continuing basis was to hold the organization together by keeping its personnel constantly active.

SELECTED BIBLIOGRAPHY ON VIETNAM AND THE HISTORICAL RECORD OF THE INTERNATIONAL COMMUNIST MOVEMENT

Against U.S. Aggression: Main Documents of the National Assembly of the Democratic Republic of Vietnam, 3rd Legislature, 2nd Session. Hanoi: Foreign Languages Publishing House, 1965.

Angress, Werner T. *Stillborn Revolution: The Communist Bid for Power in Germany—1921–1923.* Princeton, N.J.: Princeton University Press, 1963.

Armstrong, John A. (ed.). *Soviet Partisans in World War II.* Madison, Wis.: University of Wisconsin Press, 1964. For the preliminary studies by those participating in research which led to the above named volume, see the project "Alexander" monographs, War Documentation Project of the Air Research and Development Command, Human Resources Research Institute, Maxwell Air Force Base, Ala. Under this designation a series of six case studies, six monographs, a selection of Soviet sources on partisan warfare, and a bibiliography were published during the 1950's.

Barton, Fred H. *Salient Operational Aspects of Paramilitary Warfare in Three Asian Areas.* Operations Research Office (ORO) Project Parabel, T–228. Washington: April 1953. This work analyzes the Korean, Philippine, and Malayan insurgencies for similarities.

Bjelajac, Slavko K. "Anatomy of Counterinsurgency." A lecture presented to the Military Assistance Institute, February 1966.

____________. "A Design for Psychological Operations in Vietnam," *Orbis: A Quarterly Journal of World Affairs,* X, No. 1 (Spring 1966), 126, 137.

Black, Cyril E., and Thornton, Thomas P. *Communism and Revolution: The Strategic Uses of Political Violence.* Princeton, N.J.: Princeton University Press, 1964. While far from constituting a definitive statement, this volume is currently the best general survey available of the broad field of the subversive seizure of political power.

Bolloten, Burnett. *The Grand Camouflage: The Communist Conspiracy in the Spanish Civil War.* New York: Frederick A. Praeger, 1961.

Browne, Malcolm W. *The New Face of War.* New York: Bobbs-Merrill Co., 1965.

Budenz, Louis F. *The Techniques of Communism.* Chicago: Henry Regnery Co., 1954.

Bunyan, James, and Fisher, H.A. *The Bolshevik Revolution, 1917–1918.* Stanford, Calif.: Stanford University Press, 1961.

Burchett, Wilfred G. *Vietnam: Inside Story of the Guerrilla War.* New York: International Publishers, 1965. An openly Communist account of the origins and character of the conflict. Valueless as a source of factual information.

Buttinger, Joseph. *The Smaller Dragon.* New York: Frederick A. Praeger, 1958.

Cattell, David T. *Communism and the Spanish Civil War.* Berkeley, Calif.: University of California Press, 1955.

Chinese Communist Movement, July 5, 1949 (Military Intelligence Division, War Department, Washington, D.C.) in *Hearings,* Senate Judiciary Committee (Institute of Pacific Relations), 82nd Cong., Part Seven A, Appendix II. In addition to surveying the evolution of the Chinese Communist Party since the 1920's and analyzing the organizations of the movement as of the end of World War II, contains 1928 constitution of CCP.

Clissold, Stephan. *Whirlwind: An Account of Marshal Tito's Rise to Power.* London: The Cresset Press, 1949.

Conley, Michael C. "The Framework of Communist Strategy," *Orbis: A Quarterly Journal of World Affairs,* IX, No. 4 (Winter 1966), 970–84.

__________. Testimony before House of Representatives, Committee on Un-American Activities, in *Hearings,* 88th Cong., 2nd Sess., with reference to creation of a freedom commission and freedom academy, Part II, pp. 1385–1411. An attempt to define the concept "Cold War" and explain in the organizational aspects of Communist insurgency.

Dallin, David J. *Soviet Espionage.* New Haven: Yale University Press, 1955.

Dedijer, Vladimir. *With Tito Through the War: Partisan Diary, 1941–1944.* London: Alexander Hamilton, 1951.

Degras, Jane (ed.). *The Communist International, 1919–1943, Documents.* London and New York: Oxford University Press (under the auspices of the Royal Institute of International Affairs), Vol. I, 1956; Vol. II, 1960.

Devillers, Philippe. "The Struggle for Unification of Vietnam," *The China Quarterly,* IX, January–March 1962. Reprinted in Gettleman, Marvin E. (ed.), *Viet Nam: History, Documents, and Opinions on a Major World Crisis.* Greenwich, Conn.: Fawcett Publications, Inc. (1966), pp. 210–334.

Du Berrier, Hilaire. *Background to Betrayal: The Tragedy of Vietnam.* Belmont, Mass.: Western Islands Publishers, 1965. The most extreme rightist account written, contains a two-page introduction by Robert Welch.

Fall, Bernard B. "If Ho Chi Minh's Army Moves South in Force," *The New York Times Magazine,* September 5, 1965.

————. "The Choices in Viet-Nam," *The Reporter*, XXXI (March 12, 1964).

————. "Master of the Red Jab," *Saturday Evening Post*, CCXXXV (November 24, 1962), 18–21.

————. *Street Without Joy*. 4th ed. Harrisburg, Pa.: Stackpole Co., 1964.

————. *The Two Viet-Nams: A Political and Military Analysis*. Rev. ed. New York: Frederick A. Praeger, 1964.

————. *Viet-Nam Witness, 1953–66*. New York: Frederick A. Praeger, 1966.

————. *The Viet Minh Regime*. New York: Institute of Pacific Relations, 1956.

Fishel, Wesley R. (ed.). *Problems of Freedom: South Vietnam Since Independence*. New York: The Free Press of Glencoe, Inc., 1961. Contains articles by Fishel, Chief Advisor of the Michigan State University Advisory Group in Vietnam, 1956–1958; Wolfe Ladejinsky, Land Reform Expert and Technical Consultant at the Presidency, Republic of Vietnam; Tran Ngoc Lien, Commissioner General for Cooperatives and Agricultural Credit of the Republic of Vietnam; William Henderson; and others. General orientation of book is extremely complementary to the Diem regime.

Fisher, Ruth. *Stalin and German Communism*. Cambridge, Mass.: Harvard University Press, 1948.

Footman, David, *Civil War in Russia*. New York: Frederick A. Praeger, 1962.

Fundamentals of Marxism-Leninism: A Manual. Translated from the Russian. 2nd ed. Moscow: Foreign Languages Publishing House, 1963.

Galula, David. *Counterinsurgency Warfare: Theory and Practice*. New York: Frederick A. Praeger, 1964.

Gettleman, Marvin E. (ed.). *Viet Nam: History, Documents, and Opinions on a Major World Crisis*. Greenwich, Conn.: Fawcett Publications, Inc., 1966.

Gussev, Surgey Ivanovich. *Die Lehren des Burgerkrieges*. Hamburg: Verlag der Kommunistischen Internationale, 1921.

Halberstam, David. *The Making of a Quagmire*. New York: Random House, 1965.

Hammer, Ellen J. *The Struggle for Indochina*. Stanford, Calif.: Stanford University Press, 1954.

Harris, George L., *et al. U.S. Army Area Handbook for Vietnam*. Washington: The American University, Special Operations Research Office, 1962.

Hickey, Gerald C. *Village in Vietnam*. New Haven: Yale University Press, 1964.

Hoang Van Chi. *From Colonialism to Communism: A Case History of North Vietnam*. Introduction by P. J. Honey. London: Pall Mall Press, 1964.

Howe, I., and Coser, L. *The American Communist Party: A Critical History.* New York: Frederick A. Praeger, 1962.

"How the Political Commissars Should Fulfill Their Basic Duties as Leaders in Combat and Combat-Readiness Training." Editorial in *Quan Doi Nhan Dan ("People's Army")*, No. 1110. Hanoi: October 11, 1962.

Hulse, James W. *The Forming of the Communist International.* Stanford, Calif.: Stanford University Press, 1964.

Indian Communist Party Documents, 1930–1956. Compiled by the Research Staff of the Democratic Research Service, with an Introduction by V. B. Karnik. Bombay, India: Democratic Research Service and Institute of Pacific Relations, 1957.

Johnson, Chalmers A. *Peasant Nationalism and Communist Power: The Emergence of Revolutionary China, 1937–1945.* Stanford, Calif.: Stanford University Press, 1962.

Jones, F. C. *Japan's New Order in East Asia, 1937–1945.* New York: Oxford University Press, 1954.

Kaznacheev, Aleksandr. *Inside a Soviet Embassy: Experiences of a Russian Diplomat in Burma.* New York: J.B. Lippincott Co., 1962.

Krivitsky. *I was Stalin's Agent.* London: The Right Book Club, 1940.

Kelly, Maj. Joseph B. "Legal Aspects of Military Operations in Counterinsurgency," *Military Law Review,* July 1963.

Kintner, William R. *The Front Is Everywhere: Militant Communism in Action.* Norman, Okla.: University of Oklahoma Press, 1950.

Kintner, William R., and Kornfeder, Joseph Z. *The New Frontier of War: Political Warfare, Present and Future.* Chicago: Henry Regnery Co., 1962.

Korbel, J. *The Communist Subversion of Czechoslovakia.* Princeton, N.J.: Princeton University Press, 1959.

Lawyers' Committee on American Policy Towards Vietnam. *American Policy Vis-a-Vis Vietnam.* Printed without indication of publisher or date. Inserted into the Congressional Record (*Proceedings and Debates* of the 89th Cong., 1st Sess., No. 19, September 13 to September 22, 1965, pp. 24011–24018) by Senators Wayne Morse and Ernest Gruening on September 23, 1965.

Le Hong Linh *et al. Ap Bac: Major Victories of the South Vietnamese Patriotic Forces in 1963 and 1964.* Hanoi: Foreign Languages Publishing House, 1965.

Lenin, V.I. *Collected Works.* Vol. X. New York: International Publishers, 1943.

____________. Lectures at Sverdlov University, 1924; later published as *The Foundations of Leninism.*

____________. *"Left-Wing" Communism: An Infantile Disorder.* New York: International Publishers, 1934.

____________. *Two Tactics of Social-Democracy in the Democratic Revolution.* Moscow: Foreign Languages Publishing House (no date).

____________. *What Is to Be Done? Burning Questions of Our Movement.* Moscow: Foreign Languages Publishing House, 1961.

Le Quang Hoa, (Brig. Gen.). "How Company Political Officers Conduct Ideological Work." *Quan Doi Nhan Dan* ("People's Army"). Hanoi: July 11–14, 1965.

Li Wei-han. *The Struggle for Proletarian Leadership in the Period of the New Democratic Revolution in China.* Peking: Foreign Languages Press, 1962.

Lancaster, Donald. *The Emancipation of French Indo-China.* London: Oxford University Press, 1945.

Lindholm, Richard W. *Viet-Nam: The First Five Years.* An International Symposium. East Lansing, Mich.: Michigan State University Press, 1954.

Liu Shao-chi. *How To Be a Good Communist.* Adapted from the Hsin Hua text of December 1949. Peking: Foreign Languages Press (n.d.).

____________. *On Inner-Party Struggle.* A lecture delivered on July 2, 1941, at the Party School for Central China. Peking: Foreign Languages Press.

____________. *On the Party.* From the Chieh Fang Liberation Press edition of March 1950. Peking: Foreign Languages Press, 1951.

Luu Quy Ky and Nguyen Khac Vien. *Escalation War and Songs About Peace.* Hanoi: Foreign Languages Publishing House, 1965.

Mao Tse-tung. *Selected Military Writings of Mao Tse-tung.* Peking: Foreign Languages Press, 1963. Includes Mao's "Struggle in the Ching Kang Mountains" (1928); "A Single Spark Can Start a Prairie Fire" (1930); "Problems of Strategy in China's Revolutionary War" (1936); "Problems of Strategy in Guerrilla War Against Japan" (1938); "On Protracted War" (1938); "On Correcting Mistaken Ideas in the Party"); and several other of his most critical works on insurgency.

"Marxism and Insurrection." A letter to the Central Committee of the Russian Social Democratic Labor Party (Bolshevik), September 1917, in Lenin, V. I. *Collected Works,* XXVI. Moscow: Progress Publishers, 1964.

McKenzie, Kermit E. *Comintern and World Revolution, 1928–1943: The Shaping of Doctrine.* New York: Columbia University Press, 1964.

Mecklin, John. *Mission in Torment: An Intimate Account of the U.S. Role in Vietnam.* New York: Doubleday & Company, Inc., 1965.

Meyer, Frank S. *The Moulding of Communists: The Training of the Communist Cadre.* New York: Harcourt, Brace & World, Inc., 1961.

Mohr, Charles. "Saigon G.I. Billet Bombed," *New York Times,* December 4, 1965.

Molnar, Andrew R., *et al. Human Factors Considerations of Undergrounds in Insurgencies.* A manuscript prepared for the Center for Research in Social Systems, the American University, 1966.

Malnor, Andrew, R. *et al. Undergrounds in Insurgent, Revolutionary, and Resistance Warfare.* Washington: The American University, Special Operations Research Office, 1963.

Monnerot, Jules. *Sociology and Psychology of Communism.* Boston: Beacon Press, 1953.

Montgomery, John D. *The Politics of Foreign Aid: American Experience in Southeast Asia.* New York: Frederick A. Praeger, 1962.

Mus, Paul. Foreword to Gerald C. Hickey's *Village in Vietnam.* New Haven: Yale University Press, 1964.

Newman, Bernard. *Background to Viet-Nam.* New York: The New American Library, Inc., 1966.

Nguyen Kien Giang. *Les Grandes dates du parti de la classe ouvrière du Viet Nam.* Hanoi: Éditions en Langues Étrangères, 1960.

Nguyen Thai. *Is South Viet-Nam Viable?* Manila: Bauserman, 1962.

Nollau, Gunther. *International Communism and World Revolution.* Translated from the German. Foreword by Leonard Schapiro. New York: Frederick A. Praeger, 1961.

North, Robert C. *Moscow and Chinese Communists.* Stanford, Calif.: Stanford University Press, 1953.

Overstreet,. Gene D., and Windmiller, Marshall. *Communism in India.* Berkeley, Calif.: University of California Press, 1939.

Peters, J. *The Communist Party: A Manual on Organization.* Workers Library Publishers, July 1935. Reprinted in *Hearings,* App., pt. I, U.S. Committee on Un-American Activities, 76th Cong., 1st Sess., Washington (1940), pp. 650 ff. This also is an excellent source of additional documents, including the Program of the Sixth Congress of the Comintern (1928).

Pham Van Dong. *Our Struggle in the Past and at Present.* Hanoi: Foreign Languages Publishing House, 1955.

———. *Report* submitted on 16 April 1966 to the Third National Assembly, third session. Hanoi: Vietnamese New Agency International Service (in English), 28 April 1966.

Pham Van Dong *et al. Against U.S. Aggression: Main Documents of the National Assembly of the Democratic Republic of Vietnam, 3rd Legislature, 2nd Session.* Hanoi: Foreign Languages Publishing House, 1965.

Pike, Douglas. "The Communication Process of the Communist Apparatus in South Vietnam." Center for International Studies, Massachusetts Institute of Technology, Cambridge, Mass. (Mimeographed.)

Possony, Stefan T. *A Century of Conflict.* Chicago: Henry Regnery Co., 1953.

Quan Doi Nhan Dan ("People's Army"), No. 3782, August 7, 1964. Hanoi: Central Committee of the Dang Lao Dong.

Raskin, Marcus G., and Fall, Bernard B. (eds.). *The Viet-Nam Reader: Articles and Documents on American Foreign Policy and the Viet-Nam*

Crisis. New York: Vintage Books, 1965. Contains articles by George F. Kennan, Hans J. Morgenthau, W. W. Rostow, Robert S. McNamara, J. W. Fulbright, and many other prominent spokesmen.

Ravines, Eudocio. *The Yenan Way*. New York: Charles Scribner's Sons, 1951.

Ripka, Hubert. *Czechoslovakia Enslaved: The Story of the Communist Coup d'Etat*. London: Gollancz, 1950.

Rossi. A. *A Communist Party in Action: An Account of the Organization and Operations in France*. Translated from the French by W. Kendall. New Haven: Yale University Press 1949.

Rothschild, Joseph. *The Communist Party of Bulgaria: Origins and Development, 1883–1936*. New York: Columbia University Press, 1939.

Scheer, Robert. *How the United States Got Involved in Vietnam* (Report to the Center for the Study of Democratic Institutions). Santa Barbara, Calif., 1965. Reprinted in part in M. E. Gettleman (ed.), *op cit.*, pp. 235–53.

Schwartz, Benjamin I. *Chinese Communism and the Rise of Mao*. Cambridge, Mass.: Harvard University Press, 1952.

Scigliano, Robert. *South Vietnam: Nation Under Stress*. Boston: Houghton Mifflin Co., 1963.

Selznick, Philip. *The Organizational Weapon: A Study of Bolshevik Strategy and Tactics*. New York: McGraw-Hill Book Co., Inc., 1952.

Singer, Floyd L. *Control of the Population in China and Vietnam: The Pao Chia System Past and Present*. U.S. Naval Ordnance Test Station. China Lake, Calif., November 1964.

_____________. "Pao Chia: Social Control and Vietnam," *United States Naval Proceedings*, LXXXXI, No. 11, November 1965.

Snow, Edgar. *Red Star Over China*. New York: Random House, 1938.

Solemn Pledge of the Thirty Million Vietnamese People. Peking: Foreign Languages Press, 1965. Contains statement of the Central Committee of the South Vietnam National Front for Liberation of March 1965 and other comparable declarations.

Stalin, J. V. *Foundations of Leninism*. New York: International Publishers, 1939.

_____________. *Works*, VI. Moscow: Foreign Languages Publishing House, 1953.

Strausz-Hupe, Robert, *et al. Protracted Conflict*. New York: Harper & Row, Publishers, Inc., 1959.

Swearingen, R., and Langer, P. *Red Flag in Japan: International Communism in Action, 1919–1951*. Cambridge, Mass.: Harvard University Press, 1952.

Tanham, George K. *Communist Revolutionary Warfare: The Vietminh in Indochina*. New York: Frederick A. Praeger, 1961.

Tanham, George K., *et al. War Without Guns: American Civilians in Rural Vietnam*. New York: Frederick A. Praeger, 1966.

Thornton, T. P. (ed.). *The Third World in Soviet Perspective: Studies by Soviet Writers on the Developing Areas.* Princeton, N.J.: Princeton University Press, 1964.

Tran-ich-Quoc. *The Fatherland Front: A Vietnamese Communist Tactic.* Saigon, 1957.

Tran-Tam. *Communism and War in Asia: A Story of Communism in Asia.* Saigon: Free Pacific Editions, 1959. Written by the Secretary General of the Asian People's Anti-Communist League, with a Preface by Raymond J. de Jaegher, President of the Free Pacific Association.

Truong Chinh. *The Resistance Will Win.* Hanoi: Foreign Languages Publishing House, 1960. (Also available in *Primer for Revolt: The Communist Takeover in Viet-Nam.* New York: Frederick A. Praeger, 1963.)

U.S. Army Handbook for Vietnam. Foreign Area Studies Division. Washington: The American University, Special Operations Research Office, September 1962.

U.S. Department of State. Publication 7308 (Far Eastern Series 110). *A Threat to the Peace: North Viet-Nam's Effort To Conquer South Viet-Nam.* Washington: U.S. Department of State, 1961.

————————. Publication 7724. *Viet-Nam: The Struggle for Freedom.* Washington: U.S. Department of State, 1964.

————————. Publication 7839 (Far Eastern Series 130). *Aggression From the North: The Record of North Viet-Nam's Campaign To Conquer South Viet-Nam.* Washington: U.S. Department of State, 1965.

U.S. House Committee on Un-American Activities. *Hearings.* 76th Cong., 1st Sess. Washington: Government Printing Office, 1940.

U.S. House of Representatives, Committee on Un-American Activities. *Communist Conspiracy: Strategy and Tactics of World Communism.* Part I. Section D: *Communist Activities Around the World,* Report No. 2243. 84th Cong., 2nd Sess. Washington: Government Printing Office, May 29, 1956. An interesting collection of original sources, pamphlets, speeches, and other documents, drawn from all corners of the world.

USIS. "National Liberation Front's Second Congress: A Study." Saigon, 1964. (Mimeographed.)

Vanguard. October 1964. PRP insurgent publication.

Vo Nguyen Giap, (Gen.). *The Liberation War of Our People in the South Against the US for National Salvation Will Surely Be Victorious,* prepublication extracts in *Nhan Dan* ("The People"). Hanoi, 21–23 July 1965.

————————. *People's War, People's Army.* Washington: U.S. Government Printing Office, 1962.

————————. "Promote the People's War, Resolve To Defeat the American Interventionist Aggressors," *Tuyen Huan* ("Agitation and Propaganda"), Hanoi, No. 10. (October 1965), pp. 17–45. A collection of several documents drawn from the writings of Giap.

———————. *The South Vietnam People Will Win.* Hanoi: Foreign Languages Publishing House, 1965.

Vu Quang. "Making Youths into Warriors Loyal to the Fatherland." *Hoc Tap* ("Studies"), a Vietnamese language periodical, VII, July 1965.

Wang Tsan-ming, Anti-Communist: An Autobiographical Account of Chinese Communist Thought Reform. Psychological Warfare Division Human Resources Research Office (HumRRO), George Washington University, November 1954.

Warner, Denis. *The Last Confucian.* New York: The Macmillan Company, 1963. One of the best journalistic accounts of the origins and character of the conflict in South Vietnam and the person of Ngo Dinh Diem.

We Will Win. Hanoi: Foreign Languages Publishing House, 1965. Contains declarations by North Vietnamese Fatherland Front and its South Vietnamese counterpart.

Wolf, Charles. *Insurgency and Counterinsurgency: New Myths and Old Realities.* Unpublished RAND Corporation manuscript, July 1965.

"The Youth International." An editorial comment published in *Sbornik Sotsial-Demokrata,* No. 2, December 1916, in V. I. Lenin's *Collected Works,* XXIII. Moscow: Progress Publishers, 1964.

For additional references to international communism, cf. Walter Kolarz, *Books on Communism.* 2nd ed. New York: Oxford University Press, 1964; Thomas T. Hammond (ed.), *Soviet Foreign Relations and World Communism,* a selected annotated bibliography of 7,000 books in 30 languages. Princeton, N.J.: Princeton University Press, 1965; and Witold S. Sworakowski, *The Communist International and Its Front Organizations.* Stanford, Calif.: The Hoover Institution on War, Revolution and Peace, 1965.

APPENDIX A

INNER-PARTY PRACTICES AND EXTRA-PARTY ACTIVITIES OF COMMUNISTS ENGAGED IN INSURGENCY

INTRODUCTION

There are four fundamental elements at the heart of an insurgency:

(1) The overt/clandestine party command organization,

(2) A strategy of political opportunism,

(3) Techniques for the control of extra-party bodies, and

(4) A doctrine stressing the political content of military operations.

The development of these several factors into an integrated body of thought has taken many decades of reflection and experimentation. To follow the evolution of these themes in Communist literature is to examine one of the striking sagas of twentieth-century history.

In Volume I, the analysis of the tightly related subjects of mass organizational work and the political strategy of the United Front From Below alerted the reader to the meaning of political opportunism. The study of the organizational position of the PRP within both the civil front and the armed forces of the insurgency revealed the manner in which controls are maintained over these indispensable extra-party bodies. And the manner in which an armed force may be utilized as a political catalyst was treated in the three chapters devoted to the military and in the chapter on strategy and concept of operations. Regarding the party itself, attention was directed to the issues of committee and cellular structure and to the controls exercised by higher party bodies over subordinate elements of the PRP.

None of these subjects, of course, has been exhausted in the discussion to this point. This is particularly the case with respect to the party organization. Thus, despite the several chapters specifically on the PRP, little has been said as yet regarding the complex of distinctive inner-party practices which take up so many of the waking hours of the party member, already heavily engaged in one or more aspects of the insurgency itself. Consequently, the first purpose of the essay presented here as Appendix A is to incorporate additional information not included in the main text, particularly with respect to the party apparatus.

Beyond this, the essay has a second purpose. By approaching the subject on a comparative basis, one may demonstrate the close agreement between the structure, practices, and operational procedures of the PRP and Communist parties in other portions of the world. To give historical perspective to this essential agreement among Communist parties not only on how to organize, but also how to fight, the last section of the following statement will examine the contributions of Lenin and Mao Tse-tung to current practice. Finally these pages are designed to serve as an introduction to the subsequent collection of original sources acquired for the most part directly from South Vietnam. The documents relevant to each of the subjects examined in the following text have been identified appropriately to facilitate the reader's use of them. By giving attention to these sources, the reader may further pursue matters treated in both the main text and in this essay, and he may likewise analyze for himself examples of the source materials which were utilized in the present study.

CHAPTER I: THE STRUCTURE OF COMMUNIST PARTIES IN NON-COMMUNIST COUNTRIES

GENERAL STRUCTURE

Communist parties represent themselves as democratic organizations, the officers of which are elected either directly by their immediate subordinates or indirectly by delegates selected by the rank and file. Thus, most party constitutions contain stipulations for periodic branch (or local) party conferences at which the assembled membership of the appropriate cells (or units) elect the branch committee and determine who will be its secretary or principal officer. Further, a conference of several branch committees is assigned the duty, officially, of selecting the members of a district committee and its secretary. This process is supposedly repeated at the provincial, interprovincial—where such a division occurs—and national levels. Several levels of delegation are interposed in the process, and the member at the grassroots level still feels that he demonstrably influences the choice of officers in the organization; but a series of additional provisions, also incorporated into party constitutions and directives, stand in opposition to this electoral technique. In part, these supplementary arrangements deal with the authority of upper committees over subordinate bodies. Thus "the committee at the next higher level" must "approve" the elections at lower levels for both committee members and their secretaries. This principle, of crucial importance in the subordination of local parties to Moscow's will, was first introduced into the German Communist Party (KPD) in 1924 in the aftermath of the abortive uprising by the party in October of the preceding year. This practice was introduced throughout Europe and the Orient in the course of the 1920's, resulting in what was known as the "bolshevization of the member parties of the Comintern," [1] i.e., their de facto organizational and administrative subordination to the ECCI which, in turn, by the 1930's was effectively controlled by Stalin, working through his secret police (the NKVD). (In the United States the bolshevization of the CP was associated with the infighting between the Lovestone-Ruthberg and the Foster factions, 1924–1929. This factional struggle may be considered to have been resolved by the latter date.)

The principle of the confirmation of elections by the next higher echelon of the party hierarchy "eliminated for all practical purposes the remaining vestiges of democracy, and enabled the leadership to exercise a stricter control over their subordinates. Furthermore, it made it easier to suppress all oppositional trends from the outset." [2]

[1] Jules Monnerot, *Sociology and Psychology of Communism* (Boston: The Beacon Press, 1953), pp. 56–57.

[2] Werner T. Angress, *Stillborn Revolution: The Communist Bid for Power in Germany, 1921–1923* (Princeton, N.J.: Princeton Univ. Press, 1963), p. 470.

Higher bodies in the party apparatus enjoy even further discretion with respect to subordinate units. They may prorogue assemblies of lower bodies and prevent organized opposition from crystallizing. Another party procedure draws the legitimacy of party democracy into question: the right of co-optation. Without the approval of lesser bodies or the general membership, a committee may co-opt additional persons to serve in it. Finally, the central committee (CC) of a Communist party, theoretically the highest policymaking body in the organization, may reconstitute itself at its own discretion. In practice, this step presupposes the initiative of the secretary of the CC who is the party's chief executive, normally with the title of Secretary General. (See chart 1, this appendix.)

Some idea as to the numbers of individuals involved in the several conferences at higher levels can be gleaned from the arrangement followed by the CPUSA at its 8th national convention (1934). Cells (units) sent one delegate for each five members to the local (section) conference. The locals sent one delegate for each 15 members to the district conference. And the district conference sent one delegate for each 100 members to the national congress. (The slight size of the CPUSA accounts for its failure to establish a counterpart for the provincial committee.) [3]

A survey of these prerogatives in the conduct of party "democracy" leads one to conclude that authority proceeds by dictate from the top down. Direction is not generated through the series of conferences but through the system of committees and their secretaries, who are subject to removal at the will of the SG. Nomination for election becomes equivalent to promotion.

From this de facto disposition of authority follows the party principle of reverse representation treated in chapter 5 of the main text. The elected or designated leader of any organizational element of the party at every level represents among his associates the authority of the next higher party body. He is not the spokesman for the interests of his subordinates in high party councils, but rather the latter's liaison with inferiors. In this context one approaches a Communist party's organization and channels of communication.

SPECIFIC ELEMENTS OF THE APPARATUS AND THEIR FUNCTIONS

1. The Politburo and Central Committee

One must make a clear distinction between a party's central committee (CC) and its politburo (or presidium) and secretary general (SG). Party constitutions invariably represent the politburo to be simply an agency of the CC, constituted from members of the latter body and charged with supervising the execution of policy during periods when the CC is not in session. It is also suggested in such formal party documents that the SG participates in the making of policy only in his capacity as chairman of the

[3] J. Peters, *The Communist Party: A Manual on Organization* (New York: Workers Library Publishers, July 1935), in *Hearings*, Appendix, Part I, U.S. House of Representatives Special Committee on Un-American Activities, 76th Cong., 1st Sess. (Washington, D.C., Government Printing Office, 1940).

Chart 1. PARTY STRUCTURE IN THEORY AND PRACTICE

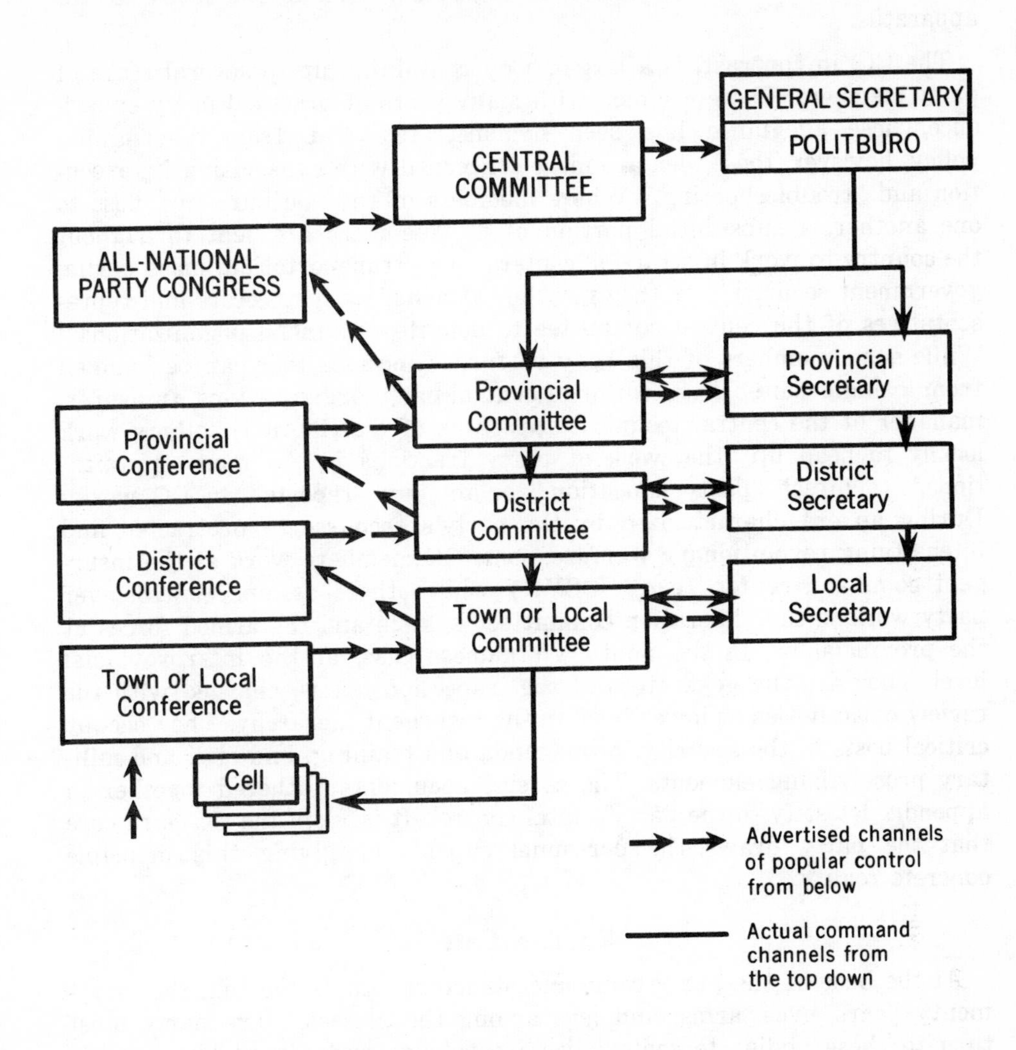

CC the *primus inter pares.* Nothing could be further from the case than this implied subordination of the politburo and SG to the CC. Rather the reverse is true.

To the extent that a national CP makes policy and determines strategy —as opposed to receiving it from some outside source such as a Soviet or Chinese embassy or, before 1943, the executive committee of the Comintern—it does so within the politburo. The SG is a member of this small body of from half a dozen to a dozen men.

The members of the politburo frequently all reside in one city, since they must be able to meet together often and at short notice. Occasionally, they are obliged to remain in session for days at a time. The politburo determines strategy and makes significant promotions in the party. The external movement of personnel is regulated. This is the heart of the apparatus.

The CC, in contrast, is a larger body containing up to several score of party members. These are men with many years of practical party experience,whose allegiance has been demonstrated. Far from determining policy, however, these men are more concerned with supervising its execution and "troubleshooting." Where members of the politburo live close to one another, a substantial portion of CC members are sent throughout the country to work in strategic centers (e.g., transportation, mass media, government security), or they may be "attached as instructors and representatives of the central committee to definite provincial organizations." While some members of this body perform functions that can be handled from a single center (e.g., editor of central party organizations, treasurer, manager of the central technical apparatus of distribution), others work locally to head up "the work of party fractions in the mass organizations," to direct "party education," or to "give reports" on CC work.[4] During an era characterized by the party's recourse to protracted and intensifying revolutionary warfare, some CC members work at the insurgent command center (e.g., COSVN) while others assume control over party work in the "liberation committee" system and the armed forces at the provincial or, in the South Vietnamese case, at the interprovincial level. They are the generators of the inspection teams, charged with the review of activities at lower level in the insurgent hierarchy. They occupy critical posts in the security, propaganda and training, and civil and military proselytizing elements. The several documents gathered together in appendix I testify to the party's total control. It is from the CC hard core that the party draws the personnel capable of giving this principle concrete reality.

2. The Cell

At the base of the party command structure stands the cell, the movement's "ears, eyes, arms, and legs among the masses." The party must turn to these bodies to materialize its policies and plans. The historic party is inconceivable without an authoritarian command center at the top. It would serve as little more than a debating society without the system of cells (in the Anglo-Saxon world, "units") at the lower extremities of its structure.

The role played by the cell is quickly revealed by the "model statutes for a CP," drafted by the organization department of the ECCI in 1925:

> The cell is the organization which connects the party with the workers and small peasants. The functions of the cell are to carry out party work among the non-party working masses by means of systematic communist agitation and propaganda: to recruit new members, distribute party literature, issue a

[4] *Indian Communist Party Documents, 1930–1956.* Compiled by the Research Staff of the Democratic Research Service, with an introduction by V. B. Karnik. (Bombay, India: Democratic Research Service and Institute of Pacific Relations, 1957), pp. 28–29.

factory newspaper, conduct cultural and educational work among the party members and workers in the factory, to work persistently and uninterruptedly to win all official positions in the factory, to intervene in all industrial conflicts and demands by the employees, to explain them from the standpoint of the revolutionary class struggle, to win the leadership in all struggles of the employees by persistent and unflagging work.[5]

Persons who naturally come into contact with one another in their daily life normally are assigned to a single cell in the legal party. Thus, the primary criteria in the determination of who will belong to what cell are objective factors, such as place of residence or work, types of professional contacts, special interests, or activities. Once this determination has been made, the manner in which the cell is structured is relatively uniform. To become active, a cell must be able to perform a predetermined minimum number of functions; it must contain at least three persons; and it must be officially "recognized" by the party committee exercising control over its immediate superior body, e.g., the district party body.

At the time the new cell is recognized, one of its members is formally designated as secretary or cell captain; he is held responsible henceforth for all cell activities. The new unit is expected to maintain regular liaison with its superiors, distribute party literature to the citizenry among which it operates, issue its own leaflets and agitational materials (including possibly a factory news sheet) and, finally, establish its own accounting section.

Once the cell has acquired a half dozen or more members it may take steps to expand the office of its cell captain. A steering or cell committee may be activated. Superior party bodies may introduce control or surveillance personnel into the cell by unilaterally ordering the appointment of one of their own numbers as a member of this executive body.

In South Vietnam, the uncertainties of protracted conflict have led party officials to place increasing importance upon providing each cell with sufficient leadership. From the moment of its activation, the new cell in the South is under pressure to name an assistant cell leader. Once a unit has reached a strength of five members, it is required by regulation to designate such an assistant cell captain irrespective of the members' wishes—a matter left optional in Lao Dong Party regulations for the North.

Second in importance only to this stipulation, which provides for a line of succession in the cell, is the matter of providing the cell with an executive or directing committee of three or more members. In South Vietnam, all basic units of eight or more members (in the North, nine or more members) must have a directing committee of at least three party members, including the cell captain or leader. Article 21 of the PRP draft regulations, and Article 22 of the subsequent official regulations (in force

---

[5] J. Degras, *The Communist International, 1919–1943, Documents*, Vol. II: 1923–1928 (London: Oxford University Press, 1960), p. 174. For one of the most effective statements on cell life in the entire body of Communist literature on this subject, see Lesson Five of the Study Document in appendix E, doc. E-4. Note particularly numbered paragraphs 2 and 3 for the functions assigned the cell as a whole.

since 1 May 1964) provide for the establishment of "provisional directing organs" where the requirements for the creation of a formal unit directing body cannot immediately be met. Such a provisional body is subject to more extensive supervision by higher party bodies than its formally constituted parallel, and its authority is sharply limited (e.g., all decisions are subject to review prior to implementation, etc.). Nevertheless, in setting up such a directing organ, leadership is strengthened at the basic level, and the organization acquires an ever firmer substructure. The imperative of assuring the party continuity in its operations in the face of possible reverses—an imperative associated with Communist party work since the early writing of Lenin—has been provided for.

As the cell expands in size, it assumes additional duties, the most important of which is mass organizational work. For the purposes of the present survey, a mass organization is defined as an officially, freely established association of persons who either serve a common ideological principle or seek to effect articulated socioeconomic aims through integrated activity. Depending upon intent and interest, the criteria for membership in a mass organization may be determined by age, sex, profession, or place of residence. Because most free-world Communist parties are relatively small bodies, they attempt to bring their message to the population, not by preaching at the street corner—an activity requiring an excessive expenditure of time and energy and producing extremely limited results—but by infiltrating mass organizations, capturing critical offices in them, and using them as amplifying devices through which larger groups, possibly inaccessible by any direct approach, may be reached. In detail, this subject is treated later (cf. ch 3, below). Here it is only important to identify the device through which this most important activity is conducted, the *fraction*.[6]

A fraction, organizationally speaking, can assume either of two forms. It may consist of not less than two persons, members of a specific cell assigned the specialized function of popularizing party themes, slogans, and program in a given nonparty organization. As an alternative, a fraction may consist of all of the members of a three- to five-member cell which specializes in infiltration and agitation/propaganda work inside other popular bodies. The fraction in the latter guise occurs frequently, and the former arrangement is also of great utility in party work. A glance at the structure of a mature cell in the Japanese CP shows how the fraction is organizationally integrated with the other elements of a cell (see chart 2, this appendix).

3. The Chapter Committee

The activities of several cells are coordinated by a local party chapter. The party chapter "is the base of the Party," declared a PRP booklet

[6] The term "fraction" as employed in the following statement is used in a fashion other than that employed in the Merriam-Webster Third International Dictionary (". . . a group within the Communist party holding views different from the approved views of the party"). Webster's definition is inaccurate. An extensive review of Communist literature reveals that what Webster calls a "fraction" is actually a "faction."

Chart 2. INTEGRATION OF FRACTION WITH OTHER ELEMENTS OF A CELL*

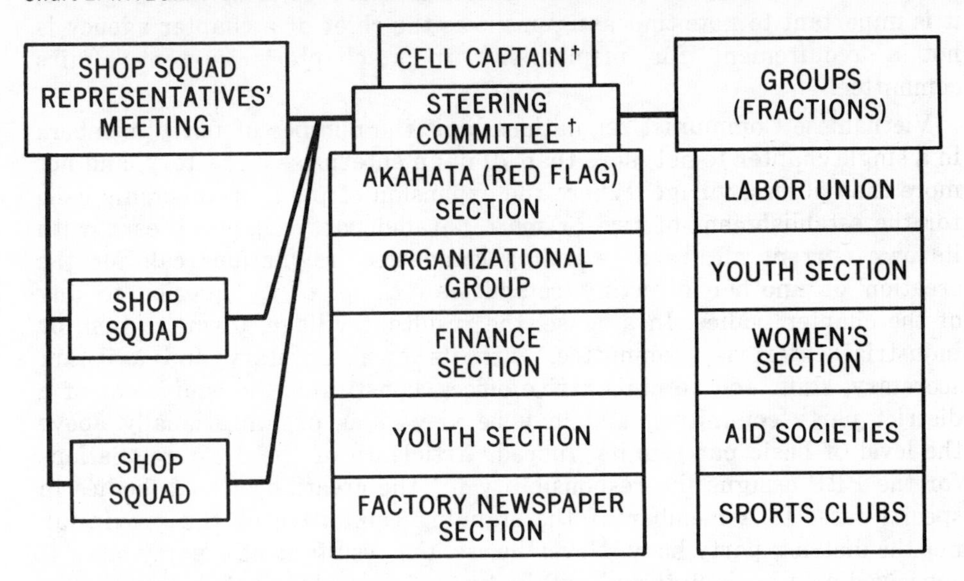

* Cf. Roger Swearingen and Paul Langer, *Red Flag in Japan: International Communism in Action, 1919–1951* (Cambridge, Mass.: Harvard University Press, 1952).

† Known together in the CPUSA as the "Unit Bureau"; cf. Peters, p. 705, a three- to five-member element. (The "Shop Squad" is a fraction specializing in work among the factory proletariat.)

issued by its Binh Long provincial party headquarters, "and the link between the Party and the people." Among the functions of the chapter, according to the booklet, were the following critical tasks:

(1) The constant conduct of political training for party members.
(2) The preparation of operational plans within the policy guidelines provided by higher offices which conform with local conditions.
(3) The guidance and indoctrination of the local population.

This body may exist in several alternate forms, depending upon the number of its members and the extent of their experience. Where the basic unit is small, there are no organizational subdivisions of a cellular character below the chapter level. All local PRP personnel are enrolled in a single body, indistinguishable from a simple cell. As membership increases, differentiation is effected through the assignment of individuals to subordinated cells or units. In its most complex form, a system of parallel chapter units may emerge coordinated through a multichapter executive body. The organizational form most frequently found is that of a single directing committee. It exists in hamlets, villages, and city wards where party cells have remained small and limited in number. Such a party unit is headed by a secretary, an assistant secretary, and a chapter committee of from three to seven persons known as the current affairs or standing committee of the chapter. In addition to constituting the chapter's deliberative body under the chairmanship of the secretary and assistant secretary, some of the members of the chapter committee preside over administrative or staff agencies of the chapter, i.e., finance, party property, agitational and mass organization work, personnel (cadre) affairs, security and counterintelligence, military affairs, etc. However, it is important to note that assignment as the chief of a chapter agency is not a requirement for membership in a chapter's current affairs committee.[7]

Vietnamese Communist regulations limit the number of party members in a single chapter to not more than 70 in an enterprise or factory, and not more than 50 in a village. Where the expansion of party membership calls for the establishment of two or more parallel party chapters, each with its own current affairs or standing committee, regulations call for the creation of another directing committee (*Dang Uy*), superior to any of the chapter bodies. In a sense, the resultant village, town, section, or industrial enterprise committee, with its own secretary and assistant secretary, staff, and administrative offices, constitutes the equivalent of a district party committee, and may be viewed as organizationally above the level of basic party units. Indeed, Article 19 of the draft regulations for the PRP assigns the responsibility for the creation of such bodies in special cases to a member of the standing committee of the provincial, not the district, party body. Nevertheless, the resultant new party office is conceived as a basic unit and will be treated as such in this report.

Keeping in mind the several alternate organizational forms treated thus far, a composite organizational chart of party structure at the basic level assumes the pattern given in chart 3 this appendix.

[7] The evidence available from captured enemy documents indicates that at the basic unit level, as throughout the party's hierarchy, many of the persons engaged in the activities of current affairs committees (or permanent standing committees) have no specifically assigned responsibility that falls clearly within the survey of any one committee agency. Again, it should be noted that persons who do not belong to the current affairs committee frequently are charged with the direction of agencies of the chapter or high bodies but are excluded from participating in the determination of policy.

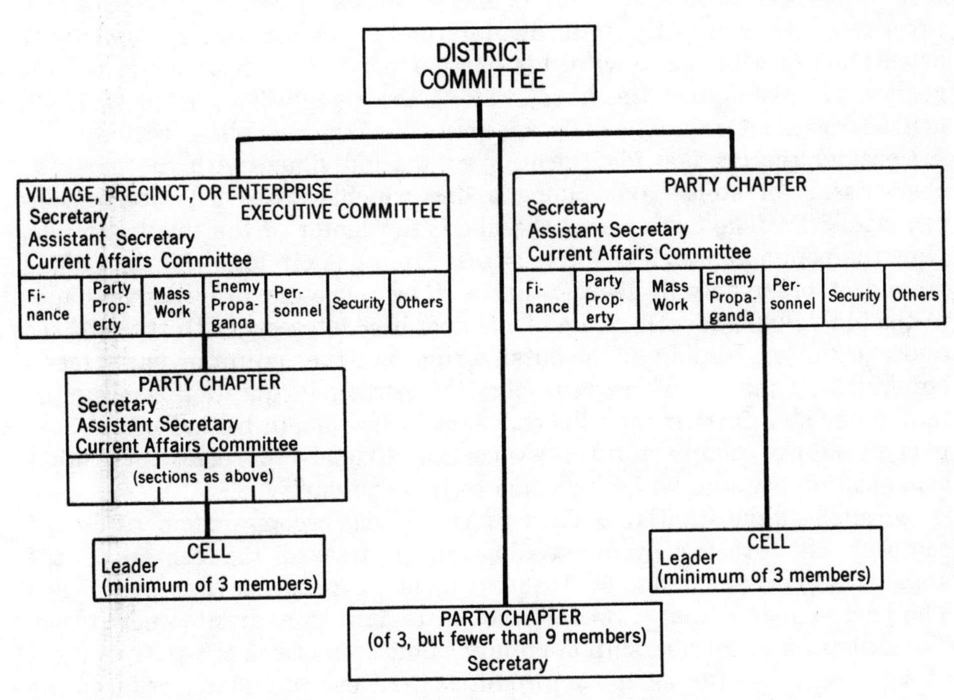

CHART 3. COMPOSITE ORGANIZATIONAL CHART OF PARTY STRUCTURE AT THE BASIC LEVEL

CHAPTER II: THE ACQUISITION OF PARTY MEMBERSHIP[8]

Membership in a Communist party, as conceived by a Communist, is a process, not a condition. The granting of a party card is not to be understood as the completion or consummation of a period of preparation after which the member may relax with the assurance of having "passed the test." The receipt of membership is only a halfway point in the course of a process whose goal is the total mental (one is tempted to say, spiritual) orientation of a person toward his party superiors. To have achieved this goal is to have joined the hard core at the center. This is most likely achieved without any externally apparent display or public ceremony.

Consider the gradual identification of the individual with the party as a succession of steps taken along a line which crosses a series of concentric circles. The terminus of the line is the center of the smallest circle. Now the points at which the line crosses from one circle to the next differ from each other only in degree, that is, they represent progressive stages in the individual's identification of his own best interests with those of the apparatus. The crossing of the outside ring, i.e., the receipt of party membership, is a matter of degree only; the person in question has simply moved one step farther than his colleagues who remain behind in the nonparty reading group, cultural association, friendship society, or other organization through which he came to join the party.

Normally, a substantial portion of those who become members do not complete the process by proceeding on in toward the center of the apparatus. Perhaps from 60 to 80 percent of party novices withdraw. The party expects this. However, enough remain to guarantee new blood. The extension of membership is an important event from the party's point of view only insofar as it compromises the new candidate, reduces his customary mental defenses, and increases his susceptibility to control through manipulation. Once officially inside the party, the task of the cadre is to compromise the novice still further, prodding him continuously, from one act to the next until he has passed the point of no return. The techniques of the struggle meeting or criticism meeting, discussed below, can become decisive instruments in provoking submission. Such experiences can have a particularly lasting impact upon the individual who has failed to develop independent initiative. That even a longtime cell captain will not be successful in this tactic with every new member is accepted beforehand. It is important only that he produce results with sufficient frequency to assure the growth of the CP.

Until the candidate has moved well along the way to total commitment, he is restricted in what he may learn. The party need not fear repercussions when the novice withdraws after two, three, or more years. He will not have been allowed to acquaint himself with the workings of the central organs of the apparatus or with its full-time illegal network.

[8] For the assortment of documentation which precedes the receipt of party membership in the DLD (or its southern branch, the PRP), see appendix C.

Given the situation in which initial membership constitutes no major dividing line, no absolute change in condition, it follows that the specific requirements listed for the potential member at any given time in any one party are strictly a matter of tactics, in accordance with (1) the broad strategy line being pursued by the national CP as adapted to (2) the social/psychological peculiarities of the particular country in which a given party is operative, and finally (3) the effectiveness of the movement's appeal to the public for support during the period in question.

The reason the apparatus can consider broad membership drives is because the new recruit, even when he holds a party card, is still on the outer fringes and not "in the know." Even when he has consciously separated himself from the public at large, he still is not yet regarded by the district or local committee as belonging to the "insiders."

To clarify this in detail, let us turn our attention to actual case studies. We will examine and contrast the requirements for membership in two Communist parties, at about the same point in time—namely, the early 1940's—but widely separated geographically. We select the Chinese Communist Party (CCP) and the Communist Party USA.

For the case of the CCP, Liu Shao-chi's *On the Party* may be cited. The author divides the mainland population into four categories, assigning detailed attributes and provisions to each as follows:

> The first category consists of workers, coolies, farm hands, poor peasants, city poor, and revolutionary soldiers. The requirements for those recommending them as well as their terms of candidature are comparatively moderate. This means that there are no special restrictions on the admission into the Party of proletarian and semi-proletarian elements. Persons brought up in our revolutionary ranks from childhood on are accorded the same treatment.[9]

These several groups—the lowest levels of society—have immediate access to the party. Why? Because they are the most readily controllable. Since they know nothing, the task of "re-educating" them demands little.

> The second category consists of revolutionaries from the petty bourgeoisie whose admission should be recommended by comparatively more experienced Party members and whose term of candidature is one year. This is due to the fact that the ideology of people from this social stratum *is usually more complicated,* and they often have misgivings about the discipline of our Party and about participation in serious revolutionary struggles.[10]

If there was any question before, Liu Shao-chi's reference to the "complicated" nature of category two persons confirms the opportunism of the CP recruiter.

> The third category consists of revolutionaries who formerly belonged to the middle and upper strata of the exploiting classes, whose ideology is even more complicated, and who find it more difficult to accept the programme and discipline of our Party. Therefore, the constitution provides that their applications for joining the Party must be recommended by experienced Party members and be approved by a relatively high Party committee, while their term of candidature in two years.[11]

---

[9] Liu Shao-chi, *On the Party* (Foreign Languages Press, Peking, 1951), p. 63. Chapter I, articles 4 through 9 in the Lao Dong Party Regulations (appendix B, doc. B–1) restates the essential principle enunciated here for the CCP.

[10] Liu Shao-chi, *op. cit.*, p. 64.

[11] *Ibid.*, p. 65.

Finally, as the fourth and most extreme group from which the CCP considers the possibility of drawing members, Liu identified those "who have accepted other political faiths and joined other political parties or groups." For persons who fall into this category, approval must be given from high in the CCP and the period of candidature is indefinite. However, with his eye upon the United Front From Below strategy being pursued by his party at the time, and desiring to attract as wide a group of the population as possible, Liu does not abandon his treatment of this category until he has added that his apparatus is prepared to acknowledge "a distinction between an ordinary member, a relatively responsible member, and a highly important and responsible member of another political party." [12]

While this highly complex recruitment policy was in force in mainland China, the fraternal American party set up entirely different prerequisites for membership:

> Agreement with the party platform in applying it where one is active. . . . Participation in somé phase of war work. . . . Reading of the party press. . . . Payment of dues and membership in a branch, but not compulsory regular attendance.[13]

The distinction from the Chinese situation is extreme. The potential U.S. candidate need not involve himself in party work—at the outset of his party career, at least—only in "war work!" Again there is no reference to the novice's class origin and, in particular, there is no indication of undergoing a probationary period prior to the granting of full membership.

With these two sets of provisions behind us, we can ask ourselves the question: "Why?" What ends were to be achieved, tactically, by pursuing such dissimilar recruitment policies? To answer these queries, one must first look to the general strategic lines being pursued on either side of the Pacific Ocean. The CCP was successfully developing a United Front From Below, identical in its intent with the public strategy pursued by the PRP in South Vietnam and discussed in the main text in chapter 7. As it acquired de facto control over increasingly large regions of China, it labored diligently to project the image of itself as the "wave of the future." What could be more appealing to the peasants than the idea of belonging to the elite within the elite? While attempting to appear attractive to the bulk of the population, the CCP was concurrently holding out the option to other groups of joining the "insiders." What line could possibly have supported the party's interests more effectively than the one chosen?

In the United States, during the same period, altogether different imperatives obtained. The CPUSA, in line with orders from the Kremlin, followed "right" strategy. To avoid projecting the image of the Communist as a sinister-looking, shabbily dressed, bomb-in-hand East European, the American Communist went all out to be clean-cut, open, and straight-talking. Recruiting policy was adjusted to fit the line pursued.

---

[12] For DLD regulations, see appendix B, doc. B–1, articles 5 and 6.

[13] Irving Howe and Lewis Coser, *The American Communist Party: A Critical History* (New York: Frederick A. Praeger, 1962).

CHAPTER III: CRITICAL INNER-PARTY PRACTICES

PERSISTENCE OF PARTY WORK

Once inside the party, the novice finds himself involved in continual meeting-going. This occupies most of his free time, leaving him almost without a private life. As soon as he has finished his regular day's work, he proceeds to one or another assembly of fellow Communists. To display annoyance or lack of interest, to make it apparent that he had retained outside involvement in matters unassociated with the CP, is to bring himself immediately under suspicion of "dilettantism" and lack of dedication to the cause of the "vanguard of the toiling masses."

The following account of the intensive activity within the CP appeared in *The Communist* in May 1931.

> There are about 3,000 members of the party in New York. Of this number. . . . there are 700 direct Party functionaries[14] [operating at the level of] District, Section and Unit, not counting auxiliary functionaries which probably number several hundred more.

The following is their schedule:

Monday: unit bureau meeting
Tuesday: unit meeting
Wednesday: department meeting (agitprop, Negro)
Thursday: school, union meeting
Friday: section committees meetings, street meeting
Saturday: free
Sunday: weekend schools, "Red Sundays" (e.g., distribution of *Daily Worker*)[15]

William S. Schlamm, a Communist Party member for several years during his youth, tells the tale of meeting Gen. Walter Krivitzki in New York some 10 years after his own break with the party and one year after Krivitzki's break with the Comintern apparatus. In the course of their conversation (which occurred in 1938) Schlamm asked Krivitzki how it came about that he [Schlamm] had never been drawn into the party's clandestine work.

Krivitzki, the leading west European Chief of the Soviet Secret Police (GPU) in the 1930's, and the chief of the Comintern's Vienna Secret Bureau in the 1920's when Schlamm had been active in the Austrian party, remembered his case quite well.

> "I can explain that to you quite clearly," he mused, "we never trusted you."
>
> "Who, me?" replied Schlamm in surprise, "Never trusted? Was I not a dedicated young fellow?"

[14] Only a few of these persons were full-time paid employees of the CP national office, also in New York. Throughout the whole country in 1934, the CP had only 190 salaried persons occupying positions at three levels plus some 230 paid (employed) functionaries in mass organizations. Howe and Coser, *ibid.*, p. 229).

[15] C. Hathaway, "On the Use of Transmission Belts in Our Struggle for the Masses" quoted in Howe and Coser, *op. cit.*, p. 220.

> "No, for us, that is just what you were not," replied Krivitzki. "When you were not yet fifteen years of age, you came to the Party in 1919 and said, 'You can have everything you want from me—except for two evenings in the week. On those evenings I have to attend concerts.' And any young fellow for whom Mozart remained more important than the Party, particularly back in the stormy revolutionary era of 1919—just such a person, we did not trust."[16]

There are any number of written reports to be read and discussed; the techniques of the struggle-meeting are employed. Attention is directed to the "ideological lives" of the cell members, and more written literature is turned out on this theme. Indeed, reading and writing are so important that one is justified in concluding that no one can become a good Communist until he is literate!

The massive flow of paper inherent in party work has its practical consequences on the insurgent battlefield. The production of written self-criticisms and ideological autobiographies, the maintenance of cadre dossiers, party reports, etc., means a continuing flow of possible intelligence for the counterinsurgent.[17]

Why this concentration on "togetherness," on provoking each and every member to articulate his feelings and join in actively in the conduct of ideological indoctrination?—because the Communist leaders see in these activities the best means to accomplish dual goals. First, the technique readily uncovers mental reservations, personal estrangement, and covert obstructionism within the party membership. Secondly, in this fashion the aberrant Communist can be provoked into condemning his own individualism and subordinating himself to the will of the CP without open recourse to intimidation, threat of expulsion, or force on the part of the cell or higher party leader. In this context one may begin to understand the dynamics of interpersonnel relationships in a Communist party.

DEMOCRATIC CENTRALISM

As originally defined by Lenin, "democratic centralism" incorporated (1) free discussion of proposed party policy at all levels of the party until a majority position crystallized and (2) unqualified loyalty and obedience by the membership to that policy at all levels of the party, once a final decision had been made. Lenin's presumption was that monolithic unity and steely self-discipline could be derived from the give-and-take of articulating new policies in response to the course of events. The abandonment of this idea came early in the history of communism. The 10th Congress of the Communist Party of the Soviet Union (CPSU) in 1921 was critical in this development; the "bolshevization" of the member parties of the Communist International (Comintern) during the 1920's and the early 1930's internationalized the reality of dictatorial controls within all parties. The phrase "democratic centralism" was retained in party jargon and quickly acquired new meaning.

[16] William S. Schlamm, *Die Jungen Herren der Alten Erde: vom neuen Stil der Macht* (Stuttgart: Seewald Verlag, 1962), pp. 61–62. Translated by M. C. Conley.

[17] The report forms, contained in appendix F, and the written self-criticisms in appendix G belong to that order of party paper work which may be exploited by intelligence.

By this term, we may understand either of two related practices. On the one hand, democratic centralism provides the party with highly effective techniques of evoking from the membership spirited support for the policies adopted by the leadership. But simultaneously in the form of the "criticism-self-criticism meeting," it is a means through which the attitudes of party cadres can be incessantly probed and the growth of separatist cliques thwarted. Let us consider each of these aspects of the practice in succession.

The Internalization of Party Orders

Even if there is no question of permitting the formulation of policy among the lower levels of the party, the leadership will demand that policies already fully elaborated at the top be discussed in all of the lower echelons of the organization. Members are compelled to discuss, overtly agree, and vote on the dictated line.

The issues submitted to a vote are not appeals to the membership to support one or another policy as is common in unmobilized and unstructured groups, but are instead specific orders and plans for future work. The member's attention is focused not on evaluation but upon personal adjustment and reorientation toward what is to be done next. Emphasis is placed upon uniformity of thought and the ultimate authority of the leadership.[18]

Discussion continues until the rank and file are not only convinced of the propriety of the policy announced but have worked out in their minds the best methods for local implementation of the orders from higher headquarters.[19] For this reason, criticism must (1) be constructive and (2) conform with the current party line and the dogma of international communism. Negative criticism could disrupt party work; consequently, if it is not constructive and does not offer a proposal for an improvement in work or a means to correct mistakes, it is not acceptable. At the same time, by unspoken accord, certain subjects are taboo. The impression is not be left with the group that the party's ideology is under examination.

> . . . basic principles and decisions, cannot be questioned in the Party. We cannot imagine a discussion, for example, questioning the correctness of the leading role of the proletariat in the revolution, or the necessity for the proletarian dictatorship. We do not question the theory of the necessity for the forceful overthrow of capitalism. We do not question the political correctness of the decisions, resolutions, etc., of the Executive Committee of the C.I., of the Convention of the Party, or of the Central Committee after they are ratified.[20]

The intent behind the group discussion may be to remind the rank and file not to impair the execution of a policy. Or the leadership may utilize

---

[18] Philip Selznick, *The Organizational Weapon*, (Glencoe, Ill.: The Free Press, 1960), pp. 30–32.

[19] J. Peters, *The Communist Party: A Manual on Organization*, Workers Library Publishers (July 1935), p. 27.

[20] Peters, *op. cit.*, pp. 26–27. For a characteristic agenda of a cell meeting and the ground rules for the direction of such a gathering, see numbered paragraphs 6 through 9 in Lesson Five of doc. E–4, appendix E.

the trappings of self-criticism to introduce formally new policy decisions to the membership. The reporting during a party session of the errors, mistakes, or weaknesses displayed by members may mean, in fact, that all are expected to redouble their efforts to realize announced goals; such criticism or analysis may also provide the occasion to dramatize the commencement of entirely new tactics.

To the extent that all criticism must be coupled with concrete proposals for improvement, the speaker, irrespective of the design behind his remarks, is provided with the means of indicating future direction. Every individual attending the session is expected to join in the discussion, criticizing his own personal conduct in conformity with the direction made apparent by the initial speaker. In the process, the individual internalizes party directives, personalizing them to accord with his distinctive needs. Since the discussion throughout its course is conducted within the jointly recognized, dogmatic bounds accepted by all members, the entire process encourages the evolution of normative behavioral patterns.

High Responsiveness as a Function of Institutionalized Incertitude

To understand the use of "democratic centralism" as a means of attitude control and enhanced responsiveness to direction, both words in the phrase require further examination.[21]

"Centralism" provides the party member with his principle of leadership: In all party bodies, irrespective of importance, size, degree of permanence, or mission, a single individual is designated to be held responsible for what happens to the rest of the group. Under no circumstances is a leaderless *ad hoc* assembly allowed to exist. The person identified as responsible conceives of himself as the local representative of the next higher level of authority. He does not associate himself with his subordinates to constitute a joint front against the higher body; he serves as the agent of his superiors.

To delegate the authority of such an office to an individual is to bring him into the dread danger of "bureaucratism." The mechanical implementation of orders received with little more motivation than the desire to "keep oneself protected," the summary overriding of objections and suggestions made by fellow cell members, the failure to imaginatively execute tasks assigned so as to maximize their impact—these and other possible byproducts of authority constitute "bureaucratism." To allow this tendency free play would rapidly lead to the petrifaction of the party organization, ultimately destroying its capability to effect the subversive, revolutionary operations for which it was specifically designed.

To thwart such a development, the Communists set against the leadership doctrine of "centralism" the second concept, "democracy," which may

[21] For a more exhaustive treatment of "democratic centralism" and the "struggle meeting," specifically in the Chinese Communist Party, see H. F. Schurman, "Organizational Principles of the Chinese Communists," *The China Quarterly*, II (April-June 1960), pp. 47–58.

be roughly translated as "participation." To participate is to be democratic. The Communists use the word continually in this context. The existence within the Communist bloc of a series of "Democratic Peoples' Republics," in which the citizenry is thoroughly regimented and engaged on a group basis in so-called free-time, voluntary duties, is an example of being "democratic." The drives, mass movements, and people's action programs assure the Communist leadership elements of the population's *participation* in desired activities through organization. Insofar as the population participates, it is—from the party member's point of view—democratic.

In the Lao Dong Party Regulations, chapter II, article 12 (appendix B, doc. B–1), the party member is assured that he enjoys democratic election rights and freedom of speech in paragraphs (a) and (b), but his ability to exercise these powers is negated by the determination in paragraph (c) that "the minority should yield to the majority; lower echelons should comply with higher echelons; the whole Party shall obey the Central Committee." Due to the hierarchical character of the party, most members will always be located in the lower echelons; in no case will they be found in the Central Committee. If a majority, democratically determined, in these lower reaches of the structure is of a different opinion from that of the leadership, then obeying the wishes of the higher offices can hardly be adjudged "democratic" as that word is understood in the free world. The absence of democratic procedure is further indicated by the provision of paragraph (d) restricting the initiative of lower bodies in the resolution of their current problems to policy lines previously set by higher headquarters. Given this situation, one is indeed obliged to assign to the word "democratic" in Communist usage the altered meaning of "participation" or "personal involvement."

Criticism-Self-Criticism

Within the party apparatus, one of the principal ways in which one acts "democratically" is by participating in criticism-self-criticism sessions (also known as mutual struggle meetings). From the point of view of the leadership, every member of a healthy party organization lives in eternal anticipation of serving as the focal point for commentary during the next cell meeting. He will fully expect each of his cohorts to exert himself to the utmost to be penetrating, comprehensive, and uninhibited in his remarks during the meeting. Every party member knows two things: (1) that if he does not make every effort to contribute seriously to the critique of his fellows, then he himself will shortly be subjected to a comprehensive dissection of his conduct, by his compatriots, to which he will be obliged to confess his guilt; (2) that in participating fully in the identifications of the others' failings, he has not escaped his own eventual subjection to the same process.

If it is concluded at a higher party level that the cell captain or another responsible cell member suffers from "bureaucratism," then the cell members will be encouraged to conduct a criticism session. The person in question will be restive, of course, but realizing that the critique has been purposely provoked he will be powerless to resist. He will submit to a thoroughgoing analysis of his conduct which can proceed into the smallest details of his life, both private and public, both intimate and generally known. He must clearly acknowledge the reproaches before the group, promising to improve himself. He will understand that an inadequate showing on his part could lead to his reduction in rank and, ultimately, even to his expulsion from the party.

This can be a traumatic experience for the individual, and it is very important for us to keep in mind that nothing resembling fraternal group identity develops among those participating in the struggle meeting against their fellows. The relationship "in-group" "out-group" can never evolve within the cell's membership; for at the very moment that they unite their talents in castigating a member of the group, each participating individual is on the defensive with respect to his associates. His aggressiveness is motivated by mistrust of his fellow cell members. The "democratic" half of democratic centralism instills in each member the need to demonstrate to his associates his unqualified responsiveness to the wishes of authority at the next higher level so that he can avoid undue attention by his cohorts, and consequently escape excessive criticism when finally his turn comes around.

What we are treating here is a high-powered, dynamic situation, well calculated to prevent the growth of grassroots opposition against the party leadership. Through this technique, a group of persons are (1) obliged to work together, while (2) each remains isolated spiritually from the next—"atomized." The orientation of each individual toward higher party authorities—a pathetic, eternal striving to find approval and solace by demonstrating obedience to the committee at the next higher level—characterizes the mentality of the party member.

In this fashion the politburo of a CP can maintain a built-in, permanent uncertainty and apprehensiveness among the rank and file. The politburo is certain of responsiveness from below and likewise is insured against the growth of "bureaucratism." Orders are implemented, not mechanically, but *"creatively," on the basis of "absolute commitment."*[22]

Liu Shao-chi had these important pronouncements to make on the struggle meeting:

> The upholding of Party discipline and Party unity does not in the main depend on the punishment of comrades (if they have to be held in such a manner it signifies a crisis in the Party), but rather on the actual unity of the Party in ideology and principle, and on the consciousness of the vast majority of the Party members.
>
> Only by achieving ideological unity can unity inside the Party be maintained and strengthened politically, organizationally and in action. . . . Problems must be solved from the angle of ideology and principle before they can be solved from the angle of organization and action. . . . This can only be achieved

[22] Schurman, *op. cit.*

through painstaking persuasion and education, through various kinds of complicated struggles and through a considerable period of education, struggle and practice in revolution.

When we are eventually fully clear regarding ideology and principle, it is very easy for us to draw organizational conclusions, if necessary. It does not take us a minute to expel Party members or announce voluntary withdrawal from the Party.[23]

In a Vietnamese setting, examples of democratic centralism and the criticism meeting are provided by docs. G–2 and G–3 in appendix G. Both documents were made up of notes prepared either by the chairmen of the respective assemblies for their meetings or by persons in attendance who kept records on the course of events. In the first of these documents an attempt is made to use criticism-self-criticism to enhance the responsiveness of those present to the will of higher party bodies. The second document in which criticism figures more prominently is oriented toward the eradication of heretical ideas and undesirable work practices. The order in which subjects were taken up for group discussion during these meetings, it should be further remarked, tends to conform to the recommended agenda outlined in paragraph six of Lesson Five in the Study Document, (appendix E. doc. E–4). In particular, the first of these collections of notes agrees with the arrangement called for by higher party authorities.

That the device of the criticism meeting can be utilized in other ways is indicated by docs. G–1 and G–4 in the same appendix G. In both of these documents, the technique of self-criticism accounts for the format in which reports to superior party offices were cast.

[23] Liu Shao-chi, *On Inner-Party Struggle* (Peking: Foreign Languages Press), pp. 30, 61. (A lecture delivered on July 2, 1941, at the Party School for Central China.)

CHAPTER IV: MASS ORGANIZATIONS AND THE PARTY FRACTION

All groups that the Communists try to penetrate are called mass organizations.[24] Stalin argued that in order to transform the Communist Party from a propaganda party to an agency of leadership the members must break from the conception that Communists work solely to direct efforts to build the Communist Party by recruiting new members.

> We must learn to set up and work through a whole series of mass organizations and in this way also develop our party work. Our chief error is our failure to understand the role and to systematically utilize mass organizations as transmission belts through the broad masses of nonparty workers. The Communist Party is necessarily composed of the most conscientious and self-sacrificing elements among the workers. These mass organizations, on the contrary, with a correct political line, can be made to reach many thousands of workers not yet prepared for party membership. Through these organizations, led by well-functioning fractions, the party must necessarily find its best training and recruiting ground. They are the medium through which the party, on the one hand, guides and directs the workers in their struggles and, on the other hand, keeps itself informed on the mood of the masses, the correctness of the party slogans, etc.[25]

In line with Stalin's guidance, Communists seek to create power by building their own controls within an organization; by seeking allies—they attempt to form new groups which they can control; or they seek out local centers of power which they can use for future operations. Whenever possible, they attempt to establish formal organizations which isolate the individuals from the governmental leadership and, therefore, create centers of local control. They attempt to subvert institutional loyalities and create new allegiances within mass organizations at the community level. They undermine old forms of authority and create new ones. They corrupt the authority upon which institutional foundations are built.[26]

The objectives of infiltrating mass organizations are to (1) neutralize existing agencies which support the government; (2) legitimize causes of the subversives; and (3) mobilize mass support. The Communists tend to avoid isolation of their party by gaining access to and penetrating organizations and institutions within the society. In order to gain support for their movement, they will attempt to neutralize any competitors and in this way monopolize mass support. The strategy of neutralization has played a large role in the relationship of the Communist to the Socialist and other left-wing organizations. They attempt to infiltrate these groups

[24] Louis F. Budenz, *The Techniques of Communism* (Chicago: Henry Regnery Co., 1954), p. 35.

[25] C. A. Hathaway, "On the Use of 'Transmission Belts' in Our Struggle for the Masses," *The Communist*, May 1931. Reprinted in *Hearings*, appendix, part I, U.S. House of Representatives Special Committee on Un-American Activities, 76th Cong., 1st Sess. (Washington, D.C.: Government Printing Office, 1940), p. 484; also Selznick, *op. cit.*, p. 118.

[26] Selznick, *op. cit.*, pp. 213–14.

and through disruptive practices attempt to neutralize their effectiveness and discredit the leadership.

In many areas of the world, communism is not a popular cause. On the other hand, there are many popular issues which the Communists may use to bring support to their movement. They seek out legitimate issues and causes within any societal structure and organize and mobilize forces around these causes. In this way they gain legitimacy for their movement.

Another major objective is to mobilize those who are not members of groups. By mobilizing the unorganized into formal organizations, they are able to create mass support for their issues.[27]

In his April 1924 Sverdlov lectures, later published as *Foundations of Leninism,* Stalin indicated the types of organziations to be infiltrated: "trade unions, cooperatives, factory and shop organizations, parliamentary fractions, non-Party women's associations, the press, cultural and educational organizations, youth leagues, military revolutionary organizations (in times of direct revolutionary action), soviets of deputies, which is the state form of organization (where the proletariat is in power), etc." Only the "Party of the Proletariat," he continued, "could guarantee 'unity of leadership' . . . in the face of such a multiplicity of organizations." The duty of the party was to: "transform each and every non-party organization of the working class into a serviceable functioning body, a transmission belt linking it with the class."

Individual members of mass organizations might eventually be enlisted in the ranks of the party, but the intent was not to take the organization into the party.

> This does not mean, of course, that non-party organizations like trade unions, co-operatives, etc., must be formally subordinated to Party leadership. It means simply that the members of the Party who belong to these organizations and doubtless exercise influence in them, should do all they can to persuade these non-party organizations to draw nearer to the Party of the proletariat in their work and voluntarily accept its political guidance.[28]

The device through which the party works to influence other organizations is the fraction, an element within the basic party cell. It will be recalled from the preceding discussions of the functional structure of the cell that specialized groups known respectively as "shop squads" and "fractions" were attached to the cell's steering committee. The first of these is to be understood as a specialized form of the second, constituting as it does the party's organizational response to Karl Marx's preoccupation with the factory proletariat. Its activities, if directed toward a specifically delimited group, do not in principle differ from those of the fraction in general.

It is through these instruments that the party penetrates into the marrow of independently organized groups. As the American Communist J. Peters has declared, these bodies are "an instrument in the hands of

[27] *Ibid.*, pp. 78–79.
[28] Joseph Stalin, *Foundations of Leninism* (New York: International Publishers, 1939), pp. 115–17.

the Party is brought which the policy of the Party is brought to the organized masses, and through which the Party gives leadership to members of the mass organizations." [29]

Section VIII (paragraphs 40 and 41) of the May 1934 "Statutes of the Communist Party of India." describes in considerable detail the procedures evolved in Communist parties about the world to achieve the ends set forth by Stalin. In all non-party associations in which three or more members of the CPI are active, declare the Statutes, "party fractions are organized which must function in an organized way, strengthen party discipline, work to increase the influence of the party, and carry party policy among non-party masses." [30] For current work, the fraction elects a secretary.

The fraction is controlled by the corresponding party committee (CC, provincial committees, town or local committees or nucleus), and on all questions must strictly and without vacillation carry out the decisions of the party organizations which lead them. The fractions of the higher bodies of mass organizations, by agreement with the corresponding party committee, may send directives to the fraction of lower bodies of the some mass organizations and the latter must carry them out without fail as directives from a higher party organ.[31]

Critical is the provision insuring control to the parent cell from which the fraction arose, or the appropriate party committee if infiltration is effected above the primary level. The universality of this principle of control is substantiated by the stipulations which were being announced almost simultaneously by the CPUSA:

> Members who belong to mass organizations must systematically report to the Unit Bureau (i.e., the cell captain and his assistants) or to the Unit meeting about their work: how they bring the various political campaigns of the Party into their mass organizations; about their experiences in recruiting members for the Party. . . . etc.[32]

For a specific example of the principles here involved, the case of an Indian peasant organization, the Kisan Sabhas, which eventually fell under total Communist control during World War II, may be cited.[33] This peasant association maintained committees at the primary, district, provincial, and all-India levels. Chart 4, this appendix, depicts the varying channels through which the CPI exercised its controls over the multiple fractions inserted into this body. As long as successful penetration was restricted to the primary level of organization within the Kisan Sabhas, controls were exercised from the Politburo of the Central Committee, down through the party apparatus to the local committee or nucleus, which in turn provided the fraction with the themes to be stressed, recommended techniques to be employed in operations, and, as necessary, provided logistic support to sustain the activities undertaken. Under no circum-

[29] J. Peters, *op. cit.*, p. 729.

[30] *Indian Communist Party Documents, 1930–1956, op. cit.*

[31] *Indian Communist Party Documents, 1930–1956, op. cit.*, pp. 33–34.

[32] Peters, *op. cit.*, p. 719.

[33] Gene D. Overstreet and Marshall Windmiller, *Communism in India* (Berkeley, Calif.: University of California Press, 1939), pp. 384–95.

stances would the party committee surrender the initiative in policy matters to the fraction or fraction secretary.

This principle of reserving to the parent body dictatorial authority over parallel units obtains in all Communist parties. Thus, the assertion in the regulations of the CPUSA:

> The policy for a mass organization is made in the party committee, but before the decisions are made on an basic question, the committee invites the representatives of the given fraction to participate in the discussion. *The fraction at this meeting has a consultative role.* After the discussion, the decision is made by the party committee.[34]

This principle of control from the party's core is universal and constant. The CPI provisions above did alter the channel through which authority was asserted over the fraction at the primary level, once organized fractions began to operate in the Kisan Sabhas at the district, provincial, and all-India levels. Thus, the fraction within the provincial committee of the peasant association "by agreement with the corresponding party committee" assumed operational control over all fractions active in the Kisan Sabhas within its province by issuing directives which carried as much weight among all lesser fractions as would have been the case if they had been issued from within the central party cadre itself. Once the all-India offices of the Kisan Sabhas were penetrated, the CPI controlled a comprehensive hierarchy of the offices, parallel to itself and completely

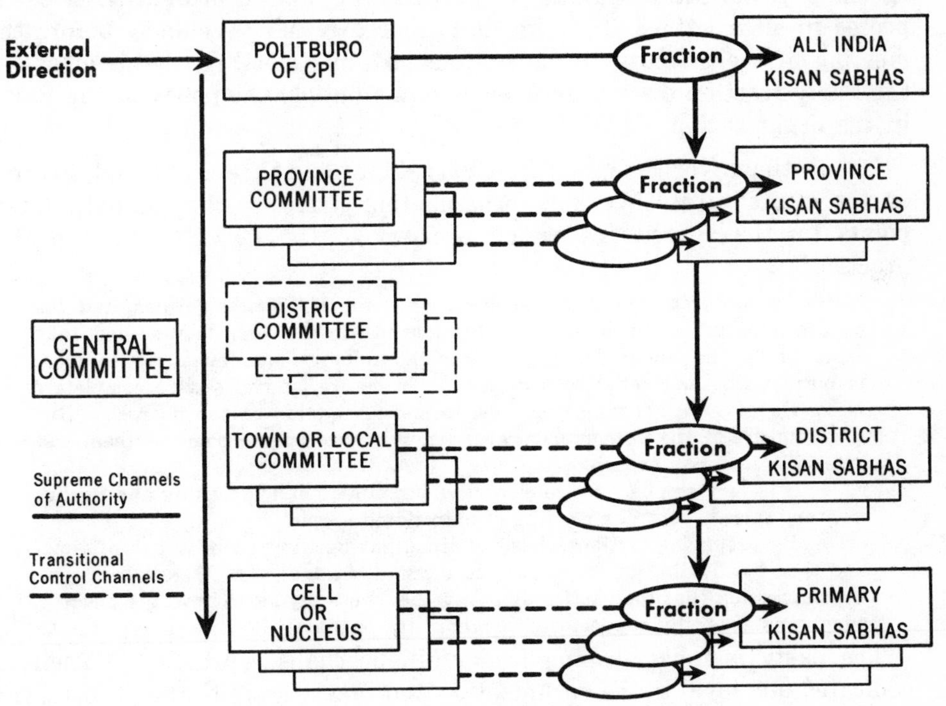

Chart 4. COMMAND STRUCTURE OF COMMUNIST PARTY OF INDIA IN A PEASANT MASS ORGANIZATION

[34] Peters, *op. cit.*, p. 729.

under its control. Policy proceeded from the politburo to its own "leading fraction" in the national offices of the peasant association (composed of designated members of the party's central committee). And from this vantage point, orders, directives, and supervisory controls flowed down through highly functional lines of command which rested upon a disciplined body of men who constituted an organization within the organization.

While relentless in pursuit of his goals, the party member carefully weighs the language with which he addresses others. The following advice was given the fraction member of a shop squad by a member of the Communist chapter of the CPUSA in the *Party Organizer* in June 1931:

> Step continually to the left in conversation, a step at a time, bringing the workers along. It will take time and patience. . . . They must see the perfect logic of your argument and you must speak, not as a soap boxer or a seasoned Communist theoretician, for they will not listen and you will be known too soon as a Communist before you have had the opportunity to get in all the necessary ground work. . . .
>
> Don't appear too insistent at first. Just be one of the workers, which indeed you are.[35]

Once party members have organized fractions successfully, they caucus and plan their tactics within the organization in advance. In his manual on organization and operational practices within the party, J. Peters specifically indicates that such pre-planning and coordination are expected in all fractions. They are to gather together "regularly before the meeting of their (mass) organizations. At this meeting, the members of the Party fraction discuss and decide how to apply the policy of the Party in the organization." [36]

The testimony of Zygmund Dobryzynski, at one time a national director of the United Auto Workers organization drive in the United States, points up the advantages which accrued to the CPUSA through this practice:

> During the first organizational days, when the UAW was formed, and the men were beginning to recognize that unionism was the thing they needed, they came in by the hundreds; the automobile industry was made up of men, primarily, who had never been in any union before, and who were completely inexperienced, not knowing even how to make a motion on the floor. . . . But the members of the Communist Party knew how to speak; some of them had extensive soap-box experience.
>
> . . . It is very simple for a man who understands public speaking and parliamentary rules to control a meeting of uninitiated people.
>
> . . . By preparing motions ahead of time, having discussions ahead of time, and then by dividing up in various sections of the hall, the CPers would give the impression that the particular policy they were trying to have the meeting adopt was generally supported throughout the membership.[37]

The party member seeking leadership positions represents himself as dedicated and loyal to the organization and takes the initiative in planning

---

[35] Howe and Coser, *op. cit.*, p. 224.
[36] Peters, *op. cit.*, p. 730.
[37] Howe and Coser, *op. cit.*, pp. 375–76.

activities and volunteering for any job, no matter how time-consuming or unpleasant. He avoids the appearance of subversive activity. His candidacy is supported by cell members in the rank and file, but close ties between the candidates and the cell collaborators are hidden from the general membership so that the candidates' support appears spontaneous and unsolicited.

That the party's conspiratorial nature assists it in mass-organizational work is apparent from innumerable specific cases. S. A. Dange, long an influential Indian Communist, called for more extensive reliance upon clandestine work in trade unions during a CPI congress in Calcutta in May 1952:

> We must learn to keep some of the cadres unexposed. Or else, victimization by the employers will throw all our best leaders and men from the real field of work that is the factory, shop and office.
>
> Some people think that because our unions are now legal, we bring all our cadres to the forefront. We have to remember that the unions are legal but the crisis of capitalism is not over. The bourgeoisie does not hesitate to attack us when we lead workers' struggles.[38]

The payoff for systematic, highly rationalized efforts of this character can be gleaned from the report of a Communist steelworker in western Pennsylvania of April 1938:

> Our party unit a few years ago had ten members, and it was the hardest job to get them to a meeting. Now our party has grown to 43 members. How was this done? When the CIO started organization work in steel, there were four of us comrades who put ourselves in the front line to help build the union. I want to say as a Communist that, with my own signature, I have signed 800 members into the CIO. Through such activity we won the confidence of the men and were able to recruit. Our branch meeting now has a weekly attendance of more than 25.[39]

Another American example of Communist party mass organization work was the infiltration and takeover of the National Maritime Union. The small Communist fraction utilized the support of the non-Communist, Joseph Curran, who was popular with the rank and file. Curran agreed to work with the Communists and become president of the union; since he had no independent machine he had to rely upon the support of the Communists. The Communists took advantage of this, for they had control of the key posts within the organization. Therefore, if 17 of the 32 top posts belong to Communists, they controlled the organization. Through the use of 500 members within the Communist fractions, they were able to establish control over union membership for approximately 50,000.[40]

In the Malayan Communist insurgency the MCP maintained its influence within the General Labor Union (GLU) through three separate control systems. The first was comprised of a president or secretary and two or three full-time organizers. They were part of the open membership of the labor union. Although they were party members, they avoided any con-

[38] Overstreet and Windmiller, *op. cit.*, p. 379.
[39] Howe and Coser, *op. cit.*, p. 376.
[40] Selznick, *op. cit.*, pp. 194–96.

nection with the party and meetings and activities which might identify them with the party. They reported to and took orders from the GLU. They were to operate within the law and to give the impression that their primary interest was the advancement and concern of trade unionism.

The second system of control was exercised through underground party work. Full-time party members who held no official office were members of the rank and file of the union. They did not seek office but served as activists among the rank and file. It was their job to recruit new members for the union and for the MCP. One tactic which they used was to present demands through the leaders as grassroots sentiment. The leader would then reluctantly announce policy on the basis of these popular demands. In this way the leader would avoid dictating to the union but would "follow" the sentiment of its members.

It was also the responsibility of this group to determine the financial status of each member and to provide information on the member's attitudes. On the basis of these reports, the MCP made policy decisions on the moves to be taken within the organizations. The underground members were responsible to and reported to the section of the party responsible for trade unionism which was separate from the regular party. These members were more trusted than the leaders of the union movement. The leaders were expendable in case they were arrested.

A third control system was provided by the regular party members who were a part of the fraction within the membership of the union. They held no official posts and they reported their activities to the regular party and were given orders from the regular party.[41]

In Latin America the Communists have created a wide range of interlocking mass organizations. They penetrate and manipulate professional societies, cultural groups, women's associations, ethnic groups and other special-interest groups. They emphasize legitimate special-interest needs and issues which appeal to special-interest group aspirations: higher wages, agrarian reform, benefits to students, equal rights. Many prominent non-Communist personalities have been attracted to these groups by the avowed objectives, such as peace, democracy, and the abolition of nuclear weapons. Other issues are also used to unite under a national front many groups which cut across class and group lines.

Nor must it be thought that a Communist party—for ideological reasons, e.g., class struggle, dictatorship of the proletariat, etc.—is uninterested in infiltrating fractions into mass organizations representing conservative or even reactionary groups in other countries. The policies pursued by international communism in the Middle East for a decade after World War II brought it to cooperate with religious fanatics who coupled a policy of anti-semitism with (1) opposition to a secular way of life and (2) hostility to Western influence in local politics.

[41] Lucian Pye, *Guerrilla Communism in Malaya* (Princeton, N.J.: Princeton University Press, 1956), pp. 77–78.

In Egypt, this produced close ties with the Moslem Brotherhood to the extent that literature, jointly sponsored, was published, and demonstrations, both unarmed and armed, were jointly conducted.

In Turkey, Communists worked through fanatical pan-Islamists who opposed Turkish nationalism and the modern inheritance from Kemal Ataturk. Of importance here were reactionary groups such as the Tijanis, pan-Islamists, and the clique associated with the periodical *Buyuk Dogu*. Investigations conducted by the Turkish Government in 1953 showed that money transfers from Egypt and Iran to back these groups had originated in an Iron Curtain country.

The infiltration of the Moslem Brotherhood in Egypt had occurred—at least in part, openly—but the tieup with Turkish reactionaries was strictly covert. A rank-and-file Turkish Communist or Tijani would have through the very idea absurd. Nevertheless, the activity of a few well-chosen people in key positions in the right-wing organizations coupled with financial assistance was enough to strengthen them and to damage the Government.[42]

The counterpart to infiltration work in areas where open associations are already in being before party fraction personnel commence their work is political organizational work where the population has not previously provided itself with popular organizations. The system of "liberation associations" in South Vietnam was of this latter type, but the PRP did not restrict itself exclusively to these kinds of bodies. The instructions and recommendations contained in docs. E–4, E–5, and E–6 in appendix E (Communist Propaganda and Training), outline the alternate procedures to be followed where organizations already exist, but likewise where the party had to take the initiative in creating them. Irrespective, however, of the dissimilar origins of the one or the other type of body, the ultimate result of fraction work, if allowed to continue, would be the fabrication of a system of overt organizations which resembled one another closely and were dominated by one and the same propaganda-indoctrination apparatus, the one outlined in doc. E–1, appendix E.[43]

---

[42] Cf. chapter XVIII in W. Z. Laqueur, *Communism and Nationalism in the Middle East* (New York: Frederick A. Praeger, 1957).

[43] For the constitution of the NFLSVN and several of the Liberation Associations, see appendix D.

CHAPTER V: MAO TSE-TUNG'S AND LENIN'S PARTY OF PROFESSIONAL REVOLUTIONARIES

The requirements for the elaboration of an insurgent structure such as that in South Vietnam are fourfold. First, a disciplined body of professional revolutionaries, an apparat, must be built, trained in the arts of manipulating human beings and made capable of surviving under conditions of illegality. This body is charged with generating the movement's ideological justification. Second, a concept of strategy must be evolved which provides the careerist in revolution with clear guidelines for his tactical operations which concurrently condoning extremes of flexibility to include open opportunism at all levels. Third, a technique through which the apparat may assure itself of unrelenting control over the associations of non-party civilians, the mass organizations which are utterly indispensable to the intensification of the insurgent effort, and over the more specifically military or paramilitary forces raised by the party in order to contend with the nation's security forces. Fourth, a military doctrine covering the tactics to be utilized by the "guerrillas," which (1) stresses their offensive role while making due allowance for their survival as operative units in the face of superior, professional national army and police organization, and (2) assures that political/psychological criteria and not military considerations are preeminent in determining the conduct of both the unit as a whole and its individual members. In other words, this last requirement treats combat units as catalysts for political organizational work.

Having already dealt with the first three of these requirements, we shall now speak of the fourth.

The founder of modern communism, Vladimir Ilyich Lenin, combined in his person the distinctive attributes of the revolutionary and the bureaucrat. The party organization he evolved became an extension of his own personality and has never lost the characteristics it inherited from the man. Since this apparatus of bureaucrats stands at the center of Communist insurgency as we know it today, Lenin himself consequently must be recognized as one of the decisive contributors of all time to the Communist doctrine of insurgency.

But one may go a step further and argue that Lenin was also the leader of communism's first successful insurgency, the Bolshevik Revolution of 1917. There are distinctions to be drawn between the protracted guerrilla wars of the last several decades and the preceding Bolshevik power seizure in Russia, and there are concurrently a number of marked similarities to be noted. Thus Lenin, with the assistance of Leon Trotsky, was the first to evolve the system of political commissar or political officer—the party member with authority coequal to that of the unit commander, inserted within operational forces, command headquarters, and staff sections. Through this organizational device, the party took command away from Colonel Polkovnikov, commander in chief of the Petrograd military district in November 1917. By maintaining the system during the subsequent years of the Civil War, 1918–1921, additional boons fell to the party. It acquired ideological control over the minds of the soldiers who were thrown against the White Armies of Denikin, Kolchak, Miller, and Yudenich, making it possible to employ safely large numbers of "military specialists" (i.e., former Tsarist officers), as operational commanders at the head of the units. This last factor, the supervision of suspect command personnel, would not apply on any comparable plane to the later military forces activated by Communist parties, but the remaining functions of the policom developed during the Civil War in Russia do not differ in intent from the role assigned today to the policom's Vietnamese counterpart in the guerrilla unit.

With respect to the multiple civil mass organizations which are called into life by the party as its impact increases among the populace at large, the first essay into such operations also dates from the period of the Bolshevik Revolution and involved the party's infiltration of the Petrograd soviet, the amorphous federation of laborers which genuinely represented the working classes of the city at the outset and enjoyed great popularity. The task before the party in the autumn of 1917 was to capture control of critical offices within the soviet and then to address the citizenry "through" and "in the name of" the soviet. In this fashion, the prestige of the soviet could be utilized to secure goals ultimately of interest only to the apparat. Trotsky revealed his effective grasp of the strategy pursued by Lenin when he declared:

> The impatient attempt to connect the party wheel directly with the gigantic wheel of the masses—omitting the medium-sized wheel of the soviets—would have given rise to the danger of breaking the teeth of the party wheel and nevertheless not setting sufficiently large masses in motion.[44]

Initially a body that had arisen spontaneously, the soviet became a parallel hierarchy competing with the formal national government, the provisional government of Prince Lvov, Kerensky, *et al.* It was Lenin's genius to be the first to grasp the potentialities of the situation. In April 1917 he wrote for the party's journal, *Pravda*:

> The highly remarkable feature of our revolution is that it has brought about a dual power. This fact must be grasped first and foremost: unless it is understood, we cannot advance. . . . What is this dual power? Alongside the Provisional Government, the government of the bourgeoisie, another government has arisen, so far weak and incipient, but undoubtedly a government that actually exists and is growing—the Soviet of Workers' and Soldiers' Deputies.[45]

The grand strategy of the Bolshevik seizure of political power became, then, essentially the following:

---

[44] Leon Trotsky, "The Triumph of the Soviet," *The History of the Russian Revolution, III* (New York: Simon and Schuster, 1932), p. 284.

[45] V. I. Lenin, "The Dual Power," *Collected Works, XXIV*. April–June 1917 (Moscow: Progress Publishers, 1964), p. 39.

(1) Infiltrate the soviet and turn it into the nucleus of a future, party-controlled government.

(2) From the base developed within the soviet, insert political commissars into the military forces which belong, in a formal sense, under the command of the ministry of defense of the provisional government.

(3) Incorporate the most attractive slogans of all the political factions active in the Petrograd region into a single political platform, in which the name Karl Marx is never mentioned, and have the soviet subscribe to it all by getting the party members who have infiltrated the policy bureau of the soviet publicly to declare themselves in its favor.

(4) Conduct agitation among the masses, solidify control over military units, carry out provocative acts against the provisional government to test its reaction capabilities.

(5) Once it has been determined that the government is no longer capable of defending itself, instigate an urban uprising to seize government installations and liquidate the hard core supporters and sympathizers of the provisional government.

The Bolshevik seizure of power serves as a case study in insurgency involving three of the four fundamental attributes of insurgency listed in the introduction to this appendix: (1) a disciplined party; (2) a concept of strategy which condones uninhibited opportunities; (3) an organizational disposition under which the party retains control of the parallel organizations, civil and military, through which it prosecutes the broad spectrum of activities adjudged indispensible to its internal struggle. Missing from this experience is the fourth listed attribute, a doctrine which assures military operations a primarly political impact. The absence of this factor from the Russian scene of November 1917 followed from the distinctive milieu in which that transfer of power occurred, followed from the unique—as opposed to general—principles involved in the Russian case history.

By the autumn of 1917, Russia was in an advanced stage of national deterioration. At the front, against the German and Austro-Hungarian Armies, casualties had passed the 10 million mark. In the rear, famine was rampant, communications, public utilities, and government administration were collapsing. The dynasty of the Romanovs had disappeared from the scene as a result of its own incompetence. There was no genuine, broadly based, popular revolt against Nicolas II. In silence, he signed the papers proclaiming his abdication. The provisional government came into being not in response to a groundswell of the populace at large, but because there was no one else to assume the functions of government; and that new government found no support among the people.

Russia at this juncture was in a situation where the resolute effort of any organized group could well lead to the capture of state authority. The drive for power did not require of the insurgent that he first destroy the channels of communication (figurative or physical) between the government and its citizency. It did not oblige him to intimidate the village notables, the teacher, the priest, or any other "key communicators." Finally, he was under no pressure to demonstrate that he represented the "wave of the future," for any commonsense proposal for a new form of government was preferable to the governmental void then existing. Given this situation, the success of the revolution did not depend upon raising up an army of guerrillas. The takeover could be effected, essentially, by the crowds in the street under the insurgent's prodding. For this reason, the Bolshevik insurgency could succeed without the guerrilla. For this tactical reason, the struggle was not protracted in the sense of stretching out over years. Specifically, it required some 7½ months, from 15 March to 7 November 1917.

Many of the Communist insurgents in the 1920's and 1930's who attempted to export the techniques of the Soviet insurgency failed to distinguish between the unique aspects of the power seizure and the general principles which might be applied elsewhere. Their efforts consequently failed. This was the case in Germany in 1921 and 1923, in Bulgaria in 1923 and 1925, in Estonia in 1924, in China in 1927. But after 1927, one Communist, Mao Tse-tung, did indeed grasp the distinction to be drawn, in the Bolshevik experience, between the unique and the general, and in adjusting his tactics accordingly to the domestic conditions inside China, he evolved the body of doctrine dealing with the guerrilla which is associated with his name. This is to say, Mao's theories are to be understood as a further elaboration of a body of thought initially set forth in the writings of Lenin.

Mao kept the heart of Lenin's thought. Indeed, he was specifically taught this in the Whampoa Military Academy built up by Soviet advisers outside Canton in the early 1920's. But he added to it. Many men would play their part in the further development of Lenin's principles. The most critical additions came from Mao Tse-tung and his close collaborator, Chu Teh. It is the synthesis of their respective work into a single body of thought which provides the basis for the modern Communist doctrine on the conduct of insurgency.

But given the dissimilar national origins of the two principal contributors, this is likewise to argue against the proposition that there is a distinctively "oriental" form of Communist insurgency. On the contrary, there is one doctrine, which may be utilized in Africa, Europe, and the Americas as well as in Asia and which is the common property of all Communist parties.

The question Mao asked himself was the following: How can a country which enjoys some degree of internal stability be made to progressively approximate, domestically, the conditions which obtained in Russia in the fall of 1917 so that the (1) disciplined party, operating through (2) a "dual power" or contending parallel hierarchy, and employing (3) an opportunistic strategy, may look forward to an ultimate seizure of power through time? Mao's answer: the guerrilla.

To the guerrilla, Mao assigned two parallel responsibilities. On the one hand, he was to cut communications between the government and its citizens, paralyze commerce between city and countryside, and decimate the nation's security and armed forces. Paralleling this effort, on the other hand, the guerrilla, through terrorism, could mobilize the population in behalf of the insurgency. He would become a new kind of catalyst of political action.

While progressively recreating November 1917 by contending with the government and its representatives, the guerrilla set the scene for unrestricted agitation by the party among the populace, leading to the activation of mass associations and liberation fronts. To this end, the guerrilla approached the citizenry with dual programs: (1) promises for the future, and enhanced status now, for those who cooperated, and (2) punishment post-haste for those who would not collaborate.

This argument suggests that the prototype of the allegedly "popular" mass front facade in South Vietnam—the "National Front for the Liberation of South Vietnam" (NFLSVN)—was the soviet which once functioned in the Russian nation under Bolshevik control in November 1917. One is encouraged to conclude further, that the prototype of the military forces of the insurgency are the units developed under the leadership of Mao Tse-tung and Chu Teh in China in the 1930's, exploiting, of course, the Russian's political commissar technique. But behind both the front and the armed unit, for Mao as for Lenin, rules the party apparat, the child of the latter's fertile brain.

To presume that Mao simply struck out on his own, pursuing goals unrelated to those of his predecessors, is to fall victim to a concept of insurgency which grossly underestimates the political and social/psychological content of this phenomenon. Mao did not work in a vacuum. His own career in the late 1920's, and even more clearly, his early writings, clearly indicate his extensive reading of Lenin.[46]

Mao did not deal extensively in those aspects of the problem which Lenin analyzed, because he implicitly assumed that the readers of his own works would necessarily read Lenin as well. His task was to add to the theoretical framework already established, not to throw it aside in favor of an alternative scheme. And, of course, among Communists this interrelationship is perfectly understood even today. The writings of both men figure prominently in the schooling of the party novice in any of the many Communist training centers around the world.

It is equally important to understand that in assigning Mao a position as one among a number of party contributors to current Communist insurgency doctrine, one is not consequently downgrading the significance of the

[46]For example, his attack upon what he deems to call the "Li Li-san line" in chapter IV of his 1936 *Problems of Strategy in China's Revolutionary War* readily reveal his careful prior reading and reflection over Lenin's *Left-Wing Communism: An Infantile Deviation.* But this is to cite only one of many passages in his writings which indicate his dependence upon the body of thought evolved prior to his own effort. *Selected Military Writings of Mao Tse-tung* (Peking: Foreign Languages Press, 1963), pp. 96–100.

legacy associated with his name or disparaging the difficulties which confronted him in the actual activation and maintenance of the Communist's first major irregular peasant armies. This accomplishment is clearly of the highest order and shows Mao to have been an administrator and policymaker par excellence. However, to place him in this larger historical context is, indeed, to suggest that without the doctrinal background provided by Lenin and others, Mao could very well have failed at his effort in the late 1920's and the 1930's, despite his own innate talents.

The extreme importance of conceiving the development of Communist insurgency doctrine in this manner follows from the fact that to read Mao without due attention to the Bolshevik foundations from which he proceeded is to read him out of context and to over-concentrate on a single segment of a complex phenomenon, a danger against which Mao himself warned on many occasions.

APPENDIX B

REGULATIONS OF THE COMMUNIST PARTY AND COMMUNIST YOUTH ORGANIZATIONS IN SOUTH VIETNAM

Note. The materials in appendixes B through I were retyped verbatim from original translations which were of such poor printing quality that they could not be reproduced. The apparent errors and discrepancies were present in the original documents from which these were retyped. Information to identify the material and to permit cross-referencing was inserted at the beginning of each document. This information, including a document number, is enclosed in brackets.

[DOCUMENT B–1]
[CONSTITUTION OF THE VIETNAM LABOR PARTY]

PURPOSES AND PRINCIPLES

The Vietnam Labor Party is the Party of the workers and all laboring classes in Vietnam. Its purpose is to develop the people's democratic regime toward socialism in Vietnam, to bring freedom & happiness to the working class, the laborers and all other ethnic minorities living in this country.

The Vietnam Labor Party takes Marxism-Leninism-Stalinism coordinated with Mao Tse Tung's revolutionary ideas and the real situation in Vietnam as its foundation and guide in every action. It considers that the present revolution in Vietnam is a people's democratic revolution, aiming at driving aggressive imperialists out of the country, abolishing feudal remnants, distributing lands to the farmers, developing economy, politics and culture on a popular basis. It creates favorable conditions for a socialization of the country. At the present time, the main mission of the Revolution is to defeat the imperialist aggression.

To do the above, the Labor Party should have a National Reunification Front uniting the workers, farmers, laborers and intellectuals under the leadership of the working class. The Labor Party should have under its flag people of all walks of life, of all standards of living, all patriotic and progressive elements to strengthen the regime and develop the People's Army.

The Vietnam Labor Party recognizes that the Vietnamese Revolution is an "integral part of the world's movement for peace, democracy and socialism," under the leadership of the Soviet Union.

The Party is organized on the concept of democratic centralism. Its discipline is very strict for the purpose of maintaining within the Party a unity of thoughts and action, eliminating opportunist and partial tendencies from its ranks. Critique and self-criticism are used by the Party as means to correct mistakes of individuals and to make progress.

The Vietnam Labor Party considers service to the people as its line of action. Therefore, each member should maintain close contact with the people to timely and suitably solve the people's problems. Bureaucracy, isolationism, demagogy is not the Party's policy.

The Vietnam Labor Party recognizes its difficult mission, but it is confident in its bright future. All members should eagerly and courageously carry out the Party resolutions to bring the Revolution to success and thus, achieve the Party's purposes and goals.

CHAPTER I

MEMBERSHIP

Art. 1.—Every Vietnamese from 18 upward, without distinction of sex, and race, who recognizes the Party goals, policy and statutes, who works in one of the Party organizations, who complies with the Party's discipline, who pays monthly dues to the Party, is accepted as a member of the Party.

Art. 2.—Every member must:

a. Participate in the Party's activities, carry out its resolutions and policies introduce new members, develop the Party's influence, eliminate all ideas or actions harmful to the prestige of the Party.

b. Have close contact with the people, work in a mass organization, seek to understand people's aspirations and needs to help them solve the problems on time. [He should] heartily serve the people and educate them.

c. Be determined to fight for the defense of world peace, and independence and democracy of the country.

d. Set example in the carrying out of Party's resolutions, comply with the regulations of the government and people's revolutionary groups. Set [an] example in all revolutionary works, in labor and in the safeguard[ing] of public properties.

e. Learn to raise one's political consciousness and broaden one's knowledge by application of Marxism-Leninism-Stalinism and Mao Tse Tung ideas.

Art. 3.—Official Party members are entitled to:

—Discuss and vote in Party affairs.

—Be elected to Party executive organizations.

—Make suggestions, express opinion in every Party organ up to the National Congress of the Party.

—In Party meetings, criticize, query on the Party policy lines, criticize any member of any echelon in the Party.

Alternate members do not have [the] right to vote in Party Affairs, to run for election as said above, but are entitled to enjoy any other rights of an official member.

Art. 4.—[An] individual who would like to be a Party member:

a. Should submit an application to the Party Chapter in his area and give his background for the Chapter to consider.

b. Should be sponsored by 2 official Party members who guarantee on his background and guarantee that he deserves to be accepted.

c. Should be accepted by the Chapter meeting and thus approved by the higher level. This acception and approbation should be done by each one applicant.

d. Should go through a probationary period.

Art. 5.—Conditions of the sponsors, of the accepting unit and the probationary period should be fixed according to the social status of the applicant as follows:

a. Workers, poor farmers or poor people in the city should be sponsored by 2 official Party members with at least 6 months seniority, accepted by the Party Chapter meeting and approved by the next higher echelon of the Chapter. [Each] should go through a 6-month probationary period before becoming an official Party member.

b. Middle class farmers, petit bourgeois or intellectuals should be sponsored by official Party members with at least 1 year seniority, then accepted by the Party Chapter meeting and approved by the Chapter's next higher echelon. [Each] should go through a one-year probationary period before becoming an official Party member.

c. Persons not included in the social classes listed above should be sponsored by 2 official Party members with at least 2 years seniority, accepted by the Party Chapter meeting, approved by the City or Provincial Party Committee and should pass a 2 year probationary period before being accepted as an official Party member.

Remarks: a. The same is applied to revolutionary troops. Those with more than 3 years of service and whose social standing is in (b) category, shall enjoy conditions in (a); if their social standing is (c) category, they shall enjoy condition of admission in (b).

b. Troops with outstanding performances will have their probationary period shortened after their acceptance.

Art. 6.—Members of other parties desiring to adhere to the Labor Party:

A member whose social standing is in category A listed in Art. 5 (workers, poor farmers etc. . .) will enjoy conditions of admission in B, i.e. conditions set for middle class farmers, petit bourgeois, intellectuals etc. . .).

If his social standing is of Category B, he will enjoy conditions C (set for those not listed in A & B).

If his social standing is of Category C or if he is a leader of province-echelon in his own Party, he must have 2 members of the Labor Party having at least 3 years seniority to sponsor him. Approval will be made by the Labor Party Central Committee. Then he must pass 2 years as a probationary member before becoming an official member.

Art. 7.—The sponsor shall be responsible to the Party for the person [he] sponsors during the probationary period. The same is [true] for the approving agency.

Art. 8.—During his probationary period, the member shall learn the basic minimum notions about the policy lines of the Party, about its work procedures and its activities. The Party Chapter shall follow the development of his knowledge, his spirit, his attitude, and his progress.

Art. 9.—At the time he ceases to be a probationary member, the Party Chapter shall consider his becoming an official member. If he does not yet fulfill the conditions required, his probationary period could be extended or doubled. At the completion of this time, if he still does not satisfy the required conditions, he shall be definitely rejected. Decision of the Party Chapter to pass a member from a probationary to an official status should be approved by the Committee echelon (which had approved his admission before) to be valid.

Art. 10.—Any member who wishes to terminate his membership must send an official request to the Party Chapter and to the next higher echelon for approval.

Art. 11.—Seniority of a member in the Party shall count from the day he is accepted as an official Party member.

If during the time he loses contact with the Party, he continued to work for the revolution, his seniority still counts.

CHAPTER II

DEMOCRATIC CENTRALISM IN THE PARTY

Art. 12.—Democratic centralism is the principle organization of the Labor Party. This means:

a. The Guidance Committee of each echelon within the Party shall be elected. In case of extreme difficulty when echelon or vote cannot be made, the committee shall be appointed by higher echelons.

When a vote is carried out, official representatives shall have the right to present candidat[es] or introduce persons they trust for same.

b. Decisions in the Party meetings shall be based upon majority of votes. Before voting members are entitled to voice their own opinions.

c. Minority should yield to majority, lower echelons should comply with higher echelons, the whole Party shall obey the Central Committee.

Members who do not agree with any resolution made shall have the right to request a revision of same. Pending this, he should comply with [the] decision.

d. The Guidance Committee at each level shall have the right to solve problems within its own jurisdiction along with [passing on] the Party policy lines and principles and policy set up by the superiors. For important problems instructions for action from higher level should be requested.

e. Lower echelons should periodically report to higher echelons on local situations, policies and achievements. The same is done by the higher echelons to the lower ones. Lower levels are authorized to ask higher echelons to explain the points that are not understood.

CHAPTER III

PARTY ORGANIZATION

Art. 13.—The organization of the Party is based on the lowest production unit, working unit or administrative unit. New Party organizations should be approved, upon [their] organization, by the next higher echelon.

Art. 14.—From top to bottom, the Party is organized as follows:

—For the whole country, there is a Party national Congress and the Central Executive Committee.

—Each Region (or Inter-Region) has a Region or Inter-Region Congress and a Region or Inter-Region Executive Committee.

—Each Province or City has a Province or City Congress and a Province or City Executive Committee.

—Each District or Provincial Chief town has the same.

—Each village, or each enterprise (factory, mine, wharf, plantation, commercial firm etc. . . or school, office, block or houses) has the same organs: a Chapter convention or council and a Chapter Executive Committee.

Remarks: In areas of economic or political importance, a special area headquarters unit (Khu Bo) can be organized with its jurisdiction to be fixed by the Central Committee.

Art. 15.—The highest leading organ of the Party is the National Congress of representatives from throughout the country. The highest leading organ of each Region, Province, etc. . . is the Congress of representatives of each area.

Between 2 National Congresses, the highest leading organ of the Party is the Central Executive Committee.

Between 2 Regional Congresses, the highest organ to take care of current problems of the Region is the Region Executive Committee.

The same is applied for lower echelons.

At each national, regional or local Congress, there must be over one half of representatives present representing more than one half of party members.

Decisions taken by each echelon shall be approved by the higher one.

Art. 16.—When decision is to be made over an important problem or when it is necessary for the Party to go over a number of operations, or to complement a number of executive members etc. . . meetings can be convened (national, regional, provincial, city, district, village).

The meetings are only valid when over one half of the representatives are present.

Decisions made by the meeting shall need approval by the convening committee echelon.

Art. 17.—When it is necessary to disseminate a resolution or when a referendum is required for certain problems, the committee echelon concerned can convene a meeting of cadre.

Art. 18.—Committee echelons can establish sections and sub-sections to assist them. Composition, responsibilities and jurisdiction of these shall be fixed by the Committee echelon concerned, along the line of a resolution made by the Central Executive Committee.

Special sections can be established to work on special problems, but they shall be dissolved upon completion of mission.

CHAPTER IV

PARTY CHAPTER OR THE BASIC ORGAN OF THE PARTY

Art. 19.—In each village, enterprise, factory, mine, port, plantation, commercial firm, school, public office, agency or block of houses, with more than 3 party members, a Party Chapter shall be established. This Party Chapter should be approved by the next higher echelon. If there are only one or 2 members, they shall temporarily work with the existing nearby Chapter.

Art. 20.—The responsibilities of the Party Chapter are:

a. To carry out instructions or resolutions of higher echelons to propagandize on the policies of the Party and the Government, to lead the people toward the implementation of this policy.

b. To assign and control the work done by the members, accept new membership, collect monthly dues, and enforce discipline.

c. To discuss and participate in problems relating to the Party policy.

d. Periodically report the local situation to higher echelons.

Art. 21.—Any Party Chapter with less than 9 official Party members shall appoint a Secretary (and an Assistant Secretary if necessary) during a general meeting of the Chapter, to handle daily problems.

When there are 9 or more official Party members, a general meeting shall be held to elect a Chapter (Party) Committee of 3 to 7 persons to take charge of daily problems. This Committee shall appoint a Secretary (and an Assistant Secretary if necessary). The Secretary should have at least one year membership. The Committee is re-elected every 6 months.

Art. 22.—Party Chapter that have numerous members can spilt into cells according to nature of the operations or the geographical conditions. The cell leader works under the direction of the Chapter Committee.

Art. 23.—A general meeting of the Chapter should be held once every month to review the situation, check the operations, discuss instructions or resolutions made by the higher echelons and assign missions to Party members. The Secretary of the Chapter Committee or representative shall attend meetings of higher echelons, if any.

For important events, a particular meeting shall be held.

The Chapter Committee usually holds a meeting every other week to review the situation and set up plans for operations.

Art. 24.—In villages, enterprises or city blocks where there are too many members, several Chapters can be set up. Each enterprise or factory Chapter shall not exceed 70 members. Each village Chapter shall not have more than 50 members. These Chapters shall be under the direction of a Village or Enterprise Executive Committee.

Art. 25.—Village or Enterprise etc. . . Executive Committees are elected every 6 months by a general meeting.

The Secretary of the Village or Enterprise Committee should have at least 2 years of seniority in the Party.

Art. 26.—The responsibilities of the Village or Enterprise Committee are:

a. To carry out resolutions made by the general meeting of the representatives of the Party in the villages and to carry out instructions of higher echelons and in the meantime, to direct the operations of various Chapters.

b. To organize and supervise the activities within the jurisdiction of the village or enterprise.

c. To supervise the activities of the associations belonging to the Party or Group.

d. Assign the cadre, and manage Party financial problems within the village or enterprise.

Art. 27.—The village or Enterprise Executive Committee will hold periodical meetings once a month and submit quarterly reports to higher echelons on activities during the period.

The Current Affairs Committee meets every other week.

CHAPTER V

DISTRICT AND CITY COMMITTEE

Art. 28.—All Party Committees in a district or in a city shall form the District or City Party Committee.

Art. 29.—The highest organ in a district or city is the general meeting of representatives of this district or city. The General Meeting is convened by the District Committee or the City Committee once a year. In particular cases, the meeting can be convened earlier or later than scheduled, with the approval of the higher echelons.

Art. 30.—The responsibilities of the General Meeting are:

—To consider and approve reports made by the District Committee etc. . .

—To discuss and decide on military, political, economic, cultural problems within the district, the city etc. . . along the lines of the Party policy.

—To discuss problems set forth by the Provincial or City Committee.

—To vote a new District Committee and assign representatives to attend the Provincial General Meeting, if any.

Art. 31.—The District or City Committee is the highest working organ during the time between two general meetings.

Art. 32.—The responsibilities of the District Committee are:

—To carry out the resolutions made by the District General Meeting and instructions from higher echelons.

—To direct activities of Chapters.

—To organize and supervise Party activities within the district.

—Assign the cadre, manage financial problems.

Art. 33.—The District General meeting appoints a Current Affairs Committee, a Secretary and an Assistant Secretary to handle daily affairs.

The Secretary should have at least 3 years of seniority in the Party.

Art. 34.—The District General Meeting shall meet once every month. Every three months, the District Committee shall report to Party Committees within the District on the general situation and on he activities wtihin the District.

Reports to higher levels should be done periodically.

CHAPTER VI

PROVINCE AND CITY PARTY COMMITTEE

Art. 35.—All District and town committees in a province and all precinct Committees in a City make up a province or a city Committee of the Party.

Art. 36.—The highest organ of the Party in a province or city is the General Meeting of the Province or of the City.

The General Meeting of the province meets once every 18 months. In particular cases, the Meeting can be convened earlier or later than scheduled, with the approval of the Region or Inter-Region Committee.

If it is deemed necessary by the Province Committee or if over one half of the Representatives attending the previous meeting, or if over one half of the District Committees, Town Committees, etc., request that a meeting be held and that the request is approved by the Region or Inter-Region Committee, a general meeting shall be so convened. It can also be convened upon request of the Region or Inter-Region Committee alone.

For the meeting's decisions to be valid, there must be over one half of the representatives present and representing over one half of the Party members.

Art. 37.—The responsibilities of the Province or City Meeting are:

—To consider and approve the reports by former province or city committees.

—To discuss military, political, economical and cultural problems of the Party in the province.

—To discuss problems brought up by Region or Inter-Region Committees.

—To vote new committees for the province or city.

Art. 38.—The Province or City Committee is the highest organ to carry power between 2 General Meetings.

Members of the Province or City Committee must have at least 3 years of seniority in the Party.

Art. 39.—The responsibilities of the Province or City Committee are:

—To carry out the resolutions made by the General Meeting and by higher echelons.

—To direct the activities of district, town committees.

—To organize and direct Party operation within the province.

—Assign cadre etc. . .

Art. 40.—The Province Committee shall assign a Current Affairs Committee, a Secretary and an Assistant Secretary to handle current affairs. Secretaries must have at least 4 years of seniority.

Art. 41.—Meeting of the Province Committee shall be convened every 3 months. Every 6 months a report should be made on the situation within the province and sent to lower echelons for notification. Report to higher echelons should be periodically submitted.

CHAPTER VII

REGION OR INTER-REGION COMMITTEE

Art. 42.—All Province and City Committees in a Region or Inter-Region shall make a Regional or Zonal Party Chapter.

Art. 43.

Art. 44.

Art. 45.

Art. 46.

Art. 47* [are all concerned with General Meeting, Committee, Current Affairs Committee, Responsibilities of same, all are like organization of a Province General Meeting, Committee, Responsibilities etc. . . except the fact that the Secretary of a Region Committee of Current Affairs Committee must have at least 6 years of seniority, and that meeting of the Region Committee shall be convened once every 6 months].

* Article 48 was missing from the original sources.

CHAPTER VIII

THE PARTY CENTRAL ORGANIZATION

Art. 49.—The National Congress of Representatives is the Party's highest organ, and meets every three years. In particular cases, the Central Executive Committee can convene the Congress earlier or later than scheduled but it must so inform all echelons down to provinces.

The Executive Committee should inform the representatives on problems to be discussed at the Congress before they meet.

Upon request of more than one half of representatives who have attended the previous Congress or if it is deemed necessary by the Central Executive Committee, a special Congress can be then convened. The same is applied if there is request of more than one half of Region or Inter-Region Committees.

To be valid the Congress must be attended by more than one half of representatives, representing over one half of Party members and of Region or Inter-Region Committees.

Art. 50.—The responsibilities of the National Congress are:

—To consider and approve the reports made by the former Central Committee.

—To make decisions or to amend the Party statutes and regulations.

—To elect a new Central Executive Committee.

Art. 51.—The Central Committee is the highest organ to handle the affairs between two National Congresses. Alternate and official members of the Central Committee are appointed by the Congress. Alternate members have no voting rights. During its term, if an official member is missing, the Central Committee shall substitute an alternate.

Art. 52.—The responsibilities of the Central Committee are:

—To execute the Party regulations and carry out the resolutions of the National Congress.

—To lead the activities of the Region and Inter-Region Committees.

—To lead all activities of the Party throughout the country.

—To represent the Party in submitting to the Government, the National Assembly, the central organs of the National Reunification Front all suggestions and recommendations made by the Party.

—To represent the Party in its relations with other Parties.

—To make assignments of cadres throughout the nation.

—To manage financial problems of the Party.

Art. 53.—The Central Executive Committee shall appoint a Secretary General, a Politburo, a Secretariat and a Central Inspection Committee.

The Politburo is the organ to represent the Central Executive Committee, to direct all activities of the Party between 2 meetings of the

Committee. The Secretariat handles all current affairs along the lines of the resolutions made by the Central Committee and the Politburo. According to the requirements, the Central Committee may have various Central organs to direct the Party activities of distant localities. Jurisdictions, composition and work procedures of these central organs shall be fixed by the Central Committee [which shall notify] the localities concerned.

Art. 54.—The Central Committee shall meet every 6 months and shall report to Province echelons on the general situation and activities achieved by the Committee every 6 months.

CHAPTER IX

INSPECTION SECTION AT EACH ECHELON

Art. 55.—The Central Executive Committee, the Region, or Inter-Region Committees and the City, Province Committees shall appoint a few members each to form an Inspection Section at each echelon.

The responsibilities of the Inspection Section are:

—To check the attitude and work of the Party cadres, to fight bureaucracy and misuse of power.

—To check the application of democracy, to maintain discipline, to consider complaints made by the members pertaining to discipline at lower echelons.

—To check financial status of the Party.

—To inspect and control activities of lower echelons.

Art. 56.—Names of members taking part in the Province and City Inspection Sections should be approved by the Region Committees and in turn, those of the Region, Inspection Section should be approved by the Central Committee. Inspection Sections work under command of the Committee echelons and their recommendations should be approved by the Committee echelons to be valid.

CHAPTER X

PARTY GROUPS [Fractions]

Art. 57.—In Government agencies, in people's organizations and groups, the Party has also party groups to operate under assignment of Executive Committees of corresponding echelons.

Art. 58.—The responsibilities of those party groups are to implement the party policies and resolutions, to strengthen the Party's influence, to study and recommend operations to be practiced in the organizations in which the group operates.

Art. 59.—Party Groups shall work under the leadership of the respective Committee echelons. Through the introduction of the Committee echelons, the Party Groups of higher and lower echelons can establish contact for exchange of views and experience.

CHAPTER XI

REWARDS AND DISCIPLINE

Art. 60.—A reward and discipline system is established by the Party to strengthen the Party, to maintain order within the Party, to educate the members and the masses. Party discipline is iron discipline, all members are required to strictly comply.

Art. 61.—Good Party members who set example to others through their courage, devotion, initiatives, achievements, fulfillment of responsibilities in difficult circumstances etc. . . shall be rewarded.

Art. 62.—Party members who act in contradiction to Party lines, sow disunity and separation within the Party, desert their responsibilities, disclose Party secrets, embezzle funds, etc. . . shall be subjected to disciplinary action according to seriousness of the faults as follows:

—Warning within the Party, or before the masses, demotion, transfer, temporary or definite purge from the Party etc. . .

Art. 63.—The power to enforce discipline is as follows:

—Against a Party Committee: The warning and dissolution of a part or of the entire element shall be recommended by an immediate higher echelon and decided upon by the next higher echelon.

—Against a Committee member: The demotion or purge from the Party shall be recommended by a same echelon, decided upon by an immediate higher echelon and approved by the next higher echelon. The warning is made by the same echelon and decided upon the higher echelon.

—Against a simple Party member: Decision will be made by the Party Chapter. Purge is to be approved by the next higher level.

Art. 64.—Purge is the most serious disciplinary measure against a Party member. When this measure is enforced, careful consideration of the case should be given, and the victim should be given opportunity to explain his case.

Art. 65.—When a disciplinary measure is taken, reasons or motives should always be given. The victim should be given the right to make appeal to higher echelons. When appeal or complaint is received from a disciplined member, immediate consideration should be given.

Art. 66.—The duration of the purge from the Party shall not count in the seniority of this member within the Party. For members who are definitely purged, they shall be considered as new members if ever they are re-accepted into the Party.

CHAPTER XII

THE PARTY'S FINANCIAL BUDGET

Art. 67.—The Party budget is made up from the dues of members, and from voluntary contributions.

Art. 68.—Monthly dues should be based upon the member's salary or income. Rate shall be fixed by the Central Committee. Poor members shall be exempted.

Art. 69.—Collection from voluntary contributions should be approved by the Central Committee.

Art. 70.—Every month, each echelon should submit one third of their collections to the next higher echelon.

CHAPTER XIII

CHANGE OF THE PARTY REGULATIONS

Art. 71.—Only the National Congress is entitled to change the Party Regulations.

[Note: On 1 January 1962 a new set of regulations were issued redesignating the Labor Party the Vietnam People's Revolutionary Party and the Labor Youth Group the People's Revolutionary Youth Association. The text of the two documents are essentially the same with the addition in the more recent regulations of the following article concerning the Party's youth organization.]

Relations Between the Party and the Vietnamese People's Revolutionary Youth Association.

Article 34: The Vietnamese Popular Revolutionary Youth Association (VNPRYA) is the great reserve force of the Party. The mission of this group is to carry out propaganda and advance the political line of the Party.

The VNPRYA is placed under the command of the Party.

The Party organization at each echelon has under its command the VNPRYA at the same echelon, which at the same time is under the command of the VNPRYA organization at the next higher echelon.
The Party organizations at the various levels have the responsibility to lend assistance to the various organs of the VNPRYA in the following activities:

Organization of the VNPRYA;
Instruction in Party policy and rationale;
Creation of a spirit of solidarity between the masses and the VNPRYA;
Building and reinforcing of Party organs;
Support of the directing cadres of the VNPRYA.

Members of the VNPRYA who become members of the Party must submit their resignations from the VNPRYA unless they have been designated to a command or other special functions within the VNPRYA.

[DOCUMENT B–2]
[REGULATIONS OF THE VIETNAMESE PEOPLES REVOLUTIONARY YOUTH GROUP]

[With the January 1962 redesignation of the Vietnamese Labor Party to the People's Revolutionary Party, the regulations of the Labor Youth Group were similarly superseded by regulations issued in substantially the same form but under the designation of Vietnamese People's Revolutionary Youth Group.]

The VPRY is an advanced organization of the masses, a helping hand and a reserve of the People's Revolutionary Party. The Group includes the brave Youth who are faithful to the Liberation of the People and to Socialism and who volunteer to fight under the Party's flag for the reunification of the country and materialization of Socialism in Vietnam.

The VPRY is a Revolutionary School for the Youth. Its main mission is to combine the revolutionary struggle with the study of Marxism-Leninism. The Group forges the Youth into awakened men of the national revolution, democracy and Marxist-Leninism.

The VPRY will incessantly strive to study and develop the glorious traditions of the Party and continue the gallant struggle by their elders. The Group will help the Party carry out successfully the immediate missions: "Unite the entire People, overthrow the MY DIEM regime, liberate SVN from a Coalition Government, materialize Independence, Democracy, Freedom, improve the people's life, distribute land to the farmers, develop trade, industry and education, provide food and shelter for everybody, reunify the country and contribute to World Peace."

The Group requires of each member an effort in his own role of Vanguard and examplary element in all Revolutionary missions. All the members must show their determination to struggle against the enemy and to overcome any obstacle in carrying out the Party policy. The members must be the soldiers faithful to the Fatherland, to the Liberation of SVN, to Socialism, to the Party and ready to fight and to die for the country.

The VPRY reinforces the unity between the people of different creeds, religions, social strata to struggle against the partition of the Country, enslavement of the people, intoxication and oppression of people and US aggression, in order to achieve the National Revolution, reunify the country.

The VPRY will maintain close relations with the masses in all activities. Each member must be an intimate friend of the people. He must continue to learn for self improvement, to respond to the people's aspirations. At the same time, he must use his examplary actions and his knowledge to convince the people.

The VPRY is organized according to the principle of concentrated democracy [?] In all its activities, it must observe democracy, encourage criticism and autocriticism, especially criticism of the superiors by lower echelons. Each member must observe Discipline and develop the unity of will and action of the Group. Under the dictatorial and fascist regime of US Imperialism and its henchmen, the Group must beware of enemy cunning plots. For this reason, its organization must be "clean" and secret.

The VPRY advocates the maintenance of friendly relations with the youths of neighboring countries and all the peace-loving youth in the world. It supports all the struggles against Imperialism and Colonialism and has decided to struggle for World Peace.

The VPRY works under the leadership of the VN People's Revolution Party. The VPRY Executive Committees at different echelons are subordinates to the Party Committee of the same echelon and to the Group cadre of the next higher echelon. The VPRY member considers the membership of the VN People's Revolution Party as his greatest honor and strives to meet the requirements in order to join the Party.

CHAPTER I.

MEMBERSHIP.

Article 1. All Vietnamese Youth from 16 to 25 years of age who recognize the Group's regulations, volunteer to work in any Group organization, to carry out the Party resolutions and mission, observe Group's discipline and pay monthly fees, can become a Group member.

The members who are over 25 years old, or who have joined the VN People's Revolution Party, can no longer be Group members if they are not elected to the Executive Committee or do not assume specialized missions. At the request by the Group, some members may remain in the Group until the age of 27.

Article 2. Each member has following missions:

1. Study the policies of the Party and Front, study Marxism-Leninism and incessantly improve his political knowledge, thoughts and missions.

2. Carry out the instructions and resolutions of the Group, Observe Discipline, participate in Group activities, pay monthly fees, propagandize and recruit new members.

3. Be absolutely faithful to the Revolution, struggle determinedly and incessantly for the Revolution, forge his own morality, preserve secrecy, tighten the internal unity, honestly criticize self and the others, avoid any thoughts or acts which may harm the Revolution.

4. Maintain close relations with the masses, awaken the non-member youths, serve as cadre for the struggle for the People's and Youth's interests.

5. Attend military training, join the armed forces to fight against the enemy.

6. Practice sports and physical training.

7. Educate and help the children.

Article 3. Each member has following rights:

1. Elect and be elected to the leading organizations of the Group

2. Discuss and vote the affairs of the Group; criticize and question the cadre of other members who do not follow the Group policies and regulations.

3. Report and recommend the Group to help carry out his initiatives on political and cultural training.

4. Complain to the Central Executive Committee on disciplinary actions taken against him.

Article 4. Following procedures must be followed for membership application:

1. Members will be adhered [sic] one by one.

2. Applicants will submit an application and background data to the Group they wish to join.

3. Each applicant should be sponsored by 2 Group members or 1 member of VN People's Revolution Party. The sponsors will be responsible for their introduction.

4. The Group or Group Committee will consider the case of each applicant to accept or reject his membership.

5. The Vanguard Youths who reach the age limit and want to join the Group will be sponsored by their Vanguard Youth Platoon.

Article 5. The Group Members who move from one area to another should be introduced by [their] former Group in order to be authorized to operate in the new area.

Article 6. The Group members who lose contact with their Group but still maintain their activities, will have their service considered as uninterrupted.

Article 7. The Group members who wish to resign from the Group should give justification to the Group. The Platoon will consider the reignation and forward it to higher echelon for approval. Those members who do not participate in Group activities or pay monthly fees for 3 months without justification will be considered as withdrawing their membership.

CHAPTER II.

GROUP ORGANIZATION.

Article 8. The VPRY is organized according to the principle of Concentrated democracy[?]

—The Leading agency of each echelon will be elected by that echelon, except under [some] circumstances, when it will be appointed by higher echelons.

—The Group's organizations at all echelons will properly observe the principle of collective leadership.

—When discussing the Group activities, everybody is authorized to express his opinion. In the vote, the minority should follow the majority. In the execution of orders, lower echelons should obey higher echelons.

—The Group organizations and Group members should properly carry out the resolutions and instructions from higher echelons.

—The Executive Committee of each echelon is responsible for the reports to the Group meeting at that echelon and for the activities between the Meetings.

Article 9. In the areas under enemy control, the Group organization should be secret and compartmented.

Article 10. The Group organizations are based on the administrative, production or mission units in parallel with the unit organization of the Party. The Group organization in the Liberation Army is a Group element of separate regulations.

Article 11. The highest leading agency of each Group echelon is the Meeting of Representatives of that echelon, and the Executive Committee of that echelon between 2 meetings. The meeting of each echelon will be called by the Group Committee of that echelon.

Article 12. The Representatives attending the Meetings at different echelons will be elected by lower echelons (except some of them who will be appointed). The number of official and alternate representatives to the Meeting will be determined by the Group Committee according to the general regulations from higher echelons.

Article 13. Between 2 Meetings when an important problem arises, the Group Committee may call a special meeting to solve the problem. The Resolutions by the Representatives Meeting should be approved by the Executive Committee of that echelon in order to be valid.

Article 14. The Executive Committee at District echelon and higher will comprise [sic] a number of official and alternate members elected by the Representatives Meeting of that echelon. The alternate members can attend the Executive Committee meetings but they cannot vote. The alternate members will replace the official members when the latter are not available. When all the alternate members have been employed but vacancies by official members are still left, the Representatives Meeting will elect, or higher echelon will appoint, new members.

CHAPTER III.

ORGANIZATION OF CENTRAL GROUP INSTALLATION.

Article 15. The organization of Group installations is the active unit of Group, connecting the Group and its leading agency with the youth.

The Group uses the Village, city block, enterprise, school, public service, agency, liberation troop Company . . . as unit for its installations. At each installation 3 or more members will form 1 Platoon [?]. If many members are available, several Platoons will be formed and each Platoon of many members will be broken into several cells with the Leaders and Asst. Leaders appointed by the Platoon Executive Committee.

Article 16. Under necessary circumstances, a number of members will serve under the direct leadership of the Party.

Article 17. The permanent mission of Group installation organization is to:

1. Educate the members of the Party policy, on Marxism-Leninism, raise their degree of political awareness.

2. Lead and supervise the executive of missions assigned by the Party and Group.

3. Conduct critiques and self-criticism, consolidate the internal unity within the Group.

4. Perform the duty of Group development, members administration, collection of monthly fees.

5. Maintain relations with Party organizations and Group at higher echelons through periodic reports.

6. Maintain permanent contact with the youth outside the Group and with the masses installations.

7. Carry out the missions toward the children.

Article 18. The Executive Committee of the Platoon (known as Platoon Committee) will be elected by the members meeting or by the Representatives Meeting. The Executive Committees of installations (enterprises, city blocks, etc.,) will be elected by the Representatives at the Platoons Meeting. The term of each Executive Committee is 6 months. The number of Executive Committee members will be determined by the convention of members or their representatives, based on the general regulations and guidance of higher echelons. In case a democratic election cannot be held, the Executive Committees will be appointed by higher echelons.

Article 19. Each Platoon with 3 to 5 members will elect 1 secretary. Each Platoon with 5 to 7 members will elect 1 Secretary and 1 Asst. Secy. Each Platoon with 7 or more members will elect a Platoon Committee, a Secretary and an Assistant Secretary (if necessary).

Article 20. The Platoons will meet once a month. In enemy controlled areas, meetings of Representatives of Detachments will be organized by the Platoons while the Detachment members will meet once or twice a month.

Article 21. The installations with 2 or more Detachments will meet once every 6 months to elect a New Executive Committee and discuss future plans.

CHAPTER IV.

GROUP ORGANIZATION AT DISTRICTS AND TOWNS, PROVINCES AND CITIES, ZONE AND SPECIAL ZONES:

Article 22. The Representatives of Districts and Towns will meet once every 18 months and the Representatives of Provinces and Cities will meet once every 2 years.

Article 23. Authority and responsibility of Representatives Meetings at different echelons:

1. Examine and approve the report from the Executive Committee of their own echelon.
2. Discuss and determine the mission of their area.
3. Elect a new executive committee.
4. Elect Representatives to higher-echelon meetings (if any).

Article 24. The District and Town Group Committees will meet once every 3 or 4 months. The Province Group Committees will meet once every 6 or 9 months. When an important problem arises, a special meeting will be called.

The mission of Executive Committee at each echelon is to lead lower echelons in carrying out the missions assigned and to report to higher echelons.

Article 25. The meeting of above mentioned Group echelons will elect the Executive Committee, Secretary and Assistant Secretary.

CHAPTER V.

ORGANIZATION OF CENTRAL GROUP COMMITTEES.

Article 26. The Nation-wide Convention of Representatives will be called once every 4 years. The number of attending representatives will be determined by the Central Committee. The number of alternate and official members of the Central Executive Committee will be elected by the nation-wide Convention of Representatives.

Article 27. Authority and responsibility of the Nation-wide Convention of Representatives:

1. Examine and approve the activity reports from the Central Executive Committee.
2. Discuss and determine the policy and mission of the Group.
3. Modify the Group Regulations.
4. Elect the Central Executive Committee.

Article 28. Mission of Central Executive Committee:

—Carry out the policies and resolutions of the Party, lead the Group activities between 2 Conventions, carry out the resolutions by the Representatives at the nation-wide Convention, lead and supervise the Group activities at all echelons, determine the Group's monthly fees.

The Meeting of Central Executive Committee will elect a Current Affairs Section, 1 Secretary and 1 or 2 Assistant Secretaries. When need be, the Central Executive Committee can designate additional Executive members but the total should not exceed 1/4 of the members elected by the convention.

The Current Affairs Section will represent the Central Executive Committee in leading the Group activities between 2 meetings of the Central Executive Committee.

Article 29. When need be, the Central Executive Committee may call an unusual nation-wide Convention of Representatives. The nation-wide Convention of Representatives can elect additional executive members but the total should not exceed 1/3 of the members elected by the previous Convention.

CHAPTER VI.

GROUP ORGANIZATION IN SVN LIBERATION ARMY.

Article 30. The VPRY Organization in SVN Liberation Army is an element of the VPRY with specified organization and mission.

The VPRY's mission in the Liberation Army is part of the political mission by the Party.

Article 31. Wherever it may be, the VPRY organization in the Army must maintain contact with local Group organization.

Article 32. The VPRY is assigned by the Vietnam People's Revolution Party to organize, educate and lead the VN Vanguard Youths. Capable and experienced Group members will be selected to be in charge of the village children. The Group will coordinate the activities of all the branches concerned to carry out a general program of education for the children.

Article 33. The mission of the Group is to teach the children to love their country, the people, the Revolution, the workers; to hate the aggressors, the traitors, the oppressors; to beware of the enemy, to preserve secrecy, to be well disciplined, to be brave, honest and active. However, in the education, measure should be taken to develop the children's initiative.

Article 34. The Group should permanently educate the children to prepare them [to be] good members of the VPRY.

* * * * * * *

CHAPTER VIII.

AWARDS AND DISCIPLINE.

Article 35. The members, cadres or Group echelons who distinguish themselves with outstanding performances in the struggle for liberation of SVN will be cited and awarded.

Article 36. The cadres and members who commit errors will be friendily critized and helped to correct themselves. When errors are committed several times disciplinary action will be taken.

Article 37. Depending on the gravity and nature of the errors, following disciplinary actions will be taken: warning, demotion to a less important position, re-education or purge from the Group. The period of surveillance and re-education is 6 months. If necessary this period can be prolonged to 1 year. If no progress is obtained after this period, the faulty members will purged from the Group. During the period of re-education, the member cannot elect or be elected to the Group's leading organization and cannot sponsor new members.

Article 38. Authorities to take disciplinary measures:

—The warning to members are up to the Detachment meeting. The detention for re-education or purge from the Group will be decided by higher echelons.

CHAPTER IX.

FINANCES.

Article 39. The Group's finances come from the monthly fees paid by the members and from other receipts. The procedures of paying monthly fees are determined by the Central Group Committee. $2/3$ of the monthly fees collected will be sent to higher echelons. The members who have become members of the VN People Revolution Party but who still remain in the Group, will not have to pay the Group's monthly fees.

The Group's finances should be properly kept and employed in accordance with the financial regulations of the Party.

CHAPTER X.

CHANGE OF REGULATIONS.

Article 40. These Regulations are temporarily applied until the [next] Nation-Wide Convention of Representatives. Only this Convention can change these regulations.

[DOCUMENTS B-3]

REGULATIONS

SOUTH VIETNAM VANGUARD YOUTH

POLICY AND PURPOSE

CHAPTER I.

Article 1: The name of the organization is South Vietnam Vanguard Youth.

Article 2: The SVN Vanguard Youth is a reserve of the people's Revolutionary Youths, grouping all male and female advanced and patriotic youth in SVN, regardless of society class, creed, or religion with the purpose of:

1. Educating the youth to love their country, their people, the workers, their friends and at the same time to hate the US Imperialist Aggressors and the feudalist regime of NGO DINH DIEM.

Forging a noble Revolutionary morality for the youth.

2. Closing the unity ties between the youth within and without the organization for mutual aid in life, in the training and in the revolution.

3. Guiding the youth in their participation in the Revolution with actions appropriate to their capabilities for contribution to the Liberation of SVN.

As a reserve of the People's Revolutionary Youth, the Vanguard Youth is under its leadership and serves the same purpose as the Revolutionary Youth.

MEMBERSHIP

CHAPTER II.

Article 3: All advanced patriotic male and female youth from 12 to 15 years of age, without distinction of classes, creed or religion, accepting the program and regulations of the organization and observing its discipline will be admitted.

The applicant should be sponsored by 2 members or 1 Revolutionary Youth, or approved by the Village Section in charge of Youth.

Article 4: The members will:

—Carry out all the missions assigned by the Organization and by the People's Revolutionary Youth.

—Propagandize and recruit new members.

—Help the youth outside the organization and help the people in their daily works. Participate in the Revolution and serve as examples for other people.

—Oppose the denegerate culture of MY DIEM, participate in cultural, political training to build up a Revolutionary spirit.

—Preserve absolute secrecy for the revolution, for the organization, never disclose any information to the enemy, be always faithful to the revolution.

—Participate in the organization's activities, pay monthly fees.

Article 5: The members will enjoy following privileges:

—Attend the classes conducted by the organization.

—Elect and be elected to the Hq. of the platoons.

—Express personal opinions, discuss, and suggest all the activities of the organization. In the vote the minority should follow the majority.

—Criticize and question other members and the cadre in charge, with a constructive purpose.

—Receive help from the organization when they encounter difficulties.

—Read the documents and newspapers of the Organization.

—Participate in the entertainments conducted by the Organization.

ORGANIZATION

CHAPTER III.

Article 6. Villages and City blocks will be basic units for the organizations. The Vanguard Youth will be organized up to Platoon echelon only. In each Village, the People's Revolutionary Youth will have a Section in charge of Young Boys and Girls.

—The platoons will be organized in accordance with the concentrated and democratic principle [?]

—All the affairs will be democratically discussed.

—The opinion of all members will be the most decisive opinion.

The Platoon Hq will be elected by its own members and approved by the Section in charge of Young Boys and Girls. When an election is not possible, the Hq will be designated by the village People Revolutionary Youth.

Article 7. The Platoon Hq is responsible for guiding, inspecting, and supervising the detachments in their execution of resolution. Periodic reports will be submitted to the section in charge of Young Boys and Girls.

Article 8. Each Village or city block with 3 members or more will form a Platoon [?]. If many members are available, several Detachments [?] will be formed.

Article 9. The Hq of Detachments will be re-elected every 3 months.

The Hq of Platoons will be re-elected every 6 months.

Article 10. Depending on the members' strength, a Hq of 3 to 5 men will be elected, as follows:

—1 Leader

—2 Assistant Leaders

—Members.

CHAPTER IV.

RELATION BETWEEN PEOPLE'S REVOLUTION-YOUTH WITH THE VANGUARD YOUTH

Article 11. Each village and city block will have 1 Section in charge of Young Boys and Girls to guide their activities in the village. This section is responsible toward its Executive Committee on the Young Boys and Girls movement in the area.

Article 12. The Section in charge of Young Boys and Girls can participate in all meetings of the Platoon and approve or disapprove organization as well as their Plan.

AWARD AND DISCIPLINE

CHAPTER V.

Article 13. The members, cadres or Headquarters which distinguish themselves with outstanding performances will be worthily awarded. Awards will vary from Platoon Citation to award from District, Province etc...

Article 14. The numbers, cadres or Headquarters which do not carry out the resolutions, compromise secrets, or lower the prestige of the Revolution will be subject to disciplinary actions. Depending on the gravity of these violations, auto criticism, warnings or confinements up to purging from the organization will be applied.

The members who do not participate in the Organization activities for 3 times or do not pay monthly dues for 3 consecutive months will have their names crossed out from the personnel list.

Article 15. The Platoon Hq. is authorized to comment, analyze and recommend disciplinary action to be taken to the village Section in charge of Youth.

The Village section in charge of Youth is authorized to pass the disciplinary actions taken against the members.

The Village Youth Executive Committee is authorized to pass to disciplinary actions taken against the Platoon Hqs and their cadre.

To ensure its entity, its revolutionary nature and its growth the Vanguard Youth must have a severe discipline. Discipline is not designed to punish the members but to educate and improve them. Therefore, disciplinary actions will be taken only when other means are no longer effective.

FINANCES

CHAPTER VI.

Article 16. The financial source[s] of the Organization [are]:

—The monthly dues paid by the members. The members who

cannot afford to pay them will be excused for a determined period.

—Contributions from the members, from their parents and from the people.

—The members' production to increase the organization's funds.

The organization's funds will be employed for the activities of the Organization.

The receipts and expenditures of the Organization will be checked by the Hq. and reported to the members.

CHAPTER VII.

CHANGES OF REGULATIONS

The above Regulations can only be changed by the Meeting of representatives of Central Group Committee or Central Committee of the Peoples' Revolutionary Youth.

APPENDIX C

ADMISSION PROCEDURE AND SELF-CRITICISM OF COMMUNIST PARTY MEMBERS

[DOCUMENT C–1]

APPLICATION FOR ADMISSION INTO THE PARTY

I, the undersigned, L___ V___ T___ 32 years old.

After 2 years of assignment with my unit, there was no change in my ideology. I have enthusiastically performed all work assigned by high echelons and lived up to the Party policy lines. This advantage is a result of the education and assistance given to me by the Party Chapter and Chapter [Party] Committee. I have read the Party Regulations and its Essential lines of Action and realized that they answered by aspirations.

I realized that the Party combat policy is consistent with Marxism and Leninism which mean that we have to struggle for the proletarian class, eliminate the regime in which men exploit one another and specifically bring about realistic interests to the masses so that ploughmen would have land to cultivate.

I realized that the combat purposes of the Party are very comprehensive. At present, it is pursuing a National and Democratic Revolution. The people are fighting against Imperialists, Feudalists and landloards to liberate the nation, bring about Peace and Reunification to the Fatherland and build up Socialism and Communism.

Since this answered to my aspirations, I pledge that I will commit myself to fight until the end under the Party Flag to safeguard the Party achievements that had been gained so far. I only wish to serve the Party and never think of my own concerns.

This application is therefore submitted to the Party Chapter and Chapter [Party] Committee for consideration. I am hopeful that I would be soon admitted into the Party to fight side by side and under its Flag.

The applicant
L___ V___ T___
[Signed]

Biographical Data

Full name: L___ V___ T___
D & POB: 1932 in T___ B___ D___ Village
Residence: ___________
Family Social class: Poor farmer

Individual Social class:	Poor farmer
Date enlisted in the Army:	____________1962
Date admitted into the Party and group:	
Father:	L__ V__ C__ Occupation: Hired hand
Mother:	N__ T__ Occupation: Hired hand
Wife:	N__ D__ Occupation: Hired hand
Children:	A son and a daughter
Brothers and sisters:	3 brothers and 3 sisters. All the sisters are married—Occupation: Hired hands The 8th [Sic] brother is married—Occupation: Hired hand The youngest brother lives with my mother — Occupation: Hired hand.

Personal history from the age of 8 and past activities for the Revolution:

I went to school from the ages 8 to 10. I had to quit School because my family was too poor as it was exploited by the French imperialists and Feudalists. My parents could hardly support the family so I had to stay home to help my parents, take care of my younger brothers and sisters and do other works in the family.

When the Resistance broke out, I still worked as a hired laborer and lived with my family. Little by little I saw the social injustice and I joined the Revolution in 1950 as a village guerrilla. After the ceasefire and restoration of peace, I got married and lived with my mother and my youngest brother. I owned only one hectare of land issued by the Revolution during the 9-year [Resistance], and could only make enough money to support my mother.

When the Revolution broke the [RVN] control, in 1960 I joined the village guerrilla unit again and was captured and jailed by the enemy for 14 months but I did not disclose any [Revolutionary] installation. Upon my release, I resumed my mission with the approval of the [Party] Chapter. On ____________ 1962 I joined the army until this date.

Current [Economic] status of my family:

Presently, my family can hardly make a living but, it tries hard to contribute much to the Revolution.

Relatives working for the Revolution:

My elder brother participated in the Revolution in 1945. However, since his regroupment to NVN the family has not heard from him again.

Relatives working for the enemy:

Though my family lived in the unjust society of the French Imperialists, and is now living under American Imperialists, none of its members has been or is working for the enemy. Instead, they only serve the Revolution.

Strong and Weak points in the past:

Since my assignment to this unit, I always carried out satisfactorily all the missions assigned. However, in 1963 I once had a deficiency because I failed to preserve common property when I worked for a production [unit]. After a critique held by my company, I immediately corrected this deficiency.

I promise to avoid deficiencies and to properly carry out all missions.

Commendation and award:

In February 1964 I was once commended by my company.

Discipline:

I have never failed to observe discipline.

[DOCUMENT C–2]

RECOMMENDATION FOR ADMISSION INTO THE PARTY

[Party] Chapter B. C.

VIETNAM—LABOR PARTY

Investigation and recommendation for admission into the Party.

—We, the undersigned:

1. T__ C__:

—Date admitted as a probationary [Party] member: 1959

—Date admitted as an official [Party] member: 1960

—Member of [Party] Chapter C__, ____ Brigade. Family social class: Share cropper.

Individual social class: Share cropper.

2. N__ D__

—Date admitted as a probationary [Party] member: ________ 1961.

—Date admitted as an official [Party] member: ________ 1962.

—Member of Party Chapter C__ — E__ — F__ [TN: __Company—Regiment—__Division]

—Family social class: Poor farmer.

—Individual social class: Poor farmer.

During the time we worked, studied together and helped each other we saw that comrade L__ V__ T__ was really eager to be admitted into the Party. We had indoctrinated him and taught him all the criteria for admission into the Vietnam Labor Party. On that ground, we introduce comrade L__ V__ T__ to Chapter [Party] Committee and [Party] Chapter to examine his case and permit him to join the Vietnam Labor Party.

First sponsor: T__ C__
Second sponsor: N__ D__

Signed
T__ C__

Signed
N__ D__

OBSERVATION REPORT OF THE 2d CELL

The 2d Cell was composed of 3 Official [Party] members and 2 Probationary [Party] members. 1 Probationary [Party] Member was absent. The entire cell agreed to discuss the biographical data of Comrade T__. Seeing that the latter's biographical data was clear, the entire Cell forwarded it to the Chapter [Party] Committee and Party Chapter for consideration so that he would be soon admitted into the Party to better serve it and the people.

Comrade T__'s past weak and strong points:

Strong points: Ideology: Comrade T__ always felt assured and performed his mission in an enthusiastic manner. Specifically he had voiced no complaint when he was assigned to do farm work for a long period of time. Inversely he appeared to be assured and displayed a good sense of duty. He was fully aware of the revolutionary mission. He was also enthusiastic after his return to a combat unit. He always encouraged other members in the unit and assisted comrades lacking capability in production work and combat. Comrade T___ proved to be confident.

Missions: Comrade T___ always proved to be enthusiastic in his mission. Although he was not very qualified, he did his best to execute difficult tasks, providing quartering and messing and guiding various units. At times he submitted a report asking for the permission to perform combat mission before he had completely recovered from sickness. He had properly implemented the policy toward the people. In addition he assisted and indoctrinated the people in religious areas on the Party's policy, thus winning the sympathy of other comrades.

Indoctrination:

Comrade T___ received political indoctrination on the Party's policy lines with a highly enthusiastic spirit. He learned many things from more experienced comrades, read newspapers on a permanent basis, and studied the Party's regulations to broaden his knowledge of Marxism Leninism and improved the class viewpoint of his own.

Unity in struggle. Comrade T___ always promoted the spirit of criticism and self-criticism and bravely engaged in struggles.

Weak points—When he served in the production [unit] he failed to protect public properties and lost a number of items. He was subjected to criticism and later on did a good job [in the protection of public properties].

As regards internal struggle he would fight to the end anything which is unacceptable to him.

______________1964 For 2d Cell
Cell leader
N___ V___

(Page 2 of original text)

—Approved by the Chapter [Party] Committee on __________ 1964. Of 5 members of the Chapter [Party] Committee, 2 were absent.

—Agreed with the observation report of the _____ 2d Cell on the clear biographical data [of Comrade T].

—Chapter [Party] Committee recommends that Party Committee___ admit Subject to Vietnam people's Revolutionary Party.

For Chapter [Party] Committee

Signature

Secretary P___ N___

—Approved by the Party Chapter on ______________ 1964.

—Party Chapter members: 17

Official: 12

Probationary: 5
—Party Chapter Members present: 13
Official: 10
Probationary: 3

Unanimously approved the biographical data and observations of the 2d Cell and Chapter [Party] Committee.

It is recommended that Party Committee approve the admission of Comrade L__ C__ T__ into the Vietnam people's Revolutionary Party.

For Party Chapter
Signature
Secretary P__ N__

[DOCUMENT C–3]
SELF-CRITIQUE

1. Ideology: I am resolved to be loyal tothe Party, I am not afraid of the enemy, and will perform my mission with calmness.
2. Solidarity: I will follow the "three together": [eat together, work together and sleep together]. I have a good attitude toward others.
3. Performance of Mission: I have performed well all missions assigned to me by the cadre.
4. Discipline: I have not been subjected to any disciplinary measures.
5. Frugality: I have not wasted my money. Strong and weak points:

I am hot tempered and, I have sometimes offended others.

Signed: T__ V__ Reconnaissance agent—1st Battalion—Comment of unit:

None.

Self-Critique of comrade B__ V__:

1/ Strong points: Calm while performing missions.

2/ I have helped the people to set up their houses.

3/ I have been cooperative with comrades in the army and with the people.

1/ Weak points: I have been hot tempered while dealing with unit members.

2 Cadre's instructions have not been properly implemented at all times.

3/ Non-observance of discipline: Sometimes opened fire without authorization of the cadre.

SELF-CRITIQUE

1. Ideology: I have been resolute in my training, in performing my work, and in fighting.
2. Solidarity: I have been pleasant with everybody, I have carried out the "three together" daily [eat together, work together and sleep together].
3. Performance of mission: Good. I have overcome every difficulty to fulfill my duties.
4. Disciplinary measures: None. I have always complied with the cadre's orders.
5. Frugality: I have not wasted my money. Weak points:

A violent temper

Signed: N__ D__, Reconnaissance Agent—1st Battalion

The unit offers no additional critique.

2 DE'S SELF-CRITIQUE

During the recent period I have exhibited the following weak points as follows:

—One night I went out with D__ and H__ N__ to T.O District and spent the whole night there without the authorization of B cadre.

Discipline: I did not observe discipline: I spent one whole night out of the camp without authorization. This caused difficulty for the cadre who did not know where I was. I realize that as a liberation soldier, I am responsible for providing guidance to the people.

On the contrary, I have set a bad example which has affected the reputation of the revolution, the B2 [2d platoon], and the 120th Company, and has caused difficulty for the cadre. Therefore, I must correct my mistakes.

Thanks to the struggle of the B2 Platoon and the clearsighted leadership of the B2 cadre I realize that my acts did not comply with unit regulations and I recognize my weak points. In front of the B2 platoon and 120th Company I promise I will resolve to correct the above deficiencies so as to continue to improve myself and to exterminate the enemy.

[Signature]: B2 member
H__ D__
7 July 1965

SELF-CRITIQUE

Self-critique of comrade C__ during the period time he performed a first aid mission in the unit.

The critique is composed of 4 principal points as follows:

I. MORALE:

Devotion to duty, clear-cut beliefs concerning the enemy, and a firm standpoint concerning the class struggle.

II. SOLIDARITY:

He has been kind to unit members, to the people and is esteemed by the people, but his internal struggle is still weak.

III. DISCIPLINARY MEASURES:

None.

IV. PERFORMANCE OF MISSION:

Has resolved to do his best for the Party and the Unit

GENERAL CRITIQUE OF CELL II

I. STRONG POINTS:

—Good planning intended to lead the unit in accordance with Party policies.

—Good cooperation [among] Party, group and the people.

—Effort made to correct the deficiencies of the people and patience shown in training.

—Good ideology aimed toward the countering of lewdness and corruption.

—No race hatred.

—Efforts made to conduct propaganda and indoctrination of the people.

—Good training given to the rural people in counterespionage and preservation of secrecy.

—Efforts made toward the prevention of diseases and in sanitation activities.

—Good examples of unit leadership.

II. WEAK POINTS:

—Party members [have not yet] studied the 1965 military and political resolution or the party regulations.

No work assignments given to each individual party member to lead the group and the people.

Let us struggle for the people and for the Party.

SELF CRITIQUE OF C— C—

Ideology: He is afraid of death, tired of labor work, and has not carried out the Party resolutions. Is authoritarian towards sick soldiers.

—Attitude is escapist and balky when confronted with hardship and misery. Is contemptuous of women and religions.

Analysis: He has ruined the honor of the troops, violated the policy toward wounded soldiers, hindered the civilian prosylytizing plan, and has affected the Party policy toward women and religions.

Conclusion: Has a landlord and private property owner's ideology.

Acknowledgement: True statement.

Action taken:

He was given six lessons on class motivation, was instructed in twenty seven precepts, and in the ethics of a revolutionary medic and his attitudes toward various agencies.

Training attitude:

He has made efforts during his training and has displayed sincerity and receptivity.

5 April 1965
For 3d cell
BA TE

SELF CRITIQUE OF COMRADE HAI (2) MINH

Ideology: Balks at hardship, and displays escapist attitudes.

He has not carried out the resolutions of the party, is afraid of death, and is undisciplined.

He has missused trophies.

Has fired into the peoples' houses.

Analysis: He has not observed the rights of the people, or adhered to the civilian proselyting policies, thus causing a bad influence on the policy covering the treatment of wounded soldiers, and ultimately hindering the development of the army.

Conclusion: Imperialist and landlord's ideology.

Acknowledgement: True statement.

Action taken: He was given lessons on thirty seven precepts, the traditions of the revolutionary troops, and class motivation.

Training attitude: He has displayed willingness and has made efforts during the training.

5 April 1965
For 3d cell
BA TE

APPENDIX D

COMMUNIST-CONTROLLED MASS ORGANIZATIONS IN SOUTH VIETNAM

[Gist Translation] [DOCUMENT D-1]

REGULATIONS
of the
NATIONAL FRONT FOR LIBERATION OF SOUTH VIET NAM
[presented to the 2nd Congress of the NFLSVN]

Article 1: Designation: National Front for Liberation of South-Vietnam

Article 2: Policy, Purpose: To unite all classes of people, groups or individuals, regardless of political tendency and place of residence, with the purpose to:

—Liberate South-Vietnam from the ruling yoke of the American imperialists and the country sellers.

—Establish a national and democratic Coalition Government in the South-Vietnam, to realize Neutralism, then attain Unification of the country.

Article 3: Primary rules and system of organization.

(a). All political parties, leagues, religious groups, and individuals in favor of the NFLSVN [which have] made a vow to implement its program, are admitted into the appropriate echelons of the NFLSVN.

(b). At every echelon there is a Front Committee appointed by the members of the respective echelon.

(c). The Front Central Committee appoints a Board of Chairmen composed of: The Chairman, the Vice-Chairman and the Commissioner. This Board will appoint a Secretariat, composed of the Secretary General, the Deputy Secretary General and the Commissioner of the Secretariat.

The Front Committee at Village echelon up to Region echelon appoints a Current Affairs Section which then appoints a Permanent (Duty) Section.

(d). A Front Committee at any level may, when required, assign additional commissioners to the Committee provided a roster of the propective additional commissioners is approved in advance by the higher Front Committee.

(e). The Congress of Representatives of the National Front is the highest authority of the Front in SVN, and is the only authority qualified to prescribe or amend the NFLSVN policies and regulations and to appoint the Central Committee of the NFLSVN.

(f). Between two convocations of the Congress of Representatives, the Front Committee at each echelon is the highest authority to prescribe necessary policies and rules within its jurisdiction. The current Affairs Section disposes of all affairs between two conferences of the respective Front Committee.

Article 4: Terms and Regional Activities of the Front Committees of different echelons.

(a). The general assemblies of the National Front and Regional Fronts are convoked every 3 years. Conferences at province level are held every 18 months, and annually at district and village levels.

(b). Regional Meetings: of the Front Central Committee are held annually; meetings are held every 9 months at Region level, 6 months at the province level, and 3 months at the district and village levels.

(c). The purpose of regional meetings is to view the situation, and make plans for activities.

Article 5: Work method:

(a). Democratic discussions.

(b). Uniformity of work performance in compliance with resolutions made.

(c). Respect of the independence of subordinate organizations of the Front.

(d). Friendly critiques and self-critiques.

(e). Notes and Reports

(f). Appreciation/Award and Discipline.

Article 6: Amendment of the Regulations: Only the Congress of Representatives of the National Front has the right to make amendments to these Regulations.

These regulations were approved on 6 January 1964 by the 2nd Congress of Representatives of the Front for Liberation of South-Vietnam.

[DOCUMENT D-2]
LIBERATED LABOR ASSOCIATION'S PROGRAM & STATUTE

A. . . . . [Omitted] . . .
B. Liberated Labor Association's Statute:

CHAPTER I.

Article 1. The Liberated Labor Association, an organization including all laborers of both sexes regardless of their nationality, race or religion, is designed to:

—Help the laborers in their daily life, their struggle against oppressive and plundering acts, their daily movement of disputing and preserving their rights.

—Cooperate with other walks of life, associations and political and religious factions in the SVN National Liberation Front's fight to liberate the SVN from the oppressive yoke of the American Imperialism and its underling NGO DINH DIEM, and to organize a Democratic (United) People's Government with the purpose of improving the standard of life of the people of all walks of life, unifying the country, liberating the laborers and making the nation prosperous.

CHAPTER II.

MEMBERSHIP — MEMBERSHIP ORGANIZATION — MEMBER'S MISSIONS & RIGHTS:

Article 2. The following are accepted as members of the Association:

a. All poor laborers of both sexes from 16 years old and up, from various branches, professions including handicraftsmen, coolies etc., regardless of nationality, race or religion, who live in SVN, recognize the Association's programs and statutes, are willing to join it and operate according to its policy and objectives.

b. Each applicant must be introduced by a veteran member and his application must be approved by the Chapter's Executive Committee.

Article 3. Each member has the missions of:

a. Implementing all instructions and decisions of the association; actively propagandizing its programs and statutes in order to enlighten the laborers about people and classes and promote the united struggle against the enemy.

b. Recruiting new members.

c. Guiding the laborers' struggle . . . to preserve their daily, essential economical and political rights and meanwhile cooperating with other associations and walks of life in their struggle to preserve the people's rights and interests.

d. Participating in the activity of the Association's cell and paying membership fees.

e. Observing the counter-espionage and secrecy preservation to prevent the enemy spies' infiltration into the Association for its destruction; conducting investigations in order to unmask them.

g. Keeping his revolutionary spirit and manner firm, and his loyalty toward the people and the association.

Article 4. Every member has the right to:

a. Discuss and vote on the Association's activities.

b. Vote and/or run the elections for an Executive Committee of any echelon of the Association.

c. Criticize and/or question the association's policies during meetings as well as criticize any other members of the association of whatever echelons they may be.

d. Read the Association's books, papers or documents and be guided by the Association in the studying of these documents.

e. Be helped by the Association when he encounters difficulties in his daily life.

CHAPTER III.

The organization[al] principles and system of the Association and its working methods:

Article 5. The "Liberated Labor Association" is organized according to the "centralized democracy" principle.

a. Every member is given the right to discuss democratically and to decide unanimously on the basis of:

—Individuals must yield to the collectivity.
—The minority must yield to the majority.
—The low-echelons must obey the high echelons.
—The regional committees must obey the Central Committee.

b. The Head Agency of whatever echelon of the Association will be elected by its proper representatives' conference, except [that] in difficult circumstances which do not permit the organization to hold election such Agency will be appointed by higher echelons.

Article 6.

a. The "Liberated Labor Association" [is to take] a square, a business firm, a labor quarter of same profession, a working place or a village in a large plantation for organizing a unit of its installation designated as a "Chapter".

b. An "Executive Committee" of the Liberated Laborer Association will be founded at each of any major business firms, or large plantations or squares, where there are many laborers [or more than three chapters].

Article 7.

a. Members are gathered into 3-man cells. Each Cell is headed by a Cell-Leader who is elected and re-elected every 2 months by members.

b. A Chapter's Executive Committee is founded at any place where there are from 3 cells or more.

c. The "Executive Committee" of the Liberated Laborer Association at a business firm or plantation or square, which is elected by a conference of its own representatives, will be re-elected every year.

d. The "Executive Committee" of the Liberated Laborer Association at province capital or city will be re-elected every 18 months.

e. There is a "Central Executive Committee" of the Liberated Labor Association for the whole territory of SVN. This Committee is elected by a conference held by all representatives of the whole territory and is re-elected every 2 years.

Article 8.

a. The head Agency of each echelon has the mission of educating its members; guiding supervising and urging its subordinates in the implementation of the Association's assertions and decisions.

b. Moreover, it must report to higher echelons the Association's completed missions as well as inform its members of the same. It [has] full responsibility towards the masses and higher echelons.

CHAPTER IV.

FINANCES:

Article 9. Receipts

The financial sources of the Association [are]:

—Contributions made by its members. (Poor members are exempted).

—Support by laborers.

Article 10. Expenses:

a. The finances of the Association will be designed [sic] to the following expenses: purchasing of office supplies, publication of documents, establishment of class-rooms, relieving members who are victims of accidents.

b. Every month, the lower echelons must take out ⅓ of their monthly receipts to give to their higher echelons.

CHAPTER V.

COMMENDATIONS AND PUNISHMENTS:

Article 11. Any members or echelons, that obtain more feats [sic] in the implementation of missions assigned by the Association, will be commended.

Article 12. Any members, who do not observe the Association's directives or decisions or compromise the Association's secrecy, or fail to pay contributions during 3 consecutive months or do not take part in meetings or compromise the Association's honor, will be — depending on the character of the mistakes—either subjected to internal critiques and/or warnings, or expelled from the Association.

—Any echelons, which do not observe the Association directives and decisions, or act against the Association's decisions, will be either warned or dissolved.

CHAPTER VI.

MODIFICATION OF THIS STATUTE:

Article 13.

—This statute is to be temporarily put into application until a new statute is prescribed.

[DOCUMENT D-3]

BY-LAWS OF THE ASSOCIATION OF LIBERATED YOUTH OF SOUTH VIETNAM

Article 1. Name: Association of Liberated Youth of South Vietnam

Article 2. The ALYSVN joins together all the boys and girls, regardless of position, race or religion, to oppose the dictatorial, fascist yoke and war-like aggression of the US-DIEM, and to struggle for the legitimate rights of all youth.

Article 3. Admitted as members of the Association are these persons:

a. All boys and girls, regardless of position, race or religion, from 16 to 25 years old, who acknowledge the program and bylaws of the Association, and who volunteer to join the Association.

b. All the patriotic youth organizations, such as student associations of high schools and universities, etc., which strongly agree on the principles, goals, program and by-laws of the association and participation in activities under the guidance of the association.

Article 4. Admission Procedure:

a. For an individual—introduction by an old member and approval of the executive committee are required.

b. For an organization—it requires the approval of the executive committee.

Article 5. Duties.

1. Execution of policies and resolutions of the Association. Try to make propaganda to awaken the young people to their rights. Stay united with the other youths who are not members of the Association.

2. Make educational activities for young people and expand the recruitment of new members.

3. Guide the young people who are non-members and struggle with them to protect their essential rights.

4. Educate and take care of the young people and children.

5. Study hard and continuously to improve knowledge of politics and culture; to keep the morale high; to fight courageously; to enhance morality in order to become exemplary and progressive young people.

6. Participate in the association's activities and pay the fees regularly.

7. Keep secret the association's works, documents, policies and resolutions, in order to prevent the infiltration of informer-agents who would destroy the organization.

8. Keep up morale and revolutionary spirit, and unanimously and faithfully serve the nation and the association.

Article 6. Each member is entitled to:

1. Attend classes and share the activities of the association.

2. Vote and run the election of the executive committee at all echelons.

3. In all conferences, criticize and question policies of the association or any person of any position in the association.

4. Read the publications and documents of the association.

5. Receive protection and aid during difficult moments.

CHAPTER III—Organizational Principles

Article 7. Organizational Units: village, businesses, city quarters and school.

Article 8. Organizational principles:

a. Democratic centralization:

—All matters are discussed democratically.
—Opinion of majority of members will be decisive.
—The majority prevails over the minority.
—Inferiors must obey their superiors.
—Local echelons obey the central echelon.

b. Leading organs will be elected by members or representatives of that echelon except in the case of difficulty where the election could not be organized, then appointment will be made by higher authorities.

c. The working principle of the association consists of collective command and individual assignments.

Article 9. Organization System of the Association.

In each village, business enterprise, city quarter or school, a sub-agency will be established with at least three members. If there are many cells of three to five members in a hamlet, an agency will be established. Each cell will have a chief in charge.

When there are three sub-agencies in an area, an executive committee for inter-subagencies will be establishd. In a district where there are three sub-agencies or more, a district executive committee will be established.

Above the district executive committee is the provincial or city committee. At the higher echelon is the regional committee. The central executive committee will be the highest echelon.

Article 10. Terms of office for the executive committee:

a. For the cell echelon, election once every two months.

b. For sub-agency level, election once every four months.

c. For district, provincial or city level, once every six months.

d. For regional echelon, election once every year.

e. For the central committee, once every two years.

Article 11. Each executive committee having three or more commissioners will elect a current affairs commission to act on the daily business. Work distribution of the executive committee is as follows:

—One secretary in charge of propaganda, training and organization.

—One second secretary in charge of struggle and competition.

—One commissar in charge of young boys; if there are girls, a female representative will be appointed.

—One commissar in charge of financial matters.

—The rest of the commissars are in charge of cells or agencies.

CHAPTER IV—Finance.

Article 12. Financial resources of the association originate from:

—Monthly contribution fees of the members; exemption for a determined period will be granted to any member who is considered by the association as very poor and unable to afford to pay.

—Benevolent and voluntary contribution of the members to increase production and husbandry in order to build up the association funds.

—Each month one-third of the total money collected at the lower echelon will be given to the higher echelon.

Expenses:

—Financial resources of the association will bear the expenses regarding costs of printing documents used in classes and aid to needy or injured members.

—Credit and debit accounts must be audited by the executive committe and the community in the conferences.

CHAPTER V: Rewards and Discipline

Article 13. Any member have a good and brilliant record in the execution of directives or resolutions of the association or in the performance of assignments of struggling nature will be praised and rewarded.

Any member who did not carry out effectively the directives of the association, revealed the secrets, caused bad reputation, sowed internal dissension, did not pay the association fees for three months, or did not attend conferences three times will be warned and criticized accordingly, and eliminated for a certain period of time or permanently.

CHAPTER VI: Amendments of By-Laws

Article 14. These By-Laws are in force and take effect until such time as new regulations will come out for replacement.

[DOCUMENT D-4]

REGULATIONS FOR WOMEN'S LIBERATION ASSOCIATION OF SVN

Regulation 1—Name of Women Liberation Association of SVN.

Regulation 2—Policy lines and objectives.

Unite women of all classes without regard to religion, political party, age and political bias in order to:

A. resist all acts of oppression, exploitation, terrorism, killing and violation committed by MY DIEM and protect the essential interests of women.

B. Coordinate with the people to destroy the MY DIEM's arbitrary Regime, establish a Coalition Democratic Government in SVN, grant women equality of rights in every respect as the male sex and achieve freedom, peace and unification of the country.

Regulation 3—Enrolment conditions

All women without distinction of religion, political bias, aged from 16 and above are invited to join the W.L.A. of SVN provided they meet the following requirements:

A. Willingly accept the W.L.A.'s regulations.

B. Positively participate in struggle of whatever form to overthrow MY DIEM.

C. Hold good records

D. [Are] recommended by an official member and approved by the executive committee.

Regulation 4—Duties of members.

Members must:

A. Carry out the Association's policies

B. Disseminate the Association's Regulations with a view to recruiting more members.

C. Agitate women to participate in a struggle designed to protect women's interests.

D. Maintain mutual support with local women

E. Participate in activities and training sessions [of] the Association.

F. Support the Association financially by paying monthly dues.

G. Preserve secrecy, protect documents and the Association from enemy subversive activities.

H. Be loyal to the revolution and [have] courage to face all adverse conditions.

Regulation 5—Rights of members

Members have the right to

A. Participate in activities and training sessions given by the Association.

B. Discuss, criticize and vote on all matters raised by the Association.

C. Elect or stand as candidates for command positions in the Association.

D. Read books, newspapers and documents.

E. Receive protection when oppressed and help when meeting with critical situations.

Regulation 6—Organization.

1. Organizational System:

A. Organizational unit. The Association takes quarter, industry, town district, village as organizational units.

B. Organization. The basic organization is the "cell" which is headed by a cell leader.

C. Cadre committees. [they are] Responsible for establishing from 5 to 7 cells in a hamlet or area.

D. Executive committees at various echelons. Executive committees are available at hamlets, areas, districts, provinces and industries. Executive Committees are of course above cadre committees.

2. Organizational principles:

A. Cell. The cell leader is elected by cell members.

B. Cadre committee. [It is] composed of committee chief and a member appointed by the local Command Staff.

C. Executive Committee. Members are elected by cell representatives.

3. Term of office:

A. Cell leaders are elected every 3 months and hold meetings once a month.

B. Cadre committee members are elected every 3 mnoths.

C. Village and District Executive committee members are elected every 6 months.

D. Provincial Executive Committee members are elected every 1 year.

E. Western and Central Zone Executive Committee members are elected for 2 years.

4. Composition of an Executive Committee:

A. Village, quarter, and industry Executive Committees [are] composed of from 3 to 5 members.

—District and town Ex. Committee from 5 to 7 members.

—Provincial and City Ex. Committee from 7 to 9 members.

—Zone and Central Ex. Committee from 9 to 10 members.

Executive Committees composed of from 6 to 7 members [are] to appoint 3 of 5 men to the Permanent Affairs Section to solve the daily problems of the Association.

B. Composition of the Permanent Affairs Section:

—Chairman

—Vice-Chairman

—Clerk

—Propaganda and Training member
—Organization member
—Social Affairs member
—Censorship member
—Finance member etc.,

Regulation 7—Working procedures

A. Working procedures are purely democratic. All matters must be discussed and decided by Association's members.

The minority must obey the majority.

Local organizations must carry out the orders from Central Agency.

B. Command Staffs at all echelons apply the collective working principle.

Regulation 8—Dues and finance.

A. Dues are decided by Association members.

B. Income derives from daily and monthly dues and from production work.

C. The Association normally spends its income for the publication of documents, conduct of classes and assistance of members having an unexpected misfortune.

D. The income and expenses are properly checked by Commnad staffs and Association Members during periodic meetings.

2. Start a monetary contribution campaign among Association members if the need arises.

Regulation 9—Reward and Discipline.

A. Reward.

Members who perform distinguished service in the implementation of the Association's revolutions, introduce new members to the Association, induce women to participate in the political struggle against the enemy, are highly rewarded. Their meritorious achievements will be mentioned in training documents.

B. Discipline:

Members who fail to do their assigned work in an acceptable manner, and execute the Association's resolutions, disclose secrecy, lack fighting spirit, refuse to pay subscription fees for 3 months and miss 3 meetings without offering good reasons will be punished accordingly. They may be warned or expelled from Association.

Regulation 10—Change of regulations.

These regulations are to be applied until new regulations are introduced.

[DOCUMENT D-5]
SUMMARIZED PROGRAM AND REGULATIONS OF LIBERATED (*) FARMER ASSOCIATION OF SOUTH VIETNAM

PROGRAM

We, the farmers comprise over ninety percent of the Vietnamese population. We are the people who produce rice, foods and other material for industry. We feed (raise) our countrymen and we make our nation wealthy. Everyday, we sweat and work hard to transform marshes and waste lands into immense green rice fields and gardens.

It is we who create these rice fields and gardens, but we are deprived of our rightful possession since they fall in the imperialist and feudalist grasp.

We work hard, but must pay heavy farm taxes. We therefore lack food, clothing and medicine. In addition to this, we are oppressed by local authorities: heavy taxes, forced enlistment, forced labor, imprisonment, torture, concentration of people into "agrovilles", "land development centers", etc. . . .

Under the dictatorial and fascist yoke imposed by imperialist America and feudalist Ngo Dinh Diem, we are forced to a miserable life.

Revolution and struggle are within the farmer's traditions. Farmers have fought against French Imperialists, Japanese, feudalists and tyrants. From 1930, we have participated in meetings and demonstrations against heavy taxes, forced labor and oppression. Under the leadership of the workers and the vanguard revolutionary Party, that is the Indochinese Communist Party and at present the Viet Nam Labor Party, we have fought to overthrow the French and Japanese during the 1940 Southern Rebellion and gained victory during the glorious August Revolution. We have heroically conducted a war of resistance against the French during nine years.

The August Revolution supplied us with the following privileges: rights on the land, food, clothing, reduction of farm taxes, cancellation of old debts as well as temporary distribution of land to farmers. In NVN, the class of land owners has collapsed while farmers become the masters in their villages. Living conditions are being continuously improved.

In SVN, Imperialist America and feudalist Ngo Dinh Diem have instigated to [sic] divide our country and suppress rights we have paid for with our blood. Diem's Law No. 57 dealing with the so called agrarian reform deprives farmers of their land. Land owners and tyrants are tacitly authorized to extort us. American money is employed to force our brothers and sons to enlist in a fascist army equipped with American weapons and assigned to repress, plunder and oppress our people. We have only two ways opened to us: to be killed under the My Diem's yoke [My Diem—VC political term for American and South Vietnamese Governments] or to

(*) Or Liberation

stand and fight for the salvation of our families and country. We have no choice but to follow the second way, the revolutionary path.

Farmers and laborers:

Our farmers' aspiration is to be the owner of our own land. This is a righteous aspiration. This is clearly recorded in the regulations of the Indochinese Communist Party, later the Viet Nam Labor Party. "Land to the farmers" and "Distribution of land to farmers". Necessary action is taken to implement such a policy in NVN. This is the reason why farmers here are ready to fight under our Party's flag.

In SVN, we need to concentrate and direct our forces on Imperialist America, Ngo Dinh Diem's family, other lackeys, landowners and reactionary elements who cooperate with the puppet government in oppressing farmers. We have therefore to fight first for the following objectives: reduction of land taxes—maintenance of the right to hire land for farming—ownership regarding land previously occupied or cleared.

While fighting for the above primary rights, farmers should unite themselves with the other people to counter My Diem's oppression, terrorism, collection of taxes, community development program, economic monopolies, forced enlistment and forced labor, activation of agrovilles, Law No. 10–59 etc . . .

Laborers:

Unite, we are determined to struggle. Our strength and our life depend on this spirit of unity.

The objective of the Farmer Association is to gather our farmers and laborers and to lead them to fight against My Diem's oppression and terrorism as well as to obtain other privileges for farmers (land and other rights). The Farmer Association also advocates a close union with other social classes and revolutionary forces affiliated to the National Liberation Front of SVN, specifically with the workers, under the leadership of the Viet Nam Labor Party. It is determined to sweep out imperialist, feudalist and reactionary elements from SVN (Ngo Dinh Diem's family rule), to install a democratic government, to restore peace and unification, to distribute land to the farmers and to make them the real masters in their villages.

The Farmers Association will cooperate with any patriotic forces and organizations. It calls on individual soldiers in the SVN Army (most of them are sons or brothers of farmers) and the SVN civil servants who seek freedom and democracy and who want to side with us in our struggle to relieve our country from the imperialist domination. It will assist the rich farmers in working out appropriate solutions to their conflict about land with middle class and poor farmers. It welcomes patriotic landowners who are against My Diem, who willingly reduce farm taxes, observe the regulations on land hiring and respect the farmers' ownership.

Farmers and laborers:

The Liberated Farmer Association is truly a revolutionary organization of your own. Affiliate yourselves with the Association.

REGULATIONS
[SUMMARY]

I. DESIGNATION: "Liberated Farmer Association of . . . . . Village", abbreviated as "Farmer Association (NÔNG HÔI)".

II. PURPOSE: Its purpose is to unite poorest, poor and middle class farmers regardless of their race, religion, age and sex, to fight against My Diem, to defend daily privileges, to win independence, democracy, freedom, peace and reunification of the country and to give land, food and clothing to farmers.

III. CONDITIONS FOR ADMISSION: Poorest poor and middle class farmers, regardless of their race, religion, age and sex, over 16, will be admitted if they recognize the Regulations of the Association and volunteer to fight against My Diem for freedom, democracy and reunification of the country and for a betterment of the people's living conditions.

—If they eagerly fight to win and preserve farmers' rights and other daily privileges.

—If they are introduced by an old member, recommended by a Cell and approved by the Executive Committee of the Association.

IV. MEMBERS' RESPONSIBILITY AND AUTHORITY:

Responsibility: Individual members are responsible for the following:

1/ Carry out policies and resolutions set up by the Association, propagandize and indoctrinate villagers on farmers' rights and mutual assistance within the village.

2/ Indoctrinate farmers for affiliation to the Association.

3/ Provide necessary guidance to farmers in their struggle for daily privileges.

4/ Preserve secrecy of the operation of the Association and keep the Association's documents, policies and resolutions secret—Prevent informers and saboteurs from infiltrating into the association—Follow up and investigate undesirable elements with the Association for necessary action.

5/ Participate in the Association meetings, pay association fees and strive to build up Association funds.

Authority: Individual members are authorized [to do] the following:

1/ Take part in the Association activities and classes.

2/ Elect and run as a candidate to the Executive Committee of the Association.

3/ Have access to the association documents and publications.

4/ Be defended by the association when oppressed and assisted when meeting with difficulties in daily life.

V. ORGANIZATION AND WORKING PROCEDURES:

—Village (XA) is considered the lowest unit of the Association. A cell with a cell leader will be organized in every village counting 3 members.

—An Executive Committee will be elected for every 3 cells. The Executive Committee, composed of 7 members, will appoint a Permanent Committee of 3 members to take charge of the current affairs of the Association.

A group will be organized for every hamlet when the number of cells reaches 5 to 7. Groups will be ruled by a Cadre Section, to be appointed by Village Executive Committee.

Cell-leaders will be elected by cell members.

Village Executive Committee will be elected either by a general assembly of all the members in village or by the cell representatives.

Cells will meet once every 15 days and the cell leader is to be reelected every 2 months.

Collective working procedures are to be observed by cells and the Executive Committees. Decisions will be made through majority of votes and individuals will be responsible for the execution.

Assignment of the Executive Committee members will be based on the following missions: propaganda, indoctrination, leadership, conduct of political struggle, production, protection of villages, development of the Farmer Association.

VI. ASSOCIATION FEES AND FINANCE:

Funds of the Association will be formed by the Association fees to be paid by members and by the money the members will obtain from farming and animal husbandry. Poor members will be exempted from association fees. Donations will be accepted when necessary.

Association funds will be used in purchase of office supplies, publication of documents, organization of classes and aid to needy members.

Receipts and expenditures will be reviewed by the Executiv Committee in periodic meetings.

VII. AWARD AND DISCIPLINE:

Members who obtain outstanding performances in the execution of the orders, in proselyting for more affiliations to the association, in promoting unity among the people in hamlets and villages as well as in the struggle against the enemy will be commended. Their performances will serve as subjects for the training of other members if it [is deemed] necessary.

Critique, warning, temporary or permanent dismissal will be applied to members who fail in observing the decisions of the Association, who disclose secret affairs of the Association, who refuse to take part in the people's struggle, who fail in paying Association fees for a period of 3 consecutive months or who miss Association meetings for 3 times.

VIII. AMENDMENT OF REGULATIONS:

The present regulations will be temporarily applied until further publication of new regulations.

END

APPENDIX E

COMMUNIST PROPAGANDA AND TRAINING

[DOCUMENT E–1]

ORGANIZATION OF PROPAGANDA-INDOCTRINATION SECTIONS AT VARIOUS LEVELS

I. *DUTY OF PROPAGANDA-INDOCTRINATION SECTION.*

1. —Propaganda-Indoctrination Section is a technical section of the Party, [in charge] of following, consolidating, and submitting recommendations to [Party] committees on propaganda and indoctrination activity.

2.—The Propaganda-Indoctrination Section is responsible for propaganda, political and ideological indoctrination within the Party and for the masses, especially in these fields: Propaganda, motivation, political indoctrination, arts and culture, press, news and broadcasting agencies, counter[ing] enemy propaganda, ideology and culture, dissemination of propaganda and culture abroad.

3.—Based on its [Party] Committee policy, the Propaganda-Indoctrination Section higher echelon provides technical guidance to its subordinate Propaganda-Indoctrination Sections, agencies and [people's] associations.

4.—Form and guide the training of Propaganda Indoctrination cadre.

5.—Command its subordinate elements.

6.—In charge of various popular organizations such as: Cultural Association, Teachers' Association, Newsmen's Association.

II. *ORGANIZATION OF PROPAGANDA-INDOCTRINATION SECTIONS AT VARIOUS LEVELS.*

A. *Composition of Propaganda-Indoctrination Sections at various levels.*

1. *Propaganda-Indoctrination Sections at various levels consist of:*

—1 section chief: Party Committee, Current Affairs Committee member.

—1 or 2 assistants: (a comrade Party Committee member is more desirable)

—A number of Committee members (minimum 2, maximum 5)

2. *The Propaganda-Indoctrination Section is composed of sub-sections.*

The number of sub-sections of a Propaganda Indoctrination Section varies, depending on its level. The sub-section leader may or may not be a member of the section committee (uy vien Ban) [sic].

Under the sub-section is a desk led by a desk chief, or cell with a cell leader, and under desk is cell.

B. *Specific organization.*

—Propaganda Indoctrination Section COSVN.

I. *Propaganda sub-section.*

1. *Duty.*

—To study all propaganda tasks, and political and ideological motivation of the masses.

—To prepare general political documents.

—To study and research on information and dissemination to the press.

—To study and research on popular culture.

—To prepare training program and documents, and train cadre in propaganda, culture, press, publication.

2. *Organization:* The propaganda sub-section consists of

a. *Propaganda desk:* with its following cells:

—Study and training cell; in charge of studying substance and form of propaganda.

—Current event and policy [dissemination] cell at the same time in charge of the editing of popular news magazines.

—Cell in charge of countering enemy propaganda and culture.

—Publishing cell.

—Party masses propaganda cell.

b. *Masses cultural desk:* comprising these cells:

—Study and Training cell.

—Motion Picture and Preservation [sic] cell (and movies studio.

—Club and Library cell.

—Amateur and Popular Arts cell.

c. *Press desk:* (concurrent, Standing Committee of Newsmen's Association) comprising the following cells:

—Cell studying newspapers published in enemy controlled areas.

—Cell studying newspapers published in the liberated areas.

—Editing cell of "CO GIAI PHONG" (Liberation Flag Newspapers)

d. *Installations subordinate to Propaganda Sub-Section:*

—Tran Phu Printing House.

—Publication Organizations.

2. *Arts and Culture Sub-Section.*

1. *Duty:*

—To study and research on Arts (except amateur and popular arts)

—To compose and guide the composition of [cultural] shows.

—To publish Arts works and magazines.

—To supervise entertainment groups, (Liberation and High landers' [Groups])
—To train and direct the training of entertainment cadres.
—To supervise Arts Association.

2. *Organization:*
—Arts and Culture Sub-Section comprises these desks:

a. *Arts and Culture desk:*
—Literature Study Cell and the office of "Van Nghe Giai Phong" Magazine (Liberation Art and Culture).
—Ancient and modern music research and study cell.
—Drama and Opera Study Cell
—Theatre classes.
—Entertainment groups.

b. *Drawing desk.*
—Painting studio.
—Painting schools.

c. *Movies desk.*
—Composing and Explanatory Cell [sic]:
—Motion picture studio
—Film projection and dissemination cell.

d. *The office and the publishing house of Liberation Arts Newspapers.*

3. *Training sub-section.*

1. *Duty:*
—To study overall training tasks of the Party
—To prepare and publish training documents for cadre and Party members.
—To study dialectics.
—To supervise Party schools from the Region down to lower levels.

2. *Organization:* Training sub-section comprises the following cells:
—Cell [in charge of training] of the Cell Leaders at Region level.
Cell [in charge of training] of the Cell Leaders at Province and District level.
—Party member Indoctrination cell
—OJT cell, concurrently supervising the training of various branches and organizations.
—Cell publishing political and dialectic documents.

4. *Education sub-section.*

1. *Duty:*
—To study the overall task of education and culture.
—To compile educational program and materials.
—To train and supervise the training of educational cadres.
—To supervise Teachers' Association:

2. *Organization:* The Education sub-section comprises these desks:

a. General education desk.

—"Nursery school and kindergarten" cell.

—"Level I" cell.

—"Levels II and III" cell.

b. Popular education desk (To settle illiteracy and to improve the education in rural areas and various enterprises).

c. Desk of pedagogy (in charge of School of Pedagogy and related schools).

d. Enemy education study cell.

e. Education publishing house.

5. *Broadcasting station.*

—In charge of broadcasting

Organization. The broadcasting station consists of:

—Editing desk

—Technical desk

6. *News Agency.*

1. *Duty:* In charge of news agency operations, photography and commentaries.

2. *Organization:* The Liberation News Agency consists of:

—The editing desk.

—Photography and commentaries desk.

—Technical desk.

7. *Abroad [Foreign] Propaganda Sub-Section:*

1. *Duty:* in charge of disseminating propaganda and culture abroad.

2. *Organization:* The Abroad [Foreign] Propaganda sub-section consists of:

—Research and study all

—Press and Information cell.

—Office of foreign language newspapers (French and English versions) "MIEN NAM TRONG CHIEN DAU" (The Fighting South).

—International cultural liaison cell.

8. *TIEN PHONG Newspaper.*

It is a political organization of the Vietnamese People's Revolutionary Party.

The editing staff [Party] committee (Bien Uy) is the propaganda indoctrination section of the newspaper office comprising these cells:

—Current news and policy cell.

—"Rural area" cell.

—"City" cell.

—"Arts" cell.

9. *Nguyen Ai Quoc Southern School.*

—To train middle level cadres of COSVN, comprising 3 elements as follows:

Indoctrination, organization and management.

The Propaganda-Indoctrination Section has an office charged with management, and a combined studies cell.

Sub-sections have their own offices charged with administration.

Propaganda Indoctrination Section at the Region: comprising these sub-sections.

1. *Propaganda sub-section:*

1. *Duty:*

—Study propaganda task, political and ideological motivation of the people in the region.

—Study newspapers and publishing operations and popular culture.

—To prepare and issue general political documents within the region.

—To train and prepare training programs and documents for cultural cadre of district and villages.

—To counter enemy propaganda.

2. *Organization:* The Propaganda Sub-Section comprises the following desks.

a. *Newspaper and Propaganda desk.*

—Study and training cell.

—"Newspaper" cell (Regional newspaper not [to be] published, only supervise and consolidate local newspapers—except in Region III and V where there is the Party Newspaper annex office).

—"Counter enemy propaganda" cell

b. *"Popular culture" office.*

—Film projection cell.

—Club and library cell.

—"Amateur and popular arts" cell.

The preservation and publication task is given to the responsibility of one comrade. No separated organization is set up for this purpose.

2. *Information sub-section*: Is an annex office of Region News agency.

—To review province news bulletins.

Entertainment sub-section:

1. *Duty:*

—To study entertainment task in the Region.

—To guide the arrangement of [cultural] shows.

—To publish cultural magazines and works.

—To supervise the Region Entertainment group.
—To train Entertainment cadre.
—To assume Entertainment Association Chapters (Chi Hoi Van Nghe)

2. *Organization:* Comprising these cells.
   a. Literary composition cell ([issuing] the cultural magazine of the Region)
   b. Drawing cell
   c. Film and photographic cell.
   d. Regional Entertainment group.

4. *Training sub-section:*
   1. The training sub-section at Region level is led by Party members and consists of three technical cells.
   —Town and district level Party cell leader [training] cell.
   —Party members indoctrination cell.
   —OJT training cell, concurrently supervising the indoctrination of various Region branches and associations, providing guidance.
   —On the reading of and disseminating Party newspapers and documents sent from higher echelons.

5. *Region Party school*

[The Region Party School] is led by a Directorate consisting of the [Region] Party Committee members, chief of the Propaganda-Indoctrination as Director, and two assistants. In addition, there are three specialized teachers and for every 15 trainees there is a cell guiding cadre, alumni of the school. Party schools of Region I, II, III, and VI are specialized in training low level cadre. In Regions IV and V, and in COSVN, the training varies with the level of cadre the school is modified appropriately [for each course.]

6. *Education sub-section.*
   —To study and guide cultural indoctrination tasks within the Region.
   —To train teachers of level I, II, and educational cadres of provinces and districts.
   Organization; comprising these desks:
   —General education desk.
   —Popular education desk (also in charge of Region Farmers-Workers) advanced school)
   —Desk of pedagogy office (In charge of Region School of Pedagogy).

The Province Propaganda Indoctrination Section comprises the following sub-sections:

1. *Propaganda sub-section.*
   —Information and Press desk in charge of publishing "Prov-

ince Liberation" [newspaper] and of operating a news agency.

—"Study and training" desk

—"Popular culture" desk in charge of recreation center and film projection.

2. *Arts sub-section.*

—"Cultural study and composition" cell.

—Popular culture cell.

—Drawing and photographic cell.

—Entertainment group.

3. *Training sub-section:*

—Province training sub-section is assumed by Party members and 2 technical cells.

—Cell helping district cadres in providing refresher training for cell-leader.

—Party members indoctrination cell.

—Cell guiding the reading of various Party newspapers and documents from above and when possible, disseminating to Party chapters experiences drawn from operations at the village.

4. *The Province Party School* is led by a Directorate consisting of a [Province] Party Committee, Chief of Province Propaganda section as School Director, and two assistants. Those three comrades are also the main instructors. Besides, every 10 to 15 students are directed by a cadre previously indoctrinated on the training program documents and plan of the Province school.

5. *Education sub-section.*

—General [education] in charge of 2d level schools in the province.

—Popular education cell (also in charge of Province Farmers-Workers advanced schools).

—Cell of Pedagogy.

Region and Province printing facilities subordinate to Region and Province Propaganda-Indoctrination Sections.

The District Propaganda-Indoctrination section comprises a section leader, an assistant and a number of members and cadres responsible for propaganda, entertainment, education and training. No subsection is organized. In particular, there are:

a. Education organization desk in charge of [district] 1st level schools and of the training of Village educational cadres.

b. District training cell placed under the leadership of a District [Party] Committee member in charge of indoctrinating Party Members and, of reorganizing when necessary refresher courses for cell leaders, and at the same time of supervising the training of various branches and associations in the district.

6. *Village Propaganda Indoctrination Section.*

It is a specialized section of Village [Party] chapter (at the same time an government organization), comprising:

—1 Chapter [Party] committee current affairs committee member as chief of the Section.

—Information Propaganda [Sub] Section.

—Cultural [Sub] Section.

—Educational [Sub] Section.

One [Party] committee member is assigned by the village committee and chapter committee [sic] to undertake the training task.

Depending upon the size of the village and the number of Party members, some Party members are assigned to help indoctrinate [other] Party members, Labor Youth [Group] members, and sympathizers about to be admitted in the Party sent by higher echelons. They also help associations and branches train their members, militia members, guerrilla members, and messengers.

There is no Propaganda Indoctrination in hamlet, only:

—Hamlet Information-Propaganda sub-section.

—Hamlet Cultural sub-section.

—Hamlet Education sub-section.

The Information Propaganda sub-section consists of:

—Various Propaganda cells:

—Information, newspaper reading, radio listening cells.

—Club administration.

The Hamlet (Psywar) entertainment sub-section consists of:

—Popular culture groups.

—Entertainment groups.

Hamlet Education sub-section comprises:

—Popular education cell, in charge of anti-illiteracy groups.

—Hamlet students' parents association.

—1 cadre in charge of the management of general education 1st level schools.

NOTICE:

1. The Propaganda-Indoctrination Sections of Regions I, III, V, VI are also charged with the Indoctrination and Propaganda among ethnic minorities.

2. The Propaganda Indoctrination Section of Saigon—Gia Dinh [Special] Region and Propaganda Indoctrination sections of other cities have a different organization.

3. Propaganda and Indoctrination sections of villages, and Province may have some more cadre but their organization should be kept to the simplest.

4. As for the [RVN] controlled villages or in disputed areas, primary emphasis is placed upon propaganda and information.

5. Region and Province Party schools are dependent upon the Propaganda Indoctrination sections of Region or Province for training program and documents. Assignment of trainees and cadre is decided by corresponding [Party] committees.

1. *Working procedures of the section:*

—The working principle of the section is collectivism. The [Party] committee member when working within the section, is only one of its members and must follow its collective working procedures. However, when he takes a decision as a [Party] committee member, the Section must comply. The assistant Section Chief has some power but still is a member of the section[sic].

The section must regularly hold regimental activities. Depending upon the conditions, the section must meet together at least once a month. Minutes of the meeting should be sent to corresponding Party committee and to Propaganda and Indoctrination sections of higher echelon.

2. *Relationship between higher and lower Propaganda-Indoctrination sections.*

The Propaganda Indoctrination section of higher headquarters provides technical guidance to Propaganda Indoctrination section of lower headquarters corresponding [Party] committee for the performance of its duties, at the same time is technically responsible to the Propaganda-Indoctrination of higher echelon, so that it must report to the latter.

3. *Relationship of the Propaganda Indoctrination section with Propaganda Indoctrination of various branches (except Propaganda Indoctrination sections of the Armed Forces).*

—Provide technical guidance toward lower Propaganda Indoctrination sections.

4. *Relationship of Propaganda-Indoctrination section with Sub-Sections.*

The Propaganda-Indoctrination section directly supervises the Sub-Sections:

The Sub-Sections belonging to the higher Propaganda-Indoctrination sections do not have direct chain of command to the Sub-Section of lower Propaganda-Indoctrination section. All relationships must go through the Section. However, both sections must exchange their experiences permanently. [sic]

5. *Relationship between Propaganda Indoctrination sections of the Party* [*and*] *Propaganda-Indoctrination sections of the Army.*

Military Propaganda-Indoctrination sections exchange technical information with the Party Propaganda-Indoctrination [sections]. However to reflect the overall Propaganda and Indoctrination situation, . . . the Propaganda Indoctrination of the Army should report to the Propaganda Indoctrination of the Party. When carrying out Propaganda-Indoctrination activity among civilians, the Army should comply with policies and concepts of the Propaganda-Indoctrination section of the Party.

Regarding Province and District units, the Propaganda and Indoctrination of the Party provides technical guidance to the political section of Province and District Units.

The Propaganda and Indoctrination Section of the Party is responsible for Propaganda and Indoctrination activities within militia and guerrilla forces.

IV. *PRINCIPLES OF ORGANIZATION.*

To answer [requirements] of new situation and missions, the organizations of Propaganda-Indoctrination sections of all levels should follow these principles:

1. Compactness: A few men with much results.
2. Practicality: Assign personnel according to work load, counter perfunctoriness [sic].
3. Quality: Reinforcement of Province and villages [Propaganda and Indoctrination] machinery.
4. Cadre assignment: Concentration on most critical tasks.

V. *THE PROBLEM OF CADRE*

1. *Responsibility for training of cadre*

The Propaganda-Indoctrination of COSVN is responsible for the training of [Propaganda and Indoctrination] Section Chiefs, Assistants and Party Committee members of Region, Province and District as well as sub-section Chiefs and assistants [in] low and middle level cadre of COSVN.

The Region is responsible for training of Province and District Section and sub-section members, village chief and assistant.

The Province is responsible [for] training of district cadre, village section and village sub-section members.

The District helps province [authorities] in training and providing refresher courses to village cadre.

The village improves [sic] Propaganda-Indoctrination cadre [in] village and Hamlets.

2. *Administration of Propaganda-Indoctrination cadre:*

The assignment and administration of Propaganda-Indoctrination cadre must be directed by the [Party] committees. But Propaganda-Indoctrination sections of various levels must have an element to control these cadre in order to recommend to the corresponding [Party] committees corrective measures to reinforce weak areas.

3. *Employment of cadre:* The corresponding Party Committee has the authority to employ cadre [as deemed appropriate] within its jurisdiction, provided that essential cadre are not affected. When necessary [to move essential cadre] opinion of higher Propaganda-Indoctrination section may be requested.

[DOCUMENT E–2]

POLITICAL SELECTION AND IDEOLOGICAL INDOCTRINATION

[Extract From a Verbatim Transcript of an Interrogation Report]

SUBJECT: Lai Van Cu, an ethnic North Vietnamese who defected in November 1965 after five months in the South. The interrogation was conducted the same month. His stated military rank was Second Lieutenant in the People's Army of North Vietnam (PAVN).

Q. What do you study in military school?

A. In general you study a lot there. Technique, tactics, politics. Politics is the main topic. In military matters you learn a lot. Attack, defense, security, propaganda. About tactics, the usual ones, shooting, grenade throwing.

Q. What about relation between officers and men?

A. They are very equalitarian. Outside working hours, they are like friends. In working hours, the inferior have to execute the orders of the superior totally.

Q. Are there any cases of close friendship between officers and soldiers?

A. In general, it is quite common, to see officers and troops off duty together.

Q. Are there any cases of discord between officers and troops?

A. No, usually, they stress the unity between officers and troops.

Q. How do they choose candidates, for officer school or NCO school?

A. They must have good loyalty record, be in good health, about 5th grade in educational level, and aged between 18–25.

Q. Are there other conditions? What about military capability?

A. No, they just choose like that. You go to school and if you pass an exam and have good political understanding you become an officer. At the end of the class you have one exam. In politics. To see what is your political view. They follow you to watch your ordinary actions, what are your attitudes toward other people, your friends. Do you make all effort in your duty. About military ability, they examined you to see whether you are good in military tactics and technique. How is your command, your ability for organization. Based on all that they give you mark at the end of the year. Afterward, they give you degree. The top ones graduate second lieutenants, the ordinary ones aspiranes. Those who are weakest, or weak from a political standpoint graduate [as] sergeant majors.

Q. Take you case for example. What conditions should a candidate fulfill and how long should he be in the army before he can be sent to NCO school?

A. The requirement for NCO school is easier. It also based on good health and your class. If your record is good then you will be a candidate.

Q. Then for example, someone who is classified as petit bourgeoisie or intellectual would not be sent to school?

A. No, even middle peasants like myself is very rare. Most of the candidates belong to the poor peasantry. They are the main classes.

Q. How do they decide that you have a good record?

A. What do you mean?

Q. How does the government decide that you are loyal and have good and right political view and ideas?

A. They base their judgment on family records and your actions in study sessions and other activities. Are you active during study sessions? Do you work hard and not complain when given a difficult task?

Q. You mean they follow you a long time?

A. Yes. Right from the time you are at home. Afterward they keep checking on you while you are in school.

Q. What about before you go to school?

A. Before I went to school, I was stationed in a unit, [and] I was checked on. When they found that I was active, always volunteering, that I have good capability for observation and good military ability, they sent me to school.

Q. Are you a member of the Party?

A. Yes.

Q. When did you join?

A. In 1963

Q. That means after you joined the army?

A. Yes

Q. Do you have to learn about Marxism-Leninism when you join the Party?

A. I was taught about the books of Marx and Lenin.

Q. Did you read any of their books?

A. Yes I did but very few. I did not like to read. I learned only the rules.

Q. What are the books you are required to read?

A. None. But they recommended that you read Marxist books. However you are free to read or not, depending on the circumstances.

Q. What do you know about Marxism?

A. A little bit. Marx taught that he will bring peace and prosperity, a peaceful and equalitarian world. Everyone equal. To each according to his needs from each according to his abilities.

Q. What are the ways to get to that brave new world? Did they teach you that?

A. They taught me to believe in Marxism-Leninism. Then there would be general rise toward Communism. First socialism then communism. What people ought to follow is the materialization of the ideology. What a peasant should do, a city dweller should do, a worker should do.

Q. Do you think it is Vietnamese?

A. This is very difficult to say. As for me I think there are many points that [are] not compatible with Vietnamese society.

Q. What are the incompatible points?

A. Well there is private property. Even in the ranks of Party members there still is a lot of private property. They are still too concerned with their own interests.

Q. What about the leaders? And those who have many years in the Party? Do they have the same ideas about this brave new world? Or are they concerned with their own interests?

A. They still are, a lot. Nothing has changed.

Q. What about in the future? Do you think the idea will disappear?

A. In the long run I don't know, but in the short run it is hard to believe. One learns that to be a good Party member, one has to bear the difficulties and get happiness only after the people do. But one does not know what will be that future happiness, one only learns that, although there are many difficulties, there also is much glory. But I don't know what kind of glory it would be later. No one knows. It's just imagination.

Q. Do you know, when you were in the North, about the clash of ideology between the USSR and China? And what did the Party say about it?

A. It explained that the Soviet Union is revisionist, that it deviated from the true path of Marxist-Leninist. They are afraid of war and concentrate on peaceful competition. Following China means follow[ing] the right path.

Q. What is your own idea? Do you think it is true?

A. What do you mean? Oh you mean the part about revisionism don't you? This is an international affair, and I am in a lower position. I don't know much about it. I cannot say who's right and who's wrong.

Q. But what is your own idea about the whole things?

A. Well, the Soviet Union signed a treaty with the US and the treaty means peaceful coexistence and no war, only economic competition. But China remains determined to destroy imperialism. There is only one side, never two. That is a fact. We observed that there can be only one side in a country. If there are two, there will always be conflict and war.

[DOCUMENT E-3]

FUTURE PROPAGANDA AND INDOCTRINATION TASK IN TOWNS

I: *PROPER CONCEPT OF PROPAGANDA TASK:*

The revolution pertains to the people.

The people undertake the revolution only when they are assimilated with the revolutionary thought which has turned itself into an aspiration and action.

In order to have the people act in accordance with the Party policy lines, it is necessary to make them thoroughly understand the Party policy, lines, guide lines and revolutionary thoughts, to transform the Party resolution into the resolution of the Revolution and of the people. Therefore the propaganda and indoctrination task plays a very important role. It constitutes the most essential link and always leads the way in the revolutionary motivation.

The propaganda task involves political indoctrination and leadership of the people's ideology, struggle against reactionary ideologies, and the crushing of enemy propaganda which poisons the people's minds.

We are to form a proper concept of the role of propaganda and indoctrination task and place it in a proper position in order to overcome the shortcomings and difficulties in the administration of facilities and leadership of cadre in an effort to expeditiously step up propaganda activity to meet the new requirements of the current revolutionary movement.

II. *REQUIREMENTS AND CONTENTS OF FUTURE PROPAGANDA INDOCTRINATION TASK:*

The requirements of the future propaganda and indoctrination task are to:

—Help everyone properly evaluate the balance of friendly and enemy forces, correctly assess the present situation. This is a golden opportunity for everyone to make a special effort to expeditiously develop the forces and readily rise up as the occasion offers.

—Confirm the standpoint on the national salvation struggle. Resolutely, fight to the end to defeat the enemy, not be pessimistic or negligent, not be satisfied with a number of great successes, not shrink back before difficult situations, not be pacifistic and passive, not balk at hardships, difficulties and death and resolutely resist the enemy.

—Resolutely struggle fiercely with the enemy, never throw down weapons or lessen the struggle while the enemy still stands firm on his feet.

—Resolutely pursue a protracted struggle in spite of all difficulties. At the same time alertly struggle for opportunity and time to score big successes and defeat the enemy.

—Foster deep resentment against the imperialist [and] feudalists, enhance the awareness of the [working] class, never live in the same sky with the enemy. Motivate the determination to fight and defeat the enemy.

CONTENTS OF THE FUTURE PROPAGANDA:

Contents of the future propaganda and indoctrination:

—1. Properly evaluate the balance of friendly and enemy forces.

a. Enemy: Point out his weak points, his isolation and his inevitable failure in SVN.

In the world, he is attacked by the revolutionary movement from many sides. The peoples in the world, including the American people, are strongly protesting against the war of aggression and are fully supporting us. In SVN, the American imperialists and their lackeys suffered serious losses and are rapidly weakening. The RVNAF sustained a serious shortage of personnel. Their troops and government employees lost their morale. There was serious friction among the lackeys. The American imperialists were stuck tactically and found no way to get out, even though they do not consider giving in and are planning new plots in order to save themselves.

Friendly situation: Early this year, we gained on the enemy in several fields. The peasants and farmers rose up and liberated large rural areas. In the cities, the people, especially the workers, are decisively struggling against the Americans and their lackeys.

The situation turns out to be very advantageous. The enemy's new photo [sic] will cause us significant difficulties, but these difficulties will make us grow up. We should multiply our effort now more than ever. We should make our one day's work equal to 20 years of work.

We struggle for time and strive to gain significant victories resulting in a great change in the balance of forces. From gaining these advantages, we will step over to the final defeat of the American imperialists and lackeys.

Rapidly and timely develop our activities in all aspects: military, political, military proselytizing, people's force. Make the workers, farmers and laborers believe that we will defeat the Americans and we are determined to win.

—2. We should be resolved to fight in a prolonged and decisive war until we defeat the American imperialists and their lackeys.

The present resistance is the revolt of the South Vietnamese workers and farmers who struggle for their lands, food, clothing, democracy and independence.

The enemies of our people are the American imperialists, revenging feudalists and trading private owners. The feudalists cherish a violent sense of revenge. They serve the Americans and turn against the people in order to restore their political position and economic interests. They try to put their yoke back on the people's neck. The cruelty of their revenge is evidenced by the daily disemboweling of many people.

Therefore, the South Vietnamese will never obtain their food, clothing, lands and real freedom, so long as the American imperialists are not defeated and their lackeys not knocked down.

To fight our powerful and tricky enemy, we cannot consider to gain on him in a short time. We should consider a long fight, but we should struggle for time and grasp all opportunities in order to gain great victories in the days to come.

Denounce the crimes committed by the Americans and their lackeys by showing the people their oppressing and homicidal acts conducted in the cities and suburban areas. Thus we arouse strong hatred until the people are resolved to drive out the enemy.

—3. Make every effort and grasp all opportunities to accomplish the immediate missions to expand their aggressive war. They strive to gain a strong military position and political stability in SVN in order to maintain their control over the people.

They are trying their best to enlarge and fortify the Danang Air-Base, conduct more terrorist and oppressive actions and create more facist and dictatorial tricks.

The resistance will become more intense and require more sacrifices. We should overcome these acts, make our sacrifices to save the great victory.

We have fundamental advantages, thus we must make our efforts in carrying out the mission prescribed here below:

—Try one's best to annihilate the enemy. Determinedly raise a protest against conscription. Motivate the youths to join the army, build up the armed forces of town people. Push the military proselytizing forward to give support to the insurrection.

—Regularly and continuously push the political struggle forward on a large scale.

—Make financial contribution to the resistance.

—4. Each target:

Among the workers and laborers: develop worker's struggle achievements. Heighten their vanguard role and responsibility. Criticize the tendencies of coming to an agreement, depending on the rural area and waiting for the time. Unite with rural people, students, intellectuals and other patriotic forces for the formation of a large front against the Americans.

As to bourgeois and intellectuals: raise up one's determination to be against the Americans to the end for the slogan: independence, democracy, peace and neutralization. Overcome the ideology of being afraid of the Americans, balking at the length of time, and willing to come to an agreement. Spoil the political, cultural influence of French and American imperialists. Have confidence in the revolution and policies of the Front. Criticize the ideology of speculation, getting rich and enjoying happiness.

As to male and female youths, raise a protest against their way of living luxuriously and tendency of following the officers and tyrants to make much money.

Conduct counter-propaganda positively: Regularly follow up and propagandize the enemy. Timely detect their treacherous arguments. Take their daily realistic actions as proof to be shown to the people.

Organization of leading and form of propaganda.

To be really successful in conducting propaganda missions, it is necessary that the machinery be set up to help party committee echelons guiding propaganda missions at various echelons.

In District [Party] Committee, Chapter [Party], Committee, [Party] Civil Affairs Committee, there is one comrade in charge of propaganda, with the following mission:

—Help the party committee echelon conduct propaganda missions in his local area.

—Study the plan to help the party committee echelon unite various groups, the core of the propaganda indoctrination in each period so that it can be concentrated and largely published to the public.

—Give a direct guidance on special propaganda missions such as dissemination of leaflets, writing of slogans, use of press and cultural information.

—All Party members, Liberation Association members and people who are sympathetic toward the revolution should be propagandists.

—The Liberation cells are propaganda cells having the mission of:

—Verbally propagating the main substance of the leaflets, papers, magazines, information [bulletins], and disseminating the mission.

—Handing over papers and magazines, information and leaflets.

—Collecting short stories and happenings in the city which relate to the enemy crime, oppression and robbery; recording the opinion of the public.

In addition to the propaganda cell, it is necessary to organize the people working in collective places [in a position] to diffuse news and create public opinion in a prompt manner, such as:

In markets: In each market, a propaganda cell should be selected among the legal and capable middle-aged female agents to propagandize victories and spread out our influence.

In hairdressers', barbers', bicycle repairmen's shops, agents should be placed to assume this duty.

—In each classroom, each enterprise, a propaganda cell should be available and placed under the guidance of the school or enterprise party chapter.

—Motivate the rural people to go to market to diffuse news on victories and on the situation of the movement in rural area and in cities.

Propaganda vehicle:

In the city, the main propaganda vehicle is by mouth. Papers, magazines, and leaflets are to be disseminated only among Party members, people agent net-work, and at a predetermined rate.

To have a wide influence, propaganda should be made verbally and transmitted from mouth to mouth among the population.

Improve the mimeograph and lithograph unit. Each district should have a unit to print logs [by] means of agar-agar or glutinous rice paste. If possible, a lithograph unit should be organized.

Propaganda form:

a. Paper; Liberation Flag:

Objective of the paper: workers, labor people, small property owners, Vietnamese property owners, (the main objective is the workers and labor people). . . .

Disseminate the guideline and the policy of the revolution; motivate the masses to stand up and struggle in accordance with the Party lines.

Disseminate specific policies of the Front toward the various strata of society, towards troops and personnel of the puppet government.

Lay bare the true face of the American invaders and the traitorous lackeys. Accuse them of their plots and policies.

Unmask the reactionary parties and factions and isolate them.

Criticize the renovated political tendencies, uncommitted and unfinished agreements, or misconception such as balking at a protracted struggle and pursuing the American way of living.

Develop the people struggle achievements in time [sic].

—Refute the enemy themes of propaganda.

—Bring up slogans of momentary [sic] struggles.

—Ameliorate the core and shell of the paper [sic].

—Publish 1,000 copies a month.

—Print 6 pages, taking the contents [of] The Liberation Flag (Co giai phong) as reference [in which] local movements are reflected.

The following special articles are mentioned.

—Monthly letters
—Roundups
—Attacks against Americans
—Uprising of the urban people.

In addition, folk ballads, poems, and attacking paintings [cartoons] are added.

As [to] appearance, the papers should be clear, multicolored, legible, varied and well presented with different sized titles.

b. Information Bulletin [to be] published every week.

—It contains an editorial or an attacking article, brief world news and news concerning South Vietnam and provinces that reflect important events.

—It is well presented, divided into columns and impressed by titles.

c. Pamphlets covering combat short stories, poems, popular ballads and songs.

d. Butterfly-leaflets covering short slogans of our successful combat.

e. Accusations of Americans' and [their] henchmen's crimes.

f. Dissemination of various leaflets to denounce the enemy crimes, appeal to every level of people to struggle, float rafts, hang flags and release dogs.

g. Spread rumors, urging the people to denounce enemy crimes.

h. [Guide] the people to listen to our broadcast to be aware of current events and the general policy lines of the party. After that, the people will legally spread the news among the masses. Propaganda agents posted in public places such as: barber, tailor, bicycle repair and coffee-shops etc . . . should [encourage] broadcast listeners to [act upon the] propaganda.

i. [Hold] discussions to talk about current events.

k. Exhibit paintings that reflect the constructive work in NVN.

l. Conduct of propaganda sessions in which topics of the resistance are presented during holidays.

m. Regular and guerrilla units should keep a roster of people to be avenged.

Carefully organize unit for common celebrations, victory [and] jubilee ceremonies, traditional holidays and ceremony of motivation for the emulation and selection of outstanding individuals [sic].

[DOCUMENT E–4]
STUDY DOCUMENTS FOR RURAL PARTY MEMBERS OF THE LAO DONG [PEOPLES' REVOLUTIONARY] PARTY OF VIETNAM

Lesson I (two days).

Struggle to Defeat American Imperialism and the Clique of Lackeys Who Betray Their Country

1) *What Is Imperialism?*

Imperialism is a group of capitalists, dictatorial in nature, who occupy our territory, while their banks specialize in oppressing and enslaving the working class and the masses of our country and turn it into a colony. Whether it was the French who oppressed our country previously or the Americans who now are interfering in South Vietnam, both are reactionary imperialists.

2) *What Kind of Imperialism Is American Imperialism?*

American imperialism is the wealthiest, the leading, the most dangerous imperialism, the most combative. American imperialism at present is the enemy of the [Viet Nam?] masses, is the enemy of the masses of the world who love peace, is the enemy of all the peoples in colonial and semi-colonial countries.

3) *How Does American Imperialism Interfere in Our Country?*

Previously, in the Resistance War, American imperialism helped French imperialism to murder our people. After the Geneva Accords of 1954, American imperialism destroyed peace, ousted French imperialism, and established the authority of the clique of lackeys of Ngo dinh Diem, occupying South Vietnam and turning it into a new kind of colony and attacking our Army. From the beginning of 1960 to the present, the revolutionary movement has developed strongly in South Vietnam. American imperialism increasingly sought to help Diem to oppress our people. From November, Vietnam in a more significant and a clearer way than before. American imperialism established a military command in Saigon.

American imperialism brought many helicopters and units of the American Army to South Vietnam. The American Army directly ordered the Army of Diem to kill and burn the houses of our people, to establish strategic hamlets, to violate the women, to tear out the insides of our compatriots. American imperialism and its lackeys are the enemy of the people of Vietnam. Together with our people we will oppose it with determination and resolution and will defeat it.

4) *Why Should Our People Oppose American Imperialism And Its Lackeys with Determination?*

Reactionary American imperialism, relying on its lackey, Ngo dinh Diem, has interfered in South Vietnam, deliberately creating many difficulties and misfortunes for our people, but we were able to understand this threat. The people's revolutionary movement of South Vietnam resolutely struck back because:

a) Our people have our Party. The leadership of our Party follows the path of the correct policy of the people. Through thick and thin the Party has functionaries and members who positively and enthusiastically fight, give good example, and go all the way with our country. They understand the people.

b) The people are united in the National Front for the Liberation of South Vietnam. Our people enthusiastically love their country and are determined to oppose America. The Americans and Diem are increasingly cruel, so the patriotic soldiers in our Army and the members of the administration will show clearly their attitude and will fight alongside the people. The great united front against the U.S. and Diem will grow increasingly broad and strong. The clique of the U.S. and Diem will be increasingly isolated and will be overwhelmingly defeated. Up to now the imperialist clique has been losing, not because it has lacked weapons, but only because it lacked the support of the people.

c) Our people have armed forces which grow larger and stronger every day and consist of three kinds of troops: the people's guerrilla army [Dan Quan Du Kich], regional detachments [Bo Doi Dia Phuong], and main force detachments [Bo Doi Chu Luc]. Our armed forces are from the people, because it is the people who fight. Our forces have determination and understanding principally because they have a highly developed fighting spirit, are determined to sacrifice, to fight, and to die for their country.

d) Our people have a very firm base in socialist North Vietnam which is growing stronger every day. Our people are on the side of socialism, positively supporting the world revolutionary movement and also opposing America everywhere. Previously, our people defeated the French. Nowadays, our people are in a more advantageous position. The revolutionary movement is deepening its material base in a decisive way. It will overwhelmingly defeat American imperialism and its lackeys. American imperialism is dangerous and oppressive, but however strong it is, it will be defeated in China, in Korea, in Cuba. It is being defeated in Laos. American imperialism will be bogged down and overwhelmingly defeated in South Vietnam.

5) *What Must We Do to Defeat Reactionary Imperialism and Its Lackeys?*

a) Increase the unity of all the people. First of all is the unity of the workers and the working peasants. Preserve the patriotic officers, non-commissioned officers, and soldiers in the enemy army and administration so that they also will fight against America and Diem. Continue to attack the enemy in political matters.

b) Expand and build the armed forces of the revolution. Push forward the armed struggle to destroy the enemy forces everywhere. We must broaden the movement of the people's armed struggle and in this way save our country.

c) Expand and build our Party. Determined to stay close to the people, Party functionaries must be the vanguard, i.e., make the people believe in them, make the people respect them, make the people love them.

d) Hold fast to the motto of continuing, in adversity, to develop the defense forces, overwhelm the enemy, press onwards till victory is achieved, until the enemy is completely defeated.

6) *Why must We Continue to Develop the Supporting Forces?*

We must continue because American imperialism is the number one imperialism, determined to hold onto South Vietnam. The U.S. does not have enough strength to make us retreat, but we also do not yet have sufficient strength to overthrow them quickly. That is, our armed forces at present are not yet strong enough. We must build and expand the forces and strengthen the political struggle and the armed struggle. It is only after a long period of time that we will have a force sufficiently superior to the enemy that we will be able to defeat him. We must hold fast and be firm because the enemy is fighting and trying hard, following a plan to oppose our people. We must struggle long and hard and develop an increased number of functionaries from our Party and from our people and be ready to put up with adversity, in order to defeat the enemy.

The defense forces, especially in the political and armed struggle, must avoid wasting ammunition, must take the weapons of the enemy, must fight with the enemy. They must develop facilities to strengthen the revolutionary forces, must lead the people to unite in producing, in studying politics and culture, while struggling against the oppression and divisive maneuvers of the enemy, the destroyers of the life of the people. They must promote thrift as against waste resulting from corruption. After reoccupation of a town, they must develop all the forces of the whole Party, of the whole Army, of the whole people, in order to be able to fight harder. We depend on increasing the strength of the Party, the strength of the military units, the strength of the people—therefore, the capacity for a long-term struggle which will lead to victory.

7) *Why Must We Overthrow the Enemy in Stages?*

If we wish to overcome the enemy army over the long term, we must accomplish this by slow stages. If we wish to defeat the enemy completely, we must defeat the enemy by stages. We are determined to overcome the imperialists and feudalists. In view of all this and of bringing our country towards compact unity, at a time when we are fighting against the enemy, our leaders are gradually working towards this end. We also need to develop the revolutionary forces even more and then they will go on to defeat the enemy. By doing this our path will encounter only the problem of making the enemy surrender to our leaders. Our Party and people must positively increase their efforts to carry on all day, all month.

Summary. American imperialism and America's lackeys are very dangerous and wicked. But in the face of the intense political and armed struggle of the people and of the armed forces led by the Party, it is certain that they will be repelled and decisively defeated.

Lesson II (one and one-half days).

Properly Applying the Party's Strategy of Unity

1) *What Is a Strategic Policy?*

To defeat the enemy the Party must have a correct strategy and a strategic policy; that is, while having a program, it also must have a plan to implement it. Strategy is a program; that is, a common idea. That is the reason for the unity of all the people to defeat imperialism and defend national independence, to preserve the land for the peasants. A strategic policy is a strategem; that is, an orientation for the concrete task. Therefore, whatever we do for the unity of the people or however much we attack the enemy, whether we attack the enemy now or later in the course of defending independence and land of the peasants, whatever we do to show prudence, to show cleverness—proper leadership above all must have a strategy, while it has many strategems.

2) *Why Do We Need Unity with the Middle-Class Peasants?*

At present the Party is proposing a strategy of unity among the peasants; namely, the organic unity of the masses, of the rich, progressive, patriotic peasants fighting for their lands, establishing safe areas, trying to establish areas free of the lackeys of the U.S. and Diem.

3) *What Is the Strategy of Unity in the Countryside?*

We must unite the middle-class peasants because the middle class of the peasants are a major peasant force in the countryside. They are the main force of the army of the revolution. If we adopt a mistaken policy which the enemy can use to divide the class of the middle-level peasants, the revolution will encounter many difficulties and losses.

While working for unity of the middle-class peasants, our Party must know how to work with the poor peasants. The poor peasants are people who have no land or have little land throughout the year and who have to pay rent or pay off debts or share the proceeds of the landlords' fields, who suffer exploitation by the landlords. They suffer the most from exploitation. The Party must sympathize with them, for only in that way will the revolutionary struggle grow strong.

4) *What Must the Party Do to Work Among the Peasants?*

To work among the peasants, our Party functionaries must:

a) Truly have feelings of sympathy for the peasants, truly believe in their revolutionary capacity.

b) [Be] close to the peasants, teach and educate them so they will hold fast to the path of the policy of the Party.

c) Be completely concerned about the life of the peasants, give priority to the peasants in resolving their land problems.

d) Strengthen the various classes of peasant, positively become veterans in the struggle, bring peasant members into the mass organizations and introduce them into the Party.

5) *How Should Our Party Act Towards the Middle-Class Peasants?*

The middle peasants are people who have enough land to plant or those who have insufficient land or those who have a little more than enough. They are people who work to live or live off the proceeds of rent or work for rich peasants who exploit them. Middle-class peasants are also workers who suffer much oppression, who also are very revolutionary in outlook but, because they have little property in the form of land by themselves, they have difficuties. The Party must clearly perceive their numerical importance in order to pay sufficient attention to their education. Apart from the matter of working with the peasants, the Party must unite physically with the middle-class peasants.

The middle-class peasants are a very important force in the countryside. The poor peasants, according to the revolution, expect to improve their lives, to have land, that is, to become middle-class peasants. As the revolution advances, the forces of the middle-class peasants will grow. If we do not properly apply the policy of unity with the middle-class peasants, whether because of narrow-minded prejudice or violence or violation of their political interests and their land, this will leave the middle-class peasants lacking in revolutionary enthusiasm. The poor peasants, seeing this, will also be worried, because they want to follow the Party in order to have land, to have a water buffalo. But once they have land and a water buffalo, they will also have a narrow and indifferent outlook, so that they will not know how to follow along any particular path. Therefore, firm unity with the middle-class peasants is an extremely dangerous matter for the revolution. Some of our comrades mistakenly believe that the way to meet the needs of the poor peasants is to instill class consciousness, while violating the interests of and more or less attacking the middle-class peasants. In reality, whatever the conflict with the middle-class peasants, it is a conflict which affects all of the working peasants, causing confusion and uncertainty among all the peasants. That is the cause of divisions in our ranks, permitting the U.S. and Diem to take advantage of them to penetrate deeply, causing further and serious losses to the revolution.

6) *Why Must the Party Unite with the Rich Peasants?*

Rich peasants are those who take part in the principal work in the fields, but at the same time a large proportion of their time is spent in devising schemes to exploit the workers or get them into debt by loaning amounts of money at interest or by exploiting their opportunity to buy cheap and sell dear the produce of the fields and rice and engage in speculation. There are rich peasants who have the status of landlords. That is, they have a little land to rent out to tenants. Rich peasants are a reactionary group among the peasants, but they also have been exploited by the U.S. and Diem. A number of the rich peasants have children who go to meetings of people's organizations or serve in the revolutionary armed forces. There are a few rich peasants who are the lackeys of the U.S. and Diem, and these must be unmasked and warned, while most of the rich peasants are against the U.S. and against Diem. Therefore, our Party needs to unite with them in period of the struggle against imperialism and feudalism. If we to unite with the rich peasants, we must:

a) Consolidate the United bloc of middle-class and poor peasants firmly. Let the rich peasants see the strength of the revolution and they will follow the revolutionary path.
b) We must educate them politically so they will see clearly that following the revolution is glorious but if they follow the U.S. and Diem, the future is dark as night.
c) When it is necessary to struggle to halt the exploitation of the rich peasants, the struggle should be limited and held firmly within revolutionary bounds and proper methods of negotiation to seizing property of the rich peasant. We cannot let the rich peasants support the U.S. and Diem and oppose the revolution.

7) *Why Must the Party Distinguish Between Landlords?*

Classifying landlords means grouping landlords who have different characteristics. Having people truly independent is the object of the revolution. The direction of the revolution is to advance towards and spill over into all areas. But at present the U.S. and Diem, because of their extreme cruelty, are helping the revolutionary movement to grow stronger and deeper. Therefore, in the landlord class there are divisions emerging which are turning into groups which differ from each other. Regarding the number of groups participating in the resistance, these are patriotic and progressive elements. We must work with them. Regarding those who are not lackeys of the U.S. and Diem and also do not participate in the revolution, we are neutral. We cannot let them follow the U.S. and Diem. Regarding those landlords who are cruel and are lackeys of the U.S. and Diem, we will isolate them and seize their property.

Our Party has such a policy to concentrate all efforts on opposing the U.S. and Diem, to isolate the U.S. and Diem, in order to defeat them.

There are comrades who say: concerning the rich peasants, they are an exploiting class. Strike them hard and get land and cattle for the working peasants. This is not a proper way to think!

Our Party has the point of view of the working class. At present this point of view opposes the U.S. and Diem. If we misapply the policy, we will be abandoning the rich peasants and the patriotic and progressive landlords and those now on the side of the U.S. and Diem. If we do this, the enemy will benefit, it will create added difficulties and hardships for the struggle against the U.S. and Diem, and it will not advance the interests of the revolution.

8) *How Should We Apply Party Policy Among the Peasants?*

Party functionaries working in the country need to uphold the Party's policy on the unity of the peasants. This can only be done by applying the policies of the Party like the national front policy and the land policy, upholding the new policy of opposing the plots of the enemy to create divisions among the peasants. Each Party member and each class of people in the countryside should enthusiastically support the struggle against the U.S. and Diem.

Lesson III

Increasing the Power of the People; Strengthening The Political Struggle Against the Enemy

1) *What Does the Political Struggle Consist Of?*

The political struggle is the struggle of the people either directly or indirectly against the enemy. It shows the mood of the people, who act with spirit and work in the ranks of the enemy, using solid arguments to struggle against the enemy. The political struggle consists of all kinds of clever arguments brought out to achieve a proper understanding of the struggle by many people in the countryside and in the world. While participating in revolutionary activity, we work to make the U.S. fear world opinion. We don't dare act openly. The political struggle also consists of the struggle to enlighten the soldiers, officers, and patriotic members of the enemy administration to join with the people in opposing U.S. imperialist interference and in opposing its lackeys. The slogans of our campaign are: "Patriotic workers, peasants, soldiers, and officers in the southern army, unite in opposing the U.S. and Diem."

2) *How Is the Political Struggle Important?*

The political struggle has a very great importance. It is aimed at the most sensitive areas of the enemy; it strikes hard at the enemy administration. It forges the idea of unity and the revolutionary struggle for the people. It concentrates on the cruel, oppressive, terrorist actions of the enemy and protects the interests of the people every day. It creates favorable conditions for the armed struggle. While always opposing the enemy, it promotes thoughts of opposition in the ranks of the enemy.

3) *What Concepts Does the Political Struggle Apply?*

In guiding the political struggle we must hold fast to these principals: the struggle must have an idea, it must have the interests of the people in mind, it must have a purpose.

Having an idea means that we must have concrete ideas for the people. The Diem faction has the weakness of only going one way down one road. We need to lead the people to hold fast to the above principle in opposing those who have sold their country to the American imperialists, to oppose cruelty, oppression, and terror directed against the people. That is having an idea.

Having the interests of the people in mind in the political struggle, whether large or small, means we must consider carefully the objective interests of the people. We must follow the concrete situation and prepare realistic slogans. In the case of opposing the enemy's construction of strategic hamlets, we must hold fast to the matter of opposing forced labor, forced protection, opprose the movement of houses, oppose forcing the people to make heavy contributions, etc. Only when the struggle has a positive meaning will the people participate enthusiastically. Only with the enthusiastic participation of the people will we be victorious. When the struggle is victorious, only then will the people feel enthusiastic. Only when the movement is growing broader and stronger every day will the political objective be achieved.

Having a purpose means we must calculate our power and the enemy's power, we must calculate the level of awareness of the people in place and time concretely and prepare realistic slogans and determine the form and pattern of the struggle appropriately. At times the struggle will go in favor of our side, and at times in favor of the enemy. By supporting these slogans we help to achieve victory and maintain morale in the ranks of our struggle.

4) *How Do the Needs of the Political Struggle Vary?*

Our countryside has many areas which differ significantly from each other in the way the people react to the struggle. They also have different composition and needs. The above, which could be said of any area, also needs to be used as the basis for considering the situation of our enemy—his physical condition, the political struggle, the military campaign in terms of the armed struggle.

The enemy zone is shrinking, so the enemy continues to oppress the people. The struggle is moving from a lower level to a higher one.

The enemy zone is establishing strategic hamlets, so we have to urge the people to be determined to stand up, to oppose and destroy the strategic hamlets of the enemy. We must stick close to the people, lead the people in the armed struggle. When the strategic hamlets are destroyed, we must prevent the enemy from rebuilding them. If he rebuilds them, we must destroy them again.

When the enemy is in an area controlled by us, we oppose him by force, but we also plan the legal struggle for a portion of the people in order to be able to stick close to the enemy, to wage a clever, political struggle againts enemy terror.

5) *Why Must We Conserve the People's Strength?*

The political struggle of our people at present cannot end with just one battle but must involve a prolonged political struggle. Since we favor a long political struggle, the Party must conserve the strength of the people, both spiritually and materially. We must:

a) Build among the people feelings of mutual love and affection, of protecting and helping each other, or believing in each other. This is a very important matter. We must absolutely oppose enemy plots to provoke dissension or division among the people.

b) Regularly promote feelings of bitterness and hate of the U.S. and Diem. We must make the people determined to avenge their village, their country, their family, not to fear the enemy.

Lesson IV

Promote Development of the Armed Forces To Strengthen the Armed Struggle

1) *Why Is It Necessary to Strengthen the Armed Struggle?*

We need to strengthen the armed struggle to accelerate the destruction of the enemy, to weaken and disintegrate the Army of the U.S. and Diem, which is the basic strength of the enemy, to defeat the enemy completely. The strengthening of the armed struggle leads to strengthening the political struggle. The strengthening of the armed struggle strengthens the effort to produce results. The strengthening of the armed struggle strengthens the confidence of the people in the long-term struggle against the U.S. and Diem. The strengthening of the armed struggle, together with the political struggle, is the only way to oppose and destroy their scheme to build strategic hamlets, is the only way to make all levels of the population believe in and be enthusiastic about the revolution and the only way to broaden the National Front for the Liberation of South Vietnam. The strengthening of the armed struggle will protect the revolutionary victories which our people have achieved, will protect the already liberated areas.

2) *How Shall We Strengthen the Armed Struggle?*

To strengthen the armed struggle we must:

a) Mobilize feelings of deep hatred against American imperialist interference and the activities of its lackeys, who are provoking a merciless war, feelings which will make our Army and people determined to struggle to save our country.

b) Mobilize the entire people in arms to wage the political struggle and the armed struggle effectively to protect their own lives. In the hamlets, fields, and plots of land we must make people participate in the political struggle at the same time they become effective guerrilla fighters. We must turn a hamlet into a fortress against the aggressors. We must organize and build the struggle on a broad basis on the foundation of the people as the followers and Party figures as the leaders.

c) Positively build the armed forces, concentrating on the regional and main force detachments. We must make the regional and main force units hold firmly to the policies of the Party, have a high combative spirit, know how to fight well and work with the people and be ready to produce well.

d) Promote the people's movement to love and respect and help the revolutionary armed forces, to promote mutual understanding between the people and the army. In order to assist the armed forces in a practical way, we need a people's emulation campaign to contribute to and support the army, an emulation campaign to provide transport service and to train the children to be ready to accompany the army.

e) Improve the leadership of the Party in the armed forces, that is, make the revolutionary armed forces hold firmly to the line and policies of the Party. Firm unity with the people, determination to fight and to win, leadership of the guerrilla movement to build combat villages—these are the roles of the Party cell, and, therefore, the Party cell must pay full attention to it, and Party members must have a feeling of high responsibility for their task. Party members and youth corps members must positively participate in the armed forces, must be the vanguard elements in the struggle to save our country.

3) *In Leading the Armed Forces, What Needs Emphasis?*

In building the armed forces, the Party must hold firm to the matters of supporting the army, teaching the army, and using the army.

In supporting the army well we must emphasize the living conditions of the soldiers, we must organize well the matters of providing food, drink, rest, and medical care.

In teaching the army well we must teach political affairs well, teach culture well, teach military technique well. We must encourage the military leaders to provide enough military training, in order to build the revolutionary armed forces, and to study political affairs, culture, and technical matters. They must do this for the people, for the revolution; study, be determined to study, to avenge one's home, to pay one's debt to the fatherland.

In using the army properly, first of all we must go into the matters of nourishing the army properly and teaching the army properly. The soldiers are strong, they are politically aware, and they have specialized capabilities, so that they can only be used properly when fighting the enemy. We must positively strengthen the leading elements of the Army, as follows:

a) A skillful leader must be loyal without limit to the Party and the people.
b) A skillful leader must exercise control over the patriotic fighters.
c) A skillful leader must know how to investigate the sources of information on the enemy situation, must be an expert on the battlefield, must hold firmly to the principles of guerrilla technique, must strike in small units decisively and quickly, must make decisions quickly.

4) *How Should the Struggle Be Conducted on Enemy Ground?*......

South Vietnam has many areas where our situation differs very much from that of the enemy. In the region where the enemy is strong and we are weak, as in the cities, villages, and towns, land development centers, plantations supervised by the enemy, etc., the most essential thing is the political struggle of strengthening the life of the people, but we also need to have appropriate armed activity to wipe out the oppressors and to build the struggle among the people, not leaving the future to be settled peacefully.

The enemy zone is constructing strategic hamlets, so armed activity should simultaneously be strong in order to protect the people against the strategic hamlets and to prevent the enemy from concentrating his forces to mistreat the people.

5) *How Did the Struggle in the People's Zone Succeed?*

The people's zone which has already been liberated must positively build armed forces and develop combat villages broadly. The armed struggle and building combat villages in the people's zone must be strengthened, but we still must leave a portion of the people able to preserve legal status. We should still allow the people to buy and sell and to visit between the enemy zone and our zone. By doing this we merely maintain a normal livelihood for the people, we make it possible to maintain armed forces on a permanent basis, to have leaders close to the enemy. To build combat villages, we must increase the leadership capacity of Party functionaries, bring up the level of awareness and the unity of the people, achieve proper use of rudimentary weapons made by the people, while seizing the weapons of enemy dead. The enemy is positively reorganizing his area administratively and materially, cleverly using his counter-espionage service. Party units must regularly, together with the people, gain experience and eliminate mistakes so that the combat villages will grow stronger with time.

6) *How Is the Armed Struggle in Forest and Mountain Areas?*

Base areas in the forests and mountains are areas where the conditions are favorable to us, our armed forces are strong, so we must make full use of our opportunities to destroy the enemy in our operations. We must arm all the people and train the people to fight as guerrillas, to take shelter against air attack. We must activate the emulation movement in the armed forces to shoot down enemy aircraft. We must coordinate the armed forces and guide them in the struggle against enemy mopping-up operations. When the enemy conducts a sweep in a base area, the people residing there and the armed forces must not resist, but the people and the armed forces in other areas must use the withdrawal of enemy forces to strengthen the struggle to destroy strategic hamlets, destroying enemy posts, etc. We must strike the enemy when he withdraws and when he is tired. This is one way of properly coordinating and strengthening the movement in the provinces.

In short, with regard to the political struggle movement, we still need to strengthen the armed struggle to wear down and destroy the enemy. Party branches must try to lead the people to build up the armed forces, consisting of the people's guerrilla army, the regional units, and the main force units, into truly stronger forces. The direct responsibility of the Party units is to provide leadership in the matter of building the guerrilla movement and the combat villages, which we must spread everywhere. In the matter of building the guerrilla movement and the combat villages we must carefully watch over the people, we must regularly have different forms of activity in our areas and in enemy areas. Under the circumstances the Party member should uphold the political line and must provide a good example in the administration.

Lesson V

Role and Responsibility of Party Units in the Countryside

1) *Who Should Represent the Working Class in Rural Areas?*

Our Party is the Party of the working class. It is only composed of the working class, which is the most compact class. It has not property, it is oppressed and exploited, it has a spirit of revolutionary awareness, it has technique and organization. It is the most representative and thus the most productive and progressive class. It is capable of organizing a Party in order to lead the revolution to realize the ultimate objectives of the Party.

Party cells at the village level are principally composed of the political representatives of the working class in the countryside.

We should not see in the countryside many Party members of humble origin who are from the peasant class or from the bourgeoisie, but our Party is the Party of the peasant class and the bourgeoisie. Such thoughts are entirely wrong. The principle of the Party is: the peasants are of humble origin, coming from the peasant class or the bourgeoisie. When they enter the Party, they must see themselves as members of the working class, always determined to study the recasting of their beliefs and their old class viewpoints, in accordance with the outlook of the working class, the source of the fighters for Communism, in order to liberate the working class. The working class can be liberated, the peasant class can also be liberated and can live its own life happily. Increasing the solidarity of the worker-peasant alliance at the level of the hamlet and village—that is, increasing the leadership role of the Party cell with regard to all of the peasants—will make the peasants believe in, love, and admire Party leaders. In that way the revolutionary movement in the countryside will grow stronger.

2) *How Do Party Cells Perform Their Important Role?*

Party cells play a very important role because:

a) The cell is the basic organization, the foundation of the Party. All Party members function in cells. All of the cells, taken together, form the Party. The Party is firm and strong whenever the cells are firm and strong.

b) The cells are the essential link between the Party and the people. The link between the Party and the People can be firm or not, depending on the cells. Therefore, the Party is like a plant. The people are like the soil that nourishes the plant. The cell is like the roots of the plant. If the roots of the plant go deeply and firmly into the ground, only then will the plant grow well and steadily.

c) The cell is the immediate place for applying the line, the policy of the Party among the people. The cell applies the line, the policy, the position of the Party, publicizes and propagandizes it among the people, links it with the fighting strength of the people. If there are no cells, the line, the policy, the position of the Party cannot be implemented. The cell is the fighting unit of the Party among the people. The cell is the daily and immediate contact with the army.

d) The cell is the best school of the Party member, the place for training functionaries for the Party. All Party members actively participate in the discussion and determination of every task of the Party in the cell. On entry into the Party as well as during the process of development of every Party member, the education department trains him. Therefore, if we wish to become good Party leaders, Party members must hold firmly to the cells and agree to training in the cell.

3) *What Is the Duty of the Party Cell?*

The Party cell has several duties, as follows:

a) To lead the people to struggle to follow the line, policy, and position of the Party. Concretely, this means that the Party cell must propagandize the line, policy, and position of the Party every day among the people; educate the people to engage in Party activity; organize people's study sessions; regularly to attend to the economic, political, cultural, and social life of the people; help to resolve problems in an appropriate way, while knowing how to lead the people in the struggle against the enemy to protect their lives.

b) Based on the policy and position of higher echelons, to stay in close touch with the concrete situation in the area so that the Party cell can elaborate plans for activity, distribute and check on the tasks assigned to Party members. The cell must urge the Party member to study, to carry on criticism and self-criticism regarding Party members in order to support the strict application of the position and tasks of the Party.

c) Regularly teach and promote care and concern for the moral and material life of the Party members. Mobilize the Party members to work enthusiastically, to struggle positively, to develop initiative on the part of Party members, to take part in the work of leading the cell.

d) Popularize and spread the influence of the Party among the people and develop new Party members.

e) Discuss and participate in resolving questions pertaining to the line and policy of the Party. Periodically and on special occasions, report local conditions to higher echelons of the Party. Let the higher echelons know about the situation and local plans in a proper way.

f) Develop and lead the worker youth and other people's organizations of the Party at the base level.

4) *What Are the Duties of the Cell Committee?*

The cell committee is composed of cell members or of other, designated levels. It is responsible before the cell for performing the tasks approved by the cell meeting. The cell committee has the following concrete responsibilities:

a) Find ways to apply the position and decisions of higher echelons and of the cell.
b) Directly provide leadership to Party organisms, to Party members in people's organizations and fronts (if they exist). In accordance with ability, provide leadership to specialized units (if they are so charged). Regarding the task of developing Party members, assign Party functionaries, distribute and check on the work of Party members, hand out Party documents and leaflets, as well as other materials.
c) Lead the people in a united struggle, achieve all of the objectives of the Party, such as: production, defense, oppose arbitrary action, carry on the political struggle, etc. Build up the national front and people's organizations such as: worker youth, farmers association, liberation youth, liberation women, guerrillas, production teams, etc.
d) Call meetings of Party cells and maintain close contact between the cells and higher echelons.

5) *What Are the Duties of Party Teams?* [1]

Party teams have many concrete duties, such as:

a) Leading Party members and the people to apply the positions and decisions of the cells.
b) Contributing ideas on plans for the monthly work of the cells.
c) Taking part in the monthly work plan of the cell and preparing a work plan covering ten days to two weeks for the team.
d) Conducting propaganda on behalf of the Party and finding people to conduct educational sessions to introduce and develop new Party members.

6) *How Do Party Cells and Teams Operate?*

Ordinarily, Party teams meet once every ten to fifteen days. Cells meet once a month. When necessary, they can call an extraordinary meeting.

At present there are places where the Party cells are bringing in new members under difficult circumstances. Therefore, depending on concrete

[1] The "party teams" referred to here are synonemous with the party "fractions" treated in the appendix A, "Structure and Inner Party practices of Communist Parties in Non-communist countries."

conditions at each level, either cells are formed or they represent Party teams which are attached to Party cells.

The meetings of the committees of the Party cells are carried on as follows:

a) Report on observation of the enemy situation: regarding the position, plans of action and activity of the enemy during the month; influence on the people.
b) Report on observation of our situation, composed of four aspects: politics, economics, military affairs, culture and social matters, the situation and position of the cell, the situation and beliefs of the people, the situation of the people's organizations, the strength and development of the Party.
c) The status of the work plan the previous month. Things which can be done. Things which cannot yet be done, the reason why, and, if clear, any shortcomings.
d) Directed discussion, decision of higher echelons (if they exist), and adoption of a plan to implement.
e) Bringing up a program of work for the following month and division of work among Party members.
f) Criticism and self-criticism of the secretary, the cell committee members, and Party members regarding execution of decisions of the cell during the month, behavior and manners in connection with the way of life among the people, the way to conduct campaigns among the people, etc. Criticism of higher echelons.
g) Collecting Party dues and remitting Party dues to higher echelons.

In order to conduct the meeting more quickly and effectively, in accordance with the above, Party members or delegates on Party teams attending meetings must prepare themselves in advance, such as the secretary of the cell committee. The Party members living near each other should seek to improve each other. The Secretary or the cell committee members open the meeting and prepare a place to eat for the meeting. All Party members or delegates of Party teams should remember the date of the meeting and arrive on time. They should not visit other Party members in other places. Whatever the reason, they should not ask to be excused. No Party member shall fail to attend a meeting unless specifically excused by a Party official. Depending on the seriousness of the matter which is reported, a member shall be disciplined within the Party or purged from the Party.

In the meeting the secretary shall act as chairman. (If it is a meeting of a Party team, it shall be the leader of the team.) The chairman shall take up the first question and guide the comrades in the discussion and the conclusion. All Party members are free to present their ideas and thoughts, advantages and disadvantages—whatever is useful for the masses and the Party shall be done. After discussion and the expression of agreement, this shall become the decision of the cell.

If there are contradictory ideas, discussion but not yet agreement, expression of ideas only—these shall be referred to higher authorities. Meanwhile, all concerned must act in accordance with the ideas which the majority of the cell has expressed. All Party members must positively apply this principle. If any Party member does not apply it or deliberately misapplies it or opposes it, criticism, repreated criticism of those who do not reform themselves is called for, depending on the seriousness of the offense, followed by a reprimand, suspension, or expulsion from the Party. We must remember the slogan of Chairman Ho chi Minh that we must hold meetings; once we've met, we must decide; once we've decided, we must apply the decision.

At a meting of a cell or Party team, or a separate meeting, we cannot let the people or working youth join in the meeting. In the enemy zone we must meet very secretly, have adequate security measures, have suitable cover taken care of, and have the means to take care of an enemy attack.

7) *What Kind of Work Plan Shall a Cell Prepare?*

In preparing a work plan of a cell for proper execution, the cell must bear in mind the enemy situation and our situation in the area. Depending on the local situation, as well as on the directives and decisions of higher echelons, the cell shall prepare a work plan for itself.

The planning should be carried out in a progressive manner.

The plan that is prepared must be within the capability of the cell, concrete, and realistic, with a center purpose, a sense of unity, and an order of priorities, each task being assigned to a certain person, with provision for the participation of all organizations, with a concrete division of labor, and clear decisions on timing and duration, etc.

8) *What Kind of Plan Serves the Interests of the People?*

All Party members have the duty to express ideas for the preparation of a work plan for the cell in the following form: The Party member considers the situation of the people as it affects the Party teams. The teams consider the situation as it affects the cell leadership. The cell leadership, in considering the situation in terms of the situation in other fields, will have regard to the directives and decisions reached by higher authority in order to prepare a draft plan for the cell. The draft plan shall be brought up at a cell meeting so that all Party members will participate in expressing their ideas. All Party members in the cell must apply it.

Preparing a plan in this way is correct, as are the people's line of the Party and the joint contribution and ideas of the cell collective. By avoiding practices which lack breadth and democracy in the cell, such as having every cell matter handled by the chairman, other Party members dependent on him, failing to study the exchange of ideas, often making mistakes, we will avoid causing harm to the people and to the Party.

9) *How Does the Party Lead the Execution of the Plan?*

To apply the work plan of the cell properly, the cell needs to observe the following:

When the cell meets to prepare a work plan, all Party members in the cell must try to fulfill that plan. Party teams must base themselves on the plan prepared by the cell and depend on the capacity of the Party members to apply it. The Party members must strive earnestly to overcome difficulties, to develop initiatives, to perform the work of the cell, to teach, not to depend on others, to decline to have a negative attitude or to use this reason or that reason not to act or to act in a distorted way, harming the interests of the revolution. Strictly applying the plan of the cell leader and the decisions of the cell is a matter of discipline of the Party member. If there is a difficulty, he should report it in time and ask for the ideas of the cell. One cannot ask for permission not to report. This is the only way to achieve the united action of the cell.

While the Party teams and Party members are applying the plan, the cell committee must always follow carefully, check, and stimulate them in order to resolve difficulties in timely fashion, and to shed light in a timely way on errors and mistakes which occur.

The cell committee needs to select a Party team to provide separate leadership in the matter of applying the plan so that the secretary of the cell committee will have the ability directly to follow these points, to gain experience and, in timely fashion, to develop experience to help other teams in the cell to move ahead in their work.

At the end of the month the teams should meet to review shortcomings in the matter of implementing the work plan of the cell during the month, which matters have been completed, which are incomplete, and the reason why. New questions are raised, new ideas developed for the next plan and reported to the cell committee. The cell committee meets and reviews and observes the matter of implementation, the matter of leading the teams in the cell and the leadership of the cell committee, develops experience, and decides to prepare a new plan, to have it ready for the regular monthly meeting of the cell.

Each time the cell meets to check into the matter of the application of the old Plan or to prepare a new Plan, afterwards the cell committee must report to higher echelons and ask for comments. In reporting, the committee must describe the situation completely, including the things the cell has done, the results of the implementation of the plan, and the program of the new plan of the cell during the next month. The report can be written or oral. The report must tell the truth as far as it is known, explain why things are as they are, not add or subtract details, not report strong points and ignore weak points. It must report properly to higher echelons so that they can provide proper leadership and be useful to the people and the Party. Reporting incorrectly will cause the higher echelons to lead incorrectly, damaging the people and the Party.

Lesson VI

The Role and Qualities of a Communist Party Member

1) *What Are the Duties of a Party Member?*

The by-laws of our Party have determined the responsibilities of a Party member as follows:

a) To be eager to fight to achieve the aims and objectives of the Party, to participate in Party life, to popularize the Party, to participate in developing the Party.
b) To be absolutely loyal and true to the Party, to serve with all his heart, with all his strength the interests of the people. To be determined to join in supporting the heroic struggle against the enemy army, to defend the existence and reputation of the Party, to ensure victory for the revolution.
c) To preserve Party secrecy. Always to be on guard against the enemy army. To be loyal to the principal responsibilities and rules of the Party. To preserve and promote unity within the Party.
d) To be in close contact with the people, to be in accord with the people, to study, with and teach the people. To seek to develop the ideas and aspirations of the people, to propagandize, organize, and lead the people to fight to preserve their interests.
e) To try to study Marxism-Leninism and the political line of the Party, ceaselessly upholding the political program, beliefs, and working capacity of the people, always serving as a model in work.
f) To apply criticism and self-criticism.

If all of our Party members perform the above responsibilities as well as they can, the cells will become very strong, they will gain the trust of the people, and with this support the revolutionary struggle will triumph. Cells like that are composed of Party members who not only have good qualities but also have talent; not only are aware of political considerations but also have a high revolutionary fighting spirit and are prepared, heart and soul, to sacrifice and struggle to serve the Party, to serve the people. They also have the talent to teach, to organize, to lead the people united around the cell in order to implement the decisions and directives of the Party.

The foregoing, in summary form, are some ideas on Party matters to bring out the responsibilities of Party members and to remind every one of our Party members that he must fully and carefully discharge these responsibilities.

At present, in many of our cells, there is a situation where, although the majority of members of the cell are good and constructive, although in their minds they want to perform the duties of Party members, still there is a minority of our comrades who merely participate in the Party. Although they enthusiastically participate in the programs of carrying out the line and policy of the Party, their experience in actual tasks is inadequate. They commit many errors, have many shortcomings in the course of performing their duties.

2) *How Should Party Members Carry Out Party and Cell Duties?*

Every decision and directive of the Party is aimed at the objective of strengthening and developing our forces in all fields, defeating enemy plots, weakening the enemy, in order to advance to his complete defeat.

The reason why decisions and directives of the Party have strength is that they are right, so that the people in their millions follow and systematically apply them. Party cells are the element which directly leads the people to implement the directives and policy of the Party. Cell leaders watch over Party members in the cell. Therefore, the by-laws have provided that the primary duty of a Party member is positively to struggle to apply every decision and directive of the Party. This is not to say that matters concerning the spirit of directives and opinions concerning them do not have to be applied and, indeed, implemented. But we need to implement correctly the decisions of the Party. They must not be applied rigidly, causing defects to appear.

Properly implementing the matter of reducing rents, paying back debts, dividing land, improving the life of the people in the villages—and, on the other hand, developing the spirit of unity in the countryside, causing the people to produce enthusiastically and struggle against the enemy—this is positively carrying out the directives and policy of the Party. If, while doing this, we do not apply the line and policy or do so in a bureaucratic and authoritarian manner, cause divisions, provoke coarse and haphazard criticism among the peasants, among the people in the villages, do not apply properly the agricultural policy of the Party, then, although we may work day and night, and run from one end of the village to the other, although we work hard, it will be useless and will not adequately discharge our duty, will not be able to apply the policy of the Party.

Therefore, an important condition for being able to apply the line of the policy of the Party is that Party members need to study, to hold firmly to the line and policy of the Party. They must have a method of working properly, in accordance with the people's line of the Party. If we wish to uphold the line and policy of the Party, the Party member must regularly participate in the life of the cell, must pay attention to Party representatives from higher echelons or cell committee members making public explanations regarding decisions or directives of the Party. The Party member must think positively, try to understand and participate in discussions within the cell, wherever they occur, pay attention to explanations by the cell committee or higher authority in order to be able to understand, to report on the decisions and directives of the Party. The Party member must understand clearly why and under what circumstances the Party has acted in that way and acted correctly in the interests of the Revolution. If we make mistakes, there are two things to say: the Party member again needs to discuss a little bit within the cell the way to apply concrete Party directives in his own village, so that, whatever happens, whatever came before and occurred afterwards, he will organize the matter of education, mobilize the organization for leading the people. The Party member also needs to discuss in the cell the matter of reviewing the directives and manner of work of the cell, whether previously there were correct areas, whether there were areas which were not in accordance with the spirit of directives of higher echelons.

All of these questions need to be considered positively by the Party member and discussed in order that they will become the matter of decisions by the cell and are positively implemented.

3) *How Should the Party Member Lead the People?*

The policy of the Party must be understood clearly by the mass of the people and positively implemented. The duty of every Party member is to make the people understand more clearly the policy of the Party, see clearly the reasons for and objectives of the policy, and, after that, lead the people in a determined way to apply the policy.

If we want to do this, every Party member must become a propaganda specialist, positively applying the policy of the Party, popularizing, discussing, and explaining it to the people. He must strengthen the people, the representatives in the liberation forces, so that these comrades will popularize the campaign for recruiting members for these forces. He must strengthen the people positively, to apply the policy of the Party and the directives of the cells.

Every Party member must keep in close touch with the condition of the people in his own village or hamlet. He must understand clearly the condition of each family, must understand their aspirations and worries, the difficulties facing the people in order to report them to the cell so that the cell will discuss them and issue directives in accordance with conditions in the villages. The Party member must be on intimate terms with the people, make the people love him. He should not have a condescending attitude towards the people or a bureaucratic or hectoring manner of work, not be unconcerned with the life of the people, not fail to pay attention to the aspirations of the people, not fail to be concerned with the difficulties of the people. He should be in close contact with the people, take the people's correct ideas on doing work, fill in gaps and correct deficiencies in himself. Regarding the people, he should not only work with people who are positively disposed but must work alongside everybody, the half-hearted and the reactionaries, as well as those who previously followed a line in conflict with the revolution. He must persuade and explain, educate them regarding the policy and directives of the Party, make these people understand the Party clearly. He must campaign among the people to help them all in their daily life, in production as well as in matters affecting morale. He must make the half-hearted become positive, the reactionaries become progressive, those opposed to the revolution to get instruction to reform them.

Party members must lead in upholding the line and policy and the campaign to lead the people positively. This is an important matter which needs to be given priority and needs to be accomplished truly well. Party members must support the basic objective of the Party, that is, make every village the material base of the revolution by means of always increasing the unity of the people in the countryside, by means of making the Party and all of the people into a solid bloc that no force can divide. If we want to lead the people, Party members must not be merely skillful propagandists but what is still needed is people who know how to lead, to provide guidance, while serving as a model, by means of making the people see clearly that Party members always work as two people.

4) *How Should Party Members Help Recruit New Members?*

Regarding the responsibilities of educating, organizing, and leading the people to implement the line and policy of the Party, our Party members have a responsibility with regard to developing and strengthening our Party. In the present struggle with the barbarian enemy of the U.S. and Diem, our comrades have made many sacrifices. The blood of our comrades has not ceased to flow, our enemy has savagely sought to destroy our Party, but our Party has not ceased to grow stronger. A member of the Party may fall, but the example of sacrifice of our comrade has led hundreds and thousands of comrades, of youth corps members, of liberation organizations, and of the working people to step forward and continue the work of the fallen comrade. Brilliant candidates will be invigorated by this example and will become Party members.

The duty of every member of our Party is to help these comrades progress rapidly and achieve a level sufficient to become Party members. Every Party member must see clearly that this is his duty and that it is not a matter of doing what he can at his convenience or not doing anything. Every Party member should choose from among a number of members of the liberation youth corps that he knows best for their part in participating in revolutionary work, a number of people whom he knows well, who have the revolutionary spirit, who have a good relationship with the people of their village, introduce them to the cell so that the cell can see whether they can be considered for entry into the Party. If the cell is attentive, our comrades will have a plan to propagandize—strengthening and helping these comrades. This kind of propaganda is needed to make these comrades understand the Party better, understand the rules and by-laws of the Party. It is also necessary to strengthen them in accordance with their work, to help them work better, to provide them with timely instruction, to imbue them with a spirit of understanding. Party members must make these comrades understand and know the policy of the Party, the directives and decisions of the cell, so that they may apply and support the line. By these means we will gradually help them to understand the Party better, clearly understand the objectives and the ideals of the Party, to see the need for striving to study to cultivate their own development and to progress towards joining the Party. The procedure of joining the Party must follow exactly as set forth in the existing by-laws and may not proceed in a manner other than provided in the by-laws.

5) *How Should Party Members Promote Revolutionary Virtue?*

If we want to discharge our duties, Party members must not cease developing and progressing, must seek the people's confidence to serve the people, to love the people. First of all, they must promote a basic revolutionary spirit, a feeling of profound hatred, a spirit of loyalty to the revolutionary work of the Party. A Party member must forge for himself a spirit of heart and soul serving the people, serving the Party. When the

Party joins in work, he must bring all of his mind and thoughts, all of his effort to try to work as well as possible. He must try to struggle at first to overcome individual difficulties. Generally speaking, people affected with individualism cannot serve the revolution well when they perform a given task if they are thinking more of themselves, thinking about social position, thinking about reputation, thinking about personal gain. The sickness of individualism is the original source of the sicknesses of negativism, dissatisfaction, corruption. It takes individual interests as its own and its own family as a matter for concern rather than the people and incorrectly executes the policy of the Party. Bad, old, degenerate habits; the practice of working in terms of a general outline; bureaucracy; petty authoritarian practices; showing one's power with the people; not thinking of the interests and aspirations of the people—these are the forms of individualism. We must try to overcome the disease of individualism, because it weakens the Party. A Party member who takes individualism as a serious matter is a person who has a high spirit of organization and discipline. Those affected with individualism always think of their own interests first, but don't think of the interests of the Party. In the Party they are envious, they select their work carefully, do not agree to follow the guidance of the organization. They want to avoid difficult and dangerous work. Individualism, in regard to Party members, provokes contradictions, does not unify, is narrow-minded, is prejudiced, is addicted to factionalism. People affected with individualism, when the revolution encounters difficulties, when it meets the increasingly terroristic enemy, when the movement in the villages temporarily withdraws, are very agitated, no longer have confidence, bring up questions of food, are only concerned with their own life, do not think of the people or the Party or the movement. They will abandon the work, even the Party cells; they will abandon the revolution.

The comrades we want are revolutionaries who are determined, hardened, who are well-forged, who have discarded individualism. They want to overcome individualism directed at themselves. They have a steady, firm, impartial spirit, absolutely loyal to the Party. They will work either morning or evening, are tested in battle, in daily work. They always think in terms of controlling their thoughts, their attitudes, their expressions in a sincere way. They always ask the question: are we doing this right, are we thinking correctly? Is this useful or harmful for the revolution? When we act and think that way, are we serving the interests of the revolution or individual interests? Have we brought to bear all of our spirit of responsibility before the Party and the people? Have we brought all of our mind and strength to bear on this task? If we see clearly, see there are still shortcomings, such as individualistic thoughts, we must try to overcome them. We must bravely carry on self-criticism, point out where we are wrong, where we are right in our work and in our thought. We should not fear losing face, fear that our comrades will belittle us, will laugh at us. Self-criticism which continues will triumph—it is a guarantee of progress. It is proof of the quality of Party members that they always are concerned to strengthen themselves in order to serve the revolution well. Hiding defects, not agreeing to self-criticism, not telling the truth to the Party in order to have the strength of the collective to help one to reform—only that is worthy of scorn.

In another sense we must be concerned about the thoughts and activities of other comrades, must see that their good efforts are praised and emulated, must see that their defects need to be treated with compassion, that the criticism of comrades is accomplished in a spirit of comradely affection. We must help comrades to correct their defects in order to progress, to serve the Party better. We must serve the interests of the Party and the revolution as well as criticism. We must not serve individual interests, for if we serve individual interests, then with regard to the person himself there will be a feeling of being confirmed in his defects, there will be no criticism, the comrade will reach the point where he will not correct his defects. Regarding the person himself, the criticism must be made in a spirit of mutual, comradely affection, helping each other to reform. But criticism in a hostile spirit does harm, causes loss of face, goes too far, etc. Criticism of this kind really causes divisions and prejudices in the Party. It is not useful for unity, for helping each other to correct defects, in a spirit of compassion, to advance together.

Finally, the matter of self-criticism and criticism should aim especially at the matter of helping Party members to implement Party policy correctly, to keep the revolutionary spirit high, to hold high organizational awareness and discipline, to overcome individualism, so that criticism will be only a material matter.

The work of our revolution is very great and glorious. We are Party members who should exhibit a high revolutionary spirit, fully stable, a powerful will to defeat the enemy, worthy Party members in the front rank, leading all of our people forward to defeat the U.S. and Diem to liberate South Vietnam, to unify the fatherland, to be worthy of our fighters for Communism.

[DOCUMENT E-5]

ESSAY ON THE FIVE STEPS IN THE OPERATION OF A REVOLUTION

In order to promote the masses to carry out an effective revolution the best thing for the revolutionary combatant is to know the "promotion method." This method is known as "Five Steps in the Operation": investigation propaganda, organization, training, struggle.

Therefore, the study on the method of controlling the five steps in the operation of a Revolution is essential for a Revolutionary.

Investigation:

1) *Why do we have to investigate?*

In order to acquire good results in any work whatever, no matter how small or big, as well as to carry out a revolution, it's essential for one to know one's work prior to initiating it.

This fact implies "investigation." If this policy is prescribed while the real motive is unknown, failure will be insured.

In order to defeat the enemy, it's necessary to make investigations to "know the enemy." "Know one's enemy, know oneself, it's certain to win over one hundred battles."

Therefore, investigation is an important mission and the first step of the propaganda, organization and struggle activities.

2) *What do we have to investigate?*

Depending upon the purpose required by the revolutionary Operation, the following points are prescribed for the investigation mission:

a) *What must we search for when investigating a person?*

Generally speaking, when investigating a person with the purpose of urging him to participate in the Revolutionary movement, we must search for the following points:

1) Social class; life and occupation status, and aspiration.
2) Family relatives, friends, faith and education, etc. . .
3) Attitude towards the Revolution, masses (through the various struggles for the People's life, democracy, peacefulness and unity).
4) Attitude towards the enemy (through the various policies of the U.S. Diem).

Based on the above facts, we can determine whether this person is for or against the Revolutionary movement. Are there any problems to be solved? We must search for his resentment with the purpose of motivating and leading him to perform his Revolutionary activity in accordance with his capabilities, etc. . .

b) *What do we search for when investigating an organization?*

When investigating an organization such as a Popular Association, we must search for:

1) Its purpose and policy—Who is its founder and leader?
2) Its program, regulations and internal rules.
3) Its membership composition—Its members' attitude towards the enemy and the Revolution.
4) What and how are its activities carried out?

Therefore, we can determine whether this organization is profitable or harmful for the population and the Revolution, thus enabling us to have a suitable attitude towards it.

Investigating a factory;

—Who is its employer? What raw goods does it produce?
—Its capital? How much does it gain or lose? and why? (due to the American aid, or any other reasons).
—The attitude of its employer towards the workers, the Revolution, the enemy.
—Number of workers. What is the workers' situation (salary livelihood, worker's system)?
—How is the workers' struggle movement? Is there any organization in this factory?
—What is the primary contradiction in the factory? (between the employer and employees or between the employer and employees on one side and the US & Diem on the other side)?

Therefore, plans can be perfected, on the basis of the above facts, to lead the struggle of the workers, to organize a union between the employers and employees to conduct a struggle against the US & Diem.

c) *What must we search for when investigating a locality?*

The purpose of making an investigation of a locality is to get the knowledge of the relative situation between our forces and those of the enemy in the locality—We can subsequently set up our plans for an accurate promotion in behalf of the Revolution. But localities are different from one another, such as 1 village, 1 community, 1 market, 1 plantation, 1 military base, etc. . . and generally speaking, when conducting an investigation on any locality whatever the following points must be known:

1/ Geographical situation (area, population, communication roads, terrain features).

2/ The enemy situation: Communal council members, police SDC, spies, national Revolutionary movement, Youth of the Republic, Female Youth of the Republic, Labor and Personalism etc. . . , their conspiracy and activities. Taxes, Fines, Forced Working without pay, anti-communist activities, spy, soldier's recruiting, etc. . . Their internal contradiction. Their attitude when carrying out orders given by higher echelons.

3/ The population situation: the enemy oppressing and plundering acts, the population's livelihood, thoughts, aspirations; political tendency of the various classes, walks; religion, tradition and custom, the population's educational level; the contradiction between the masses and the enemy. The struggle movement of the population. Special attention should also be paid to the situation of land and rice fields.

4/ Popular organizations and their activities (open, semi-open and clandestine).

d) *Investigating a school:*

1/ Public or Private? Up to what grade? Number of male and female pupils?

2/ The enemy organizational activities: the enemy curriculum.

3/ Political: thoughts, aspirations and attitude of the pupils and teachers.

4/ Contradiction between the enemy on one side and pupils, students and teachers on the other side.

5/ The struggle movement, as well as legal, illegal and clandestine organization of the pupils and students.

It's necessary to know its past and present situation, when conducting an investigation on a locality, a factory or a school. *Example:* When we conduct an investigation on the struggle movement of the population of a locality, we must search for the existing movement and check to see how wide, and strong has it been expanded or does it remain at the same level as previously. The knowledge of this situation will enable us to find out the cause and to set up an accurate plan to raise a stronger movement.

And in the investigation of a locality, a factory, etc. . . we must search for: What are, up to now, the influence and leadership of the Party?

3) *How to investigate:*

There are 3 current methods to conduct investigations:

a) *Direct investigation:*

Direct investigation is to conduct a direct conversation with the individual whom we want to investigate. When conducting an investigation on a locality it's necessary to go to this place. Asking the persons who are concerned with the matter, the locality, or the organization . . . is the best and most accurate method. We can only learn about what we want to know by making direct [contact] and conversation.

We use the indirect investigation method only when conditions for direct investigation are not available. When conducting an indirect investigation we must be very adroit; otherwise we will create misunderstanding, disunion, and make the population hate us.

b) *Indirect investigation:*

This method is to address the residents of the environment, the inhabitants of the same locality or other persons, organizations or locations in order to know the person, the organization or the locality.

The reading of reports and documents is also a method of indirect investigation. Coordination between the direct and the indirect methods are recommended in order to insure an accurate result.

c) *Typical investigation:*

Selecting persons, localities or matters symbolizing the generality to conduct the investigation, in order to find this generality. This means to investigate the main point which was apparently known. But when direct investigation on the main point is being made, it's necessary to simultaneously conduct an indirect investigation on the apparent aspect. By doing so, the situation can be more sufficiently and concretely controlled.

The 3 current investigation methods stated above should be combinationally applied one after the other and good results will be insured.

What is the Attitude of the Cadre in Charge of the Investigation?

a) The cadre must be patient in searching for the level which can be realized by action. Concreteness does not mean to be satisfied with an apparent and vague knowledge. Sometime, one investigation is not sufficient, and reinvestigation is required or supplemental investigation is needed.

b) We must stand for the interest of the laboring masses, and base our opinions on theirs. . . .

c) The attitude of the cadre must be correct and must not be subject to mak[ing] decisions without a real reason and must not be affected by personal affection, etc. . .

Propaganda Activities

1) *Why must a revolutionary member carry out propaganda activities?*

Upon the completion of an investigation on any person, locality or organization, we initiate Revolutionary promotion propaganda activities. Propaganda activities will make the population know their rights and interests.

To explain to the population why their lives become hard, to make them hate the cruel regime of the US-Diem so they will decide to join the Revolution. When the population are resolute, we must make them understand the way, policy and goal of our Front, in order for them to have confidence to willingly struggle. Propaganda activities are to make the population know the policy conspired by the enemy, and to help them not to fall into the enemy plot. Simultaneously conduct propaganda on the righteous cause of the Party, in order to gain the population's respect and sympathy for the party, and as a result the population will not dare to struggle under the Party's flag.

In short, propaganda activity is very important, because its purpose is to make up [to] the population and to show [them] the way to . . . participation in the Revolutionary movement. Therefore, as far as we are concerned, we must look for every way, even if captured by the enemy, to continuously conduct propaganda activity to educate the people, in order to implement the following slogan: "Each cadre of the Party is a Propagandist."

2) *What do we have to propagandize every day?*

1) Every day, a cadre of the Party in charge of the Masses' Propaganda must unveil the barbarous and cruel face of the US-Diem to the population, so that they can be aware of the US-Diem pitiless plot and plundering activities, warfare and eager preparation with the purpose of

eternally dividing our fatherland and turning South Vietnam into a US Colony.

2) To point out the US-Diem demagogue argument deceiving the population and distorting the revolution, the Party and the North Vietnam government.

3) The following points must be widely propagated to all the people: The purpose of arming the general uprising, the policy of political and armed struggle, and the immediate mission situation.

4) To conduct propaganda activities in order to instruct the building up of the unification has an extreme power to defeat the enemy.

5) To conduct propaganda activities in behalf of the South Vietnam liberation front, to widely disseminate its proclamation and objective and to motivate the revolutionary population to join the front.

To conduct propaganda activities praising the Party's power, influence, struggle deeds, role and steering capabilities of the workers' class. In the meantime making the people realize that socialism in North Vietnam is a good system, and the strengthening in every aspect of worldwide socialism.

3) *How to bring out accurate propaganda slogans:*

Here below is the common basic Propaganda instruction that we must apply with exactness to carry out our activities. However, good results in Propaganda activities can only be acquired when we know how to bring out the relevant slogans which are suitable to each locality, situation or person concerned and accurately profitable for the populations actual rights and interests. Therefore, we must know the method of combining the various concrete ambiances to bring out accurate slogans. Every day, we must maintain close relations with the population, and search for the population's aspirations and needs, so that exact slogans can be brought out, because these subjects will come from the population's actual rights and interests. The population will join the Revolution only when appropriate slogans are used.

4) *How to conduct effective propaganda activities?*

Following are some primary methods of Propaganda activities to reeducate the population:

A. Verbal Propaganda:

Verbal propaganda is the most important method, because it has the capabilities of performing clandestine as well as open activities, it can express in detail our requirements and solve any difficulties presented by the population.

Verbal propaganda consists of the following methods:

a) Propagating to the population the Policy and slogans of the Revolutionary Organizations by applying verbal propaganda.

b) Stirring up public opinion to make the population discuss political subjects, and previous situation experiences. Creating public opinion is a strong form because public opinion makes the enemy disappointed and they can not prevent it from being discussed. When we desire to create public opinion in a city and in favor of our installation in the city surroundings we must recruit various tradesmen who frequent Saigon every day, or families having their relatives in the city, depending on the requirements of our local installations in order to seize [upon] all timely events which occur in the locality. Or to propagate public opinion received from outside in order to create a wide movement attacking the enemy continuously, and to raise up the influence of the general uprising.

c) *To openly Progagate our Policy and Goal:*

Secret propaganda is the basic method, but attention should also be paid to the open method. The various daily events such as: idleness, losses and unmarketability in business, anti-terrorist activities, claims for free labor unions, etc. . . could be used as subjects for discussion in a crowd, on a bus, on a boat, or at a meeting of a legal public organization.

B. *To Conduct Propaganda Activities by Using Documents, at Various Points where the People are Crowded:*

To conduct propaganda activities by using secret documents such as: booklets, papers, information bulletins, leaflets, slogans, pictures, banners and megaphones, etc. . . In addition to the above activities performed by our installations we must also urge the population to write slogans, as many as possible, themselves. And there are some other propaganda forms such as: to float puppets on rafts, to send aloft balloons and birds, to errand dogs and monkeys, armed propaganda activities, meetings, demonstrations, to beat drums and rattles, etc. . .

At this moment, the revolutionary movement of the population is rising to a high level, the population are awaiting the leadership of the PARTY. Therefore, the above mentioned propaganda methods are very appropriate and effective for stimulation, mobilization and concentration of the population. But, simultaneously we must apply these methods with flexibility depending on each case, each local situation and each moment, and the use of the same methods in different situations. . . .

Good results can only be achieved when propaganda documents having concrete plans are handed over to the people.

Of course, we must not overlook the enemy and be confused [to the] damage of our installations. . . .

C. *Use of Entertainment in Propaganda Activities:*

Depending on the particular locality, we can use the following appropriate forms in our propaganda activities: Songs, musical texts, dancing parties, theatrical plays, exhibitions, etc. . .

Especially, in the areas placed under our control, we must stir up the entertainment under the various forms in order to eliminate the apprehensive atmosphere and to create a delightful atmosphere to increase production output.

Presently, in the cities we can compose healthy songs, musical texts, pictures, and particularly disseminate them within the community of youths and students. We must also take advantage of the enemy carelessness to conduct propaganda activities by using revolutionary papers, public association magazines, and liberal arts groups.

5) *What is the attitude of the Propaganda Cadre?*

Propaganda activity is the keen, complicated, long lasting and hard thought struggle—As a matter of fact, the Propaganda Cadre should be tenacious, hard and modest in listening to the people's ideas. . . .

Organizing Mission

1) *Why must a Party member carry out the organizing mission of the population?*

After the population has been subjected by and instructed in our propaganda activities, then we must organize them into a strong force to fight against the enemy and to create condition for our wider range of propaganda activities.

Presently, the population of all parts of the country are rising up, and looking for the revolutionary organizations; therefore, we come to realize that the organizing mission of the population is necessary.

2) *What organizations do we have to set up?*

We must set up secret, semi-open and open organizations.

A. *Revolutionary organizations:*

a) *What is the importance of the establishment and development of the Revolutionary Organizations?*

The Revolutionary Organization is the highest one of the population, it aims at concentrating those people who are interested in the Revolution, and have a spirit of union with other people in their surroundings in order to collectively fight against the enemy and to resolutely overthrow the enemy. The people in this organization are considered as a force which conducts a daily struggle against the enemy with the various forms of a higher level of the Revolution; moreover, it's a key-force constituted by the people of the legal and semi-legal organizations.

The recruiting of the people into the Revolutionary Organization could not be omitted if we wish to stir up the local Revolutionary movement to the strongest point and to defeat the enemy for accomplishing our Revolutionary purpose.

Based on the present situation, it is realized that the development of the Revolutionary Organization in the liberated and infested areas is a very urgent necessity. In addition, we must also set up such organizations within the various business firms, communities and schools located in an area adjacent to that of the enemy, and we can develop these organizations through the struggle movement.

b) *How to set up and develop the Revolutionary Organization:*

The settlement and development of the Revolutionary Organization depends on the following basic principles:

—We must motivate the population, make them interested in

the Revolution, make them ultimately hate the enemy, make them realize the necessity to join our organizations in order to fight against the enemy. It's advisable that careful propaganda activities should be conducted prior to the enrollment of the people into our organizations.

—We must stir up the struggle for the benefit of the peoples' daily rights and interests, in order to instruct and finally enrol them in our organization.

—We must continuously instruct, train those people in the organizations who positively and vehemently carry out their duties, with the purpose of forming them into key-cadremen. On the other hand, we must plan to introduce our Party cadre and members into these organizations to serve as key-elements to supervise the operation of such organizations.

—We must always maintain a smooth and regular operation within our organizations.

—We must continuously consolidate the union and mutual aid concept of the organizations' members as well as the non-organizational persons in their daily production and struggle activities.

c) *The Revolutionary Organization consists of:*

The front and various liberation associations:

1) *The Front:*

Education propaganda activities should be implemented to make all various people aware of the Front proclamations and statutes. Party cadre must be sent throughout the country in order to:

—Sound out public opinion.
—Solve the people's problems and anxiety relating to the Front's policy and goals.
—Gradually develop the Front's organizations, thus making the S.V.N. People's Liberation Front more influential and powerful among the population. The population will [then] recognize our organizations.

2) *Liberation Associations:*

a) Rural areas:

In rural areas we must immediately expedite the Organization of the Communal Farmer's Association, but prior to setting up such an Association, we must commence by working out the following lower committees:

—Campaigning Committee at commune [level].
—Cadre committees at hamlet [level].
—Male and female youths who have not yet been organized into proper associations can be gathered separately into male youth organizations and female youth organizations, and these organizations will be attached to the Farmer's Association in order to simultaneously implement the social classes' type of workers' operation.

—Attention must always be paid to the formation of popular cadre; the strengthening as well as the praising of the fighting capabilities and nature of the active Cadre.

—Propaganda activities must always be implemented in order to enroll as many people as possible into the Farmer's Association, but the people cannot be recruited unless they have undergone the following prescribed principles: Investigation, Propaganda Indoctrination, Challenge.

Finally they must submit their requests for admittance accompanied by their pledges to firmly . . . safeguard the organizations. We must, upon having completed any organizations, consolidate the members' thoughts and maintain good operation of such organizations. Negligent action should be avoided.

—The Farmer Association's role should be praised, because this type of association is one of the Revolutionary Organizations and of the social class which has an absolute and widespread prestige among the farmers. Moreover, the above association is considered as a key organization of the Front in rural areas and responsible for the solution of internal affairs such as: Unification, mutual aid among various farmers within the districts, communes and hamlets, and its primary mission aims at overthrowing the local enemy authorities and serving as a shock-action force and a base to support the activities of the farmers legal or illegal organizations in the commune.

B. *In Town:*

—At the present time, we must speed up our activities in recruiting the people into our organizations such as "Secret Liberation Association" and the formation of cadres necessary for such organization.

—Now, the establishment of the following associations is badly required:

—Labors' Liberation Association: This association will consist of these types of workers; workers of various business firms, handicraftsman, workers of various types, and shop owners. Business firms, working places, industrial firms and working communities will be used as a base of organization. Attention should be paid to the quality of the personnel we recruit into our organizations. Those people who are known to be patriots and volunteer to carry out, with recklessness, any missions which might be assigned to them. This is called a committee and the lower echelon will be called a cell.

—Liberated Students Alliance Association:

Students and pupils will be recruited into this association. School and college courses will be used as a base of organization and a committee will be organized at each school and college course. Each committee consists of many sub-committees, and each sub-committtee will control many cells. Each committee will be placed under the supervision of an executive board.

—As regards the other branches, various associations will be organized accordingly, such as:

—Liberated Liberal Arts Assn.
—Liberated Newsmen Assn.
—Liberated Teachers Assn.
—Liberated Industrial Tradesmen Assn.
—Liberated Women's Assn.
—Liberated Youths Assn.
—Liberated Junior's Group
—Liberated Employees Association.

In addition all individuals who do not belong to the above stated social classes and branches, but are known as patriots, will be recruited in the Liberation Association.

Note:

The Association's organization and membership development should be carefully implemented. Prior to the acceptance of any member, the individual concerned must undergo an investigation and challenge in compliance with the principles prescribed above. We must always be alert to preclude the infiltration of enemy agents into our organizations to carry out sabotage activities.

—The relations between one organization and another are strictly prohibited, in order to consolidate the moral[e] of our cadre and members.

—Preserve secrecy and maintain long existence of the organization.

—The entire membership must be thoroughly aware of the Association's program and regulations in order to correctly carry out any tasks assigned to them.

C. *What is the Popular Open Organization?*

The Popular Open Organizations are those which operate openly, aiming at protecting the people's rights and interests relating to their social classes or branches. Owing to the people's struggle, the enemy's lawful authorities are obliged to recognize the following associations as the official ones:

—Various syndicate.
—VN women's associations.
—VN language—cultural mission.
—Student's parents association.
—Student council.

Be aware of counter revolutionary organizations established by the enemy to oppose our revolution: Personalist Party, National Revolutionary Movement, Republican Youth, Republican Women, Communist Victims. We must absolutely boycott these organizations.

D. *What are the semi-public organizations?*

The semi-public organizations are based on the people's interests although not authorized by the enemy. They can operate openly like other organizations such as Worker Exchange Association, Mutual Aid Association, Soccer Association, music bands, fire fighting groups, etc. . .

The objective of these organizations is to educate, unify and assist the people in this struggle for their own rights. These organizations can be changed to meet the requirements, if necessary.

How to develop leadership for semi-public organizations?

The semi-public organizations must be established, based on the people's actual requirements, and in consistence with the people's rights and the situation to develop unity, mutual assistance, and defend the people's rights.

The organizations must struggle for the people's interests (economical, cultural, political, and social). They must develop and strengthen their ranks to achieve success in their struggle. The organization must know how to use the people's struggle to defeat the enemy, regardless of regulations prescribed by the letter. Key members of the organization must develop their secret bases and do their best to win the people's support. Party cadre must know how to maintain their legal position, work together with other members to carry out their assigned mission and struggle for the organization's interest along with other members. They must be discreet, especially underground cadre in the executive committee.

Struggle Mission

1. *Why must we struggle?*

Educating and organizing the people is to urge them to struggle against the enemy and defend their own rights. The closer they come to their end the more the enemy are fascist and tyrannical. They terrorize and rob the people, making their physical and spiritual life miserable; especially in the enemy controlled area. In the face of such a situation, our people are determined to struggle for the betterment of their life, because inactivity means death. Struggle is a way that oppressed people have adopted to preserve their life. Despite the enemy's tyranny, the people will never be subdued. The enemy's terrorism will increase the people's resentment. Premier Pham Van Dong said: "Struggle comes from repression, and the heavier the repression the stronger the struggle." To defend their rights our people must struggle. By struggling they develop their force to annihilate the enemy.

2. *What is the responsibility of the party members towards the struggle movement?*

Our people are determined to struggle. At present their resentment against the enemy increases and their struggle becomes more and more intense. As for the enemy, their end is approaching. It is impossible for them now to rise up and the collapse of their regime is certain. Before this situation, the party members must be aware of their responsibility, especially:

—They must enhance their revolutionary spirit, hold the people, know their aspirations and increasingly urge the people to organize themselves into well disciplined groups for struggle.

—They must be aware of the enemy situation and their deficiencies, timely employ the people to attack and confuse the enemy and attain their final objective of the revolution by conducting a general uprising to seize power.

3. *How to build up, develop, and support the struggle movement.*

—The best base to build up, maintain and develop the people's struggle is the cadre Party members, [who] must increasingly enhance their revolutionary will power, develop their fighting, spirit and know their responsibility to the Party and the masses. In addition they must know the responsibility of the party to increase their confidence in the Party's struggle and the people's revolutionary capabilities. Cadre and party members must do their best to spread propaganda and arouse the people's resentment against the enemy and keep the people informed of their rights. Do not start the struggle at the last moment because the loss of initiatives will adversely affect the development of the movement.

—Along with the arousing of resentment, we must educate the people, evaluate the situation and place confidence in the Party's struggle. At the same time make the people understand that their mission is to struggle against the enemy, that the enemy is weakening, their defeat is certain and our movement will be successful. Make the people believe in their strength so that they can struggle effectively.

—Educate the people and develop their unity.

—Have close contact with the people and try to understand their aspirations and attitudes towards the enemy for appropriate action. If the people are not familiar with the struggle and their morale is still weak we must at first adopt a small scale struggle to familiarize the people with it then raise it to a higher level later.

—Devise a plan to prevent the movement from slowing down at the same time develop open or secret installations and spread propaganda to enhance the movement.

a) *Slogan for the struggle.*

Oppose the enemy's terrorism, expropriation of people's land, increase of rental, amassing of the people, construction of strategic hamlets, land development centers, compulsory military service, forced labor, exorbitant taxes and contribution of any land to the enemy. Closely unify to overthrow the dictatorial, fascist regime and Diem's family rule.

In the towns and cities:

Gather the people and step up their struggle in the towns in order to:

—Overthrow Ngo Dinh Diem's family rule regime.

—Oppose the enemy's terrorism, ask for the organization of syndicates, student councils [and] press freedom; uncover reactionaries who are attempting to sabotage the mass organizations ask for the abolition of tyrannical regulations, struggle for the betterment of living conditions, such as increase of salary, protection from discharge, aid to the unemployed, full employment—reduction of taxes; and when necessary, urge the people to struggle for the abolition of the 6% production taxes.

4. *How to lead a struggle?*

1) *What is to be done prior to the struggle?*

a. *Investigation and research:*

To defeat the enemy we must know the enemy force and our own force.

Enemy forces although fascist, also have deficiencies and contradiction among themselves. We must know how to locate their weakness for attack. Our forces special attention must be paid to the motives which have urged the people to struggle—analyze the revolutionary capabilities and political prestige of the masses.

b. Set the objective, estimate the requirements, devise slogans and methods of struggle.

—Assign a level and a name for the objective. Take advantage of the contradiction among the enemy to win the support of dissatisfied people.

—Requirements and slogans must be very concise with the principal slogans and secondary slogans. The methods and the level of struggle depend upon the vigilance of the masses.

c. *Organization and deployment of the struggling force.*

In the struggle, no matter how small or large it may be there must be 3 forces: main force, support force, and self-defense force.

—*Main force.* It is the key force of the struggle [and] as a result consists of people whose rights have been involved and who are determined to struggle. In the main force is a representative committee elected to talk with the enemy and start disturbances, if necessary.

—*Support force.* It is a relatively numerous force of the masses and consists of 3 types:

1) Support force. This force struggles along with the main force. In this force each member is given a special mission such as to win the enemy soldiers' and officials' support, give support to the main force, mobilize soldiers' dependents to participate in the struggle.

2) Mutual assistance force. The mission of this force is to mobilize various classes of people to participate in the struggle, take care of the job of those members who are absent, organize welcomes and visits to members returning from the struggle, give money and medicine to members wounded during the struggle.

3) Reinforcement forces. If necessary build up this force by enlisting the relatives of those members who have participated in the struggle.

4) Self Defense force. It is deployed along with the struggle force for defense when necessary.

The struggle force must be well organized with a clear assignment for each force and each party member.

If the struggle lasts for a long period of time, a supply plan will be devised.

d. *Anti-terrorism plan.*

Take preventive measures against terrorism to be adopted by the enemy during or to after our struggle.

e. *Organization of a leadership committee.*

There are a local leadership committee and an outside leadership committee. The mission of the outside leadership cómmittee is to advise the local leadership committee. These 2 committees must coordinate closely and their members must be selected from discreet and active people.

f. *"Selling" the plan.*

Keep the struggle force informed of the struggle plan especially the leadership committee and the main force in the struggle. Teach them how to deal with the enemy and avoid the enemy's provocation.

g. Investigation is an important duty during the preparation. Closely supervise the implementation of the preparation plan. Check the preparation at the last moment before starting the struggle.

Notes:

—Speed up the struggle with preparation in advance. Conduct small and sporadic struggles daily.

—Cadre and party members must be ready for struggle, tightly hold the masses through propaganda and thoroughly know the enemy situation to start the struggle in time.

5. *What is to be done during the struggle.*

—Start the struggle at the proper time.

—Continue spreading propaganda and tightly hold the masses during the struggle.

—Closely coordinate the people in their struggle.

—Respect the people's initiatives and recognize active members.

—The leadership committee must place the main force under its command, closely supervise the unit and cleverly direct it through the cadre.

—Avoid provocation. Apply flexibility in our struggle and know how to win the cooperation of the enemy soldiers.

—Know how to face the enemy's terrorism and win the people's sympathy.

—Take advantage of the people's mind to start the struggle at the proper time and achieve success for the people (no matter how small it may be).

—Upon completion of the struggle, withdraw rapidly and do not delay, to avoid the enemy's terrorism.

6. *What is to be done after the struggle?*

—Anticipate the enemy's future attempt—Devise a plan to face the enemy's terrorism following the struggle.

—Analyze what has happened to gain experiences. Correct mistakes, encourage the people and enhance the fighting spirit. Of the mass: analyze the struggle forces. Make a report on the success achieved by each force or each individual to develop the fighting spirit of the masses. Form a unity among the force at home to strengthen the cooperation among the masses.

—Conduct an internal critique, adopt reward and punishment policies to educate the people, admit new members, look for active individuals among the masses to build up secret organizations.

[DOCUMENT E–6]

EXPERIENCES IN TURNING XB VILLAGE IN KIEN PHONG PROVINCE INTO A COMBATANT VILLAGE

Part One

SITUATION FACING US WHEN WE BEGAN.

The village of XB is entirely surrounded by water. It has a population of 6,000 and is a new village, founded during the war [i.e. late 1940's]. There were 200 Cao Dai and 100 Hoa Hao.

Land originally was owned by landlords. There was one big landowner and 50 smaller ones. During the resistance the landowners were absent and control of the land was in the hands of the farmers. At the restoration of peace the landowners returned with the troops to retake their land and collect back rent. Since the farmers were dependent on the land for their livelihood, for their survival, they were thus greatly motivated to struggle against the landlords.

XB village had a Diem government administrative office, a security section and a post of militiamen. Mobile troops [ARVN] and Civil Guards were active in the area, especially in the two neighboring villages which are on dry land.

During the first few years of peace the Party made several attempts to step up its activities. Three times its organization was destroyed by the enemy. Three Party members were killed, two secretaries arrested, more than 100 cadres and members were taken into custody. Finally only one Party member remained and he was driven onto the beach at Luc Binh. He got no help from the local people.

In 1959, cadres from the higher level arrived to gather the scattered Party members and instruct them in the reestablishment of the destroyed party base. Things were so difficult, at that time, that our comrades were forced to hide in the fields and marshes during the day and only at night could they slip into the village to do propaganda work among the farmers. Several farmers were deeply interested in the struggle to get them land and they let themselves be indoctrinated easily. A base was soon established at a farm. Our cadres went on helping the farmers fight for ownership of certain lands and for the reduction of rent on other pieces of land. Gradually our victories convinced some of the farmers and we were able to bring into being the XB Party, consisting of seven members.

Then the enemy began launching sweep operations. Battalions of troops came by land and water to clear the area. But the Party base and the Party organization were not injured. One Self-Defense Group, a three-man cell, was reduced to a one-man cell one bitter day when the two members were killed in action. Now, this self-defense group has become a real force, a platoon of armed men.

At the present time our organizational strength is as follows: the Party totals 26 members, the Lao Dong Youth 30, the Farmers Association 274, the Liberation Youth Group 150, the Liberation Women Group 119; 2,000 people, or two-thirds of the villagers, take part in Party led activities.

Part Two

MEANS AND METHODS OF OUR SUCCESS.

Elimination of Village Elders and Security Agents.

As the first step in establishing a base and fanning the fires of revolution, the Party began agitation of farmers to seek their own interests—the right of owning land or reduction of land rent. This struggle, however, remained sporadic and weak and did not constitute a mass movement. To better meet the enemy, which remained strong in the village, the Party began the elimination of influence of the village notables and local security agents. However, it failed to follow this with the development of a mass base. The cadres thought that efforts to end the authority of the village leaders alone would be enough. The enemy succeeded in maintaining the village administration. In the face of such a situation the Party called for a meeting. We explained to the villagers the evil caused by village notables and security agents. We awoke the people to the fact that if the American-Diem clique succeeded in permanently maintaining the organization of village notables and security, soon Mister H, the cruel landlord, and others would return to the village to seize land and collect back rent. For that reason, we said, the farmers must eliminate the influence of the village notables and sweep away the security agents. At the same time we sought to win the sympathy of the families of the village notables (while we were urging the masses to rise up and eliminate the influence of the notables). It was a good method. After a while certain notables refused to work for the enemy and some took the side of the people.

Thus, when our enemies tried to begin projects in the village no one would work for them. The US-Diem clique tried to win back the people by distributing drugs in the village. The offer was flatly rejected. Some of the people even debated openly and strongly with the enemy agents. Finally the Diem clique had to abandon the village, no village council could be maintained there.

The Party hailed this great success and urged other villages in the area to follow the example. Since then, in surrounding villages, we have been successful in preventing the influence of the enemy. In the area now there remains only some Diem soldiers who live in a military post.

The Struggle For Land

As I have noted, the main interest of the farmer of XB village is in land. Before, during and after the elimination of our enemy's influence, the Party in XB village always used the subject of land as a means of propagandizing the people and indoctrinating the masses.

In its political and armed struggle, in its administration of the rural area, and in other revolutionary tasks, the Party knew well how to make use of the farmers' interest in land. On it we built a mass movement. And for that reason the revolutionary movement made great progress and resulted in a great success.

At first this struggle was sporadic and weak. The farmers merely wanted land rent to be reduced and their right to farm the land maintained. Now the farmers cling to their land. The landowners remain in the cities, leaving the task of retaking the land and collecting rent to the soldiers posted in the area. But these troops can do little.

The Party Unit developed and used this slogan: *"Kill the Land Robbers."* This slogan was welcomed and used by the local people. The farmers now know they have the force to prevent the landowners from retaking their lands and can prevent the US-Diem clique from oppressing the people. Farmers are now free to farm, without paying either land rent or agricultural tax.

With respect to land, the people have scored these successes:

1. All private and public land has been distributed and ownership is now maintained except for land located near enemy army posts.
2. Land rent has been reduced by 16,000 gia of paddy [one gia equals forty liters; this is rice payment on rice producing land but to whom it is paid is not clear].

Victory came to the farmers and the people then enthusiastically joined the movement and put their confidence in the Party as the leader of the revolution.

However there were some clashes of interest, some discord. There was a dispute between two farmers over a small parcel of land and each threatened to kill the other. The Party stepped in and called a meeting of villagers to hear and solve the problem. A cadre pointed out that:

"Land comes as part of the revolution's achievements and as a result of the people's struggle. Farmers must remain united and share the good and bad. Because the American-Diem clique and the landlords plot to come back, farmers must make concessions to each other to ensure final victory. Only if these conditions are met will the farmers be able to take permanent possession of the land."

Upon hearing this the two farmers became enlightened, embraced each other and wept.

In administering the rural area, the Party seeks to settle contradictions between people, teach the people Party policy, urge the people to have spite for the Americans and Diem and seek to unit all groups and social classes in the village. If a party member or cadre makes a mistake he will be freely subjected to the criticism of the people. When the people can boldly criticize party members they will then be ready to forgive them.

Since the people are united, and since they have learned how to guard against leakage of secrets and the penetrations of the enemy, security agents and spies cannot survive.

Besides the matter of land, the Party also attends to the other needs of the people, such as public health, sanitation, education, maternity facilities, etc. Moreover, the Party helps farmers market their produce at high prices. Through organization, merchant speculators are avoided.

The Party operates a first aid station run by a public health cadre who also makes visits around to look after the health of people in the area. There is also a midwife who manages confinements. The people pay for these services and they also have a voice in the management of them.

In the matter of schools, the Party called the problem to the attention of the people at a public meeting. The Party guided the people in applying to district officials for aid of building schools and supplying teachers. This failed and the Party led the people into the task of providing a school themselves. At the last moment, the authorities approved the establishment of a school [meaning?]. A Pupil Parent Association was founded and two schools were built. Maintenance of the school is through money collected from the people. The school is managed by the people under the guidance of the Party. The people take turns observing the operation of the school and prepare to answer the enemies if they come to criticize the school operation.

In one case, as one of the schools neared completion, soldiers came to ask why. The people answered: "Admission to [nearby] public schools requires birth certificates. Our children have none and therefore cannot be admitted. Therefore we establish a special school for them." The soldiers agreed with this view. Consequently the schools established are legal. And children are educated under our guidance.

Display of the Flag.

Seeing that the Party assumes responsibility for education, seeing that Party members in XB village are devoted to the people's cause, especially with regard to land, seeing how the Party looks after the people's living standards, the people of the village became attached to the cadres and Party members and ready to support Party policy.

During a ceremony to welcome the establishment of the National Liberation Front (December 1960—ed) the inhabitants of XB village enthusiastically prepared. The walls of the houses were whitewashed, flags were made and raised of flagpoles in front of each house. In all, 600 flags were flown throughout the village—expressing the people's spirit of struggle and their support of the revolution. The Party cadres had indoctrinated the people and prepared them to debate with the enemies. When the soldiers came to take away the flags, the people said to them calmly: "This is a flag of peace. It is not a Viet Cong flag. This flag means that the people, some of whom are your relatives or even your families, have land to till."

Most of the soldiers agreed with this view and took away only a few flags.

One old man was concerned because his flag was wet. He feared this would lessen the solemnity of the ceremony. This incident proves that if the people understand the Party's goals, and become enlightened, our efforts can never fail.

In summary, the Party in SB village has established a mass movement, has enlightened the people, has made the Party's policies a great force among the villagers.

Forging Weapons and Establishing Defenses.

When we tried to get the people to forge rudimentary weapons we encountered great difficulty, for the people were not accustomed to this sort of thing. At first our own self defense troops and cadres carried the burden, unsupported by the people.

The laying of naily boards [metal or bamboo spikes set in weeds or in marsh land to pierce the shoe and foot], the forging of rudimentary weapons, the establishment of combat villages requires the cooperation of all. Unless all understand Party policy and contribute to these works, the movement in the village will be weak.

The people thought that the laying of naily boards was illegal and would result in terror and reprisals by the soldiers. In light of this the Party members laid the naily boards themselves, while endeavoring at the same time to educate the people. The Party laid more naily boards than ever. Once, during a terror sweep one of the soldiers was injured by a naily board. This caused the soldier to withdraw. Party members correctly regarded this as a success and held a mass meeting at which it was explained that laying of naily boards had prevented the entrance of the enemy. The cadres declared that if the people did not lay naily boards the enemies would come to collect land rents, levy taxes, impose corvee labor and draft young men into the army. The Party then introduced the slogan: *"One naily board for each square of land."*

The people each day were urged to oppose the Americans and Diem in order to keep their land and protect themselves.

The idea of naily boards was eventually supported by the people. Many were laid. Later three enemy soldiers were injured by naily boards. Taking advantage of this event, the Party held a meeting and reported the success to the whole village.

In one hamlet the Party cadre showed the people how to lay a barricade of thorny bamboo across a road and underneath put grenades attached to the branches. When the enemy came, however, the soldiers hooked ropes to the branches and pulled them away, exploding the grenades but not injuring the soldiers. However, the soldiers became fearful and did not do any more mopping up that day.

Encouraged by this success, our comrades urged the people to set up eleven combat gates [barricades] to prevent the entrance of our enemies.

However, the education work was not careful enough. For instance, one old farmer opposed our plan and asked permission to leave the area. But then the soldiers came and the farmer was afraid. The soldiers forced him to remove the combat gates. He removed a few.

The Party began anew its education work to explain away the damage done by the mopping up operation. The cadre explained that fencing the area, laying combat gates, laying naily boards, proselytizing the Army and engaging in political struggle all contributed to the defense of the village, protected the lives of the villagers and kept the land intact.

The Party sent its best cadre to reeducate the old farmer and in time he became enlightened, approved the setting up of combat gates and confessed his faults before the people.

The Farmers Association was put in charge of combat gates (each was given a number) and of laying naily boards. Each sub-cell of the Farmers Association is in charge of one combat gate—and closes the gate when the enemy comes and gives the alarm by means of tocsin. When a tocsin sounds each person knows which gate the enemy is entering and thus how best to cope with the situation.

The mass movement to lay naily boards, set up gates and establish a combat village had good results and illustrates how our comrades know correct propaganda techniques. They know how to make efficient propaganda that reflects the real interests of the people; they also know how to stimulate the rancor of the people.

The Party constantly studies not only the interests of each social class, but also the attitudes of each family.

In rural areas, they found it necessary to propagandize in the following way: "To keep your land and prevent landowners from collecting rent, you must lay naily boards."

With families who have youths of military age it is necessary to propagandize as follows: "The laying of naily boards prevents the Americans and Diem from recruiting soldiers by force. Soldiers taken into the Army will die, as did A and B, from this village. Those who become soldiers will be forced to participate in mopping up operations and will die of naily board injuries as we have seen here."

In a family whose members are from North Vietnam it is necessary to say: "Please lay naily boards to fight against the Americans and Diem for the restoration of peace, and for the unification of our country. When the revolution is successful you and your relatives will be reunited."

Before the start of a recent series of mopping up operations the Party worked to educate the people. They prepared by designating people to lay naily boards, engage in legal struggles against our enemies, carry on Army proselytizing efforts, etc. During the operation our enemies encountered naily boards everywhere. They tried to force the villagers to guide them but no one would accept this task. People told them that the day before, the Liberation Army forbade the inhabitants to go out so they did not know the location of naily boards and grenades. The people also urged the troops not to advance. Some persons, designated to guide our enemies, led them into swampland. Tired, after many hours, our enemies had to withdraw.

After each mopping up operation the people review the failure or the success of the resistance effort in each hamlet. A meeting is held and each hamlet makes a report, in the presence of a cadre, who then points out the experience gained. At this meeting the hamlet which showed initiative or which achieved some outstanding victory in fighting with rudimentary weapons occupies a place of honor in the front ranks. Although one group is not encouraged to outdo the other, the various groups sometimes compete with one another in laying naily boards.

One farmer even competed with his wife in laying naily boards. The husband said: "Your duty is in attending to the children. You do not have time to lay naily boards. Let me fight our enemies." "You fight against our enemies," answered the wife, "it is your duty. But as a woman I also have the task of annihilating them." So they both participated.

During one operation some of the villagers did not fight and were captured. Later they were released and when they came home, the villagers met them and berated them and told them only by fighting could the people protect their lives and property.

After each mopping up operation, various groups review the actions of each hamlet and indulge in mutual criticism. This serves to increase devotion, bring out the strong points and the shortcomings of the effort. This enables the people to convert experience into an improved organization.

In mopping up operations in mid-July our enemies sent in 600 soldiers, in motor boats, to attack XB village. The leadership of the Party was stable, however, and had prepared well the political and military struggle, so the efforts of the enemy came to nothing. Seven enemy soldiers were wounded by naily boards. The enemy soldiers withdrew before the united resistance of the people.

During this same operation it was discovered that some of the naily boards had become warped and unusable. Afterwards the people had a meeting attended by the cadre in charge of laying naily boards. It was decided that round naily boards were better than the ordinary one, also that the barbed naily boards were more dangerous for our enemies.

One farmer had invented a kind of bottle grenade using a cartridge. It was tested on a dog and the explosion disembowled him. Now people are busy making the new bottle grenade.

It should be noted that whereas the laying of naily boards was at first done by the cadres, now everyone, especially the Farmers Association, participate in the effort, under the guidance of cadres.

The people now even say to the cadres: "Take care of the documents and avoid encountering the enemy." This proves that the people place full confidence in the cadres, are devoted to them and want to protect them.

XB Village is still not yet well known. But local soldiers are fearful of it. The soldiers camped at LH and TH villages (nearby) say: "If you wish to meet your loved ones again, don't attack XB."

Part Three

LESSONS TO BE LEARNED FROM XB.

The Party at XB has scored some outstanding successes. These are due to the following:

1. Party members were determined correctly to carry out Party's policies. When the village bases were dispersed and the situation worsened, these comrades took increased resolve to surmount their difficulties. They strived at all times to get closer to the poor farmers, to keep a firm hold on, and at the same time keep a deep faith in the masses. By so taking this approach they were able to re-kindle the people's spirit and reorganize the mass movement.
2. Their attitudes and working methods were based on the Party's policy of being in close touch with the masses, of relating to the indispensable interests of the masses, especially with relationship to land. On this they built a mass movement. They not only learned how to use the interests of each class, group and circle, but also learned to study carefully the interests of each individual so they could better influence him. The experiences at XB show clearly that if one fails to base propaganda on the practical interests of the people, one cannot expect the people to stand up and face the struggle.

   Using democratic methods plus detailed planning, the Party and the people considered, debated and met all problems concerning the rights and interests of the people. This increased the people's role and interest in the struggle to protect the countryside. The Party thus was able to harness the whole of the masses. Finally, from the struggle it drew out various lessons, it overcame weaknesses and it modified working methods where necessary.
3. The Party spirit of serving the masses is correct. Party members in XB are determined to work and die for the masses. If a members or cadre commits a mistake, he openly admits it before the masses. As a result,the masses believe in the cadres more and more, and spare no effort to protect them.
4. The educational methods used by the Party in XB village are both practical and effective. The Party leaders learned how to put theory into practice; it educated the internal ranks as well as explained the situation and basic plan to the masses. It did not try to teach the masses difficult arguments by rote. After attending a course for four days, for example, Party members came back to the village and studied documents for 5–7 days more. During this time they taught themselves ways in which they could make the contents of the documents known easily to the masses through public speaking.

   Propaganda was very simple and made to fit the feelings of the people. For example, in the matter of the relative strength of ourselves and the enemies, Party members told the people: "In the past, the US-Diem clique and village notables and security agents pursued us. Right now they do not dare come against us. Therefore, who is stronger? They are. They still can return. They still have military posts and conduct mopping up operations." This is the truth and thus the masses are made aware of the true situation.

5. The Party put prime stress on leading the masses in the struggle for land. It also paid close attention to the people's daily needs by leading in the struggle for the establishment of schools, first aid stations, a maternity clinic, etc., whose expenses were borne by the people. The Party consolidated and improved relations between workers and farmers. In any revolutionary operation, the Party must always heighten the role of the masses and see they are served. Thus the people are made to know that their interests are tied to the general struggle and that the glorious revolution is theirs. Consequently, the masses will take sides with the revolution and will adopt the political ideas of the revolution.

The Party in XB Village, however, still was guilty of a number of shortcomings:

1. It has failed to make a full three-prong attack. Best progress was made in the field of the armed struggle. But the political struggle and the army proselytizing operations remain weak. The weakest effort is the Army proselytizing operations. But even the armed struggle is inadequate and the Party must stay on the defensive. It cannot take the offensive to destroy the enemy forces and make our forces supreme.

   The laying of naily boards and various counter attacks were designed only to check the enemy's operations. They were not aimed at annihilating the enemy and seizing his weapons. From a practical standpoint the whole effort was not aimed at destruction of the enemy, only injuring him. The naily boards were numerous but they only injured the enemy and we did not seize any weapons from him. The combat village still lacks many conditions for us to go on the offensive.

   The political struggle is weak and is not closely enough bound to the armed struggle. The people are not properly trained in political arguments and in standing up to the enemy. Instead of attacking our enemies politically, through denunciations and army proselytizing operations, the Party only led the people to the point where they passively opposed our enemies and were content if the latter did not terrorize the village.

   Hundreds of people left the village—but they left only to avoid enemy soldiers, not to go out and make political attacks on them. The people do not understand that this is not a form of struggle. During mopping up operations the people are responsible for trying to win over the enemy soldiers' sympathy, enlightening them, and persuading them to desert to the revolution and bring their weapons with them. This is a form of army proselytizing which the Party must teach the people and tell them to practice every day under all circumstances.

With regard to person-to-person propaganda, the method and the slogans used are still poor. They achieve little except in one case, when a village council was overthrown through agitation. The struggle of the masses is also inadequate. The political struggle is on a low level, consisting only of simple demands and denunciations. The Party lacks slogans that reflect the practical interests and the aspirations of the people. Demands relating to economic and political rights have not yet reached the proper level.

2. Concerning army proselytizing operations, the Party has paid little attention to getting agents to infiltrate into the army, to persuade the families of soldiers who have rallied to the people, and these came without guns except a few who brought cartridges and grenades; others deserted but only went home. All of this had little effect on the enemy's strength. The Party still has not tried to persuade the families of soldiers of the Cao Dai and Hoa Hao religious sects to take sides with the revolution. The local cadres, being short-sighted, have failed to enlighten soldiers whom they contact and turn them into infiltration agents, or to establish political bases in local military units.

3. The political education of the people is not yet so well organized that the people can be taught politics regularly and thus improve and increase their political knowledge and revolutionary thoughts.

   Though the Party correctly based its action on the people's interests —especially with respect to land—and persuaded them to join the mass movement, it did not know how to profit from the opportunity to teach the people that their rights and interests must be subordinated to the national interests of Independence, Peace and Reunification, or that they must focus all their resentment on, and fight against the US-Diem clique. Consequently once the people are satisfied about land, the movement degenerates. This does not fit in with the Party's objective of mobilizing the strength of the entire people for the day of the general uprising.

4. The Party did not pay enough attention, nor is it determined to get in touch with, the Cao Dai and Hoa Hao religious people who are also farmers in the area—to make propaganda and persude them to join the revolution. The enemy, on the other hand, has been resorting to every kind of trick in order to win over the religious people. The Party is strong in the great part of the village, but few cells exist in the localities where live the religious compatriots.

Part Four

SITUATION AT OTHER VILLAGES AS COMPARED WITH XB.

The above is what happened at XB Village. This is the situation at other villages:

Village N is also a combatant village. It is fenced in, has naily boards and gates, etc. It has succeeded in keeping out the enemy, especially the commandos. But the mass movement there remains weak. The struggle against the enemy was assumed by Party cadres and self-defense troops and they also laid the naily boards. The farmers did not participate in the operations.

The Party in N village does not understand that the key motive power in a combatant village comes from urging the people to stand up and fight. It failed to study the situation and work out concrete plans, and it failed to make propaganda among the people. Thus, the people, being unaware of the necessity for a combatant village, did not participate positively in its establishment. The said Party does not know how correctly to start a mass movement as was done in XB village, nor how to draw out lessons from experiences, not to attach itself to the people's struggle. Therefore the movement in N is not as strong as previously planned.

In the villages of MM, MN, MT, and LN the farmers made naily boards to be laid by the self-defense forces but the people did not take part in laying the naily boards.

In MQ village, though an enemy soldier was injured once by a naily board, the Party failed to take the opportunity to point out this success and further mobilize the people. The movement there was supported by a small number of people, and some time later it degenerated.

The cadres in a great number of villages assume the responsibility for doing work, instead of leading the masses. Thus they really do not follow the Party's policy of engaging the masses. Their educational and propaganda efforts are not based on the fundamental needs and desires of the people. The said cadres also adopt out-of-date working methods, become bureaucrats, stand in awe of the enemy, lack vigilance and wish for peace. They serve in form only and do not attack the enemy.

In summary, our movement is weak in those villages because:

Cadres do not properly grasp Party policy and consequently lack revolutionary spirit. They are not in tune with the thoughts of the people, nor are they dedicated to serving the masses and struggling in the interests of the people.

Their attitudes and working methods are too bureaucratic. They do not follow the methods which the Party has worked out, do not study their local situation closely enough. They inaugurate policies which are not rooted in the rights, interests, hopes and feelings of the people. They also attempt to indoctrinate the masses dogmatically, using materials which are not relevant to the situation.

The lessons to be learned from XB Village may be summarized as follows:

The people are all powerful. It remains only for us to harness ourselves to serving the people. With the people following us, if we have initiative and use tested Party techniques, all operations will succeed.

In the simplest terms, the Party's political line must be based on the needs and interests and rights of the people, the most vital ones. These are concrete and plain to see. On these needs and interests we must build, educating the people, mobilizing them to rise and join the revolution.

In any operation we must carefuly make specific plans, well in advance. This is particularly true in the launching the organization as a mass movement. People are not eager to join such movements unless they have carefully been made aware of its objectives and thus are enlightened. In leadership, tasks assigned should be graded from the easy to the difficult, and should be assigned with consideration of the person [who is] to execute them. . . . In XB, the Party made careful advance preparations; the people were well educated and mobilized prior to the launching of the mass movement and the start of the building of the combat village. Once started everything progressed quickly and smoothly. The day after it was started the people were in a position to repulse an enemy attack. This is the way it should be done elsewhere.

Properly containing security agents and informers depends on uniting the rural people against these enemies. This is done by showing how these agents would deny the people's rights, showing how they do damage, telling about the crimes they commit using specific examples from the local area. This is also done by promoting the spirit of secrecy among the rural people as well as getting them to commit themselves in fighting with the self-defense forces against the enemy. We must also maintain firm leadership of the various civic organizations, and set up special revolutionary groups if necessary—only then can we prevent security agents, local informers and spies from penetrating our area.

We must maintain a spirit of offense. In order to motivate the people to attack our enemies we must make them understand the validity of the Revolution's policies, and must also set up rules and working methods for them. They will not be active unless we carefully show them what they must do. Most of these efforts are political and the poor people must learn how to advance the revolution through political means, thus avoiding the risks of regrettable losses which hurt the revolution and discourage the people. Above all, we must keep the masses from becoming passive.

We must better our movement, that is the caliber of Party members, the cadres and all organizations working with us. Highly motivated people will show initiative in carrying out various tasks, making propaganda, etc. In truth, there is a tendency for the Party members to study documents in a mechanical fashion and for form's sake only. As a result the Party members and cadre are not well aware of rules and working methods. In this situation they fail to carry out plans eagerly and as a consequence the movement goes astray. Further, in some places, local policy runs unintentionally counter to Party policy. Further there are cadres with erroneous thoughts, bureaucrats whose working methods are wrong and these affect the organization very much. Our internal ranks, therefore, take top priority in training work.

We must increase our spirit of dedication, and be determined properly to carry out Party policy, always serving the people's needs. We need to develop better methods, as was done by the Party at XB. We must rid ourselves of any strong desire for peace, eliminate our fear of the enemy. We must resist adopting irresponsible attitudes. We must develop discipline. We must avoid becoming too optimistic. We must remain always vigilant. We must eliminate bureaucratic attitudes. These things still exist in the Party.

Finally, we must develop a great spirit of offense, determined to attack our enemies ever more fiercely. In this way victory over our enemies finally will be accomplished.

APPENDIX F

COMMENDATION LETTER, BASIC REPORT FORMS, TEN OATHS OF THE SOLDIER, AND RULES AND PRECEPTS

[DOCUMENT F-1]

NATIONAL FRONT FOR LIBERATION OF SOUTH VIETNAM

LETTER OF COMMENDATION

Considering Regulations concerning Awards and Punishment prescribed "R" (COSVN) Military Affairs Committee for SVN Liberation Army.

Based upon the authority and responsibility of the Commanders at all levels in the SVN Liberation Army.

Considering recommendations of ______ Commander, and the outstanding performance of duty of Comrade T______, First Aidman during the attack on enemy boats at K____ X____ on ______ 1964, the following is recorded:

This individual performed his first aid duty in a good manner, and participated in the engagement as a courageous soldier. Met with a hard-to-handle situation, this individual insisted on remaining in his position, killing 3 of the enemy, and seizing 1 TSMG and 200 rounds.

In order to encourage distinguished personnel, "D" Commander

DECIDES:

ART. 1: Grant Letter of Commendation to Comrade: I____ V____ T____, First Aidman a group member of ________.

ART. 2: This decision has been disseminated throughout "D" as subject for indoctrination class, and one copy to the family of individual concerned.

ART. 3: Political and Staff Sections, ______ and Comrade T ______ will comply with this decision as outlined.

1964

For the Commander of "D"

B____ H____

P____ V____ H____

[DOCUMENT F–2]

FORM OF MONTHLY REPORT ON OUR STRENGTH

NUMBER OF PARTY MEMBERS IN: . . ./September/64

(1) Names of hamlets having Party members	Number of Party Members in the month									Number of Party Members at month's end																								
													Strata			Social Classes					Nationalities			Religions				Behavior			Status			Remarks
	Total number of each hamlet	Purged	Defected	Surrendered	Transferred	Killed	Captured	Admitted	Recruited	Total Number of each hamlet	Officials	Reserves	Farmers	Youths	Women	Laborers	School Children	Share croppers	Poor farmers	Middle farmers	Vietnamese	Cambodian		Caodaist	Buddhist			Good	Fair	Poor	Illegal	Semi-legal	Legal	
30	3								0	4	12	2	3	1		4			4		1							1	1	2	4			Notes on each hamlet killed
40	2									2	2	1	2			2			2		2							1	1	0	2			
50	23								0	3	2	1	3			3			1	2	3							1	2	2	1		2	
60	78								+	2	2	4	2			2			2	3	2							2	2	4	2			
70	2									8	4		4	2	2	8			5	1	8							1	1	1	6	2		
80	1									3	3		2	1		3			2		3								1	1	2			
10	2									1	1		1			1			1		1								2	1	1			
BOS	3									2	2		2			2			2	1	2								2		2			
DK	1									3		3		3		3			2		3										3			
20																																		

[DOCUMENT F-2 Continued]

NUMBER OF GROUP MEMBERS IN: . . . / . . . /64

(2)		Number of Group Members in the month									Number of Group Members at month's end																					REMARKS
														Social Classes					Nation-alities			Religions				Behavior			Status			
Village	Names of ham-lets having group members	Total number of each hamlet	Purged	Defected	Surrendered	Transferred	Killed	Captured	Admitted	Recruited	Total number of each hamlet	Male	Female	Laborers	School children	Share croppers	Poor farmers	Middle farmers	Vietnamese	Cambodian		Caodaist	Buddhist			Good	Fair	Poor	Illegal	Semi-legal	Legal	Notes on each hamlet

[DOCUMENT F–2 Continued]

NUMBER OF FARMERS' ASSOCIATION MEMBERS IN: . . ./. . ./64

(3) Villages	Names of Hamlets having Farmers' Associa-tion	Number of Farmers' Association members in the month								Number of Farmer's Association Members at month's end																					REMARKS
											Strata			Social Classes				Nation-alities			Religions				Behavior			Status			
		Total number of each hamlet	Purged	Defected	Surrendered	Killed	Captured	Transferred	Recruited	Total number of each hamlet	Farmers	Youths	Women	Share croppers	Poor farmers	Middle farmers		Vietnamese	Cambodian		Caodaist	Buddhist			Good	Fair	Poor	Illegal	Semi-legal	Legal	Notes on each hamlet

[DOCUMENT F-2 Continued]

[NUMBER OF MILITIA MEMBERS IN: . . ./. . ./64]

(4)		Number of militia in the month								Number of militia at month's end																		Equipment						REMARKS
												Kinds			Behavior			Social Classes			Nation-alities		Religions									
Villages	Names of ham-lets having Militia	Total number of each hamlet	Purged	Surrendered	Defected	Transferred	Killed	Captured	Recruited	Total number of each hamlet	Women militia	Party members	Group members	Farmers' Association members	Good	Fair	Poor	Share croppers	Poor farmers	Middle farmers	Vietnamese	Cambodian	Caodaist	Buddhist			Rifles	Home made weapons	Ammunition	Grenades			Notes on each hamlet

[DOCUMENT F–3]

STRENGTH OF VILLAGE LIBERATION YOUTH ASSOCIATION

Name of Each Village	Total number of Youth				Composition of Youth Command Committee							
	Number of Youth (?)	Female	Number of grown-ups	Female	Total number of personnel in Command Committee	Number of members (female)	Analysis			Social class		
							Fair	Mediocre	Poor	Peasant	Middle Class Farmer	Small bourgeois

(Continued)

Liberat (ed/ion)

Social Class		Religion			Association Sub-Chapters and Cells					Village and Hamlet		
Landlord	Cao Dai	Catholic	Hoa Hao	Buddhist	Total No. of Sub-Chapters	Association Sub-Chapter members	No. of Association Cell	Most numerous Association Cells	Smallest number of Association Cells	How many Hamlet (s) in village	No. of hamlets having Sub-Chapter	No. of hamlet (s) having Association members

(Continued)

Social Class

				Analysis			Social Class					Religion
Number of Hamlets having no Committee members	Total No. of Asso- ciation members (?)	No. of females	No. un- compro- mised	Fair	Mediocre	Poor	Peasant	Middle Class Farmer	Small Bourgeois	Bourgeois Wealthy Farmer	Stu- dent	Cao Dai

(Continued)

Association member of the same

Religion			Disposition of Association member						Reason for decrease					No. of Associations
Hoa Hao	Catholic	Buddhist	Guer- rilla	Self- Defense	Farmer Asso- ciation	Propa- ganda Cultural Indoctri- nation	Commo- liasion	Weapons Cell	Captured	Surren-	dered	Purged	Dead	

(Continued)

District, Year

Association Chapter	Number attending courses			Association Chapter	Projected	Remarks
Date of activation	No. (of members) in Command Committee	No. (of members) in Association Chapter	No. (of members) in Cells	No. (of members) joining Group	No. (of members) to develop Association	

To: Youth Groups and Association Chapters

The attached strength format is sent to you with the following requirements:

1. Enable the comrades to establish the total number of Village Youth as they are broken into positive and non-aligned so that we may have a disposition plan for the Group, the Association, and thus lead and control the Village Youth from whose ranks we draw our strength.

2. Administer the youth we now have and indicate the number of youth in each hamlet so that we will be enabled to develop those hamlets in which the strength available is not sufficient.

3. District and province request to have the overall strength of each village with indications as to weakness in each field and action to be taken so that they will assist us.

Method of determining the number of youth available:

Convene Command Committee meetings in assigning the work to specific members of specific hamlet for a given period of time.

Conduct investigations in order to know and develop those where Groups and Associations have not been developed.

Youth Group Chapters and Command Committees have a deadline of 15 Dec ____ for forwarding reports to District Youth Command Committees and Groups who will in turn consolidate them before forwarding to province. In case of delay, 20 Dec ____ will be the suspense date. Request that Group Chapters do their best.

29 Nov.

Greetings in Anti-American Emulation.

[DOCUMENT F–4]
[RULES AND PRECEPTS]

The Ten Oaths of the Soldier

1. Defend the Fatherland, fight and sacrifice [myself] for the people's Revolution.
2. Obey the orders received and carry out the mission of the soldier.
3. Strive to improve the virtues of a Revolutionary soldier.
4. Study to improve [myself] and build up a powerful Revolutionary Army.
5. Carry out other missions of the Army.
6. Be vigilant, preserve secrecy, heighten the Revolutionary soldier's honor.
7. Help consolidate the internal unity.
8. Preserve and save public properties.
9. Work for the solidarity between the Army and People.
10. Maintain the Quality and Honor of the Revolutionary Soldier.

The Twelve Points of Discipline

1. Obey and carry out orders from superiors.
2. Strictly preserve military secrets.
3. Maintain order in the Units' location.
4. Properly maintain weapons and prevent their capture by the enemy.
5. Never take common properties for personal use.
6. Be fair and honest in business with the people, encourage the people to increase production.
7. Never take even a needle from the people.
8. Return what one borrows, reimburse for what one damages.
9. When staying in civilian houses, maintain it as if it is one's own.
10. Be polite with the people and love the people.
11. Propagandize the people to participate in the struggle.
12. Be respected and loved by the people.

[The immediate historical precedent for these two declarations are the "Rules of Discipline" and the "Point for Attention" originally formulated by Mao Tse-tung and officially restated by the General Headquarters of the Peoples' Liberation Army in October 1947 in the following modified version:]

The Three Main Rules of Discipline are as follows:

(1) Obey orders in all your actions.

(2) Do not take a single needle or piece of thread from the masses.

(3) Turn in everything captured.

The Eight Points for Attention are as follows:

(1) Speak politely.
(2) Pay fairly for what you buy.
(3) Return everything you borrow.
(4) Pay for everything you damage.
(5) Do not hit or swear at people.
(6) Do not damage crops.
(7) Do not take liberties with women.
(8) Do not ill-treat captives.*

Rules of Secrecy

1. Be always vigilant against enemy sabotage plots.
2. Never disclose unit's designation, strength, weapons and Commander's name and rank.
3. Never disclose the policy and place for the struggle and use of friendly forces.
4. Never disclose friendly locations and installations.
5. Never disclose the operation route and the roads leading to bases.
6. Do not take the unauthorized persons to the bases, units and agencies.
7. Unauthorized persons will not be allowed to enter bases, units and agencies.
8. Never disclose your name, rank and mission to anyone except to your Commander.
9. Report to your Commander upon completion of mission.
10. Never disclose the secrets and internal organization of your unit or friendly units to relatives or friends.
11. When living in civilian houses, educate the people on preservation of secrecy according to the "Three NO's motto: no hear, no see, no know.
12. Papers and documents should be carefully protected. They should not be carried along in missions and combat if they are not necessary. When they are no longer needed, they should be burned.
13. The mail should be censored by the Command Section.
14. Personnel should be permanently educated to observe the regulations on preservation of secrecy.
15. Uncover and punish the violations of these regulations.

* *Selected Military Writings*, p. 341.

APPENDIX G
UNIT AND ACTIVITY CRITIQUE

[DOCUMENT G–1]
REPORT ON THE REGIONAL ACTIVITIES OF THE K VILLAGE PARTY CHAPTER

I. *SOME FEATURES OF THE GENERAL SITUATION IN K VILLAGE*

A. *Social Organization*

K village is one of 19 villages of Dau Tieng rubber plantation. It is comprised of 126 houses and 700 people. Most of these people are contract workers and others are refugees and peasants who came from other areas. There are over 400 male and female workers, 15 foremen, 7 supervisors, 1 guard, 1 chief of village, 1 medical aide and 2 secretaries. The workers lived in tile-roof concreted rooms. One family of workers lives in one room. In revolutionary organization, we have an official basic party section which includes 7 party members; a youth association, a women's association which has 12 members, and 60 members of liberation labor association. We also have one secret self-defense cell and 3 troop-proselytizing cadres.

As legal and semi-legal organizations in the village, we have a union sub-section, 1 representative of the workers and 1 pagoda association. As far as enemy organizations, before 1959 there were a village council, a self-defense unit, a section of national revolutionary movement, a republican youth association, and a rural defense youth association. But after 1959 while the revolutionary movement was rising, the people broke up the enemy encircling pressure and the above people moved to Dau Tieng town. Presently there are only a few left in the village, who are suspected of being enemy agents. Therefore we are checking on them. Unfortunately K village is located near the main road. It is only 6 kilometers from K village to Dau Tieng town, so the enemy need only 5 or 10 minutes to come to K village to repress and terrorize the people in the village or force them to build strategic hamlets, destroy our movement or capture our cadres.

B. *Situation of the Population and Our Cadres*

After 9 years of resistance and 8 years of political struggle, the workers in the plantation are conscious of the revolution. They have a firm standpoint on class struggle and strong hatred of the Imperialists and feudalists. They are determined to side with the revolution in any way. They have absolute belief in the final victory of the revolution and our people. So in 1959, when our cadre came to work at the plantation, the workers stood up and joined our movement. They supported the revolution in spirit as well as in materials: rice, cloth, money, food, dried fish, medical supply. They supply the revolution every day and every month. When we came to the village, many workers were penniless. But they did their best and tried to borrow secretly to pay their contributions. Though U.S. Diem had agreed with the plantation owner to cut down their food rations, the workers, despite their being short of rice and everything, had come to regularly and adequately supply the revolution. Some workers gave the cadre all their rice. And our cadres were obliged to tell them to keep some rice for their families. Whenever, we are in need of something they have made efforts to give it to us. Daily they brought our cadres food stuffs such as: plums, strawberries, mangoes, pieces of rice cake, some candies, a bunch of bananas, a kg of sugar or soya-cake, or a can of milk, etc. . . When they found rounds of ammo or a hand grenade dropped by the enemy, they were not afraid of danger and brought them to our cadres. Once a female worker found a round. With delighted, faithful and sincere face she brought us the round and said, "this is a Thompson round dropped by the enemy. I picked it up and brought it to you hoping that you would use it against the American aggressors." An old man advised us, "You should try to overcome all difficulties and miseries to struggle against the enemy, as for us we are always determined to support the revolution if it is in need. We will sacrifice ourselves until the last minute of life." After only 4 years (from 1959 to now) 42 male and female workers of K village left their families and came to the secret zone to take part in revolutionary activities. This is a proof of the good will of the workers in K village. The background of our struggle teaches us that working for the revolution we can not avoid death and arrest. From April 1961 to the end of 1962: in only 20 months: there were 35 cadres, members of the Dau Tieng Party committee, who died bravely for the cause of the revolution. As for K village there were 7 comrades who sacrificed themselves.

Even so, the rest of the workers were not discouraged. Their hatred of the enemy increased and made people more brave in the struggle against the enemy in avenging their comrades. If one person died, one hundred others would stand up to continue their work.

In short, the workers have been conscious of the revolution. They hate U.S.-Diem policy and support the revolution. They have a strong belief in the victory of the revolution. Our cadre are determined to sacrifice for the liberation of the people, the independence and the unification of our country. But in times past we had no program of action, no method of work, therefore we labored much with few results.

C. *The Activities of Our Party Chapter*

Our Party Chapter has not entirely realized the importance of the investigation and research effort which has a decisive influence on our victory over the enemy. Before doing something such as recruiting a member for an association [or] a group of our party, we must investigate him carefully. We can not do like this: make acquaintance with him 2 or 3 times, then accept him into the organization; or recruit him through friendship, family relationship or by favor. A party member was said to have told a person: "try to carry out your works successfully, I would like to recruit you. All this procedure is not [necessary]." Sometimes we do investigate, but we do not investigate a recruit directly in details such as a security officer investigates a prisoner. In training propaganda our cadres often fail to investigate and research in order to know what our cadres (association members, group members, Party members) must study so that they would become able to carry out their works later. We only explain roughly what they should do while most of them don't understand clearly the Party's regulations—what their duties and interests are in carrying out their work, what are the mottos and the methods of operation in weak areas and how to keep their organizations secret for a long time.

We conduct educative propaganda in many ways such as holding meetings, scattering leaflets, hanging banners and distributing documents, etc. . . . But in those conferences they explain the general situation without details. Thus, they speak of the world situation: the socialist block under the leadership of Russia is becoming stronger day by day while the imperialist bloc under the American leadership has become weaker and weaker. Nothing is said of the local situation. Sometimes they propagandize according to their own imagination and their own thoughts. One female worker asked comrade, "Did you take part in the revolution?" He replied "Yes." In order to make the woman believe that what he said was true, he disclosed his title and started to propagandize: "To take part in revolution is glorious and just; our liberated area has become large day by day; we have vehicles and power generator there; new affiliates of whoever comes to the secret zone of the revolution will be warmly welcomed and offered bread and coffee." While the worker was becoming confused, he continued, "Do not be afraid, at present the revolutionary movement is found everywhere, you are not the only one in our village, there are over 20 people who joined the revolution." Then he started to name a number of people with their functions. Finally he told her not to report on this to anybody because: "This is a secret organization. I believe in you, he said, for letting you know this, but don't tell the 3rd person about this story." Another party member said to his cadres: "If you join the revolution you would be educated and progress or at least you would be distributed pistols, etc. . . . The K village has 6 secret organizations (the party, youth association, women association, the labor liberation association, secret self-defense unit and the troop proselytizing group). A cadre had misunderstood the meaning of the sentence he read in certain documents that "our party does not abandon any one." Therefore all workers of the village took part in secret organizations and tried to develop and gather as many members as possible. These members were recruited carelessly without investigation and not in conformity with the party regulations. Among 126 families in K village there are some wicked families which are suspected by us. So we have not admitted them into our organization yet. However, we are planning to propagandize these families to turn them into good people and urge them to join our party. If one of the 6 above-mentioned organizations finds a good worker who does not fulfil the required conditions, it introduces him to yet another one. There is a female comrade, who was first a group member then accepted into the party as chief of a party cell. She later became a member of a Party Chapter and was assigned to be a leader of a youth association. Finally she was appointed a leader of the women's association. Thus, this woman she was a member of 4 different secret organizations at the same time.

In one family which included wife, husband and one child, 3 of them took part in 3 different organizations. Whenever they came back from the meeting, they usually discussed the problems of three different organizations. Sometimes the child did the work entrusted to his mother or father.

A person can become a member of the liberation labor association after paying certain contributions to the association. Seven party members worked in the same Party Chapter. Each one takes charge of 10 other persons of different secret organizations; therefore most of them know each other pretty well.

The secretary of the Party Chapter knows all the party members in the village as well as all associations such as the labor association, secret self-defense unit and cadres of propaganda and action against the enemy. Sometimes the secretary did not wait for cadres of lower level to bring him their collection of taxes. Rather did he himself go to those associations and groups to control and collect taxes. Once he inadvertently talked with a person who formerly was the chief of the village Republican youth association under the Diem regime. The latter reported to the enemy who captured and destroyed our organizations. We often advised him to correct himself, but he did not listen to us and said, "If you can not do any difficult work, leave it to me, then go away, I will do the work myself, I am not afraid of death." Whenever a dispute arose between the cadres some of them left their organizations and changed to others. Sometimes they came to see the secretary and asked him to give up their function to work under the leadership of the secretary. Instead of rebutting him the secretary said, "If you can not work over there, come and work with me." Nearly all the cadres know the secretary. If there was any important work, one courier came to the secretary's house as many times a day as needed. Therefore all workers in the village pretty well know about the activities of the Party Chapter. People did not hesitate to gamble because they could stop when they saw the secretary coming. Sometimes the cadres committee invited the secretary to attend a meeting of criticism, the latter came but did not admit his mistakes. Whenever a meeting took place the Party Chapter recommended their cadres in advance how to report, what they should report and what they should not, etc. . . Thus no sincere reports were made and the party could not learn the exact situation of the organization. However, we can say that at the present time the revolutionary activities of our Party Chapter in K village has risen to the highest degree. Education propaganda, well conducted among the people, has had a good effect. We could divide a number of irresolute people and isolate a group of "devils" and spies. Our organization can develop very fast. Our struggle helps the masses improve their conditions and rights. Thus, our struggle has brought reductions of rice prices. We have claimed for a raise in pay and for buying rice freely without pemission, etc. . . Workers and cadre are very happy to be in such a situation. Some people realized that "within a short time there will be a general uprising which will overthrow the U.S. Diem regime. Independence and unification of our country will come very soon." So, our cadres are very happy. Besides working at the plantation they take part in revolutionary activities such as educative propaganda, recruiting of members, making requests for the struggle of the workers, collecting money and rice for the revolutions, etc. . . .

The recruiting of members was well performed. Large numbers have joined our organization. The quantity is good but the quality is not what we have desired. The training activities were conducted openly. The 3 meetings of Party Chapter, youth association and women's association took place on Sundays. Training was based on documents sent by higher levels. These documents often dealt with the general situation and general work, having no relation to the happenings in the area or with the cadres. As a result, the latter can not draw any experience from them.

Assignment, control, comment, and evaluation are not good. They assign a task to a cadre according to the general plan without considering the cadre's actual capabilities. They do not listen to his reasons and comment. The cadre does not know the importance of the job entrusted to him. Sometimes the cadre has not been trained for the task. He may not thoroughly understand the regulations of the party and realize all that is incumbent upon him. He does not have a firm grasp of the work methods, guidelines for action in weak areas, especially the guarantee of security that will permit the organization to last long. He does not know how the struggle is organized covertly and overtly.

The Chapter can not carry out the task by itself. It always relies on higher levels. In the face of the present situation where the enemy has enough machinery: a government, spies, armed forces, police, security, intelligence agents, etc . . . and imposes large encircling pressures upon the people every day and every hour. If the Party Chapter always waits for higher level's instructions, it would be in trouble whenever a break in liaison is made.

A struggle movement took place in various villages asking for a raise of salary, improvement of worker's living conditions, release of people who were forced to enlist in the army or imprisoned, and for the resignation of Diem. All these villages had prepared their requests and motions. The K village, in particular, has been informed about this matter by the

Party Chapter, but it did not prepare either requests or motions. When the workers of other villages went through the K village, the party members, group members, association members in the village were very excited. They joined the demonstration; but half way there they were called back by order of the Party Chapter, because they had neither requests nor motions. There was then a struggle for resolving the 11 days of forced idleness decided by the manager. The workers sent representatives to discuss the matter with the management board of representatives. The latter promised that the workers would be paid 11 rations of rice for 11 days of unemployment and 110$ VN a piece. They later dealt with the authorities in Binh Duong province who terrorized the representatives of the workers and paid them nothing. There was a struggle for a raise of 42$ VN in the salary given [for] every cut of rubber tree in K village. At the beginning the manager rejected the claim of the workers. The latter struggle was stronger. They went on strike. The managing board replaced them with unqualified workers. All the workers in the village came to the plantation and dissuaded new ones from working for the managers. They explained to them the manager's schemes of sowing dissension among the workers and exploiting them.

Finally the new workers agreed with the local workers to stop working and force the managing board to satisfy the workers' claim. Then came the successful struggle of 11 female workers claiming for the free purchase of rice without paying the tax of 12$ VN. The U.S.-Diemists agreed with the plantation managing board to cut down the rations of the workers from 933 gr. of rice to 700 gr 11 female workers' families which had many members did not have enough rice to eat. They had to buy rice at the market. The Diem authorities ordered them to come to the village council to get tickets for their purchase and to pay 12$ VN duty. Each time they could only buy 5 liters of rice. Before this inhuman exploitation, the above female workers came to Dau Tieng district and asked the district chief to let them buy rice freely without paying any money to the village council. Under the pretext that these workers were so induced by the Viet Cong, the district authorities arrested these women and sent them to Binh Duong province. Our cadres took 8 children from 8 to 14 years of age of these women and brought them to Dau Tieng market, to find their mothers they said. These children cried and said: "The managers of the plantation have cut down our rations, our families are lacking rice, so our mothers have gone to the market to buy some more rice. They were captured by the government. We are to young, nobody takes care of us." They were crying like this for 2 days and gave rise to a rumour among the population in Dau Tieng and among the U.S.-Diem soldiers. The latter came and gave food to the children; and they brought them ice lemon water, gave them some money to buy a bus ticket and told them to go home. Finally the U.S. authorities released the above female workers and cancelled the regulations about the purchase of rice.

Considering the situation and activities of our organization in K village from 1959 to the end of 1962 we can roughtly make these comments:

II. *THE TASK OF THE PARTY CHAPTER AND OUR AGENTS*

A. *Investigation and Research*

Our Chapter has not entirely realized the importance of this kind of task which has a decisive effect on success or failure of the movement in the future. The Chapter has not clearly understood our principles and the task of investigation and research. Investigation of personal histories is often carelessly conducted.

In training action they do not try to find out what the cadres must study in order to carry out their task successfully. They do not know the forces of the enemy and ours. In their work they usually rely on luck.

B. *Educative Propaganda Action*

In educative propaganda, our cadres used to speak of general things. They have not synthesized facts [of the situation] and activities so that our members may draw experience from them.

Propaganda is not conducted according to the Party's principles in weak areas. We have not given enough attention to the use of all the capabilities of our people. We do not differentiate between legal and semi-legal activities. So the lines and the policies of the party are not well disseminated among the workers and the masses. Sometimes our cadre carry out propaganda openly and unintentionally give the enemy opportunities for terrorizing the people and making them afraid of joining our movement.

There are many ways of carrying out propaganda. Propaganda may be carried out among the cadres. At the meetings we can stop cars and conduct spontaneous propaganda. We can scatter leaflets, hang banners, stick slogans, distribute information documents and magazines in the villages or on roads, thus allowing the workers and population to read them.

C. *Organization*

1. *Party Chapter.*

The Party Chapter is not organized according to the principles of the party in the weak area. We organized, according to our feeling, friendships, family relations or certain favors. Our cadres recruit as many members as possible without paying attention to the secrecy of the organization. They should recruit members according to their capabilities and good behaviour. A village having 300 workers of whom 7 are party members, 12 association members and 60 liberation labor association members may be considered very active. We can say that the Party Chapter in that village has done a good job. This village however has 6 covert organizations at the same time (Party Chapter, youth association, women's association, liberation association, secret self-defense unit and troop proselytizing organization). Seven party members work in the same Chapter, one party member is a member of 4 different covert organizations. Most of these party members and association members know each other pretty well, which is not advantageous for our movement.

The basic party does not understand the party's principles for selection of members. It does not investigate their personal histories carefully. A number of recruits still indulge in gambling and many wives etc . . . They were accepted as party members even without application. Candidate members also have the right of introducing new ones. The method of operation for the Party Chapter is still untidy. It has never succeeded in carrying out any action worth mentioning in its area of responsibility. For everything, it relies on help from the outside. Troubled by the situation and in the face of plots by the enemy, it becomes confused without leadership from the outside. Party Chapter members and association members have conducted extensive activities, but they can not work by themselves. They can only operate when they receive instructions from outside. So there are neither monthly program of actions nor periodic reports, but only a report after each operation. Examining the question they can only see its external appearance and not its characteristics or its nature.

The Chapter activities are still very loose. Its meetings are not held regularly. They lack in importance and attention to detail.

The Party Chapter is not organized according to a chain of command. That means the organization does not begin with one group member, one association member or one hard-core cadre then develops slowly until there are 3 people who come together to form a basic party section. Here it is not the case. Members of the Chapter are recruited one by one from the outside until 3 people are available and then united to form a Chapter. In this way these 3 members of the Chapter do not know and understand each other. So they do not trust each other. Sometimes they become jealous of each other because of their positions. These members are not trained people. They do not clearly understand every step of the activities of a cadre. Later they run into difficulties, especially when they have to deal with the organization in weak areas. Our cadres' degree of understanding of the party's policy is still very low. Their method of working is not scientific. They can not fulfil the requirements of the revolutionary movement.

2. *Activities of the party group*

The work at the party group is relatively careful. The method of carrying out its tasks is better than that of the Chapter. Its members are recruited according to the regulations of the party. People are investigated before entering the group. Group members have carried out their activities very eagerly. They attracted a good deal of youth in the village who have joined the group and behave themselves as the backbone of the revolution. But the group's organizational system is still untidy. The group has not enough experience to operate in weak areas. The group members work well together but they have no idea of our protracted and hard struggle. They do not understand that the present situation requires us to struggle more in the heart of the enemy than in our secret zone. They misunderstand when they think that they can only render service to the revolution in secret zones. So most of group members have left their families to go to the liberated areas to take part in the struggle against the enemy. In addition to this military conscription, forced labor and the obligation to join the republican youth association or rural youth association etc. . . have pushed 70% of youth into entering secret zones. Thus, very few youth remain in the village. So the party group has met with difficulty in recruiting its members.

3. *Activities of Liberation Labor Association*

Its concept on quality is very low. It considers the standard of its members equal to that of sympathizers.

Members of the association are recruited without any investigation or check on their past activities. They need only to be briefed 2 or 3 times about the principles of the party and to pay certain contributions to the association fund, and that is all. They don't have to know the regulations of the association and need not declare anything. The wishes of the association is to recruit as many members as possible.

4. *Secret Self-defense*

There is a cell of secret-defense comprised of 3 people who do not understand their important role and the responsibility of their cell. The work of the cell is careless and carried out in a disorderly manner. Cell members are entrusted with insignificant work such as that of the courier who bicycles every day from the village to the liberated area to meet certain cadres. The main job of the cell which is secret self-defense can not be carried out correctly. Self-defense members have no experience in working though they are eager to perform their duties. They never refuse to do anything and are not troubled when encountering difficulties. They are very faithful towards the party.

5. *Troop Proselytizing*

This group is organized very simply. Each cell is composed of 3 people who were taught the party's policy, and the methods of carrying out troop proselytizing.

They were assigned to go to restaurants and snack bars where U.S.-Diemist military personnel used to come, in order to get information and to carry out their troop proselytizing activities, such as to persuading enemy servicemen to cross over to the people's side. They can do better in trying to win over the enemy soldiers and use them as penetrators. However at present, this organization is still weak. Troop proselytizing has been implemented for training people to penetrate enemy ranks. But this work of penetration has met with great difficulties which the cell has not succeeded in overcoming yet. The cell has induced families of servicemen to go to see their husbands and sons and tell them that they are very miserable, they strongly need their help and must leave the enemy ranks and go home, or in case they can not do so they should put down their arms and join the people when they face them in mopping-up operations.

6. *Legal and semi-legal organizations*

The strong workers' struggle against the U.S.-Diem's regime

and plantation owners has permitted the setting up of a rubber workers union.

After 1959, the revolutionary movement came into ascendance. Thanks to the influence of the movement we won over most of the union cadre, representatives of the workers in the villages and some members of the managing board of Dau Tieng plantation. But we did not carry our struggle according to the party's principles. We usually mixed the work of legal and illegal organizations. We used cadres of covert organizations instead of workers for carrying motions to the managers. This move gave the enemy the motives to repress the workers. They threatened and captured the best workers in legal organization and other people dared not cooperate with us. Thus the enemy succeeded in sending their lackeys to the workers union to manage it. Since that day the workers' union stopped all its struggle activities and could draw no interest from the workers. The union also limited itself to collecting monthly dues. As our cadres saw that the workers union was of no use to them, they left it and led the workers to fight against it.

Our movement could not profit by our semi-legal organizations such as: the compatriots association, the pagoda association etc. . . and at had no further intentions of organizing any semi-legal organization. In the meanwhile the workers worked by teams at the plantation. They rested at the same place after eating together. Usually 1 team included 5 or 7 workers and they took their turn in cooking rice at the plantation. Small groups were formed which used to come together to talk and rest. It was a very convenient situation for us to carry out propaganda and educate these workers, so that they espouse our cause, struggle against the enemy for the essential rights of the workers.

D. *Training*

The training was based on documents given by higher levels. These documents covered the general situation of the country without mentioning any details on the local situation, so the training course had little interest and at the end of the course the students could not use anything they had studied. Members were assigned work without understanding it. So they had little chance to carry out their task successfully. The work was assigned according to a fixed plan, without any regard for the local situation. Whenever they completed any work our members did not have time to check it over, to draw experience from it or to examine the weak points. But with its eager spirit and good will the Party Chapter had found ways to train our cadres on the spot or outside. Therefore most of our cadres have grown up in the movement and have contributed very much to the cause of the revolution.

E. *Struggle Activities.*

There is a struggle of the 11 female workers for buying rice freely, and there has been success in the struggle for a raise of 4$20 [sic] in the salary given for every cut of rubber trees. Our struggle was successful because it was reasonable, and had responded to the aspiration of the workers. The majority of the people including those in the city and the military personnel of U.S.-Diem have supported our struggle. It illustrated the plots of U.S.-Diem and the plantation owners who put the workers under their pressures and exploitation. We took advantage of this struggle to denounce their rotten regime before the public. This successful struggle of the workers was a victory in the economic field. It brought an improvement to other workers' living conditions. It is also a victory in the political field. It makes the workers of the plantation in K village unite together. It showed that: "if we want to win a victory such as to improve our living condition we must unite closely." The successful struggle of K village encourages the struggle of workers in Dau Tieng city. In the above struggle, the Party Chapter showed that it had some initiative and has the confidence of all the workers.

Besides, there are some other struggles such as that of the workers demanding the resignation of Diem and compensation for the suspensions of work ordered by the managing board. However, in these struggles we did not follow the exact struggle guidance. Some struggles had not relied on the aspiration of all the workers. There was a lack of plausible reasons. Before and after a struggle we did not carefully investigate the balance of forces between the enemy and ourselves. We could not weigh all the importance of the problem. Our members have often misused the legal and semi-legal forms.

F. *The Leadership of the Operational Group and the Agent Affairs Section in Regard to the Party Chapter*

At the beginning of 1959 the Agent Affairs Section sent a member to K village under the guise of a rubber plantation worker to serve as a leader of this Party Chapter. In August 1961 he was captured by the enemy. Since that day, the Agent Affairs Section has led the Party Chapter indirectly by orders given through the operational group. Formerly the Party Chapter had relied on the Agent Affairs Cadre for carrying out its tasks. Now there was no Agent Affairs cadre, whose advice could be asked. So the Party Chapter was very troubled and did not know how to carry out its task. The operational group transmitted the orders of the Agent Affairs Section to the Party Chapter and could not solve any problem submitted by the Party Chapter. More than once was the Party Chapter bewildered by the plots of the U.S.-Diemists. The Agents Affairs Section had no time to check the activities of the Party Chapter, so they became worse every day. The evaluation of the revolution in South Vietnam made by our cadres and by the Agent Affairs Section is not exact. It had a bad influence on the work of the Party Chapter. Our members are lacking in knowledge of the enemy. They do not realize that if we want to carry out a successful revolution we must be patient and struggle very hard with the enemy. The operational group worked very eagerly. It usually came to the village to hold meetings for educative propaganda toward the people. But it did not have the party principles in mind and got in touch with the cadres in the village too. Every Sunday its members came to the road leading to the village to welcome the participants of meetings with their wives and children who came there to see them. The enemy were aware of it and laid an ambush for them. Seven cadres were thus shot dead by the enemy.

III. *THE BREAK-UP OF THE PARTY CHAPTER IN K VILLAGE*

Our cadres have made a bad appraisal of the nature of the revolution in South Vietnam at the present. They value the enemy potential too low and don't realize the important position of the South with regard to South-East-Asia and the whole world. If the Americans lost Vietnam they would lose the whole of South-East-Asia and this would have a worse effect on their influence in the whole world. Our people endured much sufferings during the 9 years of resistance, and suffered many losses at the hands of the French. When the peace was restored, 14 million people in South Vietnam have had to face the American aggressors. Compared with the French imperialists, the Americans are richer and have plenty of weapons and war materiel. The Americans have the ability of inducing other imperialist countries to join them in the dirty war which they waged against the people in South Vietnam. They are very clever and have great experience in invading other countries. Our cadres are too subjective. They do not know the balance of forces between the enemy's and ours or understand the guideline of our Party in South Vietnam. We have no other way to save ourselves but the one traced by our party. We must wage a protracted struggle against the enemy. We must undergo much suffering and hardship. This long and lasting struggle will lead us step by step to the final victory. Our cadre have badly appraised the enemy. They think the enemy are exhausted and that we have only to gather up our forces and attack the enemy to destroy them. They think the general uprising is coming with the attendant independence and unification within a short time. We are lacking in understanding about the principles of operation in weak areas. Our cadres use the legal organization in a wrong way. Sometimes they do not use it at all. Thus, they can not cover up our secret organization. Our members are so carelessly recruited that the enemy can infiltrate our organizations. Furthermore, the cadres of operational groups have so often and openly come to the village that they may easily be unmasked by the enemy. The above facts have caused us great harm. The Party Chapter in K village was broken up and 4 of the 7 party members, 2 labor youths and 1 sympathizer were captured by the enemy. This brought the movement down. The people became confused and afraid. Most of the agents were dispersed.

IV. *SOLUTION*

In short, the workers in K village have some knowledge of the revolution. Their standpoint on class struggle is firm. They have pledged to support the revolution. The spirit of our cadres, party members, and association members is very high. They have great hatred of the U.S.-Diemists. They are determined to fight the enemy until the last minute of their lives. But most of them have just grown up in the revolutionary movement and their knowledge of the party's policy is still very poor. They have not enough experience for leading the people to struggle. Their method of work is not scientific and cannot guarantee the party secrets for a long period of time. Our members do not know the way to perform their jobs in weak areas. As such they can not firmly develop the movement.

V. *STRONG AND WEAK POINTS*

a. *Strong Points*

Though the Party Committee Headquarters in Dau Tieng and the Party Chapter in K village have grown up within the revolutionary movement, they have a good knowledge of the revolution. They have a firm political standpoint; they have great hatred of U.S.-Diemists, and a strong belief in the final victory of the revolution.

The party members, group members and association members are good; they are very eager to carry out their activities in struggling against the enemy and to study for the improvement of their minds. They are determined to struggle against the enemy and to undergo all difficulties and sufferings. This is so even when they are captured, beaten, and tortured by the enemy. They resolutely keep their courage as a member of the revolution must do. They have built up the Party Chapter right in the middle of enemy areas, gathered most people and workers under the leadership of the party, propagandized on party's policy and persuaded the workers and people to believe in the party. They have led the people and workers to destroy the encircling pressures of the enemy and struggle for the interests of the people. They have carried out their financial task in detail and gotten good results in labor work and could supply the Party Committee with everything it needed.

b. *Weak Points*

The Party Chapter is not organized according to the Party's principles, that is to say from "bottom to top" from one to two, then three persons. But it is built up with 3 members brought from the outside by the operational group. Its knowledge of the party policies and lines is poor. Its methods for carrying out assigned tasks and experience in leadership are weak. The Party Chapter has not realized the importance of its role in the leadership of the masses. It does not know the principles of operating in weak areas. It has not paid attention to the preservation of secrecy. The Party Chapter did not know how to take advantage of the legal and semi-legal organizations for covering its secret activities. It has not seen how important its role is in the development of the Party.

VI. *CORRECTIONS TO BE MADE IN THE ORGANIZATION AND ACTIVITIES OF THE PARTY CHAPTER IN K VILLAGE*

After a summary of activities in June 1963, the Party Chapter in Dau Tieng rubber plantation had noticed the strong and weak points of the Party Chapter of K village, and laid down the following program of corrections.

In order to solve a number of urgent problems set up by the cadres in K village, the cadres [must] build up a new Party Chapter. The Agent Affairs Section entrusts the operational group in K village with the mission of the cadre in this village in building up a new Party Chapter. It has to educate the village cadres of the movement in political and cultural matters and teach them the guidelincs and methods of carrying out their tasks in weak areas. Before assigning a task to some cadres we must listen to their opinions, explain to them the objective we want to reach, and we must be sure that they clearly understand what we require from them. We must be careful and just in making our judgment so that the cadres may know what is right and what is wrong and draw experience from their work. At present, there remains 1 party member in this party unit. We have to recruit a new one. Later on we will add another cadre to them in building a new Party Chapter. Where we have a Party Chapter we need not organize any other group or association. . . Cells formed in threes must be kept in secret. Compartmentation rules must [be] strictly adhered to and followed. Cells including more than 3 persons must be partitioned. Make the cadres in the village understand the significance of the legal and semi-legal organizations, and, when the occasion arises, launch a movement for the union of all workers at the plantation. Urge them to struggle against the managers for the defense of their rights and interests.

[DOCUMENT G–2]

NATIONAL FRONT FOR LIBERATION OF SOUTH VIETNAM MINUTES OF MEETING OF YA 9

[Present:] Military and Civilian representatives.

Location: Hamlet 3. Time: 0230 hours on 5 July 1965.

I. *Reasons for the meeting.*

—Report on the situation of E's after recent sweep operations conducted by the enemy.

—Review activities of the past month.

II. *Introduction*

—Front's representatives: 55 men

—Military and civilian representatives of Ya, TB and E's.

III. *Report on the situation of E's in Ya.*

E.1 *Cadre.* Cadre are rather confused and shaken due to the enemy surprise mop-up operations.

The people. The people are confused and displeased with their work.

Thought evolution. It had better not liberate the area because once the latter is liberated, it should be occupied.

E.2 *Cadre.* Cadre are confused and shaken because of enemy violence.

The people. The people are demoralized and not willing to assume assigned work.

E.3 *Cadre.* Cadre are demoralized, afraid of the enemy and not enthusiastic in work.

Guerrillas. Guerrillas have attempted to desert fearing the enemy's fierce weapons.

The people. The people are confused, dissatisfied and not confident in the revolutionary success.

E.4 *Cadre.*

E.2 *Cadre.* Some cadre failed to work due to fear of the enemy.

Guerrillas. A number of them have deserted and are willing to leave our ranks.

The people. The people do not believe in the positive success of the Revolution. Some of them have created difficulties for cadre by demanding the latter to return their ID cards to them.

Worries and requirements. The people do not believe in the revolutionary success. If the revolution is powerful, the people will be willing to assume tasks.

—Generally speaking, all E's stated the same thing and brought up no other obstacles.

—Cadre from Ya to E's are all demoralized because they do not take hold of the friendly and enemy situation.

—Liaison agents from Ya to E have fled and refused to work.

Guerrillas. Guerrillas have fled with weapons, thus affecting the morale of the local inhabitants.

Self-defense corps. Self-defense members have given up guard mission after recent sweep operations.

Security. Enemy spies and administrative personnel are stimulated by a new ideology, but cadre have not taken advantage of this in time.

Worries. People are not assured, thinking it had better not liberate the area. The reason is they are not aware of the present situation.

Implementation plan.

—Liaison between Ya to E should be permanently maintained and information reported quickly.

Guerrillas. Work out a guard plan to relay warning against the enemy sweep operations or report the situation in time to avert the enemy [attack].

Warning signals. The warning for appearance of enemy tanks is 3 success strokes on the triangular iron and his sweep operations by continuous strokes. Appearance of aircraft is given by 2 successive strokes on the triangular iron.

Assignment of work to cadre in charge.

E. 2: DIEN, BAO

E.1: THUAN

E.3: QUY

E 9: ANH

E.4: PHUOC

E.5: THIEN

E. 6: THU

E. 7: TIEN

Guerrillas. Tonight, village unit members are ordered to tranquilize the people's morale and assume their tasks.

Cadre [illegible]

E.6: PHI—E1: CONG and VINH—E9: VINH. Presently cadre are required to assume missions, tranquilize the people's ideology, pursue your tasks to master the national controlled areas and coordinate production work.

About youths' enrollment: on the 6th night gather youths at E3 for E4—1 2 3 4: and on the 7th night gather youths at E5 for 5E's—56789.

Beginning on nights of 6 and 7 July 1965, tranquilize and motivate the people's ideology.

[DOCUMENT G-3]

[AGENDA OF LOCAL CHAPTER MEETING]

Plan for July [1965]

A. Develop the spirit of the offensive in determining to counter enemy mopping up operations, to attack enemy posts and to raid and ambush the enemy everywhere.

—Develop the traditions of leadership of the [Party] Chapter, so as to surpass all difficulties and hardships.

—Develop traditions of executing Party Committee resolutions.

—Develop the experiences of leadership in organizing classes [to analyze and synthesize the bad and good points in leadership].

B. Resolve to [get] rid of bad thoughts which may impede the leadership of the chapter, such as:

—Lack of internal struggle
—Lust and waste
—Irresponsible statements
—Disregard of Party leadership

C. Program for future indoctrination.

Party members will study:
—Military and political resolutions of 1965.
—Party regulations (2 hours during nighttime)
—Plan of carrying out Party leadership on [Party] groups and soldiers within the unit.
—Role and mission of the [Party] group
—Strengthen the union between group members and soldiers, during peace time as in combat.

D. Correct activities of the Masses.

—Have peace of mind about fighting
—Have peace of mind concerning political indoctrination and military training.
—Struggle against lust, licentiousness, corruption
—Fight against discord between Vietnamese and Khmer
To develop union and confidence between Khmer-born Vietnamese and Vietnamese in peace time as in combat.

E. Correct the Party leadership of the masses in the front and education of the masses in the rear.

—Contents of propaganda on the correct Party line and the front, on the role of combat hamlets in defending base areas.
—Fight against spies,
Protect the rural areas, encourage the Youth joining the Army, and pay salaries according to army standards.
—Explain to 1000 Cambodian-born Vietnamese, including 300 young men, 200 young girls, 200 teen-agers, 300 old women, the need to contribute 100 booby traps.

F. On sanitation.

Teach the people:

To preserve their health by cleaning houses and constructing proper latrines.

—To sleep under mosquito nets,

—To partake in physical exercise every morning and to drink only boiled water.

G. Development of Party.

—To admit 6 members to the Party (2 officials)

—Every Party member must lead 3 group members and 4 of the masses.

—Cell meetings to be held every 5 days, 5 times a month.

—Party chapter meeting to be held every 7 days, and 3 times a month.

—The whole Party Chapter will meet 2 times a month.

—Party members and group members guide the masses by their examples.

—Develop the offensive spirit in intensively attacking the enemy.

—Develop the traditions of good leadership.

—Have good leadership in training and indoctrination.

—Have well executed policies.

—Have good critiques of and within the internal organization.

—No lust, no waste of money and time.

—No irresponsible statements.

Program of future indoctrination

Party regulations not yet learned.

Report on activities of 2d Cell

1. *Propaganda:* 55 times. (17 times to men, 13 to women, 6 to teenagers, 19 to old women).

Contribution to construction of combat hamlet:

2. Construct 2 bridges for the people.
3. Dig 10 air-raid shelters.

Chin (9) Dung.

—Weak in internal struggle.

—Bad in getting along with other people

—Bad in executing orders.

—Seldom studies with other people.

Nam (5) Mot

—Goes out more than other people.

—Seldom studies with other people.

—Will not dig out trenches.

—Vexes other by joking.

—Weak in self-criticism.

5 Tich. Does not follow orders such as: leaves the class-room early, won't dig fortified work.

Nam (5) Vu. Goes out freely, weak in self criticism.

Critique in general

Cadre.

—Lack of coordination and methods
—Don't get along with other people
—Abandon guard duty
—Drunk
—Undisciplined
—Constructed bad fortified works
—Not participating in indoctrination

Every 2 days, cadre (from squad to platoon) to meet to report the situation of ideology and suggest ideas.

[Six pages dealing with Chinese medicinal herbs have been omitted.]

[DOCUMENT G-4]

REPORT

GENERAL POLITICAL SITUATION AT THE END OF 1963

[Consolidation of situation during the 4th quarter]

I. *POLITICAL INDOCTRINATION AND IDEOLOGICAL GUIDANCE SITUATION:*

A) *Ideology:*

According to the resolution of the entire army's Political Conference held at the end of 1962, the political indoctrination and ideological guidance in 1963 was basically and systematically carried out. The guidance movement consisted of 4 ideological systems disseminated with the content of 4 "build-ups" (xây) and 4 "oppositions" (chống).

[As] the fight raged, the battlefield grew more and more violent. The Political indoctrination and ideological guidance movement in armed units and guerrilla forces was really a permanent ideological struggle. This was very violent in some places and periods.

1/*Build up an ideology of violently fighting the enemy, patiently and bravely attacking and annihilating the enemy, oppose the ideology of balking the long-range (struggle) hardships and sacrifice/which is the main point/*

This ideological situation fluctuated and was very complex. Since the beginning of the year, the battle of Ấp Bắc which challenged the troops to solve the ideology of fearing sweep operations, and mechanized equipment. Subsequently permanent positive indoctrination strengthened the ideology of fighting the enemy. The proof was that the troops' and guerrillas' morale was very high. They patiently, bravely and continuously attacked the enemy. With that morale, our forces were twice stronger than the enemy, and our province units obtained the successes in Mỹ Tinh An, Quón Long [July 1963] Tân Thành [Sep 63], Cú Chi, Phú My, My Tinh An, Cá Quoi bridge [November 1963], An Thanh Thúy, Bińh Ninh and Cu Chi [Dec 63]. The concrete proof was that they continuously attacked posts at nights, and countered large-scale sweep operations during daytime. They endured, overcame hunger, tiresome, violent fire and bombs, and were determined to achieve victory.

After participating in struggles and training courses, the morale and endurance of the cadre, and soldiers reached a high level which ensured the fighting during 2 or 3 consecutive days and nights [such as the phases of 20 July and Dôc Lâp (Independence) which lasted for 6 or 7 days and nights] [such as the phase of attack on Phu My, Cu Chi in Nov 63 which lasted for 20–30 days].

District Local Forces always stayed close to weak areas, and strategic hamlets. They bravely attacked the enemy and scored many successes in Hòa Khánh, Mỹ Dúc Tây, Mỹ Lúóng [Cái Bè] Phúóc Thanh [Chaù Thaňh], Tàn Thành, Biñh Ân, Kióńg Phúóc [Gõ Công]. Guerrilla units bravely encircled and killed enemy troops and forced them to withdraw from their posts [Binh An, Kiong Phuoc, Hâu Mỹ and Thành Hứng etc. . .]. Workshops, commo-liaison stations . . . struggled patiently to accomplish their mission in a difficult and complex situation. Generally speaking, cadre and soldiers [armed units and guerrillas] have good ideology. They have developed the following points:

—The ideology of fighting the enemy.

—Endurance of hardship, and spirit of fighting bravely, patiently and continuously.

2/*Organization and discipline*

The ideology and obedience to the Party, committee levels, and execution of resolutions were good. This was reflected in the eagerness and proper implementation of various resolutions, especially the resolution regarding the constant penetration and close stay in the enemy areas, the removal of enemy grip, the stay in strategic hamlets, the creation of (favorable) conditions to eagerly and patiently attack the enemy, to engage in the phase of attacking enemy during several consecutive days, to overcome privations, hardships, violent (enemy) aircraft and artillery, and to accomplish the difficult and complex mission, most typical of all the various Province Infantry detachments, Go Cong Local Force Troops, and particularly the attack phase before and after the 1 Nov 63 coup.

3/*High sense of responsibility and Democratic ideology and conduct*

In comparison to last year (1962) this ideology was strengthened and developed to a certain degree. Facing the ever growing responsibility and after receiving indoctrination, most of cadre and Party members clearly realized their duties and made every effort to perform them. A number of cadre were noted for their high morale and sense of responsibility. They worked tirelessly and deserved the key role in Party Chapters and units. Therefore, the active cadre successfully commanded and developed forces quickly.

Under the leadership of the Party, generally speaking, the troops and guerrilla units could strengthen ideology and develop during a year of hard struggle.

—*Bad ideologies:*

1. Ideology of fearing long range (struggle), hardships, sacrifice and the lack of combat spirit. Through the test of the violent war, this ideology has constantly fluctuated according to the period, and place. This ideology was reflected in the fact that friendly forces dared not stay close to weak areas [district units at the beginning and in the middle of the year], to stay or unsteadily stay [Province units in the middle of the year]. Some units that previously countered sweep operations successfully, later feared to counter sweep operations [C1 province local unit] and to attack posts. They withdrew shortly after the attack started [From Jul to Oct 63]. Some were satisfied with the successes achieved and feared hardship, so they could not score great achievements. [Cấm Són on 13 Jun, Cu Chi on

6 Nov, etc. . .]. When the forces developed desertion and discharge (from armed forces) occurred monthly in province or district units. Most of deserters were recruits who were not yet accustomed to violent combats, bombings and shellings. 1 Assistant province platoon leader and Party members [3 squad cadre of province unit] deserted. After a successful counter sweep operation, 2 or 3 soldiers in each company deserted [34 deserters during the year including 3 Party members of C1 province unit]. At present, this ideology is reflected in the fact that (the troops) fear bombing and artillery fire. [The degree of fear varies with each unit and individual.] It is noted that during the fight, many soldiers wasted ammo due to lack of calmness.

2. Ideology of overconfidence, self complacency and freedom from discipline. When a unit scored many achievements, cadre and soldiers of this unit became overconfident [they more or less adopted an ideology of self-complacency]. The ideology of freedom caused the failure [sic] to strictly observe the regulations, the application of schedule of activity, the conduct of indoctrination and training which was beneficial to the development of combat efficiency. The waste of money for cigarettes was relatively widespread. The saving budget of the unit was less than 1961–1962. The request for money from families by cadre and soldiers became a common practice. In province or district organizations and units, many instances of drunkennesses, quarrels, violation of the masses' discipline took place. In some cases, squad and platoon cadre spoke ill of their commanders and failed to observe discipline. [Similar cases were noted in a number of sapper province, district commo-liaison and village militia units.] Some individuals withdrew during combat, some fired at PW's, some kept war booty as personal properties [province platoon leader].

3. Ideology of fame and bureaucracy. Determine and implement the cadre's regime and policy. The ideology of fame developed and was widespread in some respects. Some cadre showed anxiety when carrying out their work. They showed jealousy and created difficulties in internal organization.

—While a lot of Squad and Platoon cadre made progress and stayed close to the masses, a small number of others acquired a mandarin attitude due to their overconfidence and self-complacency. A number of squad and platoon cadre who were put in the charge of indoctrination, and recuperation, failed to swiftly adopt a good ideology and caused worries among the soldiers. A number of soldiers in province units deserted and requested discharge because they were indignant with squad and platoon cadre [July, August and September 63]. Particularly 1 Co cadre, 2 province platoon cadre, and some district platoon cadre failed to improve their military conduct. They beat and insulted the soldiers.

4. The additional supply of weapons including firearms and the untimely guidance of ideology caused the units to abuse and rely on weapons. They attacked posts with the main purpose of capturing weapons. They organized no raids [Sep 63]. Sometimes the influence of weapons helped

improve the moral of troops [from Jul to Sept 63]. It is also due to the dependency on weapons, that some units had to fight alone, and ignored Political and Military Proselytizing [province C1 unit, and a number of district units]. Due to the dependency on weapons that in a number of battles, the soldiers wasted too much ammo, and chased the enemy with fire. As war grew more violent, cadre and soldiers thought much of weapons [75mmRR's . . .], and they devoted little attention to the development of the moral strength of the unit.

Guerrilla Forces: Since the equipment of modern weapons, guerrilla forces neglected the construction of combat villages. Units in some areas abandoned rudimentary weapons and threw away firearms. Some others received Red stock weapons and refused to use French weapons such as MAS Rifle.

B) *Political indoctrination and ideology guidance*

Under the leadership of higher headquarters and province (party) committees, the political indoctrination and ideology guidance in various armed forces was particularly emphasized, the organization, the subjects and duration of political training better than 1962.

Besides the instructions, the documents disseminated by higher echelons, courses on the policies, instructions and communiques from province (party) committee regarding general and local problems were organized. At the same time and according to the requirements and ideology of each period and target, the Military Affairs Committee of K25 prepared a number of documents for recruits and guerrillas to study.

Documents studied during the year included:

Units and Organizations:

—Traditional nature of the armed formes [political indoctrination documents for squad cadre and soldiers, and in particular, the book entitled "Traditional Nature" . . . reprinted by the Province].

—Recruits and personnel re-studied the resolutionary [sic] lines in RVN, phase by phase.

—Studied various instructions regarding the opposition against the exchange of plastic cards, enemy Chiêu-hồi [open-arms] policy, the sabotage of strategic hamlets, commemorative days, attack phases, conduct of Ap Bac, patriotic and anti-American emulations, and the meaning of the designation of "gi-rông" [name of a beach in Cuba] of D261, etc. . . .

—Various appeals, and proclamations of the Front, and organizations of the Province (Party) Committee, the appeals of the Province (Party) Committee, Military Affairs Committee of K during each phase of attack and commemorative days. Documents were disseminated to platoons and squads for collective study.

Various religious policies [document from R (COSVN) land policy [same document], and the Front disciplinary policy [document prepared by the Military Affairs Committee of K] policy and discipline in newly liberated areas [documents prepared by K].

—Every 3 months, indoctrinated soldiers on the communiques of the

Province (Party) Committee concerning the situation of political movement, sabotage of strategic hamlets and experience gained from the sabotage of strategic hamlets in weak areas, etc. . . .

For guerrillas: Studied the question and answer document concerning the duty of guerrilla militia [prepared by the Military Affairs Committee of K, based on DQ (Militia) Resolution 63].

For recruits: Overcame the situation of verbal indoctrination conducted so far, K prepared a document concerning the armed mission and the duty of recruits to indoctrinate youths to promote an entlistment movement, and educate immediate basic things to recruits.

Co and Platoon cadre studied the directives on the ranks of 29 types of military cadre of K (region) level. 6 districts military and unit political officers were appointed to attend the on-the-job basic training conducted by Province (Party) Committee and to study the document concerning historical materialism disseminated by Higher Echelon. The individual training and study on the basic philosophy of Maxism was not conducted until the end of the year. [Some comrades read through the documents 2 or 3 times and some others carefully studied the first 2 parts of the documents.]

—CV (Company members ?] studied their responsibilities. C (Co.) Command Section studied political task in combat.

Party members studied: Regulations of the Party [basically implemented], the 6 criteria of a party member and a gallant communist fighter. Unit Chapter (Party) Committees studied the tasks of the Chapter (Party) Committee in combat [not all party-members studied].

Group members studied: Regulations of the group [then all the group members], mission of Party Chapter in the Liberation Army, the role of the youths and youth proselytizing of the Group during the present war [reserved for Chapter (Party) Committee and Chapter Group Committee].

The indoctrination brought the knowledge of a number of revolutionary basic problems of cadre and soldiers up to a higher level. They better understood the nature of the enemy, the armed role in the present liberation revolution, the disadvantages and advantages of the liberation revolution and the factors ensuring the victory and the international prestige of the revolution in RVN. In addition cadre and troops improved their combat spirit.

Party members and cadre understood better their positions, and made a step forward in their daily duty.

During 1963, the main trend of indoctrination was to guide the ideology of positively attacking the enemy. Follow the motto of recuperating loyal cadre, of leading the armed forces of Province (Party) Committee and Military Affairs Committee which paid much attention to the indoctrination of the cadre. During the year, after each phase of attacking enemy, the Province (Party) Committee held a series of critique sessions, C [Company] cadre in provinces, chiefs or deputy chiefs of province organizations, TV (?) and Political Officers of district units were entitled to join in these critique sessions. The main task was to guide ideology, eliminate the passive ideology, build and strengthen, then the attack ideology, follow policy lines, believe the Party, the people, and oneself, and continue to fight the enemy valiantly.

After each violent phase of the fight, the ideology of friendly troops was shaken. Under the direct guidance of Military Affairs Committee, various combat units initiated several phases of strengthening the internal political situation from chapter (Party) Committee to Party Chapter and down to soldiers. There were 4 main phases:

1) After the victory of Ap Bac [2 Jan 63], designed to overcome the ideology of fearing large-scale sweep operations, aircraft and artillery, strengthen the spirit of self-confidence, courageously counter sweep operations and at the same time, avoid the ideology of overconfidence.

2) Around July, August 63, the enemy troops reduced their activities, and operations. They stayed in posts, our troop could seldom engage them. We conducted only large scale attacks, [counter sweep operations]. The guidance phase was intended to enhance the unsubdued spirit, overcome the ideology of fearing attacks on posts, build up a determination to attack posts and defeat the enemy.

3) Then came the Doc Lâp (Independence) phase [Sep 63]. Most of units did not score good achievements. District units were hesitant and dared not fight courageously, [except units in Go Cong]. Province units still lacked determination in the attack on posts. Attacks on posts were continuously defeated. Cadre and soldiers were afraid of sweep operations and became pessimistic. The critique phase of the Province (Party) Committee followed the inspection of the internal organization of units which was designed to promote the unsubdued spirit and self-sufficiency, annihilate the enemy and overcome the ideology of fearing attacks on posts, large scale sweep operations, build up a determination to annihilate the enemy in fortified works, fight the enemy continuously, counter sweep operations, overcome the ideology of counting on firepower, and the support provided by major units, etc...

4) During the first days of Nov 63, province and district units rose up and took advantage of the coup d'etat to attack the enemy, and they gained some results. But subsequently, due to long range activity, they were tired and were forced to cope with enemy aircraft and artillery, therefore cadre and soldiers developed a fear of aircraft and artillery. They dared not stay to counter sweep operations and lost the courage of promoting achievements. The province Military Affairs Committee also directly conducted a phase of critique of internal organization of companies, Chapter (Party) Committees Party Chapters the masses and soldiers for 7 consecutive days.

—Military Affairs Committee directly reviewed the activities of Chapter (Party) Committee.

—The Political Section and 6 C [Company] and B [Platoon] cadre directly reviewed the activities of Party Chapter and assigned works to platoon and squads.

4 phases implemented systematically

After reviewing the activities of Chapter (Party) Committee and on the basis of the real political situation, the Military Affairs Committee submitted a letter urging and guiding party members and soldiers to take part in critique sessions and strengthen internal organization. A selection of meritorious individuals for reward and bad individuals for punishment followed critique sessions.

In general, the political activities in 1963 to guide the troops' ideology progressed with continuity and, although the ideological warfare presented difficulties and complexities, the results of the troops' ideologies and combat efficiencies were relatively satisfactory.

In addition to the above principles, the Province conducted after-action critiques, examinations for consolidation. After each successful or unsuccessful phase of activity or attack conducted by units, districts, the Province immediately sent letters evaluating the attack, bringing up the good and bad points to be examined and learned by the units. This timely guidance had good effects. One of the cases was that of an unit [Province Company 1] whose cadre and soldiers, after the exploits of 3 big anti-sweep operations in 1962 and the victory of Ấp Bắc [2 January] became optimistic and satisfied, thus neglecting self-improvement; consequently there were internal difficulties and poor discipline during the year and the unit contributed little to the 2 successful attacks [Bối Tuồng and Cầm Són]; and the more its cadre and soldiers saw that a friendly unit [Company 2] recorded achievements, the more they became pessimistic and lost their self-confidence; in addition, the political indoctrination within the unit was poor and consequently, after a number of attacks resulting in heavy losses, many cadre developed a fear of the enemy. In some attacks, a number of Party members flinched while the soldiers assaulted [the attack of Chùa Phât Dá, 23 November].

(However) during the 4th period of self-improvement [early in Dec 63], the above mentioned feelings were examined and the concerned Chapter (Party) Committee members and Party members successfully improved themselves [on the night of 31 Dec 63, the (same above) unit rose up to attack and destroy an entire enemy platoon in the town of Cú Chi, with only one soldier slightly injured].

However there still existed many such deficiencies in the political indoctrination and ideology guidance as: much indoctrination conducted but very few reports on preliminary results received by higher echelons. Some units did not evaluate and report the indoctrination results nor did they follow up and timely note the phenomena of ideologies in order to insure appropriate reform and guidance. The district and province political organizations failed to closely and timely follow and recapitulate the political and ideological situation of cadre and troops. The recapitulation reports were normally delayed and neglected and the confusion of contents in reports was not avoided.

In particular, a number of units disregarded the political indoctrination and ideology guidance or performed them in a bureaucratic manner. The cadre gave instructions in confusion (old manner) or gave free-hands to squad cadre to guide the soldiers regardless whether the former were qualified or not. The cadre failed to attach attention, to follow-up the political and ideological situations, to make reports on the recapitulation of situations or they just submitted reports based on their own subjective interpretation.

The role of collectivity [Party Chapter] in the leadership of units [in general] and in the leadership of propaganda, indoctrination and ideology reform activities [in particular] failed to satisfy the requirements. Chapter (Party) Committees were still much concerned in administrative tasks which consumed all the time while the ideology guidance was still not properly emphasized and considered as a principal task of units. There were relatively more classes and directives and little efforts to detect and correct deficiencies and guide ideologies. In addition, more emphasis was placed on the issue of orders and critiques than on the analysis and development of ideology. Most District Military Affairs Committees still did not assess the principle "Politics are the foundation and ideology must go first." Some places even neglected the indoctrination activities and principles of political activities, others neglected the Party activities within the unit [(in) Châu Thành (district)].

II. *CULTURAL ACTIVITIES*
III. *CIVILIAN PROSELYTIZING ACTIVITIES*
IV. *ENEMY PROSELYTIZING*
V. *CLUB ACTIVITIES*

} attached herewith [sic]

1) *Internal Information:*

The Province did not publish a bulletin of information within its internal organization. The units, agencies, members and guerrillas were furnished with only newsletters published by the Province Propaganda, Cultural and Indoctrination Section. Since the 3rd quarter, information on armed activities was published in this newsletter.

Organization: Information bulletins, newsletters, newspapers . . . were distributed by the province political organization which insured that each concentrated company [C] or each organization received one copy. The information was consolidated; however, the Political Officers of units and organizations failed to meet the requirements for the guidance in presenting the information [what is the key article in a paper, what is the principal point in an article; what should be developed; how to give additional explanations, etc. . .] and did not follow up to draw experiences and contribute critiques of the information. Apart from some comrades at Political Committees, Staffs, the cadre and soldiers did not contribute works to the information bulletins and newspapers.

2) *Book reading:*

There still existed a great shortage of books for troops and guerrillas. During the year, cadre and soldiers had a number of combat novels:

—*On the Great Wall* (of China) *Battlefields* [Trên Mǎt Trân Truong Thành], *The Iron Soldier on Cùù Lỹ Mountain* [Ngùoi Chién sĩ Gang Thép trên Núi Cùu Lỹ], *The Girl of the Fatherland* [Nùùoi Con Gái của Tổ Quôc]; *Stories of Military Heroes* (Truyên Anh Hung Quân Dôi]; [each squad received 1 copy].

—A few books like: *The 4-Sided Spike Pit* [Hâm Chông 4 Mǎt], *The Protection of Diem An* [Bao Vê Diên An], *The Story of the US Intervention and Invasion in Cuba* [1 copy per book, and the Political Committee reserved those books for the wounded soldiers at the Province Military Hospital].

In charge of getting books for the units, the Political Committee only made arrangements with the Propaganda, Culture and Indoctrination (Section) to reprint one book about the *Stories of Military Heroes* [Book 1] for distribution down to village guerrillas. Cadre and soldiers like short stories [such as the *Military Heroes*]; the novels with many characters and full of intricate details are hardly understood, remembered and retold by them.

3) *Listening to radio broadcasts:*

Since the 3rd Quarter each concentrated company was issued 1 radio and each cadre organization 1 to 2 radios. This program was successful; there were no more cases of listening to enemy broadcasts, and the Hanoi and Liberation stations were the 2 principal stations which were followed up and listened to by units and organizations. In general, the cadre and soldiers were able to follow-up the situation of the movement, and the international situation. However political leaders did not positively exploit the capabilities of indoctrination within units through radio broadcasts, they did not appoint personnel to follow-up radio broadcasts, to copy the slow-read news . . . for orderly and accurate dissemination to units. The news or stories retold to cadre and soldiers were sometimes incomplete.

4) *Wall newspapers, culture/arts activities:*

Due to the permanently tumultuous situation of the battlefields which caused units to continuously move from place to place and engage in combat operations, and deprived them of the determination to overcome difficulties, combat units became passive and neglected 2 following types of activities: Publication of wall newspapers and culture/arts activities:

—Wall newspapers: the medical organization, worksites and a number of commo-liaison staff organizations permanently published wall newspapers. The subjects in these wall newspapers reflected the daily activities. These wall newspapers were well constructed and made progresses in writing techniques [many good articles] and they produced the effects of urging the unanimous participation in the emulation of performance of work within the units [the case of the Province Worksite was most typical]. However some deficiencies still existed: soldiers contributed more articles than cadre and the articles contained more criticism than appreciation. The troops failed to appreciate the value of wall newspapers and their commanders did not properly use wall newspapers to serve the requirements within the units. The articles were written without coordination, concentration and did not reflect the circumstances and time.

—Culture/Arts: the youths in units and agencies like culture/arts very much; the majority of them have kept a book to copy songs and poems, with great care. Many of them enjoy composing six–eight meter poems regardless whether they follow correctly or not the principles of writing poems [2/3 of the contents of the wall newspapers are six–eight meter poems.

—The culture/arts activities of units and agencies were very limited. In the province and districts, the units and organizations were made passive by the enemy situation and by the requirements for preservation of secrecy. During the year, the movements and combat commitments of the troops in the area took 3/4 of their time but when returning to rear bases they were able to organize squad and platoon sized entertainment meetings. However, since the time the enemy increased airstrikes and artillery fire against our troops [August 1963], the principle of troop bivouac became the principle of troop concealment and all forms of entertainment stopped. We were more inclined to the protection (of troops) and disregarded their joyful and youthful activities. The story telling in squads [and] platoons could only be conducted separately and other entertainment forms such as playing the flute and the harmonica or dancing and giving shows could very possibly be realized but lacked leadership and encouragement. The units and organizations were enveloped in a melancholic and uneasy atmosphere; troops in bivouacs often wandered alone, violating the internal policies, partly because they could not bear the melancholic atmosphere.

—*Physical training, sports:*

Affected by the situation, volley-ball, soccer games were forbidden. During the year the organization of these games was planned [discussed] twice but could not be realized. Recently the habitual physical training in the morning [5 o'clock] in the units was limited due to the fact that too much time was spent in digging fortified works [on combat days troops slept immedately after digging fortified works; on movement days, troops normally arrived at the stopover site at 2, 3 o'clock in the morning and they were tired after digging fortified works, and had to do the cooking, perform guard duties, etc. . .]. The physical training could possibly be conducted in the evening in lieu but this still failed to attract our attention and there was still a lack of guidance for units.

VI. *CADRE MISSION*
VII. *SECURITY GUARD MISSION*
VIII. *COMPETITIVE EMULATION MOVEMENT:* } Enclosed herewith [sic]

During the year, the Competitive Emulation Council in Province, as well as Competitive Emulation Sections in local areas, units and agencies have not been formed yet. This is a big mistake resulting from lack of determination and efforts by command echelons. One of the three main points in the 63 CT (TN: Poss. Political) mission is the competitive emulation. However the competitive spirit of units and agencies is rather high. Following the meeting held in June 1963 to initiate a competitive emulation movement, Provinces worked out and submitted a competitive emulation plan to higher echelons which disseminated it to soldiers and personnel for training. Generally speaking, most of cadre, soldiers and personnel are well aware of the importance of the competitive emulation and are willing to respond to the emulation.

Despite the lack of technical organizations to foster, support and guide the competitive emulation movement in province units, Ấp Bắc competitive emulation reflects in every mission—specifically in combat missions. Units know how to use Ap Bac competitive emulation as a political task prior to and during combat. The troops also know how to use political task as a combat one by motivating the competitive emulation movement to promote the tradition of being determined to fight and win. During the development of the battle, one comrade said "medals of our company [C] are pinned on Phu My bunkers" [Phu My in November 63] while another seriously wounded comrade carried on a hammock said "our comrades resolutely kept their promise and won the first fanion [banner] of Ap Bac competitive emulation." The competitive spirit encouraged troops to advance. During a competitive movement conducted prior to an engagement, a soldier promised to capture 2 weapons from the enemy (RVN) and during the battle, this soldier [a recon-intel member participating in Cam Son battle on 13 June] proved to be very courageous and succeeded in capturing 2 carbines. In medical missions especially Province worksite mission, the competitive emulation slogan reflects every mission on labor, (agricultural) production, administration and economy. As compared to 1962, outputs continue to increase from 100/000 up to 300/100 and dozens of initiative are welcomed. Through the initiation of competitive emulation movement in provinces and districts, many problems have been solved such as the consolidation of political and internal organizations [unification in the execution of missions] and experience gained from hard missions which are accomplished by devoted cadre and courageous soldiers [there are 3 to 4 cases of succeeding in protection of documents during the exchange of fire with sweep operation enemy forces].

While awaiting the organization of a competitive emulation machinery under the guidance of BQS (Military Affairs Committee) the Province Political Section has concentrated its efforts in the competitive emulation movement:—Over 10 letters (of commendation) sent to victorious units after each battle and phase of combat activity to raise the patriotism against the US, Ap Bac competitive emulation, protection of the first fanion and competitive emulation to promote the tradition of units. Each letter is reproduced in many copies and disseminated to units and districts so as to promote the common movement.

The critique, election and proposal for commendation from 3-man cell and higher after each campaign and combat mission are relatively well conducted. The preparation of papers, making of decisions, issuance of letters and certificates of commendation, submission of proposal to higher echelons and furnishing of information on training in internal organizations and DK (Guerrilla) throughout the province is also relatively well conducted. In addition to reports and proposals from lower echelons, the Province Political Section has aggressively assisted units in motivating local members to carry out missions, thus enabling the promotion of competitive emulation movement to bring about good results.

—During the year, Province has made reports and recommendations to superiors on commendation as follows:

—Medals for 40 cases [23 for units and 17 for individuals].

—Certificate of commendation for Military Regions.

Province issues:

—Certificate of commendation . . . [for units and individuals] . . . in province agency . . . district units, 3 cases in district agency, 2 cases and 6 other cases in village DK.

—Letter of commendation [including . . . units . . . individuals, province units . . ., province agencies], district unit 2, district agency 2, village guerrilla 14. Districts and infantry companies frequently organize citations of (combat) achievements following each battle [not recapitulated].

—The competitive emulation movement still leaves much to be desired, and the lack of technical machinery leads to the improper initiation of movement. Province has a relatively (strong) movement, but the movements of district and village are still weak. District political agencies have not been aware of the importance and do not pay much attention to the competitive emulation movement and disregard the commendation of Troops' fighting spirit, thus weakening the movement. After a year of resistance, hundreds of units, guerrillas and individuals from districts and villages have scored many good combat achievements but have not received a commendation. Even in province, competitive emulation and commendation are only concentrated on units, troops and worksites. A number of units, agencies and sections [Commo-liaison, Medical, Base Security Guard, Staff, Political, Rear Services . . . etc. . .] have failed to give proper commendation and do not pay attention to the commendation. To sum up, the education, initiation and fostering of competitive emulation movement leave much to be desired.

IX. *FORMATION OF PARTY* X. *FORMATION OF YOUTH AND LABOR [TL] GROUP* XI. *EXECUTION OF POLICY LINES*	Enclosed herewith [sic]

Attention is paid to the training of troops and agencies on policy lines. Apart from the basic documents of superiors, Provinces prepare internal regulations, policy lines, battlefield disciplines for troops, provinces and districts, the political projects in support of campaign and combat for the training of troops. Therefore, during the year, guerrillas and troops have properly executed the policy lines on wounded, war dead, prisoners of war, defectors, war booties and populace.

—The abandoning of the killed on the battlefield and the leaving of the wounded to the care of organizations, etc. . . [such as the case of Ap Bac battle and another number of battles] is satisfactorily improved [such as the case of Quan Long battle on 20 July, Kim Son post, Câu Dó. . .] the wounded and killed were carried by their friends to the prescribed places; in addition, in Quan Long fierce battle on 20 July, all the laborers ran away and cadre and soldiers had to manage to carry the wounded and killed] . . .

—Since the troops have understood the policy on PW's and defectors they have properly executed it. During the year, most of the prisoners of war captured and released have a good impression toward the liberation policy and think that if they surrender to the liberation troops, they will not be killed. It has been noted that the policy of the guerrilla has improved and there is no secret killing of PW's as before.

—Generally speaking, troops have felt that they must protect people's lives and properties during engagements. When preparing a combat plan, the limit of fire is prescribed and every soldier must comply with this. During fierce fights, cadre and soldiers must put the covers on trenches for the people and encourage people to take shelters [Ap Bac battle on 2 January]. During and after the fight, troops must not pick up the foodstuffs left behind by civilian evacuees, and if they do so, they must leave a letter and money behind to pay for the food. Furthermore, troops [are to] put out the fire for civilian houses [Phu My battle on 4 November] and dress the injured . . . etc. . .

WEAKNESSES STILL COMMITTED

—As regards the burial of the killed, local members are [at] once assigned to bury the killed in a village but it is hard for the relatives to find the latter's graves. The procedures for the control and reporting by troops are not detailed. The name plates of the killed should be planted right on the graves to facilitate the recognition by their relatives. There is much slack and inaccurate information from troops to the armed forces and the mouth-passing information is faster than the one to family, or the armed forces do not inform their relatives thus causing much concern to the latter. A number of souvenirs [2 radios] have not been sent to addressees and a number of fountain pens and miscellaneous items are sometimes lost in mid road.

—Around the end of the year, there is a great increase of recruits assigned to units, so troops have not enough time for training on policy lines. That is why there were some violations of prescribed policy lines such as the secret firing of PW's by guerrillas which was not reported to Province unit [the investigation of this incident is underway] the beating up of enemies by guerrillas and the firing at a church which made the people lodge a complaint to the Front (NLFSVN) [Long-Dinh December 63].

For war booties, cadre and troops have made a large number of violations: cadre ask for and re-buy war booties [parachutes and strings (?) in Ap Bac battle cn 2 Jan] picked up by the people for their own use. Cadre and soldiers hid canteens, duffle bags, belts. . . etc. . . for their personal use instead of handing them over to superiors and making reports. A number of soldiers entered a (RVN) post and searched for equipment, clothing. . . [for their own use] instead of capturing weapons and ammunition. One cadre [Platoon Leader of Province unit] seized good jackets in a post and traded them for money in November 1963. The capturing and hiding of ammunition by guerrilla cadre for their own use can be discovered, but the properties captured in an attacked post such as wood, bricks, tiles, iron, barbed wires, furniture . . . etc. . . have not been under close control and are still kept in civilian houses.

XII. *POLITICAL ORGANIZATION:*

1) *Organization:*

The situation has not been improved as compared with that by the end of 1962. The Province receives an additional comrade. Assistant Political Officer of the Military Affairs Committee and also Chief of Political Section, but no additional cadre have been assigned to the province.

—Propaganda and training:—1st Assistant [Truc] for education, politics and civilian and military proselytizing.

—2nd Assistants [Ngoc] for Politic and Militia, and [Minh] for Information, Newspaper, Entertainment and Culture.

—Organization and CAB (TN. Poss. Cadre): 1 Cadre [Tuoc]

—Security Guard: 1 cadre [Dung], 3 comrades [Hong Son, Lanh and Dôi] who all are assigned other MISSIONS.

By the end of December 1963, 6 additional cadre [2 assistants for organization and cadre, 1 administrative clerk and 3 militia cadre], 4 photographers and radio operators were taken from districts and villages in compliance with a strength replacement resolution.

District: There are 2 or 3 assistants for the Military Affairs Committee Political Officer at every place, but the negligence of Political Officers and their assistants still continues. The Political Officer continues to superficially do his work and his assistants to operate separately. Thus the political agencies are still very weak. Each district has 3 Political Officer assistants except the Chau Thanh district which has only one.

2) *Activities:* The Province Political Committee cannot avoid administrative affairs activities due to shortage of personnel and poor operating procedure: cadre personnel was changed 3 times, consecutively. Most of the cadre have the sense of responsibility but they are too busy with the administrative work and sometimes mobilized for special missions [motivation of recruits, recapitulation (of the results) of the guerrilla warfare movement, work for the campaign, etc. . .]. Therefore if problems on documents, training directives, commendation studies of biographical datum for admittance into the Party or official transfers, etc. . . are solved in time, the mission of following up to improve the specialty of Chapter (Party) Committee members and the practical training of District Assistant Political Officers to realistically Control (Party) Chapter installations and of recapitulating the general situation and experiences are not satisfactorily carried out.

—The District Political agency has not carried out all its jobs. Apart from the participation in Military Affairs meetings not organized yet and specialized meetings, the cadre do not have initiative in their activities, even in the execution of directives and in the accomplishment of a separate work. Among the total number of districts, only some succeed to follow up, recapitulate and reflect a part of the situation and the political mission experiences in guerrilla units [Cái Bè, Hoà Dông and Cai Lây].

Generally speaking the political agency has not properly accomplished its mission, satisfactorily met the requirements of the study and recapitulation of the political situation and submitted any new ideas for the preparation of political plans to the local (Party) committee members and to higher echelons [as regards the Province Troops, they perform their missions in a relatively good manner].

XIII. *GENERAL OBSERVATIONS:*

After a year of fierce war, the armed forces in the Province have increased twice and made considerable achievements in every field of activities and combat, etc. . . This proves that political and Party missions are relatively well performed in the armed forces. The basic political situation [organization and ideology] of the armed forces are insured. The Party closely controls and succeeds in the leadership of the combat armed forces in compliance with the revolutionary policy which guarantees the loyalty and obedience of the armed forces in regard to the Party. There is a concrete evidence that the armed forces (VC) have a high morale in the fight against the enemy (RVN) and the hard-working spirit of laborers who succeed in overcoming difficulties.

A year of challenge is a year of success obtained by revolutionary and armed movement. . . . However the fighting spirit of cadre and soldiers against the enemy fails to reach the highest level because the cadre and soldiers cannot endure hardship and are afraid to sacrifice their lives for the revolution. The spirit of discipline is still not good [they are still fond of free life and debaucheries]; revolutionary policy and ideology and Party's Military policy leave much to be desired.

Regulations on the development of the troops [internal unity, unity between soldiers and people and division of the enemy are 3 important freedoms(?)] have been improved but have not reached the desired standard. This situation limits the strength of the armed forces and the intensive development of the requirements of local revolution.

The main reason is that the political and Party missions of the armed forces are still weak, and have not been able to meet the requirement of a fast developing force, during combat, and on important battlefields while the war becomes fiercer and more violent each day. Steering organizations [districts and villages] have not been able to closely control the armed force, hold and positively guide the cadre and soldiers' political ideology. Political organizations from provinces to districts and villages have not been well fortified. Cadre are insufficient and do not have a high special [ization]. L_3V does not have a good organization to insure a close coordination between the high and low echelons. Especially, Chapter (Party) organizations have not consolidated. The number of Party Chapters which work willingly is still small. Most of the combat and commanding cadre and party members are relatively good, but the control and guidance are still weak.

XIV. *FUTURE MISSIONS:*

Based on the battlefield and internal political situation of armed forces, and the 63 political resolution, the 3 important points [reorientation strengthening of the Party Chapter and competitive emulation of the political and Party missions in the armed forces] are:

1) To continue to carry out the ideological struggle aimed at 4 (sic) points: 4 points on construction and 4 points against concentration. In order to develop a high fighting spirit without fearing to suffer and to sacrifice, we must patiently and continuously attack the enemy and observe the military discipline and organization.

—Try to conduct on the job basic political indoctrination.

—Continue to re-educate the cadre [only 1 course composed of 17 Battalion and Company cadre has been completed.].

—Oppose the enemy Chieu Hoi [open-arms] policy and bring the number of deserters and separation down.

2) Try to implement and strengthening of Party Chapter, improve the standard of Party member, and the responsibility of Chapter (Party) Committee.

3) Closely administer, control and strengthen cadre to insure the leading role of the Party Chapter over units.

4) Establish Province competitive Emulation Boards and organize and activate various organization emulation sections. Try to expend the large-scale emulation movement to the Village Militia, and to all units and

organizations, and timely improve the system and procedures of commendation.

5) Provide sufficient personnel to the Province and district political organizations and train the political cadre to carry out their missions. Improve the specialty of platoon and company Political Officers, troops, organizations and village military units.

Military Affairs Committee (BQS)
Area 25

APPENDIX H
GUIDANCE DIRECTIVES TO SUBORDINATE UNITS

[DOCUMENT H–1]
ACTIVITY PLAN FOR AUGUST, SEPTEMBER AND OCTOBER 1965

The Party (Committee) Headquarters needs to grasp all opportunities to centralize all effort in the accomplishment of the immediate revolutionary requirements, and place emphasis on six objectives as follows:

1. Develop ideology
2. Attrite and destroy the enemy, destroy the New Rural Life hamlets and build our combat villages, expand our base areas.
3. Political struggle
4. Military proselytizing
5. Build up our forces, recruit youths, react against the RVN conscription policy.
6. Build up the rural areas, sell the Troop Support Bonds, improve security, protect the crops, apply economy, react to the new American economic policy.

I. *Ideological Development*

A. *Within the Party.*

1) Required knowledge

a—Thoroughly understand the situation and strategy, especially during the rainy season.

—Thoroughly understand the war.

—Accurately evaluate our victories, especially those gained during the first part of this year, and the serious failures of the American imperialists and their lackeys.

b—Thoroughly understand the center of importance of the resistance. Attain the two requirements. Accomplish the six immediate objectives.

c—Thoroughly understand the dual guideline of political and armed struggle, the three-front attack, the development of guerrilla warfare in tandem with the fast expansion of our forces.

2) *Required ideology*

a. Eliminate ideological divergencies such as

—Escapism, passiveness, reluctance, over-estimation of the enemy, fear of difficulty and hardship, discouragement.

—Disregarding the political struggle and the rudimentary weapons. Improper handling of the people, especially the Chinese and Cambodian-born people.

Consolidate the determination to fight, struggle for time. Grasp all opportunities. Strengthen the will to win, even to fight a prolonged war.

b. Abandon the habit of making individual or unilateral decisions causing difference in action.

c. Properly execute resolutions. Think and act boldly. Multiply efforts.

d. Definitely abandon the prospect of a peace talk which causes loss of vigilance and aggressiveness.

3) *Required attitude.*

a—Fully develop democracy. Respect the masses' initiatives. Cooperate with the people.

b—Understand the masses and deliberately steer them.

c—Make tremendous effort.

4) *Training program and subjects.*

—*Various agencies of village Party Chapter:*

a) Situation and mission (available; revised material) 1 day.

b) Guerrilla warfare (specific material not available; use the current "People's Guerrilla Warfare"): 1 day.

c) Reaction against the RVN conscription policy, and military proselytizing (specific material not available; use the current instruction available at the District Party Committee): ½ day.

d) Motivation of the people and the 5-step plan, operating procedures and organization: 1 day.

e) Troop Support Bonds, summary on instructions and operating procedures: 1 day.

f) District and village's plans of activity: 1 day.

The training duration is 5 days, during which the Regional Force troops learn the materials #1, 2, 3 and 5.

—*People's Group Chapter and Cadre:*

1) The revised material and Troop Support Bonds: 1 day.

2) Guerrilla warfare, with material available at the district Party Committee (use the "Armed Struggle" part): 1 day.

3) Motivation of the people, and the 3-Step Plan: ½ day.

4) Village's plan of activity

Training duration: 3½ days.

—*Education of the people:*

1) Required knowledge:

—Understand the situation.

—Understand the war and its military, political and economic aspects, the balance of forces.

—Understand their mission in 1965 and the local objectives to be accomplished.

—Join the hamlet and village guerrillas to build the combat villages.

—Participate in the political struggle and military proselytizing.

—Join the army, Buy Troop Support Bonds.

2) *Required ideology:*

a) Eliminate escapism, fear of war and fear of hostile activities, in order to make oneself honest to the RVN. Hold one's farm and orchard.

b) Keep vigilant and strong the hate of the Americans and feudalists.

c) Eliminate selfishness and disunity. Help each other.

Strengthen the will to fight. Contribute finance and manpower to step up the resistance.

—Strengthen hate for the imperialists and feudalists.

—Obtain unity and rally with the Chinese and Cambodian-born Vietnamese people to fight the common enemy.

—Place an absolute belief in the Party, and in one's capabilities of self aid and strengthening.

3) *Required results:*

The education and motivation of the people should result in their eager contribution of money and manpower to serve the following objectives of the resistance:

1—Participation of the people in the guerrilla war.

2—Purchase of Troop Support Bonds.

3—The people's support in building a stronger force.

—Educational materials and guide:

1) A letter from the Party addressed tothe farmers (this letter is available).

2) Apply the 7-Step Plan.

—Learn the enclosed "Basic Guide"

—The education should be given on the basis of the toiling class (in accordance with the directives on the motivation of the people.)

Training program and reporting:

—The training of the party members should be completed in late August.

—The education of the people should be conducted from 30 August to the end of September (divide this period into two phases: 30 August to 20 September completion of the first 5 steps of the 7-step plan; 20 September to 30 September, completion of the 2 last steps.)

—Initial reporting:

30 August: Training of the party members

10 September: Training of People's Group Chapter and Cadre.

7—October: Education of the people, and final reporting.

—The Propaganda and Training Section assumes the reporting, surveys and steers the training.

II.—*Armed Struggle*

1) *Combat:*

Step up guerrilla warfare. Shift it to destruction of New Rural Life hamlets and intensify the communication (axes) [sic] rear base, encirclement and destruction warfare.

One guerrilla must kill or injure one enemy troop.

—Capture the RVN rural administrative personnel, uncover spies, destroy the village bullies. Conduct aggressive attacks. Counter the sweep operations.

—The district force assumes [sic] the main element to conduct encirclement of enemy installations, attack on their flank, blocking of retreat, destruction of communications and of New Rural Life hamlets. Make full use of the rudimentary weapons.

Make full use of the terrain. Establish a strong defense system to be able to counter all sweep operations. Spread thin, or concentrate whenever possible. Each cell kills 1 enemy troop at least.

The required result is to annihilate one enemy squad.

The primary targets are Special Forces, Popular Forces and Combat Youths. Coordinate with military proselytizing to annihilate one enemy squad or seriously wear it down.

2) *Encirclement.*

Example: The district Regional Force coordinates with the guerrillas to encircle Hao Quan (RVN district installation), the village force encircles Thoi An and VHH element encircles and shells Tac Cau.

3) *Communication (axes) warfare:*

Example: The Local Forces and guerrillas of Vinh Hoa Hiep attacked one enemy vehicle and one boat.

4) *Attack on the enemy's rear base:*

Example: The City Unit conducted two attacks in the city, using grenades and explosive charges, to destroy the tyrants.

5) *Sabotage:*

Example: VHH element destroyed 100 meters of Tac Cau road. 705 unit built dirt barriers on Minh Luong highway.

Continue to sabotage the highways.

6) Destruction of New Rural Life hamlets:

Destroy the 7 hamlets planned and half of the tyrants. In each of these hamlets, organize one Farmer's Association cell, one hamlet security cell, one signal and liaison cell and one guerrilla cell.

Objectives:

Hoa Quan is to paralyze Co Khia
Binh An ″ Go Dat and An Binh
Minh Hoa ″ Cu La and Minh Hung
VHH ″ Vinh Phong and Vinh Dang

7) *Develop guerrilla warfare and build combat villages.*

A) *Essential knowledge:*

The American Imperialists fight an aggressive and counter-revolutionary war.

In reaction to it, our Party fights a people's war. It is an omnistrata [sic] and protracted war in which the people are determined to win.

For this reason, our Party has confirmed that the people's guerrilla warfare plays the basic strategic role in this revolutionary war.

—The guerillas will defeat the Americans and their lackeys.

—Master the 3-front attack.

—The further the war develops, the greater strength it requires. The guerrilla force needs to be largely expanded to be able to furnish remplacements to the regular force.

When orienting the people on the Party's war policies, their principles must not be omitted. Otherwise it will be a big mistake.

Our Party (Committee) Headquarters scored significant achievements in the people's guerrilla movement, disruption of the RVN control, destruction of the New Rural Life hamlets reaction to the sweep operations and construction of our combat hamlets. However, several shortcomings have been noted.

Our Party Headquarters realizes that the people's war policies have not been thoroughly understood. The noted deficiencies are these:

1) Little attention was paid to the motivation of the people, therefore the people's participation in the war did not reach a strong movement.

2) The rudimentary weapons were disregarded.

3) The combat hamlets and villages were not fully developed. The guerrilla training was inadequate.

4) No aggressive action was initiated. Our force only acted when the enemy came.

5) The guerrillas, especially the concentrated guerrillas, were not given enough moral or physical care.

These facts indicate a wrong concept of action, such as assumption of the defensive, more reliance on the concentrated force than the people's force, under-estimation of the rudimentary weapons, lack of self-reliance.

Reluctance, lack of eagerness, disregard of the people's initiatives should be eliminated in several places.

B) *Mission and methods of promoting the people's guerrilla warfare.*

—Mission of the guerrillas:

1) Fight the enemy and hold the villages.

2) Protect the installations and revolutionary force.

3) Furnish replacements to the concentrated force and various field units

4) Perform exemplary production and work labor mission.

—Methods of motivation:

1) Mobilize the masses to participate in the fight, to join the guerrillas, self-defense and the army, to build combat villages.

—Consolidate the hamlet and village agencies, the guerrilla and the people's groups, which serve as foundation for the movement.

—Organize an effective communication and warning system to serve the counter-operations. Closely coordinate with village security to uncover spies.

—Build combat hamlets. Push action over to the enemy controlled areas. Install protective shelters against air raids and artillery. Protect the people's lives and properties.

The combat hamlets and villages should meet the following requirements:

—Each guerrilla or self-defense troop should have one to three combat and AA positions with some spikes or booby traps installed along the designated retreat path.

—The construction of combat hamlets and villages should be carefully planned and conducted at the same time in the entire province and in phases of 10 days. Initiate the first phase from 30 August to 10 September and the next phase 30 September to 10 October.

—Encourage the youths, self-defense personnel and guerrillas to train.

—Expedite the recruitment and organization of self-defense and guerrillas to attain the following strengths required by the end of October:

—Self-Defense	200
—Hamlet guerrillas	100
—Village guerrillas	50
—Regional Force	10
—Recruits	150

These strengths do not include the present personnel.

—Train the hamlet guerrilla squad leaders on weapon firing and firing at aircraft.

—Conduct brief training for the hamlet guerrillas and the self-defense. One-third of them should have completed the training by the end of October.

III.—*Political Struggle*

A—*Required knowledge:*

—Know the present situation which is favorable to the political struggle. Know the capabilities of the people.

—Know how the political struggle plays its vital strategic role in all activities.

—The political struggle is vital because it ignites effort in the destruction of the enemy, protection of the people's lives and properties, increasing the production and safeguard of our crops.

B—*Required results: Face to face struggle.*

1) The party members and cadre operating among the people should act in consonance with the Party's policy. They should never forget that the armed and political struggles always go hand-in-hand.

2) Train the people's force. Organize them into cells and teams with a close control system from the district to hamlets. Assign the female leaders of the face-to-face struggle. The people in the districts and villages should be well prepared for the struggle at all times.

3) *Motivation of the people:* Each month, at least 20 minor incidents, including terrorism, should be initiated in each village.

The district and village agencies should grasp the most favorable time to conduct major struggle at the following rate:

—In village: once a month with a people's force of 50 to 100 persons.

—In the district: once every two months with a people's force of 500 to 1,000 persons.

—When necessary the province will concentrate a larger people's force. The people's force should be well organized and maintained [at] active [level] at all times.

4) Submit reports covering all aspects of the struggle in each phase. Draw the learned to improve the movement.

5) Promote the movement. Encourage the Chinese and Cambodian born Vietnamese troops and their dependents to participate in the struggle. When a struggle is initiated, each local place should know how to organize the people and send them to town or city.

The people's force should also be well prepared for a fire fight, and fight if they are attacked.

6) Deficiencies should be noted and corrected in all echelons.

—In order to promote the movement, the people's activities in the villages and districts should be closely supervised. Observe the Party's policy towards the political combatants. After each struggle and phase, conducts critiques and comments, and select the outstanding emulator. All persons who are killed, injured or disabled in the struggle will be regarded as combat soldiers.

—*Indirect struggle:*

Perform the indirect struggle as usual to support the face-to-face struggle. Emphasis is placed on the following points:

1) Promote unity and mutual assistance among the workers, farmers and toiling people. Every day and after an enemy raid give aid of money, rice, latania leaves, medicine to the victims. Hold gatherings to sow hate.

2) In each phase, the outstanding persons in mutual assistance, rescue of victims and holding the farms are cited.

C) *Mottoes of the struggle:*

In the RVN controlled areas:

—Against the construction New Rural Life hamlets.
—Against the conscription policy.
—Against violation of private properties.
—Against harassment, air raids and artillery fire.
—Demand the civil and democratic rights.

In the liberated areas:

—Against air raids and artillery fire
—Against violation of private properties
—Against the construction of New Rural Life hamlets.
—Against the conscription policy.

In both areas:

—Fight off the Americans
—Demand peace and non-alignment on the basis of the Geneva Agreement of 1954.

IV.—*Military Proselytizing*

A. *Motivation:*

Initiate a broad military proselytizing movement among the Party members and the masses.

Learn the letter of the Party addressed to the people.

Learn the material relative to the people's participation in the military proselytizing.

Employ a large number of troop dependents, relatives and friends from the predominantly Cambodian areas. By the end of October, 100 dependents of the troops should have been trained, and 70 of them employed.

Consecutively attack the enemy posts and patrols.

The desired result is 70 troops of Regional Force and Popular Force to rally by the end of October.

B. *Military proselytizing, attrition and destruction of the enemy.*

Double the results this year. The desired result is to put 30 RVNAF troops out of combat by the end of October.

Intensify action to attain the desired results. The district force is to destroy from one enemy cell to one squad, and attack the enemy rear installations to put 40 troops out of combat, and seize 10 weapons by the end of October.

In each village, kill one village bully.

C. *Infiltrate personnel in the enemy ranks.*

Designate three district cadre to assume penetration of officers. Complete two installations by the end of October.

Designate three village cadre to assume penetration of troops:

Desired number of penetration agents:

—Thoi An	2
—Hoa Quan	2
—Binh An	3
—VHH	2
—MH	2
—The city	2

Three Party members in charge of Signal and Liaison have to infiltrate one Signal and liaison agent in each military installation by the end of this year, and control their operation.

D. *Organization of the military proselytizing.*

—At the district, organize one section of three consisting of one section chief and two cadre.

—Each village organize one section of two cadre, one of which is sent out to contact the troops' dependents and relatives.

—Place one comrade beside each enemy installation.

E. *Observation of the Party's policy.*

—The Party Chapters and Committees should firmly hold the penetration personnel.

—Orient the Signal and Liaison cadre, people's organizations and the masses on the Party's policy.

—Military proselytizing reporting should be made once every 15 days and a complete reporting every quarter.

V. *Building of Force*

A—*Situation:*

—Timely grasp the opportunities, and struggle for time in order to shorten our fight and to save the lives of our troops and people. The building of our force is an extremely urgent and important operation which will determine the result of our fight.

Our forces are still unable to meet the situation due to the following deficiencies:

1) The development of our forces has not been undertaken in consistence with the local [illegible].

2) The class policy has not been fully observed. The cadre's attitude [leaves] much to be desired. There are many dishonest members in the various organizations. One guerrilla cell was said to be very haughty. This situation caused disunity and discouragement of our personnel and disrespect of the revolutionary organizations during the past six months.

—This situation also caused great difficulties to the development of village farmer's association and guerrillas. In some places, the guerrillas were completely inactive. The Party and various groups developed very slowly.

3) The organization and development was not specifically undertaken to suit the classes, localities aind racial origins.

4) When a person was given a mission, he was not fully educated, nor was his ideological standpoint strengthened. There was no coordination of action and of forces.

B. *Consolidation and development requirements:*

Consolidate and develop our forces, as required, to facilitate the accomplishment of our Party's political missions in 1965.

Each party chapter or branch should establish specific plans for activities in the liberated areas and the RVN controlled areas, to cover the immediate and long range requirements. Specify the mission of the party and group members.

Consolidation:

Continue to consolidate the ideological standpoint of the party and group members. Improve their attitude and performance. Correct all the mistakes which were noted during the last reorientation. Discharge the incorrigible comrades and group members.

The armed elements of the various groups should also meet the same requirements.

However, their primary mission is to consolidate their ideological standpoint and organization.

—*Development:*

Personnel should be equipped in proportion to their armed activities:

—Party members	40
—Group cadre	50
—Farmer's Association members	500

—Women's association members 300
—Youth association members 100

VI.—*CONSTRUCTION OF THE RURAL AREAS.*

Suspend the new land reform policy. Apply the old land policy of 1964. Continue to seize lands from the traitors and village bullies. Distribute the seized lands to the farmers. The other land owners should observe the established rates of land rental and loan interest.

Prohibit dropping cultivation; selling or lend[ing] lands. If the landowners are absent, we administer their land and give it to the farmers to farm on. They will not be called back. If they come back, no land rentals will be paid to them, unless they actually cooperate with us and make themselves eligible.

Continue to give government lands to the farmers in reasonable proportion.

Planned rural activities:

1) Encourage production, unity, exchange of labor, mutual assistance, low loan interests.

2) Protect the crops against enemy plundering by moving them to the liberated areas.

3) Investigate and fill out the two forms issued by the Rural Affairs section.

Economization:

—Learn the letter the Party sent to the farmers. Clarify the new economic policy of the Americans. They exploit our workers through their purchase of goods.

—Encourage economy by only buying the very essential goods.

—Calculate the expenditures wasted during the past year and show the people what we could save.

Troop Support Bonds:

The district agency will designate the village agencies to sell the bonds.

—This operation will be conducted in three steps:

1st Step: From now to 30 August, motivate the people to contribute manpower and finance. Select and train the necessary accounting cadre. Estimate the sale capabilities and draw the bonds from the province.

2d Step: 30 August to 15 October, continue the motivation and sell the bonds.

3d Step: 15 October to 30 October, close the accounts and send the funds to the province. Keep the archives in safe places.

Submit a report to the district every 10 days, and to the province every 15 days.

The desired amount of sale is 3,000,000$00 [sic] in the following proportion:

—Hoa Quan [?]
—Thoi An [?]

—Binh An 680,000$00
—VHH [?]
—Minh Huong [?]
—The City [?]

4) *Improvement of Security:*

Reinforce the existing village security agencies run by the party members.

Designate cadre to organize security in other villages.

Designate two security agents and one assistant hamlet chief concurrently in charge of Farmer's Association for each hamlet.

Some guidelines on the implementation of this plan:

Understand the situation and grasp the opportunities. Concentrate a maximum of effort on the resistance.

Initiate the ideological campaign to start with the party members and extend it to the masses.

An effective motivation of the people will result in a large contribution of their manpower and resources which are vital to the resistance.

Observe the 7-step plan. The key step is to sow hate.

Results:

The results of the 5-month plan will be evaluated according to the accomplishment of the following missions:

—Destruction of New Rural Life hamlets.
—Construction of combat villages.
—Enlistment.
—Sale of Bonds.

22 August 1965

[DOCUMENT H-2]
ECONOMY FINANCE SECTION
CIRCULAR

Issue of meal coupons to cadre and servicemen on mission and operations for payment of their messing to the people.

To comply with a Directive from the Province Finance and Economy Section providing for a timely and adequate food supply for troops in order to enable them to fight relentlessly and everywhere, at the same time to increase the solidarity between the military and the civilian, to insure that the latter would be able to feed cadre and servicemen for a lasting period, and that troops would comply to the Party's policies regarding the masses.

As the liberated areas in the lowlands are expanding daily, operational requirements increase, cadre and troops' movements become numerous. All their needs, messing and billeting are provided by the people, [who] should be properly paid to be able to feed troops and cadre for a protracted period.

In the past, cadre and troops properly effected this reimbursement but there were still some who did not pay for thousands of meals. In some instances as the people refused the reimbursement, the money was spent for banquets. Others only paid for foodstuffs and not for rice.

The people have also to pay liberation taxes. If their food supply remains unpaid, they will not be able to pay taxes.

Cadre and troops receive their daily food allowances from the Party. If they do not pay for their food, the people will be giving contributions twice. Therefore the people would complain, adversely affecting the policies of the Party, the solidarity between the civilian and the military, as well as the sources of contribution.

Instead of paying to the people or returning the money to the budget a number of cadre and troops become corrupt and greedy, keeping the money for their own expenses, smoking Virginia cigarettes at all times.

In order to stop the above practices, our Party's policy of standardized financial management should be strictly enforced.

Henceforth, the Finance and Economy Section establishes the following procedures relating to issue of food allowances for cadre and troops operating in the lowlands and payment of their messing to the people:

—When cadre, troops and government employees come to a given place, they must come to the local village or hamlet Autonomous Committee to be assigned billets and messing which are furnished primarily by the people. Messing should be reimbursed (except religious or New Year's parties and victory banquets). *"Do not take anything, even a needle or a bit of thread from the people."*

Starting June 1965, District Finance and Economy Sections will issue meal coupons to troops and cadre for settlement of their messing with the people. There will be "1-meal," "1-day" and "5-day" meal coupons.

These coupons replace money or rice in substance. The 1-day's meal coupon is the equivalent of three condensed milk canfuls of rice and RVN 2$00. The people will use these coupons to pay taxes. Village Finance Economy sections will add the coupons in the equivalent amount of rice or money, when settling with the district authorities. Tax exempted persons having these coupons will have them exempted by the village authorities for money or donate them to the Liberation funds. The donations will be acknowledged as individual achievement. If these people are too poor, village authorities will reimburse them with cash, upon presentation of meal coupons. These coupons issued to cadre and troops are exclusively used for payment of food to the people, and not for commercial transactions or settlement of accounts between agencies. Example: Comrade A from B agency receives ten 1-day meal coupons for a 10-day temporary duty. During the 10-day trip comrade A spent 8 coupons. On his return he should turn in 2 remaining coupons to his agency that will not reimburse him with money or rice.

Every month commanders of various district agencies and branches will make estimate of their needs in type of coupons then bring these to the district administrative [section] to draw the needed coupons. Any withdrawal of coupons should be accompanied by a settlement of coupons expended in the preceding month.

Starting June 1965, cadre and troops who still hold food allowances in money should exchange it for coupons.

Upon receipt of this circular, all agencies, branches and Q.15 Unit are requested to widely disseminate it to the people and troops in order to insure its proper execution.

Village agencies are also requested to clearly explain it to the people.

12 May 1965
Finance and Economy Section

—True copies of H.114 Finance and Economy Section's Circular to all units and comrades subordinate to Q.15 for action.

30 May 1965

For the Command Committee of Q.15

s/ ____________________

[DIRECTIVE]

[DOCUMENT H-3]

TO HAMLET PARTY CHAPTERS

In order to execute Directive No. 21 of higher echelon concerning the motivation of the people to perform their battlefield support obligations to gain decisive victories.

Due to present pressing requirements, Hamlet Party Chapters are requested to:

1. *Indoctrinate and encourage the masses* to work as laborers, serving the front line. First of all, make the Party and Group members, cadre and the masses to understand clearly and realize that the responsibility of each individual is to set examples in volunteering his service. Party and Group members have to act as laborers. This is to symbolize their close association with the masses and to lead them in struggles.

Thus, effective immediately, meetings should be held in hamlets and areas to motivate the masses and determine the front-line; mid-line and rear-line laborers, to activate squads and platoons with squad command committees and Platoon Command Committees. Party and Group members must be assigned to these command committees.

2. *Organization and Employment of laborers:*

Each hamlet must activate a volunteer squad for use as a principal element when needed, and to work outside the area. Laborers must be employed alternately; do not employ one man on every mission, while the others stay home as this may cause bad influence. If conditions permit, assemble the masses for public debate; attention should be paid to the small families, and those of the cadre and soldiers. Mobilization of each individual must be based on realistic and local demands to be reasonable. Each person must discharge his own responsibility and should not delegate another person to do the job for him so he can stay home.

3. *Equipment and material support:*

Laborers should be thoroughly indoctrinated so that they can help reduce the people's monetary contributions by restricting their expenses. They should be instructed that they should contribute to the Revolution, by self-providing necessary individual equipment. This equipment will be loaned by those who have completed their duty to those who are bound for it. The masses are capable of settling every problem.

—The shortest trip will take 15 days, therefore the masses should be motivated to bring their own rice, money and medicines. Material requirements of laborers who have to stay more than 15 days will be sponsored by the tactical command post.

Please discuss this and initiate immediate execution; report to Village [Party] Committee for instructions if difficulty is encountered.

TO: Hamlet Party Chapters for immediate execution

(Our greeting for efforts)
3 May 1965
For LBN: 202
B____P______

APPENDIX I
THE PARTY'S ROLE IN MILITARY FOUNDATIONS

[DOCUMENT I–1]
PARTY LEADERSHIP OVER PEOPLE'S ARMY

[Following is a translation of an article by Song Hao in the Vietnamese-language publication *Hoc Tap* (Studies), Hanoi, No. 12 December 1964, pages 17–36]*

Our army was born and grew up in the crucible of the people's revolutionary struggle; its mission was to fight for the nation's independence, to win land for the people's cultivation, and to bring socialism and communism to our country.

Under the banner of the Party our army has for the past several decades been bringing into play the nature of the proletariat and the nation's traditional courage in struggle; it has surmounted every difficulty and hardship during the barbarous war against the nation's and class enemies, defeated the Japanese fascists, French imperialists, and U.S. interventionists and their stooges. It has become an extremely powerful striking force that makes the people's foes tremble but heartens those nations in struggle for self-liberation.

The source of our army's strength is first and foremost the leadership of the Party. Without party leadership our army would not have accomplished anything and would never have become a genuine people's army.

Throughout the period of formation, fighting, and during the coming of age of the army the strengthening of the leadership of the Party has always been a question of prime importance and a determinative factor. It constitutes the army's guiding principle whether for building itself up or in combat.

The Party of the Vietnamese working class is the creator, organizer, trainer, and leader of our army. This fact amounts to an objective law and a requirement of our nation in this phase of its history. Ever since the capitalist way of production was established around the world, two antagonistic classes took shape: the capitalist class and the proletarian class, the life-and-death struggle between which demanded that each had its own political party. Leading the capitalists is their party while the proletariat is under the leadership of its vanguard—the Marxist-Leninist party.

Toward the middle of the 19th century French capitalism perpetrated aggression against our country. Our ruling feudalists first went down in surrender then colluded with the French bandits and helped them oppress

*[Concurrently, the main arguments developed here appeared in yet a second article (attributed to Song Hao) of a more popular character in *Nhan Dan* (The People) 18 December 1964, pp. 1–2.]

our people. Vietnam became a semifeudal colony. To exist and develop themselves our people had to rise up and fight for freedom and independence. This is for the nation a question of survival and also a law governing its history.

With the victory of the Russian socialist October Revolution a new era began for mankind: the transitional period from capitalism to socialism on a worldwide scale. In Vietnam the national liberation revolutionary struggle could be accomplished only if it was an integral part of the Vietnamese proletarian revolution. For this reason the leading role of the Vietnamese revolution must be assumed by the Vietnamese working class. This background provides the answer to the question why the Vietnamese working class, although young and immature, found itself in the leading role of the Vietnamese revolution when it first appeared on the political scene.

Looking at its economic and social background we can see that only the working class is genuinely revolutionary in nature, only it shows absolute loyalty toward the laboring people and possesses the capability of leading the Vietnamese revolution and our worker-peasant army in its decisive war against the class and nation's enemies. Like all other world countries' working classes, the Vietnamese working class is blessed with particularly favorable factors in waging the revolution for liberating itself along with all oppressed people, because it is bound by nothing to a society built on exploitation. Leading a life of joblessness and privation, with bare hands as its only assets, the Vietnamese working class realizes more acutely than any other classes the wretchedness of the oppressed and exploited and the humiliation of people without a country of their own. The interests of the class and nation have created in their heart an extreme hatred of imperialism and feudalism, and animated in them a determined revolutionary spirit.

Born at a time when world capitalism was well on its way toward bankruptcy and when the Russian October Revolution has scored complete success, the Vietnamese working class inherited the valuable experience of the first victorious proletarian revolution under the leadership of Lenin, the great successor of Marx and Engels. Perfectly aware of its own strength and confident in its future, it unhesitatingly went ahead with the task of eradicating the imperialists and feudalists. The working class was not the only one to have realized its own leading role in the revolution, the entire Vietnamese people, drawing from their own experience, had indeed come to conclusion that only under the leadership of the working class would they be able to win total freedom.

With a historic mission devolving upon it, with the specific historical conditions of the country, with a most revolutionary standpoint, with the great revolutionary doctrine of Marx and Lenin, the fact that the Vietnamese working class, through its Party, is providing leadership to the Vietnamese revolution is entirely consistent with the objective law and necessary requirement of history.

To achieve power is vital in all revolutions. In order to seize and maintain power the working class' party had to build up, organize, and lead a revolutionary armed force—the principal instrument of the revolution's physical strength. The greatest, most important fact in a capitalist society is that the bourgeois class is armed from top to toe against the proletariat. For this reason, unless the proletariat possessed its own armed forces and relied on the people to wage a revolutionary struggle, it would not be in a position to secure leadership, to free itself along with all other laboring strata, to eradicate classes, and to eliminate the very root cause of war. No political objectives whatever would have been attained by the proletariat had it been without the means of revolutionary violence or without armed forces in its hands. The experience of the revolutionary struggle of the French proletariat in 1848 has taught us that, when the people were without armed strength, even though they were represented in the bourgeois government, their representatives were in the end but "high priests" whose only "responsibility consisted of discovering paradise and explaining the new testament."

There are two kinds of politics in a society where classes still exist: the politics of the oppressor-exploiter class and the politics of the oppressed-exploited classes. War is the continuation of politics and the army is the main instrument for the prosecution of war. It follows that whatever aim an army is fighting for must serve the political line that has brought it about. There has never been such thing as a war without political aim and there likewise has never been a supraclass, politically independent army. On the basis of this theory our Party has, even since our people's revolutionary struggle became an armed one, always considered the organization, building up, and leadership of the armed forces as vital tasks. Facts show that the Party has set up the people's army and that, from the outset, it has always had a firm leadership over the revolutionary army.

The experiences of history have demonstrated that, if an army is in the hands of the exploiting class, it sooner or later will betray the interests of the laboring people.

In 1775 the American people organized an army to oppose the rule of English imperialism. Once the war of liberation had ended the American bourgeoisie set out to oppress and exploit the people with every known trick; what followed was that the laboring people of the north rose up in opposition. But the northern American bourgeois in collusion with the southern landlords and slave-owners used the army to repress and quell the uprising. Today the American army has become an effective tool in the hands of American imperialism which uses it against the American people and revolutionary people the world over.

In 1789 the French bourgeoisie formed an alliance with the peasants, set up an army, overthrew the feudalist autocracy, and built a bourgeois republic. With the success of the revolution, the capitalist regime was set up. The bourgeois class thereupon used the said army as an instrument to safeguard its "inviolable rights of ownership," to oppress its former allies the French peasants and laboring people, and to perpetrate aggression against other nations.

In 1911 a Chinese bourgeois democratic revolution overthrew the feudalist regime and established the "Republic of China." But in its wake the contributing armies now under bourgeois leadership became bourgeois tools for the oppression of the laboring people and against the revolutionary movement.

Another lesson of experience is that, even if it is composed of an absolute majority of oppressed and exploited men, an army which is not led by the working class becomes but a tool in the hands of the exploiting class to oppress the laboring class. We still remember that in February 1848 the proletariat chased the royalist troops from Paris and set up a bourgeois republic. The bourgeois provisional government thereupon organized 24 battalions of special guards comprising 24,000 brave men recruited from among the proletariat. Lacking experience and a seasoned staff of its own, the proletariat failed to seize command of these battalions, convinced as it was that these armed laborers were in effect proletarian troops. It consequently cheered the guards when they paraded through the streets of Paris. Barely 4 months later these very guards, on bourgeois orders, pitilessly repressed a proletarian uprising side by side with the bourgeois national guards.

In 1925, under the leadership of the Chinese Communist Party, men from the warlords' armies of Kwantung, Kwangsi, and Yunnan who had rallied to the cause of the revolution were reorganized into a national army. But Chen Tu-Hsiu, who held party leadership then, chose to compromise and surrendered to the bourgeois. He therefore failed to consolidate the party's leadership over the army and allowed the latter to eventually become a tool in the hands of the feudalists and bourgeois for oppressing the proletariat.

In some peculiar historical circumstances our Party, too, entered alliances with other classes to form a united national front or administration with a view to eliminating the enemy; it however never shared its leadership of the revolution with any other classes. The Party never held its absolute leadership over the revolutionary forces firmer. In the complicated political situation during the first days of the August Revolution when our administration was still in its infancy, the reactionaries who called themselves Vietnamese Nationalist Party and who came on the heels of the Chiang Kai-Shek troops contrived to station their men in key positions in our army hoping that they would turn it into a tool of counterrevolution. Some others sought to take advantage of the situation and set up bourgeois-style rules according to which our army was to be taken away from party leadership. The Party fought back resolutely against all schemes of sabotage on the part of the class enemies, all rightist views and unprincipled compromises, holding on firmly to its absolute leadership over the revolutionary armed forces.

The leadership of the Party is the factor that determines what the political nature of the army and what its goals of struggle should be. Formed during the climax of a national liberation revolution in a backward agricultural country, the cadres of fighters of our army are generally imbued with patriotism, revolutionary fervor, and the sense of sacrifice, and they are courageous and endure hardship well, all of which does not mean that they were already holding a good fighting standpoint, a correct revolutionary viewpoint, and a lofty ideal of struggle when they first entered the army. While they could easily see in the enemy a national enemy, they seldom saw in him a class enemy. They could have accomplished the national democratic revolution more consciously than they would the socialist revolution. Only under the leadership of the Party could our army—composed mainly of uniformed peasants—have acquired a thoroughly revolutionary spirit, the determination to exterminate all class and national enemies, an unconditional loyalty toward the Party and the people, and only under Party leadership could it have become a modern proletarian army. As Lenin has said: "Only the proletariat can create the nucleus of a powerful army—powerful because of its ideals, discipline, and heroism in combat (1)."

In order to give the army its absolute leadership, the Party constantly educates the men on what they must fight for, on the political tasks of the Party which vary with the circumstances, and on the proletarian line for conducting war and building up the army. It unremittingly arms the cadres and soldiers with the Marxist-Leninist ideological standpoint and approach for dealing with all questions relative to war and army building. Organizationally, there has been set up an entire party system from party chapters at the unit level to party committees in divisions, military zones, etc. The Party has also set up various leadership and operation rules for party committees at all levels and trained a body of cadres and party members to serve as the core for combat and army building duties.

Thanks to the Party's leadership the army progressed from being nothing to being something, from small to large, from weak to strong, and it won victory upon victory. Experience tells us that the key to solving all questions relative to building the army and conducting war is to strengthen party leadership. Wherever and whenever party leadership weakens, errors crop up in great number and in all respects. All inclinations toward curtailing or weakening party leadership over the army are therefore erroneous and harmful to the Party and people's cause of the revolution.

So that the Party may perform its historic task and so that the army may be unconditionally loyal to the interests of the class and nation we in our effort to build the army must bear in mind the following basic points:

—The Party's absolute, direct, and total leadership over the armed forces must be maintained.

To maintain an absolute leadership over the army, the Party must first of all refrain from sharing its rights of leadership with any other classes.

---

(1) Lenin: "Between two Wars," complete Russian edition, Political Literature Publisher, Moscow, 1947, Vol 9, page 431.

Because the army is the working class' sharpest instrument of struggle, it is imperative that it should be led by the working class' party if it is to remain loyal to the revolution of the class and nation.

The importance of the leadership of the Party can be felt in the fact that individual authority should not be allowed to be stressed lest it weaken party leadership. Our party-created army came into being and grew up during the revolutionary movement; it fought for the liberation of the nation and class. Building it up is a task devolving on the entire Party and people. Absolute leadership over the army should therefore be the collective leadership of the Party represented by the Central Executive Committee and party committees of all levels. Any tendencies toward promoting the authority of individuals or reducing the Party's collective leadership are contrary to the Party's principle of army leadership. Enlargement of an individual's authority in any sector of party endeavor is always conducive to despotism, arbitrariness, bureaucratism, and estrangement from the masses, all of which is contravening the Party's collective leadership principle with evil consequences upon the revolution. Allowing individuals to build up their authority at various levels of leadership and command of the army, which is a military organization, would mean militarism and arbitrariness internal relations would be adversely affected and troops could even be caused to go astray. It is for this reason that our Party has always consistently been applying the regime of "two commanders sharing responsibilities under the collective, unified, and centralized leadership of the Party committee," which is regarded as the only principle for the leadership and command of the army.

Politically, the Party has laid down its political and military lines and is using them as the guideline and principle for building the army and for combat and other party duties. The lines currently followed by our army consist precisely of socialist revolution in the North and people's national democratic revolution in the South. The military line of the Party consists in "building up the people's armed forces and waging a people's war;" it is the correct and creative integration of the Marxist-Leninist theory on war and armies with actual experiences in class and armed struggles. Its content is permeated with the spirit of revolution to the bitter end, the scientific touch of the doctrine of Marx and Lenin, and the courage and creativity of our Party, and it faithfully mirrors our country's concepts on armed struggle. In order then for the cadres and soldiers to thoroughly understand the Party's military line governing all actions taken whether in combat or army building, it is necessary for them to have a firm class standpoint and a good realistic viewpoint. Our experiences in combat and army building have proved that, to carry through its military line, the Party had to wage a persevering struggle against all influences left by bourgeois military thinking—overemphasis on individual talent, weapons, technology; downgrading of the role played by the masses, man, and politics within the military realm. The Party had to abide by and go through on its realistic viewpoint, fighting dogmatism with all its manifestations— overlooking the military and combat tasks of the army, taking no account of our country's possibilities and actual conditions, and disregarding our army's experience and magnificent traditions.

Ideologically, the Party regards Marxism-Leninism as the leading ideology for the army, it has never ceased to fight nonproletarian ideologies of all kinds which are trying to make inroads into the army. The army's standpoint and viewpoint must be those of the working class, its only ideological method must be the dialectic materialist method. All cadres and men, no matter from what class they come, must be made to consider Marxism-Leninism as the compass course of all their actions, to learn and acquire the Party's class and vanguard character, and to resolutely carry out all party political and military lines. Consequently, if a man joins the army but does not learn and train in accordance with the proletariat's standpoint and viewpoint, if he does not carry out the Party's political and military lines, he can never become a cadre or a soldier of the people's revolutionary army.

In organization, the Party adapts its own organizational principle to the army. It made the workers and peasants the core of the cadres, it strengthened the proletarian component when echelon party committees in the army were reorganized, it recruited party members from among the workers, peasants, and members of the Labor Youth Union. Such is the content of the class line of the Party as regards the organizational aspect of army building. Other leadership principles which the Party applies to the army are the principles of democratic centralization and collective leadership. Criticism and self-criticism should become a rule and a routine in the army's political life.

The army is the main instrument through which the revolution's physical strength manifests itself. It is the most potent tool in the hands of the dictatorial proletarian state for maintaining power, for safeguarding and developing the achievements of the revolution. As a result, every move and every combat action on the part of the army is entirely consistent with the Party's political line. Organizationally, our army is a very tightly knit body. It is highly centralized and unified according to a vertical system of command; it is operationally very efficient, and its sphere of action covers the entire country. For this reason, not only must the Party assume absolute leadership over the army but it also must assume direct command of it as well, not going through the intermediary of party organs as it does with the people's groups. From the point of view of the Party and army, the Central Executive Committee of the Party alone is the supreme echelon with the authority to assume direct command of the army. The Central Committee directly instructs, inspects, and supervises the building of the army in accordance with the class line of the Party and sees that the army always acts in conformity to the Party's political task. It determines the combat objectives and the strategy and tactics of each phase; it maps out plans for building up or using the armed forces which will fit each particular situation and perform specific task. Regional military organizations (provincial, municipal, district, and village units) as well as the entire regional armed strength, the people's armed police and self-defense militia must submit to the direct command of various echelon committees (provincial, municipal committees, etc.) In the main force, party organizations command directly all units and make all decisions concerning army building and combat duty.

Only through such direct, top-to-bottom leadership can the Party provide a centralized, unified, firm, and efficient leadership consistent with the nature and peculiarities of the armed forces, and only then can it secure a constant, unconditional loyalty on the part of the army for the revolution and people.

Any inclinations toward making the Party's leadership over the army an indirect one, that is, having it go through intermediary organizations, are incompatible with the nature and peculiarities of the army would hamper smooth functioning when assignments are being implemented, especially when these are army combat assignments from the Party.

Beside being absolute and direct, the Party's leadership over the army must also be total if the army is to develop harmoniously in all respects and to heighten its combat ability and readiness.

To insure that party leadership is total we must well understand that building up the Party, strengthening the army ideologically, scientifically and technologically are the three main aspects of army building. Consequently, we must combat all contentions that the Party only needs to and only can lead the army politically and ideologically but that it need not and cannot lead it as to science and technology. This is a tendency toward pure and simple technological specialization, toward severing science and technology from the Party's leadership. Science and technology are essentially classless. Using them for the promotion of certain classes' interests implies, however, a class motive, particularly when military science is put to work for class struggle. Moreover, technical equipment is an indispensable element of the army's fighting strength. For all these reasons, should the Party confine itself to political and ideological leadership while foregoing leadership on military science and technology, not only would it fail to impart to the army the physical strength with which to carry out the Party's political tasks, but military science and technology themselves could deviate from party military line and run counter to the Marxist-Leninist view on war and army and, at worst, they could stray into and adopt the view of the bourgeois class. Whenever military science and technology are not under party leadership, they can never be revolutionary military science and technology. In summary, the Party must assume total leadership over the army with stress on military science and technology. In this respect our Party is entirely capable of performing its task.

The Party's total leadership over the army is also reflected in [the fact] that full party leadership must be provided politically, ideologically, and organizationally. The political and ideological sectors are considered the most vital and far-reaching; the organizational aspect helps the ideological one, which in turn helps implementing the political tasks.

Ideological leadership consists in educating the masses to think correctly and act consciously and in the right direction. Organizational leadership, on the other hand, channels all the masses' conscious actions into a single objective as prescribed by the specific rules and principles for creating physical strength. Without organizational leadership, ideological leadership would result in uncoordinated actions on the part of the masses and, hence, failure to achieve the concerted, powerful strength expected of the army as a whole. Ideological leadership and organizational leadership are therefore two closely interwoven aspects, neither of which can be overlooked.

The Party must see that total leadership is provided to all revolutionary armed forces from the main body to the regional forces, the people's armed police, and the self-defense militia none of which is to be neglected. Only by coordinating all these troops can the Party consolidate its entire revolutionary armed forces steadily, develop them harmoniously, and generate a strength large enough to overwhelm any enemy.

For each of its armed forces the Party must reaffirm its leadership both when it is building itself up and in its combat duty. In building up and training the troops, attention must be paid to meeting all requirements for combat readiness and combatability [sic]—the objectives of all building and training works. As regards combat leadership, the Party must know how to use combat itself to keep the army expanding and training, to raise its ideological, political, technological, and tactical levels, and to make it possible for the army not only to fulfill its tasks well but also to grow and mature in every respect while in combat.

Absolute, direct, and total leadership constitutes the fundamental principle of party leadership over the army and the immutable principle for building a modern proletarian army. To struggle for reaffirming and consolidating this principle is the all-important task devolving on all party organizations within the army.

—Building a strong network of party organizations.

To establish and strengthen its leadership over the army, the Party takes the general principles on party building and the nature and peculiarities of the army as the bases for establishing within the army echelon party committees and party chapters which would serve as the nuclei of a unified, centralized leadership and, at the same time, uphold the system of "two commanders sharing responsibility under the collective leadership of the party committee" for the fulfillment of all tasks confronting the army.

Strengthening the Party's absolute leadership over the army consists in stepping up the construction of a network of party organizations within the army and in struggling against misconceptions tending to minimize this job or to separte party building and army building.

The army is strong so long as its party organizations are—an experience, learned from actual army building and combat, that has all but become a principle.

The Party provides the army with political, ideological, and organizational leadership of which the political and ideological aspects are the primordial ones. Each party organization and each party member must therefore have a good political and ideological understanding. Our Party is strong chiefly because its organizations and members have a firm viewpoint, standpoint, and ideology. Consequently, strengthening the Party ideologically has always been first and foremost in party building. A strong echelon committee calls for good members, and this calls for exemplary masses, revolutionary, class-conscious, and first of all deeply aware of the proletariat's rights and obligations. Good, exemplary masses in turn call for party members firm in their standpoint and ideology to educate and guide the masses. All of which demands that all party organizations focus on strengthening the Party ideologically. Only through field training in army building and through the test of actual combats can good members and echelon committees be formed and party organizations tempered into powerful ones. The stronger the Party and its organizations are, the better the education of the masses, and the larger the exemplary masses will become; as a result, party building will have more favorable factors working for it. Therefore, strengthening the Party ideologically always serves as the basis for stepping up the building of the Party organizationally. The more carefully we educate the party members and masses ideologically, the more favorable factors we shall have working for us in the setting up of the party organizations.

In our effort to strengthen the Party ideologically, we should adhere to our class line thoroughly when setting up party organizations, that is, when building up the Party and its committees we should follow the class line and enlarge the proletarian element in the Party and particularly in the party committees. We have brought up this question of increasing the worker and peasant element within the Party not because we want to stress the doctrine of party composition, but because we must implement correctly the class line in building up the Party organizationally in order to strengthen it and bolster its fighting potential. Here, the class line is identical to that which guides us in the selection of our cadres or new members for the Labor Youths. It is therefore entirely consistent with the class line in party building and army building to select cadres from among the best party members and new party members from among the outstanding, front-rank members of the Labor Youths, to select for the armed forces the best young men whose class composition is clean and whose personal history is clear, and to train them into soldiers of talent and strict morals.

To have a strong network of party organizations it is paramount that the Party's principle of centralized democracy be thoroughly adhered to in all aspects of party organizational or other activities in the army.

Centralized democracy is the Party's fundamental principal of organization. It is based on the fact that unity in organization is conducive to unity in party action and ideology. It transforms the Party into a well disciplined army with high fighting ability, and it gives full play to party members' initiative and creativeness.

Of the above principle democracy and centralization are the two inextricably interwoven elements. A noncentralized democracy would preclude unity, it would disperse our strength and stifle people's minds and talents. On the other hand, centralization without democracy would not result in true unity either, it would not bring the strength of the collective to the fore and it would turn into arbitrariness and onesidedness.

Applying thoroughly the principle of centralized democracy in party organizations within the army consists primarily in maintaining and consolidating the system of "two commanders sharing responsibility under the collective leadership of the party committees." Actual experiences in army building have borne testimony to the soundness of this system for maintaining the Party's absolute leadership over the army—a system fully embodying the Party's fundamental principle of organization, which is centralized democracy, and its uppermost principle of leadership, which is collective leadership with individual responsibility. Under the system the collective leadership of the party echelon committee is total, it works closer to the masses and to realities. The system is also able to coordinate all party pursuits within the army and to insure that unity prevails in ideology and action—the source of the Party's strength. It brings to bear the commanders' initiative, ingenuity, and sense of responsibility.

This system, which leaves leadership to the party committee and responsibility to the commanders, not only does not weaken in any way the orders or directives issued by the commanders, but it insures that these orders or directives are correct and fully implemented. It does not get in the way of scientific and technological pursuits, but it helps science and technology develop more vigorously and in the correct direction. The Party committee's leadership does not downgrade the role of the modern regular army in army building and actual combat; on the contrary, it is very much needed and all the more so where joint operations are essential and commanding becomes a complicated job.

To perfect the system, it is first necessary to constantly strengthen the principle of collective leadership by the party committees. The reason is that only the party committees' collective leadership can insure that party lines and policies are correctly laid down and implemented. This makes it possible for opinions from the party members and masses to be centralized; subjective, onesided errors to be reduced; the sense of responsibility, the positiveness and creativeness of party members to be brought into play; and the unity within the Party and army to be enhanced. This collective leadership must also be centralized and vested in the party committees which represent the Party. All endeavors must spring from the decisions of party committees of various echelons, all authorities must be centralized and vested in the party committees. Centralization here should be aimed at the party committees as collectives, not at individuals. It follows that all inclinations toward minimizing the party committees' collective leadership in favor of individuals' authority are contrary to the principle of centralized democracy and in violation of the principle of collective leadership upheld by the Party. Ambitious thinkings aimed at power and position, paternalism, and militarism often are the root causes of such inclinations as upgrade individual authority and downgrade party leadership. On the other hand, the absence of democracy-consciousness, ignorance of the masses' viewpoint, and lack of the sense of responsibility, initiative, and creativeness displayed by some commanders are factors that hinder collective leadership by the party committees.

While emphasizing the party committees' collective leadership we are not overlooking the responsibility of the commanders, because collective leadership must be coupled with responsibility, otherwise we shall fall into the mistake of empty talk and not follow up with action. Conversely, sharing responsibility not backed by collective leadership will lead to dispersal of strength, dogmatism, despotism, and inability to summon the total strength of the organizations.

A correct relationship between the party committees and the commanders calls for the party committees, on the one hand, to supervise closely the commanders' implementation activities and, on the other, to strive to bolster them, making them bolder, more active and more creative, and to provide them with every possibility for fulfilling their tasks. Only in so doing will party committees avoid monopolism and routineism and be able to deal with more vital, decisive questions. The party committees should always serve as fulcrums for the commanders in decision making. Consequently the commanders must realize what their duty is toward the Party's collective leadership, they must obey the party committees unconditionally and ask to be rigidly controlled by them. However, they must also know their responsibility which is to serve as experts for the party committees. They must heighten their sense of responsibility, give fuller play to their creativeness, and contribute ideas useful to the committees' collective leadership.

Abiding by the Party's leadership system, we must establish a correct relationship between the leadership and the commanders consistent with the revolutionary character of the army and the fact that it is becoming a modern regular army. Party leadership is absolute, direct, and total over the army; its political goal is the army's combat target, its resolutions are the directives of action for all cadres and fighting men. A commander, whether he is a party member or not, must therefore assume the duty of conscientiously implementing all resolutions arrived at by the party committee of his own or higher echelon; he must respect the Party's army leadership and command systems.

Under the leadership of the Party, we now have rules, orders, regimens, etc. governing the responsibility and authority of each commander. To carry them out thoroughly is essential for making the army system of command stronger. The party committee's leadership not only does not hamper in any way the commander in the execution of the prescribed regulations within his authority, on the contrary, it helps the commander fulfill his duty and carry out orders and regulations to the letter. Orders and regulations are but codified decisions concerning organization aimed at unifying our actions. So that they may be fully carried out it is necessary that their ideological and political contents are well understood. The resolutions arrived at by the party committee are ideological and political bases to insure that all orders and regulations are rigorously carried out, which in effect helps strengthen the command system. Moreover, the resolutions reached by the party committee have a much broader scope, they determine the unit's political tasks and directions of action taking into account the unit's political and ideological situation and current task. No matter how specific regulations and orders may be, they can never replace the leadership of the party committee; organizational rules cannot replace the latter's political and ideological leadership, nor can military command replace the Party's leadership. Only on the basis of strengthening the party committee's leadership can military command be asserted and all regulations and orders be carried out rigorously.

The army's role is to fight. To insure that every battle is won is the highest goal of all party organizations within the army as well as all cadres and soldiers. From this principle, all army activities and all specific regulations governing leadership and command must be derived. Whether in army building or in combat duty, the principle "all for victory over the enemy" must be observed thoroughly and the party committees must always strive to make it possible for the commanders to assert their authority, discharge their responsibilities, and fulfill the tasks assigned to them by the party committees. Such is the political responsibility of the party committees of all echelons. In view of the same requirement—to triumph over the enemy—the party committee must help the commander achieve the tasks on which he believes some initiative is necessary, and it must hold firm its leadership to insure that military command is performed correctly. All this shows that leadership and command not only do not hinder or undercut each other but that they are tightly interlocked and mutually beneficial, provided everyone concerned abides rigidly by the highest principle—to triumph over the enemy—and regards it as the goal of all actions.

In specific circumstances, particularly during the climax of a battle, our leadership and command system must be used in an appropriate manner. A distinction must be made between means and principles. Whether the commander informs the party committee of his intentions before or after the fact depends on the situation. In any case, the principle must be upheld that a commander is responsible to the party committee and subjected to its control, and that he must carry out its decisions. A party committee being the united leadership organ of a unit, nothing lies outside the sphere of its control. All technical assignments or tasks must be controlled by the party committee if technology is to serve politics, help the troops perform their job, and avoid blundering. The directives and orders issued by a higher echelon reflect the lines and resolutions of that echelon's party committee, lower echelon party committees must see that they are carried out correctly. Commanding and organizing the implementation of these directives and resolutions are always in close coordination with leadership and leadership system. It can consequently be said that, to qualify as the Party's army, a well commanded army must also have party leadership and that, to qualify as a revolutionary army, it must do active political work when its masses are themselves active.

The party branch is the basic element that insures that the Party's leadership over the army is absolute. It is deeply and firmly implanted in all army installations and constitutes the bridge between the Party and the masses, the nucleus of unity and party leadership in every army unit and installation. Strong party branches assert the role of leadership of the Party. There are no strong companies without strong party branches—a fact as cogent as a principle. The party branches' part is never more prominent nor more decisive than in time of difficulty and crisis, when commanders who know how to get help from party branches and to look up to their leadership always deal successfully with problems and fulfill their tasks. Such has become a tradition with our army. Building up and consolidating the party branch is, therefore, the key to building the Party itself. All thinking or opinions tending to overlook the consolidation of the party chapter are erroneous and contrary to the basic principle on army building—to strengthen the Party's absolute leadership.

Consolidating the party branch comprises many aspects, the most important of which is the education and training of the party members, for the branch is powerful only when its members are good ones. The member must constantly be made to improve in all respects; he must be ahead of the masses not only in viewpoint, standpoint, and ideology but he also must understand the Party's line concerning the army. He must further learn and lead the masses as to technology or other endeavors. In so doing he will become a model shock element [and] at the same time a good persuasive power over the masses. In effect, the party branch is at once the core and the brains; it is suitable and proper that it be the supreme leadership organ of a company.

It is obvious that, to have a firmly established network of party organizations within the army, a good deal of work is necessary of which, it should well be borne in mind, the most basic points are the following: it is basic to build the Party up ideologically; adhere to the class line in building the Party up organizationally; the system of leadership by the party committee and responsibility shared by the commanders must be constantly perfected; party branches—the key elements—must be built up and strengthened.

—Building an elaborate, well coordinated political network.

The Party's absolute leadership over the army is obtained through the setting up of an elaborate and well coordinated political network; for political work belongs with the Party, it stirs up the masses' awareness of the revolution and it helps thoroughly establish the Party's leadership within the army.

The Party has clearly defined the purpose of political work in the army as: to educate the cadres and soldiers as to the working class' viewpoint, standpoint, and ideology thereby making the army well understand and resolutely implement the Party's political and military lines; to strengthen unity in the army; and to struggle against the enemy on the political and ideological fronts. The entire political task being aimed at building up the Party's leadership over the army, all political work past and present must be geared to strengthening the Party ideologically and organizationally and consolidating the party committee and party chapter's leadership, all of which is for the purpose of bolstering the leadership of the Party over the army. In another connection, those who are in charge of political work must pay utmost attention to training the troops as to standpoint, viewpoint, and ideology of the proletariat, regarding these as firm bases for building and expanding the army, for making it possible for it to fulfill its missions.

Thanks to the Party's leadership and its political work our army is now magnificiently revolutionary and absolutely loyal to the cause of the revolution and the interests of the class and nation. It has built for itself glorious traditions—heroism in combat, stamina, surmounting difficulties, living a simple life, practicing internal unity, military-civilian solidarity, international solidarity, and so forth.

Thanks to political work, our army has successfully been built, it has won many battles, scored great achievements and glorious victories.

Experiences gained in the coming of age of our army have clearly demonstrated the far-reaching effect and the great role of political work, and underscored the fact that it is the source of the army's vitality and strength. Moreover, the achievements as well as the excellences of the army point up the indispensability of political work, for without political work the Party's leadership over the army would have been impossible and the masses in the army would not have been revolutionary in their actions.

Our revolutionary army is completely different from no-matter-what other armies, whether they are the imperialists', the feudalists', or the bourgeois' in that ours has a political work system, that is, a party of working class leadership. That it is utterly loyal to the interests of the people and the cause of the revolution, completely revolutionary, possessed of a high, indomitable fighting spirit is thanks to political work and party leadership. The regime of political work is what differentiates the working class' army from that of any other class, and a revolutionary from a counterrevolutionary army. For this reason our Party asserts that political work, whose purpose is to realize the Party's absolute leadership over the army, is paramount and is in effect the very soul of the army. It has become the deeprooted tradition of our army in the task of building itself, in combat, in its daily life and other endeavors. It is the basis for pursuits of any importance. Anything tending to minimize and downgrade the role of political work or antagonize it with other works is the product of misconception as to the leadership of the class, revolution, and Party over the armed forces. If not resolutely checked, such errors would lead us to building our army in the bourgeois way, with disastrous consequences affecting our efforts to build the army and consolidate our defense.

With a view to performing its political task, the Party has set up a political network with political organs and political agents at every echelon, it has laid down rules regulating the political committees and political workers. This has made the Party's leadership over the army even stronger, and the Party's lines and revolutionary tasks are being imparted more and more fully to the cadres and soldiers.

The Party also asserts that political education and ideological leadership are essential to political work, it in fact regards them as permanent, central elements of political work.

Taking the Marxist-Leninist view on the importance of the revolutionary theories and on the moral being the determinative factor in war as a basis, keeping in mind its own political task, the army's combat target, and the ideological situation prevailing among the cadres and soldiers, the Party maintains that army building must be founded upon political and ideological structures. An immutable principle in army building is: politics as the base and ideology in the lead. In whatever form war is fought, under whatever circumstance the army is built, whether it is dispersed or concentrated, composed of guerrillas or organized as a modern regular army, the human factor is still the determinative one and the political and ideological factor still occupies primordial positions. The more difficult and complex the situation and the tougher the job, the more necessary a political buildup will become. Any inclinations to minimize or weaken ideological work are errors of principle. Experience has taught us that, no matter when and where and whatever the size of the unit and the importance of the task all army pursuits and activities must be based on ideological work if good results are to be accomplished. Conversely, neglecting ideological work will lead to difficulties and even failure in the performance of our tasks.

Ours is a people's army under the leadership of the Party. It wages a struggle for national and class liberation. It must be class-conscious before it can be receptive to the doctrine of Marxism-Leninism and bring to bear the revolutionary nature of the working class. Moreover, the workers account for but a small percentage of the troops while the absolute majority belongs to the peasants and patriotic petty-bourgeois. But their class-consciousness is found to be generally merely skin deep or not well understood; the line is sometimes hazy between foes, friends, and ourselves; the old class concept still persists and nonproletarian thinking still leaves its mark. Under these circumstances, unless the Party works to bolster the proletarian standpoint on a permanent basis, to inculcate the revolutionary philosophy of life in the troops, and to resolutely and perseveringly struggle against all nonproletarian standpoints and concepts among the cadres and soldiers, then our army will not be receptive to and implement correctly the Party lines and policies. Without full class-consciousness it will not acquire a thoroughly revolutionary spirit, a spirit of sacrifice and courage and the determination to conquer difficulties and to fulfill its missions. For these reasons our Party must take class-consciousness as the fundamental content of political and ideological work, attaching importance to constantly promoting the troops' class-consciousness. Whatever the nature of education, its foundation must be class-consciousness and the proletarian ideology. Facts prove that each time class-consciousness [is] high in the cadres and soldiers, with class hatred boiling inside them and class emotions well stirred up, we can witness the troops overcome all obstacles and hardships, fighting heroically, and fulfilling all party-entrusted missions. Inculcating class-consciousness and standpoint in an army such as ours constitutes a full, constant, protracted, and tough struggle. This consists first and foremost in putting the army on the working class' standpoint where it can distinguish between enemies, friends, and ourselves—a paramount question in revolutionary struggles. Only on that basis can the cadres and soldiers clearly see the nature of the army and its goal of struggle; thoroughly understand the Party's revolutionary lines; analyse the complex problems of class struggle and determine the relationship between the individual and the collective, between the interest of the class and that of the nation; and enhance their revolutionary fervor and insure that the army never strays from the Party's revolutionary lines.

Aside from teaching the troops to distinguish between enemies, friends, and ourselves, we also have to improve their methods of thinking and raise their theoretical level. Only then can they thoroughly understand such complex questions as unity between standpoint and policies, strategy and overall design, and so forth and only then can they avoid subjectivism and bias, tell right from wrong, and be truly firm in their class standpoint.

We already know that the Party's task of political education and ideological leadership within the army consists, on the one hand, in raising the level of perception of the cadres and men as regards the Marxist-Leninist theories and the basic questions concerning the Party's political and military lines and tasks; on the other hand, in staying close to the troops in their daily life and trying to solve real building, training, and combat problems. The two aspects are closely interlinked; while the former, which is basic, serves as foundation for the latter, the latter complements and strengthens the former. Failing in or neglecting questions of political and ideological education while solely concentrating on solving problems, or vice versa, will be detrimental to political work.

However, when we are solving actual problems under specific conditions, those doing ideological work must handle as correctly as possible all problems encountered in the everyday life of the troops. There are views recently that there are at present newer and more complicated issues which warrant our attention and they are the issue of modern military science and technology, that of the putting in effect of the orders for regularizing the army, that of responsibility, regimes, etc. and that ideological work must concentrate on this particular area and handle the question in a proper manner. The foregoing view is correct, for on its way toward becoming a modern regular army, our army has found the points raised above extremely important as they contribute to speeding up the process of regularization and modernization. They have been getting our attention for the past several years and even today ideological work is being stepped up with a view to resolving them in a more satisfactory way. Nevertheless, if we confine ourselves to such new and complicated things without taking into account the equally new and complicated political, ideological, and emotional problems confronting the cadres and soldiers as the present fierce class struggle is in full swing within and without the country and as the army assumes a formidable combat duty, then our ideological work will be without a direction and without strength.

Political education currently consists in making the cadres and soldiers take further cognizance of their combat targets. While the targets were national independence, land for the tillers, preparation toward socialism, they now are socialist construction in the North, national independence and land for the peasants in the South, and steps toward national reunification, nationwide socialism and communism. Only if they are imbued with these great targets will our army possess the noble ideals, the strong will and unmatched power for annihilating all enemies of the nation and class.

Ideological work in the army must at present concentrate on stamping out negative, rightist thinking which is weakening the cadres and soldiers' fighting will, paralyzing their revolutionary alertness, causing the men to waver in the faith, to balk at difficulties in reconstruction, and to shirk danger and sacrifice in combat. Individualism, too, is a great obstacle. It is the enemy of collectivism and socialism. It causes the cadres and men to literally shrink, to think of themselves first in every endeavor, to lose sight completely of the ideal they are fighting for, and to utterly lack the soldier's aims and ambitions. Freedom is an equally great plague. It makes a confusion of the distinction between right and wrong, leaves truth unprotected, weakens discipline and organization, and saps the fighting strength of party and army organizations. All these erroneous conceptions must consequently be resolutely combated.

Ideological work must also delve in military science. Military science is the science of class struggle, it belongs to the category of social sciences, hence, it calls for a thorough understanding of the Party's ideology, lines, and guiding principles. Consequently not only must we educate the army in Marxism-Leninism and party lines and policies, but we must also prompt the cadres and men to strictly adhere to discipline, rules, and orders. At the same time, we must have a good knowledge of military science and technology, concentrate on the building and managing of the material and technological basis of the army, putting everyone firm on his feet on party standpoint, and use Marxist-Leninist viewpoint and ideological methods to understand and utilize the technical equipment and to resolve all problems pertaining to army building and combat duty.

Clearly, only by understanding the fundamentals of the Party's political and military lines and tasks, considering them as the essential elements for building up the army ideologically, and only by working closely and in every phase of army building and actual combat can we enhance the absolute leadership of the Party over the army through political and ideological work and insure that the army remains forever the sharpest instrument of struggle in the hands of the Party and the dictatorship of the proletariat.

—Forming a body of skilled cadres to serve as the core of army building and combat duty.

Ideological work, a network of party organizations, a good leadership setup are vital for establishing the Party's leadership over the army. However, they are by no means enough; a strong body of cadres is also necessary. The cadres must have a firm standpoint, a deep awareness of the Party's political tasks and the army's combat targets, a thorough understanding of the Party' viewpoint on armed struggles and armed forces building. They must have a good knowledge of theoretical military science, a high technical level, the ability to organize the masses for carrying out party-entrusted tasks, and a good working style. In order for such a body of cadres to materialize, it is necessary that first of all the Party's class line regarding the cadres be well understood: to select workers and peasants as core cadres. This derives from the Party's political and organizational lines.

Ours is a people's army and a worker-peasant army. It is the sharpest instrument in the hands of the dictatorial proletarian state. The Party's class line on organization must be made the organizational line for army building, and its class line on the cadres must be made the army's line on the cadres. If we grasp the Party's line on the cadres we shall also hold the main direction to the cource of cadres, that is, we shall select and train our cadres from among the workers and peasants, who form the most determinedly revolutionary classes. The workers constitute the leadership class, the peasants the main force of the revolution, and the majority of our army consists of workers and peasants. Clearly, the latter constitute the greatest reserves of army cadres both in quantity and quality. The army cadres must therefore come from these fighting masses of laboring people, which is consistent with the Party's political and organization lines as well as with reality. Adhering to the line on the cadres—workers and peasants as core cadres—means that we must train the good worker and peasant elements, constantly forming them into cadres and bringing their qualities to the fore, relentlessly strengthening their standpoint and raising their political, scientific, and cultural level. Under the old social regime the workers and peasants were the oppressed classes to whom cultural opportunities were denied. This was worsened by the fact that our country was a colony with a backward agriculture. To bring them to the point where they can master science and technology we must impart to them the necessary knowledge. This shortcoming must be pounded home to our cadres of whom great efforts will be demanded if the slogan "intellectualizing the workers and peasants" is to be realized.

With the line making workers and peasants core cadres as a basis, we should also train and educate those cadres who do not belong to the worker and peasant classes, intellectuals who have voluntarily chosen to fight for the cause of the Party and the rights of the laboring class, who have stood the tests of the revolution and who possess close ties with the masses. We should develop their excellences and overcome their defects especially regarding their standpoint and viewpoint, and make good the slogan "worker-peasant-izing the intellectuals," and make better cadres out of them.

Selecting and training cadres must chiefly be done among the workers and peasants in order to raise the percentage of these elements and enhance the revolutionary political nature of the cadres. By stepping up political education and conducting ideological reform on a permanent basis, we should further affirm the cadres' standpoint. Cadres from all classes must try hard to reform themselves ideologically and to strengthen their working class standpoint, because the ideological standpoint of the working class and of Marxism-Leninism did not by any means come about effortlessly and, moreover, remnants of bourgeois and nonproletarian ideologies are affecting our cadres every day and every hour. As a result, if we concentrate solely on enlarging the worker-peasant component without reforming them ideologically, we shall show a lack of revolutionary viewpoint; conversely if we concern ourselves only with making ideological reforms with no thought for the worker-peasant component, we are losing sight of objective reality.

There are contentions to the effect that the class line is no longer suitable for cadre recruiting in a society such as the North's where the exploiter class has been obliterated, and that it does not answer the requirement for building a modern regular army either. Such views are completely wrong, for the army and State are themselves products of a class society and as long as they exist the class line should be maintained in our task of building the army and recruiting cadres. Moreover, our country is performing two simultaneous jobs—a socialist revolution and a national democratic revolution—and needs only more emphasis on the class line. Right here in the North, the struggle has not ended between the working and bourgeois classes whether in the political, economic, ideological, or cultural fields. The fact that the exploiting class and its private ownership system are no longer in existence does not mean that their ideology has been eradicated along with them, it is on the contrary still very much alive. Facts from the history of the proletarian dictatorship have confirmed this point.

We cannot regard knowledge of science and technology as the content of or basis for our organizational line, because science and technology are not political in nature whereas class is. They can serve only as means for class struggle but they can never replace class struggle itself. Under socialism technology serves man's welfare, it extends man's capability in his struggle against nature and his class enemy. Under capitalism on the other hand technology tends to replace man and turn him into a slave. Technology springs from labor. Theory is born of practice. The worker and peasant are laborers and they have more practice than anybody else and, what is more, the worker-peasant cadres are culturally and scientifically no longer what they used to be. If helped, the worker and peasant can and will master science and technology. Should we deem them unfit for a modern regular army, we would be lacking revolutionary viewpoint and confidence in the great possibilities of the worker and peasant. That precisely is the viewpoint of the bourgeoisie, and that also is a way of rejecting the class line in recruiting cadres. Such a rejection points up a lack of class struggle viewpoint and the failure to grasp the key to the building of the armed forces; it would result in the impossibility of building a strong body of cadres for carrying out the Party's leadership, and would cause our army to be anything but a people's, revolutionary army, or a sharp instrument in the hands of the dictatorship of the proletariat.

To carry out the class line in cadre recruiting and to form a body of good cadres who will act as the core of the armed forces, the Party has set moral and proficiency standards to serve as direction of training and improvement for all cadres. Morals and talents are closely related and, in character, this relationship is that between politics and technology, and between standpoint, ideology and skill. A cadre must have both morals and talents, but while morals are essential, talents are only very important.

Morals mean political qualities, which are absolute loyalty toward the Party's revolutionary cause and the people's interests, determination to struggle for the annihilation of all enemies, courage in combat for the cause of the revolution, diligence in work, willingness to place public interest above personal one, the sense of organization and discipline, close ties with the masses, the spirit of unity in struggle, of criticism and self-criticism, and the desire for progress and advance. In public and personal life, the cadre must prove a person of high morals, he must be industrious, thrifty, honest, upright, impartial, humble, and simple, he must consider the common laborer's as his own standard of living. Our nation and Party have magnificent traditions, we work hard and lead a simple life. These are good qualities that must be developed. We shall not fall into other people's vices and we shall not indulge in the decadent life of the exploiter class.

High morals are not enough, however. It is also necessary for the cadre to be capable. Capability means a good knowledge in Marxist-Leninist theories, ability and experience in organization and leadership, the necessary professional proficiency and technical know-how, a sense of initiative, all of which is required for resolving the cadre's problems and performing his job. The cadres and party members in the armed forces not only must understand Marxism-Leninism in a general way, but they also must be versed in the Marxist-Leninist viewpoint on war and army. It is not enough for them to know the general outline of this viewpoint, they must understand well the problems confronting the nation in the field of war and army and resolve them in conformity to the Party's military thinking, line, and task and the realities of the country. For in our country class struggle and armed struggle, beside being governed by a general law, have also their own peculiarities. Knowledge must be transformed into skills and abilities and turned to account for resolving problems relative to war and armies. Complacency with the knowledge already acquired, unwillingness to learn, reluctance to go ahead in the face if difficulties and hardships when seeking new knowledge, absence of forbearance, lack of training, actions not motivated by the army's revolutionary requirement, non-adherence and refusal to learn from the theory and practice of armed struggles, all of them are contravening the proper viewpoint and attitude of a learning, fighting, creative Marxist. Nor is learning theories enough. Experience has abundantly proved that he who goes deep into reality, taking pains to stay close to troops in combat, and showing a high fighting spirit will distinguish himself more and more every day, show great creativeness and an ability to promptly cope with all circumstances. Conversely, he who strays from reality and actual combat will make no progress whatever, he will see his abilities gradually reduced, become destitute of intelligence, lack creativeness and quickness of thinking; he will never become a good leadership cadre or commander of the Party's armed forces.

To be a good cadre of the Party, we must also have a good work style, that is, we must connect theory to practice, follow the mass line, and practice criticism and self-criticism. Only with a good work style can we make the masses adopt the ideology, viewpoint, lines, and tasks of the Party as their own ideology, viewpoint, lines, and actions. The basic spirit of a good work style consists in staying close to the actions of the masses and having a revolutionary fighting spirit in work. Practice is the standard of truth, and the masses create everything. In real life, the new, positive always multiplies itself and stimulates progress whereas the old and negative hinders it. For the new and positive to triumph over the old and negative thereby developing the masses' creativeness to the highest degree, it is necessary to raise the revolutionary fighting spirit of the cadres in their leadership work. Facts have proved that the struggle for enforcing the practice of party work style and eliminating bad work style is in reality an ideological struggle because work style is tied to ideology and is the manifestation thereof. Lacking the Party's mass viewpoint our work style will not be one that follows the mass line; on the contrary, it [will be] one that prefers using highhanded methods and personal authority. Without a profound, realistic viewpoint, it is impossible to speak of a work style that could connect theory to practice; more often than not theory is unsupported and empty. Without a strong revolutionary fighting spirit we would not be bold enough to make self-criticism and criticism that seek out the truth and stamp out errors. For this reason we must resolutely fight bureaucratism, the tendency to drift away from the masses, estrangement from reality, lack of revolutionary fighting spirit, absence of criticism and self-criticism especially criticism directed upward, and we must oppose suppressions of criticism within the Party, because all these are in complete contradition to the Party's and army's work style.

Only by struggling in the foregoing direction can we become a good cadre, and only with a body of skilled cadres will the Party be in a position to carry out its tasks of leadership over the army.

—Handling all army relationships correctly and bolstering party leadership.

Under party leadership magnificent relations have taken shape in our army, such as can never be found in any exploiter class armies.

Depending on their morals, ability, and the requirements of the task, our cadres and soldiers are assigned different jobs and receive different treatment. All of them voluntarily stand up for revolutionary duty under the leadership of the Party, however, and fight for a common goal—national liberation, class liberation. Here lies the political basis of unity, unity of ideology and unity of action within the army. The relationship between the cadres and soldiers, upper and lower ranks, party and non-party members must and can be a relationship between comrades—a relationship founded on political equality and class love among comrades who share a common responsibility before the Party and people. Thus, ours is totally different from the exploiter classes' armies in which the relationship between the officer and the soldier is one between the oppressor-exploiter and the oppressed-exploited.

Internal unity, cadres and soldiers in full agreement, upper and lower ranks in complete accord have always been magnificent traditions in our army, they have pervaded its policies and rules and become an unshakable force. In protracted fighting, sharing the sweet and the bitter, joys and sorrows, life and death cadres and soldiers have further tightened the mutual bonds. Nevertheless, our army was born and brought up in a country for generations ruled by imperialists and feudalists, in a society in which the class concept had left heavy marks and the remnants thereof had by no means been eradicated. We therefore always emphasize political equality and make continuous efforts toward correct relationship and internal unity. No matter what his position or job is and whatever his task, the cadre must be an ordinary laborer first, then at once a commander and a comrade in arms to the soldier.

The principle of internal unity, with cadres and soldiers, upper and lower ranks in complete agreement, is expressed in many ways, the most important of which is in the relationship between democracy and discipline. In this respect, the cadres must have a correct viewpoint and they must handle the above relationship properly. Unity between discipline and democracy is reflective of the principle of centralized democracy; it is a relationship showing the class nature of our army. Discipline must be founded on democracy and aimed at promoting the interests of the revolution and people. Democracy must be guided. Both democracy and discipline's goals are to see that leadership is properly implemented and command obeyed, and that all tasks are successfully performed. Both discipline and democracy are aimed at boosting the fighting strength of the army. Reinforcing discipline must always be parallel with expanding democracy. Only in so doing shall we obtain a strict discipline and keep it in a correct direction. Democracy is at the same time a political and organization principle and a prime factor in strengthening discipline. It essentially consists of political equality, conscious and voluntary performance of obligations, discipline based on unity between leadership and command, upper and lower ranks, and cadres and soldiers, and conscious adherence to discipline by the masses through persuasion by political education. It can be said that discipline is never rigorous when democracy is not properly practiced. In our effort to enhance internal unity, we therefore resolutely reprove all acts tending to impair the dignity of persons of lower ranks or that of soldiers, along with all manifestations of dogmatism and imperiousness, and all attempts to establish personal authority, because they are contravening the very nature of our army and the principle of leadership and command of the armed forces. Parallel with efforts to combat undemocratic practices we must also fight all displays of freedom-ism. Overcoming the above-mentioned errors will result in a stronger discipline based on democracy, stronger unity between leadership and command, upper and lower ranks, and cadres and soldiers.

Proper handling of the military-civilian relationship in effect strengthens the revolutionary nature of the army and the leadership of the Party. If ours is a true people's army as the Party has decided, the unconditional support of the people will constitute an inexhaustible source of power that enables the army to accomplish anything. As President Ho has put it, ". . .we must remember that the people are the masters. The people are the water in which we, the fish, swim. All strength stems from the people." The political basis for all army-civilian relationships is a complete, mutual agreement as to rights. Our army belongs to the people and particularly the laboring people, and fights for their interests; this differentiates it from the feudalist and bourgeois armies which are tools for the oppression of the people.

For all these reasons the army finds in the people its strongest support, an inexhaustible reserve of manpower, wealth, political and moral strength. A politically and economically strong home front and political and moral unity among the people always constitute a determinative factor in victory in case of war. The history of the building of our army and its combat experiences bear testimony to the fact that no victory was ever won without the help of the people. Without the benefit of the people educating, bringing up, caring for, trusting, guarding, and protecting it, the army would never have accomplished anything. An army away from the people is tantamount to a fish our of water: the army will become sinewless. This is one of the Party's principles of army building.

Accordingly, our army always considers, and will continue to consider, the principle of complete unity between the army and the people as the basic principle in political work, party work, and other pursuits of its own. Thanks to our army-people unity, under the Party's leadership, the people and army fought and won victory in the war of resistance, they then carried out a successful land reform. Today the army's goal of fighting has changed, so has the task of building a modern regular army especially regarding its organization, regimen, etc. We must constantly enhance the army-civilian solidarity and place it on a new basis, which consists of the successful building and safeguarding of socialism in the North, struggling for the liberation of the South, and achieving national reunification.

With the people, the army must show very close ties. It must be exemplary in action and strict in discipline. It must respect, love, and help the people, show respect for the administration, and carry out conscientiously the law of the State. It must constantly gauge its relationship with the people by the yardstick of the principle of army-civilian solidarity. Looking down on the people, seeing no farther than its own province, and regarding itself as the "savior" of the people, belittling the people's part in war, in army building and defense strengthening, and so forth are all inconsistent with the Party's view of a "people's war and people's armed forces."

Strengthening international solidarity and the solidarity between our army and the armies of the countries of the socialist camp is another principle for building the army, it is an important task of the Party. Predicated upon a Marxist-Leninist view that, under capitalism and feudalism, the working class and all laboring people are oppressed and exploited; that the common enemy of the working class and laboring people the world over is imperialism, the mainstay of which is U. S. imperialism and its henchmen; that the victory of the revolution in each country is linked with the common cause of the world revolutionary movement, our Party has never ceased to hold aloft the banner of proletarian internationalism.

Ours and the armies of the sister countries are armed forces led by the working class. All of them are struggling for the interests of the proletariat and laboring people and share a common, noble ideal—to struggle for the complete, absolute triumph of socialism and communism around the world.

Socialism has become today a powerful world system. The imperialists led by the United States are nevertheless feverishly carrying out their scheme of wrecking the socialist countries, enslaving their people, preparing for war, and undermining the peace of the world. Unity based on Marxism-Leninism and proletarian internationalism among the socialist countries in general and that among their armies in particular are the surest guarantees for the victory of the world revolutionary movement.

In the struggle against imperialism and for peace, national independence, democracy, and socialism, not only do we regard the people and armies of the socialist countries as comrades-in-arms fighting for a common ideal, but we also regard the working class and laboring people of the capitalist, colonial, and dependent countries as our comrades in arms. As a result, we are constantly strengthening our solidarity with the working class and laboring people of those countries in the struggle for national independence, democracy, and socialism. This, we consider our international obligation. Speaking about the international obligations of a dictatorship of the proletariat Lenin said: "The victorious proletariat of that country (a country which has successfully carried out a socialist revolution—S. H.) having confiscated the property of the bourgeois and organized socialist production, will stand up and oppose the rest of the world, that is, the capitalist world by involving the oppressed classes of the follower countries, by urging them to rise up against the bourgeois, by using, if necessary, even military force against the exploiter classes and their state (2)." To forget this teaching is tantamount to falling into the quagmire of the doctrine of national selfishness.

Educated in the principle of proletarian internationalism our army has been giving from the outset and throughout its many hard, heroic struggles, and it will continue to give in the future, full play to the spirit of international proletarian solidarity in conjunction with true patriotism. Facts and the Party and army's experiences prove that, in order to hold aloft the banner of proletarian internationalism, it is necessary to keep our guard up against all displays of nationalism, great power chauvinism, and narrow nationalism. Should we belittle or look down upon sister nations and sister armies, as is practiced by great power chauvisnism, narrow nationalism would lead us to factionalism, schism, and national selfishness. Both the above tendencies are contrary to the nature of party-led people's armies and to the Party's principle of international solidarity based on Marxism-Leninism and of proletarian internationalism.

Being an instrument of struggle in the Party's hands the army must be made to clearly realize the relationship between the enemy and ourselves. The Marxist-Leninist theories and actual revolutionary struggle so far have pointed out that the distinction between the enemy and ourselves has always been the basic problem for the revolution and in determining its strategy and overall policy. Only when the enemy has been pinpointed can a goal be determined for rallying the masses, and only when the masses have been so rallied can the enemy be isolated and annihilated. For the armed forces—the main instrument for waging the most decisive, violent form of class struggle—the identification of the enemy is of particular importance because the slightest confusion over the boundary drawn between the enemy and ourselves could make it impossible for us to chart a correct course of action.

The principle governing the relationship between the enemy and ourselves, as far as the army is concerned, is to safeguard ourselves—the revolution, people, Party—and exterminate the enemies of the nation and class. We have worked out, however, a specific policy dealing with the

---

(2) Lenin: "On the Slogan of European Federation," *Tuyen Tap* (Selection), Vietnamese language, *Su That* (Truth) publisher, Hanoi, 1959, Vol I, part II, page 390.

enemies both as individuals and as a class. The individual can be reformed into a laborer, but from a class point of view the enemy class must be eradicated pitilessly.

Regarding the enemy army, our policy also deals differently with the soldier than with the officer-ringleader. The latter is the political representative of the enemy class, and the contradiction between him and us is an antagonistic one. As for the soldiers, they are the brothers and sons of the laboring people, forced and duped into the mercenary army; their interest essentially conflicts with that of their rulers and converges with that of the oppressed and exploited class. We therefore can use justice to put some sense into them and we can attack them politically in order to make them disintegrate. Those who lay down their weapons to surrender will be treated generously, but those who strike back at us will be resolutely exterminated.

Facts have shown that it is not a simple matter to identify the enemy, stir up hatred against him, and build up the will to exterminate him. Our army easily recognizes the enemies of the nation because they are the imperialists and feudalists who invaded our country, occupied our land, and enslaved our people. Overthrow them and we win our independence back along with the land for the tillers. It is not so easy when dealing with the class enemies—the exploiting bourgeois system—and many of us are rather slow to understand. An enemy is easy to spot on the battlefield but not in a political and ideological struggle. He is readily recognizable when he harshly suppresses the revolution, but to many the difference between friends and foes becomes hazy and confusion prevails when the enemy resorts to ruse, works under the false label of nationalism, and uses demagoguery.

Consequently, if we are to draw a clear line between friends and foes, build up the determination to eradicate all national and class enemies especially when, in this complex class struggle, they are using perfidious and machiavellian tricks of all kinds against us. We must, by political work, educate the troops and instill in them the Marxist-Leninist theories on class struggle, put them on a firm proletarian standpoint, teach them the method of class analysis for finding out the nature of the enemy and guarding themselves against the outward appearances behind which he is hiding. The basis for the hatred of all reactionary classes can spring only from class consciousness. In colonial countries the masses usually progress from national consciousness to class consciousness to socialist consciousness, but only when founded on class and socialist consciousness will patriotism and the will to fight for national liberation be firmly established. As a result, an education aimed at promoting class consciousness constitutes the basic content of political education and ideological leadership. Class consciousness is the ideological basis for examining and solving correctly all problems of army building and armed struggles. Only with a deeprooted class consciousness can we heighten the positive spirit and creativeness of the army, raise its fighting potential, make it possible for it to surmount difficulties of all kinds and to fulfill all tasks. Only with it can we build up our determination to fight and to win, eliminate all class and national enemies, protect the socialist North, liberate the South, struggle for national reunification, and safeguard peace in Southeast Asia and the world. Such are the practical meaning of and correct viewpoint on the relationship between the enemy and ourselves.

The relationship between politics and technology in the army is an extremely important one. Properly handled, it boosts the fighting strength and combat readiness of the army, because the army is the result of the combination of two elements: men and weapons, politics and technology.

The essential content of politics is class struggle, of which the army is the instrument. Politically the army has to deal with its own class nature, the Party's absolute leadership, its degree of political and ideological consciousness, its political life, and so forth.

For the army technology means weapons, equipment, skill of using and servicing these weapons and equipment, knowledge of military science and technology, professional proficiency of the cadres and soldiers, and so on.

Thus, politics are tied to society's class struggle, and technology to the development of the economy and production. Unified, politics and technology heighten the army's fighting strength for class struggle, with politics always in the leading role. Politics lay down the task for technology, act as its basis, bring out its potential for politics' interest, that is, for the revolutionary mission of the class. Technology adds to man's power, boosts the army's combat potency, serves the revolution effectively.

The coming of age of the army follows the progress of the relationship between politics and technology as this relationship is handled correctly. Today our army is becoming a modern regular army, its equipment has improved, its organizational structure has undergone many changes, but the principle of the politics-technology relationship—politics leading, technology obeying—has not altered in the least. Our Party always holds firm the creative political and ideological principles to serve as bases, it at the same time strives to improve the technological equipment of the army. It regards politics and man's revolutionary consciousness as decisive factors in war, while other very important factors are technology, equipment, and weapons. Without revolution-conscious men there can be no revolutionary army, and without technology and weapons there can be no armed forces. As a result, building the army means waging two simultaneous revolutions: an ideological and a technological revolutions, with the latter depending completely on the outcome of the former.

While resolving the politics-technology relationship we must smash all arguments which upgrade and show undue respect for weapons—especially nuclear weapons—and which downgrade the part played by politics and men and render men the auxiliaries of weapons; and we must shatter all inclinations toward pure technology or technology's independence from politics, and so on. These—the viewpoints of the bourgeois class and other reactionaries—are in complete conflict with the Marxist-Leninist theory on war and armies and the Party's viewpoint on the relationship between politics and technology and on army building and armed struggles.

Having created and organized a people's army and holding firm the leadership over it, the Party of the Vietnamese working class has performed and is performing a historic mission. Without the Party there could have been no revolutionary people's army. That the people's army has come of age and won victories is thanks to the constant consolidation and strengthening of the Party's absolute leadership.

Thanks to the Party's leadership, our people's revolutionary struggle has been victorious; our army has become a genuine people's army and a powerful force, it has overcome thousands of difficulties and hardships, and won glorious victories. It is worthy of being the reliable instrument in the hands of the Party and people.

In its efforts to achieve the Party's aim, which is to eradicate classes and end wars, our army has barely completed the first leg of this ten thousand-league highway. The revolutionary task of the Party and the combat task of the army loom formidable. For the present we must build the army up into a people's modern revolutionary regular army, ready to fight for and to safeguard the North, to fulfill its obligations toward the revolution in the South, and to contribute to the peace of Indochina, Southeast Asia, and the world.

The army's experience gained over decades of building up, fighting, and growing up has proved that efforts must be made in all respects, and that party branches in the army must acquire a firm proletarian standpoint, a rigid organization and discipline, an adequate military scientific and technological leadership, and a good understanding of the Marxist-Leninist theories if we are to guide the army toward the fulfillment of all tasks entrusted by the Party.

Region Military Party Committee*

[DOCUMENT I–2]
DIRECTIVE

Political Reorientation in 1965

I. In the past few years, during the resistance to liberate the South, our military and civilian populace has won increasingly larger victories. Our forces have and are developing at a fast pace, attacking the enemy both politically and militarily in great numbers, forcing continuous defeat after defeat upon the imperialist Americans and their lackeys. The enemy is on the verge of a total military and political crisis in South Vietnam. The danger of a disintergration of the puppet army and puppet government becomes more serious each day without the hope of any relief.

Objectively, the current situation is very advantageous. The military and the people are essential and have the capability to make a sweeping change in the Revolution in South Vietnam in 1965 to create a new situation, and from that organization to garner more [and] greater victories. Due to the requirement of the revolutionary mission during the current phase, the entire Party, the entire military and the entire populace must make a basic and more profound change in the realization and in the concept of [illegible] the ideological viewpoint in order to correctly complete the requirements of the revolutionary mission as pointed out in the directives from Central [?] and from Central Office South Vietnam.

In particular as regards our army, the mission of winning large victories is becomming greater and more pressing. The combat requirement is to annihilate more enemy forces than ever. Our cadre and soldiers must have a more profound resentment towards the imperialist Americans and their lackeys, [and] . . . a high attitude of awareness. They must have a stable proletarian viewpoint which will become the foundation of a determined combat resolve, a spirit determined to fight, determined to win, determined to annihilate the enemy. Subjectively, they will expand all efforts in continuous heroic combat, not afraid to sacrifice, not afraid of hardships and difficulties.

To fulfill the combat requirements, the problem of building a force is extremely urgent, all three types of military forces must be strongly developed. To this demand, we must consolidate and heighten the political quality and combat efficiency of our troops.

These requirements are truly great and urgent as regards our army. However in the political attitude and ideology of our troops, although having advanced and that is important, a number of faults and vulnerabilities are found such as an unstable revolutionary viewpoint and concept which is vague and full of illusions. Halfway participation in the struggle against the imperialists Americans to the final victory is an-

* [TN: Quân Ủy Miền]

other. Yet another is vagueness on the classes resulting in confusion in the standpoint and policy of the current class struggle in the rural areas. Class awareness of the individual soldier has not yet been heightened. There has been no deep realization of the status of the mission yet. There are still those who are rightist, negative, pacifist, confused politically licentious and whose individualism is not yet subdued.

Emerging from the general requirement of the current revolutionary mission in the South, the requirements of the nearing military mission and the current political ideological situation within our army, the Region Military (Party) Committee has planned a political reorientation for the entire army designed to raise the political quality and quantity of our troops up an additional step, raise the combat potential to a stronger level, and guarantee the successful completion of every mission of the Party entrusted to our army.

II. *REQUIREMENTS OF POLITICAL REORIENTATION IN 1965*

The objective of this general requirement is to make cadres and soldiers understand clearly the future mission and situation, especially emphasizing a deeper understanding of class awareness and standpoint, confirming a decisive stand against the Americans and their reactionary lackeys, positively annihilating and forcing the disintegration of the enemy, [and] finally with a political struggle of the entire people advance to larger, greater victories.

Positive Actions

1. Recognize the extreme nature of the invading reactionaries and the cunning schemes of the imperialist Americans in this special war in South Vietnam. To see clearly the past crises of the Americans all over the world, especially the current defeats and weakenings of the Americans and lackeys in South Vietnam. At the same time to see our victories and emergence into manhood, to see the strong and weak spots within us, understanding the situation and future mission. To comprehend our capability and essential requirements in changing the comperative strength between us and the enemy which will bring a large victory in the future.

2. Recognize that the current revolutionary war to liberate the South is a fierce class struggle. On the outside it is a war against the imperialist invaders and on the inside it is a war for land between the farmer and the avenging landlord class. After that, there must be full understanding of the past subjective and objective requirements of our Party on farm land and its major significance as regards the basic victory-seeking mission of the national democratic revolution in the South.

3. At the lowest level, raise their realization to a new level, consolidate their proletarian class standpoint, solidify their absolute revolutionary stand to carry out protracted war, determined to fight the Americans to the end to gain the complete victory for the revolution, confirm the complete stand to overthrow the feudalist and landlord class, swinging

the farmer and laborer over to make stable support for the realization of the Party's cultivated land policy. Clarify vague concepts which simply reduce the revolution, confusing friend from enemy, right from wrong in the enemy's scheme.

4. On ideology:

—Foster and raise higher the spirit of patriotism, class love, deepen the anger against the Imperialist Americans, avenging landlord class and their lackies. Raise the will to fight, the spirit to fight, to win, to annihilate the enemy and the continuous herioc combat spirit. Stand against all manifestations of rightist negative pacifist, confused ideology along with a fear of sacrifice, a fear of hardships, hampering the spirit of vigilance and lessening the will to fight of our army.

—Build a concept of protracted fighting, a positive concept of annihilating the enemy, a diligent and frugal concept in building the army, a concept of boundless loyalty to the Party, a concept [of] respecting and loving the people and a belief in the capability of the revolution, of the immense strength of the people, belief in the ultimate victory, optimism in the revolution, spirit of initiative and close coordination, standing against individualism and over reliance in others.

—Initiate a wide democracy, raise the critiques and self-critiques, form and train for tight organization and discipline against an ideology of freedom and loss of sense of responsibility.

—This time, through these reorientations, our army's excellent character and nature must be lifted and increased another step, gaining a major change in the political ideology within the troops. Their efforts will be invigorated, determination raised expanding their efforts in patriotism against the Americans, killing them for merit, annihilating a truly large force of the enemy. The urgency is in building our force so that the entire people can gain a larger and greater victory.

III. *CONTENTS OF THE REORIENTATION*: In accordance with the document sent down by ____ Region ____ Military Party Committee.

IV. *REORIENTATION GUIDE LINES AND METHODS*

1. *Reorientation Guide Lines:*

a. In the organization, increase knowledge, heighten class awareness emphasizing the standpoint and viewpoint of the proletarian class and overcoming all troublesome ideology in the execution of the military mission of the Party.

b. Join reason with reality and propound a high hatred of the American Imperialists, the avenging landlord class and their traitorous lackies.

c. Use persuasive indoctrination, calling for a self-examination as the principal feature, instilling a freedom of thought with a sense of patience.

d. Emphasize sincerity in critiques and self-critiques, maintain internal solidarity, encouraging one another in progressing in study.

2. *Guide Line in Implementing the Reorientation:*

a. Pay attention to the explanation and analysis of arguments which bear proof of reality. Join the individual thinking with the cell discussions. Coordinate the study of political documents with secondary studies, especially realistic supplementary reports.

b. In the indoctrination, promote a deep hatred of American Imperialists and their lackies. As regards landlords and traitors, enumerate and compare the acts committed by these persons.

c. Reorientate the cadre first and the soldiers later, ensure that the training of the cadres is truely successful.

d. With regards to the organization of the reorientation it will depend on the situation of that unit but it must be arranged in such a way as to guarrantee the reorientation will be complete, timely, and with a high quality. . . . Enemy conspiracies are extremely complicated, we must investigate them so as to evaluate them properly. We should not be over simplified and subjective, rather we should fully realize their close association in fighting with the revolution. At the same time we must study and take advantage of their internal conflict.

April 165
C.55

TRUE COPY number: 48/SY–H5: 18b/T

10 May 1965
For the Commander C.522
(Signed)
Q______ H______

[DOCUMENT I-3]
ORGANIZATION AND BUILD-UP OF INTERVILLAGE AND VILLAGE GUERRILLA FORCES.

I. *Intervillage Guerrilla Forces*

Organization and assignment of cadres for the platoon.

The Platoon Command Committee of intervillage guerrilla [forces] has 4 cadres: one platoon leader, one political officer, and 2 assistant platoon leaders.

The Platoon leader . . . or assistant platoon leader [is] assigned from district village local forces.

—The platoon political officer should be selected from a Party Committee member, and the political officer of a village unit should have military experience.

—The 2 intervillage platoon assistant leaders should be selected from 2 qualified village unit assistant leaders (Platoon political officer and platoon assistant leaders should be selected from village units of those villages encompassed in the organization and area of activities of the intervillage guerrilla unit.)

Organization and assignment of squad caches.

—Every squad has a squad leader, and an assistant squad leader. In the platoon, there are 3 squad leaders and 3 assistant squad leaders who are selected from village Units.

—Village must send squad leaders of its unit.

—In case of shortage of squad leaders [soldiers] are carefully screened then promoted to squad leaders. The excess is then assigned [to intervillage guerrilla platoon].

Organization and assignment of 3-man cells.

—Each squad has 3 3-man cells. Each 3-man cell has 3 soldiers including the cell leader.

The squad leader is with the 3-man cell. No I for regimenal [sic] activities in this cell.—The assistant squad leader is also the cell leader of cell No. 3.

Missions and Operating Procedures of Platoon Command Committee.

The Platoon Command Committee, in one hand, is responsible to the higher party Committee and the higher command Committee for the implementation of all orders and resolutions, [and on the other hand] is responsible for the command, organization, training, combat, and the maintenance of the unit; at the same time [he is responsible] for the implementation of resolutions of the chapter.

The platoon leader, being the military commander, is responsible for the command of the unit, the study of the battlefield, the planning and the command in operations, the training organization of the unit.

The political officer is the unit political commander and responsible to the development of the unit's activities, the qualitative and quantitative administration of Party and Group military-revolutionary council activities and of other activities such as political indoctrination, emulation, awards, and various [other] policies, etc.

The assistant platoon leaders are responsible for equipment, weapons and ammunition and at the same time, replace the platoon leader during his absence or TDY and participate in combat, the planning of operations and the training of the unit as the platoon leader deems fit.

Missions and operating procedures of squad cadres

The squad leader has the mission of controlling the squad; he commands his unit in combat, trains it in military tactics organizes and deploys his unit in accordance with orders and resolutions under the command of the platoon Command Committee.

The assistant squad leader replaces the squad leader during the absence of the latter, and is responsible for the execution of missions given by higher echelon, for equipment, supply and self supporting production as ordered by higher echelons, at the same time maintains discipline and internal regulations.

Missions and operating procedures of 3-man cell.

The leader of a 3-man cell has the missions of supervising and controlling daily activities, and at the same time, reviewing and submitting reports on combat situation, regimenal activities, and execution of regulations to higher echelon.

Regimenal activities of the unit:

A 3-man cell will hold daily meeting. Squads hold weekly meetings. Platoons hold bi-weekly meetings.

Contents of the regimenal activities:

a) *Platoon regimenal activities.*

The platoon command committee report on the combat and training situation and other activities of the unit.

—Review execution of regulations and policies of higher echelon.

—Propose plans for execution of resolutions for next month.

—Solve problems of the unit.

—Make criticism and self-criticism on leadership of the platoon command Committee.

b) *Squad regimenal activities.*

—Each member will report his activities during the past week.

—Review the execution of regulations and policies of the unit.

—Propose the plan for execution of the revolution of higher echelon.

—Make criticism and self-criticism to each member. (Attention should be paid to the contribution of ideas on leadership).

c) *3-man cell regimenal activities.*

—A 3-man cell is not administrative; therefore, it should not try to solve its administrative problems. Rather it is a small unit, assigned to carry out political motivation to encourage, solve problems, promote confidence in all missions and under all circumstances. Daily, in the evening, the cell will hold a meeting to review all activities, and settle ideological problems. Besides the official daily meeting, the cell leader should always follow his members and help them overcome their difficulties, at the same time reporting to A [Squad] cadre to obtain assistance for improvement.

d) *Daily reporting meetings.*

—Every everning, when the cell meeting is over, there will be a meeting of cell leaders to report the situation to A cadre.

—After the A [Squad] cadre meeting, there will be a meeting with B (platoon) Command Committee to report the daily situation of squads.

—After the report of A cadre, the platoon Command Committee will disseminate the plan and orders; settle problems and prepare for future execution upon receiving orders. Squad leaders will hold a meeting of cell leaders for dissemination of orders.

2/ *Program and contents of meetings for selection of emulators*

Each soldier must have a notebook and record the results of his daily activities in combat, indoctrination and production with specific figures. One week before the A [squad] meeting, cell members will hold a meeting to review and select an outstanding individual of the cell based upon reports of achievements, to be sent to the squad meeting.

At the Squad meeting, reports will be read loudly and examined by all the squad which would select one outstanding individual, and one cell of the squad to send to platoon. The platoon meeting will then reconsider reports and select one outstanding emulator and one cell for the platoon. The platoon command Committee then approves the selection of the platoon meeting and conducts a jubilee to welcome the outstanding emulator and the cell of the unit-of-the-month.

Remarks

Meeting for the selection at cell level should be held once a week. A [squad] meeting for selection should be held once a week.

B [platoon] meeting for selection should be held once [a month]. The A–B meeting for selection should be made with the regular weekly meeting of A and B.

In addition to these regular meetings for selection of outstanding elements, special meetings for selection of outstanding elements for each combat action will be held.

The selection will be based upon the reports on individual and unit achievements from 3-man cell to platoon.

B Command Committee will decide the elements to be awarded at the unit, and those to be sent to higher echelon for awards.

II. *Organization and Build-up of the Party*

Organization.

—At least 2 or 3 squads must be sent to Intervillage Guerrilla unit and every squad must include 2 or 3 party members.

—The party chapter and group chapter must be quickly set up as soon as the platoon completes its organization, in order to guarantee the Party leadership in the unit.

—Assignment and mission of Chapter [Party] Committee members. Assignment will be made depending upon the [number] of available party members. On the principle, if there are 3 or more party members, there must be one secretary; and one assistant secretary if the [number] of party members is 4 or 5.

One secretary, one assistant secretary, and Chapter [Party] Committee member will be appointed if the [number] of party members is from 7 to 9. The Assistant Secretary is responsible for security. Chapter [Party] Committee member will be responsible for youths, finance and production, if there are 2 or 3 Chapter [Party] Committee members. The Military Revolutionary council will be responsible to the Secretary, assistant Secretary or a Chapter [Party] Committee member. These are the most important tasks which should be accomplished by all Party Chapters.

Responsibility and mission of each Chapter [Party] Committee member.

Organization:

Responsible for listing of party members, to closely grasp the quality and quantity of party members in the chapter. Examine the personal history of personnel to be recommended to the chapter for admission into the Party. Recommend to higher echelon for admission of official members.

—Study records for execution of discipline.

—Up-date personal records of Party members.

—To study and assign party members, establish and/or improve the contents of regimenal activities.

—Establish emulation and provide awards for personnel.

Training and Propaganda:

—Conduct training for party members and group members.

—Disseminate resolutions, directives of the Party to party members.

—Direct propaganda tasks on policies of the party by newspaper and posters.

—Responsible for the conduct of cultural education.

—Closely control ideology of party members, group members and soldiers: recommend plans for correction.

Security:

—Closely control the personal history of party members, group members and soldiers by checking suspicious items.

—Study and report problems to the Party Chapter for action.

—Regularly educate personnel on the preservation of secrecy during normal time and under combat conditions.

Youths:

—Responsible for [Labor Youth] Group activities.

—Responsible for the sanitation, health, sports, games, physical training and entertainment program of the unit.

—Responsible for establishing and supervising the Military Revolutionary Council.

Finance and production:

—Responsible for the liquidation and administration of the Party Chapter's funds.

—Study plans for self-sufficient production, economy in the unit.

Assignment of Chapter [Party] Committee members, sub-cell members and Party members.

—Each A [squad] must organize a party sub-cell of 5 party members and Chapter [Party] Committee members must be assigned to the sub-cells to guide regimenal activities.

—A Sub-Cell must elect one [sub] cell leader and one assistant.

—In case of shortage of Party members for organizing a one party cell in each squad, then Party members must be assigned in such a manner that every squad must have a Party member and 2 Party cells for the platoon.

—Even if there is a large number of Party members, office cell should not be organized as there will be no office of the Command Committee. But each platoon cadre will control a squad.

Development of the party.

—Basing on the class of the party, the Party Chapter must be developed with people of the basic social class such as share croppers, poor farmer, middle farmer. Outstanding individuals of other classes may also be selected, relying on their ideology.

—Labor Youth [Group] members, outstanding emulators, and zealous soldiers should be selected with priority for admission into the party. Attention must be paid to individuals who have participated in the struggle for a long time. Newly activated units must try to have 2 party members assigned to each squad, units which have been activated for 3 months, must try to have 1 party member assigned to every 3-man cell; the cell leader must be a party member.

—Every squad must have, at all times 2 prospects for admission into the party.

Principles, regulations and working procedures in the development of the party.

Applicants for admission into the party should be processed as follows.

—Investigate their personal history records and report the results to the sub-cell; assign 2 party members to help them by indoctrinating them on Communism upon completion of the investigation.

—The sub-cell confirms their personal history records and submit them to the Party Chapter for approval.

—Upon receiving approval of the Party Chapter applicants begin to study party regulations, and volunteer to join the Party [sic].

—The Sub-Cell and 2 sponsors guide applicants to prepare personal history statements, the request for admission into the party. These papers will be sent by the Sub-Cell to the Party Chapter for approval. Personal history statements must contain clear and detailed information in order to check on the family relations, on social class of applicants.

Personal history statements, guaranteed by 2 sponsors, party members, must be confirmed by the Cell and approved by the Party Chapter.

The request for admission into the Party must be written by applicant to test the degree of his understanding.

If the Party Chapter approves the papers, they should be sent to a higher echelon.

Party Chapter regimenal activities.

The Party Chapter will meet once a month, the Sub-Cell meet four times monthly for regiminal activities, twice a month to study Party documents and twice a month to report [on achievements].

Contents of cell regimenal activities:

—Each party member will report to the cell the results of his assignment given by the Sub-Cell.

—When the report is finished, the cell will review the status and the results of its activities.

—Review on the execution of the resolutions of party members, and the party Sub-Cell.

—Recommend resolutions for the coming period, basing them the resolution of the Party Chapter.

—Party Members make Criticism and self Criticism.

—Settle internal problems.

—Contribute opinions or criticize the leadership of the Party Chapter.

Contents of Party Chapter regimenal activities:

The Party Chapter meets on:

—Reports on the Party situation, military and political activities, on equipment, production. The platoon leader will report on administration; the [platoon] political officer reports on political activities; 2 assistant Platoon leaders report on rear service and production.

—The meeting participants contribute opinions or review strong and weak points.

—Review the execution of resolution, directions of higher echelon on party activities, military, political and production activities.

—Prepares future plans for administration, Party and the self-sufficient production activities.

—Make assignments to Sub-Cells and the platoon Command Committee, carry out each resolution of the Party, solve some internal problems and provide recommendations for miscellaneous items.

—Criticize the working procedures of the meeting.

Working procedures of the Party Chapter.

—The role of Chapter [Party] Committee members, the political and military commanders (i.e. Platoon Command Committee) and the Party leadership of the Party Chapter.

—Upon receiving orders of resolutions from higher echelon, the political and military commanders (i.e. the Platoon leader and political officer) will report to the Chapter [Party] Committee members the mission assigned by the higher echelon and at the same time, their plans. Basing it on [current] disadvantages and advantages, the Chapter [Party] Committee members recommend additional opinions to improve the plan. After the Chapter [Party] Committee members have finished discussions a report on the [Platoon] resolution will be made.

At the same time, the Chapter [Party] Committee members will contribute opinions to help the Party Chapter discuss openly and sincerely all different problems such as plan of attack, deployment of forces, distribution of fire power. These matters should be discussed democratically by all the members.

When the Party Chapter has reached a resolution, assignment will be made. The Platoon leader will be responsible for the plan of combat; and military training; the political officer will be responsible for the political activities in the combat, and political indoctrination and the 2 assistant platoon leaders will be responsible for rear service and production. The Platoon Command Committee, will accordingly carry out the resolution of the Party Chapter in the unit, under combat condition or in normal times and will be responsible to the Party Chapter for execution.

The Party Chapter leads the Party Members, Group Members and troops to execute the orders and supervises A [squad] and expedites the execution of the resolution by the Platoon Command Committee.

Duration of meetings.

Prior to each session the Party Chapter will hold a meeting of the Sub-cells.

The Party Chapter meet twice a month. In addition, there are other meetings [to discuss] implementation of the resolution of higher echelons, or to discuss resolutions concerning combat, and training tasks. (The Party Chapter commands the unit in all aspects.)

The Chapter [Party] Committee meet 3 times a month.

The Chapter [Party] Committee meeting lasts 2 hours, cell meeting half a day. And Party Chapter meeting one day.—The district military affairs Committee should participate in meetings of intervillage guerrilla platoon, and the secretary of village [Party] Chapter must attend meetings of village guerrilla units.

Political program.

Contents of Political indoctrination: mission of concentrated guerrillas, 37 precepts; Regulations and policies.

Political activities in the army.

—1 entertainment-poster cell, 1 sports cell and 1 sanitation cell will be organized.

—1 cultural education cell: consisting of 3 men.

—One squad leader.

—One assistant squad leader, and one soldier.

These cells will be formed with personnel from the platoon among the qualified individuals with a squad leader as a cell leader.

These cells will be operated in all squads of the platoon and are responsible for control and supervision of sanitation and execution of regulations. All these cells are under the direct leadership of the political officer.

[DOCUMENT I–4]

THE 21 CONDITIONS [FOR A MEMBERSHIP IN THE COMMUNIST INTERNATIONAL (1919/20)]*

The 1st Congress of the Communist International did not draw up any precise conditions for the admission of parties to the Third International. When the 1st Congress was convened there were in the majority of countries only Communist *trends* and *groups*.

The 2nd Congress of the Communist International is meeting in different circumstances. At the present time there are in most countries not only Communist trends and tendencies, but Communist *parties* and *organizations*.

Application for admission to the Communist International is now frequently made by parties and groups which up to a short time ago still belonged to the Second International, but which have not in fact become Communist. The Second International has finally broken down. The in-between parties and the centrist groups, seeing the utter hopelessness of the Second International, are trying to find a support in the Communist International, which is growing steadily stronger. But in doing so they hope to retain enough "autonomy" to enable them to continue their former opportunist or "centrist" policy. The Communist International is becoming, to some extent, fashionable.

The desire of some leading 'centrist' groups to join the Communist International indirectly confirms that it has won the sympathies of the overwhelming majority of the class-conscious workers of the entire world and that with every day it is beoming a more powerful force.

The Communist International is threatened by the danger of dilution by unstable and irresolute elements which have not yet completely discarded the ideology of the Second International.

Moreover, in some of the larger parties (Italy, Sweden, Norway, Yugoslavia, etc.) where the majority adhere to the Communist standpoint, there still remains even today a reformist and social-pacifist wing which is only waiting a favourable moment to raise its head again and start active sabotage of the proletarian revolution and so help the bourgeoisie and the Second International.

No Communist should forget the lessons of the Hungarian revolution. The Hungarian proletariat paid a high price for the fusion of the Hungarian Communists with the so-called "left" social-democrats.

Consequently the 2nd Congress of the Communist International thinks it necessary to lay down quite precisely the conditions of admission of new parties, and to point out to those parties which have already joined the duties imposed on them.

---

*[Primarily the work of Lenin].

The 2nd Congress of the Communist International puts forward the following conditions of adherence to the Communist International:

1. All propaganda and agitation must be of a genuinely Communist character and in conformity with the programme and decisions of the Communist International. The entire Party press must be run by reliable Communists who have proved their devotion to the cause of the proletariat. The dictatorship of the proletariat is to be treated not simply as a current formula learnt by rote; it must be advocated in a way which makes its necessity comprehensible to every ordinary working man and woman, every soldier and peasant, from the facts of their daily life, which must be systematically noted in our press and made use of every day.

The periodical press and other publications, and all Party publishing houses, must be completely subordinated to the Party Presidium, regardless of whether the Party as a whole is at the given moment legal or illegal. Publishing houses must not be allowed to abuse their independence and pursue a policy which is not wholly in accordance with the policy of the Party.

In the columns of the press, at popular meetings, in the trade unions and co-operatives, wherever the adherents of the Communist International have an entry, it is necessary to denounce systematically and unrelentingly, not only the bourgeoisie, but also their assistants, the reformists of all shades.

2. Every organization which wishes to join the Communist International must, in an orderly and planned fashion, remove reformists and centrists from all responsible positions in the workers movement (party organizations, editorial boards, trade unions, parliamentary fractions, co-operatives, local government bodies) and replace them by tried Communists, even if, particularly at the beginning, "experienced" opportunists have to be replaced by ordinary rank-and-file workers.

3. In practically every country of Europe and America the class struggle is entering the phase of civil war. In these circumstances Communists can have no confidence in bourgeois legality. They are obliged everywhere to create a parallel illegal organization which at the decisive moment will help the Party to do its duty to the revolution. In all those countries where, because of a state of siege or of emergency laws, Communists are unable to do all their work legally, it is absolutely essential to combine legal and illegal work.

4. The obligation to spread Communist ideas includes the special obligation to carry on systematic and energetic propaganda in the Army. Where such agitation is prevented by emergency laws, it must be carried on illegally. Refusal to undertake such work would be tantamount to a dereliction of revolutionary duty and is incompatible with membership of the Communist International.

5. Systematic and well-planned agitation must be carried on in the

countryside. The working class cannot consolidate its victory if it has not by its policy assured itself of the support of at least part of the rural proletariat and the poorest peasants, and of the neutrality of part of the rest of the rural population. At the present time Communist work in rural areas is acquiring first-rate importance. It should be conducted primarily with the help of revolutionary Communist urban and rural workers who have close connections with the countryside. To neglect this work, or to leave it in unreliable semi-reformist hands, is tantamount to renouncing the proletarian revolution.

6. Every party which wishes to join the Communist International is obliged to expose not only avowed social-patriotism, but also the insincerity and hypocrisy of social-pacifism; to bring home to the workers systematically that without the revolutionary overthrow of capitalism no international court of arbitration, no agreement to limit armaments, no "democratic" reorganization of the League of Nations, will be able to prevent new imperialist wars.

7. Parties which wish to join the Communist International are obliged to recognize the necessity for a complete and absolute break with reformism and with the policy of the "centre", and to advocate this break as widely as possible among their members. Without that no consistent Communist policy is possible.

The Communist International demands unconditionally and categorically that this break be effected as quickly as possible. The Communist International is unable to agree that notorious opportunists, such as Turati Modigliani, Kautsky, Hilferding, Hilquit, Longguet, MacDonald, etc., shall have the right to appear as members of the Communist International. That could only lead to the Communist International becoming in many respects similar to the Second International, which has gone to pieces.

8. A particularly explicit and clear attitude on the question of the colonies and the oppressed peoples is necessary for the parties in those countries where the bourgeoisie possess colonies and oppress other nations. Every party which wishes to join the Communist International is obliged to expose the tricks and dodges of "its" imperialists in the colonies, to support every colonial liberation movement not merely in words but in deeds, to demand the expulsion of their own imperialists from these colonies, to inculcate among the workers of their country a genuinely fraternal attitude to the working people of the colonies and the oppressed nations, and to carry on systematic agitation among the troops of their country against any oppression of the colonial peoples.

9. Every party which wishes to join the Communist International must carry on systematic and persistent Communist activity inside the trade unions, the workers' councils and factory committees, the co-operatives, and other mass workers' organizations. Within these organizations Communist cells must be organized which shall by persistent and unflagging work win the trade unions, etc., for the Communist cause. In their daily

work the cells must everywhere expose the treachery of the social-patriots and the instability of the "centre". The Communist cells must be completely subordinate to the Party as a whole.

10. Every party belonging to the Communist International is obliged to wage an unyielding struggle against the Amsterdam "International" of the yellow trade unions it must conduct the most vigorous propaganda among trade unionists for the necessity of a break with the yellow Amsterdam International. It must do all it can to support the international association of red trade unions, adhering to the Communist International, which is being formed.

11. Parties which wish to join the Communist International are obliged to review the personnel of their parliamentary fractions and remove all unreliable elements, to make these fractions not only verbally but in fact subordinate to the Party Presidium, requiring of each individual Communist member of parliament that he subordinate his entire activity to the interests of genuinely revolutionary propaganda and agitation.

12. Parties belonging to the Communist International must be based on the principle of *democratic centralism*. In the present epoch of acute civil war the Communist Party will be able to fulfill its duty only if its organization is as centralized as possible, if iron discipline prevails, and if the Party centre, upheld by the confidence of the Party membership, has strength and authority and is equipped with the most comprehensive powers.

13. Communist parties in those countries where Communists carry on their work legally must from time to time undertake cleansing (re-registration) of the membership of the Party in order to get rid of any petty-bourgeois elements which have crept in.

14. Every party which wishes to join the Communist International is obliged to give unconditional support to any Soviet republic in its struggle against counter-revolutionary forces. Communist parties must carry on unambiguous propaganda to prevent the dispatch of munitions transports to the enemies of the Soviet republics; they must also carry on propaganda by every means, legal or illegal, among the troops sent to strangle workers' republics.

15. Parties which still retain their old social-democratic programmes are obliged to revise them as quickly as possible, and to draw up, in accordance with the special conditions of their country, a new Communist programme in conformity with the decisions of the Communist International. As a rule the programme of every party belonging to the Communist International must be ratified by the regular Congress of the Communist International or by the Executive Committee. Should the programme of a party not be ratified by the ECCI, the party concerned has the right to appeal to the Congress of the Communist International.

16. All the decisions of the Congresses of the Communist International, as well as the decisions of its Executive Committee, are binding on all

parties belonging to the Communist International. The Communist International, working in conditions of acute civil war, must be far more centralized in its structure than was the Second International. Consideration must of course be given by the Communist International and its Executive Committee in all their activities to the varying conditions in which the individual parties have to fight and work, and they must take decisions of general validity only when such decisions are possible.

17. In this connection, all parties which wish to join the Communist International must change their names. Every party which wishes to join the Communist International must be called: *Communist* party of such and such a country (section of the Communist International). This question of name is not merely a formal matter, but essentially a political question of great importance. The Communist International has declared war on the entire bourgeois world and on all yellow social-democratic parties. The difference between the Communist parties and the old official "social-democratic" or "socialist" parties, which have betrayed the banner of the working class, must be brought home to every ordinary worker.

18. All leading Party press organs in all countries are obliged to publish all important official documents of the Executive Committee of the Communist International.

19. All parties belonging to the Communist International, and those which have applied for admission, are obliged to convene an extraordinary Congress as soon as possible, and in any case not later than four months after the 2nd Congress of the Communist International, to examine all these conditions of admission. In this connection all party centres must see that the decisions of the 2nd Congress of the Communist International are made known to all local organizations.

20. Those parties which now wish to join the Communist International, but which have not radically changed their former tactics, must see to it that, before entering the Communist International, not less than two-thirds of the members of their central committee and of all their leading central bodies consist of comrades who publicly and unambiguously advocated the entry of their party into the Communist International before its 2nd Congress. Exceptions can be made with the consent of the Executive Committee of the Communist International. The ECCI also has the right to make exceptions in the case of representatives of the centre mentioned in paragraph 7.

21. Those members of the Party who reject in principle the conditions and these put forward by the Communist International are to be expelled from the Party.

The same applies in particular to delegates to the extraordinary Congresses.

[DOCUMENT I-5]

[INSTRUCTIONS FROM THE PROVINCIAL PARTY COMMITTEE OF BA XUYEN PROVINCE TO ITS DISTRICT COMMITTEES 7 December, 1961.]*

To D2 and K,

In regard to the foundation of the People's Revolutionary Party of South Vietnam, the creation of this party is only a matter of strategy; it needs to be explained within the party; and, to deceive the enemy, it is necessary that the new party be given the outward appearance corresponding to a division of the party (Lao Dong) into two and the foundation of a new party, so that the enemy cannot use it in his propaganda.

Within the party, it is necessary to explain that the founding of the People's Revolutionary Party has the purpose of isolating the Americans and the Ngo Dinh Diem regime, and to counter their accusations of an invasion of the South by the North. It is means of supporting our sabotage of the Geneva Agreements, of advancing the plan of invasion of the South, and at the same time permitting the Front for Liberation of the South to recruit new adherents, and to gain the sympathy of non-aligned countries in Southeast Asia.

The People's Revolutionary Party has only the appearance of an independent existence; actually, our party is nothing but the Lao Dong Party of Vietnam (Viet-Minh Communist Party), unified from North to South, under the direction of the central executive committee of the party, the chief of which is President Ho. . . .

During these explanations, take care to keep this strictly secret, especially in South Vietnam, so that the enemy does not perceive our purpose. . . . Do not put these explanations in party bulletins. . . .

[Another party circular† of the same date said:]

The reasons for the change in the party's name must be kept strictly secret. According to instructions of the Central Committee, one must not tell the people or party sympathizers that the People's Revolutionary Party and the Lao Dong Party of Vietnam are one. One must not say that is is only a tactic, because it would not be good for the enemy to know. . . .

---

* *Aggression From the North: The Record of North Vietnam's Campaign to Conquer South Vietnam*, Bureau of Public Affairs: Department of State Publication 7839 (Far Eastern Series 130), February 1965, p. 57.

† *Ibid.*

By Order of the Secretary of the Army:

HAROLD K. JOHNSON
General, United States Army,
Chief of Staff

Official:

KENNETH G. WICKHAM,
Major General, United States Army,
The Adjutant General.

Distribution:

In accordance with Special List.

☆ U.S. Government Printing Office: 1967—0 261-501